MORE THAN A GAME

HISTORY OF THE
WESTERN PROVINCE CRICKET BOARD
1959-1991

MORE THAN A GAME

MOGAMAD ALLIE

HISTORY OF THE
WESTERN PROVINCE CRICKET BOARD
1959-1991

CAPE ARGUS

Western Province Cricket Association, Cape Town

Editor: Dougie Oakes

Designer: Stuart Nix of Square Edge Design

stuartn@mweb.co.za

Indexer: Jeanne Cope

Reader: Neilah Miller

Special contributor: Michael Doman

ISBN 0-620-26899-9

Printed by Cape and Transvaal Book Printers, Parow, Cape Town.

Introduction

WHEN CRICKET in the Western Province was finally unified under one controlling body in June 1991, after nearly a century of playing under racially-divided bodies, many people, especially white and younger cricket followers, were completely in the dark about the rich history of the Western Province Cricket Board (WPCB).

Having played and followed cricket in the WPCB closely since 1970, I had a very close attachment to the affairs of an organisation which played a leading role in the anti-apartheid sports struggle.

Bearing this in mind, I felt the need to recognise the role of the WPCB in the non-racial sports movement, as well as to highlight the achievements of some of the top players who have been largely unrecognised, because of the head-in-the sand attitude of the white-controlled media.

The urgent need to write grew even stronger when I observed how easily black youngsters could identify with new heroes such as Jonty Rhodes and Allan Donald – and I have no problem with that, as they are fine cricketers – while being oblivious to the feats of past greats such as Lefty Adams, Dik Abed, Coetie Neethling, Owen Williams and Saait Magiet, among many others. These former greats are virtually unknown to the new generation of cricketers and cricket lovers – yet had they been given the opportunities and facilities available to their more privileged white countrymen they may well have become household names in international cricket.

Many are also unaware of the effects of apartheid on sport, and how the WPCB managed to administer and play the game under extremely trying circumstances. The convenient argument used by those who turned a blind eye to the political stance adopted by the WPCB in the face of repression and discrimination on the basis of colour, was that politics and sport should not be mixed. But try telling this to the many cricket clubs who had to close as a result of forced removals in terms of the Group Areas Act, which scattered their membership to all parts of the Cape Flats – or to the many schoolchildren who were allocated grossly inferior facilities by the National Party government.

While many are still struggling to come to terms with transformation in South African cricket, this book is an attempt to highlight the inequalities perpetrated by the apartheid system. In outlining the trying circumstances under which black people were forced to play the game, I am hoping that those who were unaware will at least develop an understanding about the need to transform in order to give the previously deprived communities a fair chance to develop their potential.

Researching the history of the WPCB was no easy exercise, although it was a thoroughly enjoyable and enriching experience. In many cases, records – especially of the early years of the board – were not available. In addition, media coverage was patchy, and I had to rely on the sometimes fading memories of people who were involved in the game at the time.

The common thread through all my interviews with former administrators and players was their willingness to share information and to speak very warmly about their experiences within the WPCB.

Without exception, people willingly parted with their treasured scrap books and photo albums – they too realised the need to record the history of the board.

What was particularly striking was the passion people had for the game under particularly trying circumstances. Administrators such as Abu Desai and Matt Segers, who had meticulously kept all the records of the initial meetings of the WPCB, were very helpful as were Cliffie Ravens and Barney Leendertz, who were also instrumental in the formation of the WPCB in 1959. I value their input.

Cliff Adams' records and photographs, and Ray Bharoochi's meticulously-kept minutes of the important unity negotiations were also invaluable. Abubakaar Haywood's encyclopaedic knowledge of Sacboc cricket was crucial as a reference point.

One must also acknowledge the tremendous efforts of Damoo Bansda and Syd Reddy, the editors of the *South African Cricket Almanack*, which proved to be a veritable mine of authentic information on Sacboc and its affiliates. Sadly, the *Almanack* was published for the last time in 1969.

Compiling the statistics was a time-consuming and, sometimes, frustrating exercise. Although I was able to find scorebooks of the early 1970s, I was forced to rely on newspaper cuttings which, often, were difficult to find; in many instances, these scorecards were incomplete or they didn't tally. However, thanks to the invaluable assistance of Krish Reddy from Durban, who had the much tougher task of finding the scorecards of all four provinces, I was able to compile the career records of all 114 players who represented the WPCB at first-class level.

I would also like to pay tribute to my editor, Dougie Oakes, and Michael Doman (my high school cricket captain), for their valuable input.

While the history of the WPCB is indeed rich, it was also turbulent at times. Through the years, administrators and players have made decisions and taken actions which they have later regretted. In relating the controversies, which may sometimes reflect negatively on certain individuals, I must emphasise that the main aim of this book is to relate the history of the WPCB as accurately as possible. It has never been my intention to use my research as a tool to discredit any individual.

I have no scores to settle with anyone. I deeply respect the tireless, unselfish work of the pioneers of the WPCB, who sacrificed their time and energy to ensure that the ideal of a democratic, nonracial South African society was finally realised.

Finally, I salute the players who ignored the lure of better opportunities to remain true to the principles of nonracialism. Their selflessness played a significant role in creating the democratic society which black South Africans had struggled to attain for so many years.

Mogamad Allie
January 2001

Contents

Foreword

The United Cricket Board of South Africa was formed in 1991, uniting all cricketers in the country in a single cricket controlling body for the first time. The Western Province Cricket Association was formed in the same year as part of the same process at provincial level.

The benefits of unity have been so great that it is difficult, especially for younger cricketers, to comprehend that cricket could have been played in any other way.

But the current situation, reinforced by a democracy that emphasises equal rights for all South Africans, is relatively new.

For more than a hundred years, South African cricketers played their cricket apart in segregated racial bodies.

In keeping with the logic of apartheid and colonialism, white cricketers excluded those classified as "non-white" from their clubs and competitions. The law and custom tied people into separate "Group Areas". At one time, there were five different bodies controlling cricket in the Western Province.

More Than a Game deals with an important part of this overall history. It tells the story of the Western Province Cricket Board, which existed between 1959 and 1991. In doing so it helps bring to life the rich tradition of cricket in communities excluded from the official record under apartheid. Moreover, it helps explain the emergence of the nonracial philosophy underpinning South African cricket today. The Western Province Cricket Board (and its mother bodies, the South African Cricket Board of Control and the South African Cricket Board) early on rejected apartheid's racial categorisations and insisted on equality for all cricketers, based on the policy of nonracialism.

This book is published by the Western Province Cricket Association (WPCA) as part of its commitment to deepening unity and transformation in cricket.

The WPCA has fully endorsed the Transformation Charter, adopted by the United Cricket Board of South Africa in 1998, which identified 10 main strategic thrusts for the future growth of the game in this country, including that of "Recording the full history of South African cricket".

The key to this thrust is to "acknowledge, record and respect" the achievements of black cricketers over the past century, "recognising our diversity as a source of strength" in the process.

The WPCA responded by setting up a WPCA History Committee in 1998 to ensure that the broad history of Western Province cricket was recorded. This book is the first step in that process. Hopefully more such histories will follow to help shed light on a story that goes back to the first recorded game of cricket in South Africa – in 1809, at the Green Point Common.

Various acknowledgements need to be made. By giving whole-hearted support and generously allocating resources, the WPCA executive has shown it understands the importance of memory and acknowledgement in the healing and rebuilding of our cricket – and, indeed, our country.

The president, Arnold Bloch, and vice-president, Sadick Emeran, did not have to be persuaded. General Manager, Peter Heeger, and Carol van Vuuren in the office were ever ready to give administrative backup. The History Committee members showed fierce enthusiasm for making a history, which too few people know about, accessible to larger audiences. Mogamad Allie, in particular, so relished the opportunity to be involved that he ran ahead and authored this part of the project by himself. He has made a big contribution to Western Province cricket.

Dougie Oakes also needs special mention. His professional input and quiet dedication has given this book the form and status it deserves.

Michael Doman, Mario Williams and Solomon Makosana gave solid support. Stuart Nix did the design and layout. Our thanks also to Shaun Johnson and his team at Independent Newspapers for agreeing to be co-publishers.

The WPCA is proud to be part of a national effort to reclaim and celebrate the past. The association hopes that this book will encourage other provinces, who have embarked on similar tasks, as well as the United Cricket Board, which has given its approval for an official history.

Finally, special thanks are due to the ex-board cricketers, who contributed directly and indirectly to this story.

More Than a Game highlights the rich legacy the former "untouchables" have left Western Province and South African cricket. It is a legacy that we can learn from and build on as cricket rethinks its future and seeks to become a dynamically South African game in the 21st century.

Prof. André Odendaal
Chairperson: WPCA History Committee

Part 1

The formation of the Western Province Cricket Board

IN DECEMBER 1953, a team of cricketers set off by lorry from Cape Town for a series of matches in the Eastern Cape and Natal.

Among the group were some of the Western Cape's finest black players – Abdul Gameed ("Happie") Noordien, Tiny and Lobo Abed, Dol Freeman, Sydney Solomons, Jackie Truter, Paddy Thomas, Adam Sobotker, Cliffie Ravens....

Theirs was a crucial mission – a mission that had little to do with on-the-field skills or, indeed, with winning or losing. Rather, the purpose of their trip was to cement a plan that had been meticulously put together over a long period – which had united cricketers from a number of ethnic and religious communities in Cape Town under the banner of the Western Province Cricket Federation (WPCF).

THE SEARCH FOR UNITY

"The narrow seats at the back of the lorry did not make for a comfortable journey," said the team manager, Matt Segers. "But we felt that this was the best way of getting the players – all of whom came from various backgrounds – to bond."

"Being thrown together like this welded the players together as nothing else could have done – whereas car travel might, perhaps, have resulted in little cliques being formed," said Segers

Although the trip was hailed as a wonderful success by the organisers, the dreams of the men driving the new federation – towards a broader unity of cricketers in the Western Cape – were quickly dashed.

The WPCF folded within two years – with a shortage of cash being one of the reasons for its premature death.

Nevertheless, the formation of the WPCF was the first step towards the drawing together of players from different ethnic and religious backgrounds into one body. It encouraged those preaching unity – and these included players, administrators and members of the media – to raise their voices just a little bit louder.

But a long and bitter fight for wider unity lay ahead – in which far too often victories seemed too tiny, and disappointments too big and too gut-wrenching for the amount of effort that had been put in.

The chief problem for those trying to build a single, united body in the Western Cape was that black cricket clubs and associations were (not surprisingly) as divided as the communities that spawned them. For every club which refused to accept African members there was one that would say "No" to Muslims; for every one that refused membership to a dark-skinned, frizzy-haired coloured, there was another with a clause in its constitution which read, "No Christians."

To complicate matters even further, the national body for black cricketers, the South African Cricket Board of Control, was made up of national ethnic organisations. representing coloured, Indian, African and Malay cricketers.

By the 1950s it had become clear that black cricket needed to be pushed in a radically new direction. But how? and by whom?

It was quickly acknowledged that what was needed to kick-start the process were men with vision and drive. Although Dol Freeman, who spearheaded the formation of the Western Province Cricket Federation, appeared to have all the credentials to lead the drive, other names began to emerge – names such as Damoo Bansda, a journalist; Hoosain Parker, a city councillor; MG Booley, a Muslim sheikh; Johnny van Harte, a school principal; and a young firebrand named Hassan Howa....

Thanks to these officials and, in later years, a host of others, black cricket in the Western Cape – represented by the Western Province Cricket Board – would, over the next three decades and more, emerge as one of the standard-bearers of the fight for nonracial sport in South Africa.

The start of a long and winding road

FOR A COUNTRY continuously swaying on the lip of political crisis, the spat which tore apart the South African Coloured Cricket Board in 1926 was, at first sight, an insignificant event – a silly fall-out among a group of anonymous officials – hardly worthy of attention or comment....

Far bigger issues had emerged to concentrate the minds of the country's racially-divided population – none more so than Prime Minister Barry Hertzog's single-minded determination to push through a package of three so-called "Native Bills", the aim of which was to remove the final vestiges of African political rights (notably in the Cape Province, where, in a throwback to pre-Union days, a "qualified" franchise clause still enabled some blacks to vote).

And yet, the decision by disaffected members of the South African Coloured Cricket Board to launch a South African Independent Coloured Cricket Board was to have serious long-term implications for cricketers from the country's black communities. It signalled the beginning of a bleak period, in which the game was played (unquestioningly, if not entirely happily) along ethnic and religious lines – in the Western Cape and, indeed, throughout South Africa. Whereas the SA Coloured Cricket Board (also known as the Barnato Board) had represented all the country's black cricketers, the split encouraged the formation of new, racially exclusive bodies – the SA Bantu Cricket Board in 1932 and the SA Indian Cricket Union in 1940. Worse, after the 1932 Barnato tournament in Bloemfontein, the SA Coloured

Cricket Board ceased to function (although it was resuscitated 12 years later).

Many years would pass before the word "unity" was raised again....

The issue re-emerged in 1945 when the SA Indian Cricket Union (SAICU) pushed its head outside its ethnic compartment long enough to call for the establishment of a single body made up of all the different ethnic and religious groupings playing cricket in South Africa.

Signor Barnato's "magnificent silverware"

FEW BLACK cricketers, in the early part of the 20th century, would have been familiar with the name, Barnett Isaacs. But if the name "Barnato" had been mentioned to them, that would have been a different story.

According to the editors of the *South African Cricket Almanack*, the Barnato Memorial trophy was a "magnificent piece of silverware" around which "the destiny of non-white cricket had taken shape in South Africa".

Barnett Isaacs was the Barnato after whom the trophy was named – and his was the ultimate rags-to-riches story. Born dirt poor in the East End of London, he left school at 14 with hardly any academic skills. He did, however, own a handy pair of fists and he showed a fine sleight of hand – ideal tools for a prize-fighter and a magician named, "Signor Barnato" (his stage name).

By the time he arrived in South Africa to try his luck on the Kimberley diamond fields, he'd changed his name to Barney Barnato – and proceeded to make a fortune.

Later, he sold his stake in the Kimberley Mine to Cecil John Rhodes for more than £5-million (sterling) – a fortune in those days. A staunch supporter of President Paul Kruger's South African Republic, he committed suicide in 1897, a year after the Rhodes-inspired Jameson Raid.

When Sir David Harris, the chairman of De Beers Consolidated Mines Ltd, presented a trophy to the Griqualand West Coloured Cricket Union, he named it after Barnato.

AE Docrat, the secretary of the SA Malay Cricket Board, warned about the dangers associated with playing cricket along religious and ethnic lines. But it was only in 1958 – four years after his warning – that the South African Cricket Board of Control voted to outlaw the racial character with which it had been associated since its formation.

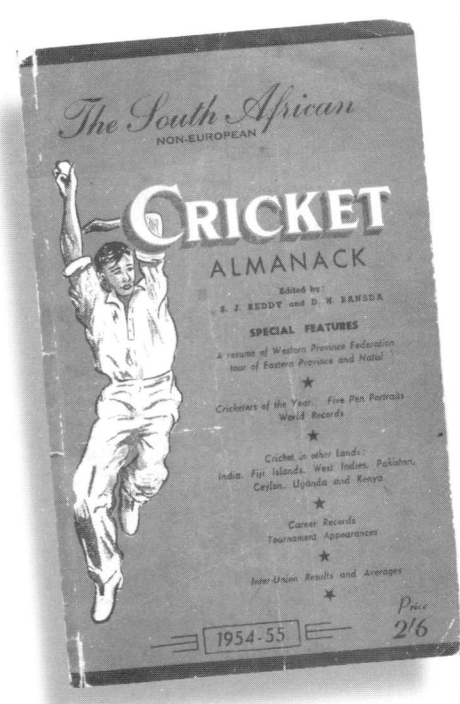

The South African Cricket Almanack was crammed with information about black cricket from throughout the country and, sometimes, even from abroad. When first published in 1953, it was advertised as an annual publication. But financial constraints limited the editors, Damoo Bansda and Syd Reddy to just two more editions – in 1954 and 1969.

It was a well-timed call: the SAICU's suggestion drew enough support to persuade other controlling bodies to elect a committee to investigate the feasibility of forming a national association to administer black cricket in South Africa.

Although there was consensus that there should be a national cricket governing body to administer the sport, it took another two years before an agreement supported by the majority of unions was thrashed out. In July 1947, the SA Cricket Board of Control (Sacboc) – an umbrella body made up of the SAICU, the SA Coloured Cricket Association (which had changed its name from the SA Independent Coloured Cricket Board) and the SA Bantu Cricket Union – was launched in Johannesburg. The SA Coloured Cricket Board, after first being excluded from the new alliance, was later allowed to join – on condition that it changed its name to the SA Malay Cricket Board.

Buoyed by pledges of support from its affiliates, Sacboc staged its first inter-race tournament – for the Dadabhay Brothers Trophy – in Johannesburg in 1951. The next two biennial tournaments were also held in Johannesburg, before Cape Town hosted what proved to be the final tournament run on an inter-race format, in 1958.

RACIAL TENSIONS

An unforeseen – and unwelcome – consequence of the inter-race tournaments of the 1950s was the imperfections it highlighted in the makeup of Sacboc.

To the supporters of the Dadabhay tourney, the opportunity to see the country's best black cricketers in action at one centralised venue was a major plus. But, to its detractors, its

glaring weakness – and this, it was claimed, far outweighed its strengths – was the ethnic makeup of the various competing teams. It was a drawback that required decisive, corrective action. And yet, the warning signs had long been flashing....

In 1954, three years after the first inter-race tourney, AE Docrat, the secretary of the SA Malay Cricket Board, confirmed in his annual report what had already been discussed and agonised over by many politically-aware observers: ethnic and racial tensions were on the increase among Sacboc's various affiliates.

Sacboc, Docrat noted, had failed to promote racial harmony among both players and spectators.

"[It] should take cognisance of this ... and endeavour to quickly remedy the same, which quite obviously will bring us to the question of removing artificial barriers that have been set up between some of the units of the Board of Control."

"The Board of Control should never have attempted to stage their initial tournament on an inter-racial basis – it should rather have been run more or less on provincial lines," he added.

Damoo Bansda and Syd Reddy, the editors of the SA Non-European Cricket Almanack, also came out strongly against inter-race tournaments. In the 1954/55 edition of the publication, they wrote: "Numerous cricket personalities with whom we have had discussions on the present set-up of the SA Cricket Board of Control, [have] indicated their disapproval of ... racial tournaments. Time alone will test the sincerity of those at the helm of affairs, whether they will agree to ... a new policy and thereby seek international recognition."

While a growing number of people were starting to campaign for unity among black cricket bodies in the 1950s, those who wielded authority in these organisations took nearly a decade to follow suit. This slow pace of change made some of the concessions which followed seem far more dramatic than what they really were.

Thus, for instance, when the SA Indian Cricket Union agreed to a proposal by one of its affiliates, the Western Province Indian Cricket Union, to allow the three Cape centres – Western Province, Eastern Province and Griqualand West – to field four cricketers of non-Indian descent at the 1953 Christopher Trophy tournament, this development was hailed by Bobby Harrypersadh, the sports editor of the Natal-based *Leader* newspaper, as "a fundamental contribution to race relations in this country". (Previously, the non-Indian players that these units were allowed to field had to be of "Malay" descent.)

This policy switch, though, could hardly be described as far-sighted. Rather, an event had occurred which had left officials with the choice of either changing the rules or looking ridiculous....

Abu Desai, at that time the secretary of the WP Indian Cricket Union, explained that the change had been forced on officials of the national body by the appearance of Farook du Preez, a coloured convert to Islam, in the WP Indian team at the 1952 Christopher Tournament in Durban. The inclusion of Du Preez as one of the allotted four "Malays" had sparked a vigorous debate about the identity of "Malays" who, in terms of the Population Registration Act, were classified as a separate South African race group.

"You had the ridiculous situation where a Christian coloured who con-verted to Islam was reclassified as Malay, yet a Hindu who converted to Islam continued to be classified as an Indian," said Desai.

"Because the South African Indian Cricket Union president, the Rev Bernard Sigamoney, understood these anomalies, he changed the rules to allow four players of non-Indian descent to represent the Cape provinces," Desai said.

While the occasional tinkering with the rules was cheered by some administrators and players, others saw it as a waste of time – and called instead for a redoubling of efforts to bring about true non-racial unity in cricket.

BIRTH OF THE WP CRICKET FEDERATION

The first attempt to unite the various unions in the Western Cape into a body in which race or religion played no part was spearheaded by all-rounder Abdol "Dol" Josef Freeman, whose efforts resulted in the establishment of the Western Province Cricket Federation (WPCF) in 1952. Freeman became the WPCF's president, with WB Lubelwana and EC Hodges his deputies. Other key founder members included journalist Damoo Bansda (secretary), Councillor Hoosain Parker (treasurer), Cliffie Ravens and Hassan Howa.

Prospects for a wider, lasting unity received a great boost when Matt Segers, an up-and-coming administrator, and a group of friends persuaded the Stellenbosch and District Union to join the WPCF – against the wishes of its powerful parent body, the Peninsula and Western Districts Cricket Board (the Coloured Union). The independent Central Union also allied itself to the new body, as did Wynberg (thanks to the lobbying of Ravens and Howa).

A rare photograph of a youthful-looking Hassan Howa, one of the key founder members of the Western Province Cricket Federation.

As moves towards nonracial unity gathered momentum, the Western Province African and Indian unions also came on board.

"Those in the country areas, especially, believed strongly that because

The Western Province Cricket Federation side which toured the Eastern Cape and Natal in 1953. Back (left to right): C Ravens, GT Holmes, S Abed, E Petersen, E Rhode, P Thomas, J Truter, I Shaik Middle: G Abed, AJ Freeman, M Segers (manager), H Noordien (captain), A Brown (assistant manager), M Coetzee (vice-captain), A Sobotker Front: I Latief, S Solomons, T Hendricks

we lived together all ethnic affiliations needed to be dispensed with. Certainly, in my case, I was never home during the Muslim festival of Eid – I was always invited to lunch by my Muslim friends," Segers said.

Abdullah Brown, the cricket correspondent for the Cape Town-based *Sun* newspaper, proved a valuable ally of those striving to destroy ethnic barriers. He argued strongly that the scrapping of inter-race tournaments would provide a great fillip to the unity process within Sacboc.

"Not only do the majority of the Non-Europeans disapprove of playing cricket on a racial system, but it has also become a source of embarrassment to many of the players who take part in the tournaments," he said.

"How can the Malay team be termed thus when a third of its side are not Malays? The Indian team has a Coloured and a Malay playing for them and the Coloured side includes a

Malay," Brown argued. While this debate continued, the WPCF quietly went about promoting itself itself by means of a series of inter-union matches involving Central, the WP Coloured Cricket Union (the Malays), the WP Bantu Cricket Union, the WP Indian Cricket Union, the Stellenbosch and District Union and the Hottentots Holland Union. The WP Coloured Cricket Union won both versions of the Moslem Progressive Society Trophy which was at stake between 1952 and 1954.

A TOUR FOR UNITY

To consolidate its formation, the WPCF arranged a goodwill tour of the Eastern Cape and Natal in December 1953, by a team led by Abdul Gameed (Happie) Noordien.

The side, which was selected after a series of trials, included such players as Tiny and Lobo Abed, and Dol Freeman of the WP Coloured Cricket Union, Jackie Truter, Paddy Thomas and Adam Sobotker of the Central Union and Cliffie Ravens of the Wynberg and District Union.

It was not a comfortable journey. A row of seats – narrow and hard – at the back of a lorry was a long way off from first-class luxury. But team manager Matt Segers said: "It was a good way of getting players from various backgrounds to bond.

"Being thrown together from the outset welded the players together as nothing else could have done. Travelling by motorcar would, perhaps, have resulted in little cliques being formed. As we already had different denominational groups in the team, this would have highlighted the differences.

"We were accommodated in private houses in Port Elizabeth and in a Muslim hostel in Durban.

"Between matches, the Muslim players liked to play cards while the Christian members wandered off on their own. On the field, however, we were united as a team," Segers wrote in his tour report.

Despite weaknesses in key areas – for instance, the touring party had just one specialist opening batsman and no reserve wicketkeeper – the team won most of the 10 games it played in 15 hectic days.

Two weeks after the goodwill tour, the WPCF played a friendly at the Vineyard in Claremont against a "European XI" led by Alan Marshall, a Western Province provincial player.

The contest proved to be less than equal – as the editors of the 1954/55 edition of the *SA Non-European Cricket Almanack* pointed out in their match report.

"This match was played on turf, where our players failed to display the form they showed on matting wickets. Although the match was lost it was invaluable insofar as experience goes, for our players now realise that it is a completely different proposition playing on turf wickets. Our bowlers, nevertheless, redeemed the poor batting display, especially Eric Petersen and Mike Coetzee who turned in creditable performances."

Despite the optimism which greeted its formation, the WPCF quickly found that noble ideals were not a guarantee for a long existence. After just two years it was dead – throttled by a shortage of cash and the refusal by the powerful Peninsula and Western Districts Cricket Board to join it. Many supporters of the WPCF were sharply critical of the decision by the board to stay outside the unity process. Others, though disappointed, could see why the board had opted for this course of action.

Cliff Ravens, a former president of Wynberg and District Cricket Union, felt that the board's stance revolved around a number of strategic issues.

"It was the strongest association in terms of playing strength; it also had the most money. Obviously then, the majority of its members were not keen to see the merging of its financial resources with those of other unions that had virtually nothing," Ravens said.

"Also, its top officials were prepared to consider participation only if they could retain their positions in a unified body – and this was a guarantee we couldn't give them."

A WPCF XI v Alan Marshall's XI

PACEMEN ERIC Petersen (5/30) and Mike Coetzee (4/19) blasted out the Marshall side's classy batting lineup for just 93 – but then saw their own batsmen negate all their good work by tamely surrendering to the white side's bowlers for a paltry 38.

A much improved second innings effort steered Marshall's XI to 113/4 declared (which, added to their lead of 55, put them 168 ahead of the WPCF).

Solid knocks by Lobo Abed (38) and his brother, Tiny (23), helped the WPCF to 134 all out – 35 runs short of their victory target.

Summarised scores:

Marshall's XI 93 (B. Killian 33; F. Bing 13; Mike Coetzee 4/19; Eric Petersen 5/30) and 113/4 dec (F. Bing 45; B. Pfaaf 25)

WPCF XI 38 (Leslie Less 15; B. Peacock 8/15) and 134 (Lobo Abed 38; Tiny Abed 23; Paddy Thomas 20; A. Marshall 4/30)

Marshall's XI won by 34 runs

Abu Desai, later to become the first secretary of a nonracial Western Province Cricket Board, suggested that the problem with Peninsula was the exclusivity of some of its urban affiliates.

"For instance, the Cape District and Central Unions, which, at that time, catered for so-called upper-class coloureds, refused to allow people with darker skins or curly hair to become members. Muslims, too, were not welcome."

Although these attitudes changed in later years, in the period before the formation of the WP Cricket Board a number of talented cricketers felt the lash of coloured racism.

One of them was a big-boned seam bowler named Eric Petersen, whom many experts believe would have played test cricket if he'd practised his craft in any country other than in South Africa....

ERIC PETERSEN'S BURDEN

In the early 1950s, Petersen, already a prodigious talent, applied to join Ridgeville Cricket Club, a member of the Central Union.

"Ridgeville accepted me," he said, "but when I appeared before the executive of the Central Union during its weekly 'passing out parade', I was turned down.

"They gave no reason for their decision, but I knew the union had a policy of not accepting players who were too dark-skinned!"

A bitter Petersen joined Pirates in the Western Province Coloured Cricket Union (also known as the Malay union), where he was given a warm reception by both players and fans.

"At every game, spectators would come with their picnic baskets, and they would invite me to have lunch with them. It was impossible to accept every invitation – and those I had to turn down always made a point of coming to me afterwards and saying how disappointed they were that I couldn't join them," he said.

"The Malay guys treated me like a brother – like one of them. They always encouraged me and were never jealous of my achievements."

There were other spinoffs for Petersen, too: the Adams family – noted tailors in the area – treated him like royalty. If he needed a trousers, they'd make it for him – free of charge. They also paid his subscription and ball fees (which, in the 1950s, amounted to one shilling).

Ironically, after Petersen had made a name for himself in the SA Malay team and, later, as a member of Basil D'Oliveira's team which toured Kenya in 1958, Central cleared the way for him to play in their union.

But by then the damage had been done. Petersen wasn't interested, and was more than happy to continue his career with Pirates.

Had he tried to join Pirates just a few years earlier, though, he would probably have been barred from playing in the very union which, he said, had made him feel so welcome.

Several clubs had constitutions stipulating that only Muslims could play for them – and they were not prepared to change this rule (not even if the surname of a prospective member was D'Oliveira).

According to Abubakaar Haywood, a schoolmate of Basil D'Oliveira at Zonnebloem High School, the future England star had at one stage been keen to join the Muslim club, Ottomans, which was located virtually on his doorstep in the Bo-Kaap. He was prevented from doing so, however, because of a clause in the club's constitution which said: "Muslims Only".

Similarly, many Christian clubs had constitutions preventing non-Christians from becoming members. Others barred Africans. Still others made it plain that they preferred applications for membership from players with straight hair and a fair skin.

BEN MALAMBA

Of course, not every coloured cricketer or club official was a racist, or supported the racist or religious bigotry prevalent in other clubs and unions.

On the contrary, there were many individuals who were prepared to tackle bigotry in cricket head on. In the Central Union, for instance, the

Eric Petersen, probably the greatest pace bowler to play in South African Cricket Board of Control competitions, once had an application for membership of a Sacboc affiliate rejected because his skin pigmentation was too dark.

fight to force a change in the admission policy which had earlier disqualified Petersen was led by a talented all-rounder named Cecil Abrahams, and other members of the Trafalgar club side.

In 1958, Abrahams and his team mates pulled off a coup when they persuaded Ben Malamba, a flamboyant allrounder in Basil D'Oliveira's Sacboc team which shortly before had toured Kenya, to join Trafalgar.

But before Malamba could play his first game, there was the question of Central's "passing-out parade...."

The facts were quite simple and the issues clear. Malamba's cricketing credentials could not be questioned – but there were one or two things over which he had no control: his skin colour couldn't be blacker, or the texture of his hair kinkier.

And that wasn't all: as a member of the African community, Malamba would have been regarded by a significant portion of the Central Union's hierarchy as being a product of the wrong side of the wrong side of the tracks. Trafalgar's activists, however, were more than prepared for an eyeball-to-eyeball confrontation with the union. As the date for Malamba's "passing-out" appointment drew closer, the club made it clear that it would quit the union if Malamba's admission to the union was not a formality.

Abrahams also arranged for a newspaper reporter and photographer to be present at the "passing-out" ceremony.

Trafalgar's careful preparations had the desired effect: the parade went off without a hitch. Union officials graciously welcomed their new African member into what had, up to then, been regarded as a fortress of the middle-class coloured community.

Malamba's victory over bigotry may seem small today, but in the 1950s, every barrier that was broken down was hailed as a major development, which added impetus to other efforts to unite black cricket under a nonracial controlling body.

In many instances, forward-looking officials adopted a dual approach to running the game. On the one hand, they were driven by what they saw as a strong moral duty to build nonracial unity; on the other hand, they strove hard to fulfill the mandate given to them by an ambitious and, often, impatient constituency – to find ways to improve the standard of the game.

In a bid to provide their top players with an incentive, the Sacboc hierarchy tried for many years to bring an international side to South Africa.

SEEKING TO BUILD INTERNATIONAL TIES

The first target was India – but Sacboc couldn't raise the cash. Later, an invitation to tour South Africa was sent to Pakistan – and this time there were sufficient funds in the kitty. But just when negotiations had reached a critical stage, the Pakistanis backed out, following a decision by cricket's controlling body, the Imperial Cricket Conference, to grant membership to the Pakistani cricketing authority.

Sacboc's big breakthrough finally came in 1956 – when a team of Kenyan Asians agreed to tour. It was the first tour to South Africa organised by a black cricketing body – and it proved to be an administrative Everest for officials.

In the end, however, they passed the test, just as the players would later pass it on the field.

Reminiscing about the tour in 1968, Bob Pavadai, the first president of Sacboc, wrote that although the news of the tour was warmly welcomed by cricket lovers, the various units did

Ben Malamba became a tremendously popular member of the Central Union, which earlier had a policy of accepting only fair-skinned coloured players.

not have the experience to arrange it. This required national officials to put in many hours of hard work to create the machinery for the smooth running of the tour.

Each province rose magnificently to the occasion, Pavadai wrote.

In the Western Cape, a board of control was formed especially to organise the Cape Town leg of the Kenyans' itinerary.

The organisers faced many problems – not least of which was an acute shortage of funds.

There was also a major difference of opinion among officials over the choice of venue for the matches – with one group wanting to accept an invitation from the white WP Cricket Union to play at Newlands and the other pushing for the use of the Hartleyvale football stadium.

Frank Brache, a member of the organising committee, and one of those favouring Newlands, said: "I was against Hartleyvale because it was a football ground – which meant that it didn't have a pitch, its boundaries were too short and the grass on its outfield was too thick."

But Brache was in the minority. Hartleyvale got the vote.

Matt Segers, who voted for playing the Kenyans at the football stadium, said: "We laid the pitch in a very short time – and despite the shortage of money, everything worked out very well for us."

Segers said that although the Kenyan tour highlighted the need for all who were interested in unity to work together, it took a long time for a united WP Cricket Board to get off the ground.

"Religious fanatics on both sides hampered the process," he claimed.

"Nevertheless, the unity process received a major boost when the head-

quarters of the SA Coloured Cricket Association was moved from Kimberley to Cape Town." [It was common knowledge that the majority of officials committed to unity were based in Cape Town.]

A WEST INDIAN CRISIS

Following the successful reciprocal tour to Kenya in 1958 by a team led by Basil D'Oliveira, strong efforts were made to increase the momentum of international contact.

But even so, the announcement that a powerful West Indian side led by Frank Worrell had agreed to tour South Africa in November and December 1959 was initially greeted with stunned disbelief.

Could it really be possible that stars such as Worrell, Everton Weekes, Clyde Walcott, Garfield Sobers, Conrad Hunte, Wes Hall, Charlie Griffiths, Sonny Ramadhin and Basil Butcher were willing to test the mettle of Sacboc's best? But black cricket fans were not dreaming. As far as Sacboc was concerned, the tour was in the bag: visas had been applied for and issued; the South African government had given its approval (because all matches were to be played against a black side).

For this tour, unlike the case with the Kenyans, there were to be no games at soccer stadiums. Agreements had been concluded with white bodies to play matches at grounds such as Newlands and the Wanderers. Indeed, so far advanced were arrangements that even the badges and ties had been made and the programme drawn up. It was just a case of waiting for Worrell's team to arrive.

But trouble was brewing – in the form of a fledgling anti-apartheid organisation named the South African Sports Association (SASA)....

Frank Brache was in favour of using white venues to play matches against touring teams such as the Kenyan Asians.

INTERVENTION BY SASA

The proposed tour presented SASA with its first major crisis – just a few months after its formation in 1958: SASA members were instinctively opposed to anything that gave credibility to the National Party government's policy of separating the races – whether this be in sport, education or residential areas.

They were convinced that, because the planned West Indian visit fitted in with government policy, it had to be opposed.

But there was an awareness, too, that the majority of black cricketers and supporters couldn't wait for Worrell and his team to arrive.

For it simply to barge in and demand the cancellation of the tour (thereby probably enraging a large number of black sports fans) would have placed SASA's ambitions of becoming a mass-based anti-apartheid organisation in jeopardy. What was needed was a carefully worked out strategy that would win the support of the majority of black people.

Dennis Brutus, SASA's secretary at the time, argued that the National Party government and its supporters were happy to support a system in which blacks played matches against blacks and whites against whites.

"This would have allowed South Africa's whites [as the country's official national representatives] to play against England, Australia and New Zealand, while South Africa's blacks [simply as blacks] would play Kenya, Uganda, Guyana, Jamaica and other black nations."

Brutus acknowledged that some South African blacks were keen supporters of this system. "To them it was a way to break into international sport. But we saw it as a backward step that would consolidate apartheid.

"The issue created major conflict. Administrators such as Rashid Varachia and Checker Jassat supported the tour because they had their own interests at heart. Jassat, for example, ran a travel agency – and would have expected the travel arrangements to be entrusted to his company."

Brutus said it took SASA almost a year to turn opinion against the tour. "Getting it cancelled was our major achievement," he said.

He acknowledged, though, that SASA would not have succeeded on its own. "The ANC also played a significant role in mobilising opposition to the visit – as did the SA Indian Congress, the Congress of Democrats and other groups in South Africa and abroad.

The future Rivonia trialist, Ahmed Kathrada came to me and promised that the ANC would call out its Youth League to take part in pitch invasions if the tour was allowed to go ahead," Brutus said. Eventually, opponents of the tour exerted sufficient pressure on both Sacboc and Worrell to force its cancellation.

"The decision to scrap the West Indies visit not only caused unhappiness among many cricketers and officials in South Africa, but, according to Brutus, it was also bitterly criticised in some significant quarters in the West Indies.

He said that CLR James, a leading Caribbean Marxist, had lashed out at him, stating that activists in the islands had been hoping to use the tour to fight racism in the West Indies – racism which at the time was so bad that it blocked a black man from being allowed to captain a West Indies cricket team.

"James argued that if Worrell had successfully captained a team in South Africa, pressure would have

Dennis Brutus played a key role in persuading the South African Cricket Board of Control to cancel a tour to South Africa by the West Indies in 1959.

been put on the West Indian selectors to appoint him captain of the official test side.

"Both of us were fighting racism, but coming from different angles," Brutus said.

Basil D'Oliveira bitterly criticised the decision to call off the West Indies tour of South Africa.

D'OLIVEIRA GOES TO ENGLAND

Basil D'Oliveira, in particular, was bitterly disappointed about the cancellation of the tour, and made his feelings known in a manner that earned him a sharp rebuke from WP cricket officials. D'Oliveira, however, had for a long time set his sights on showing off his talents in England – and from then on, everything he did, revolved around realising this ambition.

D'Oliveira's opportunity to play in the Lancashire League was made possible largely through the efforts of Adam Vasta, a local businessman, Damoo Bansda, an avid cricket fan and journalist, and Ray Robertson, an Australian journalist, who put the South Africans in contact with the influential English cricket commentator, John Arlott.

In a series of letters, D'Oliveira pleaded with Arlott to use his influence to help him secure a contract with an English league side.

Arlott persuaded the Lancashire League club, Middleton, to sign the South African. Middleton laid down one condition, though: D'Oliveira had to pay his own way from Cape Town to England.

The fare for the trip was raised through the proceeds of a series of matches, arranged by Vasta, between provincial-strength black and white teams, at the Claremont cricket ground and at the Green Point Track.

In one match at Claremont, the talented Eric Petersen, bowling off-cutters, destroyed what was virtually the entire white WP Currie Cup team. "Only Gerald Innes could play him," said Sacboc allrounder Coetie Neethling. "The rest were totally confused by Eric's unorthodox grip, and they were stunned by the amount of movement he got out of a pitch that was unresponsive to everyone else.

"Innes was impressed enough to suggest that Eric would walk into the Western Province Currie Cup side," Neethling said.

Petersen wasn't the only black player to impress. A legside stumping of Malcolm Richardson by Lobo Abed, regarded by many as the best wicket-keeper – black or white – of his generation in South Africa, was spoken of in awe for many years afterwards by all who saw it.

With their appetites whetted by the stiffer competition of inter-race tournaments and fund-raising friendlies, many top players began to ask: "Why can't matches involving the province's best cricketers be played regularly as a matter of course?"

FORMATION OF THE WP CRICKET BOARD

Certainly, among black unions there was nothing to stop a system of strength versus strength being introduced, without ethnic or religious constraints.

The crucial question, however, was: who would take the plunge and lead a shake up (if not a shake out) of the moribund group of administrators running the game at both provincial and national level? And if there were people prepared to grab the nettle, who would follow them?

As it turned out, there was no shortage of takers: thanks to the efforts of a new breed of politically - aware young administrators – people such as Abu Desai, Joe Rassool, Matt Segers, Cliffie Ravens, Hassan Howa and John van Harte – the WP Cricket Board was formed on 1 February 1959 at a well-attended meeting in a classroom of the all-girls Immaculata High School in Wynberg.

Because the new body was determined to remove all mention of race from its activities, affiliates which carried their ethnic origins in their titles were persuaded to change their names. Thus, the WP Indian Cricket Union became the United Cricket Union, the WP Bantu Cricket Union became the Langa Cricket Union, the WP Coloured Cricket Union (also sometimes known as the Malay Union) changed its name to the WP Cricket Association and the WP Cricket Association and Country (Coloured) opted to be called the Paarl Cricket Union. Others who joined were Cape District, Central, Cosmopolitan, Maitland-Parow, Paarl Prolific, Stellenbosch and District, Wynberg and District, Hottentots Holland and Somerset West.

"Central joined shortly after the inaugural meeting – and Cape District, after first deciding to stay out, changed its mind when the majority of the Peninsula and Western Districts Cricket Board's units joined," said Segers.

Van Harte was elected the first president of the new board. Other officials were Councillor Hoosain E Parker (deputy president), Desai (secretary), AW le Roux (assistant-secretary), Howa (treasurer) and Alec Anthony (match and registration secretary).

Van Harte proved to be the ideal choice for president. The principal of Athlone North Primary School, he was highly regarded by players and officials across the different racial and religious divides.

Perhaps *the* major decision at the founding meeting was the agreement by all the unions to stop participating in national racial tournaments.

It was agreed, too, that in future, units would be accepted as members only if they rejected any racial affiliations. This was regarded as a major step, since several units were members of national ethnic bodies when the WP Cricket Board was formed.

John van Harte proved to be the ideal choice for president of the Western Province Cricket Board.

"There was a great spirit in the first meeting," said Desai. "It was only later , when people realised that a job had to be done, that the reality of it all sunk in."

"Forming the board was the easy part; getting it to work properly proved to be a different story altogether," said Segers.

PROVINCIAL TEAMS

With so many disparate groupings under one roof (so to speak), the new body had to tread carefully during the first few months of its existence.

Even a bread-and-butter issue such as the selection of a provincial side carried the potential for conflict.

"For instance, in the beginning, it was not unusual for the representative of each union to insist that a player of his union be selected to the side," said Ravens.

The board generally chose the easy – and least troublesome – option: it sanctioned teams with at least one representative from each team. "At times, sides were chosen by up to eight provincial selectors," said Ravens.

In other areas, progress was much more satisfactory: from its inception, the new body displayed an impressive tolerance of religious sensitivities.

"Everybody respected the Friday observance of Muslims – so lunch would be taken between 12 noon and 2pm when matches were played on a Friday," said Ravens. "In the same vein, Sunday games were started after 11am, to allow those players who wanted to go to church to do so."

Muslim teams were also excused from playing during the fast of Ramadaan.

At the board's first annual general meeting in the City Hall on 25 October 1959, delegates recommended that all affiliates quit their respective national bodies. A motion barring any unit from participating in racial tournaments was also formally introduced and passed.

In his 1959-60 secretarial report to delegates at the annual general meeting, Desai spoke about a "very happy atmosphere at most matches".

But there were one or two matters which concerned him. Chief among these was a tendency among players to put club before union.

He believed, however, that there was a way to rectify this problem: he called on the board to introduce a Super League competition between the various unions.

A SUPER LEAGUE

A Super League , with matches played over two days, Desai argued, would be the ideal vehicle to pit strength against strength. "It is the only way of improving our playing standards."

Pointing out that under the present set-up, the benchmark for top players was a place in a provincial team that went on tour only every second year, Desai suggested that a Super League of unions would offer the better players "something more tangible to strive for on the home front – a position higher than the first team".

But, sadly, some of the founder affiliates would not be part of efforts

The cost of being a WP Cricket Board player

IN HIS annual secretarial report in for the 1960-61 season, Sheikh Ganief Booley recorded that all units had to register their players at a cost of 5 cents per player.

Late registration would elicit a fine of R2.

A total of 3 383 players were registered in the WP Cricket Board in the 1960-61 season.

Sheikh Booley reported a surplus of R40.

The board's only income was the affiliation fees and capitation tax, with most of the expenditure going to the Umpires' Association.

to improve the standard of the game. In the 1960/61 season, the Langa Union failed to register due to administrative difficulties. When top administrators such as VC Qunta and others found work elsewhere in the country, there were no ready candidates to take their places.

Although the majority of the predominantly coloured unions struggled to make headway in the face of severe cash shortages and poor facilities, they were many, many times better off than cricketers playing in the African areas.

In his secretarial report, Sheikh Ganief Booley, deputising for Desai (who was unavailable), touched on the Langa Union's plight. Langa, he reported, felt that their administration was not of a sufficiently high standard to warrant participation in a Super League competition, or, indeed, to remain members of the board.

Soon afterwards, the United and Cosmopolitan unions also threw in the towel, while Paarl Prolific and Paarl Union were instructed to merge.

A NEW NATIONAL BODY

The WP Cricket Board's success in uniting the various local bodies – and driving the process of dismantling the racial structures that had underpinned so many of these bodies for so long – encouraged officials to start campaigning for a united, non-racial national body.

In many ways, Sacboc had become an anachronism – a body consisting of a number of racial bodies which were clearly out of kilter with the realities of the country. But, following events in the Western Province, plans to drag Sacboc into a new era progressed quickly. At a conference in Johannesburg on 9 April 1960, Sacboc appointed an eight-man committee to draft a resolution calling for of a single, national non-racial controlling body. The committee's resolution was made up of four proposals:

- That Sacboc's affiliates be provincial units.
- That they be non-racial entities.
- That Sacboc demarcates the playing area of each province.
- That Sacboc should strive for international recognition.

Delegates at the conference suggested that these proposals be implemented in the following way:

- That the provincial units draft and accept a constitution to be approved by Sacboc.
- That Sacboc should convene a meeting in Cape Town in January 1961 to transfer control to the provincial units.

The unflappable Sheikh Booley

MOST WP Cricket Board meetings proceeded smoothly, but there were times when matters became quite heated.

But when that happened, Sheikh Ganief Booley, a highly respected Muslim leader proved to be something of a master of conflict resolution – using rather unconventional methods.

According to Cliff Ravens, if Muslim delegates were involved in a spat with board officials, Sheikh Booley would say: "You can't argue with me – I am the Sheikh!"

"If the disagreement was slightly more serious", said Ravens, "Sheikh Booley would take those involved outside – and soon afterwards they would return to the meeting in total agreement."

"The only person he didn't try this tactic on was Hassan Howa, who was a very stubborn character."

- That the ethnically-based national units should cease to exist immediately (but that they be given six months to conclude outstanding business).

Once these steps had been agreed upon, Sacboc threw all its energies into the establishment of provincial federations throughout the country. In 1961, a highly significant decision was taken at a meeting in Cape Town: under the new dispensation, Sacboc membership would be open only to

Damoo Bansda and his Eaglets Society

IN FEBRUARY 1961, Damoo Bansda was the prime mover in the formation of the South African Eaglets Society, based on a Pakistani model which was responsible to a large degree in developing Pakistan as a cricketing power.

Taking a leaf out of Pakistan's book, the SA Eaglets Society was devoted to the general development of young cricketers.

Among its objectives was to arrange tours to and from South Africa for players under the age of 21, and to arrange for players such as Garfield Sobers, Rohan Kanhai, Basil D'Oliveira and Cecil Abrahams to play in invitation matches throughout South Africa.

Bansda, who was elected president of the society, campaigned for support around the country.

In Cape Town, the SA Eaglets society had an indoor net in District Six, where young cricketers honed their craft under the watchful eye of official coach Basil D'Oliveira .

Sadly, a lack of interest and lack of finance saw the society flounder after a short period of existence.

provincial boards or federations which embraced nonracialism.

BOOM TIMES

During the 1950s and 60s, nonracial cricket experienced a boom. After the successful exchange of tours with the Kenyan Asians, the biennial Dadabhay inter-provincial tournaments produced cricket of a high standard – and this despite poor facilities.

These tournaments were closely watched by Lancashire League scouts and provided an opportunity for players such as Cecil Abrahams, Coetie Neethling, Owen Williams, Dik Abed, Des February, Dickie Conrad and Rushdi Magiet to secure contracts to play in England.

However, many of the top players, including those who went into the Lancashire League, were critical of what they believed to be the inaction of

Basil D'Oliveira, who, in a sense, was Sacboc's Lancashire League pioneer.

There was a unanimous feeling that D'Oliveira, who by then was playing county cricket for Worcestershire, could have done more to help Sacboc players to get to England. He had the influence, it was argued, to help players such as Abed and Abrahams, both of whom had performed well in the leagues, to secure county contracts – but he had done nothing.

D'Oliveira was aware of these criticisms. Writing in the brochure for the 1968 Sacboc tournament in Cape Town, he said: "I have always said that ability-wise there are dozens of cricketers in South Africa who have the potential to become county players if given the opportunity. People turn to me for this sort of assistance, but South Africans must realise that I play six days of the week plus charity games on Sundays, This leaves me no time ... to negotiate on their behalf. It grieves me that I cannot help, but with the added duties of test cricket for England, I have now less time even to see my family.

"However, I am confident there are responsible people in this country who can negotiate on their behalf, one of whom is my mentor (DN Bansda)."

THE GROUP AREAS ACT

In the 1960s, while the WP Cricket Board was flourishing as a nonracial organisation, more and more black people were beginning to feel the effects of apartheid legislation. In the 1965/66 season, the end-of-season function of the board had to be moved from the Claremont Civic Centre to the Railway Institute in Salt River because venues located in white areas were declared out of bounds to black organisations.

From 1965, traditionally white venues such as the Hartleyvale

Stadium, Green Point stadium and Newlands were required to be in possession of government permits to allow blacks to watch matches. Permits were granted only if the administrators of these stadiums agreed to build fences to separate white spectators from black – something which the majority readily agreed to do. This resulted in a boycott of white venues by many black sports fans.

D'Oliveira, who had gained selection to the England side which played a series against the West Indies in 1965, and who had returned to South Africa at the end of 1966 to run a countrywide series of coaching clinics, was unwittingly caught up in the furore over permits.

On 22 and 23 January 1967, many white spectators, eager to see the new England international in action, were barred from watching a match between a D'Oliveira XI and an Invitation XI at Green Point Track – because the WP Cricket Board had refused to apply for a permit.

More than 6 000 spectators turned up to watch D'Oliveira score 66 and 33 in masterly fashion, before being dismissed in both innings by the Transvaaler Tiffie Barnes. Omar Vawda, a bright young prospect from Natal, playing in D'Oliveira's XI, showed his class with a polished half-century, while Dik Abed shone with both bat and ball.

INCENTIVES FOR CLUBS
In an effort to stimulate interest in the local game and provide opportunities for club players, the Fester Trophy competition for the champion clubs in the respective unions was reintroduced in the 1965/66 season.

Oakdale of Cape District won the trophy when they beat Pirates (WP

Cricket Association) in the final. Previously, only clubs affiliated to the Peninsula and Western Districts Cricket Board competed for the trophy.

To provide more players with an opportunity to play at a higher level, a two-day Super League competition was launched in the 1966/67 season.

Ironically, the Green Point Track-based Western Province Cricket Association, which a few years earlier had campaigned so strongly for its introduction, and Cape District, did not participate because they were unhappy with the format of the competition. This left the competition without two of the WP Cricket Board's strongest units.

Matches were played over two Saturdays on a home and away basis. Maitland-Parow, led by Coetie Neethling, were the inaugural winners. The other participants were Metropolitan, Somerset West and Wynberg.

Robbie van Graan, the stylish Metropolitan batsman, became the first player to score a century in the Super League when he made 128 against Somerset West. Super League matches between the city unions and their country counterparts were always needle affairs with the country players keen on putting one over "the stiffies" as the city players were known.

JUNIOR CRICKET
The board's first junior games were organised during the 1966/67 season, and shortly afterwards the *Cape Herald* newspaper wrote: "Cricket for juniors is rapidly becoming the rule rather than the exception. Most of the leading unions have now commenced to cater for the needs of the youngsters and last Saturday Metropolitan staged their first fixtures."

Prior to that, there had been no formal cricket for juniors, and youngsters who wanted to play cricket had to play in the senior teams.

An under-21 section, which was run on the same basis as the Super League, proved a great success and was an important motivating factor for emerging players. When a WP under-21 side visited Kimberley in 1967, the value of catering for players in this age group was underlined when Gertjie Williams' team beat Griqualand West's senior side.

Although the WP Cricket Board could boast of steady growth in numbers, as well as a high degree of interest, the facilities under which their players were expected to perform were less than satisfactory – especially when compared with that enjoyed by their white counterparts.

These inequalities moved the *Cape Herald* to write on 27 February 1965: "The struggle for a fairer deal and better facilities has been long and arduous. Our sports administrators have achieved wonders during the last few years, but they have succeeded only in a small measure to alleviate the many problems ... which confront our sportsmen on all sides.

"In a few isolated instances modern facilities have been acquired, but for many the position remains unaltered, and sport has to exist under most inadequate conditions."

After the long and sometimes difficult road to achieve unity among the various religious and ethnic groups in Cape Town, the Western Province Cricket Board had by the end of the 1960s been able to organise nonracial cricket effectively in the Western Cape. But other challenges were looming on the horizon....

Part 2

The Dadabhay interprovincials

Here is a little poser for all you armchair experts. At which Dadabhay tournament did Western Province Cricket Board manager Hassiem Edross arm his players with water pistols – and why?

The answer is simple (or, rather, it ought to be, if you're a fundi who closely followed the fortunes of the South African Cricket Board of Control in the 1960s).

It was the one held in Kimberley – in 1969 – and Mr Edross was demonstrating the type of innovation that all good teams would expect from their managers: he'd dipped his hand into the petty cash envelope to buy water pistols to enable his hard-pressed players to cool themselves down.

That summer, Kimberley, the host venue for what proved to be Sacboc's final centralised

tournament, was roasting in a heatwave. It was 50°C in the middle of the bone-hard playing surface of the Eddie Williams Oval – and the tempers of many of the players were as frayed as some of the matting that covered the wickets.

Playing conditions – the heat, the uneven outfield and a powdery pitch, which the *Cape Herald* said "was kept together only by the grace of spiked boots – were sharply criticised by a host of players, led by star Western Province allrounder Dik Abed.

"I would have withdrawn from the side if I had known that we were going to play under such atrocious conditions," Abed said.

Despite the conditions, Western Province won (they were joint winners with Transvaal on this occasion) – just as they had done three times in a row before that. In fact, the Capetonians had lost out only once since the inception of the competition, finishing runners-up to Transvaal in the inaugural tournament in 1961/62.

A NEW SACBOC – A NEW BROOM

When the reconstituted Sacboc – shed of the racial trappings of the past – came into being in 1961, one of the first priorities that the new body set itself was the launch of a centralised inter-provincial tournament.

In 1961/62, the new-look Dadabhay Brothers tournament came into being.

That Sacboc was able to hold a nonracial tournament so soon after its relaunch was seen in some quarters as being "nothing short of miraculous".

"How many of us ever thought that this could be accomplished in such a short time? But things move rapidly these days," was how WP Cricket Board president John van Harte described the development.

Five biennial tournaments were held between 1961 and 1970 – in Johannesburg, Port Elizabeth, Durban, Cape Town and Kimberley.

In the beginning, the various Dadabhay representatives regarded these inter-provincial matches as the ideal opportunity for the top players to show off their talents to scouts of the growing number of Lancashire League clubs who were beginning to show an interest in Sacboc players.

The players themselves enjoyed the contact with their peers from other provinces – and for many it was an opportunity to renew old friendships as well as to test their strength against some of the best players in the country. But it soon became apparent to Sacboc that theirs was not a perfect system.

THE GOOD AND THE FRANKLY DREADFUL

The Kimberley tourney in 1969 emphasised all that was good and bad in Sacboc's centralised showpiece (although, it had become quite clear that the bad was by now far beginning to outweigh the good).

That fans of the host province had the opportunity of seeing all the country's top black cricketers together at a single venue continued to be regarded as a major plus. And even though playing conditions at the different centres varied from indifferent to bad, the classier players continued to deliver performances of a high standard.

A major criticism, though, was the duration of the tournament: two weeks away from family and work – coupled with the harsh physical punishment that a daily diet of cricket inflicted on often not very young bodies – was a sacrifice that many players started finding increasingly difficult to make.

By the time the last tournament was played in 1969, the growing number of withdrawals, had convinced Sacboc that the time had arrived for something different".

A new home-and-away competition was approved on the understanding that a round trip should cost no more than R1 000, and that the host union should provide free accommodation for their visitors.

Masters of a less than perfect competition

WITH HOME GROUND advantage, and with members of their team in compelling form, Transvaal were expected to coast to victory in the inaugural Dadabhay Brothers inter-provincial tournament in Johannesburg in 1961/62.

The confidence of the hosts was understandable: just a few weeks earlier, several members of their side had played a key role in a stunning victory by a South African Haque XI over a Johnny Waite XI loaded with big (white) names such as Ali Bacher, Russell Endean, Peter Carlstein, Jackie Botten and Mike Macauley.

Although the star-studded Transvaalers eventually took the honours, the mauling they suffered in the first innings of their opening match against their arch-rivals, Western Province, rankled them for a long time afterwards.

Western Province's early blitz was orchestrated by two old hands – left-arm spinner Owen Williams and explosive all-rounder (and captain) Tiny Abed.

Williams, whose expertise was built upon the tried-and-tested combination of deadly accuracy, subtle changes of pace and flight, and his ability to extract wicked turn from most wickets, claimed 5/37 as Transvaal stumbled to 147 in their first innings. Abed, too, gave warning that he was on song, with a workmanlike bowling performance that earned him 3/29.

Abed was in imposing form when Western Province went in to bat, plundering exactly 100 not out as Western Province fought their way (not without some difficulty) to 265. Of the rest of the batsmen, only Laam Raziet, at

the top of the order, and Williams, at the bottom, passed 30.

Transvaal, chastened by their dismal effort in their first innings, applied themselves infinitely better in their second knock, reaching 253/5 before declaring.

Western Province (24/1) were happy to bat out time – and so take first innings points.

Having outmanoeuvred the favourites, the Capetonians would have been reasonably confident of taking the honours. All that was required of them was to beat the supposedly less challenging Eastern Province, Natal and Griqualand West.

But the warning bells quickly began to ring. Although they won their second match against Eastern Province by what, on paper, seemed a comfortable 147 runs, their first innings total of 78 suggested that there were worrying chinks in their batting armour.

Their sudden dip in batting confidence continued against Natal, whom Transvaal had earlier thrashed by 122 runs....

Two mediocre batting efforts, which realised just 131 and 162, saw them tumble to defeat by 18 runs, to allow the grateful Transvaalers to sneak in through the back door.

The highlight of the tournament for Western Province, came in their last match when Ivan D'Oliveira (the younger brother of Basil) and Graham

Western Province skipper Tiny Abed scored a fine, undefeated century and took three wickets as Western Province beat arch-rivals Transvaal in the first match of the inaugural Dadabhay Brothers tournament in the 1961/62 season.

Jardine wrote themselves into the Dadabhay record books with an opening stand of 283 against the hapless Griqualand West.

Griquas were dismissed for 77 and 155 in reply to Western Province's mammoth 382/3 declared.

The Western Province team which played in the first Sacboc non-racial tournament, in Johannesburg in the 1961/62 season were:
(Standing, left to right)
I Behardien, G Jardine, N Lakay, I D'Oliveira, A Maclons, H Carelse, B Kleintjies.
(Seated, left to right)
O Williams, D Mulder, J Neethling (vice-captain), J Carelse (manager), G Abed (captain), S Raziet, J Sylvester.

There was some off-the-field drama too: Eric Petersen was sent home before the first match, after a bust-up with some members of the Western Province contingent – the culmination of a feud which apparently had its origins in Kenya in 1958.

The choice of replacement – fast bowler Pettie Dollie – served only to fan the flames of controversy caused by Petersen's expulsion. Dollie, who wasn't even in the team, and, in fact, was attending the tournament as a spectator, was pressed into action against Transvaal – much to the dismay of other squad members.

PORT ELIZABETH
In 1963/64, in Port Elizabeth, Western Province demonstrated their awesome strength in depth – again and again and... well, five times.

Under the astute leadership of left-arm spinner, Owen Williams, they crushed all-comers – traditional rivals

such as Transvaal, Natal and Eastern Province, as well as provincial debutants such as Border and South Western Districts.

In their first game against Natal, Coetie Neethling smashed 98 – his highest Dadabhay score. Together with Salie "Lobo" Abed (72), he added 121 for the fifth wicket as Western Province posted a healthy first innings total of 286. Then, to show what a fine allrounder he was, Neethling (3/10) formed a lethal right-left bowling combination with Colin (Waleed) Joshua (3/6), to skittle Natal for 63 in the first innings.

In their second innings, the Natalians continued to reel under the cosh of a relentless Western Province attack. With legspinner Norman Abrahams (the brother of South African Cricket Board of Control great Cecil Abrahams) leading the charge with 3/21, Natal were again shot out in their second innings – this time registering a paltry 77.

Western Province's easy victory against Natal set the tone for the rest of the tournament.

In the next game against South Western Districts, Owen Williams claimed seven wickets for just six runs.

Ironically, South Western District's first innings total of 22, a record low for a Dadabhay match, came just a few days after their 467 – a record high for the tournament – against Border.

Centuries by Des February (110) and Yusuf "Timmy" Lakay (103 not out), who put on 132 for the fifth wicket, took Western Province to 388/7 against Border. The Eastern Cape side, newcomers to the competition, were bamboozled by the spin of Gertjie Williams, and tumbled to scores of 29 and 47. Williams returned the incredible figures of 8/11 in 4,3 overs, in the Border first innings.

The by now rampant Western Province side then comfortably beat hosts Eastern Province by 85 runs, with February (53), Owen Williams (5/25) and Colin (Waleed) Joshua (4/6) being the stand-out performers. Set to score a moderate 154 for victory, after Western Province had made 154 and 114, Eastern Province struggled against the left-arm seamers of Joshua and were bundled out for 79 in their second innings, having made just 104 in their first knock.

Owen Williams continued his great form in the next match against Griqualand West, claiming 5/18 in the Griquas second innings as Western Province strode to victory by 10 wickets. Williams ended the tournament with 35 wickets at a cost of four runs per wicket. Another left-hander, the appropriately named Lefty Adams, also had a highly satisfactory tournament. Playing for Griqualand West, Adams claimed 22 wickets, including a haul of 5/60 against Western Province and a tournament best of 8/82 (including a hat trick) against South Western Districts.

Western Province's last match, against the defending champions, Transvaal, was an anti-climax. After holding a slender one run lead at the end of the first innings, Transvaal were bundled out for 59 in their second knock. With Neville Lakay taking 3/6 to add to his first innings haul of 5/19, and with Owen Williams weighing in with 4/14, Western Province were left with the simple task of scoring 60 for victory.

Openers Dickie Conrad and Howie Carelse put on 41 to take Western Province within 17 runs of victory. Conrad (43 not out) clouted off-spinner Gamba Johannessie for a four and a six to clinch a comfortable nine-wicket victory for his team.

Neethling, who along with fellow all-rounder Neville Lakay, was the only Western Province player to have played in all five centralised tournaments, headed the batting averages with 39,14 (highest score 98); he also took 11 wickets at a cost of 7,90.

Looking back on his career almost 40 years later, Neethling hailed the 1963/64 Western Province Dadabhay side as "the best Western Province team I've ever played in".

"We had some quality players who had great technique and skills. It was amazing to see how well they performed under extremely poor conditions," he said.

DURBAN

There was no Owen Williams in the Western Province side which travelled to Durban in 1966 to defend their title. Like Basil D'Oliveira, Goolam Abed and Cecil Abrahams before him, Williams had decided to take the foot-in-the-door opportunity that Lancashire League cricket offered – and then to play it by ear after that.

Under their new captain, Salie "Lobo" Abed, Western Province managed just one victory – an eight-wicket triumph over hosts Natal – but it was enough for them to retain the honours.

Opening batsman Dickie Conrad provided the best individual performance for the champions, compiling an exquisite 194 against Griquas in the tournament opener, before being run-out by the Joey Lambert who, according to Conrad, felt that he had batted long enough. Conrad and Neville Lakay (84) put on 210 for the second wicket as WP powered their way to 337/4 declared, in reply to the Griquas first innings total of 76.

Griquas' first and second innings were as different as chalk and cheese. The team which had found Rushdien

Dickie Conrad hit a career-best 194 for Western Province against Griqualand West

Neville Lakay was Western Province's top batsman in the 1968 tournament in Cape Town.

Alexander (6/39) unplayable in their first knock, dominated the Western Province attack in their second: spearheaded by a superb 104 from Solly Saloojee, they reached 288, to restrict Western Province to a first-innings victory.

In the next match, Des February (6/40) and Alexander (3/19) skittled Natal for 62.

Western Province, thanks to Neville Lakay (64) and Les Martin (48), replied with 220 – a big enough insurance policy against defeat. But would it be enough to set them up for victory? Although the hosts fared much better in their second innings to make 251 (Coetie Neethling 5/32), their lead of 92 wasn't enough to stop Western Province from strolling to an easy eight-wicket win, thanks to stand-out performances from Lambert (50 not out) and Martin (32).

Requiring only first innings points in their last game against Transvaal, to retain the title, Western Province overhauled the Transvaal total of 167, reaching 189, thanks to solid contributions from Joey Lambert (37), Gertjie Williams (33) and Taliep Behardien (32). Coetie Neethling recorded his best Dadabhay bowling figures of 7/58 as Transvaal struggled to 138/8 declared in their second innings, leaving Western Province with insufficient time to reach 117 to win.

CAPE TOWN

In the 1968 tournament in Cape Town, Western Province went into battle with a severely weakened team. Several key players were ineligible for selection following the decision by their parent body, the Green Point-based Western Province Cricket Association, not to participate in the inter-union Super League competition because they objected to the structure of the league.

Despite the absence of players such as Lobo and Dik Abed, as well as star opening batsman Dickie Conrad, Western Province won comfortably by 10 wickets against Natal, and by an innings against Eastern Province, Griqualand West and Southern Cape.

But their winning march was brought to a rude halt by their old rivals, Transvaal, who after scoring 262, blasted them out for 132, and then asked them to follow on.

A fine 119 by Neville Lakay, who together with Mornay "Kulu" Maclons (93), added 140 for the third wicket, and helped Western Province regain their pride with 325/7 in their second innings.

By restricting Transvaal to first innings points, Western Province completed a hat trick of Dadabhay tournament victories (since the Transvaalers could only manage first innings wins over Eastern Province and Natal).

Lakay (263) finished second to Transvaal's Tiffie Barnes (287) as the highest runscorer, while Maclons (51,50) and Johnny le Roux (51,33) occupied the first two places on the batting averages table. (Le Roux emigrated to Australia in 1970.)

Lefty Adams, with 35 wickets at an average of 7,40 per wicket, was the top wicket taker – some distance ahead of Transvaal's Solly Chothia, who claimed 23 scalps.

KIMBERLEY

The last centralised Dadabhay tournament, in Kimberley in 1969 was a bittersweet occasion for Dik Abed. Having returned from England after a superb season with Enfield in the Lancashire League, Abed simply oozed class.

Although he struck a masterful 145 – Western Province's best individual

The Western Province team which won the Dadabhay Trophy in Port Elizabeth in the 1963/64 season.
Back row, left to right: F Anthony, C Joshua, H Carelse, A Maclons, G Williams, D February, N Abrahams.
Middle: SL Abed, G Abed, Sheikh MG Booley (manager), O Williams (captain), J Neethling.
Front: Y Lakay, S Conrad.

The cricket-loving Dadabhays

The Dadabhay Brothers Trophy was first presented to the South African Cricket Board of Control (Sacboc) in 1952.

The Dadabhays, a wealthy family, who were leaders in the textile industry, had the jug-eared sterling silver trophy made in London at a cost of around £2000.

The trophy was first played for at the second Sacboc inter-race tournament in Johannesburg in 1953, and became the board's premier competition until the mid-1970s.

In the 1975/76 season it was replaced, amid much controversy, by an inter-provincial competition sponsored by Stellenbosch Farmers Winery.

Aggrieved members of the Dadabhay family said no reason was given for the shelving of the trophy.

Gertjie Williams emerged as a valuable allrounder for Western Province from around the mid-Sixties onwards.

Ivan Dagnin hit a rich vein of form in the Kimberley tournament, compiling 321 runs at an average of over 54.

performance – out of a massive 424 against Transvaal, he was far from happy with the facilities that had been provided.

And he made his feelings known in no uncertain terms....

In an interview with the *Cape Herald* newspaper, Abed said he would have withdrawn from the Western Province side had he known what the conditions would be like.

"How can anybody be expected to do his best on such wickets, in such blistering heat, with so many organisational lapses?" he wanted to know.

The *Cape Herald* correspondent, in concurring with Abed, described the wicket as "powdery, loose and crumbling. It was held together only by the grace of spiked boots," the reporter said, adding that the only consolation was that the short boundaries enabled Abed to hit the ball out of the ground so often "that it provided players with the chance to shelter from the blistering heat".

The heat – temperatures on some days were measured at 50°C – restricted the quicker bowlers to a maximum of five overs each.

In fact, on one day it was so hot that the Western Province manager, Hassiem Edross, went out to buy water pistols for his players so that they could use them to keep themselves cool on the field!

Although Western Province tied for honours with Transvaal, all the individual honours went to the men from the Cape.

Opener Ivan Dagnin, with 321 runs at an average of 64,2, was the tournament's top scorer. The batting averages table was headed by the ever-consistent Coetie Neethling, who, with two undefeated knocks in three innings, was able to post an average of 151 per innings.

Abed's 145 (he retired because of the heat) was the highest individual score at the tournament.

Lefty Adams took the most wickets (31), while his spin twin Owen Williams headed the bowling averages with 22 wickets at an average of 9,1 each.

In many ways, the chaotic events at the Kimberley tourney, swung the pendulum in favour of the argument of a growing number of South African Cricket Board of Control members, who felt that the time had arrived to scrap centralised tournaments – and replace them with a new home-and-away-competition for the senior provincial sides.

Later, Sacboc approved the new format, on the understanding that a round trip would cost no more than R1000, and that the host union would provide free accommodation for their visitors.

Great start by Western Province – but then they let it slip

WP Dadabhay scorecards 1961/62 in Johannesburg

Western Province vs Transvaal

Transvaal 147 (Owen Williams 5/37; Tiny Abed 3/29) and 253/5 declared
(R Khota 83 not out; H Abrahams 71)
Western Province 265 (Tiny Abed 100 not out; Owen Williams 34; Laam Raziet 32;
AL Barnes 3/46; A Rubidge 3/65) and 24/1
Western Province won on the first innings

Western Province vs Eastern Province

Western Province 78 (P Snyman 6/13) and 304 (Laam Raziet 93; Ivan D'Oliveira 76;
Tiny Abed 56 not out; G Connolly 3/50; P Smith 3/58)
Eastern Province 134 (G Connolly 35 not out; F Abrahams 35; Alan Maclons 4/37;
Coetie Neethling 4/43) and 101 (P Smith 38; Bennie Kleintjies 6/22)
Western Province won by 147 runs

Western Province vs Natal

Natal 195 (I Laher 44; Y Laher 33; B Seedat 33; M Boomgard 32; Alan Maclons 4/24) and
116/9 (E Laher 39; Owen Williams 3/14)
Western Province 131 (OFE Sader 4/59; T Parusaraman 3/39) and 162 (Ivan D'Oliveira 60;
Owen Williams 44; OFE Sader 4/59; T Parusaraman 3/39)
Natal won by 18 runs

Western Province vs Griqualand West

Griqualand West 77 (Neville Lakay 3/14; Pettie Dollie 3/29) and 155 (R Kader 72 not out;
Neville Lakay 6/43; Owen Williams 3/50)
Western Province 382/3 declared (Ivan D'Oliveira 145; Graham Jardine 132;
Howie Carelse 55 not out)
Western Province won by an innings and 150 runs

Transvaal won the Dadabhay Tournament

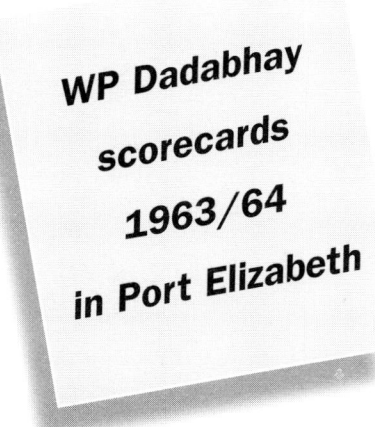

WP Dadabhay scorecards 1963/64 in Port Elizabeth

"The best Western Province team I've ever played in" – Coetie Neethling

Western Province vs Natal

Western Province 285 (Coetie Neethling 98; Lobo Abed 72; Dik Abed 31 not out; Timmy Lakay 28; Neville Lakay 25; A Kajee 3/48; T Parusaraman 3/77)
Natal 63 (E Laher 16; Y Laher 11; Coetie Neethling 3/10; Colin Joshua 3/21; Alan Maclons 2/8; Dik Abed 2/12) and, followed on, 77 (E Laher 23; B Nassiep 14; Norman Abrahams 3/21; Neville Lakay 2/7)
Western Province won by an innings and 145 runs

Western Province vs South Western Districts

South Western Districts 22 (Owen Williams 6/7) and 94 (Kulu Maclons 43; Owen Williams 4/22; Norman Abrahams 3/18)
Western Province 202 (Dickie Conrad 58; Frank Anthony 45; Howie Carelse 36)
Western Province won by an innings and 86 runs

Western Province vs Border

Western Province 387 (Des February 110; Timmy Lakay 103 not out; Coetie Neethling 55; Lobo Abed 37; Howie Carelse 34; M Jacobs 4/140
Border 29 (Gertjie Williams 8/11) and 47 (Timmy Lakay 3/10; Colin Joshua 2/3; Des February 2/10)
Western Province won by an innings and 311 runs

Western Province vs Eastern Province

Western Province 154 (Des February 53; Dik Abed 26; Coetie Neethling 23; P Snyman 4/29; N Francis 2/12) and 114 (Dik Abed 23; Coetie Neethling 20; P Snyman 5/33; N Francis 3/22)
Eastern Province 104 (M Wilson 35; A Douglas 22; Owen Williams 5/25; Coetie Neethling 4/31) and 79 (N Francis 35; Colin Joshua 4/6; Dik Abed 2/9; Coetie Neethling 2/15)
Western Province won by 85 runs

Western Province vs Griqualand West

Griqualand West 94 (K Saloojee 40; Owen Williams 3/14; Dik Abed 2/13; Coetie Neethling 2/7) and 57 (I Kajee 23; Owen Williams 5/18; Dik Abed 4/16)
Western Province 143 (Des February 54; Lobo Abed 13; Y Bhayat 4/34) and 9/0
Western Province won by 10 wickets

Western Province vs Transvaal

Transvaal 81 (S Chothia 19; I Joseph 17 not out; Neville Lakay 5/19; Owen Williams 3/25) and 59 (S Chothia 16; H Cassim 15; Owen Williams 4/14; Neville Lakay 3/6; Dik Abed 2/13)
Western Province 80 (Dickie Conrad 24; Coetie Neethling 24; H Ayob 5/30; AL Barnes 4/20) and 61/1 (Dickie Conrad 43 not out)
Western Province win by 9 wickets
Western Province won the Dadabhay Tournament

Dickie Conrad's batting is the highlight of a hard-fought Western Province triumph

WP Dadabhay scorecards 1966 in Durban

Western Province vs Griqualand West

Griqualand West 76 (D Richards 26; Rushdien Alexander 6/39) and 288 (S Saloojee 104; Gertjie Williams 4/59; Joey Lambert 3/32; Lefty Adams 3/66)
Western Province 337/4 declared (Dickie Conrad 194; Neville Lakay 84)
Western Province won on the first innings

Western Province vs Transvaal

Transvaal 167 (M Saleh 28; A Bhamjee 25; Neville Lakay 4/33; Coetie Neethling 3/57; Des February 2/12) and 138/8 declared (A Kirsten 40; A Moola 32; AL Barnes 28; Coetie Neethling 7/58)
Western Province 189 (Joey Lambert 37; Gertjie Williams 33; Taliep Behardien 32; A Moola 3/35; AL Barnes 3/49; H Ayob 3/58) and 6/0
Western Province won on the first innings

Western Province vs Natal

Natal 62 (D Asmal 14; Des February 6/40; Rushdien Alexander 3/19) and 251 (J Govender 90; O Vawda 41; M Patrick 38; Coetie Neethling 5/32; Rushdien Alexander 2/46)
Western Province 220 (Neville Lakay 64; Les Martin 48; Dik Abed 29; Coetie Neethling 26 not out; I Ebrahim 4/48) and 95/2 (Joey Lambert 50 not out; Les Martin 30)
Western Province won by eight wickets

Western Province won the Dadabhay Tournament

WP Dadabhay scorecards 1968 in Cape Town

Lefty Adams' bowling sets up victory for severely weakened home side

Western Province vs Natal

Natal 121 (M Patrick 32; Ismail Tromp 4/36; Lefty Adams 3/13) and 139 (MS Randeree 44; O Vawda 40; Lefty Adams 4/37)
Western Province 235 (Neville Lakay 44; Viccie Moodie 39; Des February 32; G Manicum 5/62) and 28/0
Western Province won by 8 wickets

Western Province vs Eastern Province

Eastern Province 165 (A Douglas 56; N Francis 36; Des February 7/40) and 97 (Lefty Adams 5/16)
Western Province 389 (Johnny le Roux 104 not out; Coetie Neethling 70; Kulu Maclons 59; Des February 47; M Wilson 3/49)
Western Province won by an innings and 127 runs

Western Province vs Griqualand West

Griqualand West 47 (Ismail Tromp 4/13; Lefty Adams 4/10) and 72 (Lefty Adams 6/25)
Western Province 227 (Gertjie Williams 68 not out; Coetie Neethling 40; AL Cader 3/11)
Western Province won by an innings and 108 runs

Western Province vs Southern Cape

Southern Cape 55 (Lefty Adams 6/21; Pettie Dollie 3/10) and 39 (Coetie Neethling 4/11)
Western Province 261 (Neville Lakay 62; Gertjie Williams 46; Kulu Maclons 43; Pettie Dollie 40)
Western Province won by an innings and 167 runs

Western Province vs Transvaal

Transvaal 262 (AL Barnes 86; S Cajee 57; S Chothia 55; H Ayob 40; Lefty Adams 4/81; Ismail Tromp 3/40)
Western Province 132 (Kulu Maclons 49; H Ayob 4/40; H Jairam 3/16) and, followed on, 325/7 (Neville Lakay 119; Kulu Maclons 93; Viccie Moodie 41; H Ayob 4/70)
Transvaal won on the first innings

Western Province won the Dadabhay Tournament

Old enemies tie for honours in last centralised Dadabhay tournament

Western Province vs Griqualand West

Griqualand West 90 (C Jacobs 44; Dik Abed 4/28; Gertjie Williams 2/11; Owen Williams 2/12) and 97 (Lefty Adams 5/25; Dik Abed 3/29)

Western Province 115 (Ivan Dagnin 26; R Engelbrecht 6/49; S Saloojee 4/56) and 75/1 (Ivan Dagnin 36 not out; Dickie Conrad 34)

Western Province won by 9 wickets

Western Province vs Eastern Province

Western Province 212 (Coetie Neethling 91 not out, E Clarke 4/74) and 201/4 declared (Ivan Dagnin 82, Lefty Adams 50 not out)

Eastern Province 159 (Lefty Adams 6/45) and 126 (Coetie Neethling 4/28; Dik Abed 4/42)

Western Province won by 128 runs

Western Province vs Natal

Natal 135 and 221/8 (J Govender 126, Coetie Neethling 5/58)

Western Province 335/6 declared (Dickie Conrad 104, Kulu Maclons 72, Kenny (Karriem) Rodriques 56)

Western Province won on the first innings

Western Province vs Transvaal

Western Province 424 (Dik Abed 145 not out; Dickie Conrad 93; Coetie Neethling 52 not out; Neville Lakay 48; Ivan Dagnin 30)

Transvaal 122 (I Garda 47; Owen Williams 6/22) and 152/8 (A Gabru 54; AL Barnes 39; Owen Williams 4/40; Lefty Adams 3/42)

Western Province won on the first innings

Western Province vs South Western Districts

South Western Districts 93 (D Walburgh 40; Owen Williams 5/27; Lefty Adams 5/40) and 77 (Lefty Adams 7/27; Owen Williams 2/23)

Western Province 204/3 declared (Ivan Dagnin 100 not out; Kulu Maclons 64)

Western Province won by an innings and 34 runs

Western Province and Transvaal were joint winners of the Dadabhay Trophy

Dadabhay statistics (1961-1969/70) and two-day interprovincials (1970/71)

Partnership records

1st Wicket: 283 – Ivan D'Oliveira (145) and Graham Jardine (132) vs Griqualand West in Johannesburg, 1961/62

2nd Wicket: 210 – Dickie Conrad (194) and Neville Lakay (83) vs Griqualand West in Durban, 1965/66

3rd Wicket: 153 – Ivan Dagnin (100 not out) and Kulu Maclons (64) vs South Western Districts in Kimberley, 1969/70

4th Wicket: 120 – Dickie Conrad (104) and Kulu Maclons (72) vs Natal in Kimberley, 1969/70

5th Wicket: 132 – Timmy Lakay (103 not out) and Des February (110) vs Border in Port Elizabeth, 1963/64

6th Wicket: 164 – Dik Abed (145 retired) and Coetie Neethling (52 not out) vs Transvaal in Kimberley, 1969/70

7th Wicket: 121 – Coetie Neethling (98) and Lobo Abed (72) vs Natal in Port Elizabeth, 1963/64

8th Wicket: 81 – Pettie Dollie and Gertjie Williams vs South Western Districts in Cape Town, 1967/68

9th Wicket: 83 – Lefty Adams (52) and Lobo Abed (29) vs Natal in Durban, 1970/71

10th Wicket: 54 – Lobo Abed (27 not out) and Gertjie Williams (33) vs Transvaal in Durban 1965/66

Centuries (1961-69) and two-day matches (1970)

194 not out – Dickie Conrad vs Griqualand West, 1966

145 not out – Dik Abed vs Transvaal, 1969/70

145 – Ivan D'Oliveira vs Griqualand West, 1961/62

132 – Graham Jardine vs Griqualand West, 1961/62

119 – Neville Lakay vs Transvaal, 1968

110 – Des February vs Border 1963/64

107 not out – Johnny le Roux vs Eastern Province, 1968

104 – Dickie Conrad vs Natal 1969/70

103 not out – Timmy Lakay vs Border, 1963/64

100 not out – Tiny Abed vs Transvaal, 1961/62

100 not out – Ivan Dagnin vs South Western Districts, 1969/70

10 Wickets in a Match

Lefty Adams – 12/67 (5/40 & 7/27) vs South Western Districts, 1969

Owen Williams – 11/28 (7/6 & 4/22) vs South Western Districts, 1963/64

Lefty Adams – 10/35 (4/10 & 6/25) vs Griqualand West, 1968

Owen Williams – 10/62 (6/22 & 4/40) vs Transvaal 1969/70

Coetie Neethling – 10/115 (3/57 & 7/58) vs Transvaal, 1966

The Adams and Williams show – with some useful performances by the supporting cast

5 or more wickets in an Innings

8/11 – Gertjie Williams vs Border, 1963/64

7/6 – Owen Williams vs South Western Districts, 1963/64

7/27 – Lefty Adams vs South Western Districts, 1969/70

7/40 – Des February vs Eastern Province 1968

7/58 – Coetie Neethling vs Transvaal, 1966

6/21 – Lefty Adams vs Southern Cape, 1968

6/22 – Bennie Kleintjies vs Eastern Province, 1961/62

6/22 – Owen Williams vs Transvaal 1969/70

6/25 – Lefty Adams vs Griqualand West, 1968

6/39 – Rushdien Alexander vs Griqualand West, 1966

6/40 – Des February vs Natal, 1966

6/43 – Neville Lakay vs Griqualand West, 1961/62

6/45 – Lefty Adams vs Eastern Province 1969/70

5/16 – Lefty Adams vs Eastern Province, 1968

5/18 – Owen Williams vs Griqualand West, 1963/64

5/19 – Neville Lakay vs Transvaal, 1963/64

5/25 – Owen Williams vs Eastern Province, 1963/64

5/25 – Lefty Adams vs Griqualand West, 1969/70

5/27 – Alan Maclons vs South Western Districts, 1963/64

5/27 – Owen Williams vs South Western Districts, 1969/70

5/32 – Coetie Neethling vs Natal, 1966

5/37 – Owen Williams vs Transvaal 1961/62

5/40 – Lefty Adams vs South Western Districts, 1969/70

5/58 – Coetie Neethling vs Natal 1969/70

Most 5-wicket hauls

7 – Lefty Adams

6 – Owen Williams

3 – Coetie Neethling

2 – Neville Lakay, Des February

1 – Gertjie Williams, Rushdien Alexander, Alan Maclons, Bennie Kleintjies

Batting averages
1961-1969/70
two-day games
1970/71

The other D'Oliveira – Ivan – tops the batting averages for Western Province

Name	Innings	No	Runs	Highest	ScoreAve
I D'Oliveira	6	0	348	145 v Griqualand West 1961/62	58,00
J Lambert	4	2	112	50 v Natal 1966	56,0
G Jardine	3	0	166	132 v Griqualand West 1961/62	55,33
G "Tiny" Abed	5	2	161	100* v Transvaal 1961/62	53,66
J Le Roux	4	1	154	104* v Eastern Province 1968	51,33
S Conrad	16	1	719	194 v Griqualand West 1964	47,93
**M Maclons	10	0	404	93 v Transvaal 1968	40,40
Y Lakay	5	1	143	103* v Border 1963/6	35,75
J Neethling	23	4	615	98 v Natal 1963/64	32,37
S Raziet	6	1	153	93 v Eastern Province 1961/62	30,60
S "Dik" Abed	15	1	418	145* v Transvaal 1969/70	29,85
I Dagnin	16	2	415	100 v South Western Districts 1969/70	29,64
AL Adams	14	4	272	55 v Transvaal 1971	27,20
F Anthony	3	1	53	45 v South Western Districts 1963/64	26,50
N Lakay	27	1	686	119 v Transvaal 1968	26,38
R Magiet	3	0	80	38 v Transvaal 1971	26,38
D February	14	1	328	110 v Border 1963/64	25,20
DV Moodie	10	0	242	41 v Transvaal 1968	24,20
G Williams	17	2	330	77* v Transvaal 1971	22,00
H Carelse	10	1	196	55* v Griqualand West 1961/62	21,77
L Martin	4	0	87	48 v Natal 1966	21,75
MS Dollie	4	1	62	40 v Southern Cape 1968	20,66
N Abrahams	5	3	36	10* v South Western Districts 1963/64	18,00
S "Lobo" Abed	14	1	205	72 v Natal 1963/64	15,78
B Kleintjies	4	1	46	25	15,33
D Mulder	6	1	75	25*	15,00
M Finnan	3	0	42	26	14,00
E Isaacs	4	0	54	23	13,50
M Pick	4	1	37	26	12,33
O Williams	14	2	125	44 v Natal 1961/62	10,41
J Sylvester	3	1	21	16*	10,50
I Tromp	3	1	19	19	9,50
C Joshua	7	1	51	16 v Natal 1966	8,50
T Behardien	13	1	77	32 v Transvaal 1966	6,41
R Alexander	3	2	4	4	4,00
A Maclons	11	1	23	7	1,77

** Note M Maclons played for South Western Districts in the 1963/64 tournament; his record is not available

Left-handers Adams and Williams head the bowling for Western Province

Bowling averages 1961-1969/70 two-day games 1970/71

Name	Runs	Wickets	Ave	Best Bowling
**AL Adams	690	92	7,50	8/82 for Griqualand West v South Western Districts 1963/64
O Williams	646	83	7,78	7/6 vs South Western Districts 1963/64
N Abrahams	65	7	9,28	3/21 v Natal 1963/63
B Kleintjies	66	7	9,42	6/22 v Eastern Province 1961/62
R Alexander	104	11	9,45	3/19 v Natal 1966
I Tromp	132	13	10,15	4/13 v Griqualand West 1968
S "Dik" Abed	268	26	10,30	4/28 v Griqualand West 1969
MS Dollie	81	7	11,57	3/10 v Southern Cape 1968
D February	349	29	12,03	7/40 v Eastern Province 1968
A Maclons	243	20	12,15	5/29 v South Western Districts 1963/64
N Lakay	453	34	13,32	6/43 v GriqualandWest 1961/62
J Neethling	826	59	14,00	7/58 v Transvaal 1966
C Joshua	182	13	14,00	4/6 v Eastern Province 1963/64
G Williams	390	26	15,00	8/11 v Border 1963/64
Y "Timmy" Lakay	15	1	15,00	1/15 v 1963/64
G "Tiny" Abed	111	6	18,50	3/29 v Transvaal 1961/62
R Magiet	48	2	24,00	2/28 v Natal 1971

** Note: AL Adams played for Griqualand West in the 1963/64 tournament, taking 22 wickets.

Western Province teams:

1961/62 tournament played in Johannesburg

G "Tiny" Abed (WP Cricket Association)(captain)
G Jardine (Cape District)
D Mulder (Cape District)
J Van Stavel (Cape District)
J Neethling (Maitland-Parow)
B Kleintjies (Wynberg)
E Petersen (WP Cricket Association)
O Williams (Cape District)
T Behardien (Stellenbosch)
N Lakay (Cape District)
S Raziet (Stellenbosch)
I D'Oliveira (Metropolitan)
A Maclons (Somerset West)
J Sylvester (Somerset West)

1963/64 tournament in Port Elizabeth

O Williams (Cape District)(captain)
A Maclons (Somerset West)
S "Lobo" Abed (WP Cricket Association)
S Conrad (WP Cricket Association)
F Anthony (Wynberg)
G Williams (Maitland-Parow)
S "Dik" Abed (WP Cricket Association)
C Joshua (WP Cricket Association)
D February (Somerset West)
J Neethling (Maitland-Parow)
H Carelse (Wynberg)
N Abrahams (Central)
Y "Timmy" Lakay (WP Cricket Association)

Western Province teams:

1966 tournament in Durban

S Conrad (WP Cricket Association)
H Carelse (Wynberg)
N Lakay (Cape District)
D February (Somerset West)
J Neethling (Maitland-Parow)
S "Dik" Abed (WP Cricket Association)
T Behardien (Stellenbosch)
G Williams (Maitland-Parow)
O Williams (Cape District)*
S "Lobo" Abed (WP Cricket Association) (captain).
R Alexander (WP Cricket Association)
D Mulder (Cape District)*
C Joshua (WP Cricket Association)
J Lambert (WP Cricket Association)
*Williams left to play Lancashire League cricket
and was replaced by A "Lefty" Adams
(WP Cricket Association).
*Mulder was suspended for disciplinary reasons
and replaced by Les Martin (Mets)

1968 tournament in Cape Town

J "Coetie" Neethling (Maitland-Parow) (captain)
M "Kulu" Maclons (Maitland-Parow)
I Dagnin (Wynberg)
E Isaacs (Metropolitan)
G Williams (Maitland-Parow)
J le Roux (Metropolitan)
M Pick (Maitland-Parow)
MS "Pettie" Dollie (Wynberg)
D February (Somerset West)
DV Moodie (Maitland-Parow)
M Finnan (Metropolitan)
N Lakay (Cape District)
AL 'Lefty" Adams (Metropolitan)
I Tromp (Worcester)

*Note: WP Cricket Association players were not
eligible for selection as they were not part of the
Super League competition.*

1969 tournament in Kimberley

J "Coetie" Neethling (Maitland-Parow) (captain)
AL Adams (Metropolitan) (vice-captain)
S "Dik" Abed (WP Cricket Association)
S "Lobo" Abed (WP Cricket Association)
K Blaauw (Wynberg)
S Conrad (WP Cricket Association)
I Dagnin (Wynberg)
M Finnan (Wynberg)
N Lakay (Cape District)
M "Kulu" Maclons (Maitland-Parow)
P Minnies (Stellenbosch)
K Rodriques (Metropolitan)
G Williams (Maitland-Parow)
O Williams (Cape District)
D Fester (Maitland Parow)

First non-centralised competition in 1969/70
Western Province vs Transvaal at William Herbert
sportsground, Wynberg – 1-2 January 1970

Western Province

I Dagnin (Wynberg)
S Conrad (WP Cricket Association)
DV Moodie (Maitland-Parow)
N Lakay (Cape District)
SD Abed (WP Cricket Association)
M Maclons (Maitland-Parow)
R Magiet (Wynberg)
J Neethling (Maitland-Parow) (captain)
G Williams (Maitland-Parow)
AL Adams (Metropolitan) (vice-captain)
O Williams (Cape District)
12th man S Meyer (WP Cricket Association)

Western Province vs Natal in Durban on 6-7 March 1970

S Conrad (WP Cricket Association)
I Dagnin (Wynberg)
V Moodie (Maitland-Parow)
T Behardien (WP Cricket Association)
SD Abed (WP Cricket Association)
J Neethling (Maitland-Parow) (captain)
R Magiet (Wynberg)
G Williams (Maitland-Parow)
AL Adams (Metropolitan)
SL Abed (WP Cricket Association)
O Williams (Cape District)

Part 3

The lure of the Lancashire League

MIDDLETON, RADCLIFFE, COLNE, Enfield and Todmorden are tiny villages nestling in the shadows of the once-thriving cotton towns and cities of Lancashire in the United Kingdom.

But to Western Cape cricketers of the 1950s and '60s, these (and others) were names of Lancashire League clubs – and to the top black players of that era, the Lancashire League spelt hope.

Basil D'Oliveira wrote a series of letters to radio commentator John Arlott, begging for help to secure a contract with one of the clubs. Cecil Abrahams, in turn, begged D'Oliveira to "fix him up" with a contract – and then when Owen Williams, Rushdi Magiet, Desmond February and Sedick Conrad arrived, helped them to settle in. Goolam Abed chose a more roundabout

route – he entered the leagues via 13-man Rugby League. Magiet had a miserable time; Dik Abed took to it like a duck to water – and became one of the league's all-time greats. Coetie Neethling would have played county cricket, had he stayed. February and Abrahams criticised D'Oliveira for not doing enough for other hopefuls "back home...."

And always in the background was Damoo Bansda, a hotel waiter, part-time journalist and full-time cricket fanatic, who was a master at keeping records, cultivating contacts, pulling strings, manufacturing exaggerated curriculum vitaes, and raising funds for the Lancashire-bound hopefuls.

Those who secured contracts had much to contend with – cold, miserable weather conditions, slow pitches and aching loneliness.

That the majority of them enjoyed successful stints with their new clubs in a new society spoke volumes for their perseverance – for the odds, quite frankly, were heavily stacked against them.

All of them were introduced to the game via street cricket (which strengthened their skills in some areas, but did them no good in others). None could claim to have had any type of formal coaching. Swing bowling was a mystery to them.

But what they didn't know, they went out and learnt – through books and newspaper strips, and by watching players they admired.

Then they went out and practised.

NEW SOUTH AFRICAN

Once they arrived in England, they had to grow in other areas, too. In many ways, they were victims of the South African political system – a system which they had played no part in creating, but which inhibited their ability to forge normal relationships in a free society. For instance, their compartmentalised existence in South Africa made it difficult for them – initially – to mix freely in England (although, to be fair to them, their hosts were far from outgoing).

In the beginning, they also found it difficult to shed the tag that labelled them "inferior" in South Africa.

But once they realised that they were at least as competent, as their more privileged white compatriots, they began to shine.

D'Oliveira, having set the ball rolling when he signed to play for Middleton in the Central Lancashire League, went on to play county cricket for Worcestershire and test cricket for England. Because his story has already been so well-documented, he is not featured here among the Western

Province Cricket Board players who made their mark in the Lancashire Leagues.

All the board players acquitted themselves well, with Dik Abed going on to be named by his club, Enfield, as their "all-time great" – ahead of legends such as Conrad Hunte and Clyde Walcott (both of whom were later knighted).

Significantly, players such as D'Oliveira, Cecil Abrahams, Owen Williams and the Abed brothers – Dik and Goolam – all opted to emigrate after having had a taste of freedom in England.

The international isolation of South Africa, coupled with the death of Bansda in 1973, closed the door on the Lancashire League to players participating in the by now strongly anti-apartheid leagues.

The effect was clearly felt: the removal of this incentive resulted in a rapid decline in standards.

But by then, of course, the destruction of apartheid had become the main priority....

Goolam Abed – a player for all seasons

IN QUIETER MOMENTS, Goolam Abed sometimes casts his mind back almost 40 years... to the country of his birth, 10 000 kilometres away... to a house in Muir Street, District Six... to team-talk nights in a sports-mad community where young men dreamed crazy dreams of rugby and cricket stardom.

Goolam Abed went to the UK in the early Sixties to play rugby league, but ended up playing Lancashire League cricket.

The memories that come flooding back remain as clear as ever: Abed can still picture the primary school on one corner of the street, Khan's animal feed supply store on another corner... and the section of nearby Aspeling Street, where countless epic games of inter-street cricket were played.

Long before the bulldozers of apartheid came rumbling into the district, Muir Street – or more accurately, the Abed home – was the headquarters of the mighty Roslyns club.

In the 1950s, the mere mention of their name struck fear into the hearts of even their most resolute rivals – and it didn't matter which time of the year it was: the sporting greats of Roslyns shone for 12 months.

In winter, they played with the letters RFC – Rugby Football Club – affixed to their name and, more often than not, swept all before them; in summer, they replaced RFC with CC – Cricket Club – and continued to heap misery on all challengers. The same cast (more or less) were in attendance throughout the year; their players were as effective in gentlemanly white flannels as they were in hard leather boots with aluminium studs.

Competition among the clubs of the area was intense. In rugby, especially, virtually every street was represented by a team (some streets even had two representatives). Each team yearned for the right to be hailed as the champions of District Six.

But even against the not inconsiderable talents of sides such as Rosendales of Rose Street, Rangers of Clifton Street, Royal Alberts of Albert Street or Watsonias of Chapel Street, Roslyns always seemed to have the knack of being able to lift their play just when they needed to – and quick, clever, brave Goolam Abed was a key member of that team.

A SUPERB SPORTSMAN

Roslyns had a simple recipe for developing star players. It was built around the belief that "if you're good enough, you're old enough".

Abed, the teenager was good enough. In fact, he was so good that, by the age of 19, he had forced his way into the Green Point-based Western Province Rugby Union side, alongside his brothers, Tiny and Lobo.

That was in 1953.

In 1957 and 1959, he played in centralised interrace tournaments for the South African Coloured team – and in 1960 he was appointed captain of the Western Province Rugby Union side.

He was as successful as a cricketer. In 1955, he won the best all-rounder award as a member of the Western Province Indian team at the South

African Indian Cricket Union's Christopher tournament.

In the 1957/58 season, he scored 102 for the South African Malay side against the South African Bantus. In fact, he was in such fine form at the 1958 interracial tournament that he was one of 18 players shortlisted for the tour to Kenya.

Although Goolam Abed is a regular visitor to his roots in Cape Town – here, he's pictured with his brothers Lobo (right), Dik (back, left) and Hymie (back, right) – he says he can no longer identify with South African sports teams.

"I thought I stood a good chance of making the side, especially since I finished fourth on the batting averages at the end of the tournament, and I was told to get my passport ready for the trip," Abed said.

"But I missed out, along with players such as Timmy Lakay and Taliep Behardien. My brothers, Tiny and Lobo, were regarded as certainties for selection – and I suppose it would have been difficult for the selectors to choose three Abed brothers for the side. I must admit though that I was very disappointed not to have been selected."

Although talk of the Abed brothers usually inevitably gravitates towards

the achievements of Tiny, Lobo, Goolam, and later, Dik, Goolam graciously acknowledged the role played by his eldest brother Babu in nurturing his (as well as the others') love of cricket and rugby.

"Babu played rugby and cricket for Roslyns and we followed him as we grew up. With the exception of Dik, who was much younger than the rests of us, we all played in the same team. For many years, we also played for the South African Malay team in the Barnato tournament."

A TASTE OF RUGBY LEAGUE...

In 1961, Abed was offered the opportunity to show off his rugby talents to a wider audience – thanks to the prompting of Jim Windsor, an English rugby league talent scout, and a regular visitor to Cape Town.

When he was invited to a Sea Point hotel to listen to a proposition from Windsor, Abed confessed that he was more than a little apprehensive, so much so that he roped in his brother Tiny and Basil D'Oliveira to provide him with some moral support at the meeting.

"Actually, Windsor had never seen me in action. He'd heard about me from Dr Louis Babrow, a former Springbok, who'd watched me playing for the Western Province Rugby Union side in the 1959 Rhodes tournament in Cape Town."

"I wasn't even all that sure that I wanted to play overseas. I was young and, quite frankly, I was worried about having to travel all the way to England. It would have meant being separated from the people who were closest to me."

"But, in the end, after much agonising, it was the support and encouragement from my family, that persuaded me to take up Windsor's offer."

The deal that Abed agreed to was far from lucrative. "Windsor made it clear that my status would be that of an amateur – because I was an unknown. Like other black players, I was in a Catch-22 situation. It certainly wasn't our fault that we didn't get any publicity.

"To the majority of newspapers of that time, 'black' and 'top class' were words that didn't go together."

There was, however, some peace of mind for Abed and his travelling companion, Louis Neumann, another leading coloured player: they were promised that if they didn't make the grade, they would be given return tickets to South Africa.

Abed's league debut was for Leeds against Hunslet – in front of 28000 spectators. "I was a bundle of nerves," he recalled. "And it didn't make me feel any better to know that my opposite number was the Great Britain fly-half.

"Fortunately, I had the Springbok, Wilf Rosenberg, playing next to me – and he helped to calm my jitters. In the weeks that followed, he went out of his way to help Louis and me to settle down in our new surroundings."

Abed did not, however, make the grade with Leeds because, as he put it, "they were a top-class team" with some exceptionally good players.

Neumann, though, proved to be a great success at the Yorkshire club.

Another Yorkshire side, Bradford Northern, saw enough potential in Abed to offer him a five-year contract worth £1000 a year, a lot of money in those days.

With the long contract offering him a measure of job security, he was able to give much more thought to his other interests – one of which was cricket.

Although it was his rugby skills that had won him the opportunity to play in England, Abed confessed that cricket had always been his first love.

So, when he was offered the chance to play competitive cricket in the rugby off-season, he grabbed it: "I played in the Bradford League for six seasons – first for Yeadon and then for Laisterdyke," he said. "In that time I scored three centuries for Yeadon and two for Laisterdyke."

"Because the rugby and cricket seasons overlapped, he usually missed the first few matches at the start and end of the season.

"But it was a situation I accepted – rugby, after all, provided me with my bread and butter.

"Nevertheless, when I finally decided to call it a day, I wasn't really sad. In fact, I was extremely relieved and grateful that I was able to bow out relatively unscathed.

"Rugby League is a hard, hard game," he said.

LIFE IN ENGLAND

When he arrived in England in 1961, Abed thought, perhaps naively, that he had escaped the racism that dictated so many facets of his life in South Africa.

"But I was wrong," he said.

"To be honest, I came across a great deal of racial prejudice while playing rugby and cricket in England. Much of it came in the form of comments passed by spectators and opponents, and although I'd be the first to acknowledge that some things were said in the heat of the moment, I found them to be hurtful all the same."

The young Abed also struggled to adapt socially to his new surroundings. "I was shy and quiet – and because of my experiences growing up in a racially obsessed South African society, I often felt inferior in the company of whites. But that's what the apartheid system did to all

Springbok rugby player Wilf Rosenberg helped Goolam Abed to settle down during the first few weeks of his stay at Leeds.

Goolam Abed shows the style of a top-order Lancashire League batsman.

black people – it was designed to make us feel inferior," he said.

"The English weren't particularly friendly either. I'll never forget my first purely social visit to someone in England, because it took place *two years* after my arrival in the UK."

The cold, wet weather of the north of England did not make it easier for him to settle down. "Shortly after my arrival, when I found the cold almost unbearable, I wore three rugby jerseys to bed – and that was in summer!

"Under these circumstances, it would have been easy to get homesick. But then something happened which changed my perspective completely: I met Jean, the woman who would become my wife.

"If I had not met her, I would have returned home to South Africa for good."

Abed's early experiences in the UK made him vow later, after he had settled down and started learning the ropes, to help make it easier for the black sportsmen who followed him in trying to break into British rugby and cricket. (Cecil Abrahams had a similar attitude.)

"I was filled with pride when fellow South Africans such as Coetie Neethling, my brother Dik, Rushdi Magiet, Baboo Ebrahim, Yacoob Omar and Des February started playing in the leagues.

"We met up with one another during the cricket season, though perhaps not as regularly as we might have wished. We lived quite far from one another – and because we didn't have motor cars, we had to travel by public transport – bus and train for our little social gatherings," he said.

Abed said he'd been apprehensive when Dik, his brother, signed for the league club, Enfield. "I'd never seen him playing senior cricket – and because I knew he was coming over as a professional, I feared that he wasn't aware enough of just how intense the pressure on a club professional can be.

"Fortunately, he was able to spend some time with me in Bradford, and I was able to give him a crash course on what to expect and what his club and fans would expect from him."

Although Dik, no doubt, appreciated his brother's advice, he certainly did not show any brotherly kindness on the field. In one match against Goolam's side, Dik smashed a hundred, and then proceeded to bowl his brother "black and blue".

For Goolam, one of the big learning experiences of playing in England was discovering the technical side of cricket, which black South Africans were largely unaware of.

"We were not coached in South Africa. We developed our skills by watching others – and by going to Newlands on the odd occasion. To improve my batting, I read many books and studied illustrations. I also spent many hours practising in front of a mirror.

"In South Africa we just took the ball and bowled. We didn't know about seam and swing bowling, or where to put your fingers and how to grip the ball. We simply held the ball across the seam and ran in to bowl."

ROCHDALE DAYS

The prospect of playing in the Central Lancashire League, where fellow Capetonians, Cecil Abrahams and Basil D'Oliveira, had achieved great success filled Goolam Abed with a great sense of anticipation.

"I was thrilled when Cecil arranged a contract for me with Rochdale in 1967," he said.

Natalians Yacoob Omar (left) and Baboo Ebrahim (right) also had stints in the Lancashire League.

"But it almost didn't happen....

"Shortly before I was supposed to be interviewed by the club, I hurt my arm playing for Batley against Bradford Northern in a rugby league match. As a result, I signed for Rochdale with my arm in a sling.

"It was not a particularly lucrative contract, but it helped to pay for the things I wanted."

Abed's association with the club proved to be a long and fruitful one: in 1969 he was the only professional in the league to record a century. That season he finished fifth on the batting averages. He also went on to set numerous records in limited overs matches, including being the only century-maker in 11 years when he scored 101 not out in 1969. Another record – 16 catches (also set in 1969) – stood for 17 years.

After three years as Rochdale's professional, Abed moved to Castleton Moor, where he twice won the Frank Worrell Trophy for the leading amateur run scorer in the Central Lancashire League – 805 runs in 1970 and 685 runs in 1972.

He also spent a season as the professional at the Nelson club.

In 1975, at the age of 40, he returned to Rochdale as an amateur.

"One of the proudest moments in my life," he said, "was opening the batting against Sir Gary Sobers, Littleborough's professional at the time. I'd idolised him as a boy – and there I was playing against him.

"I was chuffed when he came over to me after the match and complimented me on my batting."

Between 1976 and 1982, while playing for Walshaw in the Bolton Cricket Association, he scored four centuries. Later, at a special sportsman's dinner to thank him for his outstanding service to the club, Walshaw described him as a "model professional".

In 1983, he returned to Castleton Moor, where he captained the side for the next two seasons.

After retiring at 55, Abed managed Rochdale between 1990 and 1992, where one of his duties was to sign the club's overseas professional.

Among the well-known cricketers to have played for Rochdale have been West Indians, Sonny Ramadhin, Hartley Alleyne, Franklyn Stephenson and Desmond Haynes; Mudassar Nazar of Pakistan; Anton Ferreira, Dave Callaghan and Mike Rindel of South Africa; and Neil Johnson of Zimbabwe.

Although Abed said that he regularly returns to his roots in Cape Town, he confessed: "I find that I just cannot identify myself with the South African cricket team.

"I'm not bitter about what happened when I was growing up, but I am sorry that apartheid denied people like myself and others the opportunities that are available now."

The sad road to greatness of Sulaiman "Dik" Abed

IT IS ONE of life's strange little quirks that Sulaiman "Dik" Abed's search for the true happiness and freedom that was denied him in the land of his birth, should have ended in the Netherlands – the birthplace of Hendrik Frensch Verwoerd, the man who gathered together the strands of racial discrimination in South Africa, and then refined, strengthened and sold them to a doting white electorate... before having them written into the statutes as apartheid.

What's not a quirk, though, (but rather a grave injustice) is that Abed has not – up to now – featured in the records and photographs that make up the national and international cricket history of South Africa.

Though more than 30 years have passed since he first made his mark on cricket in South Africa, knowledgeable observers remain convinced that he was easily good enough to play provincial cricket for Western Province (in a team selected on merit) and probably good enough to play for the national side.

But, when Abed was in the prime of his career, the law dictated that only white South Africans could reach the pinnacle of sporting achievement.

And so he had to seek fulfilment elsewhere....

BEGINNINGS

Like so many black players in the Western Cape, Abed's introduction to cricket came via street matches - where snarling bowlers armed with a hard ball tried (and, more often than not, succeeded) in putting the fear of hell into batsmen whose only means of protection was a bat.

"Every Sunday morning between 20 and 30 players made their way to a street near my home for these matches," Abed said.

"Once you'd been dismissed, you had to wait until everyone else had had a chance to bat before you could bat again. Batsmen struggled to cope with bowlers intent on hitting batsmen in places where it hurt most. But these confrontations were invaluable: it toughened us up and helped us develop skills that we may not have developed otherwise."

In many ways, Abed was fortunate in that he grew up in a sports-mad family. "I never lacked help or advice from my older brothers, Babu, Tiny, Lobo and Goolam, all of whom were players of note," he said.

It was almost inevitable that Dik would follow in their footsteps. And yet, when his career was in its infancy, it was an outsider who inadvertently pushed him in the direction of bowling. Initially, he had no thoughts of becoming a bowler. "I hated running," he explained.

Instead, influenced perhaps by his brother Lobo, who was generally recognised as the best wicketkeeper

Dik Abed is generally regarded as one of the greatest cricketers to come out of the ranks of the South African Cricket Board of Control.

Clive van Ryneveld – the Springbok who inadvertently encouraged Dik Abed to take up bowling.

in the country, he started off with pretensions of becoming a wicketkeeper, *à la* Lobo, for the Roslyns club of District Six.

It was an ambition that he quickly revised. One day, while sitting in the scoreboard at Newlands, watching a Currie Cup match featuring Western Province, he became fascinated by the bowling action of the South African international, Clive van Ryneveld.

"Clive bowled legbreaks with his arms going all over the place," Abed said. "When I tried to copy his action, I found myself bowling at twice his speed – which, in retrospect, didn't turn out to be all that bad for me. I found that I was able to get pronounced movement off the pitch.

"Compared with Van Ryneveld's legbreaks, I was bowling leg cutters – although I wasn't aware of this at the time."

"I found this out only after my brother Goelie came up to me at a practice one day and asked, 'Do you know what you're bowling?'

"'Well, no,' I replied.

"'Do you know what a leg-cutter is?' he asked.

"Again, I had to say that I didn't know.

"Then he looked at me and said, 'Aag, it doesn't matter – just keep on bowling what you're bowling.'"

Dik did, and became an overnight sensation, picking up a rich haul of wickets against batsmen who had never come up against this type of bowling before.

NEW PASTURES

A series of fine all-round performances emphasised Abed's special talents. Each five-wicket haul or swashbuckling innings served to hammer home the point that his future lay far beyond the narrow confines of cen-

tralised biennial Dadabhay interprovincial tournaments.

Few had forgotten Basil D'Oliveira's route to international stardom (albeit in the colours of another country): it had come via a foot in the door of the Lancashire leagues, followed by a step up into county cricket and finally, the ultimate – a call-up into the England test team.

Many believed that Abed was at least as talented as D'Oliveira.

The man who took up the cudgels on Abed's behalf was Damoo Bansda, a local freelance journalist and cricket fanatic, who had worked tirelessly to help get D'Oliveira and several other Western Province Cricket Board players to England.

"Bansda phoned me one day with the news that he had written to a few clubs," said Abed. "When he divulged the nature of the information he'd supplied to his overseas contacts, I almost fell on my back. He claimed that I had scored more than 1000 runs and taken more than 150 wickets in each of the previous three seasons.

"This, of course, was an outrageous exaggeration."

But, exaggeration or not, one of the clubs, Enfield, was impressed enough to offer Abed a contract (although the terms were hardly special). "They offered me £600 for the season – and I had to find my own air ticket to England," he said.

After asking Clive van Ryneveld, who by then had become his lawyer, to check the fine print of the contract, Abed signed for Enfield.

"Quite frankly, I would have joined them for nothing, so eager was I to play on grass against test cricketers.

"My airfare to the UK could have been a problem – we were not a rich family – but then Roslyns and the Western Province Cricket Association stepped in with an offer to sponsor my trip.

"I could pack my bags...."

PREPARATIONS

Bansda was aware, however, that first impressions in the Lancashire leagues could make or break a new signing. He was determined that Abed should be as well prepared as possible, before he set off for the UK.

Having seen in the 1950s how black cricketers (who played only on gravel and matting) had struggled on turf on the rare occasions they played against white opposition, the conscientious Bansda organised a programme of practice sessions for Abed prior to his departure.

Abed said: "By the time I left in 1967, and for a long time afterwards, black cricketers did not have the luxury of playing on turf wickets in South Africa.

"Tom Reddick, a former professional with the English county side Nottinghamshire, put me through my paces at Bishops [a private school near Cape Town].

"When I bowled, my grip across the seam enabled me to cut the ball prodigiously on what was apparently a good batting wicket.

"Reddick looked at me incredulously before asking: 'Is that the way you normally grip the ball?'

"He was amazed that my grip enabled me to bowl fast leg-breaks. But, to his credit, he didn't try to interfere. 'If you're successful using this grip, don't change it,' he said.

"I agreed with him – so I kept bowling that way.

"I intended every ball I sent down to be a leg-cutter; my variation came in the form of pace, line and length. I simply wasn't interested in bowling a straight ball."

SETTLING IN

Abed's move to the colder, unfamiliar English environment was eased by the presence of his brother Goolam, who had moved to England in 1961, to play rugby league, first for Leeds and then for Bradford Northern.

"Goelie looked after me for the first few weeks after my arrival. His support and advice proved invaluable.

"When I first set foot on British soil it felt as if I was stepping into a nightmare. It was cold and wet – and as the days passed, it got colder and wetter. In my first game for Enfield, I discovered that games were not stopped simply because of a wet field and a slippery ball. I was expected to go out and perform. After about half an hour I took my first wicket for my new team – and then, mercifully, the rain came pouring down and the match was called off.

Despite his early struggles, Abed proved to be a willing learner and a determined performer. As the team's paid professional he was more than willing to accept that the buck stopped with him.

"In my first season I learnt a lot about bowling and responsibility. Although Enfield's batting was fairly strong, the team's bowling tended to be on the thin side.

"And so, aware of the team's bowling shortcomings, there was one sentence I never uttered to my captain, Ian Metcalf: 'Sorry, I'm tired!'

"When I was given that ball, I bowled and bowled and bowled. I hated making way for anyone else!"

Abed's desire to do well in England was fuelled by the league successes of Basil D'Oliveira, Coetie Neethling and Cecil Abrahams.

"Basil opened doors for many of us. He proved that cricketers from our communities could compete with the

In addition to being a fine bowler, Dik Abed was also an explosive batsman.

best in the world – and more than hold their own.

"My attitude was that if Basil, Coetie and Cecil could make it, so could I!"

TOWARDS GREATNESS

Abed did not return to Cape Town after his first season with Enfield. "I wanted to acclimatise properly," he said. "I stayed in England through one of the coldest winters I've ever experienced – but it was worth it."

In 1968, his second season with the club, Abed took 120 wickets at a superb average of 8,76 runs per wicket. He also scored 458 runs (at an average of 21,81). The best of a series of top-notch performances were bowling figures of 9/33 against Ramsbottom, 8/46 against Church, 7/23 against Colne and 6/18 against Ramsbottom in the second round. His brilliant all-round contribution helped Enfield to their first league championship success in 25 years.

To put his batting and bowling achievements into perspective, he took more wickets than Australian internationals Graeme Watson (61 wickets at an average of 15,86) and Graham Corling (64 wickets at an average of 15,53). Clive Lloyd, the West Indian great, was the leading batsman that season, with an average of 61,30.

Abed's stunning form did not go unnoticed. Two counties – Worcestershire (D'Oliveira's county) and Surrey – invited him for trials. But, although he scored 127 not out and 38 not out, for Surrey's Second XI and took 5/32 for the Worcestershire Second XI, he failed to break into the county circuit.

"The counties were not prepared to sign unknowns like myself; they wanted ready-made test players," Abed said. "Still, it was disappointing

that neither Surrey nor Worcester gave any reasons for turning me down. My feeling was that the rumpus over Basil [D'Oliveira] – when he was first omitted from the MCC side to tour South Africa, and then reinstated, and the subsequent cancellation of that tour – had something to do with it."

Abed was also offered two trial games by the Warwickshire coach, Alan Oakman. Again he performed creditably, claiming 17 wickets in the two matches, including an impressive haul of 7/38 against the Nottinghamshire Reserves.

"Oakman told me the order not to sign me came from the top. What that meant was a mystery to me," Abed said.

In 1969, Abed was included in the Lancashire League XI which played the International Cavaliers, an invitation side consisting of test players such as Fred Trueman and Ted Dexter (England), Graeme Pollock (South Africa), Roy Fredericks (West Indies) and Bobby Simpson (Australia).

"I was hoping to get an opportunity to bowl at Pollock, but unfortunately for me, he was dismissed for a single by Pat Trimborn, another South African.

In the *Sunday Times* of 25 January 1970, the respected coach Tom Reddick said Abed was ready for county cricket. "[He] hasn't quite got D'Oliveira's class, but he's a fine all-rounder who has deserved his success in the Lancashire League," Reddick said.

"I would like to see him move… to county cricket, where I am sure he would get 100 wickets a season with his medium-paced cutters, and probably hundreds of runs regularly."

D'Oliveira himself said of Abed: "… he's one of the most respected players ever to come from the (Lancashire) leagues. He is the nearest

I have ever seen to Alec Bedser, the great England seam bowler."

Abed, meanwhile, refused to let the disappointment of not winning a county contract affect his performances for Enfield. In the 1971 English season, he maintained his superb form, taking 101 wickets at 7,96 runs a wicket, and finishing with a batting average of 21,35 runs per

David Orchard and others, I tried doubly hard to come out on top – and most of the time I succeeded. I wanted the people in England and back home to see that black players could compete – and, in fact, often out-perform white players – on a level playing field," he said.

"Before the arrival in the Lancashire League of black players

"We refuse to be used for window-dressing"

IN 1970, JACK Cheetham, the president of the South African Cricket Association, nominated Dik Abed and Owen Williams to be included in the Springbok team that was scheduled to tour Australia in 1971/72.

Supporting Cheetham's action, *Manchester Post* sports writer, Frank Rostron, wrote that Abed would be a "magical solution" to South Africa's touring problems.

"Abed, a popular fellow, would pull his weight as a player and perhaps spike much of the anti-South African criticism," Rostron wrote.

Abed, who clearly recalled the incident many years later, said: "Owen and I were approached by someone who said he'd been sent by Cheetham to find out if we would be prepared to join the South African team for the tour of Australia.

"We made it clear that we were not prepared to be used for window-dressing purposes in order to save the tour.

"Ali Bacher, the South African and Transvaal captain, requested a meeting at a Claremont hotel with Owen, myself and Hassan Howa, whom we had informed about the offer.

"I think it was a rest day during the Currie Cup game against Western Province.

"In the end, the meeting did not take place because Bacher could not keep to the agreed time." The tour was called off due to international pressure.

innings, to help Enfield to another league championship triumph.

In the 1972 season, Abed took 89 wickets to bring his tally in Lancashire League cricket to more than 500 in just six seasons. In the 1973 season, he claimed 75 wickets at an average of 11,49 runs a wicket and scored 451 runs (at an average of 22,55). In the same season Clive Rice took 66 wickets and scored 531 runs for Ramsbottom.

Playing against white South Africans in the league provided Abed with an added incentive. "Whenever I played against cricketers such as Peter Swart, Pat Trimborn, Clive Rice,

such as Basil D'Oliveira, Owen (Williams), Coetie (Neethling), myself, Des (February), Dickie Conrad, Yacoob Omar, Rushdi (Magiet), Babco Ebrahim and others, people in England were not aware that cricket, other than cricket played by whites, was being played at a high standard by black people in South Africa.

"Looking back, I honestly believe that we were all pioneers and that we were mainly instrumental in bringing about the international sports boycott against South Africa."

Abed's consistently brilliant performances won him a special place in the

Enfield's "all-time great"

IN 1998, WHEN Enfield luminaries met to consider their nomination for the club's "all-time great", they looked no further than the South African who had been their professional for a record 10 consecutive seasons: Dik Abed.

Abed, who edged out test giants such West Indians Clyde Walcott and Conrad Hunte, and the Indian all-rounder, Madan Lal, as Enfield's nominee, said: "I felt a little embarrassed to have been nominated ahead of these great players."

The concept of an "all-time great" formed part of a grand exhibition by the Lancashire League's 14 affiliated clubs to commemorate the 106-year-old League.

Each club had to nominate its "all-time great". Among the nominees were legends such as Everton Weekes (Bacup), Charlie Griffiths (Burnley), Sydney Barnes (Church and Oswaldtwistle), George Headley (Haslingden), Mannie Martindale (Lowerhouse) and Sir Learie Constantine (Nelson).

"To have been named with such great cricketers is a great honour, even though I personally feel I was not in their class," Abed said.

"I never considered myself a great player. It is a description that should be reserved for those whom I followed and those who never got the opportunity to break out of the evil claws of apartheid.

"There were better players around than me, who could have made it had they been given the breaks."

Dik Abed regularly grabbed the headlines in Lancashire League matches.

hearts of Enfield's fans, which would later culminate in his being voted the club's "all-time great".

INTO EXILE

Given his awesome talent, it was inevitable that once Abed had secured a Lancashire League contract, he would not return to live in South Africa.

The "breaking-up" process, though, came slowly. He returned to South Africa to play in the last centralised Dadabhay tournament in the chaotic Kimberley tournament of 1969, and bitterly criticised playing conditions there.

He also played two matches for Western Province, in the new two-day Dadabhay Trophy competition in

Dik Abed, the reporter

IN 1970, DIK Abed became the first black man to apply for and receive accreditation to report on an all-white international – the first test between South Africa and Australia at Newlands.

He and Abe Adams of the *Post* occupied specially reserved seats in the front row of the coloured enclosure.

They declined the offer of a special press table because they didn't want to be conspicuous. Significantly, Abed's friend, Clive van Ryneveld, was the press officer for the match.

1971. But, by then, it had become quite apparent that his heart was no longer in the country which, he felt, had kicked him in the teeth.

"The only reason I played in England for 10 years was that I had nowhere to go," he said.

"Trevor Chappell, who was in his first season in the league when I was in my last couldn't believe I had been playing in the leagues for 10 years. He couldn't stand it.

"But, for me, the situation was different. South Africa had shut the door in my face.

"If I had returned I would have had to return to playing on matting and would have been subject to all the apartheid laws.

"Having experienced what life was like outside the country, there was no way that I was going to return permanently, simply to be treated like a second-class citizen.

"I did return to play for Western Province in 1969, 1970 and 1971, but I found it difficult to make ends meet. I'm not bitter about it. That's just the way things were then."

Abed said that when he decided to leave South Africa permanently, he never dreamt that apartheid would collapse.

"The government had such an iron grip on the country that it was impossible to imagine that it would ever relinquish its stranglehold.

"I decided to get married in Holland and see what I could do with my life there. I'm very happy now, and even though things have changed in South Africa, I doubt whether I would ever fit into that society again.

"My children have been brought up the Dutch way. I'm grateful that they have the freedom of choice which I never had while growing up in Cape Town."

Abed was philosophical about the psychological impact that apartheid had on the black criceters of his generation.

"Apartheid was designed to make blacks feel inferior to whites, with the result that many blacks thought they couldn't compete with whites at the highest level even though we were as good as they were," he said.

"But I've always felt that nobody can make you feel inferior without your consent.

"When we went to England our biggest problem was convincing ourselves that we were as good as the whites. Once we overcame that hurdle, we realised that we could compete on an equal footing.

"Owen (Williams) and Cecil (Abrahams) were just as good as Basil (D'Oliveira) – but he got the breaks and they didn't. Others may have achieved what Basil did had they been given the chance.

"It's strange that Ivan D'Oliveira (Basil's brother) got the chance to play for Leicestershire while great players such as Owen, one of the best spinners I have ever seen, and Cecil didn't.

"Cecil had the ability to play county cricket, but there was nobody opening doors for him from the inside. In fact, he had someone shutting doors from inside – and that was very sad," Abed said, declining to name the person whom he believed blocked the entry of black players into the county circuit.

DUTCH HONOURS

After a season playing Grade cricket in Perth, Australia, in 1975/76, Abed announced his retirement from Lancashire League cricket in 1976 and moved to the Dutch capital, The Hague, where he settled with his family. He joined the HBO club for whom he played for eight seasons. After serving his five-year-residency qualification, he was appointed captain of the Dutch national side which played in the second ICC trophy competition in England in 1981.

In an article reporting his retirement from Lancashire League cricket, *The Cricketer* wrote in its 1976/77 annual: "Abed contributed much to Lancashire League cricket and his departure will be regretted by all, who have watched a talented player go about his business of collecting wickets and runs and at the same time providing cricketing entertainment of the highest order."

In 1976, *Wisden* said: "For years there have been few better all-rounders in the Lancashire League than the... South African, Abed."

DIK ABED'S LANCASHIRE LEAGUE STATISTICS.

Year	BOWLING			BATTING			
	Runs	Wickets	Ave.	Inns	N/O	Runs	Ave.
1967	927	70	13,24	19	4	357	23,8
1968	1052	120	8,76	25	4	458	21,81
1969	1110	105	10,57	23	5	424	23,55
1970	1201	98	12,24	23	7	578	36,12
1971	804	101	7,96	23	3	427	21,35
1972	1007	89	11,31	22	1	558	26,57
1973	816	75	11,49	21	1	451	22,55
1974	640	61	10,49	20	1	496	26,1
1975	1078	100	10,78	26	6	819	41,35
1976	1055	66	15,98	26	4	605	27,50

Best Bowling: 9/26 vs Ramsbottom (29 May 1971)

Best Batting: 111 vs Haslingden (3 September 1972)

In all his Lancashire League games Abed took 885 wickets at an average of 10,27. He scored 5271 runs at an average of 27,17.

Cecil Abrahams – "Cricket in my blood"

TO CECIL ABRAHAMS, a stocky all-rounder from the dusty fields of the Cape Flats, Milnrow in Manchester was cricket paradise; to Geoff Griffin, a Springbok fast bowler, the final signpost pointing the way to cricket hell was located in the same tiny English village, halfway between the old Lancashire cotton towns of Oldham and Rochdale.

Cecil Abrahams – the chance to play Lancashire League for a club called Milnrow was a dream come true for him.

The year was 1960 – and Abrahams was about to become the second South African Cricket Board of Control player (Basil D'Oliveira had been the first) to launch a career in the Lancashire League.

Griffin's career as a test match performer, on the other hand, was about to come to a sudden, painful end.

Yet, early in that same year, the prospects for both men could hardly have looked more different: because of the pigment of his skin, the ambitious Abrahams was stuck in a dead-end world of the coloured cricketer – gravel wickets, uneven fields and the occasional representative game.

And although he had a burning desire to follow D'Oliveira into Lancashire League cricket, he was realistic enough to acknowledge that the chances of this happening were, at best, minimal.

Griffin, by contrast, had much to look forward to: a series showdown with traditional rivals England... followed in 1961 by a stint in the Lancashire League playing for tiny Milnrow.

But long before that, there had been whispers that Griffin's bowling action was, well, questionable.

During the series against England, matters came to a head – in an incredible, devastating manner....

In the second test at Lords, Griffin went from the dizzy heights of being the first South African to claim a hat trick in a test match (indeed, he was the first person to achieve this feat at Lords), to the sorry depths of being no-balled – 11 times – for throwing. In an exhibition game the next day, arranged after the test had ended early, Griffin was again no-balled. He completed the tour as a batsman, and was never picked for South Africa again.

Then, in a final humiliation, Milnrow cancelled their contract with him.

A "CAN'T-REFUSE" OFFER

Griffin's poison turned out to be Abrahams' meat – for, shortly after the South African international's virtual banishment from cricket, Abrahams received a letter containing great news from Basil D'Oliveira.

"He told me he'd organised a contract for me with a team called Milnrow," said Abrahams.

"I was stunned.

"I'd been writing to Basil every week since he left to play for Middleton, asking him to fix me up with a team. I desperately wanted to play in England.

"Suddenly it seemed that my wish would be granted.

"Actually, what had happened was that Basil had recommended me to

Milnrow after they had cancelled their contract with Griffin. But because he was new to England, they wouldn't take his word. So, for confirmation, they turned to Peter Walker, a professional with the Glamorgan County Cricket Club, who I'd met when Basil, Tiny Abed, Eric Petersen and I had played for a Johannesburg selection against a team of overseas professionals. Walker gave me a good recommendation – something for which I'm still grateful."

FIRST IMPRESSIONS

Despite his natural optimism, Abrahams struggled initially to settle down in his new surroundings.

"It was cold, it rained a lot – even in summer – and I struggled to make friends," he said.

"Having to leave behind my wife, Cynthia, and my six children because my contract with the club made no provision for bringing over my family, simply added to my loneliness.

"When I started playing, I was a little confused about what I should be doing. The move from being a pure amateur to a fully-fledged professional was a major transition for me.

"Even though I had become a paid employee of the club, I still played for the enjoyment of the game.

"It's a hard life being a professional at a club. You are the only person getting paid. At the start of my career, when I had an off day and one of the amateurs had a good day, I would imagine him giving me a furtive glance and muttering to himself: 'So, why's he getting paid?'

"On my bad days I was really down. All I wanted to do was escape to my lodgings and be by myself."

But once he started acclimatising, things began to improve rapidly.

Said Abrahams: "The first thing that struck me about cricket in the leagues was how knowledgeable the crowds are – especially the older women. Once they'd decided that I could play the game, a lot of pressure was taken off me. They'd overlook my bad days and celebrate the good ones with me."

In his first game for Milnrow, Abrahams came up against the great Garfield Sobers, who was playing for a team called Radcliffe.

"I hit his first ball, a full toss outside the off stump, for four. He dismissed me shortly afterwards. At the end of the day he came up to me and said: 'Next time don't hit one off the mark for four.'

"I didn't realise that 'one off the mark' was a tradition in the league, which dictated that a player batting in front of his home crowd for the first time is given a gentle full toss to save the debutant the possible embarrassment of being dismissed first ball."

Once he'd settled in, Abrahams displayed a massive appetite for the game in his new environment, playing for 15 seasons in the Central Lancashire League – first for Milnrow, and later for Radcliffe and Oldham.

And although the highpoints were too many to count, his best season was in 1970, when he took 89 wickets at a cost of 10,25 runs per wicket – the best bowling effort in the league that year by a professional.

SETTLING IN

The swinging ball in English conditions was a phenomenon which perplexed the newly-arrived Abrahams.

"In South Africa, I had had no experience of a ball swinging through the air – either as a bowler or batsman. I was confused initially by 16-year-old bowlers haring in at net practice and swinging the ball – both ways – through the air.

"I couldn't ask them how they managed to do it. After all, I was being paid to teach them how to bowl!"

Abrahams eventually bought a book which explained the art.

When Owen Williams joined Radcliffe, he was as perplexed.

"That's impossible," he told Abrahams – until he was taken to an open piece of ground and given a quick demonstration.

"He was as amazed as I had been," said Abrahams.

Unlike D'Oliveira, who returned to South Africa after his first season with Middleton, Abrahams decided to remain in Manchester during the British winter. He stayed the next season, too – and the next. Eventually, he made his home in the UK.

"At the end of my first season I had planned to return to South Africa with Basil – on the same boat, in fact. I remember thinking to myself, 'That's it – I've had my experience of playing in the Lancashire League.'

"But, when I conveyed my intentions to my dad, he wrote to me, saying: 'You're being very silly. What are you coming home for? What prospects are there for you in South Africa? You and your family should make England your home.'

"I took his advice and used the money Milnrow offered me in my second contract to bring my family over in 1962.

"Once the children started attending school in England it became difficult to leave. I simply couldn't just pack up and return. Besides, they were having a better life here than in South Africa."

As his Lancashire League career took off, Abrahams began to give increasingly serious thought to the idea of following D'Oliveira into county cricket.

"At one stage, Derbyshire showed interest in signing me. But I was naive. I didn't realise that they were based just a short distance from where I lived. I thought I would have to pack up the children and move – and I wasn't keen on doing that. Had I known that Derby was just around the corner, I probably would have taken up the offer," he said.

Another goal that Abrahams set himself was to open doors in the Lancashire League for other talented black cricketers in South Africa.

HELPING OTHERS

A number of Western Province Cricket Board players followed Abrahams into the Lancashire League – and, without exception, they praised the role he played in helping them acclimatise.

"I saw it as my duty to help them," Abrahams said. "I wanted to spare them the difficulties that I went through when I set foot in Manchester.

"I was thrilled to see younger players such as Dik Abed, Des February and Rushdi Magiet coming to play in England.

"When I first saw them I knew from bitter experience that their first few months in their new environment would be tough, even depressing. I tried to use my experience of local conditions to help them through their settling-in period.

"I'd invite them to my home for a meal – and we'd just talk. The big problem for any new arrival was loneliness. Cynthia and I tried to make them feel at home, and, hopefully, we succeeded.

"I was grateful for having been given the opportunity to play in England, and I was keen to create the same opportunities for other deprived cricketers in South Africa. In fact, I'd been in the UK for just over a year when I first mentioned this to Basil [D'Oliveira].

"'Shouldn't we be doing something for the cricketers back home?' I asked.

"Basil told me he'd received a letter from one of the hopefuls (Des February).

"I said, 'That's brilliant'.

"But he retorted that he'd torn up the letter.

"What on earth did you do that for?" I asked.

"His reply shocked me: 'He's never done anything for me, so why should I put myself out and do something for him,' was what he said.

"I was dumbfounded. With the influence he had, Basil could have done more to open doors in the UK, for South Africa's black cricketers."

Abrahams said that despite this disagreement with D'Oliveira, he continued to have great respect for him as a cricketer.

John Abrahams

A triumph for the family

ALTHOUGH ABRAHAMS himself didn't get the chance to play county cricket, his son, John, did. In fact, he went on to captain Lancashire.

John started playing at the age of three, in the Abrahams' backyard. By the time he turned 11, he was rated the finest player of his age by Tom Reddick, the Lancashire coach.

When Lancashire expressed interest in signing John, his proud father's advice was, "Go, go, go!"

"I wanted him to do it for all the black cricketers in South Africa who had not been given the chance to develop their talents," Abrahams said.

John went on to captain the Lancashire side to victory in the 1984 Benson & Hedges Final at Lord's against Warwickshire. Although he was dismissed for a first ball duck, he still won the Man of the Match – for his captaincy.

"I was especially proud when he was selected for England. He was a great player."

BACK TO SOUTH AFRICA

Thanks to the influence of the Western Province Cricket Board secretary, Frank Brache, Abrahams was invited to coach in Cape Town, along with the West Indian, John Holder.

"In 1974, Frank wrote to me saying that the Western Province Cricket Board were thinking of employing two coaches – would I be interested?" Abrahams said.

"As I had just received my coaching certificate, I jumped at the chance to return. I had a wonderful time in Cape Town."

Although well past his best, Abrahams played five first-class games for Western Province in the Dadabhay Trophy competition, scoring 111 runs (at an average of 15,86 per innings) and taking eight wickets at a cost of 23,62 a wicket.

It was his first contact in 15 years with Western Province cricket – and he was not at all disappointed with the standard.

"What I was extremely disappointed with – and I made no bones about this – were the facilities. They were unbelievably bad.

"On one occasion I coached on a levelled-out path, which also doubled as a pitch, in a graveyard outside Paarl. There, I came across a young left-armer with enormous potential. He could bowl just about everything. I couldn't believe it. What was even more remarkable was that no-one in his family played cricket, and no-one had taught him."

Abrahams still has a strong connection with the Central Lancashire League, though his sons Peter and Basil as well as some grandsons, who play every weekend.

But, he says, that he still feels a twinge whenever he watches test matches and sees black players such as Paul Adams and Makhaya Ntini playing for South Africa.

"It makes me wonder what might have been."

The life and times of an ambitious Cape Flats cricketer

MANY WHO KNEW him – and some of the top cricketers in Western Province counted themselves among his admirers – regarded Cecil Abrahams as a "natural", who nevertheless spent countless hours honing his skills.

Abrahams' mental toughness and confidence inevitably drew comparisons with the pugnacious Springbok all-rounder, Eddie Barlow. Abrahams himself said: "I was a very confident player. I had a strong belief in my ability - so much so that when I was on the field I thought I was the best player in the world (which I obviously wasn't!)." he said.

Confidence and a passionate love for the game were qualities that were instilled in Abrahams from an early age.

"My father, Sakkie, and my grandfather lived for cricket – and a club called Ashtondale. In those days, all the clubs had family affiliations: just as the Millers played for Heatherdale and the Tobins for Aurora, so did the Abrahamses play for Ashtondale in the Metropolitan and Suburban League."

Abrahams' cricket education was not confined to batting, bowling and fielding. His appointment as club scorekeeper at the age of nine, helped him to understand other areas of the game (such as umpiring).

"When all the other children were having fun playing cricket, I was sitting on the grass, keeping score," he said. "And my dad didn't believe in me getting paid either. I did it for the love of the game."

The scorekeeper at Ashtondale had another duty: he was also expected to double up as the team's official reserve. "I had to report to the team for scorekeeping duties, dressed in my whites. If anyone did turn up, I was drafted into the team."

"My dad didn't have to encourage us to play - cricket was in our blood.

"My friends and I were fanatics. We played cricket in every spare moment we had. In the school holidays, we played what we regarded as proper test matches in the streets near our homes. We kept batting and bowling averages – and even partnership records.

Abrahams confirmed the extent of his ability by smoothly making the the transition from street cricket to the officially organised variety, quickly becoming one of the mainstays in a very good Ashtondale side.

In 1953, Abrahams' compelling club form won him a place in the South African Coloured side which competed for – and won – the Dadabhay Trophy in Johannesburg.

And it was a string of fine all-round performances by the Ashtondale all-rounder, including 5/34 against a strong South African Indian side, that helped the South African Coloured side take the honours.

The 1953 tournament was the first and last appearance by Abrahams in an "interrace group" competition. "I didn't want to be part of any tournament s which encouraged racial separation," Abrahams said.

"I believed – as did many others – that all cricketers should be represented by one union. I couldn't see why a great player like Laam Raziet, had to play for a national Malay side, and not Western Province or South Africa, and Ben Malamba (see page 16) had to play for an African selection and not for a provincial or national team selected on merit."

Abrahams was in fine form against the Kenyan Asians. Playing for a combined Western Province team against the visitors at the Hartleyvale football stadium, he took 4/53 and 3/40, and scored 54. It was enough to earn him his first South African cap.

His form was as impressive in the tests: a top score of 55 took him to third spot in the batting averages (33,75). He also captured eight wickets for 166.

Abrahams continued his good form on an East African/Rhodesian tour by the national side. A total of 614 runs, with a highest score of 139 (against the Rhodesian Indians) and an average of 47,23, took him to the top of the batting averages (ahead, incidentally, of the great D'Oliveira). He also finished with the second highest number of wickets (37) – behind Eric Petersen and Coetie Neethling, both of whom finished with 42.

CECIL ABRAHAMS' LANCASHIRE LEAGUE STATISTICS.
MILNROW CC

	Batting		Bowling	
	Runs	**Ave**	**Wkts**	**Ave**
1961	505	21.96	60	16.92
1962	521	23.68	76	14.09
1963	823	39.19	108	10.77
1964	610	26.52	77	12.44

RADCLIFFE CC

	Batting		Bowling	
1967	518	25.90	50	14.04
1968		32.20	94	14.04
1969	574	23.91	50	13.16
1970	674	29.30	68	15.38
1971	425	15.17	89	10.25

OLDHAM CC

	Batting		Bowling	
1974	657	28.56	48	20.25
1975	674	37.44	43	16.40

Sedick Conrad – an insatiable appetite for runs

On a sweltering summer's day in November 1973, the provincial career of one of the Western Province Cricket Board's most outstanding talents – opening batsman and captain Dickie Conrad – came to a sudden, acrimonious end.

Sedick Conrad won a place in the Western Province provincial side just three years after playing his first club game for a team called Vineyards.

On the first day of a match between a Derrick Robins XI and a South African President's XI Conrad slipped into the Newlands cricket ground, through one of the "Whites Only" entrances, and settled down to watch the match.

His actions that day would earn him the dubious distinction of being the first Western Province Cricket Board player to be suspended for watching cricket at Newlands. The board's policy at the time was that the South African Cricket Union and all its affiliates were racist bodies and therefore should not be supported by any of its members.

"All I wanted to do," Conrad said many years later, "was watch my hero, the former England captain, Brian Close.

"Although I had been warned not to attend the match, I could not resist getting a close-up view of Close.

"As captain of the Western Province Cricket Board provincial side, I felt I could learn a lot by observing how he operated."

Conrad's action put him on a collision course with one of the most powerful figures in the anti-apartheid sports movement – board president, Hassan Howa.

Howa had a network of informants (in all areas of South African sport) that would have done any any country's intelligence-gathering agencies proud.

When Conrad returned to his Lansdowne home that evening, there was a message waiting for him....

It was from Howa, and it said: "Don't bother coming to Rosmead tomorrow for the Super League match against Maitland-Parow."

"I decided to call his bluff, and went along to the ground the next day," Conrad said.

"But just as I was getting ready to lead my Wynberg Super League team onto the field, Mr Howa marched into the dressing room, looked me straight in the eye and said, 'Get out!'

"I got out, but I was convinced that Mr Howa was acting illegally – and so I decided to fight him."

Advice from Conrad's lawyers suggested that he stood a good chance of being reinstated if he took the matter to court.

So he did, and he won.

The Cape Town Supreme Court ruled that his expulsion was illegal, and ordered his reinstatement.

But his relationship with players and officials wasn't quite the same again – and so he played only a few more games in Western Province Cricket Board competitions before crossing the floor to the Newlands-based Western Province Cricket Union.

Although it was as a batsman that he made his name, Dickie Conrad was also a useful spin bowler.

In March 1975, he became the first black player to play in the WP Cricket Union's first division when he turned out for the Green Point Club.

A LATE STARTER

The cricket bug bit Dickie Conrad relatively late in life – even though there were enough reminders close to him to push him in the right direction: for one thing, his father, Karriem (Kokkie), a left-arm seamer, had played provincial cricket in the 1940s; for another, he lived in a cricket-mad area, virtually on the other side of the road from the Newlands cricket ground.

"But I just wasn't interested," said Conrad. "I preferred to spend my summer weekends swimming. Real enjoyment for me was jumping onto a train with a group of my friends and heading for Kalk Bay."

It was only when he turned 18 that he began to give the game serious thought – and then only because of the constant pestering of his cousin, Rushdie Conrad.

Conrad's first club was Vineyards in the Green Point-based Western Province Cricket Association. "Having been kitted out by Rushdie, I made my debut for the club's second team as a seam bowler."

Promotion to the first team came in rather frightening circumstances. The team needed an opening batsman for a knockout-final showdown with a Roslyns team containing the fearsome Abed brothers – Tiny and Dik. "I volunteered," said Conrad, "and did quite well, getting into the twenties before being dismissed."

Taking into account his late start, Conrad's rapid progress suggested that he was a rather special talent.

Three years after playing his first competitive match, he was selected to open the innings for Western Province

at the 1963/64 Dadabhay Trophy tournament in Port Elizabeth. Being selected in a side, regarded by many as Western Province's best-ever side was in itself testimony to the regard in which he was held by the selectors.

Certainly, he was not out of place, playing in the company of top players such as Owen Williams (who led the side), Coetie Neethling, Dik and Lobo Abed, Neville Lakay, Alan Maclons, Timmy Lakay and Gertjie Williams, among others. Indeed, he more than held his own, scoring 156 runs at an average of 31,20 runs per innings.

But it was at the 1966 tournament in Durban that he emerged as a relentless compiler of runs. In the first match against Griqualand West, he smashed a career-best 194 runs.

"I was shattered when Joey Lambert ran me out so close to my double century," said Conrad. "Joey actually mocked me later, suggesting that I had been batting too long. Running me out, he said, had given others in the team a chance to bat."

Conrad ended with 719 runs in Dadabhay tournaments, at a healthy average of 47,93 per innings.

SEARCHING FOR PERFECTION

Once Conrad had made up his mind to play cricket seriously, he committed himself fully to the game.

"To improve my batting, I constructed a concrete practice pitch on an open field adjacent to my parents' home in Lansdowne," he said.

"I subsequently bought the vacant plot – and the strip now forms part of the garage floor of my house.

"But while it was an open field, I spent hours batting on my concrete strip, against the bowling of my brother, Toufiq, and cousin, Sharkey.

"Later it was used by my club, Vineyards, and even by the Eastern

Province team during the 1968 Dadabhay tournament. They were staying across the road and, when they saw the strip, they asked if they could practise on it."

The hours of practice paid handsome dividends. Conrad went on to become one of the most prolific run scorers in the 32-year history of the Western Province Cricket Board.

His average of 40,30 was the highest by a board player in three day cricket, while his 166 against Transvaal at Rosmead in January 1972 was the highest individual first-class score by a Western Province player.

Conrad also became the joint holder of the opening partnership and second-wicket partnership record for the board – 111 for the first wicket with Braima Isaacs and 232 for the second wicket with Viccie Moodie (232 is also the highest partnership for any wicket in the board's history).

"I was greedy for runs," said Conrad. "I loved to occupy the crease and I attached great value to my wicket. The night before a game I would dream about my innings and plan it in detail. I had a very close relationship with Dik Abed, who went on to become one of the top players in the Lancashire League. Dik and I spent hours discussing cricket."

Like Dik, Conrad also had ambitions of playing in the Lancashire League.

LANCASHIRE LEAGUE

In 1970, his wish was granted when Leyland Motors, a Northern Lancashire League club, offered him a contract.

"I went to them on the recommendation of Dik. Like the majority of South Africans who played league cricket, I struggled initially on the wet wickets.

"It rains all the time there during May and June. It's also extremely cold during these months. The fact that they didn't cover their wickets made things even more difficult. Because the wickets were sticky I had trouble in adjusting my timing – I often played my shots way before the ball would have reached my bat."

Later, when the weather improved, and the pitches became harder, Conrad struck his best batting form – scoring a brilliant 140 for Salford University against the Lancashire County Cricket Club's second eleven at Old Trafford.

"I really enjoyed that innings because the ball was coming onto the bat," said Conrad.

Despite his struggle to acclimatise to the conditions, Conrad argued that the experience he gained stood him in good stead.

"There was a big variation in the way the wickets played, compared with what I was used to in South Africa. Because I had never played on turf before, I was forced to work things out for myself.

"I believe this made me a better player."

Even though he enjoyed the experience of playing in the Northern Lancashire league, Conrad found that he was missing home.

"The end of the season couldn't come sooner for me. I was not happy being away from home for so long, especially with my wife Amina not being with me.

"Although I was asked to return, Amina wasn't keen on joining me, so I declined their offer."

TROUBLE AT HOME

Building on the experience he gained in England, Conrad scored heavily both in Super League and provincial cricket.

Sedick Conrad takes time off from a practice session to sign autographs for a pair of young fans. Conrad was one of two black players to be selected for the South African President's XI against the Derrick Robins XI, in March 1975.

Although he scored four provincial hundreds, Conrad rated the 99 he scored against Natal at Tills Crescent in 1973 as his most satisfying knock.

"It was a game we had to win to share the trophy with Natal. My innings helped us to do just that. In those days the Dadabhay competition was played over two seasons to allow each team a home and away match.

"At the end of the first round we were last on the log after losing all our games. I then took over as captain and we went on to win all our remaining games – a feat which helped us to win a share of the honours."

Conrad's trip to Newlands in 1973 to watch the Derrick Robins XI brought his career in the Western Province Cricket Board to a premature end, but signalled the start of a new chapter – in the Western Province Cricket Union.

BREAKING AWAY

While he was fighting his case against the Wynberg union, Conrad established contact with Gerald Mallinick, the chairman of the Green Point Cricket Club, who hinted that he should join Green Point.

"With the benefit of hindsight, my actions were selfish," said Conrad. "However, I was keen to test myself against the top white players.

"I didn't find the standard very much different to that in the Western Province Cricket Board. Certainly, board players such as Lefty Adams, Dik and Lobo Abed, and Owen Williams would have made their mark had they been given the opportunity.

Conrad felt that he had played well enough to at least have won a place in the white Western Province B side. "At one stage, Green Point wrote to the union to ask why I was not being selected," he said.

It was suggested at the time that he was not considered for selection to save the union from becoming entangled in the National Party government's apartheid legislation.

"It is something that I did not discount," Conrad said.

Later, Conrad was one of several black players – among the others were Edward Habane, Tiffie Barnes and Baboo Ebrahim – to be included in invitation teams to oppose the touring Derrick Robins and International Cavaliers teams.

Conrad felt that the invitation for him to play for the South African President's XI against the Derrick Robins side at Newlands in 1975 came at the wrong time.

Coming in at number 8, he didn't last very long before being bowled by the West Indian, John Shepherd.

"Because of my problems with the Western Province Cricket Board, I had been out of the game for six months – and suddenly, I found myself being thrust into the middle, playing against top guys.

"I was very tense, never having played in front of such big crowds and at a venue like Newlands.

"Moreover, at the age of 33, the better part of my career was over."

With the anti-apartheid struggle gaining momentum in the 1980s, pressure on his son Shukri, who represented the Western Province Nuffield team in 1982, 1983 and 1984 (when he also gained selection to the South African Schools side), resulted in Conrad having a rethink about playing in the Western Province Cricket Union.

Both father and son were cleared to play in the Western Province Cricket Board. Dickie returned to the club scene, while Shukri went on to represent the Howa Bowl team.

Desmond February – a country boy with attitude

DES FEBRUARY will never forget the first ball he delivered (or rather, did not deliver) in Lancashire League cricket....

Des February felt a great sense of pride on wearing the blue Western Province cap.

Imagine, if you can, a cold, overcast Lancashire day in 1968, a damp wicket and a curious crowd. Now, picture Werneth Cricket Club's new signing from South Africa – an uneasy mixture of nerves and high hopes – starting his run-up for the first ball of his first over in league cricket. He starts slowly, determined to build up to the proper rhythm. He picks up speed as he nears the crease. He's looking good. Into his delivery stride he goes and... oops, calamity!

February falls flat on his bum.

"It was the wet wicket that made me slip," he explained later, "but boy, was I embarrassed...."

Fortunately, everyone saw the funny side of the incident. In any event, it gave February the perfect opportunity to say, in all honesty, that he had started his Lancashire League career "from the bottom".

Throughout his impressive career, often for reasons other than cricket, February always had to work just that little bit harder to win recognition.

"BOS"

To a black cricketer of the 1960s, Cape Town and Somerset West were worlds apart. Somewhere along the national road to the Hottentots Holland mountains, cricket talent split into two versions – a city version and a country version. And the prevalent perception was that a "city"

player was always twice as good as a "country" player.

The converse perception was therefore true, too: for a player based in the country to gain selection to, say, the provincial team, he had to be twice as good as his main rivals. Des February's form for the Somerset West Board side was excellent. His performances said to the selectors: "Ignore me at your peril." Sensibly, they didn't.

In 1963, he gained selection to the Western Province team – an extremely powerful side, which swept the boards at the Dadabhay tournament in Port Elizabeth.

February, known as "Bos" (Bush) among Cape Town's cricket community (because of his origins) was not a fringe player in that title-winning team. Indeed, he had an excellent tournament, scoring 110 against Border, 53 out of 154 against Eastern Province and 54 out of 143 against Griqualand West.

"From that tournament onwards the Number 3 slot was mine," he said.

"Of course, there was no room for complacency. Everyone wanted to play for Western Province. For every position, there were about three players ready to step forward if an incumbent failed to deliver.

"That blue cap with the white WP embroidered on it was very important to us. It lifted our status in society."

Werneth-bound Des February bids farewell to his fiancée Myrtle Hurling, in April 1968.

February played in four of the five Dadabhay tournaments, scoring 328 runs at an average of 25,20 per innings (with a top score of 110 versus Border in 1963/64). He also took 29 wickets at a cost of 12,03 per wicket (with his best return being 7/40) against Eastern Province in 1968.

BEGINNINGS

A product of a cricket-mad family in a cricket-mad community, February honed his skills on the streets of Somerset West.

His was a highly portable form of cricket – all that was needed were a couple of wooden (often home-made) bats, a paraffin tin (for wickets), a tennis ball and a relatively open piece of road.

"On one occasion a group of policemen confiscated our paraffin tin. But because we regarded it as a precious possession, we went to the police station and pleaded with the cops until they returned it to us."

Even though hundreds of youngsters in dozens of township streets were hooked on cricket, there was no organised form of the game – at school or club level.

As a result, the very talented were pushed into adult sides at a very young age. It was a case of swim or sink. Many, like February, swam.

"It was the era of the family club," said February. "In my case, the family club was called Pirates. I was 15 when I made my debut for them."

Because the Western Province Cricket Board had no formal coaching structures, many board players tried to learn the finer points of the game by watching international stars or Currie Cup stalwarts in action at Newlands. February was no exception.

"We didn't have a choice," he said. "The only way that I could improve my game was by watching others and reading books. I was a regular at Newlands until Hassan Howa persuaded me (and many others) to stop going.

"When we started looking at things like segregated seating, it became easy to boycott Newlands. From then on, books – and a series of newspaper cuttings featuring Geoff Boycott's coaching tips – were to be February's sole source of inspiration.

TO THE LEAGUES

Nevertheless, the runs and wickets kept coming – so that soon February began to be described as "Lancashire League material".

Certainly, February himself was keen to follow in the footsteps of players such as Basil D'Oliveira, Cecil Abrahams, Owen Williams, Coetie Neethling and Dik Abed.

Like all the Western Province cricketers who went to play in the league, he was recommended by journalist Damoo Bansda.

"Bansda fed information about us – such as statistics – to John Kay of the *Manchester Guardian*. Bansda was our go-between. We didn't know anyone in the UK.

"Our contracts also normally came through the hard-working Bansda. The white sportswriters here took very little notice of the cricket being played by the affiliates of the Western Province Cricket Board.

"Because white cricket writers had no interest in us – as far as they were concerned, we were inferior – we also had to submit regular progress reports to Bansda. He then compiled reports and submitted them to the *Cape Times*."

After being chosen ahead of players such as Dickie Conrad, Gertjie Williams and Natal's Omar Vawda, February almost didn't make it to Werneth, a Central Lancashire League club.

"I had difficulty in getting a passport because one of my cousins, Basil February, was a member of *umKhonto we Sizwe* (MK), the military wing of the African National Congress.

"The security police were looking for Basil, a medical student who went to Russia and Yugoslavia with the late Chris Hani.

"When I enquired about the delay in providing me with a passport, I was told that Pretoria had sent instructions that I should not be given one.

"When I told Bansda what had happened, he accused me of being involved in politics. Eventually, James, my eldest brother, made representations on my behalf, and I was granted a passport."

As with all other board players who went to the Lancashire League, Bansda arranged for February to have a few net sessions on the turf wickets of the Bishops school, under the watchful eye of the school coach, Tom Reddick. This was to enable February to get used to playing on turf.

Going to England from the almost rural environment of Somerset West was a strange experience for the 24-year-old February .

"It rained for the first three weeks of my stay there. Fortunately, I was able to stay with relatives in London for the first few days after my arrival."

In addition to the difficulties of acclimatising to his new surroundings, February also had difficulty in communicating with his northern English teammates.

"I struggled to understand their accents. I found, in the beginning, anyway, that I had to sound like them to be accepted by them," he said.

"Dik Abed and I were fortunate to have the support of Dik's elder brother Goolam and Cecil Abrahams. In addition to their experience as cricketers in the Lancashire League, they had also been living in England for several years.

"Cecil and Goolam were our mentors. We took all our problems to them – and most times they were able to help us."

The "aloof" Basil D'Oliveira

WHILE SPEAKING warmly of the support he received from Cecil Abrahams and Goolam Abed, February was rather less impressed with Basil D'Oliveira.

"I found him to be aloof," said February.

"I was invited to bowl to the England team – of which Basil was a member – at a net session at Old Trafford in Manchester.

"Afterwards, Colin Cowdrey, the England captain, invited me to have lunch with the team. The players were all very friendly – except for Basil, who had very little time for me.

"Although we had played together in Cape Town, he spent only about five minutes with me.

"When I asked him for a recommendation to Surrey, with whom I had had trials, he said: 'You are your own recommendation.'"

Playing as Werneth's professional, February quickly found out the extent of his responsibilities: "I was expected to open the bowling, take the most catches and score the most runs."

In 1969, the *Cape Herald's* London correspondent described the wickets in the early part of the British season as little better than mud heaps.

"To play cricket under sullen skies and on such pitches was a task to test the patience and ability of any cricketer. Werneth knew this, and were far from despondent when February, a medium-paced bowler and big-hitting batsman met with little initial success.

"Unlike (Dik) Abed, he had not dropped into a side blessed with exceptionally good amateur players, especially from the bowling point of view – and the South African found the going tough. When the pitches hardened and the sun shone on his back, February produced better form.

"His final return of 81 wickets at 16 runs, and 492 runs for a batting average of 24 clearly showed promise and

Werneth were happy to give him a further season's engagement in 1969," the *Cape Herald* reported.

"Werneth offered me better terms after initially stating that they could not meet my demands," February said.

The club was clearly happy with their South African import.

"It's a long time since a professional scored 500 runs and took 50 wickets for us – and we think he will do even better for us next season," a club official said.

But he was wrong. February's second season didn't turn out to be anywhere near as good as his first.

The *Cape Herald* said: "Finishing midway in the league table, with their professional paying over 16 runs for his 53 wickets and aggregating only 253 runs with the bat for an average of only 14, it was obvious that in the highly competitive league cricket sphere, Werneth would have to look elsewhere for a professional in 1970."

February felt that the decline in his second season's performances was because of a change in captaincy at the club, as well as the knowledge that he would not be returning the following season. "I had become engaged, and my fiancé, Myrtle, would not have been able to come over to teach. Just before I left, a scout from Leyland offered me a contract, but I turned down the offer," said February

Leyland later engaged Western Province opening batsman Dickie Conrad as their overseas professional.

As a black South African coming from an apartheid society, players like February were the focus of much media attention in England.

"People were always curious about us and the situation in South Africa."

After returning from his first season in England in 1968, February initially refused to play for Somerset West.

"Certain players were not happy with me being in the board side. I decided not to play so as not to cause any ill-feelings.

"I attributed much of the trouble to petty jealousies. But cricket is the greatest leveller. This game is far greater than the individual, " he told the *Sports Post* newspaper.

Disillusioned by the poor facilities under which black cricketers had to play in Cape Town, February lost interest – and after captaining St Augustines for two seasons following his move from Somerset West to the suburb of Fairways in the southern Peninsula, he retired.

"I just couldn't see myself playing in sand and dust heaps," he said.

LANCASHIRE LEAGUE STATISTICS (WERNETH CC)

| Year | Batting | | Bowling | |
	Runs	Ave	Wkts	Ave
1968	492	24,00	81	16.00
1969	253	14,58	53	16.00

Rushdi Magiet – creating opportunities for later generations

IN THE HILL town of Kohima, the capital of the Indian state of Nagaland, stands a memorial, commemorating a victory by Anglo-Indian forces over an advancing Japanese army during the Second World War: "When you go home," the memorial says, "tell them of us and say – for your tomorrow, we gave our today."

Rushdi Magiet, a strong opponent of apartheid sport, was prepared to sacrifice his own cricketing career so that later generations could benefit.

Do these poignant words hold any special meaning for those involved in the struggle for equality in the southernmost part of Africa?

They do – quite emphatically so.

In many ways, the words are an affirmation that scores of ordinary men and women, everywhere, will confront evil – whether in government, war or sport – often at great cost to their own careers and ambitions.

They also serve as a reminder of the debt of gratitude owed to those who took up the cudgels against injustice by those who are today benefiting from the country's new, more democratic system.

The story of the political struggle against apartheid has been well documented. Less well known are the contributions that were made to a new South African society – often in small, but significant ways – by legions of black sportsmen and women.

Take, for example, the story of Rushdi Magiet....

KEEPING CRICKET ALIVE

In the late 1950s and early 1960s, when Magiet was growing up, the black cricket-playing communities of the Western Cape were reeling under the cosh of apartheid.

Although many of the most talented cricketers lived within a stone's throw of some of the province's finest facilities, apartheid decreed that these were for "Whites Only".

Black cricketers had to manufacture fields from open pieces of veld, using their own resources – both physical and financial (local municipalities, generally, didn't want to know the problems of those who weren't white). Practice pitches were tarmac roads; coaches were library books featuring the batting and bowling secrets of the great Australian and English players. Magiet and his generation (like generations before them) were automatically disqualified from representing their country. The mainly-white guardians of the game – both in South Africa and overseas – ignored them.

To all intents and purposes, they did not exist.

And yet, the more they were rebuffed, the more determined were they to continue playing the game to the highest standards that they could muster.

Magiet motivated himself in novel ways. Although the Newlands rugby and cricket stadiums, which were situated close to the Claremont home of his childhood, were out of bounds, they instilled in him a deep love for rugby and cricket – a love that would later win him provincial honours in both codes of sports.

Like dozens of his peers, he honed his cricketing skills on the streets near the two grounds.

"We were kids who ate and slept the game. Given the great level of interest, the ideal next step should have been the playing of organised junior cricket at schools or club level," Magiet said.

"The only problem, though, was that there were no structures for junior cricket – simply because there were no facilities.

"As a result, any youngster who wanted to play the game competively had to join a senior team. I was 11 years old when I became a senior member of the Muslims club."

In those days, there was more to cricket than simply batting, bowling or fielding. Club members also had to make sure that the field for a weekend fixture was "fit" to play on.

"One of my most vivid childhood memories," said Magiet, "was travelling by bus to Rondebosch Common with Abubakaar Taliep, a fellow youngster at the club, to prepare the pitch.

"It was a terrible ground, but it was all we had. Often, during matches, we'd lose the ball in the long grass – remember, clubs in those days could not afford lawn mowers. Once a year, a few weeks before the start of a new season, we'd start a veld fire to get rid of the long grass. That was the only time the outfield at the Common was in a manageable condition.

"The gravel pitches, on the other hand, were normally in excellent shape. In most cases, those who prepared the pitches were self-taught experts – they were artisans who applied the knowledge they gained from the building trade to pitch preparation," said Magiet.

"The procedure would go something like this: first, the wicket would be carefully scraped. Then, a few of the helpers would set off with a container to the nearby Red Cross Children's Hospital, and fill it with water. On the way back, they'd collect the roller, which was also stored at the hospital. A combination of scraping, watering and rolling would eventually result in a top-class pitch being prepared.

"It was a hard job, but the fact that we were prepared to go through all this trouble, showed how dedicated we were to the game," said Magiet.

STAR QUALITY

Magiet enjoyed a rapid rise through the ranks of, first, the Muslims Cricket Club, and, later, the Combine Cricket Club. He clearly was a special cricket talent. In 1967, he was "spotted" by Basil D'Oliveira during a fund-raising match at Green Point Track, in which he took 5/18 off 11 overs, including the wicket of D'Oliveira, himself.

"After the match, Basil announced that he wanted to take a few cricketers to England to give them an opportunity to play there," Magiet said.

"He chose Dickie Conrad, Omar Vawda and me."

To the disappointment of the three men, nothing came of the promise because, according to Magiet, "there was quite a bit of anti-Basil sentiment going around at the time, with his detractors criticising him for not doing enough to help promising Western Province Cricket Board players get to England".

But in 1969, Lancashire League club Todmorden approached Magiet with an offer of a contract after a recommendation by D'Oliveira (and references from former Nottinghamshire coach, Tom Reddick).

The terms of the contract were negotiated on Magiet's behalf by Dik Abed, who by then already had a few seasons of Lancashire League cricket under his belt.

"Dik also assisted me with preparations before my departure to England," said Magiet.

"Because I had never played on turf before, he took me to the Ohlssons ground in Newlands to show me how to bowl on turf. He dipped the ball in water to get me used to gripping a wet ball.

"'This is what you are going to have to get used to,' Dik told me."

Like all the other Western Province Cricket Board players who preceded him in the Lancashire League, Magiet struggled on arrival in the UK.

"Although I was warned that conditions would be different, I only discovered how different once I'd arrived there and started playing. To make matters worse for me, especially in my role as a bowler, Todmorden had the slowest wicket in the league.

"I bowled my fast leg- and offcutters far too short, and because of the slower pitches my deliveries were hammered.

"On the matting wickets of Cape Town, I was so accustomed to bowling shorter, that I battled to adjust to bowling a fuller length in England.

"I also struggled with my batting – for more or less the same reasons. I liked hooking and cutting in South Africa, but the combination of slower pitches and fuller bowling meant that I had precious few opportunities to play these shots – and when I did get the chance, I struggled with my timing.

"To add to my woes, I hurt my back and was sidelined for six weeks. I became so disheartened that I decided league cricket was not for me," he said.

The fact that he was following in the footsteps of the highly successful West Indian all-rounder Syl Oliver increased the pressure and expectation on Magiet to perform at the club. At the end of his first and only season, he had managed only 31 wickets at 20,09 per wicket, and 438 runs at 21,90 per innings. Only once did he pass 50 runs while batting – and he didn't manage a single five-wicket haul.

The London correspondent of the *Cape Herald*, in trying to put his performances into context, wrote: "Lacking the sort of amateur support that enabled (Dik) Abed to master his early doubts at Enfield, Magiet was a bitterly disappointed all-rounder long before the season ended."

HIGHLIGHTING THE POSITIVES

There were, however, some positives: after a stint of specialised coaching and net practice at the Old Trafford, Norman Oldfield, the Lancashire County Cricket Club coach (and a former England batsman) pronounced Magiet "good enough".

It was an endorsement, said Magiet, that did a lot to rebuild his shattered confidence.

While admitting that his overall performances for Todmorden did not come up to scratch, Magiet nevertheless felt that his bowling had benefited from his six-month stint with the club.

"I also grew in other ways," he said. "For instance, I was fortunate to have lived with the parents of Peter Lever, the Lancashire and England opening bowler.

"I found it very encouraging that Peter's family took a strong stand against apartheid – in fact, Peter himself was one of probably less than a handful of English cricketers who refused to play against South African teams touring England."

Magiet also acknowledged the role Lever played in his development as a bowler.

"On many occasions, Peter invited me to the Lancashire nets to bowl at the county side's batsmen. There, he taught me to bowl with the seam. I learnt a lot from him.

"I learnt to play on turf in the league, but overall it was hard work. As a professional my performances were pivotal to the success of the team. Most teams have just one or two good players, with the rest being, at best, ordinary club cricketers."

NEW TRICKS

A major learning curve for Magiet was coming to terms with the ball swinging through the air.

"In the Lancashire League, most pace bowlers swung the ball through the air," Magiet said, "but when I returned to South Africa, I found that I couldn't get the ball to swing in this manner.

"It was by trial and error that I discovered reverse swing. Because of the hard, rough fields and the matting wickets, the ball became scuffed very quickly. I found that if I shone the ball on one side and maintained the roughness on the other, aerodynamics caused the ball to swing.

"When the Western Province Cricket Board started playing on turf in 1977, the shine remained on the ball much longer, thus mitigating against movement through the air."

Magiet then started using "artificial" means to roughen up the ball. Often, a member of his team would have a bottle top or piece of glass in his pocket for precisely this purpose. With this additional help, Magiet was able to swing the ball prodigiously, often to the utter amazement of the opposing batsmen.

On his return from the Lancashire League, Magiet made his debut for the Western Province Dadabhay team in 1970, becoming an automatic selection for the next 11 seasons. He captained the team for two seasons – in 1977/78 and 1978/79 – before handing over the reins to Lefty Adams.

His best bowling analysis for Western Province was 7/35 against Transvaal in 1978. He made his top score of 76 against Eastern Province in 1975.

Even though he had the talent to have played at a much higher level, Magiet said he was not sad about the opportunities he and his peers had missed out on because of apartheid.

"I believe that we sacrificed our careers for the best possible reason – our children," he said.

"The process of unity which came about because of the isolation of South African teams, gave our children the opportunities we didn't have.

"I am proud of the sacrifices made by my generation of cricketers – and those before us."

"Coetie" Neethling – a gentleman and a match winner

WITH HIS FASHIONABLE gold-rimmed glasses and his natty selection of jackets, shoes and ties, John "Coetie" Neethling was the epitome of smart-casual in the late 1950s and early Sixties....

Coetie Neethling emerged as one of Western Province's best all-rounders during the early 1960s.

But there was another side to Neethling, too – that of a naturally talented sportsman who when togged out in either a striker's soccer shirt or in cricket whites could mix it with the roughest, toughest opponents, before teaching them a lesson in the finer arts of the game, which they seldom forgot.

As a striker for Nelsons football club and the Central Union board side, he ranked among the best in the Western Cape. But it was as a cricket all-rounder that he made his mark on both the local and national sporting scene.

Like all black cricketers in South Africa, Neethling's introduction to the game came via the streets – with home-made bats, tennis balls and oil-drum wickets.

"I received no coaching – I was entirely self-taught," he said.

Neethling taught himself in two ways: "I made sure that I was at Newlands whenever an international team toured South Africa. That's where I learnt to steal with my eyes.

"My wise old dad, realising what cricket meant to me, always came forward with the entrance fee to enable my brother, Poena, and me to attend these matches. And when games were on school days, he'd allow us to skip classes.

"His attitude was amazing, considering he never played cricket himself.

"His game was rugby.

"Poena and I watched all the touring teams who came to South Africa in the 1950s and Sixties. England, with greats such as Len Hutton, Cyril Washbrook, Peter May, Colin Cowdrey and Ken Barrington in their ranks, were our particular favourites. We watched like hawks – then photographed with our minds – their every bowling or batting move.

"Next, we played what we saw over and over – still in our minds – in slow motion.

"We were the ultimate copycats.

"We then tried to implement in the streets what we saw them doing on the field."

Books formed the second part of Neethling's cricket-coaching education. "I took books out of the library and used them to improve my technique. I read coaching manuals and biographies by players such as Hutton and Washbrook. I always took notes as I read.

"It was from books that I learnt how to grip the ball for inswingers and offcutters," he said.

MATCH DAYS

Practice nets were a luxury in the coloured cricket-playing community of Goodwood. But, once a week, Neethling and his team mates of the

Elma Cricket Club would put in some solid in-the-middle practice.

"It became quite a ritual," said Neethling. "On Saturday, we'd play our match; the following Thursday, we'd collect our mat from a woman who lived just across the road from our field, roll it out and then try to get as good a workout as we possibly could. The next day, we'd return to the ground to prepare the pitch and out-field for our next game."

Coetie Neethling reserved some of his best performances when playing for Maitland-Parow against the WP Cricket Association. Here, he is pictured with Lobo Abed (right) and Hassan Howa (centre) sharing the Super League trophy.

In the 1950s and for part of the 1960s, cricket was a game for men. Junior cricket did not exist. Boys – some as young as 11 – who thought they had the mental and physical strength, were drafted straight into senior teams.

This proved to be the making of some and the breaking of others.

Neethling was 15 when he made his debut in the senior leagues – and quickly showed that he would not be intimidated. "Nevertheless," he said, "it was tough, and the seniors showed us no mercy. It was a case of them saying, 'if you want to play with men, we'll treat you like men.'"

Neethling's first taste of serious competitive cricket came at the age of 16 when he was included in the Elma first team for a knockout final against Avenirs. This powerful side, boasted the likes of the great Basil Waterwitch and other top players such as the Bell brothers, Alex (who played for South Africa) and Willie, both of whom were very quick, and Lionel Daniels.

"Having been champions for 13 years, Avenirs had an awesome repu-tation, so much so that my brother Poena refused to play them. He said he was scared of them."

It was not a fairy-tale debut for Neethling – Avenirs, as everyone had predicted, crushed Elma, but Neeth-ling's 20-something out of 50 launched what was to become a glit-tering career in nonracial cricket.

NATIONAL HONOURS

A string of fine performances at club level earned Neethling selection to the Maitland-Parow board side.

The jump in standard did not inhib-it him at all. In 1956, he played so well for the board side that many tipped him as a certainty for the Western Province team to meet the touring Kenyan Asian side. But, to the surprise of everyone, he was left out.

Rather than mope about his omission, Neethling simply resolved to work harder at his game. Less than two years later, he'd hit such a rich vein of form, that the South African Cricket Board of Control (Sacboc) selectors could not ignore him, and he was included in the South African side, captained by Basil D'Oliveira, which toured Kenya.

Neethling confirmed his rating as one of South Africa's leading all-rounders by scoring 418 runs against Kenyan opposition at an average of 32,15 per innings, and taking 42 wickets at a cost of 14,14 runs per wicket.

His batting, particularly, was wonderfully consistent. Five fifties, including a fifty in each test, saw him winning a bat at the end of the tour for his all-round performances.

"The Kenyans were amazed when we told them about the poor playing conditions under which we laboured, and that we didn't have any organised coaching structures in South Africa," Neethling said.

"And the reason they were so incredulous was that, despite all these obstacles, we played some really great cricket on that tour."

Still in 1958, Neethling added to his selection of bats, by winning another one at Sacboc's inter race tournament in Cape Town: playing for the South African Coloured team, he topped the bowling averages at the tournament – his 13 wickets costing him just 9,15 runs each.

Neethling did not know it then, but his performances were being monitored from outside the country – by Colne, a Lancashire League club looking to sign a professional.

"The results of our matches in Kenya were recorded in *Wisden,* which was where Colne officials read about my all-round performances. They approached Basil [D'Oliveira], who recommended me.

"I was told later that some of the Colne members were sceptical about signing an unknown.

"Fortunately, I was able to justify the confidence that the club officials showed in me."

For someone who played with such confidence on the cricket field, Neethling admitted to being more than a little apprehensive about playing in England.

"I had serious doubts about whether I would make the grade – especially after Basil had mentioned the names of some of the players I would be opposing.

"I got cold shivers when I realised I would be playing against West Indian greats such as Wes Hall, Rohan Kanhai, Charlie Griffiths, Roy Gilchrist, Sonny Ramadhin and Basil Butcher."

But Neethling's colleagues at Maitland-Parow had no doubts about his ability: "Go for it," they urged him, "you'll make it."

Neethling, however, remained unsure – so he sought the opinion of Sydney Solomon, a teammate in Kenya, who had emigrated to the UK.

"I needed to be convinced," said Neethling, "and I was."

Solomon replied: "After playing four matches with Cecil [Abrahams] I shall now quote my words to Cynthia [Solomon's wife]: 'I think Coetie and Ben [Malamba] will do better with the ball [in England] than Cecil, and Eric [Petersen] will do even better.

'My reasons: Cecil is fast and moves the ball very little off the pitch. Here the batsmen have played against faster bowlers, though not very much faster.

'Coetie and Ben bring the ball off a height and can cut the ball when it's old – which Cecil can't do.

'Cecil to me is a very dear friend – I'm only being honest.'"

Reassured, Neethling signed for Colne in 1962.

Before leaving, he had to resign his job as a primary school teacher.

But he said: "It wasn't a difficult decision. I really wanted to play in England."

With a little help from his friends

THE MOMENT Coetie Neethling agreed to sign for Lancashire League club, Colne, both his local club, Elma, and his union, Maitland-Parow, immediately set fundraising efforts in motion to help pay for his trip.

"I was really very, very grateful for their help," said Neethling.

"I needed the money because in terms of my contract, Colne only needed to pay to get me to the UK.

"I had to find my own cash for the return trip."

Before going to the UK, Neethling had never played on turf.

"Fortunately, I knew someone who had connections with the white Alma club. He organised for me to use their nets. When I arrived for the workout, I found that just one bowler had been made available to me.

"That was the only practice I was able to get on turf before linking up with Colne."

Neethling travelled to England on the same boat as D'Oliveira, who had returned to South Africa to collect his family.

"The first thing that struck me when I disembarked at Southampton was how cold the UK was. Getting used to the cold was the first big adjustment I had to make. During my first game for Colne it snowed."

"A TRUE SPRINGBOK"

Neethling hardly had time to settle down in his new surroundings when Colne came up against a Church side, in which the great West Indian fast bowler, Wesley Hall, was an inspirational figure.

Displaying the temperament which had seen him rise to the occasion so many times in South Africa, Neethling stroked his way to an unbeaten 50 and then took 9/45. Hall, who should have been his 10th wicket, was dropped on the boundary by the Colne captain.

Nevertheless, the big West Indian was impressed enough to look up the South African after the match, with some special words of praise.

"He came up to me," said Neethling, "shook my hand, and said: 'You're a true Springbok'.

"That really was a fantastic compliment, especially since it came from such a great bowler."

After taking 59 wickets at an average of 14,86 in his first season, Neethling performed even better in his second, taking 88 wickets at a cost of 10,94 runs per wicket.

"Had three of our games not been rained off, I'm sure I would have reached the '100 wickets in a season' mark," he said.

He found batting in the English conditions slightly more difficult, though – scoring 433 runs (at an average of 24,55) in 1962 and 238 runs (at an average of 14,58) in 1963.

"I found it difficult to adjust to the slower British wickets," he explained.

In 1967, D'Oliveira told the *Cape Herald* that Roy Gilchrist, another top West Indian fast bowler, had once said to him: "Neethling is one helluva good bowler."

D'Oliveira said that Neethling had adapted to turf wickets so quickly that he could easily have been awarded a county contract had he stayed on in England.

Neethling decided to return to South Africa when, after finishing second in the bowling averages at the end of his second season, his request for an improved contract was turned down.

"Ironically, they paid the fee I had asked for to an Australian who took my place.

"Other sides were interested in acquiring my services, but by the time I had completed negotiations with Colne, the deadline, which clubs had to sign a professional had passed."

Looking back many years later on his time in the Lancashire League, Neethling said it was time that had been well spent.

"It helped me develop my game tremendously," he said.

"For a short time I was able to escape the isolation that was the lot of black cricketers in South Africa and had come into contact with some of the game's great players. I learnt a lot about moving the ball through the air and cutting it off the seam.

"I was also able to pick up invaluable tips from the many coaching sessions that were featured on British television."

Had he returned to England for a third season, Neethling would probably have been lost to South African cricket.

"I was offered a teaching post – and my family were also willing to accompany me," he said.

"But as it turned out I didn't go."

BACK IN SA

Neethling applied his improved skills effectively at provincial level. Through the Sixties, Western Province won four out of five interprovincial Dadabhay tournaments – and almost every time he featured prominently with either bat or ball (or sometimes both) in these triumphs.

Having made his debut at the 1961 tournament in Johannesburg, he was a regular until the 1974/75 season.

He was the captain of the side for the last two Dadabhay tournaments – in 1968 and 1969 – and also for Western Province's first three-day games in 1971/72.

Although he failed to score a Dadabhay century, Neethling twice made it into the nineties – 98 against Eastern Province in 1963/64 and 91 not out against Eastern Province in 1969, when he finished with a batting average of 151.

He also registered a career-best bowling return of 7/58 against Transvaal in 1966.

Asked to name his main bowling asset, Neethling said: "Variation. I was able to bowl quite a few different balls. I loved bowling into the breeze, which assisted my type of swing bowling. I accumulated most of my wickets with reverse swing."

Coetie Neethling was a member of the SA Coloured Cricket Association side which won the Dadabhay Trophy in 1958.
Back row (left to right): S Raziet, B Erickson, P January, C Pool, Coetie Neethling, O Williams, B Witten.
Centre: J de Bruyn (Assistant Secretary), H Howa (manager), B D'Oliveira (captain), J van Harte (president), A Sobotker, M Segers, GM Heneke (treasurer).
Front: K Salojee, D Hinrichsen, N Lakay, S Solomon
Absent: I Southgate

In 1968, the Sportsman's Club named Neethling their Sportsman of the Year. It was the cherry on the top of a great year for him – he'd also led Western Province to their third successive Dadabhay tournament victory in Cape Town.

In addition to his obvious talent, Neethling's rise to the top was assisted by his tough mental approach to the game.

In a column for the *Sports Post* in 1969, Dik Abed, who became a legend in the Lancashire League, likened Neethling's fighting spirit to the famed bulldog tenacity of Yorkshire cricketers.

"Yorkshire bring to the game a professional fanatacism – the fighting spirit which Springbok, Eddie Barlow, brought back with him to South Africa after he'd spent a season in the Lancashire League," said Abed.

"The best recent example of this fighting spirit came in the Maitland-Parow versus Western Province Cricket Association match. The fighter in this match was Coetie Neethling. With Western Province needing 100 runs for victory – and all afternoon to get them – Coetie put himself on and bowled us out.

"He just never gave up.

"You could almost hear him saying, 'I've got to get this team out. I will get them out.'

"And he did.

"We can learn a lot from the Neethlings, the Barlows and the Yorkshiremen," Abed wrote.

In 1974, Neethling captained one of the invitation sides which played a multiracial match at Rosmead in Claremont, in an effort to kickstart the move towards integrated cricket in the Western Province.

The England fast bowler Fred Trueman captained the other side.

"We were hopeful that it would be the start of a unity process in cricket," said Neethling, " but the political scenario made that impossible."

After a 20-year career in provincial cricket, Neethling retired at the age of 37 but continued playing club cricket for Elsies River until the age of 46.

Besides being a great performer on the field, he was also a well-liked figure off it.

He was regarded as one of the more popular teachers at Bishop Lavis High School, not only because he was a cricket star, but also because he was always willing to share his immense sporting knowledge with his pupils.

As was the case with other top players, such as Basil D'Oliveira, Owen Williams, Cecil Abrahams and Dik Abed, apartheid denied South African cricket lovers and, indeed, the world, the chance of seeing Coetie Neethling playing at the highest level.

COETIE NEETHLING'S LANCASHIRE LEAGUE STATISTICS

| | Batting | | Bowling | |
	Runs	Ave	Wkts	Ave
1962	433	24,55	59	14,86
1963	238	14,87	88	10,94

Owen Williams – striving for cricket excellence, with dignity

TO OWEN WILLIAMS, apartheid meant more than the humiliation of being ushered to a seat in the back of a bus... a separate queue in a post office... a "coloured group area"... or having to play the game he loved and excelled at on inferior fields and matting wickets....

Owen Williams honed his skills on the streets of Claremont.

It tore at him every minute of every day of his life – for it affected him in the most basic way possible: it split his family, elevating one section to a life of privilege, while dooming the other to a second-class existence.

Williams' nightmare began shortly after his 12th birthday, when the functionaries of South Africa's system of social engineering classified his mother, a brother and sister white; Williams and another brother and sister were declared coloured.

"I don't know if you understand what this means," he told the UK based *Sun* newspaper in 1971. "It means that I can only visit my mother after dark.

"She lives in a white area – and so, if I'm seen calling on her it starts the neighbours talking, saying she must be coloured.

"To save her, I stay away.

"It also means that I can't, for instance, meet my [white] brother in the city for a drink."

And yet, in the midst of this personal anguish, he still found time to shine at cricket.

Williams is considered by many, who had the privilege of seeing him play to have been one of the best left-arm spinners ever to come out of South Africa. His superb record as a provincial cricketer in South Africa and in the Lancashire League bears testimony to that.

Sadly, when he was at the peak of his career in the 1960s, at a time when there was a dearth of top-class spinners in white South African competitions, apartheid ruled him out of test cricket.

SEEKING A FUTURE

Like most of his peers, Williams learnt the game by watching others, and reading as much as he could.

"I was a sports fanatic who spent most of my time collecting newspaper cuttings of the Springbok rugby and cricket teams. And when I started playing, I modelled my style on that of 'Tufty' Mann, a well-known Springbok spinner of the 1940s," he said.

Competitive (but informal) cricket for the young Williams started with daily street games in Warwick Street, Claremont.

There, in the fiercely contested matches, the potential of the young players was acknowledged by some of the top judges of the day.

"Jack Newman, a respected local coach, said he was impressed after having watched us play," said Williams.

"And another spectator, the Springbok, Owen Wynne, said on one occasion: 'You boys have a great future – but not in South Africa!'

"I also learnt a lot from Mr Reid, my Biology teacher at the nearby Livingstone High School. He'd take us down to a pitch and put a 20c coin, which was a lot of money in those days, on the bails. Then he'd say, 'the first one to bowl me gets it.' That was a great incentive – for, in addition to wanting to win the money, we all relished the prospect of bowling out a first-league player."

POTENTIAL REALISED

Even as a youngster, Williams' philosophy was: "in order to be successful, practise, practise and practise again."

It certainly worked for him: his bowling improved in leaps and bounds and, consequently, his rise to the top came quickly.

Playing for the powerful Oakdale club side and the Cape District Union board team, he claimed more than 150 wickets a season, for three successive seasons – to set a record that was never broken.

In board games, he bowled the great Basil D'Oliveira six times in eight innings, before D'Oliveira's departure for England in 1960.

He also captained Oakdale for 10 seasons.

"I regarded being appointed as captain of the side as a great honour – especially since we had experienced players such as Archie McKinnon, Poenie du Preez and Dougie Mulder in our lineup.

"We were Western Province club champions for six successive seasons in the 1950s. The only side which came close to us were St Augustines, who also had a great side."

In the days of ethnically divided unions, Williams made his debut for the Western Province Coloured side in 1953. Five years and two tournaments later he had gained selection to the South African Coloured side.

"I regard that 1958 team, which included greats such as D'Oliveira, Laam Raziet, Basil Witten, Sydney Solomon and Coetie Neethling as the best I ever played in," said Williams. Under the leadership of D'Oliveira, the South African Coloured team easily won the tournament, which was played in Cape Town. Williams' 12 wickets came at a cost of just 14,80 per wicket – good enough to win him selection to the South African side which toured Kenya later that year.

Williams' outstanding performance on that tour was his 9/59 against the Kongonis, a white Kenyan side which had beaten the MCC that year.

Unfortunately for him, however, injury prevented him from playing a major part in the test series against the Kenyan Asians.

In the first nonracial tournament to be played under the auspices of the South African Cricket Board of Control, in Johannesburg in 1961/62, Williams finished as Western Province's top wicket taker. His haul of 18 wickets included a superb 5/37 against the powerful Transvaal side, which only a short time earlier had provided the bulk of the SA Haque XI that had beaten a Johnnny Waite XI, packed with South African test players.

At the next tournament in Port Elizabeth in 1963/64, Williams, who captained Western Province to their first Dadabhay tournament success, mesmerised the opposition in claiming 35 wickets at an incredible cost of only four runs per wicket. His bowling feats in Port Elizabeth included 6/7 against South Western Districts and 7/39 against Transvaal.

At the final centralised tournament in Kimberley in 1969/70 (he'd missed two tournaments because of Lancashire League commitments in England), he continued to weave his spell over the Transvaal batsmen, finishing with 10/62.

"Transvaal were my favourite opponents, but also my toughest," he said. "They had some good players in Tiffie Barnes, Ossie Latha and Solly Chothia. I always played my best cricket when up against good opponents."

THE LANCASHIRE LEAGUE

The immediate beneficiary of Williams' superb bowling performances was not the South African test side, but tiny Radcliffe in the Lancashire League in England.

Clearly impressed by the left-hander, and after the spadework had been done by journalist Damoo Bansda and former Nottinghamshire professional, Tom Reddick, Radcliffe signed Williams as their professional in 1966.

Prior to his departure for England, the *Cape Herald* said of him: "This left-hander, with his impeccable length and deadly accuracy, has always proved to be a decided menace to many batsmen, as even the great D'Oliveira will concede. But it is not only as a spinner that Owen Williams has made his mark. His qualities of leadership have placed him above the ordinary cricketer. His quiet, yet dynamic personality, his encouragement and advice and his perseverance and determination were all assets which stamped him as one of the greatest and most successful captains in the country."

After a slow start with Radcliffe, where he had problems adjusting to the conditions, particularly the wet wickets and wet balls, Williams came into his own, finishing with 143 wickets at a miserly cost of 7,94 per wicket.

Williams paid tribute to fellow Capetonian Cecil Abrahams, a teammate on the South African tour to Kenya, for his role in helping him find his feet in England.

"I'm deeply indebted to Cecil for his assistance in England, especially at a time when I knew no-one.

"He even joined Radcliffe to help me along."

Thirty years later (in the 1990s) they were still keeping in touch with each other – Williams from Australia, where he had made his home, and Abrahams from England.

Following his excellent performances with Radcliffe, Williams was offered a trial by Warwickshire in 1966 and was invited to join them the following season.

"I was quite keen to play," he said, "but when I heard they had signed the great West Indian off-spinner, Lance Gibbs, I decided against joining them because I felt it would have been very difficult for me to compete against someone with such a great reputation.

"Coming from South Africa, and not being a test player made things more difficult for me because I was an unknown. I had to choose between playing cricket full time and my job as a foreman with a cabinet-making factory in Cape Town. I was mindful, too, that I was already into my 30s. In the end, I decided to stick with the company," said Williams.

"But I will always be grateful for the assistance I received from Lance while I was playing for the Warwickshire second team.

"Until I arrived in England, I had never experienced a smooth, shiny ball or even a wet one. I had to learn cricket all over again – and Lance advised me on flight, spin and variations of attack."

Gibbs' advice and Williams' undoubted talent proved a lethal combination on the county second XI circuit. Williams became the scourge of countless batsmen, with his most satisfying figures being 7/37 in 29 overs against Glamorgan. In a game against the

Leicestershire second XI, in which he took nine wickets, he won a prize of £2 for being player of the match.

Basil D'Oliveira, referring to Williams in his book, *The D'Oliveira Affair*, wrote: "Perhaps by the time he came to England, in 1966, he had played too much cricket on matting wickets. He played in the Central Lancashire League for Radcliffe and took part in trial games for Warwickshire. But, although of obvious ability, he did not achieve his potential. He might still have done so had he stayed longer. As it was, there was some disappointment when he did not return from a coaching trip to South Africa a year or so later."

NOT AS A "GLORIFIED BAGGAGE-MASTER"

In 1971, Williams and Dik Abed were nominated by the South African Cricket Union president Jack Cheetham to accompany the Springbok side on their tour to Australia in that year

Both refused the offer.

"I refused to go as a glorified baggage master," Williams said later. "I wanted to be chosen on merit after having proved myself at club and provincial level against the best in the country. Unfortunately, the laws of the country didn't allow that."

A staunch opponent of the tour, Williams told the London-based *Sun* newspaper: "If this tour of Australia goes on, it will put back our cause many years.

"For God's sake, ban them. Make them feel as we are made to feel all the days of our lives – unwanted.

"Perhaps then we will get some changes in our country."

Ironically, Williams went to Australia the following year as an emigrant.

"I had a taste of freedom while playing in England," he explained. "Moreover, my daughter, Glynis, was very young – and I didn't want her to experience the same sort of humiliation that I had suffered as a result of apartheid."

On his arrival in Adelaide in 1972, Williams joined the highly respected Prospect club, and met with immediate success.

"In my first game, Prospect were up against Glenelg, who fielded Ian and Trevor Chappell in their side. I dismissed Trevor – first ball. Next up was Ian, who had just returned from a successful tour of the West Indies. He went first ball, too. He came dancing down the track, didn't read my arm ball, and was stumped. I finished with 6/12."

The experience of playing in Australia left Williams pondering over lost opportunities in South Africa. "When I played Grade cricket against some of Australia's test cricketers I often asked myself: 'Why couldn't this have happened 10 years ago?'"

Interviewed in early 2000, Williams expressed surprise that the change in government and the outlawing of apartheid, had not led to greater black representation in the South African test side.

"What has happened to our blokes?" he asked.

OWEN WILLIAMS' RECORD IN ENGLAND

	Batting		Bowling	
	Runs	**Ave**	**Wkts**	**Ave**
Radcliffe CC 1966	59	14,63	143	7,94
1967	134	16,75	11	34,09
Warwickshire Seconds				
1966	21	21,00	11	22,27
1967	68	3,77	45	23,00

Part 4

Moves towards "normal" cricket

A FEW MINUTES after 6.30pm, on Wednesday, 28 August 1968, Basil D'Oliveira stumbled into the physiotherapist's room at the Worcestershire County Cricket Club ground and began to weep uncontrollably.

The reason for his anguish was understandable. Ever since he had left his home in Cape Town, for England, in 1960, his life had changed from one of cricketing rags to cricketing riches. He had started off – and starred – in the Lancashire League for a club called Middleton; he had easily negotiated the leap in class into county cricket for Worcestershire; and he'd never looked out of place doing duty for England.

Just one part of his story remained unwritten – a triumphant home-coming to the country that had rejected his talents because of the colour of his skin.

England's national team – the MCC – were due to tour South Africa in 1968. D'Oliveira's test form on a tour of the Caribbean had been less than impressive, so much so that he'd initially lost his place in the side when Australia toured the UK a few months before the scheduled tour to South Africa. But, when he was called up for the fifth test against the Australians at the Oval, he grabbed his opportunity with both hands. A superb 158 runs flowed from his bat.

Surely, his place in the team was now secure?

But when the team was announced, D'Oliveira wasn't in it....

Over the next few weeks, D'Oliveira's name became synonymous with the words, "political football" – which, in a way, was ironic: few people tried as hard as he to "keep politics out of sport".

D'Oliveira's omission from the side, his subsequent "reinstatement" when all-rounder Tom Cartwright withdrew from the MCC side through injury and the South African government's harsh reaction to his late inclusion, changed the way that the world viewed sport and politics.

The "D'Oliveira Affair", as the episode became known, ushered in a new era for South Africa's white sportsmen and women: the era of isolation.

In many ways, it was a rude awakening – especially for South Africa's white cricketers.

For decades, they had played test cricket against the fellow white nations such as England, New Zealand and Australia, blissfully unconcerned about the plight of their black fellow cricketers who were playing under conditions which many observers would have described as primitive.

While black cricket had unified under the banner of the South African Cricket Board of Control, the ideal situation would have been to unite black and white cricket under one banner. The white South African Cricket Association's response to this opportunity was hesitant: its attempts at unity, were made in co-operation with the government, who announced a new multi-national sports policy, through the Sports

Minister, Piet Koornhof, in 1974.

But black sports people were no longer interested in crumbs. The overwhelming majority began demanding full equality in a democratic country – which the government was not prepared to accede to.

Still, continuing talks between the three cricket controlling bodies, Saca, SA African Cricket Board and Sacboc led to the formation of the SA Cricket Council, then the Committee of Nine and, eventually, of the new SA Cricket Union in 1977 under the leadership of Sacboc President Rashid Varachia.

The concept of "normal cricket" was accepted in all provinces except in the Western Cape where Sacboc's strongest affiliate, the WPCB, with the exception of a few players and administrators, decided not to join their white counterparts. This led to great acrimony and the subsequent formation of the SA Cricket Board in 1977 to continue the nonracial struggle in cricket.

Desperate measures – attempts to cling to international ties

ON 17 SEPTEMBER 1968, the South African Prime Minister, John Vorster, rose to address the Orange Free State Congress of the ruling National Party on a matter that would alter the course of South African sports history.

John Vorster's speech at the Orange Free State Congress of the National Party, in which he described Basil D'Oliveira as a political football, sparked the campaign to expel South Africa from all international sport.

The subject of Vorster's speech was Basil D'Oliveira, the Cape Town-born coloured cricketer who, just 24 hours earlier, had been chosen to tour South Africa with England's national side, the MCC – after having first been controversially omitted from the touring party.

The "D'Oliveira question" had intrigued the sporting world and political analysts for almost two years prior to the scheduled start of the MCC visit. "Will he or won't he be chosen to tour? Will he or won't he be *allowed* to tour by the South African authorities?" they'd speculated as they waited for the matter to come to a head.

As D-day approached, rumours began circulating of intensive behind-the-scenes diplomatic activity between the British and South African governments. In Britain, leaks emanating from the ruling Labour Party suggested that the Vorster government would allow D'Oliveira to tour; but in South Africa, well-placed sources indicated that they wouldn't.

D'Oliveira seemed a near certainty for selection. Bouncing back to form after an indifferent tour to the West Indies, he had scored a fine 158 in the final test at the Oval. On this performance, surely, he couldn't be left out, his supporters argued.

But they kept their fingers crossed all the same.

A few minutes after 6.30pm on Wednesday, 28 August, the MCC selectors announced their team.

D'Oliveira wasn't in it.

Reaction rained down fast and furiously. In Britain, D'Oliveira burst into tears when he heard the news. The MCC was castigated from all sides and from all quarters for bowing to South African pressure.

Radio commentator, John Arlott, the man who'd helped D'Oliveira get to England, said, "No-one will believe that he was left out for valid cricket reasons."

Australian test great, Richie Benaud, accused the selectors of not having chosen the team on merit. Former England test cricketer, the Rev David Sheppard, later to become the Bishop of Liverpool, served notice that he would sponsor a motion of no-confidence in the MCC committee.

Then, with accusation and justification toing and froing unabatedly, came a dramatic new development: all-rounder Tom Cartwright withdrew from the side because of injury – and the grateful selectors, believing they had been thrown a lifeline, immediately called up D'Oliveira.

The million-dollar question was: how would the South African authorities react to this news?

Now, Vorster was about to tell them....

The life sentences imposed on Rivonia Treason trialists Nelson Mandela (above left), Walter Sisulu (above right), Govan Mbeki (left) and Ahmed Kathrada (right) increased international opposition to the National Party government's apartheid policies.

The South African Prime Minister, a heavy-jowled, stern-looking man, had a reputation for toughness. Standing in front of 3000 defiantly expectant party faithful in the heartland of Afrikaner conservatism, his expression seemed even grimmer than usual.

He stated bluntly that D'Oliveira would not be allowed to tour South Africa. Then, to a chorus of "*hoor, hoors*", he added: "We are not prepared to accept a team thrust upon us by people whose interests are not the game, but to gain certain political objectives which they do not even attempt to hide.

"The team, as constituted now, is not the team of the MCC, but the team of the Anti-Apartheid Movement, the team of Sanroc, and the team of Bishop Reeves...."

The 3000 delegates rose as one to applaud their leader.

Vorster had drawn his line in the sand. Ten thousand kilometres away, in London, the MCC drew theirs.

Stating that they were not prepared to be dictated to regarding their selection policy, they called off the tour.

TIGHTENING THE SCREWS

The furore over D'Oliveira ushered in a new phase in the fight against apartheid – a phase in which a growing number of traditional allies of South Africa began expressing disquiet about events in the country in a much louder voice.

It didn't happen suddenly. Rather, it was the cumulative effect of a number of events. The Sharpeville Massacre of 21 March 1960, in which 60 unarmed pass-law protestors were shot and killed by police, had been a defining moment for opponents of apartheid – both inside and outside South Africa. The banning of the African National Congress (ANC) and the Pan Africanist Congress (PAC) shortly afterwards, had been another.

The conclusion of the Rivonia Trial in 1963, in which the key figures of the leadership of the ANC – including Nelson Mandela, Walter Sisulu, Ahmed Kathrada and Govan Mbeki – were jailed for life, had added to the slow build-up of opposition.

But slow – and uneven – were the operative words. Not surprisingly then, the National Party rulers did not seem unduly perturbed that traditional allies appeared to be slowly distancing themselves from some of their actions.

The South African government did, however, attempt to crush internal opposition with an even greater than (what was to them) normal show of *kragdadigheid* (literally, brute force).

At the same time, they moved quickly to implement laws aimed at underpinning their policy of separate homelands, group areas and education systems.

The D'Oliveira controversy, especially its aftermath in South Africa, confirmed one thing: sport had become the soft underbelly of the apartheid republic.

But again, attempts to isolate the republic did not occur suddenly. In 1969, a tour by an Australian cricket team led by Bill Lawry, took place as planned. But it proved to be white South Africa's last official international contact at cricket for more than three decades.

A planned tour to England in 1970 was called off following intense pressure by the British government; a visit to Australia by a South African Nuffield side in 1971 suffered the same fate.

And yet, despite these setbacks, it took a long time for white administrators to acknowledge that the writing was on the wall. Thus, stubbornly, perhaps foolishly, even arrogantly, they persevered with trying to organise a Springbok tour to Australia in 1971.

They were well aware that something needed to be done to rescue their floundering international ties. But they couldn't grasp how much the world was changing and, indeed, how much attitudes among the black have-nots of South Africa were hardening.

And so, in a desperate bid to save the Australian tour, South African Cricket Association (Saca) president, Jack Cheetham, made what he thought to be a magnanimous offer: he invited two South African Cricket Board of Control (Sacboc) players – Dik Abed and Owen Williams – to join the rest of the white side on tour.

Cheetham seemed blissfully unaware of the patronising nature of his offer: he had never seen Abed and Williams play; he didn't have the courtesy of consulting Sacboc about the offer. Nor, in fact, did he make the offer personally. Instead, he chose to send a go-between to the players, who rejected the proposal with contempt.

"I want to be selected on merit – and not as a glorified baggage master," said an angry Williams.

The tour was called off.

Although bitterly disappointed, Saca continued to seek ways to keep open or reopen international ties. With the government having changed its sports policy to allow mixed-race competition between national (as defined by them) sides, the white cricket authorities began perfecting a new tactic to secure international contacts: a key element of their new strategy was the co-opting of black players into their plans.

In 1971, former England captain, Colin Cowdrey, tried to arrange a tour by an English invitation team, of which D'Oliveira and other black players would have been drawcards. The plan was for the tourists to play separate white and black national teams.

Not only did Sacboc reject this idea out of hand, but its officials also persuaded D'Oliveira to withdraw from the project.

D'Oliveira, in fact, was instrumental in convincing Cowdrey that the time was not right for such a tour.

Realising the importance of sport in the psyche of white South Africans, the government began thinking of ways to enable mixed-race national sport to be evolved, and then to move this downwards into club and regional competitions, without, of course, tampering with grand apartheid.

START OF THE HOWA ERA

In a kite-flying exercise in 1971, Sports Minister, Frank Waring, said: "If cricketers... from club level upwards were... to state that they were in favour of racially integrated cricket and their authorities came to me and stated that this is the position, then I am fully prepared to take this matter to the Cabinet."

Waring's offer drew a measured response from Hassan Howa, who had taken over the Sacboc presidency in 1970 from John van Harte: "We do not ask to play together at club level as suggested by Mr Waring. We merely ask for South African teams to be chosen on merit.

"What I foresee is a single Western Province Association to which all clubs, white and black belong. They will play inter-club matches. Interprovincial teams will be chosen from these players in the senior divisions exactly as is now the case in their existing associations, white and non-white."

Jack Cheetham tried to save the 1971 Springbok tour to Australia by inviting two coloured cricketers to tour with the side.

Colin Cowdrey takes time off for a hit-about with some under-11 cricketers at the William Herbert sports ground in Wiynberg. In 1971, Cowdrey tried to bring an invitation side to South Africa in 1971 to play separate black and white teams.

Basil D'Oliveira's attempts to separate South Africa's politics from its sporting issues angered many of his erstwhile colleagues in the South African Cricket Board of Control.

Howa, who over the next few years would be branded an unreasonable militant by the white establishment, was, in fact, quite moderate – even by the standards of that time.

Indeed, at a Sacboc symposium in Port Elizabeth in 1971, he came under fire for suggesting that playing cricket in certain areas under permit "is preferable to not playing at all".

A delegate strongly criticised this point of view, pointing out to Howa that the nonracial policy of Sacboc did not allow for the playing of sport under permit.

Howa also locked horns with D'Oliveira. When the England international returned to Cape Town in 1972 for a lengthy visit, he was sharply criticised by Howa for his public support of the controversial tour of England by a coloured South African Rugby Federation side, the Proteas.

Later, at a specially organised symposium featuring both men, D'Oliveira pledged his support to the nonracial cause. But tensions again flared when he accepted an invitation from the Western Province Cricket Union to watch the traditional New Year Currie Cup encounter between Western Province and Transvaal at Newlands.

In defending his decision to attend the match, D'Oliveira challenged board officials to censure him for watching sport at white venues.

"There is nothing in Sacboc's constitution that prevents me from doing so," he said.

D'OLIVEIRA, THE NEGOTIATOR

In the early 1970s, D'Oliveira emerged as a key figure behind efforts to get Sacboc and Saca to negotiate a united future for the game in South Africa. He appeared to have strong credentials – notably, his long-standing emotional ties with Sacboc and his cordial relationship with officials of Saca. But his insistence on wanting to separate cricket issues from apartheid laws which blighted the lives of his compatriots, alienated him from many of the Sacboc administrators.

Little came from his efforts. The two bodies spent most of their time shadow-boxing – and outside of a number of messages carried backwards and forwards by intermediaries, progress was painfully slow.

Then, in 1972, there was a breakthrough (of sorts): the two bodies held talks for the first time, after Saca had agreed to Sacboc's demand to allow the sports media to cover proceedings.

Nothing of note came out of the talks – although Sacboc cleverly took the opportunity to reiterate its demand that the national team should be chosen on merit, following mixed trials.

Politically, the two bodies were still miles apart. While Sacboc was edging ever closer to the principle of a single national body and merit selection, Saca continued to take its cue from government policy.

In the 1972/73 season, Sacboc turned down a written invitation from Saca to select its own team to play the visiting Derrick Robins XI, led by former England international, Brian Close. In its letter, Saca invited Sacboc to play the match "in an effort to bring your cricket to a higher level"

Sacboc rejected this approach "with contempt".

In 1972, after its attempts to establish a trust fund for Sacboc was rebuffed, Saca, with the help of the South African African Cricket Board (Saacb), formed the Cricket Council of South Africa, the purpose of which was to create a loose liaison between Saca, Saacb and Sacboc, and to enable consultations on cricket to take place.

Saca insisted that each body should retain its identity and that cricket should continue to be played along ethnic lines, as in the past.

Sacboc rejected the Council, as well as the premise for its existence.

A CALL FOR A MORATORIUM

Sacboc president Hassan Howa did not trust Saca. Because he suspected that Saca's motive for seeking a unity of sorts with Sacboc was to get back into international cricket, he asked them to agree to a three-year, tour-free period.

Their compliance, Howa said, would be regarded as proof that they genuinely wanted integrated cricket in South Africa.

But Saca president, Jack Cheetham, would give no such commitment. "To do so would set cricket back," he said.

Howa's retort was: "There's nothing in tours for us. Only whites will benefit from a resumption of international ties."

The South African African Cricket Board sided with Saca. "We know which side our bread is buttered," their delegate, Lennox Mlonzi, said.

Howa was unequivocal about Sacboc's demands: "Our aim is selection on merit," he said.

He said that clubs should choose for themselves whether they wanted to throw open their doors to everyone.

Sacboc's starting point was to be mixed cricket at Currie Cup level – and then to move downwards to club level.

But Cheetham's response was to continue with efforts to get Sacboc to join the Cricket Council of South Africa.

"I believe any step forward is a step in the right direction," he told Howa. "If you don't join, the contact we have with each other will be sporadic."

One country, different worlds – the story of cricket's unequal facilities

WHEN THE BATTLE against apartheid began in earnest, black cricketers were confronted with a critical choice: Should they offer their talents as part of a broader fight for equality for all South Africans? Or should they insist that their personal development as cricketers be paramount?

The majority of those favouring the first option readily accepted that the fight for equality in cricket could not be separated from, for instance, the fight against group areas or forced removals – or the fight for equal facilities and a single education system. It wasn't easy to sacrifice personal ambition for a cause which held out little hope for short-term success. And the route they chose became even more difficult to follow once the government and rival bodies started waving "carrots" such as better facilities and cash handouts in front of their noses. But as so many who completed the course repeatedly said, "We're not doing this for us, but for our children."

STANDARD OF FACILITIES

Those leaning towards the second option argued that the priority of the game's administrators was to strive to maintain the highest standards and provide the best facilities possible. To take their argument to its logical conclusion – if the government refused to provide facilities, it was the duty of the cricket authorities to go out and find ways of providing these themselves.

The standard of facilities in Sacboc, the lack of them and the promise of them (when the government and the South African Cricket Association tried to entice black players into nominally mixed cricket structures) weighed heavily on the minds of those players who were talented enough to play at national or international level.

Basil D'Oliveira fitted comfortably into the second camp. During one of his visits to South Africa in 1972, he hit out at Sacboc's poor facilities and what he described as the refusal of players to make sacrifices and to work hard.

Facilities available to black players in the Western Province were in poor condition – but there were good reasons for this. Municipalities, generally, spent very little of their sports and recreation budgets on maintaining grounds that were not used by white sportsmen and women. While players in the rest of the world were playing on turf wickets, board cricketers were forced to perform on bouncy, matting wickets surrounded by uneven, weed-infested outfields.

COULD MORE HAVE BEEN DONE?

Whereas white cricketers could, as a matter of course, have expect to arrive for a match at a field which was well prepared and manicured, their black counterparts often had to spend the Friday prior to a game preparing a gravel wicket.

Dressing rooms and ablution facilities were nonexistent, too, with players often having to resort to changing in their cars or behind trees.

But could the board have done more to improve facilities? Former Western Province captain, Brian O'Connell, felt that they could have.

"Had they been really creative, they could have developed better facilities and raised standards. But the problem was that everything was dealt with in terms of the political argument. While this was understandable, it wasn't good enough," he said.

In 1971, the Wynberg Cricket Board set aside R800 to build a turf wicket at their William Herbert ground. Although a start was made on the wicket, a lack of expertise within Wynberg's parent body, the Western Province Cricket Board, saw the project coming to nothing.

Frank Brache, a Western Province Cricket Board official during that period, said: "We managed to secure a sponsorship, and I suggested that we approach the white Western Province Cricket Union, who were willing to offer assistance free of charge.

"But Hassan [Howa] refused to deal with them. He said he'd lay the pitch himself. He did, and made a complete mess of it."

In 1974, Essop Pahad (above) and Basil Bhana submitted an application for membership of the International Cricket Conference on behalf of Sacboc.

But Howa indicated that he was in no rush. Those sacrificing their own careers for the cause of nonracial sport, he said, were doing it for their children. "Do you think any of them will deny their children the chance of living a full, equal life in South Africa one day?" he asked.

Saca, however, reiterated its contention that mixed cricket was against the law.

In 1973, Boon Wallace, who had taken over from Cheetham as president of Saca, said: "There is nothing to stop multiracial cricket from taking place, but I have not encouraged it because I do not want to upset the government."

Wallace felt that matches involving blacks would contravene the laws relating to group areas, separate amenities and the consumption of liquor on public premises.

SACBOC AND THE ICC

In July 1974, Sacboc decided to apply to the International Cricket Conference for associate membership.

Although the government refused to grant Howa a passport to attend the ICC meeting, Sacboc's submission – in which they accused Saca about not caring about how and where, and under what conditions their less-privileged counterparts played – was tabled at the ICC conference by Basil Bhana and Essop Pahad of the London-based pressure group, the South African Non-Racial Olympic Committee (Sanroc).

Bhana and Pahad also submitted an application from Sacboc for associate membership of the ICC.

But with conservative officials of the three white countries – England, Australia and New Zealand – still wielding the power in the ICC, the application was turned down.

As South Africa sunk deeper into the trough of international isolation, the country's nonracial unions began boycotting venues which, in the past, had been used as learning grounds by many black players, who, from their segregated seats had watched and then modelled themselves on the visiting international stars.

Because its seating was segregated and because it had to apply for a permit to admit black spectators, Newlands was declared out of bounds to Sacboc members.

In 1973, Dickie Conrad, the captain of the Western Province Dadabhay Trophy team, became the first Western Province Cricket Board player to be suspended for watching cricket at Newlands. Conrad was prevented by board president Hassan Howa from leading his union, Wynberg, against Maitland-Parow in a Super League game, after he admitted watching a "mini test" between the Derrick Robins XI and a South African XI.

Although he succeeded in overturning his banning through a Supreme Court action, Conrad remained with the Western Province Cricket Board for only a few more months before joing the Western Province Cricket Union. Shortly after joining Green Point Cricket Club, he became the first black player to play in the first division of the Western Province Cricket Union. In 1975, he played for the President's XI against a Derrick Robins XI at Newlands.

MORE CHANGES

In February 1973, American tennis star, Arthur Ashe, told Howa that the National Party government had promised to introduce mixed sport within three years.

And, in another development, Saca came up with yet another scheme to bring black faces onto its fields – an international double wicket competition at the Wanderers in Johannesburg, featuring, among others, D'Oliveira.

Springbok batsman, Lee Irvine, one of the tournament organisers, pleaded with Howa to allow D'Oliveira to participate in the tournament.

"It will prove that black and white can play together," Irvine argued.

But Howa was unimpressed – and D'Oliveira, inevitably, was a nonparticipant in the event.

Sacboc, who were also invited to send players to the tournament, set out two conditions for its participation:

• Seating should be integrated; and
• Each Sacboc player should partner a white player.

The request was rejected.

Piet Koornhof, the Minister of Sport, accused Sacboc of setting the clock backwards with its "all-or-nothing attitude".

Despite the constant sniping at each other in the media, talks between Sacboc and Saca continued as the government sought to sell its concept of multinational sport (which required the different racial groups to remain in their separate organisations and to play each other at "national level").

On 25 March 1973, the presidents of Sacboc (Howa), Saca (Wallace) and the South African African Cricket Board (HM Butshingi) met in Cape Town to discuss, among a host of other things, the issue of merit selection, and of South Africa's admission to the International Cricket Conference.

After three hours of debate, they resolved to investigate the effects of the Group Areas Act on the game, the provision of satisfactory facilities for all cricketers and a system of play for a proposed new set-up.

It would take another three years of negotiation before the three bodies were able to thrash out an agreement.

In January 1976, South Africa's cricket leaders accepted the principle of playing the game under a single banner. A steering committee, known as the Committee of Nine, was charged with driving the process. Significantly, the Sacboc delegates

The formation of the South African Council on Sport (Sacos)

IN A MAJOR boost to the campaign to isolate apartheid sport, nine nonracial sports associations formed the South African Council on Sport (Sacos) in Durban on 17 March 1973.

Among the resolutions it adopted at its inaugural conference were:

• To work for international recognition;
• To try to resolve the problems of inadequate facilities and sponsorship, faced by nonracial sports organisations;
• To urge the private sector to remedy the disparate system of sports sponsorship;
• To stop the degrading and humiliating practice of having to apply for permits to play sport.

Probably its greatest success was the way it was able to garner support internationally for the isolation of white South African sports codes (and their black allies). In this respect, one of its first successes was the role it played in blocking a visit to South Africa by the Mozambique-born Portuguese international football star, Eusebio.

Although its double standards resolution was attacked in many quarters – sometimes even from within its own ranks – there can be no doubt that the resolution provided direction for the nonracial sports movement in South Africa during a crucial period of the struggle against apartheid.

Sacos' slogan, "no normal sport in an abnormal society", became the battle cry of the nonracial sports movement.

were requested by their president, Rashid Varachia (who had taken over from Howa), to ensure that discussions "were friendly and that there be no confrontation."

On 24 September 1976, the Minister of Sport, Piet Koornhof, accepted and approved the blueprint and plans for normal cricket as submitted by the Committee of Nine under the chairmanship of Varachia.

But by then, of course, the country had been torn apart by the events of June 1976....

In the 1970s, Piet Koornhof formulated and drove the National Party government's plan for multinational sport.

Koornhof's three-year plan

In March 1974, Western Province Cricket Board president Hassan Howa told the Argus newspaper that a secret meeting with Sports Minister Piet Koornhof in November of the previous year, Koornhof had outlined a new three-year plan for mixed cricket.

In the first year, Australia would play a South African multinational (mixed race) side, white provincial teams, a white test team and a Sacboc national side.

In the second year, a touring New Zealand side would play combined black and white provincial teams and a South African team chosen on merit. Trials, involving black and white teams would be held to select the provincial sides. There would also be a trial match to select the South African side.

In the third year there would be fully integrated cricket at club and provincial levels.

Blueprint for normal cricket

THE BLUEPRINT for a single controlling body in a normal cricket set-up was underpinned by three resolutions adopted by the three national bodies on 18 January 1976. These were:

(a) Sacboc, Saacb and Saca hereby adopt the principle that cricket in South Africa be played on a normal basis under the controlling aegis of one united governing body in South Africa, the name and constitution of which will be agreed upon as soon as possible. "Normal" cricket shall mean, at this stage, the participation of, and competition between, all cricketers regardless of race, creed or colour, in cricket at club level under one provincial governing body;

(b) Sacboc, Saacb and Saca shall forthwith require their provincial authorities to enter into dialogue with their opposite numbers to give effect to resolution (a);

(c) A motivating committee consisting of not more than three each from Sacboc, Saacb and Saca is hereby appointed to ensure that the resolutions as aforementioned be given effect.

The adoption of the resolution meant that each province was required to move as speedily as possible to establish new, united provincial bodies.

Staying competitive – Sacboc's efforts to improve the game

BY THE EARLY 1970s, the South African Cricket Board of Control was spiralling towards a crisis. Its membership was dropping and its standards slipping; its affiliates lacked fields and money; and its players were clamouring for coaches and competition.

The heady optimism of the Fifties and Sixties, when many of Sacboc's top performers dreamed of securing Lancashire League contracts (as a first step, perhaps, to bigger things), and its officials brainstormed ways of bringing top (black) international teams such as the West Indies to South Africa, had evaporated.

Now, the priority was survival.

Many of Sacboc's problems were caused by factors beyond its control. The Group Areas Act had forced many of its members (and potential members) to move from suburban areas to bleak, faraway townships on the Cape Flats, where no facilities existed.

Strong community bonds were destroyed overnight.

In the Western Cape, when well-established suburbs such as Vasco, Goodwood, Rondebosch, Green Point and Mowbray were declared white group areas, a number of sports grounds on which black cricketers had played for generations, were declared out of bounds.

Clubs from these areas, the majority of which could boast long, proud traditions, struggled to survive in their new surroundings.

Clearly, something had to be done – quickly.

A NEW SYSTEM

Sacboc, wisely, began its process of regeneration by opting to tackle the most easily fixable problems first.

For most of the Sixties, the centralised biennial Dadabhay tournament had served as Sacboc's showpiece national competition. It had proved to be a popular event, with the prospect of seeing all the board's top cricketers at a single venue being its main drawcard.

But by the end of the decade, the tournament had started taking strain, mainly because many players were finding it increasingly difficult to obtain leave for the two-week duration of the competition.

In an effort to improve the standard of the game, Sacboc replaced the centralised tourney at the start of the 1970/71 season with a two-day home and away interprovincial competition.

Two conditions were attached to the playing of the new competition: trips were not to cost more than R1000 each; and the competition was not to be confused with the white Currie Cup competition.

The two-day format was expanded to three days for the 1971/72 season after teams complained that two days were insufficient to get an outright result. For example, in the first game of the new competition, Western

Rohan Kanhai, the great West Indies batsman, helped Transvaal win the Dadabhay Trophy in the 1974/75 season.

Province's stranglehold on the Dadabhay trophy, by taking the honours in 1974/75.

In 1975/76, the majority of Western Province's Muslim players withdrew from the side on religious grounds. They refused to play in a competition sponsored by a liquor company – Stellenbosch Farmers' Winery. But, even then, the replacements that Western Province were able to call on – players such as O'Connell, Howie Bergins and Pinky Carelse – continued to give the side the winning edge.

THE OVERSEAS CONNECTION

In a further effort to improve the standard of their game and to provide their players with incentives beyond the Dadabhay competition and the annual North versus South clash, Sacboc decided at their annual general meeting in Cape Town in 1971 to invite New Zealand to play a series of matches against a representative side in Cape Town.

It was planned to play the matches before the New Zealanders began their tour of England later that year. However, the visit to South Africa did not materialise.

Sacboc also embarked on a programme of recruiting coaches from the West Indies. After initially seeking out big names such as Clive Lloyd, Charlie Griffith and Seymour Nurse, they eventually settled for Lancashire League professionals such as Duncan Carter (who went to Eastern Province), Keith Barker (Natal) and John Holder (Western Province).

Cecil Abrahams, a member of the Sacboc team which toured Kenya, also returned to coach and play in the Western Province in 1974/75 – his first visit since he left to play in the Lancashire League in 1961.

"We managed to get a sponsor to

Province and Transvaal, both passed 300 runs and could complete just one innings each.

Western Province, led by respectively, Coetie Neethling, Gertjie Williams, Dickie Conrad, Lefty Adams and Brian O'Connell, dominated the Dadabhay competition and its successor, the Stellenbosch Farmers' Winery competition.

Although Natal and Transvaal, in particular, usually fielded powerful teams, Western Province could call on the services of top-quality players such as Neethling, Williams, Conrad, Adams, Rushdi and Saait Magiet, Robbie van Graan, Jock Mahoney, Viccie Moodie, Braima Isaacs and Kulu Maclons, among others.

Only Transvaal, with a lot of help from the great West Indian Rohan Kanhai, managed to break Western

bring out Holder and Abrahams," said Frank Brache, who was secretary of the Western Province Cricket Board at that time.

"But the project was not a success. Our people didn't want to be taught. There was no respect and support for the coaches – and this started at the highest level," said Brache.

"On one occasion, Hassan [Howa] instructed Abrahams and Holder to come to his house – so that he could teach them about coaching."

Brache said that attempts by Abrahams and Holder to coach schoolchildren were as unsuccessful. "We didn't have a support base outside the ordinary cricketing structures – and so the programme fell flat," he said.

NOT ALL DOOM AND GLOOM

The introduction of the West Indians had a tremendous effect on the game in the other provinces. Barker performed well for Natal, while Carter was getting into his stride for Eastern Province when he had to rush back to the Caribbean because his mother had taken ill.

Basil D'Oliveira also returned in the 1973/74 season to take up a coaching engagement with the Eastern Province Cricket Association, after having turned down two offers to play Grade cricket in Australia. He'd opted for the Eastern Province offer, he said, because he couldn't turn down the chance of coaching coloured cricketers in South Africa.

D'Oliveira's contract with the association required him to coach at school, club and provincial level, as well as playing for Eastern Province in the Dadabhay competition.

Rohan Kanhai, the West Indian great, helped Transvaal to their only first-class Sacboc title in the 1974/75

season, but he left under acrimonious circumstances during the end-of-season mini test between North and South in Johannesburg.

Kanhai refused to continue batting on a dangerous wicket after his appeal for a postponement to allow the wet wicket to dry was turned down by the umpires.

He stormed off the field and flew to London the same evening.

Glad to be back – Cecil Abrahams (right), Coetie Neethling (centre) and Lennie Walsh (left) share a joke at a social function in Cape Town. Abrahams returned to Cape Town in 1974, his first visit in 13 years.

MONEY WOES

A shortage of cash was an ongoing problem for the Sacboc administration.

With the cost of travel, cricket equipment and the maintenance of facilities rising, Sacboc tried hard to obtain sponsorship from big companies – but with little success.

One leading business house commented that they didn't sponsor "non-whites" because "they are disunited and lack continuity".

A host of other reasons were cited by companies for not sponsoring black sport. These included:

• The difficulty they had in distinguishing the claims of two to three rival bodies;

• A tendency for splinter groups to form;

• Disorganisation and personality clashes in black organisations;

• A lack of continuity

"We are ready and willing to sponsor nonwhite sport to a far greater extent, but any commercial organisation wants maximum results for its money and most nonwhite unions cannot guarantee results," said a spokesperson for one company.

"We have no desire to back one group or person at the expense of another," said a marketing manager of another company, who added: "Instead of getting involved, we tell all parties to come back when they have sorted out their differences."

Nonracial sportspeople found these arguments difficult to accept – especially since they were, in many cases, the biggest consumers of products of the companies which sponsored white sport.

There were calls from time to time, for a boycott of companies which refused to sponsor nonracial sport, but these never materialised.

Official attempts at mixed cricket in Cape Town

WHILE CRICKET administrators haggled in the boardrooms, and South Africa's security police kept their ears and eyes open for any signs of "illegal" mixed matches, players from both sides of the racial divide in the Western Cape expressed a willingness to compete on the cricket field as equals.

In 1972, four members of the white Western Province Currie Cup team – Tony Whitfield, Neville Budge, André Bruyns and Mike Bowditch – accepted invitations to play in a farewell match for Basil D'Oliveira at Turfhall Park in Lansdowne.

Paul Saville, the chairman of the St Augustine club, and the chief organiser of the match, said: "Basil [D'Oliveira], who had come to Cape Town on holiday, was keen to play some cricket while here.

"After he'd played for us in a league match against Rythorn, who didn't provide much opposition, we came up with the idea of selecting a combined Western Province team, made up of players from the Western Province Cricket Board and the white Currie Cup team to play against St Augustines.

"Once the Currie Cup players had expressed their willingness to play in the match, St Augustines proceeded with arrangements.

"But it wasn't long before I received a telephone call from the Minister of Sport, Frank Waring, warning me that the proposed game – which he termed a political gathering – would be illegal because we did not have a permit for white players to play in a coloured area. He said that the

police would intervene if Barlow and company played," said Saville.

"The players themselves were warned by the WP Cricket Union president, Boon Wallace, that they would get into trouble if they played."

Later, Saville was contacted by Owen Wynne, a former Springbok opening batsman, and a member of the opposition Progressive Federal Party (PFP), who offered to play.

"I told him that at the age of 50 he was too old," said Saville, "and, anyway, we didn't want the match to be used by any organisation to score political points."

Although the white players withdrew from the match, the security police sent an officer to Turfhall anyway – just to make sure.

"While the match was on," said Saville, the policeman approached me and said: 'You people just don't want to listen. He asked: "Who is that white man you have playing over there?'. The player he was pointing to was Lefty Adams."

The withdrawal of Whitfield, Budge, Bruyns and Bowditch was slated by WP Cricket Board president, Hassan Howa. "Their decision," he said "reflected the depth of their commitment to multiracial cricket in South Africa."

But Budge hit back at Howa: "I have been against Mr Howa's attitude

After first agreeing to play in a farewell match for Basil D'Oliveira, Andre Bruyns (above), Mike Bowditch (left) and Neville Budge (right) withdrew from the match after warnings from Minister of Sport, Frank Waring, and WP Cricket Union president, Boon Wallace.

Jock Mahoney hit the top score of 57 in a farewell match for Basil D'Oliveira, between St Augustines and a WP Invitation XI.

ST AUGUSTINES VERSUS A WESTERN PROVINCE INVITATION XI

ST AUGUSTINES

L. Walsh c Fillies b Khan	26
H. Arenz c Maclons b Magiet	4
C. Kolbe b Henry	5
B. D'Oliveira c Fillies b Khan	9
K. Rodriques c Phillips b Smith	13
D. February c Smith b Adams	34
J. Mahoney c Katts b Adams	57
E. Wakefield b Adams	8
N. February c Phillips b Adams	15
C. Adams not out	5
M. September c Fillies b Adams	0
Extras	5
Total	181

Bowling: Sonn 3-0-5-0; Magiet 4-2-7-1; Katts 2-0-8-0; Khan 8-0-30-2; Henry 6-0-16-1; Smith 5-0-23-1; Fillies 5-0-23-1; Jacobs 4-0-46- 0; AL Adams 4-0-16-5; Phillips 1-0-2-0

WP INVITATION XI

L. Jacobs st Arenz b Kolbe	30
H. Phillips c Wakefield b D'Oliveira	29
A. Sonn b Kolbe	2
B. Fillies st Arenz b Kolbe	0
S. Magiet run out	31
A. Katts c Arenz b D. February	8
M. Maclons b D. February	23
AL. Adams c Arenz b Mahoney	2
O. Henry run out	6
J. Khan c Arenz b D. February	0
E. Smith not out	1
Extras	7
Total	139

Bowling: September 3,1-0-12-0; Mahoney 8-1-32-1; D. February 8-0-29-3; Adams 4-0-11-0; D'Oliveira 8-3-9-1; Kolbe 7-1-39-3

***ST AUGUSTINES WON BY 42 RUNS

all along," he said. "If he were quieter, he would get more."

MIXED-RACE COACHING

Unofficial contact between players and clubs of the two Western Province unions continued – seemingly, with the blessing of top officials of the Western Province Cricket Board.

Thus, when St Athens, a club affiliated to the Metropolitan Cricket Union, approached the Western Province Currie Cup batsman, Hylton Ackerman, to coach them, Howa had no hesitation in giving the move his (unofficial) backing.

"Ackerman will give invaluable advice to St Athens," Howa said. "Colour doesn't come into it at all."

Robbie van Graan, a member of the club during this period, said that Ackerman had been present at one of the club's meetings, "when he agreed to coach our players – with no strings attached".

"But after that meeting, we never saw him again."

In that same season, Roy Virgin, a professional with the English county side, Northamptonshire, who played for Green Point and the Western Province Currie Cup side in the British winter, was engaged by the Western Province Cricket Board to coach black youngsters.

Saca, meanwhile, continued to woo Sacboc. In August 1974, Sacboc, rejected an offer from Saca to play against the touring Derrick Robins XI. "One of the reasons for this stance is the firm belief that isolated and random playing together serves no meaningful purpose," Sacboc said.

"Instead, it helps to create a false and distorted picture of playing conditions in the local cricket world. No change of whatever nature has yet been evidenced. The evaluation of any cricketer's ability can only be assessed if normal cricket is played and merit selection is the yardstick."

Tiffie Barnes, the Transvaal all-rounder, who was selected along with the South African African Cricket

Board's Edward Habane, refused to play.

He said he would have given the matter serious thought had the team been chosen on merit.

A TINY WALK INTO HISTORY

In December 1973, Tiny Abed, a former Western Province captain, and a member of Basil D'Oliveira's side which toured Kenya in 1958, became the first board player to become a member of the white union when he joined Green Point.

Abed was 43 years old when he made the move.

Gerald Mallinick, the chairman of Green Point at the time, recalled the moment Abed decided to take the plunge: "I met Tiny in a lift in a building in Long Street – and we started talking about cricket. He said he was sick of the mess that cricket was in. He said all he wanted to do was play. I invited him to join Green Point – and he accepted.

"Although he was past his best by then, his move to us was a significant step. Shortly afterwards, a number of former Sacboc players – including Dickie Conrad, Omar Henry and Howie Bergins – joined us.

"The decision by these players created a momentum for change."

Mallinick said that the Western Province Cricket Union had exerted some pressure on Green Point, but that the club had shrugged this off.

"We did our own thing," he said.

"On one occasion, Boon Wallace [the president of the WP Cricket Union] asked us not to select Conrad for our first division match against Stellenbosch University.

"But we refused.

"Later, he asked us to switch the venue for the match from Stellenbosch to Green Point.

"Again we refused.

"The game went ahead without any problems at Stellenbosch," Mallinick concluded.

Mallinick said that Conrad had been a huge success at the club. "The fact that he was a practising Muslim, who didn't consume alcohol, meant that the liquor law excuse could never be used to ban him from any venues."

Mallinick, who was one of only a handful of white cricket fans who went to watch Rohan Kanhai when the great West Indian played for Transvaal against Western Province in

Tiny Abed, a member of a famous sporting family of District Six, became the first black player to join a white club when he joined WP Cricket Union affiliates, Green Point in 1973.

a Dadabhay Trophy match at the William Herbert Sportsground in Wynberg, said:" I could see that Sacboc had some very good cricketers, but poor facilities made it impossible for them to develop to their full potential.

In an article in the February 1975 edition of the *SA Cricketer*, Mallinick wrote: "The little master [Kanhai], in incredibly primitive circumstances – no sightscreens, gravel and mat pitch, bumpy and sloping outfield and under surveillance by a pigeon closely guarding its newly-laid eggs at short leg – obliged with a hundred."

A week after Abed joined Green Point, Freddie Trueman, the former England fast bowler, captained a mixed local invitation XI against a side led by former WP Dadabhay captain, Coetie Neethling, at Rosmead in Claremont. The two sides consisted of players from the two provincial unions.

The match was arranged by Ted Doman, the sports editor of the *Cape Herald* newspaper, who had invited Trueman to be the guest speaker at the newspaper's annual Sportsman of the Year banquet.

"There was no opposition to the game, even though it was illegal in terms of the law," said Doman.

"We decided to choose two teams – and then issue invitations to players and spectators so that, technically, the match was a private affair.

"When a reporter of *Die Burger* newspaper asked me if we had a per-mit to play the match, my reply was: 'I didn't realise it was necessary to get a permit to play a game of cricket.'"

Doman also recalled that Eddie Barlow had failed to turn up for the match – "which didn't surprise his Western Province Cricket Union team mates".

"When I phoned him, his wife said he was out on the farm sorting out a problem with the pigs."

With the prospect of cricket unity in sight, the game was seen as another step in that direction.

"Anything we did at that time was aimed at getting ahead," said Doman.

"The game, which was played in a healthy atmosphere, offered hope to the players that cricket unity in the Western Cape would not be far off.

After the game Trueman, whose first ball on the bouncy matting wicket, took off and nearly went for six byes, commented on the poor facilities *(Continued on page 108)*

NEETHLING'S XI VERSUS TRUEMAN'S XI

NEETHLING'S XI

H. Dawson run out	3
V. Moodie b Nieuwoudt	1
V. Smith c Behardien b Kolbe	16
A. Katts c Timol b Trueman	50
J. Neethling c van Niekerk b Kolbe	11
P. Swart c K van Graan b Trueman	2
G. Pfuhl c & b Abrahams	0
D. Hobson c Brache b van Niekerk	33
C. Miller c Petersen b Abrahams	24
A. Sonn not out	7
E. Smith not out	6
Extras	14
Total	167/9

Fall of wickets: 1/8; 2/8; 3/64; 4/89; 5/93; 6/93; 7/109; 8/148; 9/150

Bowling: Trueman 8-2-25-2; Nieuwoudt 7-5-4-1; Holder 3-2-5-0; Petersen 8-1-27-0; Kolbe 8-0-41-2; Abrahams 7-2-31-2; Van Niekerk 4-0-20-1

TRUEMAN'S XI

K. Van Graan c Swart b Hobson	28
N. Brache c Swart b E. Smith	27
C. Kolbe b V. Smith	12
T. Behardien b V. Smith	26
C. Abrahams c Swart b V. Smith	16
A. Van Niekerk c Hobson b V. Smith	2
J. Holder c Pfuhl b E. Smith	0
I. Timol c Sonn b Katts	12
F. Trueman c Sonn b Katts	11
A. Nieuwoudt c Moodie b Katts	1
B. Petersen not out	5
Extras	10
Total	150

Fall of wickets: 158; 2/60; 3/92; 4/107; 5/113; 6/114; 7/116; 8/130; 9/131

Bowling: Swart 4-0-15-0; Sonn 4-0-17-0; E. Smith 8-0-20-2; Hobson 9-3-20-1; Miller 5-1-17-0; Neethling 2-0-3-0; V. Smith 7-1-22-4; Moodie 3-0-14-1; Katts 1,.3-0-2-2

**NEETHLING'S XI WON BY 17 RUNS

Eddie Barlow's team which played a "mixed" match against a Coetie Neethling XI at UCT, in October 1975.
Back (left to right): Vincent Farrell, Stephen Bruce, Norman Adams, Hilary Dawson, John Farrell, Viccie Moodie, Eddie Barlow and Zac Coetzee.
Front (left to right): Hylton Ackerman, Clive de Waal, Noel Brache, Gertjie Williams and Omar Henry,

Former England fast bowler, Freddie Trueman seen here in Cape Town with his wife (far left), WP scorer Cynthia Poggenpoel and WPCB President Hassan Howa. After playing at Rosmead Trueman said the Western Province Cricket Board would have to acquire better facilities if they wished to produce world-class players.

Peter Kirsten played for Coetie Neethling's XI in a friendly against Eddie Barlow's XI at UCT in October 1975.

NEETHLING'S XI VERSUS BARLOW'S XI

NEETHLING'S XI

F. Goldstein c Henry b G. Williams 20
W. Hendricks b Farrell 0
P. Kirsten c De Waal b Ackerman 29
M. Maclons c Dawson b Ackerman 20
A. Lamb lbw Ackerman 0
D. Kohler c Bruce b Ackerman 7
C. Weeden b Brache..20
J. Neethling b Brache..4
S. Jones not out 23
J. Mahoney c Barlow b Brache 16
G. Bricknell not out 0

                 Extras.................. 4
                 Total 143/9

Fall of wickets: 1/1; 2/50; 3/56; 4/62; 5/76; 6/85; 7/93; 8/104; 9/142

Bowling: Farrell 5-1-10-1; Barlow 5-0-13-0; Henry 10-1-35-0; Williams 10-2-22-1; Ackerman 10-6-11-4; Brache 10-1-48-1

BARLOW'S XI

H. Dawson b Mahoney..0
E. Barlow c Jones b Mahoney...................................3
V. Moodie b Jones...0
H. Ackerman b Hendricks..19
N. Adams c Maclons b Hendricks 32
S. Bruce c Hendricks b Weeden 46
N. Brache not out 16
O. Henry b Mahoney...3
G. Williams c Kohler b Weeden 1
C. de Waal b Weeden 0
J. Farrell not out 9

                 Extras 15
                 Total 144/9

Fall of wickets: 1/5; 2/6; 3/6; 4/59; 5/68; 6/116; 7/131; 8/ 134; 9/134

Bowling: Jones 5-1-10-1; Mahoney 10-4-20-3; Weeden 9-5-13-3; Bricknell 10-3-22-0; Hendricks 10-2-37-2; Kirsten 6-2-27-0

★★★BARLOW'S XI WON BY 1 WICKET

at a ground which was used for Dadabhay interprovincial matches:

"That you persevere under such conditions is amazing," he said.

But he warned: "You are going to have to change to turf wickets. It is virtually impossible to produce world-class players on your matting-on-gravel wickets."

In October 1975, another match between leading players of the board and the union was played at the University of Cape Town.

The WP Cricket Union was represented by some of its most talented provincial stars, including Fred Goldstein, a hard-hitting opening batsman with a reputation for taking pace bowlers apart apart, Peter Kirsten and Allan Lamb, two of the finest players of their generation, talented left-handed batsman Hylton Ackerman and the Springbok allrounder Eddie Barlow.

Among the WP Cricket Board stars were Coetie Neethling, Jock Mahoney, Kulu Maclons, Omar Henry and Gertjie Williams.

Lamb, Kirsten, Barlow and Ackerman compiled just 43 runs between them.

Shafiek Toefy, an executive member of the board said that Howa had been reluctant to sanction the game. "He gave the go-ahead on condition that the teams were mixed, that there would be no media coverage and that no permit would be applied for.

"A few days after the game he showed me some Australian newspapers containing coverage of the match as well as advertisements trying to portray how successfully mixed cricket was being played in South Africa.

"Mr Howa had remarkable insight," said Toefy.

The advertisements had probably been placed to pave the way for a tour by the Australian national team to South Africa.

A controversial tour by Richie Benaud's International Wanderers side, did eventually take place during the 1975/76 season.

Under the axe of the Group Areas Act

GAFSA DE LA CRUZ had travelled from London to visit the museum dedicated to the people of District Six. Inside the building, which had once been a church, she wrote her name and address – 30 Ross Street – using a red khoki pen. Then she crafted her simple message on the giant roll of calico sheeting: "Fondest love for my home country."

It was yet another poignant moment in a place that had known countless other poignant moments in its short existence.

Roger Kearns' pilgrimage to his past was made from his new home in Melbourne, Australia: "My father was the projectionist at the National Bioscope," he wrote.

"Thanks for the memories."
And then there was Armien May, son of Ralie, "who stole peanuts at the Star bioscope...."

Hundreds of other messages adorn the calico sheeting in the District Six Museum – messages from former residents of the area, now settled in Paris, London, Stockholm, Rio de Janeiro, New York, Montreal....

And messages of pain, longing and loss, from those who never settled where they'd been dumped – in the windswept, soulless townships of Manenberg, Bonteheuwel, Heideveld, Hanover Park, Lavender Hill, Mitchells Plain....

From 1966 onwards, a community of more than 55000 people was eliminated in District Six – in the name of the Group Areas Act.

More than 30 years later, many residents could still remember those traumatic times – the bulldozers that came rumbling down the streets, the dust that was kicked up by demolished buildings and the never-ending procession of tearful goodbyes.

The Group Areas Act was one of three pieces of legislation promulgated in the late 1940s and early 1950s by the newly-elected National Party to underpin their policy of apartheid: the first, the Prohibition of Mixed Marriages Act, which outlawed mixed-race marriages, was passed in 1949; next, in 1950, came the Population Registration Act, which sought to define who was of what "race".

Its coming ushered in the days of the infamous "pencil test", where white bureaucrats sometimes determined a person's race by inserting a pencil into his or her hair. If the pencil fell out, it signalled straight hair – and classification, possibly, as white or coloured. If it stayed put, it signalled *kroes* (or frizzy) hair – and classification as African or coloured.

In the first few years after its promulgation, thousands of coloureds became whites, whites became coloureds, Indians became "Malays", Cape coloureds became "other coloureds" and Chinese became whites (the possibilities seemed endless) – all at the stroke of a pen (or the drop of a pencil).

Finally, in 1950, in the same year that the Population Registration Act was passed, the Group Areas Act was written into the statutes.

Like all the other laws drawn up by the National Party, the Group Areas Act was enforced with gusto by the functionaries of apartheid.

District Six was just one community that felt its effects. Dozens of other communities, throughout South Africa, were also destroyed.

Families and friends who had lived close to each other were removed to far-flung and, for a long time, unliveable places on the Cape Flats. Strong community bonds which had been built up over decades were eroded.

And, in most cases, affected people received disproportionate remuneration for the properties from which they had to move, many of which were located in prime areas.

In a book entitled *Dispossession in Black River, Rondebosch: The Unfolding of the Group Areas Act in Cape Town,* Dr Uma Mesthrie-Dhupelia argued that the Act went beyond simply allocating a separate area for each population group.

"[It] wasn't entirely about ensuring segregation, since South African cities had high levels of segregation by 1948. It was about reordering the city and reclaiming vital space for whites," she wrote.

Dr Mesthrie-Dhupelia noted that when representatives and witnesses appeared for various white interests at Group Areas Board hearings, they supported the idea behind the Group Areas Act and argued repeatedly against coloured settlements being allowed too close to white areas, because they claimed that this would affect property values and also lead to coloured penetration into the white areas.

They also objected to coloureds passing through white areas.

THE EFFECT ON CRICKET

Besides having a massive social and economic effect, the Group Areas Act also impacted greatly on the game of cricket in the black communities. When large numbers of cricketers were forced to move from suburban areas in which they had lived for generations to new, faraway townships, where there were no facilities, the standard of cricket dropped appreciably.

Grounds in recently declared white areas such as Vasco, Rondebosch, Goodwood, Green Point, Mowbray and Kromboom, were taken away from black clubs, most of which suddenly found themselves struggling to survive.

Sa-at Galant, a former member of the Claremont-based Violets club, remembered the devastation caused by the Act which, he said, had been primarily responsible for the demise of the club in the mid-1970s.

"Our club was formed by a few families – the Galants, Ganiefs and Adamses – who lived close together," Galant said. "It is impossible to describe the *belieftigheid* (love and respect) we had for one another.

Because we lived so close to one another, we would always be together, whether this togetherness meant going to the mosque on Friday, playing cricket in the streets, practising or simply socialising."

All this changed with the implementation of the Act.

"Suddenly, families in our neighbourhood moved to different areas – to places such as Lansdowne, Grassy Park and Manenberg," said Galant.

"Most of us didn't have motorcars. It became difficult to attend practices and meetings. Group Areas strangled the spirit. Violets began to disintegrate.

"The same thing happened to neighbouring clubs such as Vineyards and Combine."

Galant spoke of the strong culture of cricket in the area which, from the point of view of black lovers of the game, cut across the racial divide.

"We spent hours watching top international and provincial players practising in the nets at Newlands and at the nearby Claremont Cricket Club grounds (which were situated behind the mosque in Stegman Road)," he said.

"We never paid to watch matches at Newlands because the gates were manned by our family and friends.

"We'd pay special attention to the technique of visiting players such as Colin Cowdrey, Ken Barrington and Dennis Compton – and then, when we went home, we'd imitate them in our street games.

"Some of my friends could execute the 'Compton sweep' perfectly; some of the others could imitate exactly the actions of the bowlers they had watched at Newlands.

"A number of us worked in the Newlands scoreboard, which was run by Hadjie Mogamat Jacobs. This enabled us to watch many of the test matches and Currie Cup games."

Hadjie Jacobs, who was fondly referred to as "Buppa", operated the scoreboard from when it was opened in 1948 until his death in 1992.

Many cricketers who later represented the Western Province Cricket Board's provincial team, including the Abed brothers, Laam Raziet, Taliep Behardien, Timmy Lakay, Faiek Davids and Galant himself worked the Newlands scoreboard at one time or the other over the years.

Although Galant and his friends lived near Claremont's grounds, they were never allowed to make use of the club's facilities.

"Once or twice, on a Sunday, when everything appeared to be quiet, we'd take a chance and try to play a match there," he said. "But the police would always spot us and chase us off. Dogs were allowed to walk on that field unhindered – but not us."

PIRATES OF RONDEBOSCH

In the 1960s, there were two clubs in the part of Rondebosch known as Black River. One was Pirates, a flourishing affiliate of the Green Point-based Western Province Cricket Association. The other was Alma, powerful members of the white Western Province Cricket Union.

But, for a long time, their lack of contact was so complete that they might as well have existed on two separate planets – so little did they know of each other.

As a youngster in the 1950s, Lefty Adams, a future Western Province Cricket Board captain, used to cycle from his home in Balfour Street to Alma Road, a few blocks away, to watch white Alma practise.

"Springboks, Jack Cheetham and Gerald Innes, played for them," said Adams. "Later, they were joined by the future Springbok captain, Peter van der Merwe.

"I spent hours watching them, so that I could learn something," Adams said.

"One day, Cheetham gave me a ball and invited me to bowl at the Alma batsmen in the nets. They were quite friendly – and eventually I ended up cycling to their grounds twice a week for bowling practice."

Adams was sometimes joined at the Alma practices by his Pirates teammate Eric Petersen, who lived in nearby Mowbray. As the relationship grew, Innes agreed to assist at Pirates practices in nearby Strathallan Road.

"He always batted for much longer than our players – and he always struggled against Eric, who was a great bowler," said Gamza Adams, a former Pirates opening bowler.

With most of their members living close to Rondebosch Common, Pirates did not have the same type of difficulty many other clubs had when it came to

Brian O'Connell: "Some of my best cricketing moments come from my days with Good Hopes [of District Six]"

preparing pitches. "We'd water and roll it on a Friday afternoon and then load our mat onto a wagon, which we'd push to the ground on a Saturday morning.

"Later, it became easier still for us to transport equipment to the field, when one of our members, 'Long' Harris, offered us the use of his horse and cart," said Lefty Adams.

On several occasions, the Pirates first team consisted of 11 members of the Adams family – and all of them were in the side on merit.

Because the majority of members lived in the area, the club's meetings on Friday night were usually packed out, and often finished very late because it turned into a social gathering once the formalities had been completed.

But, as was the case with many Western Province Cricket Board clubs, the Group Areas Act eroded the membership of Pirates in the late 1960s and early 1970s.

"Forced removals broke our team," said Gamza Adams. "Many of our members were moved to distant townships, and although some of them tried to maintain ties with the club, it was difficult because everyone was scattered far and wide.

"After most of our players had moved out of the area, we merged with the Rylands-based Rythorn club, to form Pioneer. In 1976, we merged with Primrose."

Although forced removals devastated Pirates, Lefty Adams was still able to spot some positives amid the heartache. "Many thought that Group Areas removals would break our spirit. But the contrary was true: it made us stronger human beings

"When the apartheid government took away our homes and our grounds, they increased our dedication to the game. They made us even more determined to play cricket."

DISTRICT SIX

The destruction of District Six forced a number of top clubs, including Roslyns, Red Roses and Good Hopes to throw in the towel.

Brian O'Connell, who went on to captain Western Province in the 1975/76 season, started his career with Good Hopes.

"I was playing in the street one day, when an official of the club invited me to attend their next meeting.

"I went – and was immediately selected for the first team.

"'But I don't have boots and flannels,' I protested.

"No problem. Someone went into the yard of the house where the meeting was being held, and came back with a pair of boots. Then, someone else gave me some money and told me to go to the Parade to buy white material. Within an hour of my return, I had my flannels, courtesy of one of the members of the club, who was a tailor.

"The spirit and love for the game during those years was tremendous," O'Connell said.

"Some of my best cricketing memories come from my days with Good Hopes. I was even renamed 'Braim' by the predominantly Muslim membership of the club."

The closure of most of the clubs within the former Green Point Track-based Western Province Cricket Association proved to be a blessing in disguise when the new club structure was introduced in the 1976/77 season. While some clubs had difficulty in amalgamating, others – especially those which had fallen victim to the effects of the Group Areas Act – took on a new lease of life.

"It was quite easy to form the United Cricket Club from clubs within the former Western Province Cricket Association because many of the clubs that were based in District Six and

Claremont were severely affected by the Group Areas Act. Clubs such as Roslyns, Walmers, Violets and Vineyards had difficulty in continuing because their membership had been moved to far-flung areas of the Cape Flats. As a result, it became easier to amalgamate and form one strong club," said Sadick Emeran, who became United's first president.

NORTHERN AREAS

Clubs in the northern parts of the Cape Peninsula were also affected by the Group Areas Act, but perhaps not as badly as those in the southern suburbs and central Cape Town.

In 1954, when Goodwood was declared a white group area – even though fewer than 3000 whites lived in the suburb, compared with more than 13000 coloured residents – Avenirs, the champion club of the Maitland-Parow Union, was hard hit by an exodus of members.

Stuck without a home ground, the club first moved to a vacant field next to the cemetery in Johnson Road, Athlone. "But," said Bert Erickson, a former chairman of the club, "the field was in such a pathetic state that most of our opponents were not happy playing us there."

"Later, we were granted permission to use the ground at Clover Crescent in Athlone. But soon after we started playing there, the Metropolitan and Suburban Union argued that we should join them because we were using a field in their area of operation.

"Our decision to move, lost us members who wanted to remain loyal to Maitland-Parow. On the other hand, we managed to attract new members from Athlone, Lansdowne and Crawford," Erickson said.

Avenirs eventually merged with Ashtondale in 1976, to form Avendale.

Another Goodwood club, Elma, was also forced to move. But when it based itself in Elsies River, it experienced a healthy growth in membership.

"Many players who had already been forced to move to Elsies River joined us," said Coetie Neethling. Later, when Elma merged with Valiants and Elsies River-Parow in 1971, the area was represented by a much stronger club."

ST AUGUSTINES

St Augustines, the club which came into being in 1899 when Sidney Lavis, an Anglican bishop based at St Paul's Church in Bree Street, Cape Town, urged the youth of his parish to do something constructive with their free time, was also forced to move headquarters in the early 1960s – from Green Point Common to Athlone.

Harold Arenz, the president of the club at the dawn of the new millennium, was a player in the early 1950s.

"In those days, I had to travel by bus from my home in the Bo-Kaap to practices at our home venue, which was adjacent to Green Point Stadium.

"Later, we moved to the beachfront area, but when that whole part was declared a white group area, we moved to the St Francis Boys' Home in Thornton Road, Athlone. We held our meetings there – and later, after we'd put down a concrete strip, we practised there as well.

"Our next move was to Turfhall Park in Lansdowne and, finally, in 1976, to our present home in Elfindale, Heathfield.

"Even though most of our members were forced to move to far-flung areas such as Athlone, Bonteheuwel, Heathfield and Wetton, we managed to stick together – perhaps with a little help from above.

"Whereas our members could previously walk to meetings in the St Paul's

Bert Erickson, a former chairman of the Avenirs Club.

Peter January broke ties with the St Augustines Cricket Club over their refusal to condemn Basil D'Oliveira for "promoting the white cause".

Hall, after they had been forced out, they had to travel by car or public transport.

"During the 1950s and '60s, we were a very successful club – and for this reason, new players joined us every season," Arenz said.

Peter January, who opened the batting for the South African Coloured XI at the 1958 Dadabhay tournament in Cape Town, joined St Augustines in 1950, after being approached by Basil D'Oliveira's father, Lulu.

"My own father suggested that I join them because he felt that the players at Meltons, the club for which I'd been playing at the time, were drinking too much."

"I used to walk from my home in District Six to practices at Green Point. After my family moved to Athlone in the 1950s, I caught a train to Cape Town and then walked from there to the club's practice venue. But I didn't see that as a problem – I was prepared to do anything to play cricket."

January said that he had broken ties with St Augustines in 1971, in protest against the club's continued association with its most famous son – Basil D'Oliveira.

"I was very politically minded at that time and was angry that the club was still prepared to associate with Basil after he had allowed himself to be brought to South Africa in the early 1970s by the whites to promote their cause."

"I still regarded him as a great cricketer, but I couldn't agree with his actions," said January.

On the verge of a split – controversy over liquor sponsorship

IN 1974, THE South African Cricket Board of Control (Sacboc) found an unlikely fairy godfather, after years of unsuccessful knocking on the doors of the country's boardrooms in search of sponsorship.

Few would have thought that an association representing wine farmers from the Afrikaner community of Stellenbosch would ever be convinced to pump money into a cricket organisation which openly used words such as "nonracial" and "anti-apartheid".

But that's precisely what happened: Sacboc announced that Stellenbosch Farmers' Winery had become the new sponsors of the three-day inter-provincial competition. In the previous season, it had sponsored a Sacboc national one-day competition to the tune of R15000.

Western Province, the strongest unit in Sacboc, opposed the deal strenuously. Many observers, in the Western Cape, especially, viewed the sponsorship as an attempt to drag Sacboc back to the days of ethnic units.

The majority of top Muslim players in the Western Cape immediately objected to the sponsorship on religious grounds. But, in the other provinces, Muslim players expressed their intention to play.

"It was a clear attempt to divide Sacboc players," said Western Province wicketkeeper, Braima Isaacs. "Remember, the announcement came at the same time that attempts were being made to force Sacboc to water down its stand with regard to unity at national level."

Not everyone agreed with Isaacs, though.

"I did not see the potential for a split along religious lines," said Brian O'Connell, who took over as captain from Lefty Adams that season. The Muslim players had taken a principled position, which I understood and respected. It never came down to an us and them situation."

Nevertheless, leading Muslim players such as Adams, the captain of the team at that time, Isaacs and the Magiet brothers – Rushdi and Saait – declared themselves unavailable. Others – notably Omar Henry and Ismail Timol – decided to play.

"I was under pressure from the Muslim community not to play," said Henry, But I asked myself: are you working for that money? The answer, of course, was no.

"We were amateurs during those days – we weren't going to get paid from the sponsorship. All Stellenbosch Farmers' Winery was doing was to sponsor our airfare and hotel accommodation.

"But there were people, especially the players who withdrew, who felt that we'd be playing for liquor money, which is contrary to Islamic principles.

"It was left for everyone to decide for themselves. I decided to play with a clear conscience."

Braima Isaacs (top) saw the sponsorship as an attempt to split Sacboc.
Omar Henry (above) played because, he said, the money was not being used to pay him.

Following the refusal of the leading Muslim players to play in the competition, O'Connell, the former Western Province under-21 captain, was rather surprisingly chosen to take over the reins from Adams.

O'Connell, who had previously played just one match for the Dadabhay team two seasons previously, was chosen ahead of more experienced candidates such as Jock Mahoney, Kulu Maclons and Viccie Moodie.

"Because I had captained Cape District, I was arrogant enough to believe I could do the job for Western Province," said O'Connell.

"Throughout my student life, I had been placed in leadership positions. However, the captaincy of the provincial side was a different type of challenge for me, mainly because I knew very little about the provincial scene."

The first thing O'Connell did was to try to get hold of every book he could find on captaincy.

"For the first time in my life I actually began to read seriously about how to captain a cricket side – even though I had done the job at various levels for many years.

"It was only then that I began to understand the mathematics of field placings - the logic of 6-3 field placing and the daring of a 7-2 placing and what that meant for bowlers. It helped me enormously to understand the game a lot better.

"My greatest anxiety revolved around the older players such as Moodie, Maclons and Mahoney, all of whom had legitimate reasons to believe that they would be appointed to the position. I also had to deal with the fact that they had already become icons in the provincial side.

"Although there wasn't any animosity towards me, I detected a guardedness, which I understood and respected.

"I knew I had to quickly prove that I could play the game at that level."

Because the chances of the team had already been written off, there was less pressure on members of the side.

"We were able to develop a strong sense of camaraderie – and we began to enjoy one another's company," said O'Connell. "We even had one practice session at Newlands prior to our game against Transvaal in Johannesburg. The Transvaalers had a turf wicket, and it was thought that it would be a good idea to practise on the Newlands turf to acclimatise."

O'Connell said the team took their responsibility of representing Western Province very seriously – and it showed in their results. They won the competition.

The advent of normal cricket – and the WP Cricket Board splits

HOWA, HOWA… in the fascinating fight for the soul of black cricket, through turbulent 1976, into viciously repressive 1977, the influence of one man – Hassan Howa – grew ever more significant.

Described by his enemies, and even some of his friends as arrogant, argumentative, dictatorial, hot-headed and unreasonable (and these were some of the more polite adjectives), Howa muscled the message of non-racialism to the top of the sports agenda, while other aspirant standard-bearers of the ideal were being swept aside on the wave of euphoria that greeted the arrival of "normal" cricket.

And although he made mistakes - "hellish mistakes" – as he himself admitted, Howa had the remarkable ability to change tack in mid-course –and still come out of it with his reputation intact.

Thus, from the man who suggested that black cricketers would be happy to change in motorcars or behind bushes when mixed-race cricket was first mooted, he became one of the strongest proponents of "no normal sport in an abnormal society" when "mixed" cricket was indeed introduced.

But, sometimes, Howa was his own worst enemy. In late 1975, he quit the presidency of the Western Province Cricket Board in a huff because his son, Sedick, had not been chosen for the Western Province Under-19 side.

Shortly afterwards, the board stumbled into a crisis that threatened its very existence....

INTERNATIONAL WANDERERS

The cause of the WP Cricket Board's problems came from a most unusual source. Early in 1976, the white South African Cricket Association (Saca) announced that an International Wanderers side, led by the Australian great, Greg Chappell, and managed by Richie Benaud, another Aussie test legend, would be visiting South Africa for a series of friendly games. (This was after a tour by a Derrick Robins XI had been called off.)

A demonstration of goodwill

IN THE SUMMER of 1976, the South African Cricket Board of Control accepted an invitation from the South African Cricket Association to participate in a series of matches against an International Wanderers side.

The decision to play was taken "to show a measure of goodwill - since it would not be long before all cricketers were playing together under one banner".

Sacboc did, however, lay down the following conditions:
• All matches be played on a non-racial basis;
• All matches be played under the auspices of the Committee of Nine;
• All facilities be open to all spectators at these matches;
• The selection of teams be done with some measure of merit;
• The "South African XI" (the so-called national side) be selected on merit from players involved in provincial matches.

The announcement came at the time of ongoing unity talks under the auspices of the Committee of Nine, made up of representatives from the South African Cricket Association, the South African African Cricket Board (SAACB) and the South African Cricket Board of Control (Sacboc).

Sacboc was asked to allow 14 of its top players, including five from Western Province, to participate in the tour matches.

Saca made the request even though they were well aware that Sacboc's strongest affiliate, the Western Province Cricket Board, strongly opposed visits to South Africa by overseas sides. Indeed, the board's opposition to the visit by a Derrick Robins XI, which had been conveyed to Saca by Sacboc, was one of the main reasons for that tour having been called off.

But this time, to the irritation of the Western Province Cricket Board, Sacboc sanctioned the International Wanderers' visit.

A statement of solidarity

THE STATEMENT issued in support of Howie Bergins and Pinky Carelse by the majority of members of the Western Province Cricket Board provincial side read as follows:

"We demonstrate our solidarity with our fellow players, Howie Bergins and Pinky Carelse, who were selected for this match, but whose selection was vetoed by the WP Cricket Board executive.

"These fine players, who have remained faithful to the stand for nonracial cricket made by Sacboc, now find themselves snubbed for remaining faithful to Sacboc.

"Owing to the courageous work of our administrators, past and present, the demand of Sacboc that normal cricket be introduced in South Africa is known throughout the world. It is our belief that by participating in these matches the players concerned have not prejudiced Sacboc's stand in the least, but have helped to create an atmosphere wherein the implementation of 'normal' cricket will be hastened.

"We will see that cricket is but one facet of our struggle for a life based fully on the Rights of Man.

"In this respect, we contend that the political precedents set during the playing of these games will be seen to have played a role in our struggle for equality.

"The players of the Western Province cricket team reaffirm their commitment to sacrifice everything, including their personal cricketing ambitions in the fight to secure the rights of the peoples of South Africa, and we believe that at this stage in the history of South Africa, a concerted forward drive by all South Africans is imperative, and that bannings and threats are not the answer."

The board's reaction put it on a collision course with its parent body –and, indeed, with some of its own officials and players.

In the middle of March 1976, shortly after two local players, Howie Bergins and Pinky Carelse, both of whom were members of Brian O'Connell's new-look provincial side, had played in a match at Newlands against the tourists, the Western Province Cricket Board demonstrated the extent of its opposition to the visit: it suspended both players.

From then onwards, the drama unfolded at rapid speed.

The first significant response to the suspension of the two players occurred on 27 March – less than half an hour before the start of the first day's play of the three-day, end-of-season showpiece between Western Province and the Rest of Sacboc at the Oude Libertas ground in Stellenbosch.

The Western Province team – with the exception of the wicketkeeper, Kulu Maclons, Archie Sonn and the 12th man, Dolfie Engels – staged a two-minute protest next to the pitch.

Immediately afterwards, they issued a statement supporting the two players.

To emphasise their solidarity with the two suspended players, nine members of the Western Province team invited Carelse onto the field (Bergins was not present) and applauded him.

Maclons, who with Sonn and Engels, had refused to join the protest, "as a matter of principle", said, "I thought the players were wrong to play at Newlands."

Carelse said he had had no qualms about having played against the International Wanderers.

"I was given the okay to play by the Sacboc president, Rashid Varachia – in a telegram," he said.

Varachia, who was not present during the protest, expressed his approval of the players' actions when he arrived at the ground later. He told the Afrikaans weekly newspaper, *Rapport:* "I have great admiration for the viewpoint of the players. Their actions prove that they support Sacboc."

He said that the protest was proof that the players in Sacboc wanted cricket to receive priority.

"There are administrators claiming to represent the cricketers," Varachia said.

"The big question is – is that really the case?"

"DON'T TOUCH IT"
Even before the Newlands match, the International Wanderers tour – and Sacboc's attitude towards it – had sparked intense debate among Western Province Cricket Board players.

Brian O'Connell, the board's provincial captain, said: "We were flying back to Cape Town after playing a match against Natal in Durban when some players admitted that they had been approached to play.

"I can still clearly remember my words to them: 'Don't touch it with a barge pole.'

"It then emerged that Pinky [Carelse] and Howie [Bergins] had already agreed to play.

"And hard though I tried, I couldn't persuade them to change their mind."

Shortly after the aircraft landed in Cape Town, O'Connell himself received an invitation – via Ken Adams, a well-known freelance journalist – to play against the International Wanderers at Newlands.

"'What is the board's standpoint?' I asked him.

'They want nothing to do with the match,' he replied.

"'Well, then, there you have my answer,' I told him."

Many people found O'Connell's stance puzzling.

On the one hand, he expressed strong opposition to the tour, and to playing in any of the tour matches; but on the other hand, he freely admitted to having played a leading role in the drawing up of the statement expressing solidarity with Bergins and Carelse, and in the protest action that preceded the start of the match at Oude Libertas.

"To me it was simple," O'Connell said. "I believed that Pinky and Howie were wrong to accept an invitation to play, but I couldn't convince them that they had erred. And that is where I left it."

"Of far more concern to me was the board's stance," O'Connell said

"Sacboc's support for the tour and the board's opposition to it, meant just one thing – the board's position within Sacboc had become untenable.

"They should have quit Sacboc.

"By not getting out, they had made themselves guilty of turning the issue of playing against tourists into a regional sin.

"They were, in effect, saying that while Western Province players would not be allowed to play against the International Wanderers – and would be punished if they did – it was okay for players from the other provinces to play in these matches. In fact, they were also saying that, not only could players from other provinces play against the International Wanderers, but they could also be selected for the Rest of Sacboc side – and play against Western Province.

"It didn't make sense."

Omar Henry, who attended the meeting at which the majority of the provincial team had decided to back Bergins and Carelse, said: "We discussed a memorandum drafted by O'Connell and the senior players – and all of us agreed that a walk-off at Oude Libertas would send a clear message to the executive of the Western Province Cricket Board.

But executive members of the board were themselves far from united:

some of them were strongly opposed to the International Wanderers' visit; others supported the Sacboc line on the tour.

The initial reaction of the board, then, was to do nothing.

Matt Segers, who had taken over as board president, following Howa's resignation, defended the decision to allow the game and the protest to proceed.

"I felt that it would have been unwise to stop the match," Segers said.

"There was a tense atmosphere at the ground. Some of the spectators expressed support for the players; others booed them."

ACTION

A few days after their protest, O'Connell and his team were called to face the board's executive committee at a disciplinary meeting, at the Swanees Inn in Bellville.

Henry, Bergins and Viccie Moodie were notable absentees, sparking speculation about their future in the board.

A stream of rumours about mass defections by leading board players to the Western Province Cricket Union began circulating.

The tension was palpable as the meeting got underway.

Later, it was reported that Percy Sonn, Barney Leendertz, Vincent Farrell, Shafiek Toefy, Neville Hartel and Ian Saunders had voted for the players to be disciplined.

Neville Marais, Frank Brache, John Carelse, Suleiman Patel and Moosa Patel had voted against any action being taken against them.

In what was seen essentially as a damage-control exercise, a compromise was reached....

To satisfy those officials calling for disciplinary action, the players apologised for their actions; to mollify those wanting no action, a statement

was released supporting the quest for normal cricket (as "championed" by the Western Province Cricket Board).

But neither apologies nor promises of support could hide the fact that the board was under siege – both from within and without.

At stake were two prizes: the province's top black players – and, ultimately, the board itself....

TARGETING THE MAGIETS

The jewel in the crown of both the Western Province Cricket Board and Sacboc was Saait Magiet – a dashing batsman and venomous fast bowler who, even as a teenager, had been held up as a player with the talent to play "international" cricket.

Magiet and his older brother, Rushdi, were prime targets of those seeking full Sacboc participation in the International Wanderers tour.

According to Rushdi Magiet, attempts to get them to play came right from the top – from Rashid Varachia, the Sacboc president.

"Varachia and his supporters were desperate for us to play," Magiet said.

"They dangled large sums of money in front of us – but Saait and I rejected these approaches with contempt. Neither of us had any interest in playing against the Wanderers."

Magiet's version was rejected by Cliff Adams, a journalist who, like his brother, Ken, had been closely involved in the recruitment of Sacboc players for the International Wanderers tour.

In an article for the *Rapport* newspaper, Adams said that Saait Magiet had been keen to play, but couldn't – because of pressure from his older brother.

"Saait would have made history in Pretoria and Cape Town had he played," Adams wrote.

Magiet confirmed having been sent an air ticket to get him to Pretoria, where the Wanderers were scheduled to play one of their matches.

"I took the ticket to a meeting of the Wynberg Cricket Board, where officials instructed me to return it.

"Since I hadn't asked for it, I was quite happy to comply," he said.

Natal opening bowler Goolam Allie also rejected an offer from Varachia to play against the International Wanderers.

"Varachia approached me at the Western Province versus Rest of Sacboc game, but I told him that I was not prepared to sell my nonracial principles," Allie said.

"The organisers offered good money to those who were selected to play in these matches, but there was no way that we – as people involved in the liberation struggle – could simply discard our beliefs and play."

While Sacboc, headed by Varachia, became enthusiastic supporters of the International Wanderers tour, many black cricketers, officials and supporters questioned whether the Sacboc Council had the power to override the clause in its constitution which stated that nonracial cricket had to be implemented at club level before it could be played at national level.

Inevitably, some of Sacboc's critics were ready to demonstrate their opposition in more concrete ways....

The first person to nail his colours to the mast was Vincent Farrell, the secretary of the Western Province Umpires' Association.

Farrell, a schoolteacher, refused to officiate in the Western Province versus Rest of Sacboc match because he objected to the presence of Tiffie Barnes and Yassien Snyders in the Sacboc side – because they had played against the International Wanderers.

Sacboc immediately replaced him with Paul Crainer, a member of the white Western Province Umpires' Union.

Later, an unrepentant Farrell said, "I wanted to show how strongly I objected to Sacboc players being involved in the International Wanderers tour.

Cecil Abrahams' advice

A BEWILDERING amount of advice – often from expert quarters – placed many of the Western Province Cricket Board's top players under intense pressure during the era of "normal" cricket.

Often, the advice would fail to take cognisance of the political realities of playing sport in South Africa.

Thus, in March 1975, Cecil Abrahams, the Lancashire League professional, writing in his weekly column in the *Cape Herald* newspaper, advised Magiet to join Green Point Cricket Club in the white Western Province Cricket Union.

"He would be a strong contender for a place in the Western Province Currie Cup team, and is the player who would be able to test the sincerity of those shouting for merit selection," Abrahams wrote.

"His other option would be to go overseas and play professional cricket.

"It would be a great waste if a player with all his natural ability did not experience playing in England, where his ability would show even more. He must do it now, or he may regret not giving himself the chance."

Abrahams subsequently organised a contract for Magiet with Strathmore in Scotland.

Magiet said: "I signed the contract and posted it to Cecil's old address in Manchester, not realising that he had moved.

"But frankly, I wasn't all that keen to play in Scotland; I'd just got married."

"And I think I succeeded."

Farrell admitted that in October 1975, he had officiated in a match at the University of Cape Town between a Coetie Neethling XI and an Eddie Barlow XI, but he said: "It was a game which had the full blessing of the Western Province Cricket Board, including Hassan Howa."

Farrell's strong opposition to apartheid resulted, a few years later, in his being banished by the state to a school in the small rural town of Sutherland.

The harassment of anti-apartheid activists such as Farrell drew attention to the farcical nature of "normal" sport.

Government policy was brutally simple: those who toed the line were okay; but those who stood up against state policy ran the risk of having the full toolbox of the state's security apparatus thrown at them – including detention without trial and banning orders.

The security police were regular visitors to the home of Howa, and many other anti-apartheid sports officials.

The trials of Vincent Farrell

FOR THREE hellish months towards the end of 1981, Vincent Farrell was given a small taste of how the South African government treated those who opposed its policies.

Farrell, a primary schoolteacher, was an enthusiastic participant in the activities of a number of sports organisations and local civic organisations, the Athlone Primary Schools Sports Union and the South African Primary Schools Sports Union.

His activities put him on a collision course with the apartheid authorities.

Farrell's punishment for becoming too involved in anti-apartheid activities was banishment to Sutherland, a little town located in the back of beyond, some 300km from Cape Town.

"Just before Christmas 1981, Chris Heunis, the minister responsible for coloured affairs sent me a letter informing me where my new home would be," said Farrell.

"In it, he vowed that I would never again be allowed to teach at a school in a metropolitan area."

In the course of his dealings with the authorities, Farrell was given an indication of the type of activities in which he had been involved, and which the state security apparatus did not like.

"I was surprised at how much information the security police could gather on an ordinary person like me," he said.

"I was shown a list of telephone calls I'd made and received; they knew exactly which meetings I'd attended... it was astounding."

Farrell's stay in Sutherland lasted just three months.

"I made up my mind that I'd rather quit teaching than stay there," he said

"With respect to its residents, I found the town to be a backwater, with an environment I just couldn't relate to. Apartheid had completely dehumanised the local black people. For instance, I could never accept the principal of the school telling me to get the children ready – because the *baas* [a local farmer] would be coming to pick them up."

On his return to Cape Town, Farrell cut his ties with cricket.

"I was too busy looking for a job," he explained.

In 1982, he eventually found one – with Kentucky Fried Chicken.

THE COMMITTEE OF NINE

Prior to the arrival of the International Wanderers, the Committee of Nine, consisting of three members each of the South African Cricket Association (Saca), the South African Cricket Board of Control (Sacboc) and the South African African Cricket Board (SAACB) had started formulating the ground rules for the implementation of "normal cricket" – from club level upwards.

Matt Segers, one of the Sacboc representatives, said the committee had chosen 1 October 1976 to launch a new era of mixed-race cricket in South Africa.

It hadn't been an easy road, he said – and it wasn't about to get any better.

Segers said that the Sports Minister, Piet Koornhof, had tried his hardest to persuade committee members to moderate their aspirations.

"Koornhof said he foresaw difficulties if we continued along the path we'd chosen," said Segers.

"It was a path that could lead to our cricketers being arrested for playing mixed sport. But we were determined to ignore his warnings.

"We had a plan which we were convinced would work. Unity was within our grasp.

"And then Varachia sold us out...."

Saca brought the International Wanderers to South Africa – and then asked him to persuade black players from around the country to play. Despite several Sacboc conditions for participation having not been adhered to, Varachia agreed to help them.

"Varachia's actions left me with no alternative but to resign from the Committee of Nine," said Segers.

"Shortly after I'd tendered my resignation, Varachia requested a meeting with me.

"I remember the day well. The International Wanderers were playing at Newlands – and Cliff Adams had picked me up to take me to the match.

"He'd also picked up Varachia.

"We stopped outside one of the gates at the ground, and Adams got out and entered the ground. For a long time, Varachia and I talked about developments in cricket. He wanted me to withdraw my resignation.

"But, I had made up my mind."

Segers' resignation provided the group of Western Province Cricket Board officials who opposed the International Wanderers tour with a welcome boost – and shortly afterwards, they'd be given an even bigger fillip....

HOWA'S COMEBACK

Hassan Howa's self-imposed exile ended as suddenly as it had begun.

With the Western Province Cricket Board wracked by division, emphasised by disagreements over the International Wanderers tour, Howa made a dramatic appearance as a delegate at a board meeting in the Landdrost Hotel in Lansdowne.

The arm-twisting that had prompted him to change his mind had been done by a delegation led by Percy Sonn.

"The situation called out for someone like Hassan," said Sonn, "so we asked him to return."

Howa didn't let his supporters down.

It was Howa, the streetfighter, who stepped into the Landdrost Hotel on the evening of the meeting. His hand was behind a motion of no-confidence in the whole board executive, which included officials such as Segers, Frank Brache, Neville Marais, Suleiman Patel and Johnny Carelse – and which was carried.

Brache was furious.

"The actions of Hassan's group was unconstitutional," he said.

"They had no authority to act in this way – and, to make matters worse, Hassan wasn't even an accredited delegate."

"He and his cronies simply took over the meeting."

Segers, who by then had broken ranks with the rest of the executive, resigned. But none of the rest would follow him.

As an impasse loomed, Segers closed the meeting and immediately started a special meeting, to elect a new executive.

Amid uproar, Howa was voted in as the new president.

"The deposed executive wanted to take the matter to court," said Segers. Their advocate said they would have a case only if I (as the president before the special meeting) supported them."

For a short time, there was a bizarre situation, in which two groups of officials laid claim to running the board.

Both groups turned up for a meeting at the Benvenuto Hotel in Stellenbosch.

Said Segers: "We [the deposed executive] sat, and they [the new executive] sat. Then they simply turned the chairs around and started their own meeting.

It was at this meeting that Segers decided to join the Howa camp.

Members of the previous executive (and, in their opinion, the legitimate one) were not impressed with Segers.

A bitter Brache called him a fence-sitter. "We took legal advice before

The board after the Howa coup

The newly-elected Western Province Cricket Board officials were:
President: Hassan Howa
Vice President: Percy Sonn
Secretary: Barney Leendertz
Recording Secretary: Roy Wolhuter
Treasurer: John Martin
Match & Registration Secretary: Lionel Smith
Trustees: Neville Hartel and Len Walsh
All of the above formed the executive of the Western Province Cricket Board.

the meeting – and we were assured that we had the law on our side," said Brache.

As board president, it was Segers' duty to tell Hassan and his group that their actions were unconstitutional.

"But he didn't. First, he allowed them to kick him out – and then he accepted life-membership from them as a reward for going over to their side.

Howa was elected unopposed as president of the newly constituted Western Province Cricket Board. He was also elected delegate to Sacboc.

TALKS CONTINUE

Despite the takeover of the board by the Howa faction, plans to introduce normal cricket in the 1976/77 season continued as envisaged.

In fact, Howa fully supported the agreement between Sacboc and the other bodies – reached in Johannesburg in January 1976 – to introduce mixed cricket at club level.

Indeed, so determined was he to see normal cricket introduced that he uttered what would become one of his most famous quotes: "We will undress in our cars and behind the bushes if necessary – as long as we play cricket. Our fight will be of a nonpolitical and nonreligious nature."

A resolution proposed by the Saca president, Billy Woodin, gave the process further impetus: "Normal cricket shall mean, at this stage, participation of all, and competition between all cricketers – regardless of race, creed or colour in cricket at club level, under one controlling body."

There was yet more encouragement when the Transvaal Cricket Federation agreed to join their white counterparts in July 1976. Natal followed suit and Howa gave the okay for normal cricket to proceed in the Western Cape.

On 27 July 1976, under a front-page headline, "Thumbs Up From Howa", the *Cape Herald* reported that the board had approved a plan for normal cricket to start on 1 October 1976.

At the heart of the plan, which was discussed and approved at a board meeting on 25 July, was a three-point agreement:

- The Western Province Cricket Board would disband and all its members would join the formerly white Western Province Cricket Union;
- The Western Province Cricket Union accepted the principle of normal, nonracial cricket from club level upwards;
- Cricketers who had formerly played for the nonracial Western Province Cricket Board side would be eligible for Currie Cup matches.

"We have compromised in the interests of cricket," a delighted Howa told the *Cape Herald*.

Howa promised that all board teams would be registered with the Western Province Cricket Union before 1 October.

"Our only conditions are that all teams be open [to everyone] and that we administer only cricket and worry about nothing else.

"We must get the assurance from the Committee of Nine and the Minister of Sport that our players will not be interfered with."

Shortly afterwards, the board abolished the Super League structures in favour of a club system – in order to fit in with the system used by the Western Province Cricket Union. The board was also happy to comply with another stipulation – that premier league teams have a membership of at least 60 and that they field an under-16 team.

"We prepared for unity by instructing the clubs to affiliate directly to the board instead of through their unions," said Barney Leendertz, the secretary of the board in 1976.

It quickly became apparent that the only way for many of the smaller clubs to survive would be to amalgamate.

"These were difficult times," said Leendertz. "Some of our clubs had histories and traditions that stretched back many decades."

A NEW CLUB SYSTEM

Even the discussions around amalgamation proved a painful exercise for many of the board's clubs.

"Some of them had family associations that went back for generations – and so, understandably, they were not prepared to surrender these identities," said Stan Abrahams, another board member of that period.

"It took many hours of debate and discussion before agreement was reached on the new system."

Although the original idea was for the former unions to transform themselves into clubs, the proposal did not draw universal support. Clubs such as St Augustines, Victoria, Ottomans and Montrose were big enough – and, they felt, confident enough – to retain their identities.

The inaugural Premier League consisted of Metropolitan, Paarl, Tygerberg, Primrose, United, Victoria, Helderberg, Rosmead and St Augustines – all of whom (with the exception of St Augustines) were the products of amalgamations.

While some clubs had difficulty in amalgamating, others, especially those which had fallen victim to the effects of the Group Areas Act, received a new lease on life.

"It was relatively easy to form United from the clubs within the former Western Province Cricket Association because many of the clubs that were based in District Six and Claremont had been severely affected by the Group Areas Act." said Sadick Emeran, the first president of the United club.

"Clubs such as Roslyns, Walmers, Violets and Vineyards had difficulty in continuing because their membership had been moved to far-flung areas of the Cape Flats. It was in their interest to amalgamate and form one strong club."

Ottomans decided at the last moment to remain on their own; Montrose were not affiliated to any union, having left the Western Province Cricket Association at the end of the previous season.

As clubs began finalising their plans for the start of cricket's great new era, cracks began to appear in the relationship between the Western Province Cricket Board and the Western Province Cricket Union.

HICCUPS

Leendertz said: "We viewed the concept of normal cricket as a means of defeating apartheid."

"Unfortunately, the Western Province Cricket Union did not see things this way. Boon Wallace, the union president, insisted that every new step had to be okayed by the government.

"Although it didn't matter to us what the government thought, or what laws were in the statutes, these were of vital importance to them.

"All we wanted was unity. They said they wanted it too – but only to the extent that the government allowed it.

"To say we were disappointed was putting it mildly. In one of our reportbacks, we predicted that unity on the terms that we had originally agreed to would not take place because Wallace was not sincere about the process."

Leendertz claimed that Wallace's reluctance to drive the process with any sort of enthusiasm, was not shared by many of the Western Province Cricket Union's affiliates.

"At the union's annual general meeting, which I attended as an observer, I distinctly remember the delegate of Stellenbosch University getting up and asking, 'When are we going to play?

"But Wallace couldn't provide them with the type of brave leadership that was required."

Board vice-president Percy Sonn accused officials of the union and their parent body, the South African Cricket Association of agreeing to one thing, and then going out and doing something completely different.

"We went into the unity process because we knew we didn't have a monopoly on what is right," said Sonn.

"When our colleagues in the white unions indicated that they were prepared to fight for the same things that we were fighting for, we were happy to join with them.

"But then they started going behind our backs, and doing things that we could never agree to.

"For instance, we made it clear from the start that we abhored the permit system – that we would never apply for a permit to play mixed-race sport or attend a venue which had applied for one. But they didn't seem to want to listen – or perhaps they just didn't care. Thus, at a meeting in Johannesburg, Joe Pamensky, a Saca official, blithely announced that he had applied for a permit to allow matches to take place.

"What was his reaction when we objected?

"'Oh, I didn't realise how you felt about the matter.'"

As members of the Western Province Cricket Board became increasingly disillusioned, Sacboc president Rashid Varachia flew in from Johannesburg to address officials at the Swanees Inn in Bellville.

"But it was too late," said Sonn. "We had made up our minds that we were not going to form part of the normal cricket set-up – and we told him so.

"Varachia was furious. During one exchange of words with me, he said

that he would see to it that I'd get beaten up should I ever set foot in Johannesburg again.

"As far as we were concerned, Varachia had lost all credibility. He operated in much the same way as the Saca officials.

"In fact, the night before he met us, he had summoned officials of United and Primrose to a 'secret' meeting – and there, tried to persuade them to take their clubs to the Western Province Cricket Union."

TAKING ON APARTHEID"

Lionel Smith, the Western Province Cricket Board's match and registration secretary in 1976, and Neville Hartel, another official, participated in the drawing up of fixtures for the first season of "normal" cricket in the 1976 season.

But it proved to be an exercise in futility.

"We wanted to take on apartheid," said Smith.

"But just as Barney Leendertz had discovered earlier, officials of the Western Province Cricket Union made it clear that they would do nothing to antagonise the government.

"As far as I was concerned, that was the end of the story. Moreover, the Soweto uprising, and its aftermath, drove home the point that sport in South Africa could not be played in a vacuum – separate from all the discriminatory legislation that blighted the lives of black people."

Last-ditch efforts were made to retrieve the situation. One of the more significants attempts to get the two bodies to speak again was made by Gerald Mallinick, chairman of the Green Point club.

Mallinick, who met with Howa at the latter's home in Heathfield, said: "I could see that Mr Howa was keen on unity, but he wanted a unity on terms that would not demolish his structures. He came across as a highly-principled man – a man who could not be bought.

"When I left his home, I realised that South African society was too abnormal for there to be any chance for cricketers to forge a significant unity."

Rushdi Magiet, who attended the meeting between Howa and Mallinick as a representative of the board's players, said: "Mr Howa was keen on joining the Western Province Cricket Union – but he backed off when I told him that he and his officials could go, but the players would certainly not."

By now it had become quite clear that there would be no unity in the Western Cape – not on 1 October... not in the immediate future.

REJECTING SACBOC

At the annual general meeting of the board on 10 September 1976, delegates formally signalled their rejection of the plan for "normal" cricket by an overwhelming majority.

They voted, too, (also by a great majority), not to participate in Sacboc's interprovincial competition.

Having made his leap of faith – and having been kicked in the teeth for his troubles – Howa was in a scathing mood when he delivered his presidential address.

"For the past few months I have been involved in an exercise in futility with our franchised counterparts, discussing the introduction of normal cricket," Howa said.

There was a unanimous view among delegates that the concept of "normal" cricket had been overtaken by recent political events, such as the Soweto uprising – and that cricket could not be isolated from the rest of life in South Africa.

Delegates voted, too, to abort the board's relationship with the white body – until such time that they indicate a willingness "to meet us on our terms".

Sonn, taking his cue from the powerful new slogan that had been coined by the South African Council on Sport (Sacos) said he could not reconcile himself to playing normal cricket under the present abnormal conditions.

Sacos's slogan succinctly summed up where the unity process had moved to: it was no longer simply a question of uniting white and black cricketing bodies. The struggle for liberation from the yoke of apartheid had entered the sporting arena.

Sport was about to become a powerful, nonviolent tool in the liberation struggle of the oppressed masses.

The abnormal conditions that Sonn was referring to related to the effects of the Group Areas Act, unequal education for blacks and whites, job reservation, separate amenities and the severe government repression of those who opposed its apartheid policies.

JUNE 1976

Several other developments impacted on the unity process, not least the June 1976 uprisings, which had started in Soweto, near Johannesburg, and had spread to other parts of the country.

In the Western Cape, schools and university students had started boycotting classes while many people had been killed in instances of police brutality.

In August 1976, 23 people had died in unrest in the townships around Cape Town.

Events outside the country had also hardened the attitudes of those opposed to apartheid.

In the Caribbean, Jamaica and Guyana banned cricketers who had played in South Africa. Then, at the

Percy Sonn called on the Western Province Cricket Board to abort its relationship with the Western Province Cricket Union because it had become quite clear that it was not possible to play normal sport in an abnormal society.

biggest sporting spectacle of all, 29 countries walked out of the Olympic Games in Montreal, only hours before the opening ceremony, in protest at the New Zealand All Blacks rugby tour of South Africa.

In addition to the international sports boycott, protest action by the oppressed majority began to gain momentum, placing the "normal" sport initiative into perspective.

"After the 1976 uprisings, people began to realise that cricket unification was a total farce," said Rushdi Magiet, a top cricketer of that period

"As the security forces of the South African government continued killing our children, we repeatedly asked how anyone with a shred of dignity could agree to playing with whites on a Saturday and then accept having their children shot on every other day of the week by policemen and soldiers of a government voted into power by the majority of white South Africans.

"Of course, some black cricketers were prepared to play with white cricketers under those conditions – but they were selfish, and thought only of themselves."

Howa said his supporters would not agree to "normal" cricket as outlined by Saca and Sacboc until the game was run in the interests of all South Africans. He said that this meant the formation of unified provincial bodies affiliated to a unified national body.

Despite the dramatically changed political scenario of the late 1970s, Howa did not shut the door completely to the possibility of unity between the country's cricketing bodies.

But if cricketers of all South Africa's communities were to get together, a number of things needed to be agreed to. These included:

• The formation of a single, controlling body for all cricketers;

• The go-ahead for clubs to decide for themselves who they wanted to admit as members;

• The opening up of facilities – and seating arrangements at all grounds to all spectators;

• A moratorium on all tours to and from South Africa, and the putting on hold of any application for membership of cricket's world body, the ICC, until a single controlling body had been formed.

Varachia pointed out that all these conditions had been accepted by Sports Minister Koornhof.

There was, of course, a wide enough gap between acceptance of a policy and its implementation for a busload of good intentions to fall through – and officials of the Western Province Cricket Board did not hesitate to point this out.

The relationship between Howa and Varachia, which had never been cordial, became progressively worse.

After one particularly vicious verbal barrage in which Varachia and board officials freely traded insults, Varachia referred to his Western Province Cricket Board critics as "urban terrorists".

In accusing "certain individuals" in the Western Province of having never stopped threatening him through the press, Varachia said: "Had it been possible, a criminal charge would have been laid against those perpetrating these mischievous and character-assassinating falsehoods, a characteristic that has of late become second nature in the Western Province."

He claimed that an autocratic group of people had taken control of cricket in the Western Province.

"Where else in the country, but in the Western Province Cricket Board, would you be able to declare a UDI [Unilateral Declaration of

Independence] and 'murder' the legitimate administration in the middle of
the season?

"Where else, but in the Western
Province, would you be able to preach
rebellion and subversion against a
democratic decision of Sacboc?

"Western Province have never
raised their objections to normal
cricket at a Sacboc meeting," he
fumed.

"If they don't want to play, they
won't, but they will have no future,"
he told the *SA Cricketer* magazine in
December 1976. Who is going to play
with or against them?"

CONFUSION

Despite the euphoria in some areas
over the introduction of normal sport,
there was general confusion in government circles about its implementation.

Koornhof appealed to sports bodies,
administrators, and sportsmen and
women not to implement the new
sports policy without first consulting
him, or the Department of Sport.

This, he said, would ensure that the
playing of sport between the various
population groups would be conducted in an orderly way – and unneces-
sary problems would be eliminated.

The preamble of the government's
new sports policy, as set out by the
Federal Council of the National Party,
alienated the Western Province
Cricket Board even further from the
unity process.

The Federal Council claimed that
the interests of South Africa and "all
its peoples" would best be served by a
sports policy in which "white,
coloured, Indian and black sportsmen
and women belong to their own clubs
and control, arrange and manage their
own sporting affairs".

Beyers Hoek, the Secretary of Sport
said that government policy did not
provide for mixed sports clubs, but for
competition between separate clubs of
different groups. Hoek warned that
legislation on separate facilities would
still be enforced.

"The Group Areas Act and Liquor
Act has not been changed," he said.

"A sports team from one race group
will still have to apply for a permit to
play in another group area.

"The aim is to have separate but
equal facilities for the different race
groups."

In a development that put a further
strain on the relationship between the
Western Province Cricket Board and
Varachia, intervention by police in
Kimberley stopped a planned multiracial trial match, in which five coloured
cricketers were due to play.

"It appears that we jumped the
gun," Des Schonegevel, a Griqualand
West selector, said afterwards.

Later, two coloured players – Keith
Hartzenberg and Des Summers – were
chosen to play for Griqualand West.
But no sooner had their selection been
hailed as a breakthrough for "normal"
cricket, when yet another problem
arose: in terms of government legislation, Hartzenberg and Summers could
not stay in the same hotel as their white
teammates, or travel in the same train.

Attempts to get around such problems by way of applying for permits,
was sharply criticised by Howa.

"I certainly will not be prepared to
play under such conditions," he said.

In another blow to "normal" cricket, the Balfour Park club stopped
Edward Habane, an African cricketer
who had participated in a multiracial
double-wicket competition in 1974,
from playing for their reserve side.
Ruby Orin, the secretary of Balfour
Park, said the request to axe Habane
had come from the Department of
Sport.

To add more fuel to the fire, Paul Marsh, the organising secretary of the Nuffield Cricket Week for white schoolboys, said there was no question of the competition going multiracial.

"We do not envisage contravening government policy, particularly as our schools are state-aided," Marsh said. (He claimed later that he had been misquoted.)

OFFICIAL WITHDRAWAL

On 10 October 1976, the Western Province Cricket Board formally and finally decided not to join forces with the Western Province Cricket Union.

Twenty of the board's 21 clubs voted against joining the union. the remaining club – Avendale – abstained.

"All the conditions set out for unity had not been met," the board pointed out.

Howa said too much emphasis had been placed on the government's sports policy – and not enough on other oppressive laws in the country.

"We are ready to play in any association which believes in playing cricket on a nonracial and free basis," he said.

However, just a day earlier, on 9 October, the relationship between the board and the union had deteriorated even further, when Howie Bergins, a pace bowler in Brian O'Connell's championship-winning provincial side, turned out for the Western Province Cricket Union side, Green Point, without a clearance.

The board said it would refuse to have any dealings with its white counterpart – "until such time as the union ceases to harbour board renegades".

Also on 10 October, the same weekend that the first "normal" cricket games commenced around the country, eight white rugby players, including Springbok triallist Dan "Cheeky" Watson and his brother Valence, played in a nonracial SA Rugby Union fixture between the Eastern Cape sides Kwaru and Sedru – in defiance of warnings from the government that the match was illegal.

Koornhof expressed annoyance at this "flouting of government policy".

Then, to add to the uncertainty, Saca president Billy Woodin told the *Rand Daily Mail* that Koornhof had never agreed to multiracial teams.

"Dr Koornhof has spelled out the new policy several times," Woodin said.

"We [Saca] and the Minister agreed to club cricket matches between clubs of different races. We never agreed to multiracial clubs."

Statements such as these proved unhelpful to Sacboc affiliates, many of whom were trying hard to make sense of how they fitted into the new scheme of things. Following a hastily arranged meeting, Varachia, Woodin and Koornhof emerged to say that their differences had been sorted out.

But they gave little details.

REACTION

On hearing that the Western Province Cricket Board had withdrawn from unity talks, the union president, Boon Wallace, issued a statement in which he expressed surprise and disappointment at the board's decision.

He said an application for membership of the Western Province Cricket Union had been tabled by the board and acknowledged by the union.

But Howa, now a staunch opponent of unity, denounced "normal" cricket as simply an attempt by Saca, its affiliates and its supporters to get back into international cricket.

In discouraging Western Province Cricket Board members from joining the "normal" cricket set-up, Howa said: "Obviously, it is not possible for us to offer the same facilities and financial arrangements that the Western Province Cricket Union is able to offer. We can, however, guarantee that while you play with us you will retain your self-respect and dignity."

HOWA'S CHANGE OF HEART

Frank Brache felt that the board had no reason to withdraw from the unity process.

Other pressures, from within the board itself, must have come into play, he suggested.

"Initially, there were one or two matters that Hassan [Howa] wanted sorted out," Brache said, "but these were not insurmountable.

"For instance, he wanted third division matches – which among whites were regarded as one-day social gatherings – to be played over two Saturdays.

"Hassan argued that because black schools did not have an established league structure, the third division should be the arena in which talented black youngsters could begin to establish themselves.

"To try to accommodate Hassan's request, Keith Griffiths, the Western Province Cricket Union's match and registration secretary, had to find grounds on which to play third division fixtures over two Saturdays.

"It took Griffiths two weeks to come up with a solution.

"Everything was formalised at a meeting at the Old Mutual building in Darling Street, Cape Town. Howa was convinced that there would be a single body administering the game by the start of the new season."

Brache said that shortly after the meeting in Cape Town he was invited to the home of Ebrahim Dawood, one of the board's main financial benefactors.

"When I arrive at his home in Heathfield, he and Hassan were having koeksisters and tea," Brache said.

"Both of them were excited about the prospect of normal cricket being played in the Western Cape in the new season."

But then, according to Brache, trouble arose.

"Barney Leendertz called me to say that Boon Wallace had gone to the government to apply for a permit to allow normal cricket to be played.

"This was a blatant lie," said Brache.

But, lie or not, it sparked angry reaction among members of the board – and the effects were quickly felt.

"The next person to call me," said Brache, "was Griffiths."

"He said: 'The Western Province Cricket Board has pulled out of the agreement.'

"'Rubbish,' I said. They haven't even had a meeting to discuss withdrawal.'"

Brache then got back to Leendertz, who repeated his claim that Wallace had applied for a permit.

By this time, news of the crisis had reached Varachia. Sensing the gravity of the situation, the Sacboc president flew to Cape Town, where he summoned Brache to a meeting at the Heerengracht Hotel in Cape Town, with Wallace and Koornhof.

"Varachia, Wallace and I were adamant that there was no way that we would apply for permits to play cricket," said Brache.

"We asked Koornhof to use his political clout within the National Party cabinet to allow cricket to be played without the necessity of having to apply for permits.

"'You guys – just watch me, Koornhof had promised. 'I am in charge here.'

"Look, we knew that whatever the National Party government did, they

Barney Leendertz accused Boon Wallace of having gone to the government to apply for permits to allow "normal" cricket.

did to suit their own political ends. But, I felt that once we were in, we would be able to change things from the inside.

"I've always believed you can't change things from the outside. I decided to stay in the unity process because I felt that I could change the situation from the inside."

A NEW DISPENSATION

Brache's first meeting under the new dispensation highlighted the type of problems that needed to be confronted and dealt with.

"The venue was the Rand Club in Johannesburg," said Brache. "All the officials walked in, and I followed last with Geoff Dakin of Eastern Province. When the clerk of the club saw me, he said, 'Sorry, we don't allow coloureds in here.'

"Dakin took me aside and said, 'F—k them!'

"We moved the meeting to the Rand International Hotel."

In many ways, Brache had become the "prize catch" of the Western Province Cricket Union. As one of the most senior officials of the board to cross to the union, it was not surprising that he was pushed to the forefront of "normal" cricket developments.

He certainly had pulling power: after leading a team consisting of provincial players such as Omar Henry, Willie Hendricks, Lawton Jacobs and Ismail Timol against a SACS/VOB team, his telephone started ringing... and ringing.

A flood of board players wanted to link up with him.

"I had 64 ex-board players ready to play in Western Province Cricket Union competitions," Brache said.

"I formed a club called Cavaliers. Clem Druker, the chairman of SACS/VOB, offered us their grounds

– and within two years, we had eight mixed teams playing in the union leagues."

Brache's next step was to get onto the Western Province Cricket Union's executive committee.

"I succeeded – but through rather unconventional means," he said.

"I proposed and then seconded myself. It was unconstitutional, I readily acknowledged, but at that stage it was the only way that I could get onto the executive."

THE BOARD'S NEW HARD LINE

Amid much confusion, and an exodus of some of their top players to the Western Province Cricket Union, the Western Province Cricket Board proceeded with its new, interclub competition in October 1976.

The competition did not, however, enjoy an auspicious start. Due to misunderstandings, there were no fixtures on the first weekend at Rosmead, Somerset West and Bellville.

Hopes of the board joining the "normal" cricket set-up were briefly raised again, shortly after the start of the season, when Howa called on Varachia to address a board meeting on 14 November 1976 – to clarify the implications of "normal" cricket.

But Howa's demands had changed by then – to accommodate the changing political climate which had been precipitated by the unrest sweeping the country.

Varachia turned down the invitation, saying: "Mr Howa will never be satisfied. He belongs on a political platform not on a cricket field.

"At a meeting on 2 October he asked for assurances on seven points, which I gave. "Suddenly there are other demands.

"Mr Howa jumps from spot to spot. It is impossible to conduct relevant dialogue while he persists with his negativist approach. In any case, who the hell does he think he is, demanding that we see him?"

Varachia's outburst was typical of the animosity that followed the split in the ranks of the Western Province Cricket Board.

Many long-standing relationships between players and administrators were severed. Those who crossed to the Western Province Cricket Union were dismissed as "renegades", "sellouts" and "deserters".

"I found it regrettable that people such as Frank Brache and Bert Erickson jumped onto the normal cricket bandwagon," said Leendertz.

"I had always considered Frank to be a great friend, but when he defected we simply ignored each other."

After initially supporting the unity process, Howa himself, clarified his change of heart in an article written in 1977, in André Odendaal's book, *Cricket in Isolation*.

"I admit that what I have been fighting for for twenty years has come about now and that I have modified my stand," he said.

"However, only recently did I become aware that to think only about cricket was wrong. Also, what we did last September and previously – to sit down with Saca – was wrong. I make no bones about this. I have made mistakes in my life, hellish mistakes, and this was one of the biggest.

"On the eve when what I had fought for together with all Sacboc was about to be realised, I decided: No! I have been wrong. I admit now that I should not have fought from a cricket angle, I should have fought from a completely humanitarian angle. I should have carried the fight right down the line.

"I saw my nephew who had been shot to death just behind his shop. And

I knew in my own mind that this boy was not connected with the riots. He was not made that way. His interests were opening his shop in the morning, running his business and closing up at night. He was shot dead.

"What upset me was that the evidence in court showed that the policeman who shot that boy admitted to killing 15 other children that same night. Fifteen! One policeman!"

While the Western Province Cricket Board held onto the majority of their players, most of Brian O'Connell's successful 1975/76 team joined clubs in the white Western Province Cricket Union. One of them was Omar Henry.

"There was so much confusion regarding the future of South African cricket at that stage," said Henry.

"On the one hand there were people using the slogan, 'no normal sport in an abnormal society', and on the other hand these same people were saying, 'we will change behind trees as long as we can play together'.

"Everything was happening so quickly, and behind closed doors – without the knowledge of the players. We didn't know what was happening.

"Many players were at their peak, and they wanted to see how good they really were."

Henry said that his decision to cross over was not based on wanting to play in matches involving the International Wanderers side. He decided to leave following an incident in Durban, in which he and some other members of the Western Province Cricket Board side had slipped into Kingsmead to have a quick look at a Currie Cup match taking place there.

"When we returned to Cape Town, word got out that we had been to Kingsmead. We were instructed to appear before the board's executive.

"It was like a kangaroo court."

Goolam Allie accused black cricketers who joined the "normal" cricket setup of having "sold out".

Henry said that he had refused to apologise when asked to do so. "I didn't believe that I was guilty of anything."

While players such as Henry and others crossed the floor to advance their cricket careers, others such as George van Oordt stayed loyal to the nonracial ideals of the board.

"For us, it was a case of using cricket to achieve our political aims – which we eventually did." said van Oordt.

"All those who were interested in only cricket should have gone to the 'boere', as we called them. We believed that there were much greater issues at stake. That is why so many talented players sacrificed what could have been lucrative careers on the other side."

Rushdi Magiet, one of the top all-rounders of the board during the 1970s, said: "I was extremely bitter towards those who decided to play normal cricket – and for many years, I refused to even speak to them.

"It was only much later that I began to mellow."

Explaining why he had been such an enthusiastic supporter of the campaign to isolate white South African sport, Magiet said, "At the very least, it made white people aware of how apartheid had blighted the lives of black people. Before the sports boycott, South Africa's white population had been living very comfortably in their ivory towers.

"Few of them were concerned about the plight of their black compatriots.

"Isolation kick-started the process of making them aware – primarily because it was a process which also deprived them of something – international sport," said Magiet.

Goolam Allie, another provincial player, was as forthright: "We were involved in a two-pronged struggle – sports and political," he said.

"We realised that the South African Council on Sport [Sacos] had visions of the type of democratic, nonracial society we were yearning for – and we supported them. To realise these ambitions, we were quite prepared to sacrifice our cricketing and financial ambitions within the game itself.

"As much as we loved the game, no self-respecting nonracial cricketer could have condoned the normal cricket set-up. It was a set-up designed to get white South Africa back into international cricket.

"Those who left showed a weakness of character – they sold out.

"If we look back at our struggle now, we can sit back with pride – especially when we consider the role that the international isolation of white sport, which we helped to bring about, played in our struggle for liberation."

Part 5

"No normal sport in an abnormal society"

ALL SA-AT Galant wanted to do was spend a lazy day at the beach with his son, Achmat. Clovelly, an intimate little spot, nestling just around the curve of the mountain between Kalk Bay and Fish Hoek, seemed an ideal choice.

BUT IT WASN'T

The biggest mistake Galant made that Sunday morning in 1976 was to ignore the "Whites-Only" signs that had been placed at strategic points along the beach.

A policeman saw the two "trespassers", and ordered them to leave.

"I felt humiliated," said Galant, who only a few weeks earlier had become part of the normal cricket setup when he joined

the Claremont Cricket Club, an affiliate of the WP Cricket Union. "I told the policeman that I played for Claremont - and I asked him why I couldn't use the beach in the same way that I used the cricket facilities of white people," he added.

But the policeman wouldn't listen to his story. He told Galant that the laws that allowed him to play cricket with whites, did not apply to beaches.

Soon afterwards Galant returned to the nonracial Western Province Cricket Board.

THE GREAT DEBATE

Few events in the history of South African sport sparked as much debate as the advent of "normal" sport. It was welcomed by many of the Western Cape's – and, indeed, South Africa's – top administrators and players. "It was," they claimed, "the beginning of a new era – a foot in the door."

To administrators such as Frank Brache and Bert Erickson, change had to come from "within".

"Nothing will ever be achieved by standing outside and shouting," they told their detractors.

But far, far more cricketers and officials rejected the concept of "normal" sport in a country with a political system that was far from normal. A seven-word slogan – "no normal sport in an abnormal society" – became one of the most effective battle cries in the fight against apartheid sport.

Certainly, Sa-at Galant's experience, and countless similar experiences by sportsmen and women throughout the country, seemed to justify the stance of those favouring the complete isolation of the predominantly white sports bodies – until the eradication of apartheid.

In the Western Cape, black cricketers who opted to play normal cricket became the lepers of their communities. They were totally shunned – often by people with whom they'd been friends for many years and, sometimes, even by family members.

Later, noncollaboration was taken a step further, when the South African Council on Sport unveiled its double standards resolution which barred their members from playing nonracial sport in one season and normal sport the next, or from attending matches at venues requiring a permit to admit blacks.

A NEW NATIONAL BODY

The decision by Rashid Varachia to take the South African Cricket Board of Control into the normal cricket setup – and the decision by a number of players and administrators in the Western Cape to follow him – came as a bitter blow to the holders of the nonracial flame.

Although a new national body – the South African Cricket Board – vowed to provide a home for cricketers who believed in the creation of a true nonracial society, it was not an easy task, especially since very few companies were prepared to sponsor them.

Picking up the pieces – the rebirth of the WP Cricket Board

BROTHER CURSED brother, neighbour shunned neighbour and old friends became sworn enemies in the tense weeks and months that followed the advent of "normal" cricket in the Western Cape.

The year was 1976 – and in spite of a strong appeal by the executive to members of the Western Province Cricket Board to stay loyal, large numbers – including the rump of Brian O'Connell's provincial side, which had won the Stellenbosch Farmers Winery trophy just a few months earlier – crossed over to the Western Province Cricket Union. Among those who left were Howie Bergins, Pinky Carelse, Viccie Moodie, Willie Hendricks, Omar Henry and Jock Mahoney.

In the immediate aftermath of the arrival of "normal" cricket, the board lost more than a thousand members. Although many joined the union, the majority simply lost interest and stopped playing as a result of the confusion.

The major consequence suffered by those who went to the union, was the way their move split their families, neighbours and, in some instances, even their communities. These "defectors", as they became known, were totally shunned by relatives, friends and acquaintances. In some instances, friendships which had been built up over many years, were ended in seconds, amid the angry swopping of insults.

The tense political atmosphere in the country, which was precipitated by increasing anti-apartheid protests from, particularly, the student and labour sectors, emphasised that change in sport could not be separated from the need for change in the general living conditions of the majority of South Africans.

Universal suffrage, equal education, the Group Areas Act, job reservation and the draconian pass laws, had become far more important issues than the mere normalising of sport.

Touching on the subject of "normal" cricket in André Odendaal's book, *Cricket in Isolation*, Howa said: "The normal cricket we hear about nowadays is rubbish. For true merit selection [to take place] everyone has to be given the same opportunities to develop his latent talent."

Comparing the living conditions and life experiences of a child of a migrant labourer living in Soweto with that of a child of an affluent family living in Houghton, Howa pointed out that there was no way that the black child could ever compete as an equal with his white counterpart.

Howa argued that his hypothetical black child would probably be living illegally in Johannesburg in conditions of near starvation, in constant fear of harassment by the white authorities. Unlike his white counterpart, he would not be getting the right

Gerald Mallinick questioned whether equal opportunities in sport were possible in a society where there were no equal opportunities in other spheres of life.

food; and unlike his white counterpart, who would take the availability of facilities and the possession of equipment for granted, the black child's hard-pressed mother would probably be unable to buy him even ordinary shoes for school (if he went to school) – let alone luxuries such as cricket shoes.

"The best time to start teaching a youngster about cricket is when he is about six or seven years old," said Howa.

"At the age of 13 he should have learned the basics of the game. Then you develop what he has.

"Not so with this chap. He doesn't get any coaching because his teachers know nothing about cricket – and there are no facilities. As a result his technique is hopeless...."

UNEQUAL FACILITIES

Howa could also have mentioned the massive inequalities in facilities between white, coloured and African schools.

For instance, there was no way that the pupils of Belhar High, on the Cape Flats, or those of Fezeka High, in the African township of Guguletu, could even dream that their schools would one day be able to provide the type of facilities being offered by Rondebosch Boys High.

Located in a magnificent setting, in the shadow of Devil's Peak, Rondebosch Boys High could offer (indeed, can still offer) its pupils more than 20 hectares of sports facilities, including seven rugby fields, eight cricket pitches, an athletics track, a swimming pool, a sports hall, a shooting range and several tennis courts.

Belhar High didn't have (and, in the year 2000, still didn't have) a school hall. While it did have a playground, this had to be shared between girls playing netball and boys playing rugby, soccer and cricket.

All Fezeka High could offer its pupils was an irregularly shaped piece of ground at the back of the school. In the year 2000, this same patch of ground was still being used by pupils.

The priority for most pupils who studied at black high schools was to leave as quickly as possible, in order to find a job to sustain their families.

Given the vast inequalities in facilities, and the increasingly desperate socio-economic conditions in the black communities, it was almost laughable for anyone to speak about equal sporting opportunities for schoolchildren.

Gerald Mallinick, the chairman of Green Point, the Western Province Cricket Union club which attracted the most black players at the advent of "normal" cricket, spelt out the problems of unequal opportunities in an article in the January 1977 edition of the *SA Cricketer* magazine.

"...[If] any meaning is to be given to the term 'multiracial cricket' ... everyone has [to be given] equal cricketing opportunities," Mallinick wrote.

He questioned whether equal opportunity and merit selection in sport were indeed possible in a situation where whites had extensive opportunities from primary school level, right up to university, while blacks had hardly any.

And then he answered the question himself: "No!"

"There must be proper schoolboy coaching and facilities for all races at all levels of the game," he wrote.

"Only when this happens can it truly be said that we have afforded equal opportunities for all, so that there may be merit selection for all."

These sentiments, so true of the situation in the 1970s, could equally be valid for the first decade of the 21st century.

A closer look at the disparity in government spending on education during the heyday of "normal" sport was equally revealing. A SA Institute of Race Relations survey on education between 1982-83 showed that the government spent R1385 on every white pupil; R871 on every Indian pupil; R593 on every coloured pupil and R192 on every African pupil.

These figures clearly highlighted the tremendous burden black pupils, in particular, had to labour against. It also exposed the myth that apartheid offered the opportunity of equal (though separate) opportunities for all in South Africa. The reality was that black pupils hardly had any educational facilities and provisions – let alone sporting facilities.

Writing in 1993 in a PhD thesis relating to the management and development of cricket in South Africa, Logan Naidoo reflected the thinking in nonracial sporting circles: "The problems encountered in sport were a reflection of the problems encountered in society as a whole. The government's stand on the Group Areas Act, Separate Amenities Act and Criminal Law Amendment Act were just a few of the policies which were aimed at separating people. These repressive policies not only affected sport, but totally undermined the nonwhite population in society."

But despite the many compelling arguments by its detractors, that "normal" cricket could benefit only the formerly all-white cricketing bodies – by allowing them to resume international ties against traditional rivals such as England, Australia and New Zealand – strong efforts were made to sell the concept to the black communities of the Western Cape.

SELLING "NORMAL" CRICKET

One of these public relations exercises – organised by Sa-at Galant and Dickie Conrad – featured a match, in February 1977, between a Claremont XI and a Conrad XI. Among the participants were Western Province Cricket Board players such as Galant and Taliep Behardien, and ex-board players such as Viccie Moodie, Omar Henry, Willie Hendricks, Lawton Jacobs and Ismail Timol.

Behardien was subsequently suspended by his club, United, for playing in the match; Galant quit the board to join Claremont.

Meanwhile, Rashid Varachia, well aware that the strength of Sacboc cricket was concentrated in the Western Province, tried to woo Primrose and United, the two leading Muslim clubs in the board, to the "normal" cricket fold.

He held a secret meeting with executive members of these two clubs, including Solly Nosarka and Mohammed Patel of Primrose, in the Heerengracht Hotel in Cape Town. Although Nosarka, whose family enjoyed close personal ties with Varachia, took the proposals back to Primrose he was told in no uncertain terms that the club was committed to the nonracial cause.

"The conviction of the office-bearers of the majority of board clubs was far too strong for them to contemplate playing normal cricket," said Sadick Emeran, the president of United at that time.

"Varachia might have had some friends in the two clubs, but he would never have been able to convince our clubs to leave the board," Emeran said.

Varachia also met the board's executive in February 1977. After initially threatening to walk out of the meeting because of the presence of former

Sa-at Galant decided to return to the WP Cricket Board after he and his son were ordered off a "Whites-Only" beach.

executive members, Frank Brache, Enver Matthews, Neville Marais and Cliff Adams, in the Varachia delegation, the board's executive agreed to continue discussions after they were given an assurance that Brache and his group would not be allowed to address the meeting.

During the tense, acrimonious discussions, the board insisted that the Committee of Nine fulfil the terms of the resolution adopted at a summit meeting in January 1976 – to work towards establishing nonracial clubs under nonracial provincial bodies.

At a meeting of Sacboc in February 1977, delegates rejected the draft constitution of the newly-formed South African Cricket Council. The composition of the new body according to the draft constitution gave the impression that an "umbrella body" comprising "population groups" would control cricket in South Africa. The sponsors of the constitution were named as the South African Cricket Union, the South African African Cricket Board and Sacboc.

In rejecting the draft constitution, Sacboc delegates proposed that the offending wording be substituted by a clause which read: "The union shall consist of the official provincial units or associations conducting their sport in such a way as to enable participation in it of all clubs without discrimination on the basis of colour, race or creed, and loyal in all respects to the principles of nonracialism."

Attempts by the Western Province Cricket Board to call further meetings of Sacboc were unsuccessful. Varachia eventually stated that a meeting of the organisation could not be called because of the introduction of "normal" cricket.

"All the units are dormant," he told the *Cape Herald*.

Despite the euphoria which greeted its introduction in some quarters, "normal" cricket was fraught with problems.

The contradiction of playing "normal" sport on a weekend and then returning to an abnormal life governed by apartheid legislation dawned on many who initially crossed the floor to the Western Province Cricket Association. One of them was Sa-at Galant, a talented Western Province Cricket Board batsman, who had won provincial honours at B team and Under-23 level....

GALANT'S LESSON

Galant, who joined Claremont, his neighbourhood side, which was out of bounds to him for all of his formative years as a cricketer, said: "I went over because I felt I was being treated unfairly by the Western Province Cricket Board selectors.

"I had topped the batting averages at a B tournament in Mossel Bay, as well as the averages in the Golden Yolk competition – and yet I wasn't considered good enough to play for the A side.

"I joined Claremont to prove to myself and others that I was good enough to play cricket at a higher level."

Galant confessed, however, that during his four-month stay with the club, he had never felt completely at ease.

"I sensed that I was being viewed as a lesser person – although that was never openly manifested."

On a warm Sunday morning, Galant was personally confronted with the contradiction of playing "normal" sport and living in an apartheid society when he and his son, Achmat, were chased off the "Whites-Only" Clovelly beach by a policeman.

"Achmat was shocked when the policeman told us to leave the beach," Galant said.

"He couldn't understand why we could not use the beach, while other lighter-skinned people could go on enjoying themselves.

"I told the policeman that I played cricket for Claremont. 'Why can't I use the beach like I use the cricket facilities of white people?' I asked him.

"But he wasn't interested in my story. He simply told me that changes to the laws that allowed me to play cricket for Claremont did not apply to beaches. That was the final straw for me. I immediately decided to return to the Western Province Cricket Board.

"But even before that incident, I saw the disparity in facilities. For example, the white schools had facilities that we [members of black clubs] could only dream of; even the fields of the white primary schools were of a much higher standard than the fields on which board affiliates played provincial cricket.

"I thought to myself that if only we had had the facilities that these white kids had at their disposal we would have produced many international players."

Like many of the other former Western Province Cricket Board players who joined the "normal" cricket fold, Galant found it difficult to cope with being ostracised by his community. "It was awkward going to mosque or social functions – and then being ignored by people who used to be my friends. I found it difficult to come to terms with this rejection by family and friends. This also played a huge part in my decision to return."

As was the case with all defectors, Galant had to appear before a Western Province Cricket Board disciplinary committee before being allowed back into the nonracial fold. "When I decided that I wanted to return to the board I went straight to Mr Howa and

told him about my experiences and how my conscience would not allow me to play normal cricket. When he heard my story, it was a straightforward process to come back."

Dissatisfaction with the provincial selectors also led to Clive Kolbe, the the leg-spinning all-rounder from the St Augustines club, moving to Cape Town, in the Western Province Cricket Union, for a short spell.

"I was already 34 years old when I went over – too late to go any further in my career," said Kolbe.

"Nevertheless, I enjoyed my time with Cape Town, and I learnt a lot about coaching techniques. Players such as Richard Knowles and Neil Lotter went out of their way to make me feel welcome, while Peter Kirsten was also a great inspiration. At least, I was able to impart the knowledge I gained to my club, St Augustines, when I returned to the Western Province Cricket Board."

Despite losing many friends because of his decision to play normal cricket, Kolbe was determined to see for himself what life was like on the other side, and to prove to himself and others that he could hold his own in the Western Province Cricket Union's first division competition.

Although players who defected to the normal cricket setup were ostracised by their former Western Province Cricket Board colleagues, their performances were followed and often discussed with great interest around the fields of the Cape Flats. In a perverse way, if an ex-board player performed well in the Western Province Cricket Union leagues, it provided a sense of satisfaction to his former colleagues in the board who saw it as a yardstick for the standard of their own game.

The realisation that "normal" cricket, with all its contradictions, was not

Clive Kolbe joined the "normal" cricket set-up to prove that he could hold his own in the Western Province Cricket Union's first division competition.

appropriate in the prevailing political setup, soon spread to other former Sacboc provinces. Problems with liquor laws, segregated facilities and the structure of local leagues saw the Natal Cricket Board withdrawing from the "normal" cricket setup midway through the 1976/77 season.

At a symposium held at the William Herbert Sportsground in Wynberg in January 1977, the influential South African Senior Schools Sports Association (Sasssa) said it would withdraw from Sacboc because it felt its interests had been neglected. It also did not accept that "normal" cricket was completely nonracial.

After the symposium, the board issued a statement in which it laid down a number of basic essentials for cricket to be brought to the people of South Africa on a normal and proper basis. Among these were:

• The abolition of all racial, tribal, religious and other labels that divide people;

• Equal facilities for all;

• Equal opportunities for all cricketers and potential cricketers to develop their game;

• The remedying of the socio-economic conditions that denied large numbers of South Africans the right to enjoy a game of cricket.

In lashing out at black players and administrators who had thrown in their lot with the "normal" cricket setup, the compilers of the statement said: "Those who can today, in spite of the morally correct stand of our board, be prepared to participate in the kind of cricket as laid down by the government and its stooges, do so only to feed their own selfish individual needs.

"These people are opportunists who are taking part... in that hideous system of discrimination."

The SA Cricket Board fills the void left by Sacboc

IN MARCH 1977, a group of sports administrators meeting in a tiny dressing-room at the Tills Crescent cricket ground in Durban, made a solemn vow to "recapture" the South African Cricket Board of Control from the man who had become nonracial sport's public enemy number one – Rashid Varachia.

Present at the gathering, which took place during a friendly match between the Western Province Cricket Board and the Natal Cricket Board, were representatives of the two provincial bodies, as well as officials of the South African Council on Sport (Sacos).

The mood in the dressing-room was grim – but determined – and the comments passed were, in many ways, predictable (it being a gathering of like-minded people): "Normal" cricket was a farce; Rashid Varachia and the leadership of Sacboc had betrayed the cause of nonracial sport by capitulating to racial cricket [meaning, "normal" cricket as defined by the South African Cricket Union].

The challenge, of course, was how to move the issue beyond rhetoric. And, in this respect there was absolute unanimity: in the light of Sacboc's failure to explain its actions to rank and file members, it had become imperative for those who carried the flame of equality in sport and society to ensure that a true nonracial national cricket body continued to exist.

The plan was to resuscitate Sacboc under the name of the South African Nonracial Cricket Board of Control.

On 25 September 1977, the process was taken a step further when representatives of the Western Province Cricket Board, the Natal Cricket Board, the Eastern Province Cricket Association, the newly-formed Transvaal Cricket Board and the Griqualand West Cricket Union, held a summit in Kimberley.

Delegates, buoyed by what they claimed to be the total opposition of the majority of players and officials of Sacboc to the actions of Varachia and his group, resolved to form the South African Nonracial Cricket Committee, with a mandate to investigate "re-forming" or "recapturing" Sacboc.

A NEW NAME

At the inaugural meeting of the new body, in Johannesburg on 13 November 1977, it was decided that the entire executive committee should be made up only of officials from the Western Province Cricket Board.

This decision was taken to save on administration costs – and because the board had been least affected by the "normal" cricket process.

"We had the same problems that we faced under the banner of Sacboc – a lack of resources and finance due to a

A new national body

THE INAUGURAL meeting of the South African Cricket Board was held at the AEL Centre in Johannesburg on 13 November 1977, where it was unanimously decided to form a new non-racial cricket body.

Delegates from the Western Province Cricket Board, the Natal Cricket Board, the Eastern Province Cricket Association, the Transvaal Cricket Board, South Western Districts and Griqualand West Cricket Union attended the meeting. The schools organisations, the South African Senior Schools Sports Association and the South African Primary Schools Sports Association were also given full membership of the SACB.

The elected officials were: president: Hassan Howa; vice-president: Sheikh Ganief Booley; secretary: Wahied Kazi; treasurer: Barney Leendertz; records clerk: Lionel Smith.

lack of sponsorship," said Lionel Smith, the records clerk of the new body.

"But, despite these drawbacks we were quickly able to get onto our feet, and were soon able to provide inter-provincial cricket at A and B section level, as well as for our Under-21, Under-19 and Under-16 players."

A warning by Varachia's legal advisors that the name "Sacboc" could not be used for any new organisation, sparked lengthy debate among office-bearers of the new body.

Some officials felt that efforts to stop them from using "Sacboc" should be resisted – on the grounds that Sacboc had achieved world renown for its fight against racism in sport.

But, another group, led by the influential Hassan Howa, favoured a name change, to prevent energies being diluted "in fighting interdict after interdict". Howa's group won the argument. As a result, Sacboc's successor in the fight against racist sport, was named the "South African Cricket Board".

SACB quickly found its feet. It immediately served notice that it would continue the fight to isolate white South African cricket – and Sacboc, of course, was now seen as being part of the white cricket setup – from the international arena.

In its memorandum to the International Cricket Conference in 1978, SACB stated that whatever optimism existed after the discussions of 18 January 1976 between representatives of the various national cricket bodies and the Minister of Sport, had been shattered with the announcement in September 1976 of the government's new sports policy, which continued to take the ethnic origins of sportsmen and women into account.

In another memorandum, in June 1979, SACB laid down what it saw as minimum requirements for nonracial sport. Among these were open membership for all sports clubs, the formation of single, nonracial controlling bodies for sport at local, provincial and national level, the creation of equal opportunities for all sportsmen and women and the utilisation of sponsorship to enable all participants in sporting events to benefit equally.

Having successfully blocked attempts by the South African Cricket Union (Sacu) to gain admission to the ICC, SACB itself applied – unsuccessfully – for associate membership of the world body in 1985. (Sacu had come into being following the merger between the South African Cricket Association, Sacboc and the South African African Cricket Board.)

REBEL TOURS

Sacu's response to its failure to gain membership of the ICC was to arrange a series of "rebel tours" to South Africa by players from various countries.

By offering visiting players large sums of money, Sacu was able to entice teams from England (led by Graham Gooch), Sri Lanka, the West Indies (led by Lawrence Rowe) and Australia (led by Kim Hughes) to tour South Africa.

SACB lashed out at Sacu for organising these tours.

"They have shown total disrespect for the future of... cricketers. They do not care about the ethics of sportsmanship. Their only interest seems to lie in their selfish and aggressively unprincipled attempts to get back into international cricket," SACB said.

Western Province – undisputed champions of the Howa Bowl

AVONWOOD PARK, Westridge, Elfindale, Green Point Track, Florida Park, Turfhall, Rocklands... it didn't matter where the Western Province Cricket Board side chose to make its base: it turned all its home grounds into impenetrable fortresses.

And although away games were slightly more difficult – accusations of "home town" decisions sometimes came to the fore – Western Province picked up enough victories in places such as Durban, Bosmont, Gelvandale and Zwide to lay a close-to-permanent claim to be the masters of the South African Cricket Board's interprovincial competition.

Against the often feeble competition of Transvaal and Natal, and the tougher challenge of Eastern Province, Western Province won the Howa Bowl (the trophy named in honour of Hassan Howa) 11 times in 14 attempts. (B-Section teams played for the Booley Bowl, named in honour of Sheikh Ganief Booley, one of the founder members of the Western Province Cricket Board and of Sacboc.)

Of course, the Transvaalers and the Natalians – such tough opponents in the pre-1976 era – would have reminded everyone that the exodus of their top players to the "normal" cricket structures virtually wiped them out. To an extent, this was probably true – but Western Province seemed to have a never-ending conveyor belt of players to call upon, even when stalwarts who would have been thought of as irreplaceable decided to retire.

Led by Rushdi Magiet, and spoilt for choice with players such as Lefty Adams, Braima Isaacs, Armien Jabaar, Saait Magiet, Kosie Williams and George van Oordt, as well as newcomers such as Charlie van Schalkwyk, Munsoor Abdullah, Cyril Martin, Rashaad Musson, Michael Doman and Yunus Thomas, Western Province swept aside all opposition.

EASTERN CAPE CHALLENGE

Only Eastern Province managed to peg them back (but then only slightly). In January 1978, the Eastern Cape side put aside the loss of experienced campaigners such as Imraan and Zakie Hendricks, Bravo Jacobs, Jeff Frans, Steven Draai and Devdas Govindjee to the "normal" cricket set-up, to beat Western Province by 34 runs in Port Elizabeth.

It was the beginning of a pattern – a straight fight for Howa Bowl honours between Western Province and Eastern Province, with Natal and Transvaal following far behind.

If anything, the introduction of turf wickets in Cape Town during the 1978/79 season saw Western Province tighten its grip on the interprovincial scene – even though they did not have a home ground. Like a band of gypsies, the provincial side flitted

Braima Isaacs was generally regarded as the best wicketkeeper in the country. Remarkably quick behind the stumps, most of his 42 stumpings were legside efforts, standing up to fast bowlers. Isaacs was also a wonderfully entertaining batsman, although he never quite fulfilled his rich potential as a top-order stroke-player.

Vincent Barnes, the Western Province Cricket Board's top fast bowler of the 1980s, said underprepared wickets helped him a lot.

between Avonwood Park in Elsies River, Westridge in Mitchells Plain, Elfindale, the Green Point Track, the University of the Western Cape, Florida Park, Turfhall and Rocklands – but kept on winning with monotonous ease.

LOSS OF INTEREST

"Most of the wickets available to the board were underprepared," said Vincent Barnes, who emerged as SACB's top fast bowler of the 1980s.

"For me, as a bowler, it was great. But, for the batsmen, it was always a struggle. We never played at set provincial venues where the groundsmen could work on the wickets. Every time we played a provincial match, it was at a different venue, which wasn't very helpful."

Barnes took a phenomenal 250 wickets in 53 matches for Western Province, including a personal best of 9/46 against Natal in 1980.

Significantly, spectator interest in provincial cricket dwindled in Cape Town. Whereas crowds of up to five thousand were the norm at Dadabhay Trophy games in the pre-1976 era, only a few hundred turned up during the late 1970s and the 1980s to watch Western Province destroy opposition, which would probably have been comfortably beaten by local Premier League clubs.

Western Province captain Rushdi Magiet suggested that there were sound reasons for the loss of interest in the game during the "normal" cricket era.

"Spectator interest declined because the other provinces were badly affected by defections," he said.

"From 1976 onwards, it became extremely frustrating playing against the other provinces because they were so weak. They provided no opposition. However, as we entered the 1980s, they improved – especially after the return of many defectors.

"The Group Areas Act also contributed to the drop in interest. New clubs had to be started in areas in which people had been dumped, but where no facilities were built for them.

"Because our provincial opposition was so weak, our top players stagnated. They had nothing to play for, and no incentive to work at their game. More often than not, it was a case of them simply having to turn up to beat the opposition inside two days," said Magiet.

Sadick Emeran echoed these sentiments in his presidential report at the annual general meeting of the board on 11 September 1988.

"Without wishing to detract from the fine achievements of many teams and players, I think you will all agree that there was definitely a drop in the overall standard of the game," he said.

"The circumstances which prevailed in some SACB units undoubtedly affected the performance of their provincial players, which had a negative effect on raising the standard of our own participants."

TOO FEW INCENTIVES

Barnes added that the lack of opportunities stagnated his development. "It was frustrating not being able to play against better players. I lost interest in playing long before unity, simply because I had nothing to play for."

The only incentive for SACB's top players was the opportunity of winning Sacos colours – Sacos held festivals in 1982 and 1988 – and the end-of-season matches when SACB teams were selected.

Western Province's domination was reflected in the composition of the Sacos XI in 1982; they supplied seven players, including the captain, Charlie van Schalkwyk. The Sacos XI consisted of: Enver Mall (Natal), Braima Isaacs (WP), Neil Fortune (WP), Munsoor Abdullah (WP), Khaya Majola (EP), Charlie van Schalkwyk (WP), Saait Magiet (WP), Mustapha Khan (Natal), Armien Jabaar (WP), Jeff Frans (EP) and Vincent Barnes (WP).

While representative matches such as those played during the Sacos festival and the SACB 10th anniversary games offered the players some incentive, it could not arrest the slide in standards. Barnes suggested that the retirement of several stalwarts contributed to the decline. "Players such as Lefty Adams, Braima Isaacs and Rushdi Magiet hated losing and played the game very hard. When they called it a day in the late 1980s, the game was never quite the same again."

Referring to his own ambitions, Barnes said: "I always knew I was never going to play for South Africa," Barnes said.

"But shortly before unity, when coaching had become part of our game I quickly made up my mind that this was the area of the game in which I wanted to become involved.

"I realised that this was where I could make a contribution – simply because no-one had coached me. Like dozens of other children from facilities-starved backgrounds, I was never told how to hold a ball. I taught myself to play the game. Although I learnt a lot from various people, there was not one particular person who specifically helped me.

"In the period just before unity, many players became terribly spoilt – they didn't have to work very hard to get into the provincial side. Previously players had to work their butts off to win provincial caps. When I first started playing in the Premier League I

took lots of wickets at club level, but still couldn't get into the side. Towards the latter part of my career, it became much easier," said Barnes.

George van Oordt agreed with Barnes. "When we had the Super League in the pre-76 era you first had to make your Board side before even coming into consideration for the A team," he said.

"You had to be very good to make the provincial side then.

"But, when the club system was introduced after 1976, it meant that players missed one step. In the new scheme of things, they only needed to do well for their clubs to get noticed by the selectors. It cheapened the whole concept of provincial colours," said Van Oordt.

A problem facing most Western Province Cricket Board players was getting time off from work in order to play away games. Many companies

The irrepressible Lefty Adams

EVEN TODAY, Lefty Adams is still remembered as the South African Cricket Board's greatest character (and he was a superb matchwinner, too).

Few other Western Province captains – and there were some good ones – had Adams' powers of motivation. He had the uncanny ability to turn what seemed like lost causes into glorious triumphs.

His finest moment? There were many – but perhaps the events at Elfindale, in March 1980, stand out just a little bit more than some of the others.

It's a simple story, really. Western Province, as usual, were playing their main rivals, Eastern Province, in a Howa Bowl decider. Not quite usual was the fact that the home team seemed to be facing a thrashing: EP, needing 62 to win, appeared to be coasting to victory, at 26/2.

But then Adams, with a characteristic piece of gamesmanship, picked up a piece of paper blowing across the ground and read a fictitious message to Khaya Majola, the key EP batsman. "I told him we'd bowl them out for 42 – my age – and we did," Adams said later. Of course, his bowling (6/7) and that of Saait Magiet (4/18) were key factors.

Adams' remarkable match analysis of 10/15 allowed him to leave the provincial stage in a blaze of glory.

were reluctant to give the players leave forcing some, like Vincent Barnes, Deon Kemp, Mervyn Theron and Neville Booysen, among others, to withdraw from the team.

"I had to miss several provincial games because of my job in the naval dockyard in Simon's Town," said Barnes.

"Usually, I only asked to get off the Friday (most Howa Bowl games were played on a Friday, Saturday and Sunday).

"My requests were often turned down, though. It was always a fight for me.

"What made the whole thing so unfair was that white sportsmen working in the naval dockyard never had the problems we had. On one occasion, a white exponent of karate was given special leave."

Rather than becoming downhearted, Barnes said he resolved to try doubly hard to be treated equally.

"I was openly told by officials of the dockyard that I ought to be playing in the Western Province Cricket Union," he said.

Playing in the UK – Part 2

IN 1985, CLINTON Ravens became the first Western Province Cricket Board player in 15 years to play in England, when he turned out for South Woodford in the Essex League.

The last WP Cricket Board cricketer to play competitively in the UK had been Dickie Conrad, who played for Leyland Motors in the Northern Lancashire League in 1970.

Cliffie Ravens, the father of the Bluebells and Montrose all-rounder, said: "I suggested to Clinton that he go to England – to learn to play properly.

"He was keen, but didn't know how to go about it or where to go – so I told him: 'Go knock on the gates of Lords, and ask whoever answers your call.'

"Fortunately, it didn't come to that. A family friend, who had been studying in Essex, put Clinton in touch with a priest, who knew someone, who knew someone.

"Eventually, Clinton ended up playing in the Essex League.

Besides playing for South Woodford, Ravens found time to complete an NCA course, which made him one of the few qualified coaches in the Western Province Cricket Board.

Fast bowler, Barney Mohammed, also played overseas – for Pollok in the Scottish League. The following season, he was joined by Vincent Barnes, who signed for a club called Ferguslie. Before leaving, Barnes sought the blessing of board president, Hassan Howa. "I told him that I would probably be playing against players from the South African Cricket Union. But he didn't have a problem with that at all."

The first person to contact Barnes once he had signed to play in Scotland, was Omar Henry (a defector in the eyes of the Western Province Cricket Board).

"He offered me some advice and encouragement – and when I arrived in Scotland, made a point of meeting me."

Barnes stayed two seasons with Ferguslie.

Other board cricketers who played in the UK during this period were Nazeem White, Shamsu Ahmed and Deon Kemp.

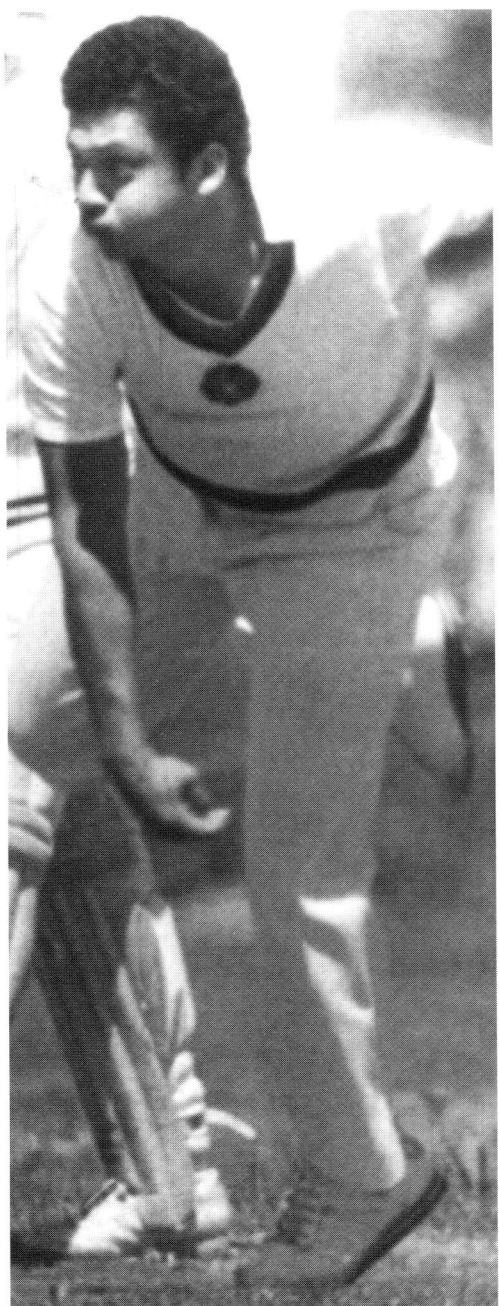

In 1985, Clinton Ravens became the first WP Cricket Board player after Dickie Conrad, in 1970, to play in the UK.

The resolution that became nonracial sport's big stick

"NO NORMAL sport in an abnormal society"... "sell-outs"... "renegades"... "defectors"... "stooges".... It was a time of slogans, insults and biting criticism. Certainly, in the bitter aftermath of the introduction of "normal" cricket, thousands of words were written, spoken and shouted about the process – and those who chose to participate in it.

But, beyond allowing those who felt betrayed to let off steam, the barrage of criticism and the mouthing of *that* famous slogan, did little to deter others from following the path to "normal" sport.

Even more confusing to the ordinary sportsman or woman, many of whom instinctively believed that real change in sport was impossible without change in other facets of life, were the number of people who played "normal" sport in one season and nonracial sport, governed by the South African Council on Sport (Sacos), in the next.

What was needed was a clear policy guideline – a guideline that would leave sportsmen and women in no doubt as to what was required of anyone who belonged to a nonracial sports organisation.

In April 1977, Sacos unveiled its "double standards resolution", one of its most controversial policies.

In terms of the resolution, any stadium for which a permit was required to allow black people to attend sports events, was ruled out of bounds to Sacos members. Among the better-known venues to immediately fall foul of the resolution were the Newlands rugby and cricket stadiums, and the Green Point and Hartleyvale soccer stadiums.

With refinement (and tweaking here and there), the double standards resolution began to touch on various

Drawing the battle lines

THE RESOLUTION on "double standards", first proposed in April 1977, stated that: "Any person, whether, he or she is a player, administrator or a spectator, [and who is] committed to the nonracial principle in sport, shall not participate in, nor be associated with, any other code of sport which practises, perpetrates or condones, racialism and multinationalism."

When the Western Province Cricket Board decided to add the resolution to its constitution, it adapted it to read as follows:

"Any club or member of the Western Province Cricket Board or any individual associated with the Western Province Cricket Board or its units, who in any way condones, fosters or advocates racialism, or discrimination in any form shall be guilty of misconduct."

In terms of this clause, anyone who participated in, or associated with government bodies designed to entrench and/or promote separateness would be deemed to have infringed the double standards resolution – and would be liable for expulsion from a nonracial body.

Government bodies which fell within the ambit of the resolution included the Coloured Persons Representative Council, the Indian Representative Council, local affairs committees and ethnic management committees.

other aspects of the lives of Sacos members. Thus, contact with players and officials from the "normal" sports setup became unacceptable; so-called international hotels, restaurants which applied for a permit to serve clients of all races, and theatres which did likewise, were all declared out of bounds.

HOWA AND SACOS

In October 1977, Hassan Howa took over as president of Sacos from Norman Middleton, the chairman of the powerful South African Soccer Federation. Middleton had become unacceptable to the movement because of his affiliation to the Labour Party, which participated in the discredited Coloured Persons Representative Council.

Sacos became the major force in isolating white South African sport, through its association with international anti-apartheid groups such as New Zealand's Halt All Racist Tours, the United Nations Committee Against Apartheid and the South African Nonracial Olympic Committee (Sanroc). The organisation's international profile was further boosted when it was granted associate membership of the highly influential Supreme Council for Sport in Africa.

With top schools administrators Philip Tobias and Richard Rive playing prominent roles, the Western Province Senior Schools Sports Association took a tough stance against pupils who participated in "normal" sport, banning them from any activities of the South African Senior Schools Sports Association.

In the first signs of tension, Hewat Training College refused to play a cricket match against a St Columba High School team which included Varsity Old Boys/Cavaliers players Glen Hendricks, Julian Fester, Derek and Greg Forbes, and Lee Schouw.

JOCK MAHONEY

Towards the end of 1977, Blue Bells Football Club refused to play a match in the Cape District Football Association's summer tournament against Glenville, because Jock Mahoney had been appointed to referee the game. In terms of the double standards resolution, Mahoney, who also played cricket for Pinelands in the Western Province Cricket Union, was a defector. There was just one problem, though: Cape District was an affiliate of the South African Soccer Federation, which, at that time, was not a member of Sacos.

Although Mahoney was later expelled by the Cape District Football Association, he appealed to the South African Soccer Federation who ordered his reinstatement.

Mahoney was at the centre of further controversy when his application to return to his former club, St Augustines, was rejected. He then joined and coached the club side of the University of the Western Cape (UWC) – and after several months of wrangling was reinstated as a member of the Western Province Cricket Board.

But it didn't take long for him to again fall foul of the double standards policy. In 1978, he played in a friendly match involving members of Frank Brache's Varsity Old Boys/Cavaliers.

George van Oordt, who in 1978 was an executive member of UWC, said the club was in the process of working out how best to defend Mahoney when they read in the newspapers that he had joined Avendale.

"I was shocked," said Van Oordt. "When Jock came to visit me a few days later, I slammed the door in his face. That was the end of what had been a close friendship."

During the first few years, a number of other players were found guilty of transgressing the double standards policy. One of the most publicised cases was that of Brian "Bollie" van Reenen, who having played baseball for VOB and hockey for Lions in the white leagues (which made him a "double defector"), joined Westridge, a Western Province Cricket Board affiliate, in 1982.

Problems arose, however, when Athlone Cricket Club, with Abe Adams and Percy Sonn at the helm, refused to play against Westridge, because of the presence of the double defector, Van Reenen.

Howa, who had cleared Van Reenen to play, was furious with Athlone. But the club refused to back down, citing the Sacos policy on defectors as a reason for its actions.

Howa, however, was adamant about clearing defectors with a minimum of fuss. "We are an autonomous body and what we do in this regard has nothing to do with ... Sacos. They have no right to tell us what to do," he told the *Cape Herald* newspaper.

After the mess around the Van Reenen affair, defectors had to apply for readmission through the codes from which they defected.

While Howa was defending the case of returning defectors such as Van Reenen, he could also be uncompromising on other "transgressors", such as George Freddy, the hardworking former secretary of the Cape District Union, as well as Kosie Williams, the former Western Province opening bowler, both of whom were banned from the board because they sent their children to private "white" schools.

"I sent my son, Lindsay, to St Joseph's College because I felt he would get better education there," said Williams.

"He did not play any sport at the school. I was still very much committed to the ideals of the board, but was forced out because I'd sent my son to a private white school. I felt it was no different to sending your child to a white university like UCT, which also

required a permit. Many members of the Western Province Cricket Board were doing this without any action being taken against them," said Williams.

Freddy, who founded the Lilies Cricket Club in Hanover Park in 1982, said, "I was asked in April to withdraw my son, Nigel, from Christian Brothers College. But I refused. How could I be expected to take my son out of a school midway through the year?"

Sadick Emeran, the match and registration secretary of the board, disagreed with the way the Freddy case had been handled. "Mr Freddy's son had won a scholarship to do Biblical studies at Christian Brothers College, the only school offering such a course in the Western Cape. I felt the case merited consideration, but Mr Howa would not allow Mr Freddy to stay in the board if his son took up the scholarship.

"As much as I respected Mr Howa, he wasn't always consistent in terms of his principles. After his removal as president of the South African Cricket Board in 1984, he started attacking personalities. It lost him support and eventually caused his downfall."

Those who transgressed the double standards resolution by playing normal sport were given a tough time, especially at school, according to Vincent Barnes. "My school, Livingstone, was tough when it came to nonracial principles. Some pupils who had joined Avendale were kicked straight out of our school teams – and ostracised."

Political events such as protests and boycotts had a significant effect on many players who had left to play "normal" cricket. During the unrest between 1984 and 1985, more than 100 players returned to the board.

Among the more significant

Sadick Emeran disagreed with the way Hassan Howa handled the controversy over George Freddy and Kosie Williams.

returnees during this period were Dickie Conrad who had left in 1974, and his son, Shukri, who represented the South African Nuffield side, alongside Daryll Cullinan and Allan Donald in 1984.

MANAGEMENT COMMITTEES

Problems with venues started in October 1981 when the Bellville South Management Committee disbanded the Bellville Sports Board, against the wishes of the community and installed the Proteaville Management Committee to take control of the sports facilities in the area.

Two years later, Elsies River Cricket Club was refused permission to play at their Avonwood Park home ground by the Elsies River Sports Board of Control. The decision was taken after Sacos affiliates campaigned to stop Lawrence Rowe's rebel West Indian tourists from playing a match at Avonwood Park in 1983.

Elsies River took legal advice and won the case on a technicality. Although they were reinstated onto the Elsies River Sports Board of Control, they were confronted with more problems when a number of members broke away to form Avonwood Cricket Club, which joined the Western Province Cricket Union. The new club was granted membership of the Elsies River Sports Board of Control, leaving Elsies River Cricket Club without a home ground.

The use of "ethnic" university sports facilities such as those at the University of the Western Cape (UWC) also caused friction between Sacos affiliates.

The Western Province Cricket Board and the South African Rugby Union were attacked by Sacos in 1980 for "embarrassing" the organisation by "persisting" in wanting to play on the UWC campus. However, Howa left the decision on whether to use the facilities at institutions like UWC and Hewat Training College to the students themselves.

During the 1980/81 season the UWC club which had played in the Premier League decided to move off campus and play under the name of Tigers.

Indeed, UWC was later accepted as "the home of the left" and became an integral part of the nonracial sports movement. Not only did the sports clubs become part of the Sacos fold, but the sports facilities were used for the South African Cricket Board's 10th anniversary day/night game in 1987 as well as for the Sacos festival in 1988. UWC was also the venue for two day/night Premier League Grand Challenge finals which were played there in 1990 and 1991.

Even Elfindale, the home of St Augustines, which was at one stage favoured as the Western Province Howa Bowl team's home base, was the subject of controversy in 1980 when the then board secretary, Stan Abrahams, argued against the venue being used for interprovincial matches, on the grounds that the club had taken a loan from the Urban Foundation. The Foundation was frowned upon by Sacos because it was said to dispense "conscience money from big business, rather than direct sponsorship of nonracial sport by those businesses".

"Mr Howa was well aware of the loan we had taken from the Urban Foundation and he had no problems with it," said Paul Saville, the chairman of St Augustines in 1980. "We eventually repaid the loan, which amounted to R10000 plus interest."

Using the system...

SUCH WAS the ubiquitous nature of the apartheid system that a puritanical observance of the double standards resolution was virtually impossible.

While the double standards resolution clause in the Western Province Cricket Board constitution specifically outlawed contact with bodies such as the coloured management committees, clubs were forced to negotiate with them to secure use of venues which they controlled. The impressive development of Florida Park in Ravensmead was a case in point.

"We decided to use the management committee to our advantage," said George van Oordt, who served on the Florida Park Sports Board for 30 years.

"Although we didn't agree with his politics, Hansie Christians, the Labour Party MP in the area, was a good community worker. He, and the management committee, played a key role in developing Florida Park to the impressive state it is presently in."

Greener pastures – the movement of clubs to the WP Cricket Union

WITH STICKS and stones, the youths of the townships of the Cape Flats squared up to the guns of the guardians of apartheid in those desperate days of 1976. It was an uprising of the poor, of the unemployed and, in many cases, of the sons and daughters of victims of the Group Areas Act.

And, perhaps, it was precisely because of this – that they were poor and marginalised – that their protests failed to strike a chord with many of the Western Cape's black – and, in the main, very middle-class – cricketers.

Certainly, there was more than a touch of the bizarre about the debate that raged among members of the Western Province Cricket Board in 1976....

"Should we – or should we not – play normal cricket [as defined by the South African government]?" was the question that was asked countless times, and argued over with increasing intensity.

And yet, at first glance, it seemed that there was just one reply that a black cricketer could give to what was essentially an invitation to become an honorary white for a few hours every Saturday: a loud, contemptuous "No!"

Despite the government's tweaking of its sports policy (mainly to try to ward off international sanctions by some of its traditional sporting allies), the reality of being black in South Africa had not changed. It was still synonymous with an inferior education, with not being able to vote, with being denied certain jobs, with the Group Areas Act and with the Population Registration Act, among a host of other daily humiliations.

True, some members of the Western Province Cricket Board were scathing in their rejection of "normal" cricket. But others argued that the advent of "normal" sport was a breakthrough – a precursor to more change, in both sport and society.

It was an argument that found favour in unlikely quarters.

CLUB LOSSES

In the Western Cape, the first black players and administrators to throw in their lot with "normal" cricket went over as individuals. Among this group were some of the Western Province Cricket Board's top players – Howie Bergins, Pinky Carelse and Viccie Moodie, to name just a few.

But, in the second year of the new dispensation – the 1977/78 season – several Western Province Cricket Board clubs joined the Newlands-based Western Province Cricket Union – amid bitter accusations that they had been bribed with promises of better facilities.

As far as the Western Province Cricket Union was concerned, the big cheese was undoubtedly Avendale, the club which had been formed especially for unity, through an amalgamation of Avenirs and Ashtondale, two clubs with a proud history in the Western Province Cricket Board.

The decision by some clubs in the Rylands Cricket Association to join the Western Province Cricket Union led to fights over the use of pitches between rival groups of cricketers.

But the loss of other clubs, such as Gatesville, Junction Rovers and Tramway, to the Western Province Cricket Union, also led to a barrage of criticism and counter-criticism between club members and members of the board.

The departure of Tramway, a club formed as a result of a merger between Glenville, Tramway and Fernwood, but sponsored by the Tramway bus company, led to particularly acrimonious exchanges.

After playing in the Western Province Cricket Board during the 1976/77 season, Tramway was left with a *fait accompli* by its parent body, the Tramway Sports Club, who took the club over to the Western Province Cricket Union.

Denis Cunningham, the chairman of the Tramway Sports Club, told Reuben Petersen, the chairman of the Tramway Cricket Club, that the company would recognise only the faction of the club that belonged to the union.

"We have poured a considerable sum of money into the club and now we have no way of getting it back," an agitated Petersen told the *Cape Herald* newspaper.

PROBLEMS IN RYLANDS

The departure of the Rylands Cricket Association to the Western Province Cricket Union was greeted with accusations that officials and clubs had been bribed to leave the Western Province Cricket Board.

According to Ray Bharoochi, the then secretary of the association, clubs were called to a hastily convened meeting, at which Rashid Varachia, Selwyn Myers, Frank Brache and Boon Wallace were present, at the Heerengracht Hotel in Cape Town.

"They offered to assist us with 75 percent of the cost of developing our grounds and clubhouses – if we disassociated ourselves from the board," said Bharoochi.

"Yusuf Sonday, the chairman of the association, told delegates they had to make a decision that same evening. We told him that we couldn't – we didn't have a mandate from our clubs.

"Boon Wallace then gave us a few days to make up our minds.

"Of the 10 clubs affiliated to the Rylands Cricket Association, four voted against accepting the offer, three were in favour and three abstained.

"Sonday then unilaterally decided that an abstention meant 'yes'. 'Gentlemen,' he told club delegates, 'we're going.'"

Bharoochi said that the clubs which stayed loyal to the Western Province Cricket Board decided to continue with their own fixtures. But almost immediately, trouble broke out between what had now become rival groups.

"The problem revolved around facilities, with the City Council being deeply involved in fanning the rivalries. The council decreed that only Sonday's teams could play at the Johnson Road sportsgrounds," said Bharoochi.

"When our teams turned up to play matches, he called the police, who chased us off, using police dogs."

Two pitches were damaged in altercations between opposing factions.

AVENDALE

Few teams supported "normal" cricket with a greater passion than the Avendale Cricket Club. And even though the club decided to stay in the Western Province Cricket Board during the 1976/77 season, the overwhelming majority of players in the club wanted to play "normal" cricket.

At a board meeting, called to discuss unity with the Western Province

Cricket Union, club delegates, Lionel van der Horst and Graham Adams, both abstained from voting – even though club members had given them a mandate to vote for unity.

"Van der Horst said his conscience would not allow him to vote that way; Adams refused to differ with his co-delegate, and so he also abstained," said Bert Erickson, the president of the club.

According to Erickson, Avendale's decision to quit the Western Province Cricket Board followed a nasty clash between the club's premier league side and the team of United, which ended with a United player threatening to drive his car over the pitch.

"That, more or less, was the final straw," he said, "because we also had longstanding problems with the board's poor administration.

"Once we took the decision to resign from the board, we could only go to the Western Province Cricket Union," said Erickson.

"Cliff Adams, the former Sacboc executive member, suggested that I speak to Boon Wallace, the president of the Western Province Cricket Union. I met Mr Wallace at his office at the SA Perm in Cape Town. He advised me to go back to the board and to tell them to keep their promises with regard to the unity agreements.

"But I told him that we had already left the board. Soon afterwards, we were accepted as members of the Western Province Cricket Union."

Board president, Hassan Howa, slammed the move: "I'm happy that they're leaving," he said, "otherwise we would have been forced to throw them out."

TROUBLE ON THE CAPE FLATS

With the political struggle having intensified and student boycotts and protests leading to a tense atmosphere on the Cape Flats, Avendale's move to play normal cricket, while operating from their Field Crescent base in the heart of the unrest area, was not viewed very kindly by the community of Athlone.

"The pressure on us was enormous," said Erickson. "We had to contend with numerous threats. Our clubhouse was petrol bombed and tyres of motor vehicles belonging to some of our players were slashed when they played a friendly on the day of a funeral of someone who had been killed by police.

"On a personal level, former board colleagues avoided me; others refused to talk to me; still others even went as far as saying that if they ever saw me walking on a pavement towards them, they would cross the road and walk on the other side.

"The *Cape Herald* newspaper also gave us a hard time," said Erickson.

"My wife asked me if it wouldn't be better to get out of the normal cricket set up, but I said, 'No!'.

"I believed that normal cricket offered a better future for our players. We had to get a foot in the door and stand up to be counted. I never stood back for anything. We were a mixed club. We had mixed juniors – and our doors were open to all.

"All our members had to do was pay their subscriptions. There were no questions asked – and no politics." In rejecting the Sacos slogan of "no normal sport in an abnormal society", Erickson argued that contact was more important that boycotts.

"To change a situation, it is imperative to have contact with the other party," he said.

Following Avendale's move to the Western Province Cricket Union, the white Cape Town City Council was accused of favouritism, by making the Field Crescent venue available to the club.

But Erickson said that the Metropolitan Cricket Union had only themselves to blame for this situation having developed.

"While we were playing in the Metropolitan union, our home ground was at the adjacent Clover Crescent. When Avendale was formed, we continued playing there. During the unity talks we were told that if we wanted to play first division cricket we needed a turf wicket.

"Although our request for a turf wicket at Turfhall was granted, we were told that we wouldn't have first call on the pitch.

"We also applied for a turf wicket to be constructed at Clover Crescent, but the Council felt that the ground wasn't suitable for such a wicket. They offered to develop a turf wicket at Field Crescent, which wasn't being used, even though the Metropolitan Cricket Union held the lease."

Paul Saville, a former executive member of Metropolitan, confirmed that the union had given written permission for Avendale to take over the lease permit – in order to save costs.

"But that was while they were members of the Western Province Cricket Board," Saville said.

"When they crossed the floor to the Western Province Cricket Union, we asked the council to rescind the request."

Stan Abrahams, the then chairman of the Metropolitan union, said that Avendale obviously had some good contacts in the City Council. "Not only did the club get Field Crescent, but they also managed to persuade the council to develop and maintain it for them.

"It was something the council would never have done for any of the clubs affiliated to the Western Province Cricket Board club.

"When we looked at what Avendale had, and what we were given, we had good reason to feel angry and resentful," Abrahams said.

Former Western Province Cricket Board captain, Rushdi Magiet, agreed with Abrahams.

"I negotiated annually with the City Council – and they made things very difficult for us," he said.

"They showed absolutely no interest in helping us to develop our sport – and as a result, our facilities were terrible."

St Augustines and "normal" cricket

SHORTLY AFTER the departure of Avendale to the Western Province Cricket Union, St Augustines, one of the oldest and strongest clubs in the Western Province Cricket Board, flirted with the "normal" cricket setup. Because of his dealings with the Garden Cities development company, Paul Saville of St Augustines had been in contact with Selwyn Myers, the Western Province Cricket Union president, who was also the managing director of Garden Cities.

"Selwyn told me we didn't need permits to play against white teams in the Western Province Cricket Union," said Saville.

"He even sent me to the Department of Sport for confirmation. I foolishly believed him. Club secretary, Willie Kriel, and I were subsequently invited to watch the traditional New Year's Currie Cup match between Western Province and Transvaal at Newlands.

"Before the game, we canvassed the opinion of our membership. They approved our visit to Newlands.

"The Western Province Cricket Union's executive committee offered us money to develop our ground at Elfindale and for other projects – on condition that we quit the board.

"We were seen at Newlands by Western Province Cricket Board members; on the very evening that I returned from the ground, I received a call from Abe Adams, one of the board's executive members, who wanted to know whether I had been to Newlands.

"Hassan Howa wasn't very pleased with our actions, and he summoned our entire club to appear before the board's executive committee.

"At the meeting, I raised the matter about where a Sacos meeting had been held the previous week. I knew that it had been held at a permit-venue, the Airport Holiday Inn in Johannesburg. After five minutes, the meeting was over with no action being taken against us."

The have-nots of sport introduce a new weapon – buying power

HAD SIMBA Quix replied to the request for sponsorship in the way that most companies responded – with a "We regret..." – the matter may well have rested there. After all, the South African Senior Schools Sports Association (Sasssa) and, indeed, other affiliates of the staunchly anti-apartheid South African Council on Sport had seen many similar requests turned down in the past.

But in 1978, for reasons known only to itself, it decided to be generous: it offered Sasssa two boxes of potato crisps!

The schools' body, mindful that Simba Quix had just announced that it would be sponsoring the South African Grand Prix to the tune of R110000, was furious. Within days, a nationwide boycott of Simba products had been launched by black schoolchildren, by a number of shops in the Western Cape and by supporters of the South African Council on Sport.

This bout of muscle-flexing proved to be highly effective. Soon, worried Simba Quix executives were flying around the country, trying to undo the damage.

"We have made some of our customers unhappy, which is something we did not want to do," said Manie Bekker, of Simba Quix.

The company subsequently withdrew its sponsorship of the Grand Prix and offered Sasssa a sponsorship of R3000. But, by then, the damage had been done. The offer was turned down.

PRESSURE TACTICS

The success of the Simba Quix boycott changed the way anti-apartheid sports bodies saw themselves. Now, more mindful than ever of the enormous economic power they wielded, they set out much more confidently in search of sponsorship. Their main targets were those companies who sponsored predominantly white rival bodies – and those who displayed reluctance were left in no doubt about the consequences of saying "No".

The word "boycott" forced a drastic rethink of sponsorship practices by many company decision makers in the late 1970s and early 1980s.

When the supermarket chain, Checkers, offered the Western Province Cricket Board R100, after sponsoring the white Transvaal Cricket Council to the tune of R100000, they were threatened with a boycott.

After talks, Checkers executives and board officials announced a sponsorship of more than R100000, over three years. It was the board's biggest ever sponsorship.

Markhams, a well-known clothing company, also felt the wrath of non-racial cricketers, following its decision to sponsor the Western Province Cricket Union to the tune of R10000 and turning down an application for financial help from the Western

---

A man of many parts

IN ADDITION to securing many sponsorships, Western Province Cricket Board secretary, Stan Abrahams, was also instrumental in establishing the Luyolo Cricket Club in Guguletu.

"Using some of our sponsorship money, we erected two practice pitches in Guguletu," said Abrahams.

"Our members canvassed youngsters in the area to play for the club. It was not an easy task – the Western Province Cricket Union were also active in the area – and it had more resources at its disposal.

After joining the Western Province Cricket Board, Luyolo used Turfhall as its base.

"The club ran fairly well, although we never started our matches on time," said Abrahams.

"Work commitments made it extremely difficult for most of the players to be punctual."

Luyola operated for two years.

The club was resuscitated in the mid-1980s.

Removing Ali Bacher's face

IN THE LATE 1980s, Western Province Cricket Board treasurer, Peter Heeger, held a secret meeting at the Newlands Hotel with Barry Fowle of Bakers Biscuits.

"My intention was to secure sponsorship for the board's junior development programme," said Heeger.

"At the time, Bakers had come in for a lot of criticism because of its heavy involvement with the South African Cricket Union's development programme.

"They were prepared to sponsor us with mini-cricket sets, but Sadick Emeran, our president, had a problem with having Ali Bacher's face and autograph on the bats.

"Apparently Bacher, when approached by Fowle, agreed to our request to have his face and autograph removed.

"We had to do it ourselves, though – with turpentine," said Heeger.

Province Cricket Board. The board reacted by passing a resolution asking members not to buy from Markhams, its sister company, American Swiss, and its parent company, Foschini. The following year Markhams agreed to sponsor the board.

This sponsorship, which lasted until unity in 1991, enabled the board to introduce junior coaching clinics; the Premier League competition also bore the sponsor's name.

In the 1982/83 season, Honda International put up R5000 for the board's limited overs competition. The Wembley group also injected R10000 into the board's coffers.

Earlier, the Golden Yolk egg company, owned by Ebrahim Dawood, one of the board's main financial benefactors, and Tiger Oats had sponsored the limited overs competition.

Pick 'n Pay was also subjected to a brief consumer boycott after it had put up R10000 for coaching clinics run by Western Province Currie Cup team members, Eddie Barlow, Garth le Roux, Allan Lamb and Peter Kirsten – and then turned down an application by the board for sponsorship.

After a meeting between Hassan Howa and Pick 'n Pay's managing director, Raymond Ackerman, in which the company pledged a similar amount to coaching clinics run by the South African Cricket Board, the boycott was called off.

Stan Abrahams, the board secretary during this period, played a major role in securing sponsorship.

"It was tough. We first had to threaten some of them with boycotts before they relented," said Abrahams.

"We learnt that it was easier to approach the companies with a specific object in mind. Most companies were prepared to give us money for particular undertakings. This was how we were able to gather enough money in our sponsorship fund to be able to lay turf wickets at Surrey Estate, Turfhall, Allenby Drive, Rosmead and Green Point Track.

"I started the first turf wicket at Turfhall myself. Being an avid reader, I read up everything I could about turf wickets. I got into trouble with Sacos for talking to Selwyn Myers, the Western Province Cricket Union president, about getting bulli for our turf wickets."

"Increased sponsorship meant that we were able to purchase equipment we'd never have dreamed we'd be in a position to get a few years earlier – such as bomag rollers and covers for our turf wickets.

Later Benson and Hedges, who sponsored the national limited overs series, also donated equipment to board clubs.

SAME OLD STORY

When Peter Heeger took over as treasurer of the board in 1987, he bought a copy of the book, *Who owns Whom in South Africa,* and proceeded to write about 500 letters to potential sponsors.

"I particularly targeted companies that were big sponsors of the South African Cricket Union," said Heeger.

"But all of them turned us down.

"Fortunately, we later received R20000 from the Mobil oil company for the development of the Elfindale ground, the laying of pitches and for junior coaching."

In the period just before unity, black-owned companies such as Gatti's Ice Cream and the Wembley Group who had sponsored the board since 1982, also started pumping more money into nonracial cricket.

Under exposed – the WP Cricket Board and the media

JIMMY ATKINS was working at the London Bureau of the Argus group of newspapers in 1976 when Soweto exploded – and horrifying television footage of police firing on schoolchildren beamed its way into millions of British homes.

Jimmy Atkins' coverage of sports-political events in the Western Cape caused a stir among both fellow journalists and the general public.

"I was sickened at the level of police brutality, as was the British TV commentator," said Atkins, an outspoken sports editor and, later, deputy editor of the *Cape Herald* newspaper.

"While we stood transfixed around a TV set, one young white reporter from the *Daily News* of Natal turned to a colleague and said: 'Well, what does the world expect the police to do? These kids should be in school.'

"I was the first person of colour to be seconded to the *Argus* bureau in 1975. Apparently, my white peers had been given several lectures on racial sensitivity prior to my arrival. The aforementioned reporter had actually befriended me. We attended sports events together and shared a few pints after work as well.

"But after his outburst, there was not much left of our 'friendship'. For, it dawned on me then that the schizophrenic nature of apartheid South Africa made friendships across the colour line artificial, at best."

Atkins said that when he returned to South Africa later that year, he'd been amused at how semantics had wormed its way into sport.

"Instead of nonracial or integrated, the favoured term was now 'normal' sport," said Atkins.

"Hassan Howa was prepared to sanction cricket with whites even if his players had to strip in their cars, since the law did not allow mixed change-rooms. This didn't strike me as normal.

"I penned an editorial in which I used the phrase, 'no normal sport in an abnormal society'. To my everlasting delight, it was picked up by several leading lights in Sacos. It became a mantra for those who felt that white sports bodies were merely trying to persuade the regime to tailor apartheid for the benefit of white sportsmen, while retaining the status quo for the rest of society.

"That particular stand did not go down well with white sports reporters at the *Argus*, sister newspaper to the *Cape Herald*, and elsewhere. While they were careful to keep their comments to a minimum, there's little doubt that they saw us, not as sports writers, but as frustrated hacks, dabbling in an arena best left to politicians."

And yet, white reporters, in the main, made very little effort to report on black sport. The stories of black achievement on the sports fields of the Cape Flats were recorded by a group of reporters whose commitment to "getting the story" often went far beyond the call of duty.

UNREPORTED CRICKETERS

A lack of media exposure was a major problem for the Western Province Cricket Board and, indeed, during the

Ted Doman – under his baton, the Cape Herald newspaper threw its weight behind the Sacos-inspired nonracial sports movement.

apartheid era, for all nonracial sports codes. Cape Town's mainstream dailies – the *Cape Times*, the *Argus* and *Die Burger* were all white-controlled and staffed almost exclusively by whites, who showed as much interest in covering the nonracial game as an arts correspondent in Iceland would have had in covering a korfbal tournament in South Africa.

The cricket correspondents at these newspapers, hardly (if ever) bothered to watch, let alone report on, Western Province Cricket Board interprovincial games. Not even the appearance of international greats such as Basil D'Oliveira and the West Indian, Rohan Kanhai, could lure them to board venues. Instead, they were happy to leave the job to largely untrained black freelance reporters, who had to battle for space in the newspapers.

Although newspapers such as the *Sun,* the *Standard* and the *Golden City Post* provided regular coverage of black cricket from the late 1940s onwards, the *Cape Times* and the *Argus* only started reporting on black

cricket in the 1950s, mainly through the representations that were made by the intrepid and resourceful Damoo Bansda, who was involved as an administrator with the South African Indian Cricket Association.

But, in the same way that blacks and whites were not allowed to mix on the sports fields, they were kept apart on the sports pages of newspapers. Certain sections of a newspaper were reserved for black sport, while white sport, no matter how insignificant, always appeared in the main sports section.

TED DOMAN

Shortly after Bansda became a regular contributor to the *Cape Times*, Ted Doman started writing for the *Argus*.

"In 1960, the *Argus* sports editor, Percy Kirk, asked me to write a weekly column on black sport," said Doman.

"I agreed – but only on condition that there would be no heading stating 'nonwhite sport'. He agreed.

"For about two years I wrote a column about the sport of the season. Thereafter, the *Argus* asked me to oversee the compilation of results for its Saturday evening edition. I assembled a team of correspondents to phone in the scores to me. Because the network of freelancers was so small, I used most of Bansda's correspondents," said Doman.

The Afrikaans-language newspapers were not slow to recognise the circulation-growing potential contained in the coverage of black sport.

Beeld, which was published on a Sunday in the 1960s, introduced an eight-page supplement of sports stories and results, which sometimes went up to 12 pages because it was so popular among readers on the Cape Flats.

Reporters for all seasons

DAMOO BANSDA wrote a midweek column on black cricket and soccer for the "Cape Flats" edition of the *Cape Times*. He also provided a results service for the "*Ekstra*" editions of *Die Burger* and *Rapport*, by using a network of correspondents. Through his various media outlets, Bansda campaigned strongly for the end of racially-based unions among South African Cricket Board of Control affiliates, an ideal which was finally realised in the Western Province in 1959.

"Bansda would normally sit in an office at *Die Burger* and collect scores from his correspondents around the peninsula," said Cliff Adams, one of his correspondents. Other reporters involved in the Bansda network were Mervyn Ford, Ken Adams, Reggie Clarke and Lennie Kleintjies.

Later, Gasant Toffar, who became one of the best-known faces at sports grounds around the Cape Flats, also started supplying newspapers with match reports.

"When I started reporting, I didn't have a car, so I took a bus from District Six, where I lived, to Rondebosch Common. After watching a match there for a while, I'd rush over to the nearby Red Cross Children's Hospital, to phone through the score, before catching a bus to my next venue."

Later in the week, if space allowed, Toffar would compile a summary of all the Western Province Cricket Board games in the various unions.

"*Die Burger*, too, indicated that they wanted to cover more black sport – and in 1968, they contacted me to write for them," said Doman, who then started writing for them under the pseudonym, *Die Snuffelaar*.

"Albert Crafford was in charge of their *Ekstra* section, with Jaap van Wyk as his number two," said Doman.

"Although Crafford supported the National Party, he was genuinely interested in black sport. I wrote in English, and he was excellent in translating the articles.

In 1971, Cliff Adams also started writing a weekly column for *Die Burger "Ekstra"*, under the pseudonym, John Collins. But after a short while most sportspersons knew who Collins really was.

Later, Adams was sharply criticised for using his column to canvass votes for Abel Jordaan in his battle for the presidency of the the Western Province Cricket Board against the incumbent, Hassan Howa. Although he went into the race in 1971 as favourite, and despite the help he received from Adams, Jordaan still lost against the wily Howa.

Following the death of Bansda in January 1973, Ken Adams took over responsibility for the coverage of black cricket and soccer for the Cape Flats edition of the *Cape Times*. In 1976, Yunus Agherdien, a former cricket umpire and administrator from Port Elizabeth, became the first full-time black sports writer to be employed by the *Cape Times*, who by then had discarded their Cape Flats edition.

Things started changing slowly – and for the first time, following the introduction of the Howa Bowl in 1977, reports on Western Province Cricket Board interprovincial matches sometimes made it onto one of the bottom corners of the back page of the *Argus* and *Cape Times*.

Later, full scorecards were published – initially on a Tuesday morning and afterwards in the Monday morning edition of the *Cape Times*, alongside those of the Western Province Cricket Union club matches. These were compiled by freelance reporters, Goosain Abrahams and Sedick Martin. Gasant Toffar, who by then had acquired a car, did the rounds all on his own for the *Argus* on a Saturday afternoon.

After Agherdien's death in 1976, Dennis Cruywagen, his successor, began to push for more column space in the *Cape Times'* sports pages. Previews of provincial and club matches became regular features. Cruywagen even began featuring profiles of top players. The *Cape Times* suddenly began to realise that there was a big readership on the Cape Flats – a readership whose needs had been ignored for far too long.

Dickie Martin – "Mr Everywhere"

IT DIDN'T matter whether it was a soccer tournament in Ocean View, a presentation of trophies ceremony in Paarl or a cricket interprovincial in Gelvandale, Port Elizabeth, Dickie Martin would find his way there.

He didn't have a motorcar (and, indeed, couldn't drive) – but this was only a minor irritation. Martin, 6 foot-massive and with a booming voice to match, always made a plan. And since he was a master in the art of gentle arm-twisting, getting to sports events was seldom a problem for him.

Martin, who worked for a variety of newspapers, took enormous pride in his work. Even when called on to provide a match report for four different newspapers, he'd resist the temptation to supply exactly the same report to all his employers. He'd always be on the lookout for a new angle.

Later, Martin was employed by the *Cape Herald* (although he continued to report for *Die Burger* under the pseudonym, Clive Arendse, as well as for several other newspapers).

Martin was popular among the players – and one of the reasons for this was that he usually had packed inside his trademark satchel piles of action photographs, which he would proceed to hand out to eager players. It proved an excellent way to cultivate contacts.

In time, he acquired such a broad knowledge of the workings of the Western Province Cricket Board, that he was co-opted onto the board's executive, as a member of the match and registration committee, in the 1979/80 season.

Martin died in 1989 in a minibus taxi accident.

A "REVOLUTIONARY" STEP

On 31 December 1980, Archie Henderson, the sports editor of the *Cape Times*, surprised everyone when he chose a story about Rashaad Musson scoring his first Howa Bowl century as the back-page lead (complete with an action picture).

To say that Henderson's decision caused a stir, would have been an understatement: reaction ranged from snide comments from some journalists in the *Cape Times* newsroom, to enquiries from several white readers wanting to know "what are you up to?", and to a call from a representative of a liquor company, threatening to withdraw his company's advertising from the newspaper.

Reflecting on his decision, and the reaction to it, almost 20 years later, Henderson said: "I look back on those times with a deep sense of regret. I think of wasted opportunities and an inability to think laterally about the whole situation in sport.

"Generally, South Africa's English-language newspapers operated in a wonderful comfort zone.

"On one level, they could easily criticise the National Party government – after all, they were never short of subject matter. As a result of this, they had a certain credibility and standing within the black community because they were regarded as the only flame-bearers of the liberal cause.

"But, on another level, the English-language press was useless in developing black talent. It simply did not make an effort to find black talent to break the logjam of covering news from a white Anglo-Saxon perspective."

CAPE HERALD

The introduction of the weekly *Cape Herald* in 1965 provided a major boost to the coverage of black sport in Cape Town. Although rejected in some quarters because it was aimed specifically at the coloured market, the *Cape Herald* filled a major gap in highlighting the achievements and activities of black sportspeople and their organisations – at a time when such exposure was extremely limited.

By the 1970s, it had become something of a paper of record, publishing full scorecards of all provincial matches, as well as the top division of local league matches.

The exploits of cricketers and the actions of administrators featured prominently. As sports-political issues

Archie Henderson's decision in December 1980 to use a report on a Western Province Cricket Board match as his main sports story caught many people by surprise.

began to come to the fore, increasing amounts of space were devoted to boardroom issues.

The *Cape Herald* enjoyed a golden period for much of the 1970s and part of the 1980s. In addition to providing extensive coverage of black sport, it began to take up the cause of nonracial sport with increasing outspokenness.

Ted Doman, whose appointment as sports editor in 1971, coincided with the *Cape Herald's* growing support for nonracial issues, hit out at white journalists for their head-in-the-sand attitude towards black sport, in an editorial in May 1974: "The sheer irresponsibility of most white sportswriters is frightening," he wrote.

"It is not unusual to find an article slamming Mr Howa in the white section of a newspaper, and another article supporting him in the coloured section of the same newspaper.

"When they are not attacking Mr Howa, they are fobbing us off with a little column headed, 'Nonwhite Sport' – and a few results in small type.

"Our white sportswriters persist in ignoring black sport, snubbing our administrators and failing even to try to understand the issues involved."

In many ways, the *Cape Herald* set the tone for what would become an increasingly bitter debate over sports-political issues between black and white journalists.

When Doman became, deputy editor and then editor of the *Cape Herald*, his place as sports editor was taken by Jimmy Atkins, a hard-hitting, in-your-face type of sportswriter, whose weekly sports columns became required reading for anyone interested in the goings-on in nonracial sporting circles, and the often hilariously funny – and, sometimes, tragically sad –

attempts by those trying to create a system of mixed-race sport in a racially divided society.

Not everyone liked what Atkins wrote – and especially among some white journalists, there was a feeling that the sword ought to be mightier than the pen, just so that he could be taught a lesson.

In 1973, Atkins had a narrow escape when he marched up to the American tennis star, Arthur Ashe, outside a house in Rondebosch, near Cape Town, and asked him: "Don't you feel like an Uncle Tom for breaking the sports embargo?"

Before Ashe could reply, Atkins was set upon by a reporter and a photographer from one of the Afrikaans-language newspapers.

"I don't recall which newspaper they were from," said Atkins, "but both employees threatened to beat me up on the spot.

"Wiser heads prevailed, but I was told to leave, anyway," he said.

Later, Atkins was attacked with fists and feet at Newlands cricket ground by a bunch of thugs who, he said, he'd seen talking to a white photographer minutes earlier.

An unrepentant Atkins said later: "Such incidents confirmed that the so-called hardliners in the South African Council on Sport (Sacos) were pursuing the right strategy.

"In South Africa, the playing field was definitely not level. By denying South Africa the oxygen of international sports contact, Sacos helped to slowly asphyxiate the beast of apartheid."

When Atkins moved up the *Argus* hierarchy, Dougie Oakes took over as the *Cape Herald's* sports editor (after Lennie Kleintjies had briefly held the position). By then, the debate over "normal" and nonracial sport had

Dougie Oakes urged Sacos to use the pages of the Cape Herald to express their views

Ways of seeing

Newspaper coverage of black sport in South Africa fitted into two categories – match reports and previews, and policy matters and political views.

In time, most newspapers – even those who openly supported the National Party – were more than happy to run match reports and previews.

What they baulked at – and English-language newspapers fell into this category, too – was giving any sort of positive publicity on the policy decisions and political views of the black sports codes (especially those who belonged to the South African Council on Sport).

And so, they tended to use only stories which portrayed the anti-apartheid sports organisations as unreasonable, even slightly crazy, ogres.

This was the picture that most white readers and, indeed, many black readers had of Sacos.

degenerated into an angry, all-out war of words.

Oakes quickly nailed his colours to the mast....

WAR OF THE MEDIA

One of the first things he did was to go to Sacos officials with a special invitation: "I want you to use the sports pages of the *Cape Herald* as a forum for expressing your views, was how I put it to them," said Oakes.

"Many Sacos officials were not comfortable with the thought of playing footsy with what was seen as a coloured newspaper. The problem for them, though, was that the only other person they could turn to was Abe Adams, who provided *Muslim News*, a newspaper with a small circulation, with sports copy.

"And so they came to me regularly with statements in reaction to events in the normal sports setup. These statements were usually far too long – and written way above the constituency they were trying to impress. When I cut their copy to make it fit into the available space, they'd suggest that the Argus Company was deliberately deleting the most important parts of their statements, because the *Argus* supported normal sport."

Over time, Oakes forged a strong relationship with Hassan Howa. "We got on so well together, that I often issued statements in his name. He'd say to me, 'If I'm not available, you know the way I feel about things. Use your discretion.'

"I only ever issued statements on his behalf when reaction was called for in regard to something done or said by the Western Province Cricket Union or the South African Cricket Union. I knew and understood what the Western Province Cricket

Board's policy was in this regard. I stayed well clear of problems within the board.

"Of course, what I did ran totally contrary to what I'd learnt about objectivity in the Argus Cadet School for journalists," said Oakes.

"But very early in my journalism career, I discovered what objectivity really meant in the South African media industry....

"In 1982, while working in the London office of the *Argus*, I started filing stories relating to the South African Non-Racial Olympic Committee (Sanroc). Cliff Scott, an editor with an awesome reputation in the company, called me into his office one day and said: 'Every statement issued by Sanroc must be balanced by a statement issued by the Committee for Fairness in Sport.'

"Of course, he did not insist that every statement issued by the Committee for Fairness in Sport be balanced by a statement from Sanroc. I couldn't help smiling to myself a few years later when it transpired that the Committee for Fairness in Sport was a South African government front company."

Oakes was well aware that his, and the *Cape Herald's* views were not generally well-received by their white counterparts in the *Argus* group. "There were journalists in the *Argus* sports department who couldn't understand why the *Cape Herald* was pushing such a strong anti-apartheid line," he said.

According to Archie Henderson, the white perception of Oakes and the *Cape Herald* sports department was that they were unpatriotic.

"Oakes wrote very provocative pieces. They used to read these articles and say, 'Frankly, this is bloody annoying.'"

ROBERT HOUWING

The appointment in 1988 of Robert Houwing as cricket correspondent of the *Argus*, provided a refreshing change in the paper's coverage of the Western Province Cricket Board.

Shortly after his appointment, he became the first white cricket writer from an English-language daily newspaper to attend a Western Province Cricket Board provincial match when he covered the game between Western Province and Eastern Province.

"I took it upon myself to broaden my cricket horizons because I realised there was another side to the game in Cape Town beyond the Western Province Currie Cup team and Alma Marist," Houwing said.

"As the *Argus* cricket writer, I felt duty-bound to cover the Western Province Cricket Board games as well.

"Previously, board officials would phone Gasant Toffar in the hope that he would be able to get the story into the paper.

"I think what helped me was the stint I had in the *Argus* newsroom, which made me more aware of the issues outside cricket. I developed something of a struggle feel in the 1980s, which helped me a lot in covering cricket issues."

Houwing said that he was made to feel very welcome by officials such as Abe Adams, the board president, and Rushdi Magiet, the manager of the provincial team.

"I also befriended players such as Nazeem White and Faiek Davids. This, I believe, gave me an inside track when I covered the unity talks which followed soon afterwards.

"The editor of the *Argus*, Andrew Drysdale, who was mindful of the needs of the Cape Flats readership, was happy with the coverage,

Reporters who were worlds apart

IN THE YEARS before unity, white sportswriters, generally, appeared to have little perception of the broader issues which affected the daily lives of people outside cricket.

"In most cases, they ignored black sport by adopting the argument that sport and politics should not be mixed," said Dougie Oakes, the sports editor of the *Cape Herald* newspaper in the 1980s.

"Even journalists at the London office of the *Argus* used this argument. Alan Robinson, for instance, couldn't understand why anyone would want to see South African sport isolated.

"His attitude was, 'You guys aren't good enough, so support the guys who are.'

"The general feeling among white sports reporters was, 'Hey, let's get on with the game.'"

It was an attitude typified by Michael Owen-Smith in an article of the *Cape Times* of 6 February 1990. Reacting to reports of widespread resentment and protests against Mike Gatting's English rebel cricket side, Owen-Smith wrote: "Of the 30-odd representatives of radio, television and newspapers from overseas for the current tour, only three or four can be regarded as specialist cricket writers.

"In the 15 years in which I have been covering international sport, I have never been involved in an event in which there has been so much antagonism between the players and certain elements of the media. Hopefully, cricket will come into its own in the next few weeks.

"Mike Gatting, in particular, has not been given a fair hearing – and fair play does not seem to be a prominent feature of the coverage of this tour."

WORD GAMES

In the "normal" cricket era, some journalists came up with the mind-boggling theory that Sacos-aligned administrators who rejected "normal" sport were probably grateful for apartheid.

Sy Lerman outlined this theory in an article in September 1985, in Business Day, in which he lashed out at South African Cricket Board official, Ahmed Mangera.

"When it comes to maintaining his position on the cricket stage, Ahmed Mangera can be thankful for apartheid," Lerman wrote.

"Once it disappears, he will surely disappear as unlamented as the system he fights tooth and nail."

Describing Mangera as "the intransigent, lightweight secretary of the South African Cricket Board", Lerman ranted that Mangera "survives as much as an artificial product of apartheid as Chief Lennox Sebe [the one-time leader of the former Ciskei homeland]".

Lerman's anger followed a rejection by Mangera of a call by Ali Bacher, the managing director of the South African Cricket Union, "for cricketers of all colours to unite to help sweep racial segregation down the drain".

In explaining his rejection of the call by Bacher, Mangera said: "Dr Bacher and his colleagues, through the benefit of their legalised position of privilege, have a monopoly of cash in sports and the best facilities, and they understand nothing of the harassment that comes from laws like the Group Areas Act, influx control, pass laws and separate education. How can anyone compete on equal terms under these circumstances?"

Lerman argued that "great sportsmen have thrived since time immemorial in areas of the underprivileged. The handicaps and hardships, it seems, have only added to their resilience and spurred them to greater achievements".

Not so Mangera's ilk. And one needs to ask oneself why.

"As a cricket administrator and personality, Mangera pales into insignificance against Bacher. And he hides his inadequacy by shielding behind apartheid."

Robert Houwing changed the way that the Argus covered Western Province Cricket Board matches.

although Peter McKenzie and John Waters, my two sports editors, were fairly indifferent. They didn't encourage or dissuade me."

Houwing also attended provincial net practices, which again helped him to build up a relationship with key people in the board.

Looking back to his time as a cricket correspondent, Houwing suggested that the *Argus* covered Western Province Cricket Board club cricket in a token way.

"They covered board cricket similar to the way they covered the Western Province Cricket Union's second division leagues.

"Gasant Toffar would go to a few matches and then phone various people around the peninsula to get the rest of the scores.

"In contrast, the *Argus* would assign a freelance reporter to each of the Western Province Cricket Union club games – and even to the white schools games. With respect, the reports on the Western Province Cricket Board games inevitably ended up as a dog's breakfast, with the scorecards not even tallying on many occasions."

As he got into the beat, Houwing started attending board meetings. "I found the sincerity and passion of debate in their meetings very refreshing," he said.

"The delegates certainly weren't afraid to speak their minds. It was certainly different to Western Province Cricket Union meetings, where things were run more professionally. There wasn't that much debate around issues, as in the Western Province Cricket Board."

In the early 1990s, when the unity process became irreversible, Houwing was invited to the launch of the new, Sacos-affiliated Cricket Board of Western Province.

"It was because of my contacts with Abe Adams, a former board president," Houwing said.

"I was surprised when the Argus ran the story as a back-page lead. That same day, I received a call from an angry Ali Bacher.

"He had a real go at me for publicising the new body. He suggested the story was counter-productive, and that I should help in crushing the splinter body. I was astonished by his response," said Houwing.

Part 6

Conflict and Unity

IT WAS a declaration of pride, expressed in the trademark Hassan Howa way – but its consequences would go far beyond the house in middle-class Heathfield, where Howa and a group of his most-trusted lieutenants were engaged in supposedly secret talks with nonracial cricket's public enemy number one, Ali Bacher.

The meeting between Howa and members of his Western Province Cricket Board executive, and Bacher revolved around cricket development – more specifically, around the issue of funds for the provision of facilities in black areas.

But during an interlude in the discussions, Howa boasted about the strength in depth of the South African Cricket Board's Under-19 players, who were engaged in a national tournament in Rocklands, Mitchells Plain.

And then, incredibly, given the deep-seated animosity towards Bacher – the architect of a number of rebel tours to South Africa, by the majority of leading lights in the anti-apartheid sports movements – Howa invited the South African Cricket Union managing director to Rocklands to watch some of the cricket.

Bacher's visit to the grounds, and the media reports of his meeting with Howa, caused an uproar far beyond the Western

Cape – and led to a crescendo of calls for Howa's head.

Over the years, Howa had made some powerful enemies within the Western Province Cricket Board – but he had always managed to whip them into compliance.

This time, however, things would prove to be different.

THE END OF AN ERA

South African Council on Sport luminaries such as Frank van der Horst led the attack in which words such as "sellout" were liberally used. Some board officials openly canvassed support for a proposed vote of no confidence; others swore to stand by Howa. Reports of secret meetings by anti-Howa factions abounded.

On Sunday, 18 January 1987, matters came to a head at a stormy, often chaotic, board council meeting at the University of the Western Cape....

Howa and the majority of his executive committee were removed in the promised vote of no confidence.

It was a sad departure for a man who'd served the board since its inception in 1959.

But, if board members believed that Howa's removal – and a reiteration of their commitment to the principles of non-racialism – would usher in a more focused period, they were about to be sadly mistaken.

To begin with, Howa's acrimonious departure saw the board battle to find its feet as the deposed president's supporters tried to make life as difficult as possible for the new executive.

And then, just when the board seemed to have safely negotiated the rough waters, thanks to the diplomatic stewardship of Sadick Emeran, a new crisis arose following the emergence of the National Sports Congress (NSC) towards the end of the decade.

Described by many of its followers as "the ANC in tracksuits", the NSC proceeded to erode the power base of the South African Council on Sport (Sacos), which had been the torchbearer of the nonracial sports struggle since its establishment in 1973.

This development saw the board lurch into yet another crisis as Abe Adams, who had succeeded Emeran as president of the board, quit amid accusations that his executive had "stabbed him in the back" with regard to aligning itself with the NSC.

Adams, a Sacos executive member, together with several other Sacos members including former secretary Willie Adams, later formed their own Sacos-aligned cricket body, when the board and the Western Province Cricket Union formed a united organisation.

Ironically, the much maligned rebel tours served as a catalyst for cricket's unification process. It was the demonstrations against Mike Gatting's rebel English touring team in January 1990 that forced the curtailment of the tour. But coming as it did, when FW de Klerk unbanned the ANC, PAC and the South African Communist Party, and released leading figures such as Nelson Mandela, Walter Sisulu, Govan Mbeki and Ahmed Kathrada from prison, the demonstrations against the Gatting tour led to NSC-brokered unity talks in 1991.

Although the WP Cricket Board took much longer than even their parent body, the South African Cricket Board, to agree to all the smallprint of the unity process, cricket in the Western Cape finally huddled under one umbrella on 25 June 1991.

Howa, Bacher talks lead to a crisis in the WP Cricket Board

LATE IN DECEMBER 1986, Frank Brache, the secretary of the Western Province Cricket Union telephoned Ali Bacher, the managing director of the South African Cricket Association, with a stunning piece of news: "Hassan Howa has agreed to meet you," he said.

It was the beginning of an amazing sequence of events that would see some of the most powerful heads in the Western Province Cricket Board rolling, including the most powerful head of all – Howa, himself....

Bacher, only too aware of how quickly things could change in South African sport, listened carefully to Brache's report of a meeting between him, Howa and Ebrahim Dawood, a long-time benefactor of the board.

Howa did indeed seem amenable to discussions – but both men agreed that any approaches had to be conducted with extreme patience, and sensitivity.

By the late 1980s, the battle between the predominantly white South African Cricket Union (Sacu) and the nonracial South African Cricket Board (SACB) had reached virtual stalemate.

Sacu had been cut off from almost all international contact (with the exception of the unsatisfactory rebel tours) following a highly effective campaign of lobbying by SACB and its powerful international allies; but, the cash-strapped SACB's campaign to isolate the predominantly white sporting organisations, deemed unpatriotic by many, resulted in them being refused sponsorship by the majority of the country's business houses.

In many ways, both national bodies were fighting for survival.

FRANK BRACHE'S ROLE

In public, Brache, would have been dismissed by board supporters as a "sellout" for having thrown in his lot with the "normal" cricket setup.

But, in private, a slightly different story emerged....

"I was in regular contact with Hassan during the late 1970s and early 1980s," Brache said. "Whenever top members of international sporting organisations came to Cape Town, I'd phone him to arrange meetings between him and them."

Given his relationship with Howa, Brache was mandated by the South African Cricket Union executive to establish contact with the board.

"Hassan agreed to meet with me at Dawood's home in Heathfield," said Brache.

"I told him that 20 top companies in South Africa were prepared to donate a total of R1-million for the development of cricket facilities throughout the country – and they weren't concerned about which organisations would be involved. He was sufficiently interested for us to agree to take the matter further. It was then that I contacted Ali [Bacher].

A meeting between Ali Bacher and Hassan Howa in January 1987 sparked outrage among Western Province Cricket Board supporters.

"Shortly after our telephonic discussion, Ali flew to Cape Town – and we drove out to Dawood's house for the meeting. Practically the whole excutive committee of the Western Province Cricket Board was there. Everyone knew what was going on.

"During the talks, Hassan boasted about the quality of SACB's juniors. It led to him inviting Ali to spend some time at the SACB under-19 tournament in Rocklands, Mitchells Plain," said Brache.

UPROAR

The meeting between Bacher and Howa at the Rocklands cricket grounds on 5 January 1987 received wide newspaper coverage – and it led to a major outcry by top officials of the South African Council on Sport (Sacos).

Krish Mackerdhuj, the president of the South African Cricket Board, responded angrily. "Bacher should never have been allowed inside the ground," he said.

Then, to show just how seriously he viewed the events at Rocklands, Mackerdhuj said that he would fly to Cape Town from his base in Durban to sort out the matter.

Howa, of course, jumped to no-one's tune.

When Mackerdhuj suggested a meeting during the match between the SA under-19 side and the WP under-21s at Green Point Track, Howa flatly refused.

Neither the time nor the place were appropriate, he said.

Responding to hints from Mackerdhuj that disciplinary action might be taken against him, Howa said: "No one is going to dictate to me who I should allow into our grounds."

At the awards dinner for the under-19 tournament at the Samaj Centre in Gatesville, Frank van der Horst, the president of Sacos, lambasted Howa.

When Van der Horst referred to "sell-outs" in his speech, the audience was left in no doubt as to whom he was referring.

Howa listened impassively.

Later, in an interview with the *Argus,* Howa was more forthcoming about his meeting with Bacher: "We need each other," he said.

"They [the South African Cricket Association] can't get into international cricket without us, but we can't realistically think of going it alone without them."

Howa also claimed that Bacher had accepted that there could not be change in sport without change in the country's political situation.

SETTLING OLD SCORES

For more than 10 years, a growing number of officials in the Western Province Cricket Board had been trying to remove Howa from the presidency. But they had been outwitted at almost every turn by his effective mixture of bluff, bluster and superb administrative skills.

But now, as the storm over the talks intensified, they could hardly believe their good fortune.

Willie Adams, chairman, in 1987, of the Bishop Lavis Cricket Club, said: "There was intense lobbying in the period leading up to the board's monthly council meeting. We were determined to gather enough support for a motion of no confidence in Howa.

"I personally contacted several clubs, all of whom assured me of their support. I called Barney Leendertz and Neville Hartel and came straight to the point: 'Did you know about the meeting with Bacher?' I asked.

"'We didn't, and we're not happy about it,' they replied.

"As the time for the meeting drew nearer, we had it all worked out," said

In a thinly disguised attack on Hassan Howa, Frank van der Horst, the president of the South African Council on Sport, described those who held talks with "normal" sports administrators as sellouts.

Adams. "Willie Kriel of St Augustines would propose the motion of no confidence; I would be the seconder. We were confident...."

Willie Adams and his group were not the only ones who wanted to oust Howa: Lefty Adams, a Howa loyalist, accused Rushdi Magiet of holding secret meetings at his Grassy Park home with another anti-Howa faction.

"But Howa knew everything that was going on," said Adams.

"Everytime Magiet held a meeting, someone would leak the information to him. Howa knew exactly who his opponents were, what they were saying about him and what their plans were to oust him."

Howa's son, Rustum, said: "My father was updated on a regular basis about what the other side had discussed at their secret meetings.

"My father took calls in the middle of the night from people who attended those meetings."

Magiet denied hosting any of the meetings referred to by Lefty Adams.

"I only became involved in the affairs of the Western Province Cricket Board when members of the new interim committee [who took over the running of the board after Howa had been ousted] approached me for help in securing air tickets for the provincial side to play a Howa Bowl match in Port Elizabeth," he said.

Mogamat Sambo, the chairman of Blue Bells in the 1980s, and a close associate of Howa, suggested that Magiet might have wanted to settle a score with Howa after a furious disagreement in 1980 over the captaincy of the Howa Bowl team.

"Mr Howa told me that Rushdi was not happy with Charlie van Schalkwyk being appointed captain of the board side in 1980," said Sambo.

"It led to a blazing row, with Mr Howa telling Rushdi that he would never play provincial cricket again."

But Magiet said: "True, I was unhappy about Van Schalkwyk's appointment, but I wasn't interested in the captaincy. My career was drawing to a close, anyway."

Shafiek Mowzer, a close associate of Magiet in the 1980s, said that at least two meetings were held at Magiet's home.

"We definitely met to devise a strategy to get rid of Howa," said Mowzer, who became a member of the interim committee which took over the running of the board after the Howa executive had been deposed.

SHOWDOWN

The board's monthly council meeting, held at the University of the Western Cape on 18 January 1987, lived up to all the predictions: it was punctuated by angry exchanges between an unrepentant Howa and a group of delegates determined not to let him off the hook.

Willie Adams said: "Howa reacted to our questions in the only way he knew – he tried to steamroll and bulldoze his questioners. We didn't like that at all.

Asked by Kriel whether he had had any prior meetings with Bacher, Howa responded in typically blunt fashion: "That's none of your business," he said.

"Do you have the right to withhold information from us?" was Kriel's next question.

"No, but I take full responsibility for everything. I don't stab people in the back," Howa shot back.

Three members of Howa's executive, Ebrahim Dawood, Denzil Barry and Mohammed Patel admitted that they knew about Howa's previous meeting with Bacher.

Willie Adams (top) openly lobbied for the removal of Hassan Howa as president of the Western Province Cricket Board. Rushdi Magiet (above) was accused of holding secret meetings in which plans to remove Howa were discussed.

Howa's explanation

ON 19 JANUARY 1987, in an interview with the *Argus* newspaper, Hassan Howa provided details of his talks with Bacher.

He said that Frank Brache, the secretary of the Western Province Cricket Union, had arranged for him to meet Kevin Commins, the director of the union.

"If there are a million rands available for sponsorship, would we accept?" they asked.

"I referred them to ... Krish Mackerdhuj [the president of the SA Cricket Board]."

"Later they came back to me and said Mackerdhuj had not replied."

Howa said that about two weeks later, he had met four or five members of the SA Cricket Development Fund, who felt they could accomplish something ... with us because of the black areas we controlled.

"The offer was for 2000 sportsfields with turf wickets at black schools at a cost of R5000 each.

"It sounded good to us because we were broke."

However, Howa said he told them that he did not accept public handouts. He again referred them to Mackerdhuj, who again did not reply.

"Eventually I was asked to meet Dr Ali Bacher [managing director of the SA Cricket Union] which I did informally at our under-19 tournament."

"Kriel proposed the motion of no confidence on the basis that Howa had refused to give us proper answers about his meetings with Bacher – he had evaded the issues," said Willie Adams.

"We also argued that he had met Bacher without consulting all the members of the executive.

"When it came to the vote, Howa showed just what a shrewd character he could be," said Adams. "Instead of calling for a closed ballot, which would almost certainly have resulted in him losing by a large margin, he ruled that the matter be settled by an open vote.

"As a result of this, some delegates who had promised us that they would vote against him, backtracked.

"Those in favour of the motion had to stand on the left side of the hall; those against had to move to the right. Kriel's motion against the executive did not include Barney Leendertz and Neville Hartel, both of whom had distanced themselves from the actions of their fellow members."

The voting was chaotic.

Some delegates tried to stay in the centre of the hall, unable to bring themselves to move left or right. Accusations and insults were thrown around like confetti.

Nabeal Dien, a delegate for the Western Province Senior Schools Sports Union, said: "Everyone was shouting. People were hurling insults at executive members. I saw Ngconde Balfour take a batch of Sacos newsletters and throw it across the room."

Amien Jacobs, the match and registration secretary of the board, said, "Because of the confusion, the vote had to be recounted several times.

"I was highly suspicious of the count. It had become quite clear that there were some people in the meeting who wanted Howa out at all costs."

When the result of the vote was announced – the motion was carried by four votes – Howa closed the meeting, and walked out.

"When he left, we followed him," said Jacobs.

LOOKING AHEAD

Immediately after Howa had walked out, delegates reopened the meeting, and elected an interim committee, consisting of Hartel, Leendertz, Shafiek Mowzer, Willie Adams, Armien Fredericks and Willie Kriel, to run the board.

The committee immediately issued a statement attacking Bacher for organising rebel tours, and the South African Cricket Union "for its latest attempt to split our ranks by offering us R1-million [for the development of sports fields]. The Western Province Cricket Board will not forsake its stand on nonracial sport...."

Hassan Howa's departure marks the end of an eventful era

HASSAN HOWA had quit cricket before – but always of his own volition. Many believed that his occasional bust-ups with fellow officials of the Western Province Cricket Board – and the furious walkouts which followed – had been carefully orchestrated events, designed either to deflect criticism from one or other of his less popular actions, or to consolidate his powers.

Hassan Howa seriously underestimated his opponents in the Western Province Cricket Board, following his talks with Ali Bacher of the South African Cricket Union.

But he never stayed out of the game for long. He always came back – and, like a knight in shining armour, he was always ready to respond to calls to extricate the board from a crisis.

In January 1987, however, the crisis was of his own making – and although he always had an unshakable belief in his ability to overcome the biggest obstacles, the wave of anger which greeted the news that he had held talks with Ali Bacher, suggested that this was one fight which he would have difficulty in winning.

And so it proved – although, to give him his due, he went down fighting.

After serving cricket and nonracial sport for 40 of his 69 years, Howa finally bowed out under acrimonious circumstances. The morning after he was ousted – Monday, 19 January – he told the *Argus* newspaper: "I will relish my new freedom. I awakened this morning and said to my wife, 'For the first time in forty years you've got me all to yourself.'"

ABRASIVE HOWA

Howa's abrasive and straightforward style often saw him being described as an autocrat and a tyrant by his opponents. Ray Bharoochi, an executive member of the board in the 1980s, recalled an incident in 1983, when two top executives of the Benson and Hedges cigarette company, Bruce Edmunds and Rauch van Reenen, came to Turfhall Park, near Cape Town, to negotiate the second year of sponsorship for the SACB limited overs competition.

"Hassan, who was organising the Turfhall Fair, made us wait for about 30 minutes before meeting us in the tiny hall at the ground. There were no chairs, so we sat on boxes. The two executives had brought the sponsorship cheque, but Hassan, after glancing at the amount, simply returned it to them and left. He wanted a similar amount to what Sacu had been given.

"Later, after a meeting in Johannesburg, we managed to reach agreement."

One of Howa's strengths was his determination to see something through once he had started it.

"Once he had made up his mind about something, he wouldn't allow anyone to stand in his way," said Willie Adams, a board executive member.

For many years, a mixture of strong-arm tactics, sweet talk, street fighter instincts and guts had helped

Stan Abrahams lost badly when he challenged Hassan Howa for the presidency of the Western Province Cricket Board in 1983.

Howa to weather the storms of his reign. In 1984, at the board's annual general meeting he alluded to the regular challenges to his authority.

"I think with amusement of the many annual general meetings ... and the attempts to take away my powers. A suggested change to the constitution here; a resolution there; a challenge over some 'undemocratic' act somewhere else; a threat of legal action by someone else....

"'Let's put Howa in his place' is an annual occurrence and many house visits are held to do this. To get me out of this chair must surely be very easy. You only have to nominate someone, who is concerned about cricket and those who play it, and then get most people to vote for that person.

"Well, I am getting tired of all this. I am saying to you, I am not going to tolerate this kind of nonsense any longer.

"I am prepared to head Western Province, only if I get the co-operation from officials and delegates to do their best for the cricketers. I am no longer going to waste time in squabbles in meetings, to the detriment of the players," Howa said.

ABRAHAMS' CHALLENGE

In May 1983, Stan Abrahams convened a meeting of 23 leading board members in an effort to unseat Howa. After conceding that Howa had played a major role in the nonracial sports struggle, they gave the following reasons for wanting to remove Howa:

• The board's administration was too concerned with petty clashes;

• Fixtures had fallen into total chaos;

• Opportunities to obtain sponsorship had been lost;

• The once flourishing umpires association was no longer operating;

• The board had not done enough to discourage division in nonracial sport.

Howa, of course, loved challenges. He welcomed Abrahams' attempt to win the presidency from him.

Howa won easily. In conceding defeat, Abrahams said: "Howa is a brilliant tactician. I thought I stood a great chance when I heard that the voting would be done by ballot. However, I still lost." That was the end of his stint as a board executive member.

Sadick Emeran felt that Abrahams had miscalculated badly by opposing Howa at such a critical period in the history of the board. "Stan did a marvellous job in acquiring sponsorships for the board. He was also an extremely competent secretary. But I thought

Howa in a nutshell

HASSAN HOWA gave the best years of his life to cricket. Having first been voted onto the Western Province Cricket Board executive in 1959, he continued to hold an executive position – mainly president – until 18 January 1987. On that day he, and the majority of his executive, were removed by a vote of no confidence in a board council meeting at the University of the Western Cape..

In many ways, Howa was the best-known face – both nationally and internationally – of the anti-apartheid sports struggle.

He did so much to popularise the Sacos slogan, "No normal sport in an abnormal society," that many people mistakenly believed that he had coined the phrase.

Some knowledgeable observers have suggested that Abel Jordaan, Howa's vice-president in the mid-1970s, was the author of the slogan (although journalist Jimmy Atkins claimed that he first used the term in an editorial for the *Cape Herald* newspaper).

After serving as treasurer on the inaugural board executive in 1959, Howa became vice-president two years later. He became president in 1963 and held the position (with the exception of a few walkouts) until his removal in 1987.

He was also president of the South African Cricket Board of Control (Sacboc) between 1970 and 1974 when he resigned and was replaced by Rashid Varachia.

To say that Howa and Varachia didn't like each other would be putting it mildly. Upon his resignation as president of Sacboc, he said: "I will return to Sacboc only when Cliff Adams, Syd Reddy and Rashid Varachia leave."

Howa was instrumental in forming the new South African Cricket Board, which he headed from its inception in 1977, until 1984, when he was replaced by Krish Mackerdhuj.

Such was the threat that Howa was deemed to pose to the future of apartheid sports, that he was denied a passport on numerous occasions.

Even Ali Bacher, who was reviled in nonracial sports circles for organising rebel tours, conceded that with the benefit of hindsight Howa and SACB were correct in their uncompromising stance. "History will record that Mr Howa was right in saying there can be no normal sport in an abnormal society – he was spot on."

it was a mistake for him to oppose Mr Howa – we needed his expertise at that stage of our struggle.

"No-one in the Board was capable of playing the role that Mr Howa chose to play. He was the icon of the nonracial sports movement. Someone else might have done a reasonable job as president, but playing the public role was even more important."

A journalist summed up Howa's larger than life stature in board cricket when he wrote: "Cricket without Hassan Howa is like the Cape summer without the south-easter. You may love him or loathe him but you certainly cannot ignore him."

Even after his departure from the scene, many nonracial sports administrators continued to visit him at his Heathfield home, to seek advice and to draw on his many years of experience in sports administration.

Despite their wide-ranging differences with him over the years, his opponents continued to stress how much they respected him.

"I was sorry to see Mr Howa leave the board on a successful motion of no confidence," said Emeran.

"I respected him, and I will continue to respect him, for the part that he played in nonracial sport, not only in cricket. The South African Council on Sport was at its strongest when he was president. He must be saluted for his contribution," said Emeran.

Rushdi Magiet, while admitting that he and Howa always had differences of opinion, also expressed regret at the nature of his departure from the board.

"I had great respect for him because he devoted his entire life to cricket. In the 1960s, he would be at the William Herbert sportsground in Wynberg preparing the wickets and fields for the juniors to play when no-one else

was prepared to help. He made a number of tremendous personal sacrifices for the game, and it's a pity that he distanced himself from the unity process. I know and appreciate how hard he fought to have unity in cricket."

Ray Bharoochi, who worked alongside Howa as a cricket administrator from the late 1960s onwards, also paid tribute to the feisty anti-apartheid campaigner.

"I think that it's a great pity that the community – both black and white – who now benefit from the freedom of being a united people, who now benefit from the freedom of playing sports with one another other, and who now enjoy the freedom of playing international sports, should have forgotten the man who made so many sacrifices and played his part, in his own way, to help bring down apartheid.

"I knew Hassan in his many moods. He was humble in his greatness, joyful in achieving success, very hospitable when entertaining guests and, at times, could be aggressive when people failed to understand him."

NO TO LIFE MEMBERSHIP

Recognising the tremendous contribution Howa had made to cricket in South Africa, former board members within the new unified Western Province Cricket Association, were keen to honour him with a life membership, according to Emeran.

"We tried to sound him out after the unity process, but he said he was not interested. It was pointless offering it to him when we knew that he would turn it down. But we felt if anyone deserved that honour it was Hassan," said Emeran.

Howa's rejection of the offer of life membership from the new Western

In the 1970s, Hassan Howa (right) often put aside cricket administration for a short while to supervise the erection of stalls at the annual Mardi Gras, at the William Herbert Sportsground.

Province Cricket Association wasn't surprising. After all, he regarded the architects of the unity process as the very people who had kicked him out.

He was never really convinced that the unity process agreed to between SACB and Sacu, in August 1991, was what he had fought for. "My personal integrity will not allow me to support the unity process. Do not get me wrong. I am not opposed to the formation of single controlling bodies in sport. This is the very thing I have been advocating all my life as an administrator," Howa told *South* newspaper in June 1991.

"However, the unity we are confronted with now is cosmetic.

"Surely our aim should be to get apartheid removed in all its forms, and to concentrate on development instead of international competition," he said.

Howa died on 10 February 1992, at the age of 69.

Tough times – but the WP Cricket Board rises to the challenge

WHEN TIMES are tough – and, in January 1987, they were for the Western Province Cricket Board's interim committee – the tough dig deep into their pockets.

Such was the level of ill-feeling within the board after the successful motion of no confidence in Hassan Howa and the majority of his executive, that the interim committee had to alter the board's letterheads to read, "Western Province Cricket Board Interim Committee", because they had been warned that there would be legal implications if they used the official board letterhead.

"There was a great deal of disruption from those who supported Howa," said Willie Adams, the interim committee secretary.

"Those in the Howa bloc were heavily against us. They even went as far as putting a freeze on the board's finances. We had to dig into our own pockets to keep nonracial cricket going in the Western Cape."

Adams said that at the interim committee's first meeting after Howa's removal, Howa supporters had arrived in force, and had again tried to disrupt proceedings.

"It was an extremely difficult time for all of us," Adams said.

"They found fault with everything we did.

"When I delivered correspondence to their houses, I was not at all well received. Some tore up letters in front of me. But we persevered."

The money problems of the board, especially, seemed insurmountable.

A fund-raising car raffle appeared to be heading for failure. Moreover, they owed SACB, their parent body, R20 000. And if this wasn't bad enough, the board's next three Howa Bowl matches were scheduled to be played away from home – which meant that air fares and hotel accommodation had to be found quickly.

The departure of Ebrahim Dawood, the board's main financial benefactor, who was part of Howa's executive, meant that the board no longer had a guarantor, without whom Flywell, the Board's travel agency, refused to issue tickets.

The matter was satisfactorily resolved when Rushdi Magiet, who had been asked by the interim committee to assist them, contacted Flywell's managing director, Usman Ahmed, in Greece, where he was on holiday, to secure bookings for the provincial team.

Neville Hartel and Barney Leendertz, the only survivors of the Howa executive, agreed to be the guarantors.

Some clever thinking by the interim committee helped to turn the annual car raffle into a financial success.

"We hired cars similar to the one which we were offering as the prize, and arranged to have them parked in shopping malls around the peninsula," said Magiet.

Losers, all?

AFTER OVERCOMING the initial rough ride in the aftermath of the departure of Hassan Howa and his executive, the Western Province Cricket Board started to function smoothly again, under the leadership of Sadick Emeran.

But many believed that the board was still the overall loser – because it could ill afford the loss of such officials as Amien Jacobs, who with his wife, Ferose, computerised the board's match and registration portfolio; Ebrahim Dawood, who had for so long been the board's financial benefactor; and, of course, Howa who had given virtually his entire adult life to the cause of nonracial cricket.

But such was the depth of administrative talent within the board that administrators such as Emeran, Abe Adams, Rushdi Magiet, Neville Hartel, Willie Adams, Peter Heeger, Percy Sonn and Willie Kriel, among others, managed to safely negotiate the turbulent waters which at one stage threatened to split the organisation.

True to his word, Emeran handed over the leadership reins to Abe Adams, after having promised on his election that he would stay in the position for only two years.

"We employed students to sell tickets – and eventually we made a healthy R30 000 profit."

OLD HANDS RETURN

Prior to the elections for a new executive, old hands such as Percy Sonn and Magiet had returned to administration to play prominent roles in the rebuilding process of the board, alongside members of the interim committee.

"We held many meetings in Sonn's office in Woodstock to discuss who we should nominate as office bearers," said Adams.

"We identified Sadick Emeran as the most suitable candidate to lead the board in what had become a critical stage of its history.

"It proved to be a wise choice. Sadick had impressive credentials: he was a person of standing in the community, he had been a long-serving match and registration secretary of the board, and he had delivered outstanding service to nonracial cricket."

Howa, surprisingly, decided to stand for selection against Emeran.

"Under normal circumstances, I wouldn't have wanted to stand against Mr Howa, because of the contribution he had made to nonracial cricket," Emeran said.

"I really thought that he would not make a bid for the presidency. I believed, perhaps naively, that since a motion of no confidence had been passed in him, he wouldn't stand again.

"I was surprised when he was nominated for the post."

Howa's supporters were unfazed by the criticism of his decision to stand for election.

"He had every right to stand," said Amien Jacobs, the match and registra-

tion secretary in the deposed executive. "And when he lost, he was gracious in defeat; he congratulated Sadick on his victory."

Emeran said that although he won by a comfortable margin (58-25), he made it clear that he would only serve as president for a short period.

"It's in-no one's interest for anyone to serve in such a position for too long," Emeran said.

Emeran's cabinet consisted of Willie Kriel (vice-president), Willie Adams (secretary), Peter Heeger (treasurer), Armien Fredericks (match and registration secretary) and Rushdi Magiet (chairperson of the selectors).

Ironically, Emeran returned to the board's executive in the same way that he had started his second term as match and registration secretary in the 1979/80 season. Then, he had taken over in mid-season from Jock Mahoney, who had left to join Avendale in the "normal" cricket setup.

Emeran was well aware of the deep scars that had been left by the acrimonious departure of the previous executive.

"I was watched very closely by Howa supporters for any slip-ups," he said.

"Later some members of the board felt, that because Mr Howa continued to attend meetings, he ought to be made to explain his actions in meeting with Ali Bacher.

"I wasn't comfortable with that," said Emeran.

"I felt that the motion of no confidence had taken care of this matter. But, before any finality could be reached on the subject, Mr Howa severed all ties with cricket."

Adams versus Magiet – power struggles in the WP Cricket Board

THE FIGHT for supremacy between the South African Council on Sport (Sacos) and the National Sports Congress (NSC), at the end of the 1980s and the beginning of the 1990s, was won relatively quickly by the NSC – but bitterness, arising from Sacos allegations of underhand tactics and backstabbing, lingered for a long time afterwards.

Abe Adams fought against the odds to keep the Western Province Cricket Board in the Sacos camp.

In many ways, it was an unequal contest: Sacos, although projecting an image of being a "tried and tested", highly principled organisation, also had a reputation for being staid and uncompromising, to the point of being unable to adapt to changing political circumstances; the NSC, by contrast, was regarded by its supporters as vibrant and innovative – an organisation willing to adapt and to compromise, if necessary, in order to secure victory against apartheid. But the biggest advantage it had over Sacos was its political connections: it was the robust offspring of the most famous political organisation of all – the ANC.

The ANC connections of the NSC was the password to the constituency that Sacos most coveted – the sportsmen and women of the African townships. Sacos, to be fair, had tried doggedly to sell itself in the townships. But, leaders such as Frank van der Horst had been evicted from African areas more than once by the apartheid police.

The NSC, boasting a membership that was far more representative of the South African population than that of Sacos, did not have this problem.

Sacos, believing that its highly principled stand on sport-apartheid issues, would beat off the NSC challenge, woke up too late. Certainly, by the time it tried to fight back, its position had already been usurped.

One of the last bodies to change from a staunchly Sacos allegiance to the NSC, was the Western Province Cricket Board. Ironically, it changed allegiance while under the stewardship of an uncompromising Sacos diehard – Abdurahmaan "Abe" Adams.

ABE ADAMS AND THE NSC

Some would say that Adams was unlucky to have been elected president of the Western Province Cricket Board – in September 1989 – at more or less the same time that the NSC began to emerge as a viable alternative to Sacos.

Others would contend that it was Adams' rigid, "it's set in concrete" approach that played right into the hands of the NSC.

The looming conflict between Sacos and the NSC was highlighted by both Sadick Emeran, the president of the board, and Willie Adams, the secretary.

Emeran predicted in his 1989 annual report that problems would arise between the two organisations, while Adams, in his secretarial report, bemoaned the fact that certain board members, who had no problem attending NSC conferences in Johannesburg, could not find the time to attend a monthly meeting of the Western Province Council on Sport, on their doorstep in Cape Town.

Rising Tensions

SADICK EMERAN touched upon the growing possibility of an ideological clash within the Western Province Cricket Board, in his presidential report of 1989.

"On the national sports front, we are aware that the emergence of the National Sports Congress (NSC) has caused ... consternation within the progressive sports organisations – and many questions are being asked," he said.

"Unfortunately, no one has been able to give concise answers to certain sensitive questions.

"We would normally draw our lead on this type of issue from the South African Council on Sport (Sacos). Although the Sacos executive decided not to attend the recent NSC conference in Johannesburg, they ... did not follow up that position with a clear statement as to how they saw the NSC's position in the nonracial fold.

Emeran pointed out that the Sacos decision to stay away from the NSC conference did not enjoy unanimous support.

"Many senior officials from a number of sports codes, including the president of the South African Cricket Board [Krish Mackerdhuj], attended the conference.

Emeran said that with all the confusion that had arisen, and with individuals clamouring for action to be taken against those who attended the NSC conference, a split within the Western Province Cricket Board had become a distinct possibility.

His words were to prove prophetic....

"Suddenly, the double standards resolution has become a stumbling block [to the extent] that it has to be 'redefined, or reinterpreted', or ... 'adapted or watered down" said Adams.

And he pointed out: "This has become the viewpoint of officials who, for years, have sat in judgement of others for transgressing this very resolution, without wanting to redefine, reinterpret or adapt it. What has changed in the hearts and minds of the ... racists for us to even think of adapting this cornerstone of nonracial sport?"

The emergence of the NSC came amid a change on the political landscape, with previously outlawed organisations such as the ANC, the PAC and the South African Communist Party being unbanned, and Nelson Mandela, long regarded as the icon of the liberation struggle, being released from prison in 1990.

But even before the momentous events of February 1990, several delegations had visited the ANC in exile. At the same time, the ANC-aligned Mass Democratic Movement (MDM) had started making its presence felt around the country with a series of mass marches. Even at this stage, it had already become evident that a strategy to replace Sacos with the NSC, as the torchbearers of nonracial sport was being evolved.

This was confirmed by Moosa Sydow, the most vocal proponent of the NSC in the Western Province Cricket Board's executive.

"Sacos was stifling progress," Sydow said.

"Their arguments, justifying things such as the double standards resolution had become stale and outdated."

"The NSC strategy was to engage in dialogue with the establishment sports organisations – with the intention of taking control of them."

Sydow said that, given the political leanings of its members, the executive of the Western Province Cricket Board was always going to split.

"Those leaning towards the NSC felt that the sooner this happened, the better. My feeling was that if we explained the situation to rank-and-file members of the board, we'd take them along with us.

"The ANC, who saw sport as a microcosm of the society they envisaged for South Africa, gave us a year to sort out the sports unity process. We had to act quickly.

"The NSC-aligned executive members agreed to nominate Rushdi Magiet for the vice-presidency of the NSC in the Western Cape," said Sydow.

"We chose Rushdi because cricket was a high-profile sport in the region, and he was a well-known and respected figure in the game.

"Rushdi accepted the nomination after we assured him of our backing should there be any problems within the board from officials such as Abe Adams, Neville Hartel and Willie Adams."

Magiet said: "Some of us were members of both Sacos and the NSC. We certainly didn't see the NSC as a threat to Sacos. All we did was change our approach in the light of changing circumstances.

"The people in the townships wanted something more – and the emergence of the United Democratic Front in 1983 helped towards meeting this need. Perhaps Sacos should have reassessed the situation. Under Sacos, the Western Province Cricket Board had no access to the townships. The emergence of the NSC offered a way around this problem," Magiet said.

On 24 July 1990, Sydow called on the board's executive to seek associate membership of the NSC. But with the president, Abe Adams, and assistant-secretary, Armien White, arguing that such a decision could only be taken at a general council meeting – and the next one was scheduled for September 1990 – the call was rejected.

FURORE OVER MAGIET

Magiet's election, in August 1990, as vice-president of the NSC's Western Cape region – in defiance of a board decision not to have official representation at the NSC launch – infuriated Sacos diehards in the board.

Three other officials with board connections – Ben Tengimfene of Luyolo (president), Humphrey Reid of Rivertonains (treasurer) and André Odendaal of United (education and training) – were also elected onto the regional NSC executive.

Board president, Abe Adams, demanded a meeting to discuss this turn of events.

Later, a special meeting was indeed called – but to discuss Adams' position as president after he had informed Magiet telephonically that he had resigned from the Western Province Cricket Board with immediate effect – because of Magiet's decision to accept a senior position on the NSC Western Cape executive committee.

Adams also accused the NSC-leaning members of the board of having "stabbed him in the back".

Insults flew around freely at the meeting. An angry Adams accused Magiet of having been "dishonest" with the board. "I am no longer prepared to work with you," he said to Magiet.

Asked if he had resigned from the board, Adams said that he had not. However, he said that he had decided to suspend all activity within the board, until the council meeting on 30 September.

"I'm not prepared to work with dishonest people," he said.

EXTREME FORM OF PROTEST

On 21 August 1990, Adams issued a circular in which he gave notice that he had decided to suspend all activity within the board – from Tuesday, 7 August 1990, to Sunday, 30 September 1990, the date of the next council meeting.

He described his decision as "the most extreme form of protest".

He pointed out how, through hard work and sacrifice, the executive had managed to "pull the board out of its embarrassing financial crisis".

"The interest and promotion of cricket was being served above all else," he said.

"My personal position, as an executive member of Sacos, is absolutely clear. I became a member of Sacos –

as did most of you – through cricket. I did not allow my position in Sacos to cloud my judgement of cricket matters – and, in fact, I agreed to subjugate the interest of Sacos to the service of cricket. I even agreed with you – to 'work with' both the NSC and Sacos," Adams said.

Adams said that the executive had discussed at length an invitation to attend the local launch of the NSC on Sunday, 5 August 1990.

"Only Mr Moosa Sydow insisted that the board should accept, at least, associate membership of the NSC. But, the executive had felt that an important policy decision such as affiliation could only be decided by the full general council meeting of the Board.

"This decision was accepted by all, including Mr Sydow.

"As president, I told the meeting that I could not prevent anyone from attending the NSC launch. However, the decision of the executive was that the question of membership had to wait until the general meeting decided one way or the other.

"All members present were obviously bound by this decision.

"Mr Armien White informed the executive that the NSC would not accept individuals as members. Neither would it accept clubs where provincial bodies existed. We accepted this as a procedurally correct position.

"Without wanting to pass judgment on the NSC, I would find it difficult to accept that they could change the above position as a matter of expediency – and so undermine the due democratic procedure of a representative body such as the WP Cricket Board.

"On Tuesday, 7 August 1990, I read in the *Cape Times* that Mr Rushdi Magiet had been elected 'vice-president' of the local NSC.

"I immediately telephoned him to find out who he had represented. He said he accepted the position in his 'personal capacity'.

"I find Mr Magiet's position totally unacceptable and intolerable because he directly contravened a fully discussed decision of the executive and thereby undermined the authority of the executive and the democratic procedure of our board.

"I told Mr Magiet that he obviously placed his personal ambition and the interest of the NSC above our commitment to put the interest of cricket above all else.

"I said to him that I found his behaviour, in this respect, deplorable and dishonest since he was part of our decision.

"The board will have to make a decision on whether it wants to affiliate to the NSC or not. That will have to be your decision, and you will have to decide what to do with those people who accepted positions in the NSC without prior permission of the Board."

On 27 August 1990, matters deteriorated even further when the executive (without Adams) met at Magiet's home to discuss "The position of the president."

Adams was deeply upset at not having been invited, but Magiet explained that because Adams had suspended himself from board activities, it had not been necessary to invite him.

Executive members who supported the NSC unanimously supported Magiet's contention that he could serve cricket in the Western Cape as a whole through his position as vice-president of the NSC.

The executive committee also argued that "the self-imposed suspension" of the president was unconstitutional. They agreed to discuss Adams' status at the special general council meeting on 30 September 1990.

Commenting on the meeting at Magiet's home, Adams said: "I, as president of the Western Province Cricket Board, was not invited to attend the executive meeting.

"Even though my actions were aimed at protecting the integrity and autonomy of the board, and the general council in particular, the executive committee has sought to ignore Mr Magiet's deliberate violation of a democratic decision."

Adams repeated his accusation that Magiet had placed the interests of the NSC above those of the Western Province Cricket Board. He also slated the NSC for seeking to "undermine and invalidate" the democratic procedures of the board.

Adams said that he could not see how accepting a position on the executive of the local region of the NSC could advance the interest of cricket – especially in Magiet's case. "He played and enjoyed his cricket under the banner of Sacos," Adams said.

"But, not once during the past 17 years did he even express an interest to attend a Sacos conference – "to advance the interest of cricket". This must prove that it is not so much cricket, but rather the NSC that Mr Magiet wants to advance."

AN EXECUTIVE RESPONSE

By now, the relationship between Adams and the majority of his executive had reached breaking point.

On 13 September 1990, the executive responded to Adams' allegations.

They sharply criticised him for continuing his own, self-imposed suspension because of problems with fellow executive members – Rushdi Magiet, in particular.

"If he had any problems, he should have raised it in an executive committee meeting, or in a council meeting," they said.

"The entire dispute raised by Mr Adams negatively affects the administration of the board, in that disruption occasioned by his unilateral action retards the progress which was envisaged for this season."

The executive committee rejected as unacceptable and "defamatory" Adams' accusations that Magiet had been dishonest and that his behaviour had been deplorable.

The executive reiterated its decision that it would remain a member of Sacos while seeking to have a working relationship with the NSC.

Matters were further complicated when the national body, the South African Cricket Board, affiliated to the NSC.

The long-awaited general council meeting, at the University of the Western Cape, on 30 September 1990, began on a fiery note when Adams refused a request by the executive committee for a special general meeting to discuss his position with regard to his self-imposed suspension.

Adams then suspended Magiet and ordered him to leave the meeting for accepting the position of vice-president of the NSC's Western Cape region – in defiance of a board ruling that its members were not to make themselves available for positions on the NSC executive.

A proposal for Adams to recuse himself so that his position could be discussed was narrowly defeated by 32 votes to 29.

However, Magiet was allowed back into the meeting following a unanimous backing of a proposal from the floor.

Surprisingly, the meeting backed a proposal by Willie Adams that the board reject an invitation to affiliate to

Howa's continuing influence

WILLIE ADAMS revealed that the strategy to expel Rushdi Magiet from a Western Province Cricket Board meeting on 30 September 1990 was taken on the advice of former president, Hassan Howa.

"Abe Adams, Neville Hartel and I went to seek advice from Mr Howa on what to do about the Rushdi Magiet issue.

"He advised us to expel Magiet from the meeting because he went against the mandate of the board not to align itself with the NSC"

the NSC, and that it remain an affiliate of Sacos. Adams' motion was carried by 35 votes to 34.

"After winning the vote, Abe adjourned the meeting because he was feeling tired. This gave NSC supporters time to lobby for the next meeting, scheduled for two weeks later," said Willie Adams.

The acrimony spilled over at the adjourned meeting, with Abe Adams calling on the executive to resign. Adams also called on Magiet to resign for "violating a decision of the exco."

But, after the proposal was defeated by 49 votes to 19, Adams indicated that he would reconsider his position within the board. After opening the second session of the adjourned meeting on 11 November 1990, Adams resigned as president of the board.

REACTION

Magiet was not happy with the accusations levelled against him by Abe Adams. "I practically ran Sacos on the cricket field. I arranged all the junior coaching clinics under the Sacos banner," he said Magiet.

"It's a pity that Sacos refused to look at things differently. We lost two excellent officials in Abe Adams and Willie Adams. They would have been a great asset in the unity process.

Some board clubs who were concerned about the South African Cricket Board's strong links with the NSC, proposed that the Western Province Cricket Board sever all links with SACB. However, the motion was defeated by 31 votes to 12.

Despite being in the same Sacos camp as his namesake, Willie Adams felt that perhaps Abe Adams was not ideally suited to leading the board through that critical period.

"The executive under Abe never really gelled. Abe couldn't bind people behind the ideology like Hassan Howa could.

"It was only under the laedership of Sadick Emeran that we operated smoothly. Thereafter, things hit a rocky patch with the executive being split along ideological grounds. With the benefit of hindsight, I think I may have made a mistake in leading the charge to oust Mr Howa, especially in view of how things turned out later when the NSC hijacked the unity process."

Despite reservations within the board – some clubs called for proportional representation within SACB to reflect the status of Western Province as the strongest affiliate, in terms of playing strength, numbers and finance – the unity process marched ahead at a frantic pace to meet the ANC and NSC deadlines.

At a SACB meeting in Port Elizabeth on 1 December 1990, the organisation decided to conduct unity talks at national level, and to involve the regional bodies only when specifics needed to be discussed.

At a Western Province Cricket Board meeting at UWC on 13 January 1991, Percy Sonn, who was unanimously elected president, succeeded in passing a motion to review and rescind the resolution binding the board to Sacos. The resolution was rescinded by 37 votes to 18.

The NSC had succeeded in its goal of loosening the Sacos stranglehold on the Western Province Cricket Board, the most powerful affiliate of the SA Cricket Board.

The way was now open to pursue unity with the Western Province Cricket Union....

Unity between the WP Cricket Board and the WP Cricket Union

PERHAPS IT was fitting that the turning point in the long, long war of attrition against apartheid sport should have occurred in the Northern Cape city of Kimberley. For it was here that some of the most momentous developments in South African sport – especially from within the ranks of the black have-nots – had taken place over the past century.

In the late 1800s, cricket was the sport of the African population of the diamond fields; the first national cricket body for blacks was formed in Kimberley; the South African Rugby Union (Saru) had its origins here. It was in Kimberley, too, that a split among black cricketers had ushered in the era of ethnic cricket bodies.

But, that was in the past. In the last decade of the 20th century, all the talk revolved around nonracialism....

In late-January 1990, with rapidly unfolding political events having pushed South Africa to the brink of an abyss (or so it seemed to many), two developments in Kimberley drew the country's warring sports factions closer together.

The first – an appeal by Ali Bacher to the South African police to allow a demonstration by the National Sports Congress (NSC) against Mike Gatting's English rebel tourists to go ahead, softened the stance towards Bacher of many who, otherwise, despised his role in arranging rebel cricket tours to South Africa; the second – brutal police action against antitour protesters – sparked widespread anger among tour opponents, and induced a sense of shock among tour organisers.

Hope and anger – who would have thought that such a strange combination of emotions would draw such long-standing foes together? But, over the next few years, South Africans would show that they still had many more surprises up their sleeves....

THE GATTING TOUR

Like the majority of fellow South Africans, Bacher was caught out by the rapid pace of political change in that eventful year of 1990 – otherwise, he would probably not have arranged the Gatting tour.

But then, having seen the mood change in the country, following the release from prison of political icons such as Walter Sisulu and Ahmed Kathrada – and, shortly afterwards, Nelson Mandela – he appeared to err badly in not immediately calling off the visit by the English rebels.

And although he tried to redeem himself by appealing to the police to allow a protest by the NSC against the tour, outside the De Beers Country Club, to go ahead, he might have guessed what the police reaction would be.

Under the full glare of the international media, they gave a demonstration of just how brutal they could be.

Mike Gatting's arrogant dismissal of demonstrators fanned the flames of protest against his team of rebel cricketers.

Two days after the Kimberley protests, an antitour gathering in Manguang township, outside Bloemfontein, was also forcibly broken up by the police.

Gatting, too, did more than his bit to provoke the anger of the anti-apartheid movement, by arrogantly dismissing the protesters as "a small group of people who were singing and dancing".

Still, the unforeseen result of Bacher's attempted intervention, police action and protester anger was sober reassessment by both organisers and protesters.

It set in motion a series of intense negotiations with Thabo Mbeki, a senior ANC official, later to become deputy-president, and then, president of South Africa, as the high-profile mediator.

Both sides agreed to the Mbeki compromise suggestion – that the tour be reduced to four one-day matches, in return for the protests being called off. Moreover, no matches would be played in Port Elizabeth and Cape Town, where opposition to the tour was strongest.

This agreement, though, was not unanimously accepted by NSC affiliates in the Western Cape; some members vowed to continue their protests until the tour in its entirety was scrapped – and a proposed second leg, scheduled for the following season, was immediately cancelled.

On 12 February 1990, the extent of opposition in Cape Town was emphasised when an explosive device was set off at the entrance to the Newlands cricket ground.

The negotiations with the NSC leadership culminated in Bacher addressing a media conference at the Wanderers on 13 February 1990, where he expressed a view much more

ANC mediator, Thabo Mbeki, managed to thrash out a compromise over Mike Gatting's rebel cricket tour.

in tune with the reality of the South African situation. "This is a time for reconciliation, a time for compromise," he said as he conceded that the tour had been "overrun by the politics of the day".

"In the interests of the country, we must acknowledge that the tour has been divisive; it has split communities, and the stage has come when we must back off. There are wider things happening in South Africa at the moment.

"There have been dramatic political changes, of which we approve – and, ultimately, the board has taken cognisance of this."

The second leg of the rebel tour, scheduled to take place early in the 1990/91 season was cancelled.

Significantly, Sacu backtracked from its hitherto obstinate stance regarding rebel tours and issued the following statement on 30 March 1990. "In the present political climate, tours are counterproductive to the medium- and long-term aims of the South African Cricket Union – and to the wider interest of South Africa as a whole."

UNITY TALKS

There was to be sunshine after the stormy weather generated by the Gatting tour: despite the anger of the preceding months, Sacu and the South African Cricket Board decided to open dialogue.

The ANC, the main power broker in sports unity talks, played a key role in getting the two bodies around the table, with Steve Tshwete, its sports spokesperson, later being dubbed "Mr Fixit" for his role in getting black and white sports bodies to unite under one banner.

On 4 August 1990, the South African Cricket Board took its first steps towards talks with Sacu when a majority of delegates voted to respond positively to a request by Bacher for dialogue.

Western Province Cricket Board president, Abe Adams, a staunch Sacos supporter, said that he was not against talks, but warned participants to be careful "not to be taken in by any [Sacu] trick".

The meeting, nevertheless, decided unanimously that the full executive of the board would meet with their Sacu counterparts for unity talks.

The first official contact between the two bodies took place on Saturday, 8 September 1990, at the Holiday Inn in Durban. At the meeting, chaired by Tshwete, the South African Cricket Board insisted that any relationship between it and Sacu should be based on Sacu's acceptance of a moratorium on all tours to and from South Africa.

On 16 December 1990, at a follow-up meeting between the two bodies, a steering committee was appointed, consisting of Geoff Dakin (president of Sacu), Krish Mackerdhuj (president of the SACB), Ronnie Pillay (secretary of the SACB), Percy Sonn (vice-president of the SACB), Peter van der Merwe (vice-president of Sacu) and Ali Bacher (managing director of Sacu).

The meeting also adopted a "declaration of intent", which was to form the basis for unity.

The steering committee directed that unity talks at provincial level should be initiated when the SACB and Sacu met again on 20 January 1991. The ambitious aim was to have unity at provincial level by early May 1991, and national unity by mid-June of the same year.

At the January 1991 meeting, matters had progressed to such a satisfactory extent that the national steering committee issued a directive that joint development committees be formed immediately within the provinces to direct the development of cricket at grassroots level within their respective areas.

Khaya Majola, the Eastern Province all-rounder, was appointed by the SACB to work with Ali Bacher on a national development project from 1 February 1991.

On 1 March 1991, the two bodies moved even closer together, when a SACB XI played against a Border Invitation XI at Buffalo Park in East London, a venue which had previously been out of bounds to SACB members.

Cricket's "declaration of intent"

HAVING REGARD for the future of South Africa, the South African Cricket Board and the South African Cricket Union declare that it is their intention to:

A. Form one nonracial democratic controlling body under a single constitution. The vision of nonracialism in a future South Africa shall include equality, irrespective of race, colour, creed, sex, religion, and shall mean equality in every sphere of life.

Nonracialism shall be the guiding principle in our endeavour to achieve unity, peace and harmony in cricket in our country.

B. To develop, administer and to make available opportunities for all those who wish to play cricket at all levels as soon as possible.

C. To immediately form a committee comprising members of the South African Cricket Union, the South African Cricket Board and the business community to formulate urgent strategies to urgently redress imbalances in regard to separate educational systems, sponsorships and facilities.

D. To contribute through cricket to the creation of a just society in South Africa, where everybody, democratically, has a common say and a common destiny.

E. To respect the sports moratorium against cricket tours to and from South Africa. To respect existing individual contracts pertaining to overseas professional cricketers playing in South Africa at present.

It will be the responsibility of the newly-formed national body, thereafter, to determine the desirability of overseas professional cricketers playing in South Africa.

F. To have respect for, and obtain recognition from, and membership of, the International Cricket Council.

G. To establish a working relationship with Sanroc and the Supreme Council of Sport in Africa.

H. To administer and share, with immediate effect, the resources within the development field.

I. To undertake to school the respective constituencies of the South African Cricket Board and the South African Cricket Union, of the spirit and letter with immediate effect.

WP CONCERNS

Nothing, of course, is ever simple — and while unity talks were proceeding

Being prepared

TO ENSURE that it would be well prepared for its first meeting to discuss unity with the Western Province Cricket Union, the Western Province Cricket Board established a number of committees to look at various aspects of administering cricket.

Constitutional committee: Sadick Emeran, Paul Saville, Norman Arendse and Donny Jurgens;

Schools and junior cricket committee: Abubakaar Taliep, Goosain Abrahams, Nazir Adam, Cliff February and Armien White;

Competitions and demarcation committee: Yunus Adams, Harold Arenz, Rodney Inglis and George van Oordt;

Coaching committee: Cyril Martin, Saait Magiet, Clinton Ravens and Beresford Williams

Facilities committee: Shafiek Mowzer, Solly Nosarka and André Odendaal;

Finance committee: Rushdi Magiet, Len Walsh, Gasant Jakoet, Eddie Harris, Abduragmaan Kamaar and Peter Heeger;

Selection committee: Rushdi Magiet, Coetie Neethling and Gertjie Williams.

Umpires: Humphrey Reid, Mohammed Bagus, Lionel February and Ray Bharoochi.

The committees were established to formulate the board's position in their respective areas of administration, before commencing negotiations with their Union counterparts.

smoothly at national level, SACB representatives in the Western Cape quickly demonstrated that they would not follow their parent body blindly.

Western Province Cricket Board clubs – notably Garlandale, Bishop Lavis, Malmesbury, Helderberg, Blue Bells and Victoria – expressed reservations about unity. They argued that the political changes in the country had not been sufficiently significant to warrant the SACB rushing into unity talks. Furthermore, clubs questioned whether Sacu had met all the preconditions for unity.

Krish Mackerdhuj and Geoff Dakin, the leaders of the two national bodies, were also criticised for submitting a joint memorandum to the International Cricket Council, in which it appeared that they were already making preparations for South Africa's readmission to test cricket – even though the unity process had only just begun.

Frank Brache, the secretary of the Western Province Cricket Union in 1991, revealed that the ANC leadership had warned the Western Province Cricket Board that they would be left behind if they did not come on board.

"The South African Cricket Union had direct contact with the ANC," Brache said.

"The ANC guaranteed that we would be in international cricket within 3-6 months if we played ball," said Brache.

Many of the Western Province Cricket Board's executive members stated privately that the SACB's long-standing preconditions for unity had not been met – but that they had been left with little alternative.

"I thought unity came too soon," said Sadick Emeran.

"We always discussed policy decisions at grassroots level in the SACB, but I don't think that this took place during the unity talks.

Emeran doubted, however, whether anything could have been done to rectify this situation. "Political organisations were in charge – and a sports organisation would not have been able to stop that drive," he said.

Rushdi Magiet said that he had been aware of objections from Sacos-aligned clubs, but he felt that events in the country such as the release from jail of Nelson Mandela and other leaders of the liberation struggle, and the initiation of talks between the government and the ANC, had set the pace for sporting bodies to follow.

On 20 February 1991, the Western Province Cricket Board executive was finally granted authorisation to proceed with unity talks with the Western Province Cricket Union.

Two days after being given the go-ahead to pursue unity, the executive of the board held an informal "break the ice" gathering with their Western Province Cricket Union counterparts at the Newlands Hotel.

"It was quite a strange feeling meeting them for the first time, but we got along well," said Emeran.

The first official meeting of the executive committees of the two bodies took place on 4 March 1991 at Newlands. The meeting adopted the "declaration of intent" agreed to by the SACB and Sacu, to put the unity process in the Western Province on track.

Representatives also elected a steering committee made up of Fritz Bing, Kevin Commins, Clem Druker, Percy Sonn, Ray Bharoochi and Moosa Sydow to drive the unity process.

A week later, on Sunday 10 March 1991, the process took another step forward when a successful minicricket festival, attended by 2 000 children, was jointly organised by the board and the union at the Stephen Reagon Oval in Mitchell's Plain

On the same day, Rushdi Magiet was appointed joint director of development, with the Western Province Cricket Union's Freek Burger.

The various committees also began a series of regular meetings to negotiate a common position.

Percy Sonn summed up the initial feelings of the respective delegations in his final president's report for the Western Province Cricket Board, in June 1991.

"Our counterparts initially displayed the same apprehensive anxiety as we did, in respect of the unknown quality of the opposition. I am, however, glad to say that the anxiety has been all but obliterated by the sincere wish of all and sundry to make unity work and thereby make cricket's contribution to the normalisation of our race-torn society."

HORSE-TRADING

As would be the case in any negotiations, more especially those involving participants from such vastly different backgrounds and experiences, there was a great deal of horse-trading between the two organisations.

Ray Bharoochi said that on one occasion he was called to a private meeting with the Western Province Cricket Union president, Clem Druker.

"He pointed out the financial and resource imbalances between our bodies, and suggested that this should be expressed in the constitution of our new executive," said Bharoochi.

"He tried to push the line that the union's superiority in the areas of finance and resources was an indication of overall superiority – and that this should be reflected in the composition of the new body.

"Of course, we did not agree with this point of view at all."

From their side, board representatives asked for the new body to be called the Western Province Cricket Board and for an official from the board to be chosen as president for the first two years.

This, board members argued, "will be a symbolic acknowledgment of historical injustices, and a visible sign that unity will involve a genuine marriage (instead of incorporation). It will loudly signal the start of a new era of nonracial cricket and reconciliation in the Western Cape".

However, through the process of negotiation, Druker of the Western Province Cricket Union was elected president, while the unified body was named the Western Province Cricket Association.

Board delegates did, however, manage to convince the Western Province Cricket Union to have a 50-50 representation at executive level, and on all committees. They also managed to push the issue of development and the redressing of imbalances in facilities to the top of the agenda.

Moreover, they succeeded in forging an agreement whereby the status quo, as far as the composition of the executive committee and the premier league was concerned, would remain for two years. There was also agreement that the presidency would be rotated.

The board was adamant that the first constitution should recognise the blatant inequalities of the past, and commit itself to addressing these inequalities, and to actively combating racism.

There was also an element of realism in the board's approach. The administration commission had decided at a meeting on 28 February 1991 that, "for historical and political reasons, the Western Province Cricket

Clem Druker became the first president of the united Western Province Cricket Association.

Into a new era

WITH ALL negotiations more or less completed, the Western Province Cricket Board elected a 10-man team for the new Western Province Cricket Association executive committee, at their final meeting on Tuesday, 18 June 1991, at UWC.

Those chosen were Percy Sonn (president), Peter Heeger, Abubakaar Taliep, André Odendaal, Yunus Adams, Shafiek Mowzer, Donny Jurgens, Rushdi Magiet, Sadick Emeran and Ray Bharoochi.

The Western Province Cricket Union was represented by Clem Druker (president), Erik van Vlaanderen, Bruce Anderson, Mickey Giles, Dave Martin, Richard Morris, Cyril O'Connor, Gavin Pfuhl, Eric Saxon and Chris Shutte.

Board has not been able to operate on the same professional lines as the Western Province Cricket Union, and therefore we accept in principle that the structure of the new unity body should be based on the lines of the union's structure, subject to possible amendments.

"For similar reasons, Newlands is the obvious choice to be the headquarters of the new body".

On Tuesday, 25 June 1991, the new Western Province Cricket Association was inaugurated at the Protea Suite, Newlands.

Fritz Bing, the immediate past president of the Western Province Cricket Union, told the gathering: "We never wanted two bodies – they were forced on us. But they are, hopefully, a thing of the past – and I am delighted that the process has gone so smoothly."

In his first address as president of the new Western Province Cricket Association, Druker said: "Gathered here are those who have sacrificed much – and who are the logical leaders of our unified body. We are... destined to guide the game into the 21st century. It is a task which must fill us with awe.

"That which brings us together will also serve as the cement which will bind us, which will engender feelings of mutual respect. In order for cricket to benefit, we have to put aside our differences. We must work in the present, for the future, drawing from the past only those elements which will unite us, and abandoning forever those which would serve to undermine unity. Let us not work under constant reminders of past injustices and inequalities – rather let our labours be such so that there shall be no chance of ever repeating the errors and omissions of the past."

Percy Sonn, the first vice-president of the new body, assured Druker of the unstinting support of all the ex-board members. "We have committed ourselves to new ideals and I don't doubt for a minute the sincerity of the union people we have met."

Unity in Western Province cricket was particularly welcomed by Matt Segers and Barney Leendertz, both of whom were part of the formation of the Western Province Cricket Board in 1959.

For Segers, unity was a dream come true – "the greatest day" of his life. "At last we can see what we have struggled for being realised," he said.

Leendertz concurred: "Our struggle over so many years has not been in vain," he said

Segers and Leendertz were both made life-members of the new body.

NEW CHALLENGES

Uniting the two organisations under the banner of the Western Province Cricket Association did not mean utopia had arrived. In fact, the new body was immediately faced with a number of thorny issues.

One of the first challenges facing the association was the deadlocked situation relating to the status of the Defence, Police and Prisons teams – regarded as non-negotiables by both the board and the union.

Ex-board clubs saw the members of these clubs as part of the oppressive state machinery, which played a major role in the brutal suppression of anti-apartheid protests.

Members of the former Western Province Cricket Union, however, were adamant that they would stand by their teams. In agreeing to disagree on the issue, the two groups referred the matter to the national body, the United Cricket Board for a decision.

The UCB subsequently referred the matter back to the Western Province

Cricket Association, who, in turn, left it up to individual clubs to decide what to do. Initially Westridge, Primrose and Victoria refused to play against Defence – a decision which was respected by the association. The matter was finally resolved after the first democratic elections in April 1994, when the security forces became part of the new, democratic state.

FACILITIES

Given the vast imbalances in resources between the board and the union, the issue of facilities was given immediate attention.

The financial disparity between the two unions was clearly illustrated in their respective cash reserves. Figures presented to the inaugural meeting of the two bodies' finance committees in June 1990, had shown that the Western Province Cricket Union had R970 000 and the Western Province Cricket Board R15 000. The union had liabilities of R250 000, and the board had none.

Another problem confronting the new association was the initial rejection of the unity process by the Western Province primary schools and senior schools sports associations, both associate members of the board.

"We withdrew from the board, following a conference in Pacaltsdorp, where we decided that unity was being used to get white South Africa back into international sport," said Robbie van Graan, cricket convenor of the primary schools union.

The Western Province Senior Schools Sports Union also felt that it could not become part of any unity process until a single education department had been set up. However, the NSC started to attract increasing numbers of schools to their fold, until, eventually, after a few years all schools

had become part of the Western Province Cricket Association.

The first combined net practices, which took place at Pinelands indoor nets in July 1991, did not meet with the unanimous approval of all the ex-board players. Ismail Behardien, a member of the 1991 SACB XI, complained that coach, Hylton Ackerman, had completely ignored the board batsmen, while giving all the union players the first opportunity to bat.

"It was fine for the bowlers because they were always needed, but it was frustrating to see only the ex-union batsmen being called to pad up. Eventually, Ebrahim Gafieldien, an ex-board opening batsman, got tired of hanging around. He padded up and went into the nets without invitation. Some of us were really demotivated and didn't return for the next session," said Behardien.

TOURS

While many former board members were under the impression that the United Cricket Board of South Africa was still committed to the sports moratorium, they were faced with the reality of a tour to India by a South African team shortly after the country was admitted to the ICC on 10 July 1991.

The executive was called to a specially arranged meeting on 2 November 1991, where the issue of the tour was raised. Eleven of the 12 Western Province Cricket Association executive members voted for the tour; only Ray Bharoochi voted against it.

After the meeting, Clem Druker, the president of the association, said in a statement that tours generated finance, which was sorely needed to develop cricket in all communities.

Later, Norman Arendse and Moosa Sydow objected to South Africa's application to play in the 1992 World

Cup in Australia and New Zealand, but were told it was a UCB matter.

"What worried me was the movement within the corridors of power," said Sydow. "It seemed as if people were only interested in getting themselves into positions. I put up resistance to this to such an extent that I was seen as a threat and eventually sidelined."

Magiet attacked – again

MOOSA SYDOW was particularly critical of the role played by Rushdi Magiet in the unity process. Writing in his WP Cricket Board secretarial report for the 1990/91 season, Sydow questioned "the role of the treasurer (Magiet) during the whole process".

Sydow said that Magiet had served on practically all committees, "where he became encamped within the confines/corridors of the WPCU".

Responding to allegations that he was jockeying for position through his presence on a variety of committees, Magiet said that he practically ran the Western Province Cricket Board on a full-time basis during its last few years of existence.

"I was treasurer, convenor of selectors and manager of the Howa Bowl team. I also organised junior coaching clinics.

"I didn't receive a cent for doing this. In fact, I delegated the managership of the Howa Bowl side to George van Oordt during the last season because I could not cope with my workload. Because I was so heavily involved I found myself floating between committees," said Magiet.

Magiet served on the facilities, finance, selection, development and the competitions committees. He also represented the board on the national steering committee involved in the unity process.

"We certainly did not compromise. Everything we asked for that was realistic was agreed on. We certainly never compromised on our principles. In fact we blocked the NSC on many issues, such as equal representation on the executive – a matter on which they wanted us to compromise," Magiet added.

Donny Jurgens, who served on the WPCB executive agreed with Magiet that they had not sacrificed anything at the altar of unity. "I don't buy the notion that we sold out. We met all the conditions of our mandate," he said.

A NEW SACOS BODY

While the majority of clubs in the board agreed to a united provincial body, nine clubs opted to form their own Sacos-aligned cricket organisation, the Cricket Board of Western Province. The organisation lasted two years before folding. "To us society was still not normal," said Willie Adams, who, almost a decade after unity, still refused to go to Newlands.

"We felt that the time was not yet right for unity. We said, 'let all the things that were promised, such as a universal franchise, the abolition of the Group Areas Act, and the end of segregated education first be implemented – and then let's talk about unity.'"

"It was not so much unity that we fought against, but the method in which unity was forged," said Amien Jacobs, the chairman of Garlandale Cricket Club.

"Your principles are too rigid" – the end of the road for Sacos

FOR THE South African Council on Sport (Sacos), the changing of the guard in South Africa during the early 1990s was a painful, bitter, humiliating experience....

After having spent more than a decade helping to shut all routes to apartheid South Africa's participation in international sport, Sacos suddenly found itself being pushed more and more into the background.

"Too rigid" – "not innovative enough" – "unwilling to compromise" – "too much coloured and Indian, too little African" – were some of its shortcomings, according to its detractors.

What was needed was a sports body that would appeal to all South Africans.

Sacos watched with a growing sense of disbelief (and, let it be said, helplessness) as many officials and participants who, just a few months earlier, would have been considered sworn enemies of nonracial sport, embrace the new sports and political set-up.

Addressing the 10th annual biennial general meeting of the organisation in Cape Town on 27 March 1993, Sacos president Joe Ebrahim conceded that the previous two years had been the most difficult in the history of Sacos.

"Never before has the organisation and, in particular its principles and policies, been the subject of such an intensive, comprehensive and sustained attack," Ebrahim said.

"But in contrast to the position which prevailed previously, those now in the forefront of these attacks are... from the ranks of the oppressed.

"Ironically, amongst them are individuals who, at one time or another, were fairly vociferous in their support for Sacos and nonracial sport.

"They are now the new promoters of multinational sport and, in their efforts to win the confidence of their newfound allies, are even more condemnatory than the latter have been of nonracial sport and what it epitomises."

Ebrahim was critical of the leadership of nonracial codes who had decided to participate in the unity process.

"We are witnessing the emergence of what can only be described as an insatiable thirst for power on the part of certain people, especially those who hold prominent positions in organisations," he said.

Ebrahim lashed out at former nonracial sports bodies for unconditionally accepting apartheid sports authorities.

"Even more damning has been the effusive praise showered on administrators of racist sport, who were instrumental in organising rebel tours – tours during which members of the oppressed who demonstrated against them taking place were imprisoned and even killed. How such individuals could be lauded for having contributed towards the 'normalisation' of South African sport defies comprehension."

Ebrahim defended the contentious double standards resolution (DSR)

Joe Ebrahim noted in 1993 that the most virulent critics of Sacos came from within the "ranks of the oppressed".

Self-examination

AT A MEETING in Cape Town on 21-22 September 1985 Sacos had already recognised some of its shortcomings.

"Sacos claims to be the sportswing of the liberation movement. If there is agreement that we have to build or extend our mass base, one of the concrete issues that need urgent attention is to examine ways and means of how to organise sport more effectively and efficiently. There is therefore a need to attract sportspeople from the townships and also to try to prevent the continual defection of Sacos members to the multinational sports organisations," Sacos said in a statement.

Some of the key areas that needed urgent attention, the meeting noted, were coaching schemes, sports facilities and sponsorships.

Frank van der Horst, in his presidential address at the 6th biennial general meeting of Sacos on 27 April 1985 in Durban, remarked: "We have to guard against being characterised a bureaucracy by dictating highfalutin policy to our players. We have to guard against alienating our players by propounding ideas which are way above them. We should rather take note of the development of our players at club level. We have to encourage them and take them further."

Unfortunately, Sacos, for a variety of reasons, did not address these shortcomings as the organisation was overtaken by the wave of political changes which engulfed South Africa in the late 1980s and early 90s.

saying "it has proved an exceptionally effective means of distinguishing the sincerity of people".

NSC

Sacos' main critic was the National Sports Congress. In a discussion document dated September 1990, the NSC set itself up as the "progressive alternative" to Sacos, stating that the latter had not moved with the times.

"When the struggles of the 1980s laid the foundations for mass action that went beyond mere protest, sport started lagging behind other sectors of the struggle in making the change from reactive to power, to transformational politics.

"Sacos (which had become the leader of the nonracial sports struggle after the banning of the early organisations) continued to hold onto strategies and tactics which were becoming static, outdated and counterproductive. Its actions started becoming more and more out of tune with those of the ANC, the United Democratic Front, the Congress of South African Trade Unions, and other organisations which were spearheading the mass struggles.

"It was against the background of sportspeople demanding change from Sacos that the NSC emerged in an attempt to locate sport more squarely with the broader liberation struggle.

"In 1988, pro-Mass Democratic Movement supporters within the ANC formed an interim committee of the NSC. Unable to reform Sacos from within, the NSC launched itself as a formal organisation in May 1990," the document states.

The NSC claimed credit for stopping all rebel tours through its programme of mass action, and also claimed to have replaced Sacos as the recognised representative of nonracial sport. "Establishment sport, having

realised that the NSC holds the key to the future, has been falling over its feet to discuss unity," the NSC said.

"The NSC grabbed the initiative regarding the future of South African sport by hosting unity talks in soccer and several other codes, something which Sacos was incapable of doing because of its rigid principles. This strengthened the position of nonracial sport in the sports struggle within the country."

The NSC criticised Sacos' inability to penetrate the African townships and rural areas. "Sacos tried hard to unite oppressed sportspeople, but was hampered by its policies and its location in the so-called coloured and Indian Group Areas," NSC officials said.

The NSC decided to align itself with the ANC/MDM

"The relationship between the NSC and Sacos is at this stage strained, to say the least. Sacos has declared us a rival body.

"Sacos fulfilled an important role in the past, But, we believe, it has played out its role. It has been overtaken by history. Its inability to become based in the townships, its preference for talk rather than action and its ideological rigidity are fatal barriers to progress."

Sacos supporter, Willie Adams, admitted that with the benefit of hindsight, some strategic mistakes made by Sacos had lost it a great deal of support.

"Perhaps we were too rigid in applying the double standards resolution. We were interfering in the household affairs of people by prescribing to them where they could or couldn't go.

"We should also have concentrated much more on developing our sport. We should have sent our sportspersons overseas on coaching courses and to play in order to provide them with incentives and to improve their sport," said Adams.

Part 7

Local competitions

SO WHERE were you when Owen Williams was turning them sideways on balmy Saturday afternoons at Rosmead in ... was it 1968? Or, do you remember Dik Abed taking Metropolitan – or was it Wynberg – to the cleaners in 1969?

"Hmmm, those were the days," the old-timers, who used to follow the fortunes of the Western Province Cricket Board's top players will tell you.

"Local cricket was a serious business in those days."

And, indeed, it was.

The Williamses, the Abeds, the Behardiens, the Neethlings, the Van Graans and a host of others were wonderful value for money – because they prepared themselves well and never gave less than a one hundred percent effort.

Even on sub-standard pitches.

Small wonder then that they attracted droves of spectators wherever they played.

INTRODUCTION

Although the respective unions played each other on a regular basis after the formation of the Western Province Cricket Board in 1959, the first major inter-union competition was only introduced in the 1966/67 season – and then only after much discussion.

Prior to that, a "champion of champions" club competition, with the Fester Trophy at stake, was the most prestigious inter-union event in the Board.

The Fester Trophy pitted the champion teams of all 13 affiliated unions against one another on a round robin basis.

The Cape District side, Oakdale, led by Williams, proved to be the most successful team. They took the honours for six successive seasons, with only St Augustines of the Metropolitan union looking remotely capable of mounting any sort of challenge to their superiority.

Even when the much discussed inter-union competition – known as the Super League – was finally introduced in the 1966/67 season, two of the board's top unions did not particpate. Cape District (home of the champion club, Oakdale) and the Western Province Cricket Association (the South African home union of Dik Abed) had strong objections to the structure of the competition. They later relented, with Cape District joining the following year, and the Western Province Cricket Association coming on board in the 1968/69 season.

The Super League and the Fester Trophy, which was later played for by the unions on a limited overs basis, proved to be popular competitions, attracting large and colourful crowds at the various venues around the peninsula.

The cricket was of a high quality and the toughness of the competition was reflected in the success of Western Province in the South African Cricket Board of Control interprovincial competitions.

After the failure of the unity process with the Western Province Cricket Union in the 1976/77 season, a new club structure was introduced, with the unions falling away. Many smaller clubs merged to form bigger and stronger entities.

By the 1980/81 season, all premier league matches were played on turf; prior to this, most board matches had been played on rather dangerous matting wickets.

In 1986/87, day-night cricket was introduced, first at the Athlone Stadium and, later, at the much better UWC Stadium in Bellville. The board's last two limited overs finals before unity were played under lights at UWC.

The board's senior competitions were dominated by three clubs – Primrose, United and Montrose. It may not have been a coincidence that all three clubs had considerably more financial muscle than their opponents, which enabled them to attract the top players in the board (although they also had thriving junior sections, a part of board activities which had been neglected for far too long.

Vintage cricket – inter-union competitions (1966-1976)

IN THE late 1960s and early 1970s, in the golden years of the Western Province Cricket Board's inter-union competition, spectators – of which there were many in those days – were spoilt for choice.

A trip to Rosmead, in Claremont, often offered the tantalising prospect of Cape District left-arm spinner, Owen Williams, tormenting batsmen from other unions across the peninsula; at Green Point Track, Dik Abed was as much of a hero among doting supporters of the Western Province Cricket Association as he had become among supporters of Enfield, in the Lancashire League. Those who followed the fortunes of Maitland-Parow, had their own answer to Abed – a fellow by the name of Coetie Neethling. And Metropolitan had a k-handed spinner, appropriately named Lefty (Adams), who had an awesome reputation for turning lost causes into glorious victories....

Cape District versus Western Province Cricket Association – Williams versus Abed; Maitland-Parow versus Metropolitan – Neethling versus Adams; Wynberg versus Somerset West – Ivan Dagnin versus Des February; Braima Isaacs, Saait Magiet, Robbie van Graan ... the combinations were endless, the possibilities mouth-watering.

A WINNING FORMULA

The Super League competition, introduced in the 1966/67 season, provided the major local competition for the Western Province Cricket Board's top players. With teams divided into A and B sections, according to their strength, the cricket played was of a high standard.

Getting into their respective board teams represented a major challenge for the province's top players – board honours, after all, was just one step away from the ultimate (for board players) – provincial honours.

In the 1967/68 season, the Fester Trophy was changed from an inter-club to an inter-union competition. Played initially by teams divided into two sections, with the winner of the A-section meeting the winner of the B-section in the final, the competition underwent several changes: first, in the 1970/71 season, a knockout format was introduced; then, from the 1972/73 season onwards, it became part of the trend towards instant cricket, when it was changed into a limited overs competition.

The Fester Trophy competition had first seen the light of day as the culmination of a championship battled out between the top sides of each union.

The powerful Oakdale Cricket Club of Cape District had won the competition for six years in succession. During this period, only the Metropolitan side, St Augustines, had posed any threat to Owen Williams' team.

Limited-overs cricket among board affiliates was first introduced in competitions by the Wynberg union in 1971.

The first matches were played over 30 overs, with each bowler limited to five overs and no more than five fielders being allowed to be more than 30 metres from the bat.

Super League and Fester Trophy cricket generated a tremendous atmosphere at matches. The Green Point Track, Rosmead, William Herbert sportsground and Turfhall, as well as grounds in Bellville and Somerset West, were always packed.

HIGH STANDARDS

"The standard of Super League cricket was very close to that of the provincial game," said former Western Province wicketkeeper, Braima Isaacs, a member of the Metropolitan side which won the competition for three consecutive seasons, from the 1971/72 season onwards.

"The banter among the crowd was something I looked forward to. Although the fans were very partisan, they always ribbed the opposition in a good natured way. This added to the atmosphere at the games," Isaacs said.

Sometimes the rivalry would extend to religious affiliation, without causing any friction, according to Omar Henry.

"When I played for [the mainly Muslim] WP Cricket Association in the Super League against [the mainly Christian] Maitland-Parow, the religious divide became very obvious by the type of comment made on the field," said Henry.

"There wasn't friction, but it was very competitive.

"The Super League was a good place to play in, because it provided players with a tough mental test.

"It helped me grow as a cricketer. It made me tougher. If it wasn't for my Super League experiences, I probably would have fallen by the wayside when I went over to the white side," said Henry, who became the first black player to represent South Africa in test cricket, when he played against the touring Indian team in 1992.

Maitland-Parow, under the leadership of the great Coetie Neethling, won the inaugural Super League in 1966/67, as well as the Fester Trophy.

However, two of the strongest unions, Cape District and the Western Province Cricket Association did not participate because they disagreed with the structure of the competition.

Robbie van Graan, the tall, stylish Metropolitan top-order batsman scored the first Super League century – 128 against Somerset West.

Cape District, captained by the star left-arm spinner, Owen Williams, joined the Super League the following year – and won the competition at their first attempt.

By the beginning of the 1968/69 season, the Western Province Cricket Association had sorted out their problems with the board. And, like Cape District and Maitland-Parow, they also won the title at their first attempt.

Led by Gasant "Tiny" Abed, regarded by many as one of South Africa's greatest all rounders, the Western Province Cricket Association proved to be a major force in the competition. When Tiny reached the end of his illustrious career, his mantle was taken over by his younger brother, Sulaiman, better known by his nickname, "Dik", who provided the team with class – and steel.

It was not only Abed's performances with bat and ball that proved crucial to the success of the Western Province Cricket Association side –

his tactical knowledge also proved decisive.

One of the most amazing spells of bowling in Super League cricket came from the Maitland-Parow off-spinner, Gertjie Williams, who claimed an incredible six wickets for one run against the champions, the Western Province Cricket Association, at the Green Point Track in the 1968/69 season. Maitland-Parow won the match by two wickets to avenge a first-round defeat.

In the same season, Coetie Neethling returned amazing figures of 6/5 for Maitland-Parow against Wynberg, who were dismissed for 33 in their first innings.

Reggie Bowers, the Metropolitan opening bowler, also turned in one of the season's outstanding performances – 8/16 against the strong Cape District side.

In the 1969/70 season, the Western Province Cricket Association shared the Super League with Maitland-Parow – thanks to Abed's all-round performances.

Soon afterwards, Abed decided not to return to South Africa. It signalled the beginning of a rocky patch for the association: hard though they tried, they never again won a trophy in board competitions.

After losing to the Western Province Cricket Association in the Fester Trophy final in the 1969/70 season, the Turfhall-based Metropolitan side, under the astute captaincy of Lefty Adams, gained revenge the following season, albeit under controversial circumstances. The Western Province Cricket Association, thanks to an outstanding allround performance by Dik Abed (64 and 5/25), fought back brilliantly from a first innings deficit of 117, to set Metropolitan a victory target of 105 in 140 minutes.

Although they managed to stave off defeat, Metropolitan were accused of time-wasting and using "unconventional" tactics; when bad light stopped play, they were tottering at 92/9. Metropolitan's Fester Trophy triumph was its first success in its 12-year history.

Having broken the ice, went on to win a hattrick of Super League titles – thanks mainly to its explosive batting lineup consisting of players such as the Van Graan brothers, Robbie and Kitty, Kenny Rodriques and Braima Isaacs. Their bowling, spearheaded by the fearsome St Augustines opening pair of Jock Mahoney and Marshall September, was complemented by the left-arm spin of Lefty Adams and Basil Petersen, and the leg-spin of Clive Kolbe.

In the 1971/72 season, the Super League hours of play were extended by one hour per day. Instead of playing between 12.30pm and 6.30 pm, the starting time of matches was brought forward to 11.30 am, to allow the teams more time to get results.

Metropolitan's third Super League success came in the 1973/74 season – with a little help from the Western Province Cricket Association. Off-spinner Shamiel Jassiem, with an inspirational spell of bowling, which saw him bagging six wickets for 10 runs (including a hattrick), played the leading role in helping the Green Point-based side to a draw against Cape District, Metropolitan's closest rivals. Prior to his rich haul, Jassiem had the rather less impressive figures of 1/64. To complete a fine allround performance, Jassiem then scored a fine, unbeaten 52 to to help hold Cape District at bay.

Wynberg, under the captaincy of Dickie Conrad, won their first (and only) trophy when they beat the favourites, Maitland-Parow, by 26 runs in the 1972/73 Fester Trophy final at Somerset West. For the first time, the competition had been played on a 40-overs-per-side basis.

The victory was a fitting finale for Wynberg, who amalgamated with their neighbours, Cape District, the following season. The two units, playing under the banner of the Claremont-based, Cape District, proved to be too strong for the opposition – they won the next three Super League titles until the competition's demise in the 1975/76 season.

Cape District, under the leadership of Rushdi Magiet, won the last Super League trophy in 1975/76, by beating Maitland-Parow by an innings in the last game of the season. Metropolitan, their nearest challengers, were held to a draw by the Western Province Cricket Association. Cape District, strengthened by the acquisition of Metropolitan stalwarts, Braima Isaacs and Lefty Adams clinched the double by also winning the Fester Trophy (which was played on a round robin format). The inter-union competition was played for the last time in the 1975/76 season. The following season, the long-awaited club competition was introduced.

Even though the Super League inter-union competition proved popular and provided a high standard of cricket, questions about its future were already being asked in 1971, during talks that had been called to find ways of improving the game.

With the board stating that it had 13 unions and 130 clubs, calls were made for clubs to amalgamate.

THE BIG EIGHT

The introduction of the Big Eight limited-overs tournament in the 1972/73 season was the first indication that an inter-club competition might replace the union structure, which up to then had provided the leading competition for the top board players.

St Augustines, one of the most enthusiastic supporters of a club championship, invited other leading clubs in the board to discuss the matter. The talks among clubs yielded much common ground. Soon, agreement was reached on the inauguration of an inter-club limited-overs competition – played for among the board's eight leading clubs, on a Sunday.

The first eight participants were: Ottomans (Western Province Cricket Association), Victoria (Cape District), Pioneer and St Augustine (Metropolitan), Wynberg and Primrose (Wynberg), Tygerberg (Maitland-Parow) and All Saints (Somerset West).

The first competition was won by St Augustines, with Primrose finishing runners up.

In its second season, the Big Eight tournament was rocked by the withdrawal of Muslim clubs, who objected on religious grounds to the competition being sponsored by the Smirnoff liquor company. The limited-overs tournament, which attracted the top clubs in the board, was watched by large crowds at the centralised venue of Turfhall in Lansdowne.

Although the Big Eight continued for another season, a new 50-over competition – sponsored by Golden Yolk, an egg company owned by Ebrahim Dawood, one of the board's main financial backers – was launched in December 1974, at Rosmead. Participants were Bellville, Walmers, Primrose, Vineyards, Pioneers, Blue Bells, Elsies River and Ottomans. This competition also proved popular among players and spectators.

The battle to be the WP Cricket Board's top club

PRIMROSE AND United threatened to turn the Western Province Cricket Board's new inter-club competition into a two-horse race in the first few years after its inauguration in 1976. This wasn't surprising – both sides were packed with players with provincial experience.

Primrose, especially, could call on the services of Rushdi and Saait Magiet, Lefty Adams, Braima Isaacs, MZ Allie, Yusuf "Gogs" Adams, Cyril Martin, Shadley Martin, Ronnie Witbooi and Goolam Allie.

United, too, boasted an abundance of talent, with Armien Jabaar, Seraj Gabriels, Mogamat Galant, Baby Damon, Munsoor Abullah and Yusuf Abed giving them the edge over most teams. Primrose won the inaugural Premier league in 1976, as well as the limited-overs Grand Challenge (round robin) and the Golden Yolk (knockout) competitions.

UPSETS

United, led by Armien Jabaar, snatched league honours from under the noses of their arch-rivals, Primrose, in the 1977/78 season, thanks to St Augustines holding the champions to a draw.

Still, Primrose did not finish the season empty-handed. They beat United by eight wickets in the Golden Yolk limited-overs final at the Green Point Track – and then offered to share the title with United after MZ Allie was found to have contravened Sacos' double standards policy.

In 1979, the first division side, Hottentots Holland, pulled off what must rank as the biggest upset in the history of the Western Province Cricket Board, when they beat the star-studded Primrose in the 1979 Golden Yolk final at Westridge in Mitchells Plain.

Playing in front of a vociferous crowd, the underdogs from the Strand made a modest 132/9 in their 40 overs, thanks mainly to Yunus Thomas (28*) and Sheraat Arnold (27) who put on a precious 53 for the eighth wicket.

Medium-pacer Anwar Daniels then ripped out the heart of the Primrose middle-order batting to finish with 4/27, as Primrose crashed to 89 all out to give the Strand side their most famous victory.

Primrose continued to dominate the board's senior competitions for two more years – until the youthful Victoria side, led by Charlie van Schalkwyk, broke their stranglehold.

THE RISE OF VICTORIA

In the 1980/81 season, Victoria claimed their first and only senior trophy, by comfortably winning the league title.

Spearheaded by a superb pair of strike bowlers in Vincent Barnes and Johnny Kleinveldt, Victoria destroyed the rest of the opposition. They

The move to turf wickets

"WHEN I look back now,I find it hard to believe that we played on matting wickets – without helmets," said Vincent Barnes, who often proved unplayable on this type of wicket.

"All of the matting wickets were extremely lively and bouncy. The Rosmead matting wicket, especially, was very dangerous – and some players got badly hurt there. I remember hitting Saait Magiet, who had a very good eye, on the head in a match against `Primrose at Rosmead.

In 1981, turf wickets were laid at Rosmead and Turfhall, to add to the existing wickets at Elfindale, Avonwood and Westridge. Elfindale was the only ground to be owned by a club (St Augustines)

"We managed to get the ground, which was probably the worst available in the new area of Elfindale, from the city council," said the St Augustines' chairman, Paul Saville.

"Thanks to the generous assistance of Garden Cities and Murray and Roberts, we managed to work it into a playable state."

Later, a turf wicket was also laid at the Green Point Track. Board matches were also played at the Rocklands complex in Mitchell's Plain, where conditions were far from ideal. There was hardly any discernible difference between the outfield and the green pitches, which inevitably favoured the bowlers.

In addition, the venue being located close to the coastline, lent itself to blustery conditions which was not conducive to good cricket.

emphasised their dominance by humiliating Primrose, the defending champions – beating them by an innings in the last match of the season. Barnes took 9/13 and 5/10 as Primrose collapsed to totals of 59 and 49.

Montrose, soon to establish themselves as the team of the Eighties, provided a sign of things to come when they annexed the limited overs Tiger Oats competition in 1980/81. Having just won promotion from the first division, and led by the newly-recruited Armien Jabaar, they surprised their more experienced opponents, Metropolitan, beating them by 28 runs.

The following season Montrose went on a strong recruitment drive, signing provincial players such as Munsoor Abdullah, MZ Allie, Nasser Antulay and Reggie February to bolster the side. Later, when other provincial players such as Vincent Barnes, Clinton Ravens, Mark Rasmus, Leon Roberts, Jacko van Graan, Nilton Muller and Nazeem White joined the club, Montrose had virtually the entire WP Howa Bowl team on their books.

After winning the league at their first attempt in 1981/82, Montrose went one better the following season when they claimed the league and limited-overs double – the first of two such successes. United began re-establishing themselves in the limited overs competitions from the 1985/86 season onwards. In the space of five years they played in four finals, winning two of them. Their two successive final encounters against Montrose must rank as the most tense matches ever played in the board. In the 1985/86 final, United scraped home by one run. The following year, Montrose turned the tables, squeaking in by two runs in a low-scoring match.

After being well-beaten by Primrose in the 1987/88 final, United, strengthened by the acquisition of the star all-rounder, Faiek Davids, and provincial opener Rashaad Musson, came back two years later to beat Rivertonians in a day/night final – another first for the board. In the 1989/90 season, the most successful in its history, United won the double.

Stellenbosch denied Montrose their third double by beating the favourites with surprising ease in what was to be the board's last limited overs competition final. Stellenbosch reached their victory target of 188 with six wickets and more than six overs to spare. Despite their defeat, Montrose (six league and five limited overs titles), together with Primrose (six league and six limited overs titles) and United (two league and five limited overs titles) will go down in history as the most successful sides in the Western Province Cricket Board's premier league, which lasted for 15 seasons.

Only Victoria managed to break their dominance by winning the league once, while Stellenbosch and Hottentots Holland won the limited overs titles once each – but very much against expectation.

Trophy winners Inter-union competition

1966/67

Super League: Maitland-Parow

Fester Trophy: Maitland-Parow

Scores in Final:

Paarl First innings 96 (G. Roux 22*; H. Arendse 20; Ralph van der Heuwel 3/10; Coetie Neethling 2/9; Derek Fester 2/11; Kosie Williams 2/14)

Second innings 106 (Gertjie Williams 5/39; Ralph van der Heuwel 3/26)

Maitland-Parow 210 (Gertjie Williams 56; Coetie Neethling 54; Ralph van der Heuwel 32; Kosie Williams 31; E. Bastiaan 3/31; A. Fortuin 2/21; S. Davids 2/25; L. Lawrence 2/41)

Maitland-Parow won by an innings and 8 runs

1967/68

Super League: Cape District

1968/69

Super League: WP Cricket Association

Fester Trophy: Stellenbosch Cricket Union

1969/70

Super League: WP Cricket Association/Maitland Parow (shared)

Fester Trophy: WP Cricket Association

Scores in Final:

Metropolitan First innings 99 (Kenny Rodriques 38; Lefty Adams 21; Dik Abed 4/26; Sep Davids 3/33; Zak Davids 2/24)

Second innings 153/9 dec (Basil Petersen 55*; Ivan van Rooi 26; Basil Witten 20; Sep Davids 3/4; Dik Abed 2/43)

WPCA First innings 128 (Taliep Behardien 30; Colin Joshua 21; Lobo Abed 20; David Lamb 3/25; Basil Petersen 2/17; Johnny le Roux 2/26)

Second innings 125/6 (Salie Meyer 43; Zaghlul Adams 37; Dik Abed 20*)

WP Cricket Association won on the first innings.

1970/71

Super League: WP Cricket Association

Fester Trophy : Metropolitan

Scores in Final:

WPCA First innings 80 (Colin Joshua 35; Basil Petersen 4/20; Lefty Adams 4/31)

Second innings 221/7 declared (Dik Abed 64; Colin Joshua 43; Zaghlul Adams 41;Taliep Behardien 38; Lefty Adams 5/81; Basil Petersen 2/104)

Metropolitan First innings 197 (Horatio Phillips 53; Norman Adams 26; Gerald Poggenpoel 23; Jumannah Khan 3/59; Colin Joshua 2/30; Dik Abed 2/32)

Second innings 92/9 (Gerald Poggenpoel 26; Dik Abed 5/25; Zak Davids 2/25)

Metropolitan won on the first innings.

1971/72

Super League: Metropolitan

Fester Trophy: Cape District

Scores in Final:

WPCA First innings 203 (Mogamat Jumat 59; Armien Jabaar 23; Taliep Behardien 21; Reggie Petersen 3/21; Willie Londt 3/44)

Second innings 140/8 declared (Zak Davids 42; Taliep Behardien 24*; Willie Londt 4/24)

Cape District First innings 262 (Tubba Andrews 83; Brian O'Connell 40; Jumannah Khan 5/75)

Second innings. 83/1 (Tubba Andrews 42*; Brian Roman 33*)

Cape District won by 9 wickets.

1972/73

Super League: Metropolitan

Fester Trophy: Wynberg

Scores in Final

Wynberg 171 (40 overs) (Dickie Conrad 79; Ivan Dagnin 22; Coetie Neethling 3/12; David Jantjies 3/47; Archie Sonn 2/22)

Maitland-Parow 142 (39 Overs) (Coetie Neethling 48; Kulu Maclons 23; Rushdi Magiet 3/11; Sydney Snyders 2/14; Pinky Carelse 2/22)

Wynberg won by 29 runs

1973/74

Super League: Metropolitan

Fester Trophy: Cape District

Scores in Final:

WP Cricket Association (40 overs) 149 (Karriem Kahaar 58; Munsoor Abdullah 22; Armien Jabaar 21; Jacko van Graan 5/32; Charlie van Schalkwyk 3/25)

Cape District (37,4 Overs) 150/9 (Mohammed Bagus 30; Ivan Dagnin 29; Ismail Timol 23; Ebrahim Damon 3/29; Shamiel Jassiem 3/26)

Cape District won by one wicket

Day/Night games

DAY/NIGHT cricket in the Western Province Cricket Board was pioneered in 1986 by Rashid Paleker, the hard-working chairman of the Combine Cricket Union, who organised a match between a Combine XI and a Western Province XI at the Athlone Stadium.

Although the lights were nowhere near the required standard, there was enough interest to ensure that day/night cricket would become a permanent feature in the Western Province Cricket Board.

1974/75

Super League: Cape District

Fester Trophy: Cape District

Scores in Final:

Cape District (57,2 overs) 210 (Saait Magiet 113*;
Reggie Bowers 3/41; Basil Petersen 2/37; Jock
Mahoney 2/37; George van Oordt 2/37)

Metropolitan (53,1 Overs) 168 (George van Oordt 32;
Mike Finnan 31; Braima Isaacs 20; Kim Blaauw 5/33)

Cape District won by 42 runs

60 overs competition

1975/76

Super League: Cape District

Fester Trophy: Cape District (round robin basis)

New inter-club structure

1976/77

League: Primrose

Grand Challenge (round robin): Primrose

Golden Yolk: Primrose

Scores in Final:

St Augustines 87

Primrose 89/6 (Rushdi Magiet 45)

Primrose won by 4 wickets

1977/78

League: United

Grand Challenge (round robin): Primrose

Golden Yolk: Primrose/United (Primrose won match, but
agreed to share after protest from United against MZ
Allie, who played soccer for Glendene at Green Point
Stadium in contravention of Sacos' policy)

Scores in Final:

United 118 (Armien Jabaar 52)

Primrose 120/3 (MZ Allie 56*)

Primrose won by 7 wickets

1978/79

League: Primrose

Grand Challenge (round robin): Primrose

Golden Yolk: Hottentots Holland

Scores in Final:

Hottentots Holland 132/9 (40 Overs) (Yunus Thomas
28*; Sheraat Arnold 27; Anwar Daniels 23; Rushdi
Magiet 2/19; Cyril Martin 2/35)

Primrose 89 (32,4 Overs) (Shadley Martin 31; Rushdi
Magiet 19; Anwar Daniels 4/27; Sheraat Arnold 2/14;
Moutie Arnold 2/21)

Hottentots Holland won by 43 runs

1979/80

League: Primrose,

Grand Challenge (Tiger Oats): United

Scores in Final:

Blue Bells 113 (32 Overs) (Clinton Ravens 37; Faried
Martheze 18; Armien Jabaar 3/32; Ebrahim Damon
2/15; Farouk Gamieldien 2/18)

United 114/7 (37,1 Overs) (Armien Jabaar 28;
Mohammed Ebrahim 25; Clinton Ravens 3/22;
Faiz Williams 2/17)

United won by three wickets

1980/81

League: Victoria ;

Grand Challenge (round robin): Primrose

Tiger Oats: Montrose

Scores in Final:

Montrose 152 (40 Overs) (Joey Lambert 66; Anthony
Meyer 4/44; Glen Maclons 2/14; Norman Arendse 2/31)

Metropolitan 124 (36,4 Overs) (Darryl Roelf 25;
Randall Cupido 15*; Armien Jabaar 2/17; Mervyn
Theron 2/17; Hassiem Noordien 2/21)

Montrose won by 28 runs

1981/82

League: Montrose,

Fester Trophy: United

Scores in Final:

Tigers 65 (31 Overs) (Tommy September 16; Mogamat
Galant 3/22; Seraj Gabriels 2/5; Billy Stander 2/9; Yusuf
Abed 2/13)

United 66/8 (27.3 Overs) (Yusuf Jacobs 17*; Charlie
Brown 5/28)

United won by 2 wickets

1982/83

League: Montrose

Wembley Grand Challenge: Montrose

Scores in Final:

Montrose 181/9 (50 Overs) (MZ Allie 67; Reggie
February 35; Armien Martin 22; Stuart Hendricks 21;
Hansie van Oordt 4/35; Colin Moodaley 2/21; George
van Oordt 2/36)

Tigers 159 (49,1 Overs) (George van Oordt 51; Fred
Cruywagen 31; Vincent Barnes 2/11; Nasser Antulay
2/37; Mervyn Theron 2/39)

Montrose won by 22 runs

1983/84

League: Primrose

Grand Challenge: Primrose

Scores in Final:

Victoria 86 (33,2 Overs) (Mark Haupt 20; Trevor le
Roux 16; Saait Magiet 5/14; Barney Mohammed 2/15;
Faiek Davids 2/25)

Primrose 89/6 (35,5 Overs) (Faiek Davids 34*; Chinky
Pentiah 3/15; Charlie van Schalkwyk 2/18)

Primrose won by 4 wickets

1984/85

League: Montrose

Grand Challenge: Montrose

Scores in Final:

St Augustines 144/9 (50 Overs) (Gerry Miller 31; Tony
Holt 25; Armien Jabaar 4/57; Jacko van Graan 3/13)

Montrose 145/7 (41 Overs) (Armien Martin 45; MZ
Allie 37; Robin Poggenpoel 3/18; Jeremy Arenz 3/43)

Montrose won by 3 wickets

1985/86

League: Montrose;

Honda Grand Challenge: United

Scores in Final:

United 178/8 (50 Overs) (Jainu Sandan 29; Shukri
Conrad 23; Ebrahim Damon 22*; Mallick Slamang 18;
Jacko van Graan 2/31; Leon Roberts 2/52)

Montrose 177 (48,1 Overs) (Stuart Hendricks 44; MZ
Allie 28; Nazeem White 27; Mark Rasmus 22; Shamsu
Ahmed 20*; Mogamat Galant 3/34; Shukri Conrad
2/19)

United won by 1 run

1986/87

League: Primrose;

Grand Challenge: Montrose

Scores in Final:

Montrose 71 (33 Overs) (Jacko van Graan 18; Ebrahim
Damon 2/12; Salie Green 2/15; Shukri Conrad 2/16;
Mogamat Galant 2/19)

United 69 (36,5 Overs) (Goosain Lutta 19*; Mallick
Slamang 17; Reggie February 5/11; Vincent Barnes 3/11)

Montrose won by 2 runs

1987/88

League: Montrose

Grand Challenge: Primrose

Scores in Final:

Primrose 228/5 (50 Overs) (Saait Magiet 55*; Waleed
Achmat 54; Faiek Davids 46; Yunus Thomas 29*)

United 132 (46,4 Overs) (Mogamat Galant 33; Munsoor
Abdullah 22; Salie Green 17; Riyaad Abrahams 3/19;
Seraj Gabriels 3/27; Fuad Benjamin 2/34)

Primrose won by 96 runs

1988/89

League: Primrose;

Grand Challenge: Montrose

Scores in Final:

St Augustines 95 (36 Overs) (Rohan Petersen 25; Gerry
Miller 18; Ashraf Karriem 5/24; Johnny Kleinveldt 2/12;
Nilton Muller 2/24)

Montrose 97/4 (34,3 Overs) (MZ Allie 45; Gerry Miller
2/17)

Montrose won by six wickets

1989/90

League: United

Grand Challenge: United

Scores in Final:

United 188 (43,5 Overs) (Faiek Davids 83; André
Odendaal 59; Shafiek Isaacs 19; Quinton Loggenstein
3/35; Owen Williams 3/12)

Rivertonians 85 (38,3 Overs) (Jacques Loggenstein 24;
Mario Williams 15; Faiek Davids 3/12; Salie Green
2/14; Adnaan Mohammed 2/21)

United won by 103 runs

1990/91

League: Montrose

Grand Challenge: Stellenbosch

Scores in Final:

Montrose 187 (40 Overs) (Nilton Muller 37; Adnaan Meyer 29; Reggie February 27; Andre van Kerwel 2/14; Aubrey Isaacs 2/28; Tyrone Williams 2/48)

Stellenbosch 190/4 (33,3 Overs) (Deon van Kerwel 46; Andre van Kerwel 45*; Raymond Jumat 42; Brian Minnis 27; Ashraf Karriem 3/30)

Stellenbosch won by 6 wickets

Title Winners:

Inter Union competition (1966/67-1975/76)

Maitland-Parow

Super League champions – twice (1966/67; 1969/70)

Fester Trophy – once (1966/67)

Double Champions – once (1966/67)

Cape District

Super League champions – 3 times (1967/68; 1974/75; 1975/76)

Fester Trophy – 4 times (1971/72; 1973/74; 1974/75; 1975/76)

Double Champions – twice (1974/75; 1975/76)

WPCA

Super League champions – 3 times (1968/69; 1969/70; 1970/71)

Fester Trophy – once (1969/70)

Double Champions – once (1969/70)

Metropolitan

Super League champions – 3 times (1971/72; 1972/73; 1973/74)

Fester Trophy – once (1970/71)

Stellenbosch Cricket Union

Fester Trophy – once (1968/69)

Wynberg

Fester Trophy – once (1972/73)

Inter-club competition (1976/77 - 1990/91)

Primrose

League Champions – 6 times (1976/77; 78/79; 79/80; 83/84; 86/87; 88/89)

Grand Challenge – (Limited Overs) 6 Times (1976/77; 77/78 (2 titles); 1978/79; 1979/80; 80/81; 83/84; 87/88)

Double Champions – 3 Times (1976/77; 79/80; 83/84)

United

League Champions – twice (1977/78; 89/90)

Grand Challenge – 5 times (1977/78; 79/80; 81/82; 85/86; 89/90)

Double Champions – once (1989/90)

Montrose

League Champions – 6 times (1981/82; 82/83; 84/85; 85/86; 87/88; 90/91)

Grand Challenge – 5 times (1980/81; 82/83; 84/85; 86/87; 88/89)

Double champions – twice (1982/83; 84/85)

Hottentots Holland

Grand Challenge Champions (Golden Yolk) – 1979/80

Victoria

League Champions – 1980/81

Stellenbosch

Grand Challenge Champions – 1990/91

Primrose and United shared Golden Yolk in 1978/79;

Note: Between 1976/77 and 1980/81 there were two Grand Challenge competitions: A round robin for premier league teams only and a Sunday League knockout competition for premier league and first division teams.

Limited Overs Finalists:

United: 7 (1977/78 s; 79/80 w; 81/82 w; 85/86 w; 86/87; 87/88; 89/90 w)

Montrose: 7 (1980/81 w; 82/83 w; 84/85 w; 85/86; 86/87 w; 88/89 w; 90/91)

Primrose: 5 (1976/77 w; 77/78 s; 78/79; 83/84 w; 87/88 w)

St Augustines: 3 (1976/77; 84/85; 88/89)

Tigers: 2 (1981/82; 82/83)

Hottentots Holland: 1 (1978/79 w)

Blue Bells: 1 (1979/80)

Metropolitan: 1 (1980/81)

Victoria: 1 (1983/84)

Rivertonians: 1 (1989/90)

Stellenbosch: 1 (1990/91 w)

Key:

w - won

s - shared

Building for the future – junior cricket in the Western Cape

FROM THE 1950s, into the early 1960s, cricket was a man's game – literally and figuratively. So what choices did this leave, say, a promising 12-year-old batsman? Or, a breathtakingly exciting 13-year-old legspinner?

None, unfortunately.

Teenagers were thrown straight into the deep end of senior cricket – where they were offered no favours by their much older opponents. Many cocky stroke players and big-turning spinners had their spirits broken in countless uneven contests around the peninsula.

The first, tentative steps, in the early 1960s, towards creating structures for junior cricketers were warmly welcomed by the more forward-looking of the Western Province Cricket Board's officials.

By the early 1970s, the future of junior cricket seemed secure.

Unfortunately, the split in the South African Cricket Board of Control in 1976 reversed all the gains made in junior and schools cricket. Even though the WP schools team produced some top-notch players – including Vincent Barnes, Nasser Antulay, Michael Doman, Eddie Harris, Randall Cupido, Barney Mohammed, Fuad Benjamin, Faiek Davids, Ismail Behardien, Mark Rasmus, Nazeem White and Nilton Muller – who went on to win South African schools honours and, eventually, Howa Bowl caps, competition at inter-schools level never quite reached the same level of organisation and competitiveness.

After the confusion in the ranks of the Western Province Cricket Board,

following the defection of several players to the normal cricket setup in 1976/77, junior cricket also suffered an exodus of players. However, under-16 cricket continued to flourish as one of the prerequisites for admission to the new premier league was that clubs had to field an under-16 team.

By the 1979/80 season, 37 teams, representing 15 clubs, were playing in the under-12, under-14 and under-16 divisions. In his annual report to the 1979/80 season, junior convenor Ian Saunders appealed for representative matches to be organised for juniors. "Our boys have reached the stage where they are demanding incentives," he said.

This request was realised the following year when three junior sides – an under-12, under-15 and an under-17 side – led by Lander Kriel, Ian Felix and Beresford Williams, respectively, undertook a tour to Durban for a series of friendlies against Natal.

Thereafter, junior cricket continued to grow, especially at clubs such as Primrose, United, St Augustines and Crusaders, whose dedicated administrators worked hard to give young players the best possible support to play the game.

By the 1984/85 season the number of junior teams had grown to 52 – and benefactors such as Ismail Parker of

Starting junior cricket

FORMALLY ORGANISED junior cricket was introduced in the WP Cricket Board in the 1970/71 season, when an inter-union competition involving under-16 teams from Metropolitan, Wynberg, Maitland-Parow, Worcester, WP Cricket Association and Stellenbosch was inaugurated.

Although junior cricket had been played in some unions from as early as the 1961/62 season, its purpose primarily had been to bridge the December school holidays.

The first inter-union junior match was played on Boxing Day, 1966, when Wynberg's under-16s played their counterparts from Metropolitan at William Herbert sportsground.

Cricket at high schools and primary schools was also fairly well organised during the late 1960s, with centralised national tournaments being played annually.

The juniors received a boost in the 1972/73 season when under-16 teams from affiliated uunions started playing in a competition sponsored by Clover dairy products.

A Western Province under-19 side, captained by Kevin Muller, won the two national South African Cricket Board of Control tournaments, played in Durban and in Cape Town in 1973 and 1974 respectively.

Innovative Garlandale

THE ESTABLISHMENT of Garlandale Cricket Club in 1984 provided a big boost to junior cricket. Spearheaded by a young and dynamic administration, the club focused most of its energies on developing young players.

"We felt that there was a special need to develop cricket among the youth because many parents saw junior cricket as a convenient place to leave their sons on a Saturday morning. We were prepared to let our club be a nursery for the top senior clubs by devoting our energies towards producing good junior cricketers through a structured coaching programme," said Nabeal Dien, a former Garlandale executive member.

One of Garlandale's big successes was its annual six-a-side tournament, the first such event for juniors, which was inaugurated in 1987. Such was the popularity of the tournament that in just two years, it grew from humble beginnings, when it was staged in Kromboom Park for 16 teams, to an event catering for 40 teams.

In 1989, the tournament gained more prestige when it became what is believed to be the first junior tournament in the world to be played under floodlights.

Parker's Trust helped to boost interest with various sponsorships, and by donating more than 100 trophies to junior cricket.

As a further incentive for junior cricketers, the South African Cricket Board introduced annual centralised tournaments at under-16 and under-19 level in the 1984/85 season. These tournaments, which proved very popular, provided young cricketers with an incentive to represent their province against the best nonracial cricketers from other parts of the country. The under-21 side, in particular, playing in the B-section Booley Bowl, provided a rich reservoir of talent for the senior provincial side.

FORMAL COACHING STARTS

Attempts at establishing a formal coaching scheme within the Western Province Cricket Board started as far back as 1961 with the formation of the SA Eaglets Society. Unfortunately that project was shortlived due to a lack of interest and finance.

The next attempt came in 1974/75 when former Sacboc star Cecil Abrahams, who had a successful stint in the Lancashire Leagues, and the West Indian overseas professional, John Holder, were imported to conduct clinics around the peninsula in 1974/75. The clinics were only moderately successful, due to a lack of interest and planning by the schools and clubs.

In 1980, part of a sponsorship acquired from Checkers was allocated for a coaching scheme run by former provincial captain Lefty Adams. The scheme, which involved top provincial players such as Armien Jabaar, Braima Isaacs and Charlie van Schalkwyk, also did not last very long.

Organised coaching eventually took its rightful place in the Western

Province Cricket Board Junior Board when sponsorship from Mobil led to the introduction of a coaching programme, with Rushdi Magiet as the convenor.

The programme was initially introduced under the guidance of Vincent Barnes and Clinton Ravens, both of whom had returned from a spell in England, where they successfully completed National Cricket Association coaching courses.

"Things went quite well during the two years I was in charge. But then, suddenly, Rushdi, who was director of coaching, sidelined me," said Barnes.

"He subsequently used everything that Clinton and I had devised, and put Cyril Martin, who had no coaching experience, in charge. I wasn't very happy about this, because Cyril had no coaching experience. It became a Primrose thing."

Still, under the new guidance of Martin, the coaching programme was extended to teaching coaches at the Hewat College of Education, the University of the Western Cape, high and primary Schools as well as to the African township of Guguletu

Although he did not have the formal NCA qualifications of fellow coaches Barnes and Ravens, Martin was a keen enough student of the game to have successfully studied the Keith Andrew NCA coaching manual. "I realised that as juniors we did not have the luxury of formal coaching so I was determined to redress that situation," said Martin.

The coaching committee extended its operations to 200 primary schools in 1991. The board also extended their services to the SA primary schools tournament in Paarl when Shukri Conrad and Martin coached the teams which were on bye.

Interprovincial scorecards

Conrad's hundred not good enough for brave Western Province

Transvaal vs WP
26-28 December, 1971
at Natalspruit
Johannesburg

SEDICK (DICKIE) Conrad recorded the first century in the new format Dadabhay Trophy competition – a masterful 139 against arch-rivals Transvaal at the Natalspruit grounds, near Johannesburg.

After the early loss of Ivan Dagnin for 5, Conrad and Braima Isaacs (50) added 101 for the second wicket to set Western Province on their way to matching Transvaal's first innings total of 369.

A middle order collapse to the spin of Hira Jairam saw the visitors tumble to 166/4 before the allrounders, Rushdi Magiet (25), Coetie Neethling (35) and Gertjie Williams (31), hauled their side back into the game.

Just when a stubborn last wicket stand between Owen Williams and Kosie Williams seemed set to guide Western Province to a first innings lead, a controversial lbw decision by the home umpire against Owen Williams shortly before the close of play, saw Western Province dismissed for 332 – a deficit of 37.

Transvaal had scored 369 in their first innings on a placid wicket, thanks to an opening partnership of 146 between Ismail (Morris) Garda (68) and Abdul Bhamjee (75).

With the Western Province pace bowlers, Rushdi Magiet and Kosie Williams, toiling without any joy on a graveyard of a pitch, it was left to the left-arm spinners Owen Williams and Lefty Adams, and off-spinner Gertjie Williams, to make inroads into the opposition's powerful batting lineup.

After the Williamses had pegged Transvaal back to 167/5, the experienced Tiffie Barnes (88) and Solly Rubidge (42) added 91 for the 6th wicket, to put their side back in control. Moosa Mangera's 36 helped the home side to a total well in excess of 300.

Any doubts about whether the Sacboc teams would be able to play over three days were disspelled as both teams had managed only one innings each at the end of the final day.

TRANSVAAL FIRST INNINGS

I. Garda run out		68
A. Bhamjee c Dagnin b O. Williams		75
A.L. Barnes b Neethling		88
S. Chothia c & b G. Williams		0
M. Saleh c Neethling b O. Williams		0
Y. Noorbhai c Neethling b G. Williams		8
S Rubidge c & b G. Williams		42
M. Mangera c Isaacs b Adams		36
A. Moola c & b Adams		9
H. Ayob c Isaacs b Neethling		5
H. Jairam not ou		0
	EXTRAS	38
	TOTAL	369

FALL OF WICKETS: 1/146; 2/153; 3/154; 4/155; 5/167; 6/258; 7/346; 8/359; 9/369

BOWLING: R. Magiet 7-0-31-0; J. Williams 23-8-44-0; Adams 17-2 79-2; O. Williams 28-4-87-2; Neethling 10-2-29-2; G. Williams 23-4-61-3

WP FIRST INNINGS

I. Dagnin c Rubidge b Moola		5
S. Conrad c Saleh b Ayob		139
+E. Isaacs c Mangera b Jairam		50
V. Moodie lbw Jairam		20
J. Lambert c Bhamjee b Jairam		1
R. Magiet run out		25
*J. Neethling c Bhamjee b Ayob		35
G. Williams b Barnes		31
A.L. Adams b Ayob		1
J. Williams not out		6
O. Willliams lbw Barnes		6
	EXTRAS	13
	TOTAL	332

FALL OF WICKETS: 1/5; 2/106; 3/150; 4/166; 5/250; 6/250; 7/317; 8/317; 9/321

BOWLING: Ayob 26-6-63-3; Moola 2-0-16-1; Rubidge 2-0-9-0; Chothia 14-3-60-0; Jairam 26-8-84-3; Barnes 37,3-11-87-2;

MATCH DRAWN – TRANSVAAL WON ON THE FIRST INNINGS

key
* captain
+ wicketkeeper

WP vs Natal,
1-3 January
1972
at William Herbert,
Cape Town

Manicum, Ebrahim set up historic Natal victory in Cape Town

DICKIE CONRAD, unable to get off work, was missed as Natal spin twins Gopaul Manicum (5/32) and Baboo Ebrahim (3/25) wrought destruction to turn 51/1 into 108 all out in the Western Province first innings.

Middle-order men Michael Patrick (51) and Ismail Timol (44) made the difference with a 100-run stand for Natal in their reply and, facing a 114-run deficit, Western Province again disappointed in making 164 in their second innings.

Only Gertjie Williams, with a swashbuckling 67, emerged with reputation enhanced, and the Natalians completed a convincing victory after an early scare, in which they lost both openers for just 15 runs. It was to be their only victory ever against Western Province in Cape Town.

WP FIRST INNINGS

I. Dagnin b M.Govender	2
+E. Isaacs c Patrick b Manicum	31
N. Lakay c Timol b Omar	14
V. Moodie c Patrick b Manicum	2
R. Magiet c J. Govender b Ebrahim	4
S. Magiet lbw Manicum	21
*J. Neethling c Hoosen b Ebrahim	16
G. Williams c Randeree b Manicum	5
B. Petersen c J. Govender b Ebrahim	2
J. Williams c Huri b Manicum	4
O. Williams not out	0
EXTRAS	7
TOTAL	108

FALL OF WICKETS: 1/10; 2/51; 3/56; 4/56; 5/64; 6/89; 7/99; 8/101; 9/108

BOWLING: M. Govender 7-2-14-1; Patrick 3-1-4-0; Omar 8-1-26-1; Manicum 21-6-32-5; Ebrahim 16,4-4-25-3

WP SECOND INNINGS

I. Dagnin b Omar	19
E. Isaacs c Huri b M. Govender	4
V. Moodie lbw Omar	23
N. Lakay b M. Govender	0
J. Neethling c Khan b M.Govender	0
R. Magiet c Patrick b Omar	2
S. Magiet lbw Patrick	10
G. Williams c Hoosen b Ebrahim	67
J. Williams st Timol b Ebrahim	10
B. Petersen c Timol b Ebrahim	12
O. Williams not out	9
EXTRAS	8
TOTAL	164

FALL OF WICKETS: 1/8; 2/49; 3/50; 4/52; 5/54; 6/55; 7/72; 8/99; 9/135

BOWLING: M. Govender 22-6-35-3; Patrick 11-6-17-1; Ebrahim 20,6-2-60-3; Manicum14-3-31-0; Omar 6-2-13-3.

NATAL FIRST INNINGS

J. Govender c S. Magiet b O. Williams	13
P. Huri c O. Williams b Petersen	13
Y. Omar c Isaacs b J. Williams	10
Y. Randeree c Isaacs b J. Williams	1
I. Timol c Isaacs b G. Williams	44
M. Patrick lbw G. Williams	51
I. Ebrahim c & b R. Magiet	25
M. Khan c J. Williams b R. Magiet	6
G. Hoosen c Moodie b S. Magiet	16
G. Manicum c Isaacs b O. Williams	13
M. Govender not out	11
EXTRAS	19
TOTAL	222

FALL OF WICKETS: 1/23; 2/41; 3/43; 4/43; 5/143; 6/150; 7/178; 8/191; 9/198

BOWLING: R. Magiet 11-2-24-2; Neethling 7-1-25-0; S. Magiet 11-1-30-1; O. Williams 19.7-6-36-2; G. Williams 16-3-41-2; Petersen 8-1-15-1; J. Williams 11-3-27-2; Lakay 1-0-5-0

NATAL 2ND INNINGS

J. Govender b S. Magiet	1
P. Huri b J. Williams	8
Y. Omar not out	29
Y. Randeree not out	12
EXTRAS	2
TOTAL	52/2

FALL OF WICKETS: 1/2; 2/15

BOWLING: S. Magiet 6-0-21-1; J. Williams 7-1-13-1; R. Magiet 2-1-7-0; G. Williams 1-0-6-0; Petersen 0,4-0-3-0

NATAL WON BY EIGHT WICKETS

Record partnership between Williams and Magiet rescues Western Province

SENT IN, Western Province had another poor start – until salvation came in the form of a record eighth-wicket partnership of 133 between Gertjie Williams (80) and Saait Magiet (89), which ensured a good first innings total of 320.

Under a new captain, Lefty Adams, Western Province protested against local umpire Attie Piedt's four lbw decisions, going as far as on-field finger-wagging.

A stubborn ninth-wicket stand of 84 got Eastern Province to within 20 runs of Western Province's total, and the home side then shot out Western Province for a paltry 104 in 39,4 overs.

Western Province bowled only 13 overs in the remaining 75 minutes and Eastern Province had to be satisfied with a draw.

WP FIRST INNINGS

E. Isaacs c Hendricks b A. Snyman	4
I. Dagnin c Barry b Langson	15
J. Lambert st Hendricks b Langson	8
V. Moodie lbw Wilson	45
+M. Maclons c P. Snyman b Houlie	31
G. Williams c Hendricks b Govindjee	80
R. Magiet lbw Abrahams	9
C. Kolbe lbw Wilson	0
S. Magiet c A. Snyman b Govindjee	89
J. Williams lbw Houlie	9
*A.L. Adams not out	25
EXTRAS	5
TOTAL	320

FALL OF WICKETS: 1/8; 2/28; 3/34; 4/82; 5/122; 6/138; 7/151; 8/284; 9/284

BOWLING: A. Snyman 7-1-31-1; P. Snyman 12-3-39-0; Langson 16-4-39-2; Abrahams 12-2-50-1; Govindjee 18-2-63-2; Houlie 17,6-2-56-2; Wilson 11-2-34-2; Francis 2-0-3-0

EP FIRST INNINGS

K. Barry c R. Magiet b G. Williams	58
T. Hendricks c S. Magiet b J. Williams	1
A Snyman b J. Williams	2
M. Wilson c sub b G. Williams	64
N. Francis c Isaacs b G. Williams	38
C. Houlie not out	58
R. Kisten c Maclons b Adams	2
F. Abrahams b Adams	10
D. Govindjee b G. Williams	5
P. Snyman c S. Magiet b Adams	40
C. Langson c Moodie b S. Magiet	2
EXTRAS	20
TOTAL	300

FALL OF WICKETS: 1/7; 2/12; 3/ 108; 4/168; 5/179; 6/182; 7/200; 8/207; 9/291

BOWLING: S. Magiet 11,5- 2- 25-1; J. Willliams 12-5-32-2; G. Williams 26-5-99 4; R. Magiet 5-1-9-0; Adams 31-3-75-3; Kolbe 7-0-30-0

WP SECOND INNINGS

I. Dagnin c Govindjee b A. Snyman	0
E. Isaacs c Wilson b A. Snyman	24
J. Lambert b Govindjee	13
V. Moodie run out	13
M. Maclons b Langson	17
G. Williams c A. Snyman b Houlie	5
R. Magiet c Houlie b Langson	8
C. Kolbe b Langson	6
S. Magiet not out	6
A.L. Adams st Hendricks b Langson	5
J. Williams lbw Langson	0
EXTRAS	7
TOTAL	104

FALL OF WICKETS: 1/0; 2/30; 3/54; 4/57; 5/62; 6/76; 7/95; 8/96; 9/102

BOWLING: A. Snyman 6-1-18-2; P. Snyman 5-3-10-0; Wilson 1-0-9-0; Houlie 9-3-17-1; Govindjee 16-5-23-1; Langson 6,4-0-20-4

EP 2ND INNINGS

A. Snyman c Isaacs b Adams	30
M. Wilson b J. Williams	1
R. Kisten b S. Magiet	2
N. Francis c R. Magiet b S. Magiet	18
D. Govindjee not out	3
C. Houlie not out	6
EXTRAS	3
TOTAL	63/4

FALL OF WICKETS: 1/2; 2/7; 3/51; 4/55

BOWLING: S. Magiet 6-1-26-2; J. Williams 4-0-20-1; Adams 2-0-8-1; Dagnin 1-0-6-0

MATCH DRAWN – WP WON ON THE FIRST INNINGS

WP vs Transvaal, 30 Dec 1972- 2 Jan 1973 at Rosmead, Cape Town

Another Conrad hundred – and Transvaal crash to an innings defeat

DICKIE CONRAD was made the third Western Province captain in four matches as the second round of the two-season home-and-away competition began, and four changes were made to a team struggling to find consistency.

The imperious Conrad, with a first-class best of 166, added a record 232 for the third wicket with Viccie Moodie (100) – and with Robbie van Graan (57), Gertjie Williams (28) and Lefty Adams (20 not out) also weighing in with useful scores, WP were able to reach a mammoth 424/8 declared in reply to Transvaal's modest first innings total of 109.

Transvaal were even worse second time around. Unable to cope with the left-arm spin of Adams (4/14) and the offbreaks of Gertjie Williams-(2/12), they were rolled out for 86 to succumb by an innings and 229 runs.

TRANSVAAL FIRST INNINGS

I. Garda c Isaacs b Sonn...23
S. Bulbulia c Isaacs b Sonn....................................10
A. Rajah b S. Magiet...6
S. Chothia c Neethling b Sonn...............................21
A. Wadvalla run out 17
I. Kara ret hurt...0
A. Manack c Khan b Adams 5
B. Fazel c Isaacs b S. Magiet...................................2
I. Sader c & b G. Williams......................................12
M. Akhalwaya c R. van Graan b Adams...................2
H. Jairam not out 2
                              EXTRAS.................9
                              TOTAL...............109

FALL OF WICKETS: 1/38; 2/39; 3/41; 4/56; 5/69; 6/72; 7/105; 8/107; 9/109

BOWLING: September 5-0-18-0; Neethling 5-1-11-0; Sonn 15-9-19-3; Adams 16,2-4-23-2; G. Williams 6-0-11-1; S. Magiet 9-2-18-2

TRANSVAAL SECOND INNINGS

I. Garda c G. Williams b September 8
S. Bulbulia c September b Sonn 29
A. Wadvallah c S. Magiet b Khan............................0
A. Manack c Khan b Adams 18
A. Rajah c September b G. Williams.......................14
S. Chothia st Isaacs b Adams 10
B. Fazel b G. Williams..3
I. Sader c Moodie b Adams......................................1
M. Akhalwaya c September b Adams.......................0
H. Jairam not out..2
I. Kara absent injured...
                              EXTRAS.................1
                              TOTAL................86

FALL OF WICKETS: 1/12; 2/22; 3/50; 4/54; 5/67; 6/72; 7/74; 8/74; 9/86

BOWLING: September 5-2-15-1; Neethling 2-2-0-0, S. Magiet 7-2-11-0, Khan 6-2-20-1, Adams 12-5-14-4; Sonn 3-1-13-1; G. Williams 7,3-4-12-2

WP FIRST INNINGS

*S. Conrad c Manack b Jairam 166
+E. Isaacs c Fazel b Jairam.....................................11
V. Moodie c Chothia b Akhalwaya 100
R. van Graan b Chothia..57
S. Magiet c Bulbulia b Chothia.................................6
A. Sonn b Jairam...17
G. Williams c Sader b Jairam..................................28
M September c Rajah b Chothia................................0
A.L. Adams not out...20
                              EXTRAS 19
                              TOTAL   424/8 dec

FALL OF WICKETS: 1/26; 2/258; 3/300; 4/308; 5/333; 6/401; 7/419; 8/424

BOWLING: Manack 3-0-25-0; Fazel 2-0-10-0; Chothia 32,3-3-151-3; Jairam 34-6-129-4; Akhalwaya 14-3-47-1; Garda 8-0-43-0

WP WON BY AN INNINGS AND 229 RUNS

Not even Dolly can halt Western Province's surge to the title

WP vs EP
27-29
January 1973
at
Rosmead

ENGLAND TEST PLAYER Basil D'Oliveira scored 23 and a duck – Archie Sonn and Gertjie Williams got his wicket – and Western Province's batting depth pushed the team to a five-wicket victory, which set up a grand finale against Natal in Durban.

Western Province's first innings lead of 28 was largely down to half-centuries by Viccie Moodie (56) and Coetie Neethling (53), in the face of a fine 7/47 by paceman Phillip "Bunny" Snyman.

Eastern Province collapsed to 137 in their second innings, but, chasing 110 for victory, Western Province stuttered to 69/5 and had to rely on the experience of Neethling (29 not out) and Williams (11 not out) to get them home.

EP FIRST INNINGS

A. Douglas not out	69
A. Snyman c Mahoney b Neethling	1
M. Wilson c Isaacs b Mahoney	10
N. Francis c Moodie b Sonn	20
B. D'Oliveira b Sonn	23
D. Jacobs lbw Adams	8
J. Vaghmaria c Sonn b Mahoney	19
D. Govindjee c Khan b Mahoney	5
C. Houlie b Sonn	5
T. Hendricks b Sonn	7
C. Langson run out	2
EXTRAS	11
TOTAL	180

FALL OF WICKETS: 1//4; 2/18; 3/46; 4/88; 5/103; 6/123; 7/132; 8/149; 9/169

BOWLING: Mahoney 18-4-33-3; Neethling 6-2-5-1; Sonn 33-9-57-4; S. Magiet 6-1-19-0; Adams 29-11-46-1; G. Williams 5-3-4-0; Khan 1,5-0-5-0

WP FIRST INNINGS

+E. Isaacs c Francis b Snyman	0
*S. Conrad lbw Snyman	13
V. Moodie lbw Houlie	56
R. van Graan c Hendricks b Snyman	19
J.Neethling b Snyman	53
S. Magiet c Vaghmaria b Snyman	4
G. Williams lbw Wilson	16
A. Sonn c D'Oliveira b Snyman	9
J. Mahoney c Govindjee b Snyman	2
J. Khan lbw Jacobs	10
A.L. Adams not out	8
EXTRAS	18
TOTAL	208

FALL OF WICKES: 1/0; 2/31; 3/102; 4/109; 5/115; 6/138; 7/164; 8/168; 9/189

BOWLING: Snyman 17-3-47-7; Houlie 14-5-27-1; Wilson 7-2-18-1; Langson 13-1-37-0; Govindjee 11-6-20-0; D'Oliveira 7-3-18-0; Jacobs 3-0-12-1; Vaghmaria 3-1-11-0

EP SECOND INNINGS

A. Douglas c G. Williams b Mahoney	4
T. Hendricks c S. Magiet b Khan	8
M. Wilson b Adams	24
N. Francis lbw G. Williams	27
D. Jacobs lbw G. Williams	42
B. D'Oliveira c Isaacs b G. Williams	0
J. Vaghmaria c R.Van Graan b Khan	4
A. Snyman c Neethling b G. Williams	0
D. Govindjee c Isaacs b Adams	9
C. Houlie not out	5
C. Langson c Sonn b Adams	6
EXTRAS	8
TOTAL	137

FALL OF WICKETS: 1/4; 2/35; 3/41; 4/88; 5/97; 6/97; 7/104; 8/121; 9/127

BOWLING: Mahoney 8-0-28-1; Sonn 4-2-10-0; Adams 16,4-6-22-3; Khan 17-4-44-2; Williams 12-3-25-4

WP SECOND INNINGS

S. Conrad c Douglas b Snyman	24
E. Isaacs c & b Snyman	10
V. Moodie b Langson	12
R. Van Graan c Houlie b Jacobs	9
S. Magiet lbw Langson	0
J. Neethling not out	29
G. Williams not out	11
EXTRAS	18
TOTAL	113/5

FALL OF WICKETS: 1/35; 2/41; 3/65; 4/65; 5/69

BOWLING: Snyman 8-1-44-2; Houlie 5-3-9-0; Jacobs 3-1-10-1; Langson 9,3-6-14-2; Govindjee 4-1-15-0; Francis 2-1-3-0

WP WON BY FIVE WICKETS

Lefty's 11 help clinch it for Western Province in the dark

TWO FIVE-WICKET hauls by left-arm spinner Lefty Adams were instrumental in Western Province claiming the outright win they needed to share the Dadabhay Trophy with Natal.

Adams' 6/54 restricted the Natalians to 167, batting first. For Western Province, openers Dickie Conrad (99) and Braima Isaacs (54) kept the ball rolling with a stand of 111, and although the rest of the order didn't really capitalise on this fine start, the visitors finished with 298 – a lead of 131.

A three-hour stoppage for rain threatened to spoil WP's chances, but Adams weaved his magic to claim 5/83 and leave his side 59 to get in 40 minutes.

They got the runs in eight overs – for a six-wicket victory and a share of the trophy.

NATAL FIRST INNINGS

J. Govender b Sonn	20
G. Francois c Mahoney b Adams	19
Y. Randeree c Isaacs b S. Magiet	0
Y. Omar c Neethling b G.Williams	52
I. Timol b Khan	4
M. Patrick c S. Magiet b Adams	3
K. Barker c Khan b Adams	31
I. Ebrahim not out	18
G. Manicum c Moodie b Adams	11
M. Vawda c Isaacs b Adams	0
M. Govender c Isaacs b Adams	0
EXTRAS	9
TOTAL	167

FALL OF WICKETS: 1/28; 2/32; 3/53; 4/66; 5/71; 6/136; 7/140; 8/165; 9/167

BOWLING: Neethling 4-1-13-0; Williams 13-5-27-1; Sonn 14-1-30-1; S. Magiet 8-2-15-1; Mahoney 7-2-14-0; Adams 20.7-4-54-6; Khan 6-2-5-1

WP FIRST INNINGS

*S. Conrad lbw Patrick	99
+E. Isaacs c Omar b Ebrahim	54
V. Moodie b Vawda	24
R. Van Graan b Manicum	15
J. Neethling ht wkt b Manicum	8
S. Magiet c Randeree b Ebrahim	26
G. Williams c Manicum b Ebrahim	17
A.L. Adams b Patrick	0
J. Mahoney lbw Ebrahim	22
A. Sonn not out	6
J. Khan not out	13
EXTRAS	14
TOTAL	298/9 dec

FALL OF WICKETS: 1/111; 2/164; 3/185; 4/201; 5/221; 6/253; 7/257; 8/257; 9/285

BOWLING: J. Govender 2-1-4-0; Patrick 29-4-78-2; Barker 1-0-16-0; Ebrahim 22-1-81-4; Vawda 7-0-40-1; Manicum 18-5-49-2; M. Govender 2-0-16-0

NATAL SECOND INNINGS

J. Govender c Adams b G. Williams	33
G. Francois b Mahoney	1
Y. Randeree c Isaacs b G. Williams	25
Y. Omar st Isaacs b Adams	26
I. Timol lbw Adams	16
M. Patrick c Khan b Adams	81
K. Barker c Moodie b Khan	0
I. Ebrahim c G. Williams b Adams	3
G. Manicum c Khan b Adams	0
M. Vawda c Neethling b G. Williams	0
M. Govender not out	0
EXTRAS	4
TOTAL	189

FALL OF WICKETS: 1/38; 2/74; 3/100; 4/107; 5/108; 6/155; 7/157; 8/162; 9/185

BOWLING: Mahoney 5-0-31-1; S. Magiet 2-0-17-0; Sonn 8-1-18-0; Adams 28.5-5-83-5; Williams 11-2-14-3; Khan 15-1-22-1

WP SECOND INNINGS

S. Conrad b Ebrahim	6
G. Williams b Patrick	20
R. Van Graan c Omar b Ebrahim	0
S. Magiet c Timol b Ebrahim	16
E. Isaacs not out	14
V. Moodie not out	3
EXTRAS	0
TOTAL	59/4

FALL OF WICKETS: 1/18; 2/18; 3/39; 4/42

BOWLING: Patrick 4-0-34-1; Ebrahim 4-0-25-3

WP WON BY SIX WICKETS - THEY SHARED DADABHAY TROPHY WITH NATAL

Rushdi Magiet vindicated and D'Oliveira sizzles in end of season showpiece

RECALLED FOR Western Province in place of Jock Mahoney, Rushdi Magiet's 5/29 justified his inclusion as the strong invitation side were dismissed for 199.

Magiet then top scored with 48 to ensure a lead of 22 for the home side.

Morris Garda (106) was the first in the match to 50, and to 100, in the Rest's second innings of 314/7 declared.

But the batting standout was Basil D'Oliveira (100 not out), whose second 50 – including three consecutive sixes off Rushdi Magiet – took a mere 15 minutes.

Western Province had four hours to get 293, but the swashbuckling Saait Magiet (50) apart, the batsmen disappointed, with the next best at the top of the order being Viccie Moodie (28). The hosts ended on 200/9.

WP vs Rest of South Africa 3-5 March 1973, at Green Point Track, Cape Town

REST OF SA FIRST INNINGS

I. Garda c Neethling b Sonn	34
K. Barker b Khan	17
S. Chothia c Khan b Adams	34
Y. Omar b R. Magiet	40
B. D'Oliveira lbw R. Magiet	18
I. Timol c Isaacs b R. Magiet	0
A. Snyman b R. Magiet	15
G. Manicum not out	25
I. Ebrahim run out	2
R. Engelbrecht run out	1
D. Malgas c Isaacs b R. Magiet	0
EXTRAS	13
TOTAL	199

FALL OF WICKETS: 1/45; 2/89; 3/106; 4/153; 5/153; 6/156; 7/196; 8/198; 9/199

BOWLING: S. Magiet 8-0-18-0; R. Magiet 13,6-3-29-5; Adams 24-6-43-1; Khan 14-1-40-1; Williams 21-6-46-0; Sonn 6-1-10-1

REST OF SA SECOND INNINGS

I. Garda run out	106
K. Barker run out	29
Y. Omar c S. Magiet b Williams	26
S. Chothia lbw R. Magiet	23
B. D'Oliveira not out	100
I. Timol c Isaacs b R. Magie	8
A. Snyman c Isaacs b Sonn	4
G. Manicum b R. Magiet	1
I. Ebrahim not out	3
EXTRAS	14
TOTAL	314/7 decl

FALL OF WICKETS: 1/57; 2/161; 3/170; 4/199; 5/225; 6/242; 7/252

BOWLING: Sonn 9-1-45-1; S. Magiet 2-0-11-0; Adams 19-0-80-0; R. Magiet 18-4-65-3; Khan 12-1-45-0; Williams 16-2-45-1

MATCH DRAWN

WP FIRST INNINGS

*S. Conrad c Barker b Ebrahim	28
+E. Isaacs c Chothia b Snyman	0
R. Van Graan b Chothia	31
V. Moodie b Chothia	27
J. Neethling c Timol b Snyman	37
S. Magiet c Engelbrecht b Manicum	2
R. Magiet lbw Ebrahim	48
G. Williams c Ebrahim b Barker	15
A. Sonn c Chothia b Snyman	22
J. Khan not out	1
A.L. Adams c Timol b Barker	0
EXTRAS	10
TOTAL	221

FALL OF WICKETS: 1/8; 2/58; 3/86; 4/91; 5/95; 6/173; 7/190; 8/220; 9/220

BOWLING: Snyman 12-2-44-3; Engelbrecht 10-2-44-0; Malgas 4-0-15-0; Ebrahim 21-6-41-2; Chothia 13-4-28-2; Manicum 11-3-23-1; D'Oliveira 8-2-15-0; Barker 0,6-0-1-2

WP SECOND INNINGS

R. Van Graan c & b Snyman	15
V. Moodie run out	28
S. Magiet c sub b Ebrahim	50
G. Williams run out	19
E. Isaacs c Chothia b Ebrahim	5
S. Conrad c Ebrahim b Malgas	17
R. Magiet run out	3
A. Sonn c Engelbrecht b Malgas	20
J. Neethling c sub b Ebrahim	11
J. Khan not out	23
AL Adams not out	0
EXTRAS	9
TOTAL	200/9

FALL OF WICKETS: 1/25; 2/63; 3/111; 4/116; 5/135; 6/143; 7/152; 8/175; 9/179

BOWLING: Snyman 5-0-33-1; Engelbrecht 5-0-21-0; Barker 7-3-17-0; Chothia 14-4-30-0; Manicum 3-0-7-0; Ebrahim 14-4-34-3; Malgas 9-0-49-0

WP Cricket Board First Class Averages 1971/73

BATTING

Name	Matches	Inns	NO	HS	Runs	Ave.	50	100
Dickie Conrad	5	8	0	166	492	61,50	1	2
Viccie Moodie	7	8	1	100	353	50,42	1	1
Jumannah Khan	4	4	3	23*	47	47,00		
Gertjie Williams	7	12	1	80	315	28,64	2	
Coetie Neethling	5	8	1	53	189	27,00	1	
Saait Magiet	6	11	1	89	230	23,00	2	
Robbie van Graan	4	7	0	57	146	20,85	1	
Ebrahim Isaacs	7	12	1	54	207	18,82	2	
Archie Sonn	4	5	1	17	74	18,50		
Owen Williams	2	3	2	9*	15	15,00		
Lefty Adams	6	8	4	25*	59	14,75		
Rushdi Magiet	4	7	0	25	99	14,14		
Jock Mahoney	2	2	0	22	24	12,00		
Ivan Dagnin	3	5	0	19	41	8,20		
Joey Lambert	2	3	0	13	22	7,33		
Kosie Williams	3	5	1	10	29	7,25		

Also Batted: Neville Lakay (14 & 0); Basil Petersen (2 & 12); Clive Kolbe (0 & 6); Marshall September (0); Mornay Maclons (31 & 17)

FIELDING:

Wicketkeeper: 24 – Ebrahim Isaacs (22ct, 2 st); 1 – Mornay Maclons (1 catch)

CATCHES:

7 – Coetie Neethling, Saait Magiet, Jumannah Khan; 6 – Viccie Moodie, Gertjie Williams; 3 – Marshall September, Rushdi Magiet; 2 – Lefty Adams, Jock Mahoney, Archie Sonn, Robbie van Graan; 1 – Ivan Dagnin, Kosie Williams, Owen Williams

BOWLING

Name	Overs	Mdns	Wkts	Runs	Ave	Best Bowling	5i	10m
Rushdi Magiet	57	11	10	175	17,50	5/29 Rest of SA	1	
Archie Sonn	92	25	11	202	18,36	4/57 v EP		
Lefty Adams	219.2	46	28	527	18,82	6/54 v Natal	2	1
Gertjie Williams	162.3	38	21	400	19,04	4/25 v EP		
Jock Mahoney	39	6	5	99	19,80	3/33 v EP		
Kosie Williams	57	17	6	136	22,67	2/27 v Natal		
Saait Magiet	70.4	10	8	211	26,37	2/18 v Tvl		
Coetie Neethling	34	9	3	83	27,66	2/29 v Tvl		
Jumannah Khan	71.5	11	6	181	30,17	2/44 v EP		
Owen Williams	47.7	10	4	123	30,75	2/36 v Natal		

Also bowled: Clive Kolbe 7-0-30-0; Neville Lakay 1-0-5-0; Basil Petersen 8,4-1-18-1; Marshall September 10-2-28-1; Ivan Dagnin 1-0-6-0

Lambert's century seals it for WP – despite D'Oliveira's heroics

JOEY LAMBERT struck a superb 137 to help Western Province to a crucial first innings lead over an Eastern Province team strengthened by the inclusion of the England international (and Cape Town old boy), Basil D'Oliveira.

The visitors, batting first, struggled to a first innings total of 181, with only D'Oliveira (81 not out) and Alec Douglas (58) batting with any authority.

Pick of the Western Province bowlers was Lefty Adams, who took 5/53 in 26 overs.

With D'Oliveira continuing his scintillating form– this time striking a superb 99, before being castled by Coetie Neethling – and with excellent support coming from Maurice Wilson (40) and Imraan Hendricks (51), Eastern Province reached 302 in their second innings, a comfortable insurance against defeat.

**WP vs EP
16-18
November 1973
at Rosmead
Cape Town**

EP FIRST INNINGS

A. Douglas c van Graan b Adams............................58
K. Barry st Isaacs b Adams.....................................11
Z. Hendricks b Magiet 1
M. Wilson b Magiet 0
B. D'Oliveira not out..81
J. Vaghmaria c Neethling b Williams.......................0
S. Draai st Isaacs b Adams.....................................16
I. Hendricks c Mahoney b Adams..............................3
T. Williams c Isaacs b Adams 0
G. Cuddembey run out...0
C. Langson run out...0

| | EXTRAS ....11 |
| | TOTAL ....181 |

FALL OF WICKETS: 1/31; 2/40; 3/42; 4/113; 5/121; 6/148; 7/168; 8/168; 9/174

BOWLING: Mahoney 7-2-12-0; Neethling 6-2-16-0; Adams 26-5-53-5; R. Magiet 12-1-41-2; Williams 13,7-7-48-1.

EP SECOND INNINGS

A. Douglas b Mahoney 14
K. Barry lbw Magiet 19
Z. Hendricks run out 21
M. Wilson c Moodie b Magiet..................................40
B. D'Oliveira b Neethling...99
J. Vaghmaria c Isaacs b Adams 10
S. Draai lbw Williams...21
I. Hendricks c Hendricks b Adams 51
T. Williams not out...11
G. Cuddembey st Isaacs b Lambert 2
C. Langson c van Graan b Adams 0

| | EXTRAS ....14 |
| | TOTAL ....302 |

FALL OF WICKETS: 1/7; 2/56; 3/60; 4/114; 5/142; 6/160; 7/262; 8/290; 9/299

BOWLING: Mahoney 11-1-42-1; Neethling 21-1-82-1; Adams 26,3-7-59-3; R.Magiet 21-5-60-2; Williams 23-9-37-1; Lambert 2-0-8-1

WP FIRST INNINGS

*S. Conrad c Cuddembey b I. Hendricks 0
W. Hendricks c I. Hendricks b Langson 28
V. Moodie c I. Hendricks b Williams.......................1
R. van Graan lbw Williams 11
+E. Isaacs c Draai b Williams..................................1
J. Lambert c Cuddembey b I. Hendricks 137
J. Neethling c sub b I. Hendricks 29
G. Williams b Langson..9
R. Magiet c Z. Hendricks b I. Hendricks...............12
J. Mahoney not out..6
A.L. Adams b I. Hendricks 0

| | EXTRAS..............19 |
| | TOTAL ....253 |

FALL OF WICKETS: 1/0; 2/4; 3/21; 4/35; 5/71; 6/168; 7/185; 8/247; 9/252

BOWLING: I. Hendricks 21,7-6-45-5; Williams 21-5-2-3; D'Oliveira 14-6-29-0; Langson 15-0-61-2; Wilson 12-0-37-0; Draai 1-0-10-0

WP SECOND INNINGS

W. Hendricks not out..11
R. van Graan not out 15

| | EXTRAS.................1 |
| | TOTAL..............27/0 |

BOWLING: Williams 3-0-7-0; Vaghmaria 1-0-11-0; Wilson 3-0-8-0

WP WON ON THE FIRST INNINGS

WP nemesis, Tiffie Barnes, hits a century to make sure the visitors play second fiddle

Transvaal vs WP
26-28
December 1973
in Johannesburg

RUSHDI MAGIET, coming in at number eight, was the only Western Province batsman prepared to graft for runs against a Transvaal attack that gave nothing away. Magiet's gutsy 64 helped the visitors to a moderate 154 in their first innings.

Western Province's hopes of a quick haul of wickets were dashed by Tiffie Barnes, who, over the years, has shown a great liking for their bowling. Barnes' 104, coupled with a some useful performances from Abdul Bhamjee (36), Moosa Mangera (27), Solly Chothia (44) and Aboo Manack (26) steered the Transvaalers to 314/9 declared– a lead of 160.

Western Province's second innings – a back to the wall effort – to ward off outright defeat, was not a pretty sight. Neither was it all that impressive. Their top-order batting again lacked authority – and, at 35/3, the looked in some danger of being easily beaten

But sensible batting by Robbie van Graan (35) and Kulu Maclons (49), both of whom were dismissed in similar fashion – hit wicket – by Gamba Johannessie, steered them to safety. First innings honours, however, went to Transvaal – by a comfortable margin.

WP FIRST INNINGS

W. Hendricks c E. Bhamjee b Ayob		0
E. Isaacs b Manack		1
V. Moodie b Chothia		18
R. van Graan b Chothia		5
+M. Maclons c Barnes b Ayob		1
J. Lambert c sub b Barnes		6
J. Neethling lbw Johannessie		13
R. Magiet c Chothia b Rubidge		64
*G. Williams c Mangera b Rubidge		13
A. Sonn c E. Bhamjee b Chothia		15
AL. Adams not out		8
EXTRAS		10
TOTAL		154

FALL OF WICKETS; 1/0; 2/2; 3/26; 4/27; 5/27; 6/42; 7/65; 8/119; 9/138

BOWLING: Ayob 14-7-22-2; Manack 5-0-15-1; Chothia 18,4-10-28-3; Barnes 15-5-31-1; Johannessie 8-0-24-1; Rubidge 5-0-24-2

WP SECOND INNINGS

W. Hendricks c Mangera b Ayob		16
E. Isaacs c Gabru b Ayob		4
V. Moodie c Barnes b Chothia		3
R. van Graan ht wkt b Johannessie		35
M. Maclons ht wkt b Johannessie		49
J. Lambert lbw Chothia		1
J. Neethling not out		19
R. Magiet b Rubidge		2
G. Williams not out		8
EXTRAS		11
TOTAL		148/7

FALL OF WICKETS: 1/7; 2/14; 3/35; 4/92; 5/95; 6/128; 7/131

BOWLING: Ayob 15-5-34-2; Chothia 29-18-22-2; Johannessie 18-9-22-2; Barnes 10-9-3-0; Manack 8-3-18-0; Rubidge 13-1-38-1; Mangera 1-1-0-0

TRANSVAAL FIRST INNINGS

A.Bhamjee c Maclons b Williams		36
A. Gabru c Isaacs b R.Magiet		14
AL. Barnes b R. Magiet		104
M. Mangera b Neethling		27
M. Saleh c & b Sonn		2
S. Rubidge c Moodie b R.Magiet		22
S. Chothia st Maclons b Williams		44
A. Manack c Neethling b Williams		26
E. Bhamjee not out		19
G. Johannessie st Maclons b Adams		2
H. Ayob not out		3
EXTRAS		15
TOTAL		314/9 dec

FALL OF WICKETS: 1/30; 2/76; 3/138; 4/147; 5/205; 6/215; 7/253; 8/296; 9/307

BOWLING: Sonn 17-6-43-1; Neethling 23-7-40-1; Adams 37-9-84-1; R. Magiet 21-8-44-3; G. Williams 28-3-88-3

TVL WON ON THE FIRST INNINGS

Saait Magiet, Neethling set up an easy victory for Western Province

NEWCOMER REGGIE Simpson took more than five hours to score 43 as the Western Province batsmen again failed to impress – this time against a naggingly accurate Natal attack.

Without Simpson's marathon stint at the crease, and quicker contributions from Joey Lambert (34) and Saait Magiet (44) in the middle of the order, the Western Province scorecard would have made for sorry reading. As it was, 174 hardly seemed a matchwinning total – until Natal went in to bat.

They had no answer to Western Province's opening attack of Coetie Neethling (5/51) and Saait Magiet (4/21), and crashed to 85 all out.

A still out of sorts home side struggled to 156/8 declared in their second innings. But Natal never looked likely to reach 246 for victory, and were dismissed for 125. Lambert (4/18), with his leg spinners, did the most damage.

WP FIRST INNINGS

W. Hendricks b Naidoo	1
R. Simpson c Patrick b Naidoo	43
R. van Graan c Roberts b Barker	6
M. Maclons c Ebrahim b Naidoo	0
J. Lambert b Naidoo	34
S. Magiet c Naidoo b Patrick	44
J. Neethling lbw Barker	7
+E. Isaacs b Barker	0
R. Magiet c Patrick b Barker	11
*G. Williams c Omar b Barker	5
B. Petersen not out	5
EXTRAS	18
TOTAL	174

FALL OF WICKETS: 1/2; 2/10; 3/11; 4/58; 5/130; 6/149; 7/149; 8/151; 9/162

BOWLING: Barker 17,1-4-39-5; Naidoo 16-6-42-4; Omar 7-4 11-0; Ebrahim 10-4-16-0; Patrick 12-3-31-1; Vawda 5-0-17-0

WP SECOND INNINGS

W. Hendricks c sub b Naidoo	0
R. Simpson c Roberts b Omar	25
+E. Isaacs b Barker	15
R. van Graan c Francois b Ebrahim	31
M. Maclons c Omar b Patrick	23
J. Lambert c Patrick b Ebrahim	15
S. Magiet ret hurt	5
B. Petersen c Hiraman b Ebrahim	17
*G. Williams c Omar b Patrick	0
R. Magiet not out	11
J. Neethling not out	0
EXTRAS	14
TOTAL	156/8 dec

FALL OF WICKETS: 1/3; 2/31; 3/64; 4/107; 5/107; 6/135; 7/135; 8/147

BOWLING: Barker 7-1-25-1; Naidoo 5-0-13-1; Omar 9-2-23-1; Patrick 15-3-33 2; Vawda 2-0-9-0; Ebrahim 9-1-39-3

NATAL FIRST INNINGS

G. Francois c Maclons b Petersen	16
G. Sewpersadh c S. Magiet b Neethling	6
K. Hiraman c S. Magiet b Neethling	0
Y. Omar b Neethling	9
M. Patrick c Maclons b S. Magiet	7
J. Govender c R. Magiet b S. Magiet	17
K. Barker c Isaacs b Neethling	6
T. Roberts c R. Magiet b S. Magiet	2
I. Ebrahim b Neethling	2
MS. Vawda c Petersen b S. Magiet	6
LS. Naidoo not out	5
EXTRAS	9
TOTAL	85

FALL OF WICKETS: 1/26; 2/27; 3/28; 4/40; 5/46; 6/68; 7/68; 8/72; 9/72

BOWLING: Neethling 16-2-51-5; S. Magiet 13,1-3-21-4; R. Magiet 2-2-0-0; Petersen 2-1-3-1; Williams 2-1-1-0;

NATAL SECOND INNINGS

G. Francois b Neethling	8
G. Sewpersadh b R. Magiet	2
K. Hiraman c Neethling b R. Magiet	0
M. Patrick b Neethling	0
Y. Omar c Williams b Lambert	36
J. Govender c Simpson b Neethling	8
K. Barker c Neethling b Williams	33
T. Roberts st Isaacs b Lambert	19
I. Ebrahim c Petersen b Lambert	2
M. Vawda st Isaacs b Lambert	4
L.S. Naidoo not out	3
EXTRAS	10
TOTAL	125

FALL OF WICKETS: 1/4; 2/11; 3/11; 4/11; 5/19; 6/65; 7/111; 8/113; 9/116

BOWLING: Neethling 10-1-24-3; R. Magiet 15-8-16-2; Petersen 15-5 28-0; Lambert 5,4-0-18-4; Williams 15-2-29-1

WP WON BY 120 RUNS

Mahoney softens up EP enough for Adams to finish them off

EASTERN PROVINCE were pummelled by the lanky Western Province opening bowler, Jock Mahoney, after batting first in this Dadabhay Trophy match in Port Elizabeth.

With the lively Mahoney gaining sharp lift, EP never really recovered from 46/6 – and were dismissed for 89. Mahoney, who finished with 5/39 was given excellent support by Archie Sonn (2/41) and Lefty Adams (3/4).

Although Western Province were not at their scintillating best when they went in to bat, they nevertheless reached 152, thanks to useful contributions from Robbie van Graan (35), Mahoney (30) and Joey Lambert 23, and 35 extras (of which 30 were for no-balls for overstepping against the West Indian import, Duncan Carter, who nevertheless took 5/53).

Eastern Province fared only marginally better in their second knock, reaching 138, with the left-hander, Devdas Govindjee (33), again doing best with the bat.

Western Province made heavy weather of getting 75 for victory, reaching 76 for the loss of six wickets. Robbie van Graan (25) again looked the pick of the visiting batsmen.

EP FIRST INNINGS

A. Douglas c Neethling b Mahoney		4
K. Barry c Isaacs b Sonn		12
Z. Hendricks c Isaacs b Mahone		2
N. Francis c Adams b Mahoney		14
D. Carter b Sonn		4
D. Jacobs c Williams b Mahoney		8
M. Wilson c Lambert b Mahoney		2
I. Hendricks not out		15
D. Govindjee c Lambert b Adams		18
S. Draai b Adams		0
T. Williams c Neethling b Adams		5
EXTRAS		5
TOTAL		89

FALL OF WICKETS: 1/4; 2/21; 3/24; 4/40; 5/40; 6/46; 7/53; 8/80; 9/81

BOWLING: Mahoney 15-2-39-5; Sonn 18-2-41-2; Adams 4-2-4-3

EP SECOND INNINGS

A. Douglas st Isaacs b Adams		6
K. Barry b Adams		18
Z. Hendricks b Williams		23
N. Francis c & b Williams		31
D. Jacobs c Mahoney b Williams		8
D. Carter c Mahoney b Adams		0
M. Wilson c Neethling b Adams		0
I. Hendricks c Maclons b Adams		1
D. Govindjee c Lambert b Adams		33
S. Draai c Mahoney b Williams		6
T. Williams not out		8
EXTRAS		4
TOTAL		138

FALL OF WICKETS: 1/8; 2/21; 3/75; 4/88; 5/88; 6/90; 7/90; 8/92; 9/127

BOWLING: Mahoney 4-3-1-0; Neethling 12-2-26-0; Adams 24-12-50-6; Williams 33.4-8-53-3; Lambert 2-0-4-0

WP FIRST INNINGS

W. Hendricks run out		3
R. Simpson lbw Williams		3
+E. Isaacs b Williams		0
R. van Graan c & b Carter		35
M. Maclons c Barry b Govindjee		15
J. Lambert c Govindjee b Carter		23
J. Neethling c Douglas b Carter		0
*G. Williams lbw Carter		0
A. Sonn run out		8
J. Mahoney c & b Carter		30
AL. Adams not out		0
EXTRAS		35
TOTAL		152

FALL OF WICKETS: 1/16; 2/16; 3/60; 4/60; 5/97; 6/98; 7/101; 8/117; 9/152

BOWLING: Carter 26-6-53-5; Williams 21-11-29-1; Draai 2-0-7-0; Govindjee 14-8-17-1; I. Hendricks 11,4-4-11-0

WP SECOND INNINGS

W. Hendricks c Draai b Francis		12
R. Simpson lbw Williams		5
E. Isaacs c Barry b Francis		8
R. van Graan not out		25
M. Maclons c Wilson b Carter		2
J. Lambert st Wilson b Govindjee		13
J. Mahoney c Wilson b Hendricks		1
J. Neethling not out		3
EXTRAS		7
TOTAL		76/6

FALL OF WICKETS: 1/14; 2/27; 3/37; 4/44; 5/63; 6/64

BOWLING: Carter 11-6-15-1; Williams 5-3-3-1; Govindjee 19,3 6-26-1; Francis 11-4-17-2; I. Hendricks 9-5-8-1

WP WON BY 4 WICKETS

Great batting by Van Graan and Kolbe – but Western Province almost throw it away

ROBBIE VAN GRAAN maintained his rich vein of form, compiling a workmanlike 67, as Western Province, replying to a Transvaal first innings total of 169, reached 265 all out.

Other useful contributions for the home side came from Clive Kolbe (50) and Lawton Jacobs (33).

The Transvaal second innings was highlighted by the number of batsmen who went out when they seemed well set. Abdul Bhamjee, Tiffie Barnes, Yassien Snyders and Aboo Manack all reached either the twenties or thirties, before contriving to lose their wickets.

Set to make 100 to win, the Western Province batsmen were back to familiar ways in their second innings, struggling to reach 105/7. The top order batsmen, Joey Lambert (22) and Jacobs (20) were both dismissed when looking well set.

WP vs Transvaal February 16-18 1974 at Green Point Track Cape Town

TRANSVAAL FIRST INNINGS

A. Bhamjee c Adams b Mahoney	4
A. Gabru c Maclons b R.Magiet	15
AL. Barnes c Neethling b R.Magiet	15
M. Mangera c Magiet b Neethling	2
S. Chothia c Maclons b R.Magiet	1
Y. Snyders c Hendricks b Adams	21
M. Saleh handled ball	25
A. Manack c Mahoney b Williams	43
E. Bhamjee lbw Williams	13
G. Johannessie run out	2
H. Ayob not out	12
EXTRAS	16
TOTAL	169

FALL OF WICKETS: 1/14; 2/40; 3/44; 4/44; 5/45; 6/78; 7/110; 8/149; 9/153

BOWLING: Mahoney 14-4-23-1; Neethling 15-1-42-1; R.Magiet 16-3-47-3; Adams 7-0-23-1; Williams 9,4-3-18-2; Lambert 1-1-0-0

TRANSVAAL SECOND INNINGS

A. Bhamjee c Maclons b Kolbe	20
I. Gabru c Maclons b Adams	12
AL.Barnes c Maclons b Kolbe	20
M. Mangera c Lambert b Kolbe	10
Y. Snyders c Mahoney b Adams	31
S. Chothia st Maclons b Kolbe	6
A. Manack b R. Magiet	26
M. Saleh b R. Magiet	19
E. Bhamjee lbw R. Magiet	13
G. Johannessie c Van Graan b Adams	4
H. Ayob not out	7
EXTRAS	27
TOTAL	195

FALL OF WICKETS: 1/44; 2/48; 3/63; 4/84; 5/98; 6/125; 7/161; 8/176; 9/181

BOWLING: Neethling 13-4-22-0; Mahoney 7-4-4-0; Adams 21-5-35-3; R. Magiet 13,3-6-27-3; Williams 13-5-22-0; Kolbe 20-2-52-4; Lambert 2-0-6-0

WP FIRST INNINGS

W. Hendricks c Manack b Ayob	0
L. Jacobs c Gabru b Johannessie	33
C. Kolbe st E Bhamjee b Johannessie	50
R. van Graan b Chothia	67
+M. Maclons c Chothia b Johannessie	14
J. Lambert lbw Manack	19
J. Neethling c E.Bhamjee b Johannessie	0
R. Magiet b Manack	9
*G. Williams c E Bhamjee b Ayob	16
J. Mahoney not out	14
AL. Adams c A. Bhamjee b Manack	19
EXTRAS	24
TOTAL	265

FALL OF WICKETS: 1/0; 2/83; 3/116; 4/130; 5/172; 6/175; 7/196; 8/232; 9/236

BOWLING: Ayob 13-1-44-2; Manack 18-5-45-3; Barnes 16-4-34-0; Chothia 21-7-47-1; Johannessie 23-3-63-4; Snyders 1-1-0-0; Mangera 1-0-8-0

WP SECOND INNINGS

W. Hendricks run out	11
L. Jacobs c Gabru b Ayob	20
C. Kolbe run out	13
R. van Graan run out	0
M. Maclons c Ayob b Manack	4
J. Lambert c Ayob b Chothia	22
J. Mahoney not out	23
R. Magiet b Chothia	8
J. Neethling not out	3
EXTRAS	1
TOTAL	105/7

FALL OF WICKETS: 1/24; 2/45; 3/45; 4/51; 5/64; 6/72; 7/82

BOWLING: Ayob 8-2-28-1; Manack 15,1-3-45-1; Chothia 8-1-31-2

WP WON BY THREE WICKETS

**Natal vs WP
16-18 March
1974
in Durban**

Williams' magic keeps WP in the hunt – but poor batting continues to be a problem

GERTJIE WILLIAMS grabbed 5/43 as Western Province restricted Natal to a first innings total of 208. But the visitors' hopes of a substantial first innings total were quickly dashed by Natal's West Indian fast bowler, Keith Barker.

Working up a good head of steam, Barker, fellow paceman Sweetie Naidoo and left-arm spinner Baboo Ebrahim had Western Province tottering at 62/7, before a one-man rescue act by Kulu Maclons (75) steered them to a highly unsatisfactory 136 all out.

Barker continued to be a thorn in the Western Province side when Natal went in to bat for a second time, smashing 56 out of a total of 158. The wickets were shared between Jock Mahoney, Coetie Neethling and part-timer Lawton Jacobs, each of whom took two.

Set to make 231 for victory, Western Province took their time in getting to 51/2 at the close, with Robbie van Graan (24 not out) faring best.

NATAL FIRST INNINGS

G. Francois b Mahoney	5
M. Vahed c R. Magiet b Williams	29
R. Reddy c Maclons b Neethling	8
Y. Omar run out	4
M. Patrick c Neethling b Williams	81
K. Barker c Maclons b Mahoney	21
V. Ellery b Mahoney	4
I. Ebrahim not out	22
T. Roberts c Maclons b Williams	9
G. Montgomery st Maclons b Williams	16
LS. Naidoo b Williams	0
EXTRAS	9
TOTAL	208

FALL OF WICKETS: 1/5; 2/22; 3/30; 4/76; 5/149; 6/161; 7/161; 8/184; 9/208

BOWLING: Neethling 11-2-46-1; Mahoney 12-2-33-3; Williams 12-2-43-5; Henry 6-1-35-0; R. Magiet 4-1-22-0; O'Connell 2-0-20-0

NATAL SECOND INNINGS

M. Vahed c Maclons b Neethling	0
G. Francois b Neethling	1
R. Reddy run out	21
Y. Omar c Arenz b Mahoney	1
M. Patrick c O'Connell b Mahoney	0
K. Barker b Williams	56
V. Ellery run out	32
I. Ebrahim c Arenz b Henry	3
T. Roberts st Arenz b Jacobs	14
G. Montgomery c Henry b Jacobs	18
LS. Naidoo not out	1
EXTRAS	11
TOTAL	158

FALL OF WICKETS: 1/1; 2/2; 3/3; 4/3; 5/55; 6/118; 7/123; 8/124; 9/157

BOWLING: Mahoney 10-2-27-2; Neethling 6-1-28-2; Williams 10-2-43-1; Henry 10-1-46-1; Jacobs 0,4-0- 3- 2

WP FIRST INNINGS

L. Jacobs c Francois b Naidoo	10
+H. Arenz c Montgomery b Barker	0
C. Kolbe b Barker	11
R. van Graan c Barker b Ebrahim	8
M. Maclons not out	75
B. O'Connell c Roberts b Ebrahim	0
R. Magiet c Ebrahim b Barker	0
J. Neethling lbw Barker	0
*G. Williams lbw Ebrahim	2
O. Henry b Naidoo	13
J. Mahoney c Ellery b Ebrahim	2
EXTRAS	15
TOTAL	136

FALL OF WICKETS: 1/3; 2/28; 3/28; 4/60; 5/60; 6/62; 7/62; 8/68; 9/118

BOWLING: Barker 13-4-27-4; Naidoo 11-3-28-2; Ebrahim 14-4-29-4; Omar 5-2-8-0; Montgomery 1-1-0-0; Patrick 7-2-29-0

WP SECOND INNINGS

L. Jacobs c Ebrahim b Naidoo	3
H. Arenz c Montgomery b Ellery	10
R. van Graan not out	24
B. O'Connell not out	6
EXTRAS	8
TOTAL	51/2

BOWLING: Barker 5-1-9-0; Naidoo 5-1-9-1; Ebrahim 6-0-17-0; Ellery 5-1-8-1

MATCH DRAWN

WP Cricket Board First Class Averages 1973-74

BATTING

NAME	MATCHES	INNS	NO	HS	RUNS	AVE	50	100
Joey Lambert	5	9	0	137	270	30,00	1	
Robbie van Graan	6	12	3	67	262	29,11	1	
Clive Kolbe	2	3	0	50	74	24,67	1	
Mornay Maclons	5	9	1	75*	183	22,88	1	
Reggie Simpson	2	4	0	43	76	19		
Jock Mahoney	4	6	2	30	76	19,00		
Lawton Jacobs	2	4	0	36	63	15,75		
Rushdi Magiet	5	8	1	64	117	16,71	1	
Coetie Neethling	6	10	4	29	74	12,33		
Lefty Adams	4	4	2	19	27	13,50		
Willie Hendricks	5	10	1	28	82	9,11		
Gertjie Williams	6	8	1	16	53	7,57		
Viccie Moodie	2	3	0	18	22	7,33		
Ebrahim Isaacs	4	7	0	15	29	4,14		

Also batted: Sedick Conrad (0); Saait Magiet (44 & 5 not out); Basil Petersen (5 not out & 17); Archie Sonn 2 matches (15 & 8); Henry Arenz (0 & 10); Brian O'Connell (0 & 6 not out); Omar Henry (13)

FIELDING:

Wicketkeepers: 17 – Mornay Maclons (13ct & 4st); 12 – Ebrahim Isaacs (6ct & 6st); 3 – Henry Arenz (2ct &1st)

CATCHES:

9 – Coetie Neethling; 6 – Jock Mahoney; 4 – Joey Lambert, Rushdi Magiet; 3 – Gertjie Williams, Robbie van Graan; 2 – Viccie Moodie, Saait Magiet, Basil Petersen, Lefty Adams, Willie Hendricks; 1 – Reggie Simpson, Archie Sonn, Brian O' Connell, Omar Henry

BOWLING

Name	Overs	Mdns	Wkts	Runs	Ave	Best Bowling	5i	10m
Lefty Adams	142,3	40	22	308	14,00	6/50 v EP	2	
Jock Mahoney	77	20	12	181	15,08	5/39 v EP	1	
Rushdi Magiet	94	27	15	257	17,13	3/27 v Tvl		
Gertjie Williams	160,1	42	17	382	22,47	5/43 v Natal	1	
Coetie Neethling	133	23	14	376	26,85	5/52 v Natal	1	
Archie Sonn	35	8	3	84	28,00	2/41 v Tvl		

Also Bowled: Joey Lambert 11-1-36-5; Basil Petersen 17-6-30-1; Saait Magiet 27,1-4-43-4; Clive Kolbe 20-2-52-4; Lawton Jacobs 0,4-0-3-2; Omar Henry 16-2-85-1; Brian O'Connell 2-0-20-0

WP vs EP
23-25 November
1974 at
Green Point Track
Cape Town

Eastern Province go-slow earns them first innings points against Western Province

"JOB DONE," the Eastern Province brains-trust would have pointed out after their team's first innings victory over the home side, at Green Point Track. But, 23 overs bowled in more than two hours of play, as Western Province tried to chase 100 runs for victory, wasn't quite cricket.

Western Province, as has been their wont in recent matches, appeared to go out of their way to make things difficult for themselves. Chasing a moderate Eastern Province total of 184, they made an awful hash of things after being sent on their way in positive fashion, with an opening stand of 38 between Lawton Jacobs (21) and Willie Hendricks (50). But then the rot set in, and the innings closed 163/9 (the injured Basil Petersen was unable to bat).

Hendricks, a part time bowler at the best of times, then took an incredible 5/9, as Eastern Province crashed to 79 all out. Western Province finished the match at 73/7.

EP FIRST INNINGS

K. Barry c R. Magiet b S. Magiet	1
G. Abrahams c S. Magiet b Abrahams	13
Z. Hendricks c S. Magiet b Abrahams	8
N. Francis st Maclons b Williams	15
J. Vaghmaria c R. Magiet b Kolbe	37
M. Wilson b S. Magiet	14
I. Hendricks run out	30
D. Govindjee b S. Magiet	32
F. Abrahams c S. Magiet b Williams	4
T. Williams not out	6
J. Frans st Maclons b Petersen	10
EXTRAS	14
TOTAL	184

FALL OF WICKETS: 1/1; 2/23; 3/25; 4/60; 5/87; 6/97; 7/160; 8/164; 9/171

BOWLING: Holder 14-4-33-0; S. Magiet 29-13-27-3; Abrahams 24-7-45-2; R. Magiet 13-5-15-0; G.Williams 15-5-31-2; Petersen 9,3-3-17-1; Kolbe 2-0-2-1

EP SECOND INNINGS

K. Barry c Kolbe b S. Magiet	0
G. Abrahams c R. Magiet b S. Magiet	0
Z. Hendricks lbw Kolbe	9
N. Francis run out	25
J. Vaghmaria b Hendricks	15
M. Wilson c R. Magiet b Hendricks	11
I. Hendricks c Holder b Hendricks	2
D. Govindjee st Maclons b Hendricks	6
F. Abrahams c Williams b Hendricks	1
J. Frans c S. Magiet b Kolbe	4
T. Williams not out	0
EXTRAS	6
TOTAL	79

FALL OF WICKETS: 1/0; 2/3; 3/28; 4/42; 5/64; 6/65; 7/68; 8/74; 9/75

BOWLING; Holder 2-2-0-0; S. Magiet 11-2-13-2; R. Magiet 8-4-7-0; G. Williams 27-14-21-0; Abrahams 6-3-5-0; Hendricks 12-5-9-5; Kolbe 11,2-5-12-2; Petersen 6-4-6-0

WP FIRST INNINGS

W. Hendricks c Abrahams b I. Hendricks	50
L. Jacobs c Wilson b Govindjee	21
C. Kolbe c Vaghmaria b Wilson	8
R. van Graan c Francis b Wilson	5
C. Abrahams run out	1
+M. Maclons c Wilson b Frans	29
S. Magiet run out	22
R. Magiet c Vaghmaria b I. Hendricks	4
*G. Williams not out	6
J. Holder c Vaghmaria b Wilson	3
B. Petersen ret hurt	0
EXTRAS	14
TOTAL	163/9

FALL OF WICKETS: 1/38; 2/54; 3/67; 4/73; 5/110; 6/149; 7/153; 8/153; 9/160

BOWLING: Frans 15-9-15-1; Williams 9-4-12-0; Govindjee 33-9-62-1; I. Hendricks 21-7-33-2; Wilson 18,3-6-27-3

WP SECOND INNINGS

L. Jacobs c Frans b Williams	14
R. van Graan c Govindjee b I. Hendricks	11
C. Kolbe c Wilson b Williams	15
J. Holder run out	4
S. Magiet c Vaghmaria b Williams	8
C. Abrahams run out	3
R. Magiet c Abrahams b Williams	8
M. Maclons not out	7
G. Williams not out	0
EXTRAS	3
TOTAL	73/7

FALL OF WICKETS: 1/18; 2/28; 3/33; 4/47; 5/52; 6/63; 7/67

BOWLING: Williams 12-4-23-4; Frans 4-0-22-0; I. Hendricks 7-1-25-1

EP WON ON THE FIRST INNINGS.

Saait Magiet's batting and bowling heroics is not enough to save Western Province

*Natal vs WP
14-16
December 1974
in Durban*

AT 4/18 Western Province again seemed to be courting disaster. But along came Saait Magiet (52) and new cap, Armien Jabaar (48), to help steer them to a first innings total of 154 – which seemed like a matchwinning effort after Natal had slumped to 113 all out in their first knock. Pick of the bowlers was Saait Magiet, who followed up his batting heroics, with 4/24 (exactly the same figures as his brother, Rushdi).

The Western Province second innings was a disastrous effort. At 36/7, they appeared in real danger of failing to reach 50. Rushdi Magiet, a man with a reputation for reserving his best batting performances for crises, hit 21 – and with help from Jock Mahoney (17) and Gertjie Williams (16), steered the visitors to 88.

Set to make 130 to win, Natal reached this target for the loss of seven wickets. The Magiet brothers, with three wickets apiece, were again the pick of the Western Province bowlers.

WP FIRST INNINGS

L. Jacobs c J. Govender b Naidoo	3
W. Hendricks c Williamson b Naidoo	11
S. Conrad c Govender b Naidoo	0
R. van Graan b Naidoo	1
+M. Maclons c Francois b Omar	6
A. Jabaar lbw Patrick	48
S. Magiet c Ebrahim b Patrick	52
R. Magiet b Naidoo	8
*G. Williams b Naidoo	0
J. Mahoney c Govender b Patrick	16
AL. Adams not out	0
EXTRAS	9
TOTAL	154

FALL OF WICKETS: 1/12; 2/12; 3/17; 4/18; 5/51; 6/102; 7/119; 8/119; 9/148

BOWLING: Naidoo 21-7-50-6; Allie 13-5-23-0; Omar 12-5-16-1; Ebrahim 6-0-21-0; Patrick 10-2-35-3

WP SECOND INNINGS

W. Hendricks c Govender b Naidoo	0
L. Jacobs c Randeree b Allie	4
S. Conrad c Francois b Patrick	16
R. van Graan c Randeree b Naidoo	2
M. Maclons c Ebrahim b Allie	0
A. Jabaar b Patrick	6
S. Magiet c Patrick b Ebrahim	2
R. Magiet c & b Ebrahim	21
G. Williams b Govender	16
J. Mahoney c Francois b Ebrahim	17
AL. Adams not out	0
EXTRAS	4
TOTAL	88

FALL OF WICKETS: 1/0; 2/6; 3/9; 4/9; 5/29; 6/30; 7/36; 8/59; 9/82

BOWLING: Naidoo 8-3-18-2; Allie 17-8-21-2; Patrick 10-5-10-2; Ebrahim 18-3-28-3; Govender 7-4-6-1; Randeree 1-0-1-0

NATAL FIRST INNINGS

G. Francois run out	1
P. Singh c Maclons b S. Magiet	4
Y. Omar b S. Magiet	9
Y. Randeree not out	57
M. Patrick c Mahoney b S. Magiet	0
J. Govender c Hendricks b Williams	11
T. Roberts b R. Magiet	0
I. Ebrahim c Hendricks b R. Magiet	0
G. Allie b R. Magiet	8
K. Williamson b S. Magiet	3
LS. Naidoo c Van Graan b R. Magiet	2
EXTRAS	18
TOTAL	113

FALL OF WICKETS: 1/10; 2/17; 3/20; 4/20; 5/58; 6/61; 7/61; 8/99; 9/102

BOWLING: S. Magiet 14-8-24-4; R. Magiet 14,3-3-24-4; Mahoney 8-4-13-0; Adams 6-1-20-0; Williams 9-6-12-1; Hendricks 2-1-2-0

NATAL SECOND INNINGS

G. Francois b S. Magiet	4
P. Singh c Jabaar b S. Magiet	1
Y. Omar lbw R. Magiet	0
Y. Randeree c Maclons b S. Magiet	0
M. Patrick c Maclons b R. Magiet	8
J. Govender not out	65
T. Roberts b Jabaar	20
I. Ebrahim c Mahoney b R. Magiet	5
G. Allie not out	13
EXTRAS	14
TOTAL	130/7

FALL OF WICKETS: 1/4; 2/6; 3/6; 4/6; 5/68; 6/77; 7/87

BOWLING: S. Magiet 24-4-40-3; R. Magiet 18-6-28-3; G. Williams 5-0-19-0; Adams 18-13-6-0; Hendricks 5-0-13-0; Jabaar 4-2-9-1; Conrad 1-0-1-0

NATAL WON BY THREE WICKETS

Kanhai shows WP how it should be done in exciting Transvaal triumph

ROHAN KANHAI, making the most of an early life, treated the large crowd at William Herbert in Wynberg, to a majestic batting display as Transvaal snatched victory by 27 runs against their arch-rivals.

Kanhai scored 104 in even time as Transvaal posted the rather moderate total of 214. Western Province never looked like matching the visitors' total – and with only Willie Hendricks (44) and Cecil Abrahams (40) looking remotely capable of playing a long innings, they slumped to 165 all out.

A fine spell of bowling by Lefty Adams (4/36) restricted the Transvaalers to 160 in their second knock. Defiant batting by Rushdi Magiet (38) and Jock Mahoney (68 not out), carried WP to 182, still well short of victory.

TRANSVAAL FIRST INNINGS

I. Garda b R. Magiet	8
A. Gabru run out	34
A. Manack c Jacobs b Mahoney	3
R. Kanhai c Maclons b Williams	104
M. Mangera c Williams b Adams	8
S. Chothia st Maclons b Williams	18
A. Bhabha lbw Adams	2
S. Rubidge c Mahoney b Williams	20
I. Kara c Abrahams b Adams	1
E. Bhamjee b Hendricks	4
H. Ayob not out	4
EXTRAS	8
TOTAL	214

FALL OF WICKETS: 1/8; 2/13; 3/100; 4/122; 5/173; 6/186; 7/199; 8/203; 9/203

BOWLING: Mahoney 13-2-45-1; R. Magiet 16-3-39-1; Adams 25-9-52-3; Abrahams 15-1-37-0; Williams 13-4-30-3; Jabaar 1-1-0-0; Hendricks 0,2-0-3-1

TRANSVAAL SECOND INNINGS

I. Garda c Mahoney b Adams	1
A. Gabru c Abrahams b Mahoney	0
M. Mangera c Jacobs b Adams	18
R. Kanhai c Jabaar b Adams	0
A. Manack b Mahoney	21
A. Bhabha st Maclons b R. Magiet	35
S. Chothia c Maclons b Williams	46
H. Ayob c Van Graan b Adams	18
S. Rubidge b Hendricks	7
I. Kara lbw Hendricks	0
E. Bhamjee not out	3
EXTRAS	11
TOTAL	160

FALL OF WICKETS: 1/1; 2/2; 3/2; 4/44; 5/50; 6/114; 7/142; 8/152; 9/152

BOWLING: Mahoney 17-8-25-2; Adams 29,2-11-36-4; R. Magiet 10-1-32-1; Williams 12-2-22-1; Jabaar 7-5-6-0; Hendricks 11-2-23-2; Abrahams 4-2-5-0

WESTERN PROVINCE FIRST INNINGS

W. Hendricks c Kanhai b Manack	44
L. Jacobs c Bhamjee b Manack	11
S. Conrad c Gabru b Ayob	11
+M. Maclons b Ayob	4
K. van Graan c Garda b Chothia	19
A. Jabaar lbw Manack	14
C. Abrahams c Bhamjee b Ayob	40
R. Magiet c Bhamjee b Kara	0
*G. Williams b Ayob	3
J. Mahoney not out	2
AL. Adams c Bhamjee b Ayob	3
EXTRAS	14
TOTAL	165

FALL OF WICKETS: 1/32; 2/58; 3/60; 4/100; 5/101; 6/120; 7/134; 8/160; 9/161

BOWLING: Ayob 18,2-5-41-5; Chothia 30-15-39-1; Manack 19-8-29-3; Kara 12-3-14-1; Babha 6-3-7-0; Rubidge 6-2-16-0; Kanhai 1-1-0-0; Mangera 1-0-5-0

WESTERN PROVINCE SECOND INNINGS

W. Hendricks c Garda b Kara	23
S. Conrad c Mangera b Ayob	4
L. Jacobs run out	10
M. Maclons c Bhabha b Kara	19
K. van Graan c Kanhai b Ayob	8
A. Jabaar b Kara	2
C. Abrahams c Mangera b Ayob	0
J. Mahoney not out	68
R. Magiet c Bhabha b Manack	38
G. Williams run out	0
AL. Adams c Garda b Ayob	0
EXTRAS	10
TOTAL	182

FALL OF WICKETS: 1/5; 2/31; 3/43; 4/56; 5/59; 6/64; 7/88; 8/178; 9/180

BOWLING: Ayob 26,5-8-53-4; Manack 10-4-13-1; Chothia 23-9-29-0; Kara 31-7-56-3; Rubidge 1-0-4-0; Kanhai 3-1-6-0; Bhabha 2-0-11-0

TRANSVAAL WON BY 27 RUNS

Magiets, Mahoney shine as WP coast to victory over EP

A RECORD 9th wicket partnership of 93 between Rushdi Magiet (76) and Jock Mahoney (32) set Western Province up for an easy 10-wicket victory over Eastern Province – and wiped out the memory of their first innings loss to their arch-rivals in Cape Town earlier in the season.

Chasing 254, Eastern Province never recovered from a miserable start, in which they lost their first four wickets for just 16 runs, and were dismissed for 92. The destroyer-in-chief for Western Province was Saait Magiet, who took 5/25 in 14 overs (and three balls) of fast, sharp bowling.

Asked to follow on, EP fared much better, reaching 184, thanks to stubborn batting from Desmond "Bravo" Jacobs (43), Jaysugh Vaghmaria (39) and Garth Cuddembey (47). However, in the end, they were again undone by the pace of Magiet (3/39), while Mahoney, Armien Jabaar and Lefty Adams weighed in with two wickets each. Western Province knocked off the 23 needed for victory without loss.

WP FIRST INNINGS

W. Hendricks b Frans	8
L. Jacobs c Govindjee b Frans	33
N. Brache c Govindjee b Frans	3
C. Abrahams c Vaghmaria b Wilson	35
K. van Graan c & b Govindjee	10
S. Magiet c & b Wilson	32
A. Jabaar c Vaghmaria b Wilson	8
+M. Maclons c Cuddembey b Govindjee	1
R. Magiet b Langson	76
J. Mahoney b Govindjee	32
*AL. Adams not out	4
EXTRAS	12
TOTAL	254

FALL OF WICKETS: 1/19; 2/39; 3/57; 4/78; 5/107; 6/124; 7/131; 8/153; 9/246

BOWLING: Pono 17-2-40-0; Snyman 3-0-6-0; Frans 14-2-37-3; Govindjee 25-5-65-3; Wilson 18-2-71-3; Langson 8,1-0-18-1; Majola 2-0-5-0

WP SECOND INNINGS

W. Hendricks not out	4
L. Jacobs not out	19
EXTRAS	0
TOTAL	23/0

BOWLING: Pono 4-0-10-0; Frans 3,1-0-13-0

EP FIRST INNINGS

K. Barry c Hendricks b Mahoney	6
D. Jacobs lbw S. Magiet	4
K. Majola b S. Magiet	2
J. Vaghmaria c Abrahams b S. Magiet	0
A. Snyman c Jacobs b Jabaar	14
M. Wilson b S. Magiet	7
D. Govindjee b S. Magiet	2
G. Cuddembey b Adams	25
J. Frans not out	18
T. Pono c & b Jabaar	1
C. Langson run out	2
EXTRAS	11
TOTAL	92

FALL OF WICKETS: 1/8; 2/15; 3/15; 4/16; 5/28; 6/30; 7/69; 8/73; 9/76

BOWLING: Mahoney 12-5-11-1; S. Magiet 14-3-25-5; R. Magiet 2-0-2-0; Adams 10,4-2-22-1; Jabaar 6-2-21-2

EP SECOND INNINGS (FOLLOWED ON)

K. Barry c van Graan b Mahoney	1
D. Jacobs c Maclons b Jabaar	43
K. Majola c Maclons b Mahoney	4
J. Vaghmaria c S.Magiet b Jabaar	39
A. Snyman b Adams	12
M. Wilson c &b Adams	20
D. Govindjee b S. Magiet	6
G. Cuddembey b S. Magiet	47
J. Frans b S.Magiet	0
T. Pono run out	2
C. Langson not out	0
EXTRAS	10
TOTAL	184

FALL OF WICKETS: 1/8; 2/18; 3/89; 4/96; 5/116; 6/127; 7/135; 8/140; 9/152

BOWLING: S. Magiet 17,4-6-39-3; Mahoney 9-1-25-2; Abrahams 11-3-26-0; Jabaar 15-2-28-2; Adams 20-6-38-2; Hendricks 1-0-7-0; R. Magiet 4-0-11-0

WP WON BY TEN WICKETS

Bowlers call the shots as Western Province scrape home by three wickets

NATAL HAD good reason to rue the name "Magiet" in this Dadabhay Trophy match at Green Point Track. Batting first, they were made to toil for the rather meagre return of 131 by the miserly Rushdi Magiet, in particular, who finished with 3/13 in 15 overs. Jock Mahoney (2/15) and Cecil Abrahams (2/21) were also effective.

Although Western Province made an encouraging start – Willie Hendricks and Lawton Jacobs put on 39 – the bowlers continued to dominate. Baboo Ebrahim (6/70) and Michael Patrick (3/11) kept their team in the hunt by dismissing WP for 143.

Natal, though, were blitzed in their second knock by another Magiet – the younger, faster, infinitely more menacing Saait – who took 6/24 in another fine spell of sustained fast bowling. Dismissed for 137, and thus leaving WP to make just 126 for victory, Natal fought bravely. With Ebrahim (5/54) again bowling magnificently, they had the home side tottering at 110/7, before Abrahams and Rushdi Magiet steered them home.

NATAL FIRST INNINGS

G. Francois c Isaacs b Mahoney	1
M. Ebrahim c S. Magiet b Mahoney	6
K. Barker c Moodie b R. Magiet	19
Y. Omar c Isaacs b Abrahams	6
T. Roberts b R. Magiet	7
M. Patrick lbw Abrahams	6
J. Govender c & b R. Magiet	36
I. Ebrahim c S. Magiet b Khan	1
G. Allie not out	23
K. Williamson run out	1
LS. Naidoo c Hendricks b Adams	8
EXTRAS	17
TOTAL	131

FALL OF WICKETS: 1/3; 2/28; 3/32; 4/43; 5/55; 6/56; 7/61; 8/110; 9/120

BOWLING: Mahoney 13-7-15-2; S. Magiet 10-2-23-0; R. Magiet 15-10-13-3; Abrahams 14-4-21-2; Khan 7-2-31-1; Adams 5,2-2-11-1

NATAL SECOND INNINGS

G. Francois b Khan	25
M. Ebrahim c S. Magiet b Khan	15
K. Barker c S. Magiet b Adams	12
T. Roberts c Mahoney b Khan	5
M. Patrick c Isaacs b S. Magiet	14
J. Govender b S. Magiet	24
Y. Omar c Moodie b S. Magiet	7
G. Allie c Isaacs b S. Magiet	16
I. Ebrahim b S. Magiet	2
K. Williamson c Isaacs b S. Magiet	2
LS. Naidoo not out	3
EXTRAS	12
TOTAL	137

FALL OF WICKETS: 1/45; 2/46; 3/62; 4/64; 5/98; 6/103; 7/116; 8/128; 9/134

BOWLING: S. Magiet 18,2-5-24-6; Mahoney 8-2-15-0; R. Magiet 8-3-9-0; Adams 18-5-39-1; Khan 12-2-25-3; Abrahams 1-0-4-0; Hendricks 2-0-9-0

WP FIRST INNINGS

W. Hendricks c Govender b I.Ebrahim	35
L. Jacobs lbw Patrick	20
N. Brache b Patrick	1
V. Moodie c Williamson b I.Ebrahim	0
+E. Isaacs c Roberts b I Ebrahim	0
S. Magiet c Omar b I.Ebrahim	32
C. Abrahams c Williamson b Patrick	12
R. Magiet c Francois b I.Ebrahim	9
J. Mahoney not out	9
J. Khan c M. Ebrahim b I.Ebrahim	10
*AL. Adams run out	4
EXTRAS	11
TOTAL	143

FALL OF WICKETS: 1/39; 2/43; 3/44; 4/44; 5/90; 6/107; 7/115; 8/119; 9/137

BOWLING: Barker 10-3-21-0; Naidoo 8-1-14-0; Allie 3-1-10-0; I. Ebrahim 27-6-70-6; Patrick 20-15-11-3; Omar 2,3-0-6-0

WP SECOND INNINGS

W. Hendricks c Omar b I. Ebrahim	13
L. Jacobs c Roberts b I. Ebrahim	26
V. Moodie c Govender b I. Ebrahim	16
N. Brache c & b Omar	1
E. Isaacs c Govender b Allie	19
J. Khan c Naidoo b I. Ebrahim	11
S. Magiet c Omar b I. Ebrahim	10
C. Abrahams not out	17
R. Magiet not out	3
EXTRAS	11
TOTAL	127/7

FALL OF WICKETS: 1/44; 2/53; 3/54; 4/82; 5/94; 6/102; 7/110

BOWLING: Barker 8-1-20-0; I. Ebrahim 25.4-8-54-5; Naidoo 6-2-8-0; Patrick 6-3-4-0; Govender 3-1-4-0; Omar 7-2-9-1; Allie 14-7-17-1

WP WON BY 3 WICKETS

Transvaal get the draw they need to win the Dadabhay Trophy

**Transvaal vs WP
15-17 March
1975 in
Johannesburg**

ALL TRANSVAAL needed to win the Dadabhay Trophy was a draw against Western Province. And a draw is what they played for and got. In truth, though, the visitors, needing an outright victory to retain the trophy, hardly looked the part of prospective champions.

Batting first, the Transvaalers compiled a useful, but hardly a matchwinning, 219. The best bowler for the visitors was the ever-reliable Rushdi Magiet (4/52).

Western Province quickly threw away their already slim chance of victory with an inept batting display that saw them dismissed for a paltry 90. Just three batsmen – Braima Isaacs (13), Jock Mahoney (15) and Jumannah Khan (10) posted double figures.

Transvaal then batted out the remainder of the match with no real intention of going for a win. With Tiffie Barnes scoring 104, they declared at 254 for 7.

Cecil Abrahams, Western Province's overseas professional, was the pick of the visiting bowlers, claiming 3/18 in 11 overs.

TRANSVAAL FIRST INNINGS

I. Garda lbw Abrahams	26
A. Gabru run out	45
AL. Barnes c Isaacs b S. Magiet	6
A. Bhamjee b R. Magiet	14
A. Manack c S. Magiet b Khan	20
S. Chothia b R. Magiet	14
R. Cajee c Abrahams b Khan	17
M. Mangera lbw R. Magiet	34
E. Bhamjee b R. Magiet	23
I. Kara c S. Magiet b Mahoney	3
H. Ayob not out	1
EXTRAS	16
TOTAL	219

FALL OF WICKETS: 1/18; 2/47; 3/57; 4/72; 5/96; 6/113; 7/184; 8/207; 9/210

BOWLING: Mahoney 14-6-23-1; S. Magiet 20-6-42-1; R. Magiet 22,5-8-52-4; Abrahams 19-4-27-1; Khan 10-2-26-2; Adams 8-0-33-0

TRANSVAAL SECOND INNINGS

I. Garda lbw Abrahams	32
A. Gabru b Abrahams	44
A. Bhamjee b Abrahams	4
A. Manack b S. Magiet	10
AL. Barnes c S. Magiet b Hendricks	104
S. Chothia c Moodie b Van Graan	39
R. Cajee c Isaacs b Van Graan	7
M. Mangera not out	2
EXTRAS	12
TOTAL	254/7 dec

FALL OF WICKETS: 1/83; 2/86; 3/92; 4/102; 5/162; 6/198; 7/254

BOWLING: Mahoney 6-1-21-0; Adams 20-4-79-0; R. Magiet 9-0-20-0; S. Magiet 15-2-35-1; Hendricks 6,4-1-25-1; Khan 3-0-7-0; Abrahams 11-3-18-3; Van Graan 12-4-17-2; Moodie 2-0-20-0

WP FIRST INNINGS

W. Hendricks b Ayob	5
L. Jacobs run out	20
V. Moodie lbw Chothia	4
R. van Graan c E.Bhamjee b Chothia	3
+E. Isaacs c Manack b Barnes	13
S. Magiet c Kara b Barnes	3
R. Magiet c Mangera b Barnes	7
C. Abrahams c Manack b Chothia	3
J. Mahoney b Barnes	15
J. Khan c Mangera b Chothia	10
*AL. Adams not out	1
EXTRAS	6
TOTAL	90

FALL OF WICKETS: 1/14; 2/20; 3/32; 4/34; 5/39; 6/39; 7/48; 8/71; 9/85

BOWLING: Ayob 11-5-10-1; Barnes 39-16-44-4; Chothia 29-14-30-4

**MATCH DRAWN
TRANSVAAL WON THE DADABHAY TROPHY**

WP Cricket Board First Class Averages 1974-75

BATTING

Name	Matches	Inns	NO	HS	Runs	Ave	50	100
Jock Mahoney	5	7	3	68*	159	39,75	1	
Willie Hendricks	6	10	1	50	193	21,44	1	
Saait Magiet	5	8	0	52	161	20,13	1	
Rushdi Magiet	6	10	1	76	174	19,33	1	
Lawton Jacobs	6	11	1	33	181	18,10		
Cecil Abrahams	5	8	1	40	111	15,86		
Armien Jabaar	3	5	0	48	78	15,60		
Keith Van Graan	2	3	0	19	37	12,33		
Mornay Maclons	4	7	1	29	66	11,00		
Ebrahim Isaacs	2	3	0	19	32	10,67		
Jumannah Khan	2	3	0	11	31	10,33		
Dickie Conrad	2	4	0	16	31	7,75		
Viccie Moodie	2	3	0	16	20	6,67		
Gertjie Williams	3	6	2	16	25	6,25		
Robbie van Graan	3	5	0	11	22	4,40		
Lefty Adams	5	7	4	4	12	4,00		
Noel Brache	2	3	0	3	5	1,67		

Also batted: John Holder (3 and 4); Clive Kolbe (8 and 15); Basil Petersen (0*)

FIELDING:

Wicketkeepers: 12 – Mornay Maclons (7ct and 5st); 7 – Ebrahim Isaacs (7ct)

CATCHES:

12 – Saait Magiet; 7 – Rushdi Magiet; 4 – Willie Hendricks, Cecil Abrahams; 3 – Lawton Jacobs, Armien Jabaar, Jock Mahoney, Viccie Moodie; 2 – Gertjie Williams, Keith van Graan; 1 – Clive Kolbe, Robbie van Graan, John Holder, Lefty Adams

BOWLING

Name	Overs	Mdns	Wkts	Runs	Ave	Best Bowling	5i	10m
Willie Hendricks	40	9	9	91	10,11	5/9 v EP	1	
Saait Magiet	173	51	27	292	10,81	6/24 v Natal	2	
Armien Jabaar	33	12	5	64	12,80	2/21 v EP		
Jumannah Khan	32	6	6	89	14,83	3/25 v Natal		
Rushdi Magiet	140,2	43	16	252	15,75	4/24 v Natal		
Gertjie Williams	81	31	7	135	19,29	3/30 v Tvl		
Jock Mahoney	100	36	9	193	21,44	2/15 v Natal		
Cecil Abrahams	105	27	8	188	23,50	3/18 v Tvl		
Lefty Adams	160,2	53	12	336	28,00	4/36 v Tvl		

Also Bowled: Clive Kolbe 13,2-5-14-3; John Holder 16-6-33-0; Basil Petersen 15,3-7-23-1; Robbie van Graan 12-4-17-2; Dickie Conrad 1-0-1-0; Viccie Moodie 2-0-20-0

WP keep their nerve to snatch a dramatic victory in Port Elizabeth

**EP vs WP
22-24 November
1975 in
Port Elizabeth**

NEW WESTERN Province skipper, Brian O'Connell, did more than his bit against tough Eastern Province, to ensure that his tenure got off to a winning start.

Batting at number 9, O'Connell struck an undefeated 46 to help Western Province reach 181 in their first innings. His knock followed a middle-order collapse, which saw five wickets falling for just 43 runs.

Eastern Province, after a bright start, were destroyed by the pace of Jock Mahoney (6/42) and Howie Bergins (3/49).

The WP second innings was anchored by Viccie Moodie, who made up for his first innings duck, with a studiously compiled 65. Helped by smaller, but, as it turned out, significant knocks by a number of other players, WP reached 178 in their second turn at bat.

Set to make 217 for victory, EP came tantalisingly close, falling for 205 – just 11 short.

WP FIRST INNINGS

W. Hendricks b Frans	8
L. Jacobs lbw Kadi	48
H. Dawson c Govindjee b Pono	28
V. Moodie c Jacobs b Davids	0
+M. Maclons b Kadi	6
K. van Graan run out	12
W. Carelse c & b Davids	4
O. Henry c & b Davids	6
*B. O'Connell not out	46
J. Mahoney run out	5
H. Bergins c Frans b Davids	9
EXTRAS	9
TOTAL	181

FALL OF WICKETS: 1/18; 2/76; 3/78; 4/91; 5/106; 6/112; 7/119; 8/122; 9/161

BOWLING: Frans 8-1-26-1; Pono 15-3-40-1; Kadi 13-0-39-2; Davids 21,5-5-48-4; Govindjee 10-4-19-0

WP SECOND INNINGS

W. Hendricks c Majola b Pono	6
L. Jacobs c Davids b Govindjee	13
V. Moodie c Govindje b Frans	65
H. Dawson b Davids	3
M. Maclons c Majola b Govindjee	17
K. van Graan c Felix b Frans	16
W. Carelse c & b Davids	2
O. Henry run out	17
H. Bergins lbw Pono	4
B. O'Connell not out	11
J. Mahoney b Pono	3
EXTRAS	21
TOTAL	178

FALL OF WICKETS: 1/7; 2/44; 3/53; 4/83; 5/126; 6/130; 7/134; 8/151; 9/173

BOWLING: Pono 13-5-47-3; Frans 22-10-27-2; Davids 17-4-39-2; Govindjee 22-15-19-2; Barry 1-0-1-0; Kadi 6-0- 18-0; Majola 1-0-6-0

EP FIRST INNINGS

K. Barry c Maclons b Bergins	25
J. Sandan c Moodie b Mahoney	57
K. Majola st Maclons b Hendricks	4
D. Jacobs c Moodie b Mahoney	14
H. Felix c Maclons b Mahoney	5
Z. Davids c Maclons b Mahoney	3
G. Cuddembey not out	17
D. Govindjee c O'Connell b Mahoney	3
T. Pono b Bergins	5
J. Frans b Mahoney	1
T. Kadi b Bergins	0
EXTRAS	9
TOTAL	143

FALL OF WICKETS: 1/46; 2/86; 3/107; 4/108; 5/112; 6/117; 7/125; 8/135; 9/140

BOWLING: Mahoney 22-8-42-6; Bergins 20,4-5-49-3; Carelse 8-1-18-0; Henry 3-3-0-0, Hendricks 6-1-25-1; Van Graan 1-1-0-0

EP SECOND INNINGS

K. Barry st Maclons b Hendricks	37
J. Sandan c Mahoney b Henry	33
K. Majola c Dawson b Hendricks	24
D. Jacobs c Dawson b Hendricks	9
H. Felix c Maclons b Henry	5
D. Govindjee run out	31
G. Cuddembey c Maclons b Hendricks	6
Z. Davids c Maclons b Henry	4
T. Pono lbw Mahoney	20
J. Frans not out	13
T. Kadi run out	7
EXTRAS	16
TOTAL	205

FALL OF WICKETS: 1/65; 2/85; 3/103; 4/110; 5/137; 6/155; 7/159; 8/176; 9/192

BOWLING: Mahoney 17-3-38-1; Bergins 14-1-30-0; Carelse 5-0-17-0; Henry 25,3-5-47-3; Hendricks 31-4-57-4

WP WON BY 11 RUNS

**Transvaal vs WP
26-28 December
1975 in
Johannesburg**

Once-mighty Transvaal are thrashed on home turf by confident WP

SO, THE question every one was asking after Transvaal were blitzed by the new-look Western Province side was: Has Father Time finally caught up with Morris Garda, Tiffie Barnes, Moosa Mangera, Solly Chothia...?

Once their batsmen had hoisted the white flag in their first innings – an innings which realised just 95 runs – Transvaal were always going to have their backs to the wall. Pick of the WP bowlers was Howie Bergins (6/27), who exploited the damp conditions.

WP, mind you, were far from impressive when they went in – and, but for the efforts of Viccie Moodie (48), Willie Hendricks (24) and Kulu Maclons (24), they would have scored even less than the home side.

And to those who argued that the Transvaal second innings couldn't possibly be as bad as their first.... it was worse. Two players reached double figures in a total of 70.

Set to get 33 for victory, Western Province reached 34 without loss, with Lawton Jacobs striking a breezy 34.

TRANSVAAL FIRST INNINGS

I. Garda run out	26
A. Gabru c Hendricks b Bergins	24
AL. Barnes c Maclons b Bergins	7
M. Mangera b Bergins	0
S. Chothia b Bergins	2
R. Cajee c Maclons b Bergins	10
S. Garda st Maclons b Hendricks	10
S. Rubidge c Jacobs b Bergins	0
E. Bhamjee c van Graan b Carelse	10
N. Abrahams c Mahoney b Carelse	0
F. Omar not out	0
EXTRAS	6
TOTAL	95

FALL OF WICKETS: 1/35; 2/43; 3/43; 4/45; 5/ 63; 6/63; 7/77; 8/94; 9/95

BOWLING: Mahoney 13-3-32-0; Bergins 14-2-27-6; Hendricks 8-2-16-1; Henry 1-1-0-0; Carelse 5,4-1-14-2

TRANSVAAL SECOND INNINGS

I. Garda run out	6
A. Gabru c Henry b Bergins	19
S. Garda c van Graan b Bergins	2
S. Chothia c Dawson b Hendricks	1
R. Cajee c Maclons b Hendricks	15
M. Mangera c Maclons b Bergins	8
AL. Barnes c van Graan b Hendricks	0
S. Rubidge lbw Bergins	1
E. Bhamjee c Bergins b Mahoney	4
N. Abrahams b Bergins	1
F. Omar not out	0
EXTRAS	13
TOTAL	70

FALL OF WICKETS: 1/13; 2/26; 3/29; 4/45; 5/59; 6/62; 7/64; 8/64; 9/70

BOWLING: Mahoney 11-3-17-1; Bergins 19,1-6-24-5; Hendricks 17-8-16-3

WP FIRST INNINGS

W. Hendricks c & b Barnes	24
L. Jacobs c Bhamjee b Barnes	14
H. Dawson c & b Chothia	1
V. Moodie c S. Garda b Chothia	48
K. van Graan lbw Barnes	0
+M. Maclons c Barnes b Rubidge	24
W. Carelse not out	10
O. Henry b Chothia	3
J. Mahoney run out	1
*B. O'Connell b Barnes	2
H. Bergins b Barnes	0
EXTRAS	6
TOTAL	133

Fall of wickets: 1/37; 2/38; 3/77; 4/77; 5/91; 6/102; 7/104; 8/127; 9/131

Bowling Barnes 44.3-31-26-5; Chothia 43-17-57-3; Abrahams 5-0-13-0; Cajee 1-0-4-0; Rubidge 7-1-22-1; Mangera 3-0-5-0

WP SECOND INNINGS

W. Hendricks not out	6
L. Jacobs not out	28
EXTRAS	0
TOTAL	34/0

BOWLING: Barnes 5-1-18-0; Chothia 6-2-10-0; Mangera 2-0-6-0

WP WON BY TEN WICKETS

Natal have no answers to the Western Province pace attack

WP vs Natal 1-3 January 1976 at Turfhall Cape Town

JOCK MAHONEY in full flight is not a sight to be relished by chicken-hearted batsmen. Which is not to say that Natal's batsmen were chicken-hearted. But they didn't play him well at all – in fact, they hardly played him at all.

Mahoney grabbed 5/37 as Natal crashed to 111 in their first innings – and from then onwards, Western Province had this Stellenbosch Farmers' Winery inter-provincial more or less in the bag.

The home side, for once, made a reasonable start. And for once, Willie Hendricks occupied the crease for as long as a good batsman ought to. Of course, old habits die hard – and after Hendricks (60) and Lawton Jacobs (23) had put on 59 for the first wicket – along came that all too familiar middle-order collapse, which saw the total suddenly tumbling to 69/4. In the end, WP reached 212, 101 runs more than Natal, who again succumbed to pace – this time to Pinky Carelse (5/15) – and were bowled out for 130 in their second innings. WP knocked off the required runs without loss.

NATAL FIRST INNINGS

G. Francois c Katts b Carelse	23
Y Omar b Mahoney	7
P. Moodley b Mahoney	2
Y. Randeree lbw Mahoney	1
T. Roberts c O' Connell b Mahoney	2
J. Govender run out	1
M. Khan run out	17
Z. Omar c Maclons b Mahoney	19
G. Allie b Van Graan	2
I. Ebrahim b Van Graan	22
D. Desplace not out	0
EXTRAS	15
TOTAL	111

FALL OF WICKETS: 1/25; 2/27; 3/38; 4/42; 5/47; 6/48; 7/83; 8/85; 9/110

BOWLING: Mahoney 23-10-37-5; Bergins 17-8-21-0; Carelse 11-6-13-1; Hendricks 8-3-19-0; Henry 8-5-6-0; K van Graan 2,3-2-0-2

NATAL SECOND INNINGS

Y. Omar st Maclons b Carelse	56
G. Francois b Bergins	3
Z. Omar b Mahoney	6
Y. Randeree c Henry b Mahoney	2
T. Roberts c Hendricks b Bergins	2
J. Govender lbw Henry	22
G. Allie b Carelse	16
P. Moodley c Hendricks b Carelse	0
I. Ebrahim c Mahoney b Carelse	13
D. Desplace not out	3
M. Khan c sub b Carelse	0
EXTRAS	7
TOTAL	130

FALL OF WICKETS: 1/5; 2/20; 3/22; 4/27; 5/69; 6/106; 7/106; 8/117; 9/130

BOWLING: Mahoney 19-6-37-2; Bergins 9-0-29-2; Carelse 20,4-11-15-5; Henry 16-8-21-1; Hendricks 5-1-9-0; K. van Graan 4-1-12-0

WP FIRST INNINGS

W. Hendricks c Roberts b Desplace	60
L. Jacobs c Govender b Allie	23
H. Dawson c Allie b Y. Omar	0
A. Katts c Govender b Allie	0
K. van Graan c Khan b Allie	0
+M. Maclons run out	37
O. Henry c Allie b Govender	2
W. Carelse st Roberts b Ebrahim	30
*B. O'Connell c Desplace b Y. Omar	13
J. Mahoney st Roberts b Ebrahim	1
H. Bergins not out	22
EXTRAS	24
TOTAL	212

FALL OF WICKETS: 1/59; 2/60; 3/65; 4/69; 5/112; 6/128; 7/152; 8/174; 9/176

BOWLING: Allie 33-16-44-3; Desplace 18-6-33-1; Y. Omar 30-16-37-2; Ebrahim 30,2-13-39-2; Khan 4-2-8-0; Govender 7-1-13-1; Moodley 5-1-14-0

WP SECOND INNINGS

L. Jacobs not out	17
H. Dawson not out	14
EXTRAS	0
TOTAL	31/0

BOWLING: Allie 1-0-2-0; Desplace 1-0-9-0; Y. Omar 3-1-7-0; Randeree 2-0-9-0; Timol 2-0-4-0

WP WON BY TEN WICKETS.

Western Province's lower-order batting shines, but EP hold out for a draw

WESTERN PROVINCE had good reason to thank the contribution of their tail-end batsmen in this drawn game against Eastern Province.

Certainly, they wouldn't have come close to their eventual first innings total of 190, without the more than useful contributions from Pinky Carelse (36), Brian O'Connell (43) and Howie Bergins (27).

The EP batting effort – 145 – against the WP pace attack of Jock Mahoney (2/55), Bergins (3/31) and Carelse (3/27) was not all that impressive. Best of their batsmen were Bravo Jacobs and Zak Davids, both of whom scored 33.

WP again made merry low down the order, with Carelse (61), O'Connell (79) and Mahoney (22), the prime reasons for their team reaching 287, after at one stage being 90/6.

EP were never really going to make 333 for victory, but they comfortably avoided outright defeat, reaching 142/4 by the end of the third day.

WP FIRST INNINGS

W. Hendricks c Govindjee b Williams.....................4
L. Jacobs b Govindjee..23
H. Dawson c Majola b Pono 2
V. Moodie run out 1
+M. Maclons c Cuddembey b Pono..........................1
K. van Graan c Wilson b Govindjee 17
O. Henry c Jacobs b Fischer 5
W. Carelse c Pono b Fischer 36
*B. O'Connell c Sandan b Wilson 43
J. Mahoney b Govindjee 13
H. Bergins not out 27

EXTRAS...............18
TOTAL...............190

FALL OF WICKETS: 1/9; 2/14; 3/16; 4/25; 5/53; 6/62; 7/62; 8/127; 9/149

BOWLING: Pono 13-2-29-2; Williams 9-2-16-1; Davids 13-3-31-0; Govindjee 18-8-22-3; Fischer 15-4-41-2; Wilson 13-5-20-1; Majola 6-1-13-0

WP SECOND INNINGS

W. Hendricks b Davids 6
L. Jacobs c Francis b Pono 7
H. Dawson c Cuddembey b Pono 1
V. Moodie c Majola b Wilson 42
M. Maclons c Francis b Wilson 1
K. van Graan c Sandan b Williams 44
O. Henry c Pono b Wilson 5
W. Carelse not out...61
B. O'Connell c Davids b Jacobs 79
J. Mahoney c Davids b Fischer 22
H. Bergins st Cuddembey b Govindjee.....................1

EXTRAS...............18
TOTAL...............287

FALL OF WICKETS: 1/10; 2/15; 3/47; 4/48; 5/70; 6/90; 7/140; 8/258; 9/286

BOWLING: Pono 9-3-27-2; Williams 18-3-40-1; Wilson 14-1-39-3; Davids 18-5-49-1; Fischer 15-1-56-1; Govindjee 11,3-2-34-1; Majola 5-2-7-0; Jacobs 2-0-17-1

EP FIRST INNINGS

D. Jacobs c Carelse b Mahoney 33
J. Sandan c Maclons b Bergins 14
K. Majola c van Graan b Mahoney..........................5
N. Francis c O'Connell b Bergins............................0
M. Wilson c Henry b Bergins 0
W. Fischer c Maclons b Carelse...............................18
Z. Davids c & b Henry 33
D. Govindjee b Carelse 0
G. Cuddembey c & b Henry 14
T. Pono not out 10
T. Williams b Carelse 8

EXTRAS...............10
TOTAL...............145

FALL OF WICKETS: 1/32; 2/50; 3/50; 4/52; 5/53; 6/105; 7/105; 8/109; 9/126

BOWLING: Mahoney 20-6-55-2; Bergins 19-5-41-3; Carelse 14,4-5-27-3; Hendricks 1-1-0-0; Henry 15-8-12-2

EP SECOND INNINGS

D. Jacobs b Van Graan..6
J. Sandan c Van Graan b Hendricks..........................8
K. Majola c Maclons b Van Graan 0
N. Francis not out 27
M. Wilson c Maclons b Bergins..............................28
W. Fischer not out 7

EXTRAS...............6
TOTAL............142/4

FALL OF WICKETS: 1/71; 2/73; 3/79; 4/121

BOWLING: Mahoney 3-1-4-0; Bergins 13-3-41-1; Carelse 11-3-30-0; Henry 18-8-17-0; Van Graan 12-5-16-2; Hendricks 9-4-16-1; O'Connell 2-0-7-0; Jacobs 2-1-2-0; Moodie 1-0-3-0

MATCH DRAWN

Western Province find their feet too late against grateful Transvaal

WP vs Transvaal 21-23 February 1976 at Turfhall Cape Town

WESTERN PROVINCE seemed hellbent on presenting Transvaal with the opportunity of wrapping up this game inside two days – although, mind you, they batted through almost 45 overs to reach their embarrassing first innings total of 67.

Transvaal were no great shakes either when they went in to bat – slumping to 85/7, before some tail-end heroics by Ebrahim Bhamjee (41) and Solly Rubidge (27) carried them to 177.

Western Province overcame the early loss of Willie Hendricks for a duck, and batted with much greater resolution in their second innings. Standout innings by skipper Brian O'Connell, who compiled a dogged 77, Pinky Carelse (40), Omar Henry (a fluent, undefeated 62) and the ever-reliable Jock Mahoney (25), carried them to 303 – 193 runs ahead of the Transvaalers.

A fine spell of bowling by medium-pacer Carelse (4/9) took the home side tantalisingly close to an unlikely victory when Transvaal slumped to 81/7 by the close.

WP FIRST INNINGS

W. Hendricks b Ayob 2
L. Jacobs c S. Rubidge b Chothia 14
V. Moodie c Saleh b Chothia 4
+M. Maclons c Barnes b Mangera..........18
W. Carelse run out....................10
K. van Graan st Bhamjee b S. Rubidge 7
A. Katts c Barnes b S. Rubidge 0
*B. O'Connell c Barnes b S. Rubidge 5
O. Henry run out 0
J. Mahoney not out.....................4
H. Bergins c Barnes b S.Rubidge 0
                     EXTRAS.............3
                     TOTAL.................67

FALL OF WICKETS: 1/3; 2/22; 3/23; 4/51; 5/58; 6/58; 7/59; 8/60; 9/67

BOWLING: Ayob 8-3-12-1; Chothia 15-7-18-2; Akoojee 7-3-5-0; Barnes 5-1-11-0; Mangera 7-2-12-1; S. Rubidge 2,4-0-6-4

WP SECOND INNINGS

W. Hendricks b Ayob 0
L. Jacobs st Bhamjee b Mangera 25
V. Moodie c sub b Mangera.................28
M. Maclons c Saleh b Mangera 12
B. O'Connell c Bhamjee b S Rubidge 77
W. Carelse c & b Chothia 40
K. van Graan st Bhamjee b S Rubidge 9
A. Katts c sub b Mangera 9
O. Henry not out 62
J. Mahoney c Akoojee b Chothia............25
H. Bergins b Ayob........................2
                     EXTRAS..............14
                     TOTAL...............303

FALL OF WICKETS: 1/4; 2/49; 3/56; 4/73; 5/166; 6/194; 7/201; 8/227; 9/287

BOWLING: Ayob 28,5-7-58-2; Akoojee 9-3-16-0; Barnes 33-14-40-0; Mangera 43-7-92-4; Chothia 27-7-49-2; S. Rubidge 17-4-30-2; Y. Rubidge 3-1-4-0; Bhamjee 1-1-0-0

TRANSVAAL FIRST INNINGS

I. Garda lbw Bergins 15
AL. Barnes c Katts b Carelse...................40
Y. Rubidge b Bergins 6
A. Manack c O'Connell b Carels...........11
S. Chothia c Van Graan b Carelse............3
M. Mangera run out 12
M. Saleh c Van Graan b Carelse...............0
S. Rubidge c Jacobs b Bergins.............27
I. Akoojee b Carelse........................0
E. Bhamjee c Mahoney b Bergins...........41
H. Ayob not out 0
                     EXTRAS..............22
                     TOTAL..............177

FALL OF WICKETS: 1/23; 2/46; 3/60; 4/79; 5/79; 6/85; 7/85; 8/142; 9/174

BOWLING: Mahoney 25-7-39-0; Bergins 23,1-6-41-4; Henry 15-6-15-0; Carelse 33-16-37-5; Hendricks 6-2-12-0; Van Graan 4-2-11-0

TRANSVAAL SECOND INNINGS

AL. Barnes c Jacobs b Carelse................14
Y. Rubidge c & b Carelse........................13
A. Manack c Mahoney b Carelse.............0
M. Mangera b Bergins 8
S. Chothia b Bergins 6
M. Saleh run out 13
S. Rubidge not out..........................2
E. Bhamjee c Moodie b Carelse..............1
I. Garda not out 1
                     EXTRAS..............13
                     TOTAL..............81/7

FALL OF WICKETS: 1/18; 2/18; 3/49; 4/57; 5/69; 6/79; 7/80

BOWLING: Mahoney 11-3-18-0; Bergins 12-5-17-2; Carelse 14-9-9-4; Hendricks 9-3-17-0; Henry 6-3-7-0

MATCH DRAWN

Natal vs WP
13-15 March
1976
in Durban

Tame draw, but first innings points are enough for WP to take the honours

GEORGE VAN OORDT, batting at number 10, struck a face-saving 37, to steer Western Province to a narrow first innings lead over Natal – enough to enable his team to annexe the Stellenbosch Farmers' Winery interprovincial championship.

For Western Province, this was a significant achievement – they began the campaign without some of their top players, who refused to play in a competition sponsored by a liquor company.

Natal's first innings was anchored by Graham Francois, who compiled a stylish 57. The best of the rest was Trevor Roberts' 25 and Baboo Ebrahim's 22. Pick of the Western Province bowlers was Van Oordt, who gave hardly anything away in taking 3/32 in 23 overs.

The Natal second innings was a disaster. They never recovered from a poor start, which saw them lose their first innings batting hero, Francois, for just 6 – and with Howie Bergins (2/11), Van Oordt (2/23) and Willie Hendricks (3/21) bowling well, they struggled to 92/8 by the close.

NATAL FIRST INNINGS
G. Francois c Timol b Van Oordt 57
Y. Omar ret hurt 6
G. Sewpersadh c Jacobs b Bergins 1
Y. Pillay run out..10
Y. Randeree c & b Mahoney 0
J. Govender run out.. 6
T. Roberts c Timol b Van Oordt 25
S. Geldenhuys lbw Van Oordt 1
I. Ebrahim b Bergins 22
G. Allie lbw Hendricks 4
M. Govender not out 7
EXTRAS...............19
TOTAL............158/9

FALL OF WICKETS: 1/10; 2/48; 3/48; 4/80; 5/121; 6/123; 7/124; 8/140; 9/158

BOWLING: Mahoney 19-4-22-1; Bergins 10,5-0-26-2; Carelse 13-3-30-0; Van Oordt 23-10 32-3; Henry 13-5-16-0; Hendricks 6-3-13-1

NATAL SECOND INNINGS
G. Francois c O'Connell b Bergins...........................6
G. Sewpersadh c Henry b Bergins 10
Y. Randeree run out..17
Y. Pillay c Maclons b Van Oordt...............................0
J. Govender b van Oordt 9
T. Roberts c Henry b Hendricks...............................1
S. Geldenhuys not out...33
I. Ebrahim lbw Hendricks 0
M. Govender c Mahoney b Hendricks......................9
G. Allie not out..0
EXTRAS.................7
TOTAL.............92/8

FALL OF WICKETS: 1/17; 2/22; 3/31; 4/42; 5/46; 6/46; 7/ 50; 8/72

BOWLING: Bergins 6-3-11-2; Van Oordt 12-6-23-2; Mahoney 6-1-21-0; Hendricks 7-2-21-3; Henry 2-0-9-0

WP FIRST INNINGS
W. Hendricks lbw Allie 10
L. Jacobs b M. Govender 0
V. Moodie b M. Govender 8
H. Bergins b Allie..18
+M. Maclons b M. Govender 1
I. Timol c Pillay b Allie..29
W. Carelse c Pillay b M Govender..........................38
*B. O'Connell c M Govender b Ebrahim................13
O. Henry b Allie...0
G. van Oordt lbw M. Govender 37
J. Mahoney not out..0
EXTRAS...............15
TOTAL 169

FALL OF WICKETS: 1/4; 2/20; 3/22; 4/25; 5/68; 6/73; 7/98; 8/99; 9/151

BOWLING: Allie 34-11-56-4; M. Govender 15,1-3-35-5; Ebrahim 35-17-47-1; J. Govender 5-2-12-0; Sewpersadh 2-1-4-0

MATCH DRAWN
WP WON THE SFW COMPETITION

"Normal" cricket protest overshadows Sacboc's easy victory over SFW champions

WP vs Rest of SACBOC 27-29 March 1976 at Oude Libertas Stellenbosch

A PROTEST by the majority of the Western Province team, in support of suspended players Howie Bergins and Pinky Carelse, overshadowed the Rest of Sacboc's easy nine-wicket victory over the interprovincial champions.

Bergins and Carelse were suspended for playing in a match (with the permission of Sacboc) against the touring International Wanderers.

Western Province, batting first, scored 151 in their first innings, with only Lawton Jacobs (50), George van Oordt (27 not out) and Ismail Timol (22), looking the part.

With Morris Garda compiling a classy 112, and with excellent supporting innings coming from Solly Chothia (52), Graham Francois (34) and Yacoob Omar (33) the Rest reached 312, a substantial lead of 161.

Thanks mainly to Viccie Moodie (55), Western Province managed to ward off an innings defeat – but only just. The Rest knocked off the winning runs in a little over three overs.

WP FIRST INNINGS

W. Hendricks b Allie	4
L. Jacobs c Allie b Barnes	50
V. Moodie c Pono b Barnes	19
+M. Maclons lbw Barnes	0
C. van Schalkwyk st Bhamjee b Ebrahim	2
I. Timol c Bhamjee b Allie	22
C. Miller lbw Barnes	1
*B. O'Connell c sub b Ebrahim	4
G. van Oordt not out	27
O. Henry c Chothia b Ebrahim	13
A. Sonn b Ebrahim	3
EXTRAS	6
TOTAL	151

FALL OF WICKETS: 1/10 ; 2/53; 3/59; 4/66; 5/80; 6/81; 7/86; 8/109; 9/136

BOWLING: Allie 14-2-28-2; Pono 6-2-14-0; Chothia 10-2-29-0; Barnes 25-15-23-4; Ebrahim 27,3-14-51- 4

WP SECOND INNINGS

L. Jacobs b Barnes	27
W. Hendricks b Barnes	19
V. Moodie c Snyders b Chothia	55
C. Miller lbw Govender	11
I. Timol c Govindjee b Pono	16
B. O'Connell lbw Barnes	9
C. van Schalkwyk st Bhamjee b Barnes	0
G. van Oordt st Bhamjee b Barnes	3
O. Henry run out	2
M. Maclons not out	2
A. Sonn c Pono b Barnes	0
EXTRAS	23
TOTAL	167

FALL OF WICKETS: 1/56; 2/57; 3/88; 4/141; 5/155; 6/159; 7/161; 8/167; 9/167

BOWLING: Allie 14-4-32-0; Pono 15-3-25-1; Barnes 30,5-13-44-6; Ebrahim 12-4-15-0; Chothia 14-8-19-1; J. Govender 7-4-9-1

REST OF SACBOC FIRST INNINGS

I. Garda c Miller b Van Schalkwyk	112
G. Francois run out	34
Y. Omar lbw Henry	33
Y. Snyders run out	23
S. Chothia b Hendricks	52
A. Barnes st Maclons b Henry	2
J. Govender c Maclons b Van Oordt	0
E. Bhamjee b Hendricks	6
I. Ebrahim lbw Hendricks	3
G. Allie not out	7
T. Pono c Maclons b Hendricks	1
EXTRAS	19
TOTAL	312

FALL OF WICKETS: 1/95; 2/182; 3/210; 4/219; 5/223; 6/224; 7/293; 8/299; 9/310

BOWLING: Sonn 18-8-28-0; Van Oordt 25-10-48-1; Van Schalkwyk 32-9-65-1; Henry 34-10-79-2; Hendricks 11,4-0-50-4; Miller 6-1-21-0; Jacobs 1-0- 2-0

REST OF SACBOC SECOND INNINGS

I. Ebrahim c & b O'Connell	0
G. Francois not out	5
I. Garda not out	3
EXTRAS	0
TOTAL	8/1

BOWLING: O'Connell 2-1-1-1; Moodie 1,3-0-7-0

REST OF SACBOC WON BY 9 WICKETS

WP Cricket Board First Class Averages 1975/76

BATTING

NAME	MATCHES	INNS	NO	HS	RUNS	AVE	50	100
Brian O'Connell	7	11	2	79	302	33,56	2	
George van Oordt	2	3	1	37	67	33,50		
Winston Carelse	6	9	2	61*	232	33,14	1	
Viccie Moodie	6	10	0	65	270	27,00	2	
Lawton Jacobs	7	13	2	50	291	26,45	1	
Ismail Timol	2	3	0	29	67	22,33		
Willie Hendricks	7	12	1	60	149	13,54	1	
Keith van Graan	5	8	0	44	105	13,13		
Mornay Maclons	7	11	1	37	119	11,90		
Omar Henry	7	11	1	62*	115	11,50	1	
Howie Bergins	6	9	2	27*	74	10,57		
Jock Mahoney	6	9	2	25	74	10,57		
Hilary Dawson	4	7	1	28	49	8,16		
Arthur Katts	2	3	0	9	9	3,00		

Also batted: Charles van Schalkwyk 2 and 0; Cedric Miller 1 and 11 and Archie Sonn 3 and 0

FIELDING:

Wicketkeeper: 23 – Mornay Maclons (18c and 5st)

CATCHES:

7 – Omar Henry; 6 – Keith van Graan, Brian O'Connell and Jock Mahoney; 5 – Lawton Jacobs; 3 – Hilary Dawson, Willie Hendricks and Viccie Moodie; 2 – Winston Carelse, Arthur Katts and Ismail Timol; 1 – Howie Bergins, Cedric Miller

BOWLING

Name	Overs	Mdns	Wkts	Runs	Ave	Best Bowling	5i	10m
Keith van Graan	23,3	11	4	40	10,00	2/0 v Natal		
Winston Carelse	133	55	20	210	10,50	5/15 v Natal	2	
Howie Bergins	177,3	44	30	357	11,90	6/27 v Tvl	2	1
Willie Hendricks	134,4	36	18	265	14,72	4/50 v S'bocXI		
George van Oordt	62	26	6	104	17,33	3/33 v Natal		
Jock Mahoney	189	55	18	362	20,11	6/42 v EP	2	
Omar Henry	156,3	62	8	229	28,63	3/47 v EP		
Charles van Schalkwyk	32	9	1	65	65,00	1/65 v S'bocXI		

Also Bowled: Archie Sonn 18-8-28-0; Cedric Miller 6-1-21-0;

Lawton Jacobs 3-1-2-0; Viccie Moodie 2,3-0-10-0; Brian O'Connell 4-1-8-1

Bowlers call the shots as Western Province crush Eastern Province

WP vs EP
26-28 November 1977
at Avonwood Park
Cape Town

SAAIT MAGIET confirmed his rating as the WP Cricket Board's top strike bowler with another rich haul in this low-scoring match at Avonwood Park in Elsies River, near Cape Town.

Both teams were severely weakened by the exodus of top players to the "normal" cricket setup – and it showed. Eastern Province, batting first, poked and scratched their way to 134, with only Wilbur Fischer (23) looking the part. Magiet (4/53) was the most successful of the Western Province bowlers, although Charlie van Schalkwyk (2/22), Armien Jabaar (2/12) and George van Oordt all bowled with their customary accuracy.

The Western Province first innings was shored up by a fine debut half-century by Cyril Martin (56). The only other batting of note was provided by Mike Finnan (21), on his return to provincial cricket after a 10-year absence.

Rushdi Magiet (4/14) and Van Oordt (3/11) were the chief destroyers in a dismal Eastern Province second innings of 60. The home side reached the required 51 for victory, for the loss of four wickets.

EP FIRST INNINGS
K. Majola c Isaacs b S. Magiet 14
N. Sain run out 13
S. Kruger b Van Schalkwyk 16
F. Abrahams b Van Oordt 1
W. Fischer lbw S. Magiet.......................................23
M. Davids c Jabaar b S. Magiet................................9
D. Booysen b Van Schalkwyk..................................13
M. Kara c Jabaar b S. Magiet 2
T. Pono c Salie b Jabaar 16
C. Moodaley st Isaacs b Jabaar 9
T. Kadi not out 6
EXTRAS..............12
TOTAL...............134

FALL OF WICKETS: 1/16; 2/44; 3/52; 4/52; 5/82; 6/89; 7/ 99; 8/105; 9/120

BOWLING: S. Magiet 14-0-53-4; Allie 5-1-14-0; Van Schalkwyk 15-5-22-2; Van Oordt 14,4-4-18-1; Jabaar 8-4-12-2; Arendse 2-1-3-0

EP SECOND INNINGS
K. Majola b S. Magiet...5
N. Sain b S. Magiet 1
S. Kruger lbw Van Schalkwyk 13
F. Abrahams c Isaacs b van Oordt.............................4
W. Fischer st Isaacs b R. Magiet 12
M. Davids c Isaacs b van Oordt 2
D. Booysen c & b R. Magiet....................................4
M. Kara b R. Magiet 4
T. Pono c Isaacs b R. Magiet 4
C. Moodaley st Isaacs b van Oordt............................1
T. Kadi not out 2
EXTRAS................8
TOTAL.................60

FALL OF WICKETS: 1/4; 2/11; 3/22; 4/34; 5/40; 6/45; 7/49; 8/50; 9/55

BOWLING: S. Magiet 9-3-12-2; Allie 9-4-9-0; Van Schalkwyk 2-1-6-1; Van Oordt 9,5-3-11-3; R. Magiet 8-2-14-4

WP FIRST INNINGS
M. Finnan c Fischer b Pono....................................21
R. Salie c Kruger b Moodaley 8
N. Arendse c Sain b Pono 0
C. Martin c & b Davids...56
A. Jabaar lbw Kara...18
+E. Isaacs lbw Pono...16
G. van Oordt b Fischer...5
C. van Schalkwyk b Fischer....................................2
S. Magiet lbw Fischer 0
*R. Magiet c Booysen b Davids 0
G. Allie not out..4
EXTRAS..............14
TOTAL 144

FALL OF WICKETS: 1/27; 2/27; 3/38; 4/79; 5/112; 6/124; 7/128; 8/130; 9/131

BOWLING: Pono 25-11-26-3; Moodaley 15-3-34-1; Davids 20,4-8-24-2; Kadi 9-3-17-0; Kara 8-1-15-1; Fischer 11-5-14-3; Majola 1-1-0-0

WP SECOND INNINGS
M. Finnan c Pono b Kadi 31
R. Salie b Pono..2
N. Arendse b Pono 3
A. Jabaar c Booysen b Moodaley 1
S. Magiet not out...10
C. van Schalkwyk not out 2
EXTRAS................2
TOTAL..............51/4

FALL OF WICKETS: 1/2; 2/20; 3/21; 4/46

BOWLING: Pono 8,1-2-19-2; Moodaley 6-2-20-1; Kadi 2-0-10-1

WP WON BY SIX WICKETS

Transvaal vs WP
26-28 December
1977
in Johannesburg

"New" Transvaal fail to top 100 in two attempts against WP pace attack

WHAT IS there to say about a team that gets blasted out for totals of 53 and 43 – on home turf? Out of their depth, would probably be putting it kindly.

Perhaps the one positive to come out of this match, was that the Transvaalers, in dismissing Western Province for 124, showed that they have a fairly decent attack. But, several Western Province batsmen would have been kicking themselves after getting into the twenties – and then getting themselves out.

Transvaal, batting first, were swept aside by the pace of Saait Magiet (4/19) and Baby Damon (4/21). The underrated George van Oordt again weighed in with a fine display of support bowling, taking 2/4 in eight overs.

Western Province would have been terribly disappointed with their reply of 124, especially since Braima Isaacs (22), Armien Jabaar (21) and Saait Magiet (26) all contrived to get themselves out when well set. Charlie van Schalkwyk was undefeated with 21.

Although hard to imagine, Transvaal's second innings was even more disastrous than their first. Saait Magiet (4/13), Rushdi Magiet (3/9) and Van Oordt (2/2) combined to shoot the home side out for 43 – to take their team to victory by an innings and 28 runs.

TRANSVAAL FIRST INNINGS

E. Amod b Damon......................................4
S. Nana c van Graan b S. Magiet.............13
Z. Baatjies c R. Magiet b S. Magiet.........1
O. Visser c Isaacs b S. Magiet..................0
N. Edwards c Martin b Damon 10
N. Okkers c Van Schalkwyk b Damon.......2
D. Jacobs c S. Magiet b Damon................0
I. Bhagalia b Van Oordt.............................2
M. Abed c Van Oordt b S. Magiet 7
N. Abrahams c Martin b S. Magiet............1
T. Hassen not out......................................4

EXTRAS.................9
TOTAL..................53

FALL OF WICKETS: 1/12; 2/17; 3/17; 4/35; 5/39; 6/39; 7/40 8/44; 9/48

BOWLING: S. Magiet 9-4-19-4; Damon 14-4-21-4; Van Oordt 8-5-4-2

WP FIRST INNINGS

M. Finnan c Okkers b Abrahams 3
R. van Graan c Bagalia b Jacobs.............13
A. Wadvalla lbw Abrahams.......................0
C. Martin lbw Jacobs 2
+E. Isaacs c Okkers b Amod.....................22
A. Jabaar b Edwards.................................21
S. Magiet c Baatjies b Amod 26
C. van Schalkwyk not out 21
G. van Oordt c Visser b Edwards.............0
*R. Magiet lbw Amod.................................0
E. Damon b Jacobs....................................7

EXTRAS.................9
TOTAL...............124

FALL OF WICKETS: 1/5; 2/5; 3/18; 4/19; 5/47; 6/89; 7/97; 8/97; 9/102

BOWLING: Abrahams 10-3-24-2; Jacobs 7,3-1-32-3; Amod 9-3-36-3; Edwards 11-3-23-2

TRANSVAAL SECOND INNINGS

E. Amod lbw R. Magiet 6
S. Nana b S. Magiet 2
Z. Baatjies c Damon b S. Magiet.............0
O. Visser c van Oordt b S. Magiet 1
N. Edwards b R. Magiet............................2
G. Okkers c Martin b Jabaar 4
D. Jacobs c van Oordt b S. Magiet 1
I. Bagalia b R. Magiet..............................2
M. Abed lbw van Oordt 18
N. Abrahams c Martin b van Oordt..........0
T. Hassen not out.....................................0

EXTRAS.................7
TOTAL.................43

FALL OF WICKETS: 1/9; 2/9; 3/9; 4/12; 5/ 12; 6/17; 7/20 8/42; 9/42

BOWLING: Damon 4-0-10-0; S. Magiet 14-8-13-4; R. Magiet 8-3-9-3; Jabaar 6-4-2-1; Van Oordt 3,2-2-2-2

WP WON BY AN INNINGS AND 28 RUNS

Jabaar's 11-wicket haul steers WP to an easy innings victory over Natal

**WP vs Natal
Dec 31, 1977-
Jan 2 1978 at
Mitchells Plain
Cape Town**

GUESS WHO couldn't play legspin – or, at least, Armien Jabaar's version of that wonderful craft? Natal, who like Transvaal, were cruelly hit by defections to "normal" cricket, were brushed aside with contemptuous ease by Western Province.

They made a reasonable enough start, though, when they went in to bat. With openers, Yacoob Omar and Graham Francois taking the total past 20, and looking reasonably comfortable against the dangerous Western Province pace attack, they must have had visions of a reasonable score. But once the openers had departed, Jabaar grabbed centre stage. In nine overs and two balls, he returned the incredible figures of 6/9 – and that, as they say in the movies, was that.

Jabaar showed that he is no slouch with the bat, either, compiling a useful 48, before hitting a return catch to Omar. With fellow allrounders, Saait Magiet (54) and Charlie van Schalkwyk (49 not out) making useful contributions, Western Province reached 241 in their first innings.

Jabaar (5/36) was again the chief destroyer in Natal's second innings of 117 – 68 runs short of making Western Province bat again.

NATAL FIRST INNINGS

Y. Omar c R. Magiet b van Oordt	15
G. Francois c R. Magiet b Damon	16
R. Julius b Jabaar	8
K. Hiraman c Finnan b Jabaar	0
T. Roberts c Finnan b Jabaar	9
A. Bawa b Jabaar	0
J. Govender c R. Magiet b Van Oordt	1
M. Khan b van Oordt	1
R. Rogers c Van Schalkwyk b Jabaar	0
L. Esterhuizen c S. Magiet b Jabaar	3
H. Moonilal not out	0
EXTRAS	3
TOTAL	56

FALL OF WICKETS: 1/22; 2/41; 3/41; 4/42; 5/43; 6/48; 7/52; 8/53; 9/53

BOWLING: Damon 12-4-17-1; S. Magiet 7-3-9-0; Van Oordt 16-7-18-3; R. Magiet 2-2-0-0; Jabaar 9,2-4-9-6

NATAL SECOND INNINGS

Y. Omar c R. Magiet b Damon	19
G. Francois b S. Magiet	5
R. Julius c Martin b S. Magiet	9
K. Hiraman b Van Oordt	20
T. Roberts c Isaacs b Jabaar	37
A. Bawa not out	18
J. Govender c Isaacs b Jabaar	1
M. Khan st Isaacs b Jabaar	1
R. Rogers c Van Schalkwyk b Jabaar	2
L. Esterhuizen c Van Oordt b Jabaar	0
H. Moonilal c & b Van Oordt	0
EXTRAS	5
TOTAL	117

FALL OF WICKETS: 1/17; 2/33; 3/35; 4/89; 5/95; 6/101; 7/106; 8/108; 9/108

BOWLING: Damon 9-2-18-1; S. Magiet 8-2-23-2; Van Oordt 11,2-3-21-2; Jabaar 17-5-36-5; Van Schalkwyk 1-0-7-0; R. Magiet 7-4-7-0

WP FIRST INNINGS

M. Finnan c Govender b Rogers	21
R. van Graan b Rogers	5
A. Wadvalla lbw Rogers	5
C. Martin c Khan b Rogers	0
+E. Isaacs b Govender	9
S. Magiet c Rogers b Omar	54
A. Jabaar c & b Omar	48
C. van Schalkwyk not out	49
*R. Magiet c Govender b Khan	2
G. van Oordt c Roberts b Rogers	36
E. Damon run out	3
EXTRAS	9
TOTAL	241

FALL OF WICKETS: 1/21; 2/28; 3/28; 4/38; 5/42; 6/149; 7/164; 8/225; 9/231

BOWLING: Esterhuizen 9-2-43-0; Rogers 18,5-4-55-5; Govender 13-1-56-1; Omar 17-1-42-2; Khan 9-1-30-1; Moonilal 3-0-6-0

WP WON BY AN INNINGS AND 68 RUNS

Western Province crash – despite bowling heroics by Jabaar and Van Oordt

A MEDIOCRE batting display by Western Province led to their downfall by 34 runs in this Howa Bowl match against arch-rivals Eastern Province in Port Elizabeth.

Although Armien Jabaar again bowled brilliantly, taking 5/33 in the Eastern Province first innings, and Georgie van Oordt (5/50) did likewise in the second innings, Western Province's first innings effort of 176 (in reply to EP's 209) cost them the match.

The best batting for the visitors was provided by makeshift opener, Armien Jabaar (35) and allrounders, Shamiel Jassiem (43) and Charlie van Schalkwyk (29).

Van Oordt's impeccably tidy bowling kept Western Province in the hunt as Eastern Province, rather fortunately, reached 208 in their second innings.

Fine batting by Munsoor Abdullah (45), Braima Isaacs (62) and Saait Magiet (48) kept Western Province in the hunt, until a middle-order collapse took the match Eastern Province's way – by 34 runs.

EP FIRST INNINGS

H. Lorgat b S. Magiet	1
S. Kruger st Isaacs b S. Magiet	7
K. Majola c & b Damon	41
F. Abrahams c Isaacs b Jabaar	83
M. Philander c Isaacs b Damon	10
V. Malgas c sub b Jabaar	12
W. Fischer run out	19
T. Pono c R. Magiet b Jabaar	11
M. Wicks c S. Magiet b Jabaar	3
M. Kara c R. Magiet b Jabaar	0
T. Kadi not out	1
EXTRAS	21
TOTAL	209

FALL OF WICKETS: 1/4; 2/18; 3/106; 4/134; 5/171; 6/182; 7/201; 8/207; 9/207

BOWLING: Damon 14-2-52-2; S. Magiet 10-3-24-2; R. Magiet 6-2-16-0; Van Oordt 16-7-27-0; Jabaar 17,2-1-33-5; Van Schalkwyk 4-3-6-0; Jassiem 18-5-30-0

EP SECOND INNINGS

S. Kruger c Van Oordt b Damon	1
H. Lorgat b R. Magiet	48
K. Majola lbw Van Oordt	15
F. Abrahams c Isaacs b Van Oordt	41
M. Philander c S. Magiet b Van Oordt	4
V. Malgas c Isaacs b S. Magiet	10
W. Fischer st Isaacs b Van Oordt	0
T. Pono not out	46
M. Wicks c Isaacs b S. Magiet	14
M. Kara c S. Magiet b Van Oordt	8
T. Kadi c Isaacs b S. Magiet	0
EXTRAS	21
TOTAL	208

FALL OF WICKETS: 1/6; 2/59; 3/72; 4/78; 5/128; 6/129; 7/132; 8/194; 9/207

BOWLING: Damon 4-1 - 19-1; S. Magiet 17,5-5-49-3; R. Magiet 14-3-27-1; Van Oordt 24-6-50-5; Jabaar 6-0-25-0; Van Schalkwyk 3-0-17-0

WP FIRST INNINGS

M. Finnan c Lorgat b Pono	2
A. Jabaar c Abrahams b Kara	35
F. Solomons b Kadi	8
M. Abdullah c Fischer b Pono	7
+E. Isaacs b Fischer	15
S. Magiet b Kara	5
C. van Schalkwyk lbw Pono	29
S. Jassiem not out	43
G. van Oordt b Kadi	0
*R. Magiet lbw Kara	19
E. Damon b Fischer	0
EXTRAS	13
TOTAL	176

FALL OF WICKETS: 1/3; 2/27; 3/48; 4/70; 5/70; 6/80; 7/122; 8/125; 9/175

BOWLING: Pono 17-3-57-3; Kadi 16-4-49-2; Kara 10-1-30-3; Fischer 9.4-0-25-2; Malgas 2- 1- 2- 0; Majola 2- 2- 0- 0

WP SECOND INNINGS

M. Finnan b Kadi	4
E. Damon c Abrahams b Pono	5
F. Solomons c & b Kara	7
M. Abdullah c Abrahams b Kara	45
E. Isaacs c Kara b Wicks	62
S. Magiet lbw Malgas	48
C. van Schalkwyk c Fischer b Pono	0
A. Jabaar lbw Kara	23
S. Jassiem b Kara	5
G. van Oordt c Abrahams b Malgas	3
R. Magiet not out	0
EXTRAS	5
TOTAL	207

BOWLING: Pono 17-2-40-2; Kadi 17-5-52-1; Wicks 14-4-28-1; Malgas 2,1-0-12-2; Kara 18-4-41-4; Fischer 4-0-15-0; Majola 3-1-14-0

EP WON BY 34 RUNS

Rushdi Magiet's 10-wicket haul sees off the challenge of much improved Transvaal

WP vs Transvaal 11-13 February 1978 at Avonwood Park Cape Town

THE TEAM that failed to top 100 in two attempts at the crease, in their first round match against Western Province in Johannesburg just a few weeks ago, fared much better this time around.

But, they still found the allround strength of the home side too much to handle. Batting first, they compiled 130, with Owen Visser (55) topscoring. WP's "king of swing", Rushdi Magiet, fared best with the ball, taking 5/23. Armien Jabaar, too, continued his rich vein of form. Another impressive display of legspin bowling earned him 2/25.

Top scorers in the WP reply of 226 were Saait Magiet (62) and new cap, Faghme Solomons (40). Rushdi Magiet picked up five wickets for the second time in the match, as the Transvaalers struggled to 140 all out, with the best contributions coming from Visser (32) and Duncan Stamper (40)

WP made heavy weather of getting 45 for victory, reaching 46 for the loss of five wickets.

TRANSVAAL FIRST INNINGS

E. Amod lbw R. Magiet		5
S. Nana b R. Magiet		4
H. Naik run out		27
O. Visser c Van Oordt b Jabaar		55
D. Stamper c van Oordt b Jabaar		6
N. Edwards c Van Schalkwyk b Van Oordt		8
S. Gabriels run out		6
N. Bismillah b R. Magiet		1
E. Choonara st Isaacs b R. Magiet		0
D. Jacobs b R. Magiet		6
N. Abrahams not out		3
	EXTRAS	9
	TOTAL	130

FALL OF WICKETS: 1/8; 2/15; 3/80; 4/102; 5/102; 6/115; 7/119; 8/119; 9/120

BOWLING: S. Magiet 7-1-25-0; R. Magiet 13,3-6-23-5; Van Oordt 11-4-17-1; Van Schalkwyk 8-1-28-0; Jabaar 14-5-25-2; Jassiem 7-5-3-0

TRANSVAAL SECOND INNINGS

E. Amod c & b Jabaar		6
S. Nana run out		3
H. Naik lbw Jassiem		19
O. Visser c S. Magiet b R. Magiet		32
D. Stamper c Solomons b R. Magiet		42
N. Edwards run out		3
S. Gabriels b R. Magiet		1
D. Jacobs c Van Schalkwyk b R. Magiet		4
N. Bismillah c Van Oordt b R. Magiet		16
N. Abrahams b Jabaar		3
E. Choonara not out		0
	EXTRAS	11
	TOTAL	140

FALL OF WICKETS: 1/9; 2/19; 3/53; 4/71; 5/79; 6/81; 7/116; 8/120; 9/140

BOWLING: S. Magiet 4-1-4-0; R. Magiet 19-7-33-5; Jabaar 24,2-3-55-2; Van Oordt 10-5-12-0; Jassiem 8-0-25-1

WP FIRST INNINGS

V. Smith lbw Jacobs		14
F. Solomons lbw Gabriels		40
M. Doman b Abrahams		12
M. Ebrahim b Gabriels		19
+E. Isaacs lbw Gabriels		9
S. Magiet c Naik b Abrahams		62
C. van Schalkwyk b Gabriels		15
A. Jabaar c Stamper b Gabriels		19
G. van Oordt lbw Gabriels		4
*R. Magiet c Gabriels b Stamper		11
S. Jassiem not out		3
	EXTRAS	18
	TOTAL	226

FALL OF WICKETS: 1/34; 2/53; 3/78; 4/94; 5/110

BOWLING: Abrahams 13-2-36-2; Jacobs 10-2-29-1; Amod 11-3-18-0; Stamper 24-8-45-1; Gabriels 31,5-6-80-6

WP SECOND INNINGS

V. Smith b Nana		1
F. Solomons run out		5
M. Doman b Nana		0
M. Ebrahim lbw Gabriels		10
E. Isaacs c Abrahams b Gabriels		0
S. Magiet not out		18
A. Jabaar not out		8
	EXTRAS	4
	TOTAL	46/5

FALL OF WICKETS: 1/5; 2/8; 3/10; 4/15; 5/30

BOWLING: Abrahams 2-0-5-0; Nana 8-3-9-2; Gabriels 7-1-20-2; Amod 1-0-8-0

WP WON BY FIVE WICKETS

Natal vs WP

4-6 March

1978

in Durban

Despite a tame draw in Durban, Western Province take the Howa Bowl

WESTERN Province's batsmen again flattered only to deceive, in their final match of the season against Natal, in Durban.

Armien Jabaar (30), Shamiel Jassiem (22), Faghme Solomons (26) and Charlie van Schalkwyk (23) all got into, or past, the twenties – and then, as Western Province players have done so many times over the past few seasons, they proceeded to throw their wickets away.

When, oh when, are they going to learn to turn solid starts into big hundreds?
Given their recent record of batting frailties, Natal did reasonably well in their first innings – to reach 209. Western Province debutant, Sheraat Arnold, was the pick of the visiting bowlers, picking up 4/50 in a lengthy 22-over bowling stint. The rest of the attack bowled accurately, if not particularly penetratively.

As mentioned earlier, the Western Province batsmen's penchant to commit *harakiri*, saw them dismissed for 145.

Natal, after using up 38 overs of batting time, declared at 80/4, inviting Western Province to make 145 for victory.

The invitation was not accepted. After the early departure of Vaughan Smith (2) and Faghme Solomons (9), they reached 20/2 by the close.

NATAL FIRST INNINGS

G. Francois run out	23
Y. Omar c Isaacs b J. Williams	0
A. Bawa st Isaacs b Arnold	11
Y. Randeree b Jabaar	5
T. Roberts c van Schalkwyk b Arnold	30
M. Khan run out	22
J. Govender b van Oordt	34
L. Lawler run out	1
R. Rogers c Martin b Arnold	32
B. David c Jabaar b Arnold	22
M. Govender not out	0
EXTRAS	29
TOTAL	209

FALL OF WICKETS: 1/5; 2/33; 3/43; 4/71; 5/94; 6/143; 7/154; 8/207; 9/209
BOWLING: J. Williams 16-5-23-1; R. Magiet 25-15-20-0; Van Schalkwyk 4-2-2-0; Van Oordt 21-7-39-1; Arnold 22,2-6-50-4; Jabaar 23-6-46-1

NATAL SECOND INNINGS

G. Francois c Isaacs b Williams	0
Y. Omar c Smith b Williams	33
A. Bawa lbw Williams	28
J. Govender b R. Magiet	5
Y. Randeree not out	2
EXTRAS	12
TOTAL	80/4 dec

FALL OF WICKETS: 1/0; 2/65; 3/74; 4/78
BOWLING: Williams 18-8-21-3; R. Magiet 14-5-24-1; Van Oordt 6-3-23-0

WP FIRST INNINGS

A. Jabaar c Bawa b M. Govender	30
V. Smith run out	5
J. Williams c David b M. Govender	4
C. Martin lbw M. Govender	0
+E. Isaacs lbw David	14
S. Jassiem c Roberts b Omar	22
F. Solomons b J. Govender	6
C. van Schalkwyk c J. Govender b Khan	23
G. van Oordt c Roberts b Khan	3
*R. Magiet c & b J. Govender	10
S. Arnold not out	1
EXTRAS	7
TOTAL	145

FALL OF WICKETS: 1/21; 2/40; 3/40; 4/41; 5/78; 6/80; 7/109; 8/113; 9/138
BOWLING: M. Govender 12-0-45-3; Rogers 11-1-24-0; J. Govender 8,5-2-12-2; David 12-3-19-1; Omar 10-5-8-1; Khan 12-2-30-2

WP SECOND INNINGS

V. Smith c Roberts b M. Govender	2
F. Solomons c Roberts b Rogers	9
A. Jabaar ret hurt	1
C. Martin not out	6
E. Isaacs not out	0
EXTRAS	2
TOTAL	20/2

BOWLING: M. Govender 5-2-11-1; Rogers 7-6-1-1; David 4-3-5-0; Khan 2-1-1-0

MATCH DRAWN
WP WON THE HOWA BOWL

WP Cricket Board First Class Averages 1977/78

BATTING

Name	Matches	Inns	NO	HS	Runs	Ave	50	100
Saait Magiet	5	8	2	62	223	37,17	2	
Shamiel Jassiem	3	4	2	43*	73	36,50		
Charles van Schalkwyk	6	8	3	49*	141	28,2		
Armien Jabaar	6	10	1	48	204	22,67		
Ebrahim Isaacs	6	9	1	62	147	18,38	1	
Cyril Martin	4	5	1	56	64	16,00	1	
Faghme Solomons	3	6	0	40	95	15,80		
Mike Finnan	4	6	0	31	82	13,67		
Robbie van Graan	2	2	0	13	18	9,00		
George van Oordt	6	7	0	36	50	7,14		
Rushdi Magiet	6	7	1	19	42	7,00		
Vaughan Smith	2	4	0	14	22	5,50		
Ebrahim Damon	3	4	0	7	15	3,75		
Aziz Wadvalla	2	2	0	5	5	2,50		

Also batted:Rashaad Salie 8 and 2; Norman Arendse 0 and 3; Mohammed Ebrahim 19 and 10; Goolam Allie 4*; Kosie Williams 4; Sheraat Arnold 1* and Munsoor Abdullah 2

FIELDING:

Wicketkeepers: 23 – Ebrahim Isaacs (15ct and 8st)

Catches:

10 – George van Oordt; 8 – Rushdi Magiet; 6 – Charles van Schalkwyk, Saait Magiet; 5 – Cyril Martin; 2 – Mike Finnan, Ebrahim Damon; 1 – Rashaad Salie, Robbie van Graan, Vaughan Smith, Faghme Solomons

BOWLING

Name	Overs	Mdns	Wkts	Runs	Ave	Best Bowling	5i	10m
Saait Magiet	100,2	30	21	231	11,00	4/13 v Tvl		
Charles van Schalkwyk	37	10	3	86	28,67	2/22 v EP		
George van Oordt	147,3	53	20	242	12,10	5/50 v EP	1	
Armien Jabaar	125	32	24	243	10,10	6/9 v Natal	3	1
Rushdi Magiet	116,3	49	19	173	9,10	5/23 v Tvl	2	1
Ebrahim Damon	57	13	9	137	15,22	4/21 v Tvl		
Shamiel Jassiem	26	10	1	58	58,00	1/25 v Tvl		
Kosie Williams	34	13	4	44	11,00	3/21 v Natal		
Sheraat Arnold	22,2	6	4	50	12,50	4/50 v Natal		

Also bowled: Goolam Allie 14-7-23-0; Norman Arendse 2-1-3-0

Jabaar's spin sets WP up for a comfortable victory over their Eastern Cape rivals

ALTHOUGH FAGHME Abrahams (60) and Devdas Govindjee (42) batted well for Eastern Province, a first innings total of 178 was never quite going to be enough to beat Western Province.

And so it proved. With Saait Magiet weighing in with what has become a customary cameo knock in the middle of the Western Province batting order, and with other familiar faces – Braima Isaacs (26), Armien Jabaar (34) and Charlie van Schalkwyk (27 not out) – also batting well, the home side reached 207 in reply.

Eastern Province had little answer to Jabaar's legbreaks in their second knock – and with only Ashwell Frans (31) and Imraan Hendricks getting beyond the teens, they crashed to 132 all out.

Western Province knocked off the required runs for the loss of five wickets.

EP FIRST INNINGS

K. Majola c Isaacs b S Magiet	7
A. Frans lbw S Magiet	0
D. Jacobs lbw van Oordt	7
F. Abrahams c Barnes b Jabaar	60
M. Philander c S Magiet b Jabaar	19
V. Malgas b R Magiet	0
W. Fischer run out	21
I. Hendricks c & b R Magiet	0
D. Govindjee c van Oordt b Jassiem	42
M. Kara not out	4
T. Kadi b van Oordt	0
EXTRAS	18
TOTAL	178

FALL OF WICKETS: 1/12; 2/13; 3/44; 4/95; 5/98; 6/114; 7/119; 8/162; 9/172

BOWLING: S Magiet 7-1-13-2; Barnes 7-2-13-0; R Magiet 12-1-38-2; Van Oordt 8,6-1-22-2; Jassiem 9-0-27-1; Jabaar 10-2-28-2; Thomas 4-0-11-0; Van Schalkwyk 3-1-8-0

EP SECOND INNINGS

K. Majola st Isaacs b Jabaar	15
A. Frans c Isaacs b Jabaar	31
I. Hendricks b van Oordt	26
F. Abrahams c Isaacs b Jabaar	0
D. Jacobs b R Magiet	17
W. Fischer c S Magiet b R Magiet	0
M. Philander b Jabaar	12
D Govindjee b Jabaar	17
V. Malgas lbw R Magiet	0
M. Kara not out	2
T. Kadi b R. Magiet	1
EXTRAS	11
TOTAL	132

FALL OF WICKETS: 1/43; 2/52; 3/52; 4/97; 5/97; 6/99; 7/128; 8/129; 9/129

BOWLING: Barnes 3-1-9-0; S. Magiet 4-1-5-0; Jabaar 21-9-28-5; Van Oordt 13-4-37-1; Jassiem 6-1-15-0; Thomas 7-4-8-0; R. Magiet 10.7-2-19-4

WP FIRST INNINGS

R. Salie b Jacobs	31
A. Jakoet lbw Hendricks	2
K. Thomas b Hendricks	1
+E. Isaacs b Fischer	26
S. Magiet st Abrahams b Jacobs	45
A. Jabaar run out	34
S. Jassiem c Kadi b Jacobs	11
C. van Schalkwyk not out	27
*R. Magiet b Jacobs	12
G. van Oordt lbw Jacobs	2
V. Barnes st Abrahams b Jacobs	0
EXTRAS	16
TOTAL	207

FALL OF WICKETS: 1/9; 2/11; 3/48; 4/105; 5/134; 6/161; 7/168; 8/203; 9/207

BOWLING: Kadi 5-1-6-0; I. Hendricks 13,3 3- 33-2; Govindjee 17-4 -34-0; Fischer 4-1-16-1; A. Frans 6-0-17-0; Kara 3-0-11-0; Jacobs 16-1-52-6; Malgas 8-0-22-0

WP SECOND INNINGS

A Jakoet c Fischer b Kadi	0
R. Salie c Kara b Kadi	10
K. Thomas lbw Kara	31
G. van Oordt b Jacobs	6
S. Magiet run out	14
A. Jabaar not out	32
C. van Schalkwyk not out	5
EXTRAS	6
TOTAL	104/5

FALL OF WICKETS: 1/10; 2/21; 3/32; 4/57; 5/91

BOWLING: Kadi 6-2-10-2; Hendricks 3-1-6-0; Malgas 2-0-6-0; Jacobs 9-0-38-1; Govindjee 9-4-10-0; Fischer 4-1-10-0; Majola 2-0-12-0; Kara 2,5-1-6-1

WP WON BY 5 WICKETS

Omar, Francois destroy Western Province with a record opening stand for Natal

Natal vs WP 26-28 December 1978 in Durban

NATAL OPENERS, Yacoob Omar (149) and Graham Francois (85), piled on the misery for Western Province with a record opening stand of 178. And although Natal lost their way slightly, later in their innings, they still managed to post 334.

Given Western Province's batting frailties, this was always likely to prove a winning total – and when the visitors lost their first three wickets for just 17 runs, the big question was: for how long could Western Province delay the inevitable? Despite heroics at the bottom of the order by George van Oordt (18), Rushdi Magiet (33) and Ronnie Witbooi (28), Western Province could manage only 177 – and were forced to follow on.

After a promising 55-run start by openers, Noeg Martin (37) and Rashaad Salie (24), the Western Province second innings was even more disappointing than their first – ending at 132, 25 runs short of making Natal bat again.

NATAL FIRST INNINGS

Y. Omar b R. Magiet 149
G. Francois c Thomas b Arnold 85
R. Julius lbw Van Oordt 23
C. Nicholson b Van Oordt..........................1
A. Bawa lbw R. Magiet...............................5
R. Compton lbw R. Magiet..........................0
M. Khan c Isaacs b Sonn 20
R. Rogers run out 22
M. Govender b Witbooi...............................1
G. Singh not out 0
P. Pillay lbw Witbooi...................................0

EXTRAS..............28
TOTAL 334

FALL OF WICKETS: 1/178; 2/214; 3/222; 4/244; 5/244; 6/298; 7/328; 8/330; 9/334

BOWLING: Van Oordt 15-2-76-2; R. Magiet 15-2-58-3; Thomas 3-0-20- 0; Witbooi 8,5-2-27-2; Sonn 11-2- 42-1; Arnold 15-0-81-1; N.Martin 1-0-2-0

WP FIRST INNINGS

R. Salie c Pillay b Govender 2
N. Martin b Govender 0
MZ. Allie b c Singh b Govender...................6
F. Solomons b Govender 18
+E. Isaacs lbw Govender 17
A. Sonn c Nicholson b Compton 17
K. Thomas lbw Compton 5
G. van Oordt c Pillay b Khan.....................18
*R. Magiet lbw Nicholson 33
R. Witbooi run out.....................................28
S. Arnold not out 7

EXTRA 26
TOTAL 177

FALL OF WICKETS: 1/2; 2/8; 3/17; 4/41; 5/64; 6/82; 7/93; 8/114; 9/167

BOWLING: Govender 18-3-48-5; Rogers 11-4-22-0; Nicholson 6-1-16-1; Compton 9-2-20-2; Singh 7-2-15-0; Khan 11,4-0-30-1

WP SECOND INNINGS (FOLLOWED ON)

N. Martin c sub b Nicholson.....................37
R. Salie b Omar 24
MZ. Allie b Nicholson 1
F. Solomons lbw Nicholson 0
K. Thomas b Khan 6
E. Isaacs c Pillay b Nicholson 36
A. Sonn c Pillay b Compton 2
R. Magiet b Nicholson 2
G. van Oordt b Omar 3
R. Witbooi c Govender b Omar 3
S. Arnold not out 4

EXTRAS..............14
TOTAL..............132

FALL OF WICKETS: 1/55; 2/56; 3/56; 4/65; 5/68; 6/117; 7/122; 8/123; 9/125

BOWLING: Govender 7-2-12-0; Rogers 6-1-14-0; Nicholson 24-5- 41-5; Compton 9-3-21-1; Omar 17,2-2-26-3; Khan 7-5-2-1; Singh 2-1-2-0

NATAL WON BY AN INNINGS AND 25 RUNS

WP vs Transvaal
30 Dec 1978-
1 Jan 1979 at
Avonwood Park
Cape Town

Rushdi's magnificent seven sets up a Western Province victory

THERE WAS little to choose between the two teams after the first half of the match: Transvaal, boosted by Seraj Gabriels' 43, gave themselves a fighting chance by getting to 153. Although Noeg Martin (43) batted well at the top of the Western Province batting order, most of their batsmen struggled to advance beyond the teens. Still, they managed 176/9, before declaring.

The Transvaal second innings was dominated by Rushdi Magiet, who, in 16 magnificent overs of swing bowling, took 7/35. The Transvaal total of 107 was never going to be enough to beat Western Province– even taking into account the number of inconsistent performances by the home side over the past few seasons.

An opening stand of 62 by the Ottomans pairing of Rashaad Salie (23) and Martin (40) more or less wrapped it up – although a minor collapse saw them losing four wickets before they were able to post the winning total.

TRANSVAAL FIRST INNINGS

E. Amod c sub b Mahoney		4
R. Musson lbw Van Oordt		22
H. Naik c & b Mahoney		6
S. Gabriels c & b Jassiem		43
D. George b Mahoney		1
O. Latha b Arnold		15
N. Edwards b Jassiem		10
YI. Gangat lbw R. Magiet		0
E. Choonara not out		24
E. Dindar b Jassiem		16
N. Abrahams b Jassiem		5
	EXTRAS	7
	TOTAL	153

FALL OF WICKETS: 1/6; 2/30; 3/34; 4/35; 5/78; 6/103; 7/103; 8/103; 9/143

BOWLING: Mahoney 12-3-24-3; Witbooi 9-3-21-0; Van Oordt 8-0-23-1; Arnold 17-4-38-1; R. Magiet 6-2-13-1; Jassiem 7,3-1-27-4

TRANSVAAL SECOND INNINGS

E. Amod b R. Magiet		21
R. Musson c Arnold b R. Magiet		3
H. Naik b Arnold		3
S. Gabriels b R. Magiet		16
D. George b R. Magiet		0
O. Latha lbw R. Magiet		7
N. Edwards c Arnold b R. Magiet		6
YI. Gangat b Arnold		3
E. Choonara c Van Oordt b R. Magiet		13
E. Dindar b Jassiem		5
N. Abrahams not out		20
	EXTRAS	10
	TOTAL	107

FALL OF WICKETS: 1/4; 2/16; 3/36 ; 4/42; 5/47; 6/59; 7/62; 8/64; 9/74

BOWLING: Mahoney 5-3-3-0; R. Magiet 16-3-35-7; Witbooi 3-1-2-0; Arnold 20-2-47-2; Martin 2-1-7-0; Jassiem 1,3-0-3-1; Van Schalkwyk 1-1-0-0

WP FIRST INNINGS

R. Salie c Musson b Abrahams		0
N. Martin b Gabriels		43
F. Solomons lbw Edwards		11
+E. Isaacs c Edwards b Gabriels		21
C. van Schalkwyk c Musson b Abrahams		14
S. Jassiem c Musson b Abrahams		22
*R. Magiet c Dindar b Gabriels		24
J. Mahoney c George b Gabriels		1
G. van Oordt c Musson b Abrahams		4
R. Witbooi not out		15
S. Arnold not out		4
	EXTRAS	17
	TOTAL	176/9 dec

FALL OF WICKETS: 1/9; 2/61; 3/65; 4/82; 5/111; 6/138; 7/154; 8/157; 9/157

BOWLING: Abrahams 17-3-40-4; Amod 3-1-10-0; Edwards 13-4-42-1; Gabriels 17-4-54-4; Dindar 4-1-13-0

WP SECOND INNINGS

R. Salie c Latha b Gabriels		23
N. Martin run out		40
F. Solomons c Abrahams b Gabriels		2
C. van Schalkwyk not out		8
E. Isaacs lbw Amod		1
S. Jassiem not out		7
	EXTRAS	4
	TOTAL	85/4

FALL OF WICKETS: 1/62; 2/66; 3/71; 4/76

BOWLING: Abrahams 8-1-21-0; Dindar 5-0-13-0; Edwards 2-1-2-0; Gabriels 9-1-37-2; George 1-0-4-0; Amod 4-2-4-1

WP WON BY 6 WICKETS

The gentle spin of Jacobs and Majola destroys Western Province

EP vs WP
20-22 January
1979 in
Port Elizabeth

WESTERN PROVINCE have never quite felt the full force of a Bravo Jacobs onslaught – not until this match, that is.

It was not a pleasant experience.

Batting first, Eastern Province scored a high satisfactory 294/8 declared, thanks to a classy knock of 81 by Jacobs and other useful contributions from Jainu Sandan (59), Wilbur Fischer (33), Faghme Abrahams (26), Imraan Hendricks (24) and Khaya Majola (22).

The Western Province first innings was a disaster. Five runs on the board for the loss of four wickets set the tone early on. And although Saait Magiet tried his best with a typically belligerent 28, the innings folded for 67, with Jacobs ending with 4/7.

Although Western Province fared better in their second innings, none of their batsmen were able to take charge and score a big hundred. In fact, the top score of 43 was compiled by their number 10 batsman – Jock Mahoney.

This time the chief destroyer for Eastern Province was Khaya Majola (6/69).

EP FIRST INNINGS

J. Sandan st Isaacs b Adams 59
H. Lorgat c Ebrahim b Mahoney 7
G. Cuddembey lbw S. Magiet 0
F. Abrahams c Isaacs b Adams 26
D. Jacobs c Salie b R. Magiet 81
K. Majola c Isaacs b Adams 22
M. Philander run out 1
W. Fischer not out 33
I. Hendricks b Jassiem 24
S. Draai not out 17

EXTRAS 24
TOTAL ....294/8 dec

FALL OF WICKETS: 1/15; 2/16; 3/72; 4/139; 4/183; 6/202; 7/228; 8/266

BOWLING: Mahoney 11-1-35-1; S. Magiet 10-2-40-1; Adams 23-1-74-3; Ebrahim 6-0- 40-0; R. Magiet 16-2-66-1; Jassiem 4-0-15-1

WP FIRST INNINGS

R. Salie b Frans 2
N. Martin c & b Jacobs 0
Y. Ebrahim b Majola 0
J. Mahoney lbw Draai 0
N. Fortune lbw Hendricks 13
+E. Isaacs b Hendricks 5
S. Magiet c Draai b Jacobs 28
C. van Schalkwyk c Frans b Jacobs 1
*R. Magiet not out 6
S. Jassiem c Lorgat b Jacobs 4
AL. Adams run out 4

EXTRAS 4
TOTAL 67

FALL OF WICKETS: 1/0; 2/3; 3/3; 4/5; 5/22; 6/49; 7/53; 8/54; 9/61

BOWLING: J. Frans 7-3-7-1; Draai 12-5-27-1; Hendricks 11-7-22-2; Jacobs 6-1-7-4

WP SECOND INNINGS (FOLLOWED ON)

R. Salie lbw Lorgat 5
N. Martin b Draai 4
N. Fortune st Abrahams b Majola 33
E. Isaacs lbw Majola 16
S. Magiet c Abrahams b Fischer 24
C. van Schalkwyk c Philander b Majola 14
S. Jassiem c & b Majola 1
R. Magiet c Abrahams b Jacobs 5
Y. Ebrahim c Jacobs b Majola 21
J. Mahoney c Frans b Majola 43
AL. Adams not out 1

EXTRAS 7
TOTAL 174

FALL OF WICKETS: 1/14; 2/18; 3/59; 4/73; 5/90; 6/102; 7/107; 8/109; 9/160

BOWLING: Frans 4-1-7-0; Draai 10-4-14-1; Hendricks 2-0-7-0; Jacobs 14-4-33-1; Majola 22,4-4-69-6; Fischer 9-1-27-1; Lorgat 3-1-10-1

EP WON BY AN INNINGS AND 53 RUNS

WP v Natal
17-19 February
1979
at Avonwood Park
Cape Town

Western Province middle order makes merry after an uncertain start against Natal

WITH THREE down for 20, things were not looking good for Western Province – but then, a superb revival led by their middle order, took them to a highly satisfactory 262/8 declared.

The recovery was led by Neil Fortune (38) and Braima Isaacs (32). But, lower down the order, things got even better. Cyril Martin struck a superb 60, while Saait Magiet was bowled by Richard Compton when just four runs short of 50. Charlie van Schalkwyk and Rushdi Magiet, with 23 apiece, heaped further misery on the hapless Natal attack.

Although Graham Francois laboured away manfully, Natal could manage only 116 – 146 behind. Chasing runs in their second innings, Western Province lost wickets regularly, and when they declared at 94, it was for the loss of seven wickets. Set to make 241 for victory, Natal were bowled out for 176, with Lefty Adams (4/86) faring best with the ball for Western Province.

WP FIRST INNINGS

N. Martin c Francois b Compton 11
A. Jakoet b M. Govender 0
F. Solomons c Compton b Omar 7
N. Fortune c & b J. Govender.................................38
+E. Isaacs c Singh b Nicholson 32
C. Martin lbw Compton 60
S. Magiet b Compton 46
C. van Schalkwyk not out 23
*R. Magiet c S. Govender b Nicholson 23
A. Sonn not out 1
                         EXTRAS...............21
                         TOTAL.....262/8 dec

FALL OF WICKETS: 1/7; 2/16; 3/20; 4/71; 5/110; 6/201; 7/217; 8/257
BOWLING: M. Govender 16-4-37-1; Compton 13-2-42-3; Omar 9-4-13-1; S. Govender 5-1-13-0; Nicholson 12-1-37-2; Singh 5-0-28-0; Khan 8-2-19-0; J. Govender 8-0-39-1; Francois 1-0-13-0

WP SECOND INNINGS

N. Martin lbw M. Govender 2
A. Jakoet run out...13
E. Isaacs b Omar 14
S. Magiet b M. Govender...38
C. van Schalkwyk c sub b Compton 2
A. Sonn lbw Omar 0
R. Magiet b Compton...10
N. Fortune not out 6
                         EXTRAS 9
                         TOTAL.......94/7 dec

FALL OF WICKETS: 1/4; 2/34; 3/36; 4/41; 5/41; 6/58; 7/94
BOWLING: M. Govender 7-1-28-2; Compton 8-1-33-2; Omar 4-1-15-2; Nicholson 1-0-9-0

NATAL FIRST INNINGS

G. Francois st Isaacs b R. Magiet 51
Y. Omar lbw S. Magiet 0
R. Julius c R. Magiet b Adams 1
C. Nicholson c Adams b S. Magiet 3
S. Govender b S. Magiet..3
J. Govender c R. Magiet b Adams 10
R. Compton b R. Magiet 0
M. Khan b Van Schalkwyk 3
Y. Moorad lbw R. Magiet 19
G. Singh b R. Magiet 4
M. Govender ....not out 5
                         EXTRAS 17
                         TOTAL 116

FALL OF WICKETS: 1/3; 2/13; 3/21; 4/24; 5/36; 6/39; 7/46; 8/104; 9/105
BOWLING: R. Magiet 14,5-3-24-4; S. Magiet 12-4-20-3; Sonn 10-5-9-0; Adams 19-9-32-2; N. Martin 2-1-3-0; Van Schalkwyk 5-0-11-1

NATAL SECOND INNINGS

G. Francois c & b Martin...26
Y. Omar lbw S. Magiet 11
R. Julius c Isaacs b Sonn...19
C. Nicholson c Sonn b Adams 40
S. Govender c Solomons b Martin 0
J. Govender b S. Magiet...39
Y. Moorad c & b Adams 5
M. Govender b S. Magiet 1
M. Khan b Adams 14
R. Compton not out..3
G. Singh c & b Adams 0
                         EXTRAS...............18
                         TOTAL 176

FALL OF WICKETS: 1/17; 2/47; 3/74; 4/74; 5/128; 6/150; 7/153; 8/172; 9/176
BOWLING: Adams 21,7-2-86-4; Sonn 8-1-21-1; S. Magiet 8-0-25-3; N. Martin 8-1-19-2; R. Magiet 2-0-6-0; Van Schalkwyk 1-0-1-0

WP WON BY 64 RUNS

Western Province turn Potchefstroom into a happy hunting ground

Transvaal vs WP
17-19 March
1979
in Potchefstroom

EVEN AT unfamiliar Potchefstroom, Western Province were still far too strong for Transvaal, easily beating them by an innings and one run .

Batting first, Western Province were given a solid start of 46 by Abdurahman Jakoet and Noeg Martin. After Martin had been dismissed for 21, Faghme Solomons (28) looked comfortable in helping Jakoet take the total to 97. Solid lower order contributions from Braima Isaacs (38) and Archie Sonn (28) took the visitors to 225 all out.

The Transvaalers were all at sea against the swing bowling of Rushdi Magiet, who took 4/9 in eight impressive overs, and collapsed to 75 all out. Lefty Adams (2/23) and Sonn (2/9) also bowled well.

Asked to follow-on, Transvaal fared only slightly better, reaching 149.

The wickets were shared among Charlie van Schalkwyk (3/7), Sonn (3/12) and Adams (3/39).

WP FIRST INNINGS
A. Jakoet b Gabriels 64
N. Martin c & b Edwards..........................21
F. Solomons c Gopal b Gabriels 28
N. Fortune c & b Abrahams 12
C. Martin b Gabriels 7
S. Magiet c Gabriels b Abrahams 4
C. van Schalkwyk b Gabriels....................12
+E. Isaacs lbw Gopal 38
*R. Magiet lbw Abrahams 2
A. Sonn c Latha b Amod.......................28
AL. Adams not out 1

EXTRAS................8
TOTAL 225

FALL OF WICKETS: 1/46; 2/97; 3/122; 4/133; 5/135; 6/143; 7/157; 8/160; 9/211

BOWLING: Abrahams 18-0-51-3; Edwards 13-0-33-1; Amod 14-2-49-1; Gabriels 24-7-54-4; Gopal 0,7-0-8-1; Okkers 2-0-22-0;

TRANSVAAL FIRST INNINGS
E. Amod c Isaacs b S. Magiet 0
R. Musson c Adams b R. Magiet 3
C. Vergie c Fortune b R. Magiet 6
S. Nana b Sonn 7
Y. Gangat lbw Sonn 4
N. Edwards b Adams 5
O. Latha not out 17
S. Gabriels run out 5
G. Okkers c N. Martin b Adams 4
R. Gopal b R. Magiet 7
N. Abrahams c Isaacs b R. Magiet...........................4

EXTRAS..............13
TOTAL 75

FALL OF WICKETS: 1/0; 2/4; 3/12; 4/22; 5/31; 6/31; 7/38; 8/47; 9/58

BOWLING: S. Magiet 8-3-21-1; R. Magiet 8,3-4-9-4; Sonn 11-9-9-2; Adams 12-4-23-2

TRANSVAAL SECOND INNINGS
E. Amod c Isaacs b Van Schalkwyk...........................9
R. Musson b R. Magiet 8
C. Vergie c Isaacs b Van Schalkwyk 8
S. Gabriels c Isaacs b Van Schalkwyk 0
O. Latha c Isaacs b Sonn.......................34
S. Nana c Isaacs b Sonn 34
R. Gopal lbw Adams....................5
G. Okkers c Adams b Sonn....................0
N. Edwards b Adams....................15
Y. Gangat not out 6
N. Abrahams b Adams 0

EXTRAS..............30
TOTAL...............149

FALL OF WICKETS: 1/17; 2/25; 3/25; 4/36; 5/112; 6/128; 7/128; 8/128; 9/149

BOWLING: S. Magiet 7-1-11-0; A. Sonn 10-4-12-3; R. Magiet 7-3-14-1; Adams 18,3-4-39-3; Van Schalkwyk 7-4-7-3; N. Martin 2-0-4-0; C. Martin 3-1-15-0; Jakoet 1-0-2-0; Fortune 2-0-15-0

WP WON BY AN INNINGS AND 1 RUN

WP Cricket Board First Class Averages 1978/79

BATTING

Name	Matches	Inns	NO	Hs	Runs	Ave	50	100
Cyril Martin	2	2	0	60	67	33,50	1	
Saait Magiet	4	7	0	46	199	28,43		
Neil Fortune	3	5	1	38	102	25,50		
Ronnie Witbooi	2	3	1	28	46	23,00		
Charles van Schalkwyk	5	9	4	27*	106	21,20		
Ebrahim Isaacs	6	10	0	38	206	20,60		
Abdurahman Jakoet	3	5	0	64	89	17,80	1	
Noeg Martin	5	9	0	43	158	17,56		
Jock Mahoney	2	3	0	43	44	14,67		
Rushdi Magiet	6	9	1	33	117	14,63		
Archie Sonn	3	5	1	28	48	12,00		
Shamiel Jassiem	3	5	1	22	45	11,25		
Faghme Solomons	4	6	0	28	66	11,00		
Rashaad Salie	4	8	0	31	87	10,88		
Kelvin Thomas	2	4	0	31	43	10,75		
George van Oordt	3	5	0	18	33	6,60		
Lefty Adams	2	3	2	4	6	6,00		

Also batted: Armien Jabaar 34 and 32*; Vincent Barnes 0; MZ Allie 6 and 1; Yusuf Ebrahim 0 and 21; Sheraat Arnold 7* and 4*; 4*;

FIELDING:

Wicketkeepers: 11 – Ebrahim Isaacs (8ct and 3st)

Catches:

3 - Lefty Adams, Rushdi Magiet

2 - Saait Magiet, George van Oordt, Sheraat Arnold

1 - Rashaad Salie, Vincent Barnes, Noeg Martin, Faghme Solomons, Shamiel Jassiem, Archie Sonn, Jock Mahoney, Yusuf Ebrahim

BOWLING

Name	Overs	Mdns	Wkts	Runs	Ave	Best Bowling	5i	10m
Charles van Schalkwyk	17	6	4	27	6,75	3/7 v Tvl		
Armien Jabaar	31	11	7	56	8,00	5/28 v EP	1	
Rushdi Magiet	108	22	27	282	10,44	7/35 v Tvl	1	
Shamiel Jassiem	27,6	2	7	87	12,43	4/27 v Tvl		
Archie Sonn	50	21	7	93	13,29	3/12 v Tvl		
Saait Magiet	56	12	10	135	13,50	3/20 v Natal		
Jock Mahoney	28	7	4	62	15,50	3/24 v Tvl		
Lefty Adams	94,1	20	14	254	18,14	4/86 v Natal		
Ronnie Witbooi	20,5	6	2	50	25,00	2/27 v Natal		
George van Oordt	44	6	6	158	26,33	2/22 v EP		
Sheraat Arnold	52	5	4	166	41,50	2/47 v Tvl		

Also bowled: Vincent Barnes 10-3-22-0; Kelvin Thomas 14-4-39-0; Noeg Martin 13-2-32-2; Yusuf Ebrahim 6-0-40-0; Cyril Martin 5-2-18-0; Abdurahman Jakoet 1-0-2-0; Neil Fortune 2-0-15-0

Draai's pace and swing too much for Western Province

EP vs WP
17-19 November
1979
in Port Elizabeth

STEVEN DRAAI twice knifed his way through Western Province's brittle batting lineup to guide the home team, Eastern Province, to an easy 123 run victory over their Howa Bowl rivals.

Eastern Province, defending a modest total of 150, grabbed a narrow first innings lead of three – thanks to Draai's 4/19, and some excellent support bowling by Jeff Frans (3/36) and Khaya Majola (3/29).

Set to make 238 for victory, after EP had declared their second innings at 234/9, Western Province collapsed to 114 all out, with the only worthwhile contributions coming from Rushdi Magiet (39) and Saait Magiet (37). Draai, with 5/40, again took the lion's share of the wickets.

EP FIRST INNINGS

J. Sandan lbw S. Magiet...13
H. Lorgat c Van Oordt b S. Magiet 1
D. Jacobs c R. Magiet b S. Magiet 16
F. Abrahams c Y. Adams b Van Oordt 16
K. Majola run out...7
W. Fischer c Richards b AL. Adams.........................4
V. Malgas b AL. Adams..42
I. Hendricks b J. Williams..10
S. Draai lbw Van Oordt.. 7
J. Frans not out 21
T. Kadi b AL. Adams.. 0

EXTRAS...............13
TOTAL.............. 150

FALL OF WICKETS: 1/7; 2/27; 3/35; 4/54; 5/57; 6/69; 7/90; 8/106; 9/150

BOWLING: S. Magiet 10-0-23-3; Kleinveldt 10-2-44-0; J. Williams 10-5-12-1; Van Oordt 15-1-43-2; A.L. Adams 7,3-4-13-3; R. Magiet 2-0-2-0

WP FIRST INNINGS

V. Smith lbw Frans..0
Y. Adams c Hendricks b Frans.................................55
N. Fortune st Abrahams b Majola............................13
T. Richards c Jacobs b Majola 2
G. van Oordt lbw Majola 3
S. Magiet c Abrahams b Frans 6
R. Magiet c Abrahams b Draai.................................40
J. Kleinveldt lbw Draai 3
+N. Kemp lbw Draai 3
J. Williams lbw Draai 4
*AL. Adams not out...5

EXTRAS...............13
TOTAL...............147

FALL OF WICKETS: 1/0; 2/65; 3/67; 4/73; 5/82; 6/95; 7/121; 8/133/ 9/138

BOWLING: Frans 13-2-36-3; Kadi 3-1-5-0; Draai 9,4-5-19-4; Hendricks 8-1-23-0; Jacobs 11-1-22-0; Majola 7-0-29-3

EP SECOND INNINGS

J. Sandan c R. Magiet b Kleinveldt...........................5
H. Lorgat b Kleinveldt 0
D. Jacobs c Kleinveldt b Van Oordt 40
F. Abrahams lbw AL. Adams 21
K. Majola c Kleinveldt b AL. Adams 37
W. Fischer c R. Magiet b J. Williams 63
V. Malgas b S. Magiet..17
I. Hendricks b S. Magiet 21
S. Draai not out 5
J. Frans c Richards b J. Williams 0

EXTRAS...............25
TOTAL .....234/9 dec

FALL OF WICKETS: 1/2; 2/19; 3/69; 4/84; 5/141; 6/194; 7/214; 8/233; 9/234

BOWLING: S. Magiet 11-2-37-2; Kleinveldt 13-5-33-2; J. Williams 19-4-45-2; Van Oordt 10-0-35-1; R. Magiet 2-0-11-0; AL. Adams 21-4-48-2

WP SECOND INNINGS

V. Smith c Hendricks b Draai 14
Y. Adams lbw Hendricks...4
N. Fortune c Hendricks b Frans 0
T. Richards c Abrahams b Hendricks.........................3
S. Magiet c Fischer b Draai 37
G. van Oordt c sub b Draai 0
R. Magiet c & b Majola 39
J. Kleinveldt c Hendricks b Majola............................1
N. Kemp b Draai 3
AL. Adams lbw Draai 5
J. Williams not out 2

EXTRAS................6
TOTAL...............114

FALL OF WICKETS: 1/10; 2/15; 3/20; 4/30; 5/32; 6/101; 7/104; 8/105; 9/107

BOWLING: Frans 7-1-13-1; Kadi 2-0-5-0; Hendricks 6-3-9-2; Draai 10-1-40-5; Malgas 2-1-1-0; Jacobs 2-0-14-0; Majola 6-1-26-2

EP WON BY 123 RUNS

Isaacs' ton helps WP to a nail-biting victory over Natal

BRAIMA ISAACS at last played the type of innings he's always looked capable of, but, for reasons known only to himself, has delivered far too seldom. His 103 against the Natalians was the first time he'd passed three figures in a provincial match – and it was the first century by a Western Province player since Joey Lambert hit 137 against Eastern Province in 1973.

The Western Province scorecard of 223 had a strange – some would say, familiar – look about it. With the exception of Isaacs and Neil Fortune, who scored a fine 71, none of the other batsmen got going (the next highest score was 12 by Georgie van Oordt).

Natal were dismissed in their first innings for 161, with Johnny Kleinveldt (3/40) faring best with the ball. Western Province were fortunate that they had the insurance of a 62-run first innings lead, because they crumbled in their second innings for 119, with only Saait Magiet (54) getting among the runs. Lefty Adams took 5/38 to help dismiss the Natalians for 177, to steer Western Province to victory by four runs.

WP FIRST INNINGS

+E. Isaacs st Moorad b Khan	103
V. Smith c Khan b Barnard	2
N. Fortune run out	71
S. Magiet lbw J. Govender	5
T. Richards st Moorad b Khan	8
R. Magiet c Asmal b Khan	8
G. van Oordt run out	12
J. Kleinveldt run out	2
Y. Adams c Pillay b Khan	1
C. Martin c Moorad b J. Govender	6
*AL. Adams not out	1
EXTRAS	4
TOTAL	223

FALL OF WICKETS: 1/2; 2/146; 3/153; 4/188; 5/195; 6/212; 7/212; 8/215; 9/216

BOWLING: Rogers 10-2-26-0; Barnard 9-2-15-1; Khan 16-0-74-4; S. Govender 2-0-23-0; J. Govender 12,4-0-54-2; Asmal 5-1-27-0

WP SECOND INNINGS

V. Smith c Moorad b Barnard	8
Y. Adams b Rogers	7
N. Fortune c Moorad b Khan	28
C. Martin c Moorad b Barnard	0
T. Richards c J. Govender b Barnard	2
E. Isaacs c Moorad b Khan	5
S. Magiet c J. Govender b Khan	54
G. van Oordt b Barnard	0
R. Magiet c Moorad b Khan	4
J. Kleinveldt run out	3
AL. Adams not out	1
EXTRAS	7
TOTAL	119

FALL OF WICKETS: 1/12; 2/16; 3/17; 4/19; 5/44; 6/63; 7/72; 8/85; 9/118

BOWLING: Barnard 14,5-1-55-4; Rogers 4-0-10-1; Asmal 4-2-6-0; Singh 2-1-2-0; Khan 8-0-39-4

WP WON BY 4 RUNS

NATAL FIRST INNINGS

P. Pillay b S. Magie	3
P. Moodley c Isaacs b Kleinveldt	7
P. Compton lbw Kleinveldt	20
S. Govender c Isaacs b Kleinveldt	4
M. Khan c Isaacs b S. Magiet	2
J. Govender st Isaacs b AL. Adams	27
Y. Moorad lbw AL. Adams	5
R. Rogers b Van Oordt	42
G. Singh c Martin b Van Oordt	3
GM. Asmal run out	0
L. Barnard not out	0
EXTRAS	28
TOTAL	161

FALL OF WICKETS: 1/15; 2/17; 3/74; 4/77; 5/84; 6/113; 7/120; 8/153; 9/157

BOWLING: S. Magiet 13-7-20-2; Kleinveldt 12-2-40-3; Van Oordt 7,4-1-21-2; R. Magiet 10-4-13-0; AL. Adams 16-9-15-2; Richards 2-0-24-0

NATAL SECOND INNINGS

P. Pillay c AL. Adams b S. Magiet	3
P. Moodley b AL. Adams	15
P. Compton lbw AL. Adams	18
S. Govender c Kleinveldt b AL. Adams	12
J. Govender c Fortune b Kleinveldt	41
M. Khan c Kleinveldt b AL. Adams	37
Y. Moorad c AL. Adams b Kleinveldt	1
R. Rogers b Kleinveldt	9
G. Singh c Y. Adams b Kleinveldt	7
GM. Asmal c & b AL. Adams	2
L. Barnard not out	1
EXTRAS	31
TOTAL	177

FALL OF WICKETS; 1/8; 2/39; 3/58; 4/73; 5/133; 6/160; 7/168; 8/172; 9/176

BOWLING: S. Magiet 11-2-25-1; Kleinveldt 17-2-35-4; R. Magiet 6-3-24-0; AL. Adams 28,4-13-38-5; Van Oordt 8-2-24-0;

Cyril Martin's 66 is the highlight of the WP batting in their draw against Transvaal

**Transvaal vs WP
4-6 January
1980
in Johannesburg**

CYRIL MARTIN emphasised his claims as one of the Western Province Cricket Board's rising young stars with a thoughtfully compiled 66 in a not entirely satisfactory Western Province first innings total of 228 against Transvaal.

Over the past few seasons, the Western Province batsmen have been criticised for their lack of commitment. "To get big scores consistently, you have to graft hard – and contentrate," they've been told often enough. Martin apart, there was very little evidence at the top of the order, that this advice has been taken to heart.

Sa-at Galant, a talented batsman, reached 19, but just when he needed to kick on, he fell leg before wicket to Seraj Gabriels. Yusuf Adams, Neil Fortune and Braima Isaacs also departed just when it seemed that they were about to blossom.

Western Province's best batting (after Martin's knock) was provided by old hands, Rushdi Magiet (39) and Georgie van Oordt (32).

Transvaal, who've done a superb job in rebuilding their side, after losing most of their stars to "normal" cricket, batted really well – even though the crafty Lefty Adams proved as much a thorn in their side as he's been to just about every other team in the Howa Bowl over the past few seasons. Adams' 6/54 was not enough to prevent the Transvaalers from gaining a slender one run lead on the first innings.

Western Province reached 19/2 in their second innings when the match was called off as a draw.

WP FIRST INNINGS

S. Galant lbw Gabriels	19
Y. Adams lbw Jacobs	10
N. Fortune c Choonara b Kimmie	7
+E. Isaacs b Edwards	12
C. Martin b Jacobs	66
T. Richards b Kimmie	19
S. Magiet c Choonara b Patel	8
R. Magiet lbw Patel	39
G. van Oordt lbw Jacobs	32
J. Kleinveldt b Kimmie	1
*AL. Adams not out	0
EXTRAS	15
TOTAL	228

FALL OF WICKETS: 1/18; 2/30; 3/48; 4/56; 5/94; 6/105; 7/173; 8/227; 9/228

BOWLING: Kimmie 14,2-3-43-3; Jacobs 16-1-37-3; Edwards 12-0-36-1; Gabriels 17-4-35-1; Patel 12-2-56-2; Francis 2-0-6-0

TRANSVAAL FIRST INNINGS

C. Vergie c Galant b Van Oordt	34
S. Gabriels run out	41
R. Cassim b AL. Adams	11
H. Naik b AL. Adams	23
N. Edwards b AL. Adams	14
O. Visser b AL. Adams	8
F. Kimmie c Kleinveldt b AL. Adams	44
E. Choonara c Fortune b R. Magiet	5
D. Jacobs c Y. Adams b R. Magiet	24
A. Francis not out	5
F. Patel b AL. Adams	1
EXTRAS	19
TOTAL	229

FALL OF WICKETS; 1/61; 2/87; 3/103; 4/119; 5/133; 6/144; 7/ 176; 8/214; 9/227

BOWLING: S. Magiet 12-4-29-0; Kleinveldt 15-3-43-0; AL. Adams 32,5-10-54-6; R. Magiet 19-5-34-2; Van Oordt 18-3-43-1; Fortune 1-0-7-0

WP SECOND INNINGS

S. Galant c Naik b Jacobs	9
Y. Adams b Naik b Jacobs	5
N. Fortune not out	2
C. Martin not out	0
EXTRAS	3
TOTAL	19/2

FALL OF WICKETS: 1/12; 2/ 19

BOWLING: Kimmie 2-0-8-0; Jacobs 5-3-5-2; Edwards 3-2-3-0; Gabriels 1-1-0-0

MATCH DRAWN

Superb batting by Doman helps Western Province overwhelm Transvaal

MICHAEL DOMAN provided the middle-order stability that Western Province have lacked for most of the season (and, indeed, for the past several seasons) with two confident batting displays against the outclassed Transvaalers, who lost the match by 222 runs.

Coming in at number 5, shortly after another up-and-coming talent, Cyril Martin, had departed for a duck, Doman batted well for his 64. Other useful contributions from Rushdi Magiet (26), Georgie van Oordt (22) and Lefty Adams (21) took Western Province to 207.

Transvaal were taken apart by Vincent Barnes, whose 6/32, was the prime reason for their tumble to 120 all out. The Western Province second innings was dominated by the contributions of Doman (62 not out) and Neil Fortune (59). Other useful contributions came via the bats of Rushdi Magiet (32) and Cyril Martin (30 not out).

Adams (4/31) was the chief wicket taker for the home side as Transvaal slumped to 107 all out in their second innings.

WP FIRST INNINGS

Y. Adams b Kimmie 0
+E. Isaacs b Edwards 22
N. Fortune c & b Kimmie 32
C. Martin b Gabriels 0
M. Doman b Kimmie 64
K. Van Graan b Kimmie........................8
R. Magiet c Edwards b Kimmie............26
G. van Oordt lbw Edwards....................22
J. Kleinveldt lbw Kimmie 0
*AL. Adams b Gabriels............................21
V. Barnes not out.....................................1

EXTRAS..............11
TOTAL...............207

FALL OF WICKETS: 1/0; 2/31; 3/40; 4/66; 5/83; 6/155; 7/170; 8/174; 9/201

BOWLING: Kimmie 16-5-47-6; Edwards 11-2-44-2; Amod 7-1-37-0; Gabriels 14,2-1-45-2; Patel 2-0-19-0; Abed 1-0-4-0

WP SECOND INNINGS

E. Isaacs b Amod.....................................22
Y. Adams lbw Gabriels...............................4
N. Fortune c Visser b Abed 59
C. Martin run out....................................30
M. Doman not out..................................62
K. van Graan b Naik 4
R. Magiet c Abed b Patel 32
G. van Oordt not out 14

EXTRAS..............15
TOTAL.....242/6 dec

FALL OF WICKETS: 1/24; 2/29; 3/94; 4/154; 5/161; 6/222

BOWLING: Kimmie 2-0-15-0; Edwards 11-1-40-0; Gabriels 16-3-44-1; Amod 5-2-12-1; Patel 8-1 44-1; Abed 6-1-33-1; Naik 8-0-39-1

WP WON BY 222 RUNS

TRANSVAAL FIRST INNINGS

C. Vergie c Isaacs b Barnes......................5
S. Gabriels b Kleinveldt 9
R. Cassim c Isaacs b Barnes 40
H. Naik c Van Graan b Barnes..................6
O. Visser c Van Graan b Van Oordt........13
F. Kimmie b Doman................................22
N. Edwards c Fortune b Doman................6
E. Amod not out 1
M. Abed c Isaacs b Barnes.......................3
E. Choonara c AL. Adams b Barnes 0
F. Patel b Barnes.......................................0

EXTRAS..............15
TOTAL...............120

FALL OF WICKETS: 1/12; 2/16; 3/29; 4/62; 5/102; 6/116; 7/117; 8/120; 9/120

BOWLING: Barnes 16.5-4-32-6; Kleinveldt 11-4-28-1; Van Oordt 7-2-12-1; Adams 8-3-13-0; R. Magiet 2-1-4-0; Doman 6-0-16-2

TRANSVAAL SECOND INNINGS

C. Vergie c Isaacs b Barnes.......................2
E. Amod c & b Doman 6
R. Cassim b Kleinveldt 1
S. Gabriels c R. Magiet b Kleinveldt 2
O. Visser c R. Magiet b AL. Adams...........9
H. Naik run out 15
F. Kimmie c AL. Adams b Doman 45
N. Edwards c R. Magiet b AL. Adams 10
M. Abed lbw AL Adams 11
E. Choonara c Van Graan b AL. Adams 1
F. Patel not out..3

EXTRAS.................2
TOTAL...............107

FALL OF WICKETS: 1/2; 2/3; 3/5; 4/21; 5/21; 6/69; 7/88; 8/98; 9/102

BOWLING: Barnes 9-3-13-1; Kleinveldt 7-1-14-2; Doman 14-0-47-2; AL. Adams 12.6-2-31-4

Western Province bowlers shine with bat and ball as Natal crash

WP vs Natal
16-18 February
1980
at Elfindale
Cape Town

VINNIE Barnes (41) and Lefty Adams (39) showed what can be achieved by playing straight and concentrating hard – even by players occupying numbers 10 and 11 in the batting order.

A record last-wicket stand of 82 by these two took Western Province from a more than modest 167/9, to a much better looking 249 all out. The value of the tailend heroics by Barnes and Adams quickly became apparent when Natal began their reply. With Adams doing what he was picked for – claiming wickets – the Natalians were soon in deep, deep trouble. They didn't really recover, mainly because Adams (6/24) wouldn't let them – and their innings closed at 153.

With a precious 96-run lead in the bank, Western Province's second innings run chase, led by Saait Magiet (63), Georgie van Oordt (34) and Keith van Graan (31), realised 194/7. Set to make 291 for victory, Natal collapsed to 141, with Rushdi Magiet finishing with 6/23.

WP FIRST INNINGS

+E. Isaacs b Sathar	23
R. Magiet c Moorad b Sathar	26
N. Fortune c Rogers b Sathar	2
C. Martin c Vahed b Sathar	7
S. Magiet c Rogers b Sathar	15
M. Doman b E. Govender	25
K. van Graan b Sathar	6
G. van Oordt c Moorad b Ramsaroop	25
J. Kleinveldt c Rogers b Ramsaroop	25
V. Barnes not out	41
*AL. Adams c Khan b E. Govender	39
EXTRAS	15
TOTAL	249

FALL OF WICKETS: 1/28; 2/32; 3/60; 4/71; 5/80; 6/91; 7/130; 8/156; 9/167

BOWLING: Rogers 13-1-54-0; Sathar 15-2-70-6; E. Govender 10.5 -2-31-2; Khan 7-0 34-0; J. Govender 3-1-13-0; Ramsaroop 9-0-32-2

WP SECOND INNINGS

E. Isaacs c Moorad b Rogers	31
R. Magiet c J. Govender b Francois	20
N. Fortune c Moorad b Rogers	3
C. Martin c & b Francois	0
M. Doman b Francois	1
S. Magiet c Moorad b Ramsaroop	63
G. van Oordt lbw Francois	34
K. van Graan not out	31
J. Kleinveldt not out	9
EXTRAS	2
TOTAL	194/7 dec

FALL OF WICKETS: 1/33; 2/53; 3/53; 4/55; 5/55; 6/127; 7/ 177

BOWLING: Rogers 13-0-66-2; Sathar 3-0-25-0; Francois 16-3-63-4; J. Govender 6-0-30-0; Ramsaroop 2-0-8-1

WP WON BY 149 RUNS

NATAL FIRST INNINGS

G. Francois run out	14
K. Hiraman lbw Kleinveldt	18
M. Vahed c Kleinveldt b Adams	23
R. Rasmsaroop st Isaacs b Van Oordt	12
S. Govender st Isaacs b Adams	2
J. Govender c Doman b Adams	4
Y. Moorad c Fortune b Adams	9
R. Rogers c Kleinveldt b Adams	17
E. Govender not out	13
A. Sathar c Van Graan b Adams	4
M. Khan absent injured	
EXTRAS	37
TOTAL	153/9

FALL OF WICKETS: 1/31; 2/55; 3/90; 4/99; 5/103; 6/106; 7/122; 8/145; 9/153

BOWLING: Barnes 7-3-10-0; S. Magiet 8-3-15-0; R. Magiet 7-1-15-0; Kleinveldt 5-1-11-1; AL Adams 15-6-24-6; Doman 5-0-23-0; Van Oordt 9-2-18-1

NATAL SECOND INNINGS

G. Francois b AL Adams	53
K. Hiraman lbw Van Oordt	5
M. Vahed lbw R. Magiet	8
R. Ramsaroop b R. Magiet	0
S. Govender b R. Magiet	0
J. Govender c Isaacs b R.Magiet	1
Y. Moorad st Isaacs b R. Magiet	4
R. Rogers c Fortune b AL Adams	21
E. Govender not out	14
A. Sathar b R. Magiet	3
M. Khan absent injured	
EXTRAS	32
TOTAL	141

FALL OF WICKETS:

BOWLING: Barnes 7-5-7-0; Kleinveldt 4-2-5-0; Van Oordt 6-4-10-1; AL Adams 22-11-27-2; Doman 5-0-13-0; S. Magiet 3-2-4-0; R. Magiet 15-9-23-6; Fortune 8-1-17-0; Isaacs 2-0-3-0

Lefty Adams destroys Eastern Province in a low-scoring shocker at Elfindale

OH, THERE'S no doubt about it – this was Lefty Adams' match. Well, you can't argue with a match analysis of 10/15....

But, after the batting debacles of both sides, serious questions were raised about the commitment of both sets of batsmen.

Batting first, Western Province limped to 70/6 – and then declared (to prevent Eastern Province from picking up any further bonus points). The best batting was provided by Neil Fortune (26) and Faghme Solomons (21).

With Saait Magiet (5/25) bowling penetratively, Eastern Province could manage only 88, thanks primarily to Zakie Hendricks (40) and Wilbur Fischer (23). The rest of the batting made sorry reading. Western Province, seemingly determined to be generous, were blown away for 79, with Imraan Hendricks (3/14) and Steven Draai (3/21) faring best with the ball. Set to get 62 for victory, Eastern Province were destroyed by Adams' 6/7, and were dismissed for 42.

WP FIRST INNINGS

+E. Isaacs c Majola b Frans......................................4
R. Magiet b Frans...1
F. Solomons b Govindjee...21
N. Fortune not out...26
M. Doman b Govindjee..0
S. Magiet run out..3
A. Jabaar c Cuddembey b I. Hendricks 8
EXTRA 7
TOTAL.......70/6 dec

FALL OF WICKETS: 1/5; 2/7; 3/49; 4/49; 5/57; 6/70
BOWLING: Frans 6-2-11-2; Draai 8-1-11-0;
I. Hendricks 9.5-2-18-1; Govindjee 8-3-23-2

WP SECOND INNINGS

E. Isaacs b Frans 21
R. Magiet c Abrahams b I. Hendricks......................0
F. Solomons c Fischer b Draai 2
N. Fortune c Majola b Draai 10
M. Doman b Frans 19
S. Magiet b Frans 10
A. Jabaar b Draai...3
G. van Oordt run out 2
Z. Davids lbw I. Hendricks 0
*AL. Adams lbw I. Hendricks 4
V. Barnes not out...6
EXTRAS.................2
TOTAL.................79

FALL OF WICKETS:
BOWLING: Frans 9-4-33-3; I. Hendricks 8,5-3-14-3;
Draai 8-1-21-3; Jacobs 2-0-3-0; Govindjee 2-1-1-0;
Majola 2-0-5-0

EP FIRST INNINGS

J. Sandan c Jabaar b S. Magiet 5
G. Cuddembey c Davids b S. Magiet 0
Z. Hendricks c Isaacs b S. Magiet 40
K. Majola b S. Magiet...1
D. Jacobs c Davids b S. Magiet 3
W. Fischer lbw Adams 23
I. Hendricks c Davids b Adams 6
F. Abrahams lbw R. Magiet 1
D. Govindjee b Adams 0
S. Draai b Adams 0
J. Frans not out..0
EXTRAS.................9
TOTAL.................88

FALL OF WICKETS: 1/5; 2/6; 3/10; 4/17; 5/74; 6/80;
7/86; 8/86; 9/88
BOWLING: Barnes 8-2-25-0; S. Magiet 14-6-25-5;
Adams 7,2-5-8-4; Davids 3-0-9-0; Van Oordt
3-0-12-0; R. Magiet 1-1-0-1

EP SECOND INNINGS

J. Sandan b Adams 6
G. Cuddembey b S. Magiet....................................16
D. Jacobs c & b S. Magiet 0
K. Majola b Adams 8
W. Fischer c Van Oordt b S. Magiet 0
I. Hendricks b Adams...6
F. Abrahams lbw Adams 0
Z. Hendricks lbw Adams 0
D. Govindjee c R. Magiet b S. Magiet 0
S. Draai not out 0
J. Frans b Adams...0
EXTRAS.................6
TOTAL.................42

FALL OF WICKETS: 1/27; 2/27; 3/28; 4/28; 5/37; 6/37;
7/37; 8/38; 9/42
BOWLING: Barnes 2-0-11-0; S. Magiet 7-1-18-4;
AL. Adams 6-3-7-6

WP WON BY 19 RUNS – TO TAKE THE HOWA BOWL

WP Cricket Board First Class Averages 1979/80

BATTING

Name	Matches	Inns	NO	HS	Runs	Ave	50	100
Michael Doman	3	6	1	64*	171	34,20	2	
Ebrahim Isaacs	5	9	0	103	243	27,00		1
Neil Fortune	6	12	2	71	253	25,30	2	
Rushdi Magiet	6	11	0	40	235	21,36		
Saait Magiet	5	10	0	63	201	20,01	2	
Lefty Adams	6	8	4	39	76	19,00		
Keith van Graan	2	4	1	31*	49	16,33		
George van Oordt	6	10	1	34	144	16,00		
Cyril Martin	4	8	1	66	109	15,58	1	
Sa-at Galant	1	2	0	19	28	14,00		
Faghme Solomons	1	2	0	21	23	11,50		
Yusuf Adams	4	8	0	55	86	10,75	1	
Terence Richards	3	5	0	19	34	6,80		
Armien Jabaar	1	2	0	8	11	6,50		
John Kleinveldt	5	8	1	25	44	6,29		
Vaughan Smith	2	4	0	14	24	6,00		
Jacobus "Kosie" Williams	1	2	1	4	6	6,00		
Nasser Kemp	1	2	0	3	6	3,00		

Also batted: Vincent Barnes: 48 runs in 3 innings (3 not outs – highest score 41 not out):

Zak Davids: 0 runs in 1 innings

FIELDING:

Wicketkeeper: 15 – Ebrahim Isaacs (11ct & 4st)

Catches:

7 – Rushdi Magiet, John Kleinveldt; 5 – Lefty Adams, Neil Fortune; 3 – Yusuf Adams, Keith van Graan; 2 – George van Oordt, Terence Richards, Michael Doman; 1 – Armien Jabaar, Saait Magiet, Cyril Martin, Sa-at Galant

BOWLING

Name	Overs	Mdns	Wkts	Runs	Ave	Best Bowling	5i	10m
Lefty Adams	177,2	70	40	277	6,93	6/7 v EP	4	2
Saait Magiet	89	27	17	196	11,53	5/25 v EP	1	
Rushdi Magiet	64	24	9	126	14,00	6/23 v Natal	1	
Vincent Barnes	49	17	7	98	14,00	6/32 v Tvl	1	
George van Oordt	83,4	15	11	218	19,82	2/18 v Natal		
Jacobus "Kosie" Williams	29	9	3	57	19,00	2/45v EP		
John Kleinveldt	94	22	13	253	19,46	4/35 v Natal		
Michael Doman	30	0	4	99	24,75	2/16 v Tvl		

Also Bowled: Neil Fortune 9-1-24-0, Ebrahim Isaacs 2-0-3-0; Terence Richards 2-0-24-0, Zak Davids 3-0-9-0

Transvaal vs WP
15-17 November
1980
in Johannesburg

Musson's the man of the moment as Western Province whip Transvaal

RASHAAD MUSSON took the Transvaal attack apart – twice – as Western Province began their defence of the Howa Bowl on a winning note.

Transvaal are not the pushovers they were a season or two ago. While their batting still occasionally lets them down, their attack has often kept them in the hunt – even when they have had to defend meagre totals.

Musson's first inning effort of 98 was compiled against the likes of Faizel Kimmie, a pretty decent opening bowler, and Seraj Gabriels, a clever, naggingly accurate spinner, who will take a lot of wickets this year.

In addition to Musson, Braima Isaacs (34), Rushdi Magiet (57) and Zak Davids (32) also batted well, helping Western Province to 276/8 declared – in reply to Transvaal's 172.

Trailing by 94 runs, Transvaal reached 237 in their second innings. Set to make 134 to win, Western Province were guided home with seven wickets to spare, by Musson's undefeated 64.

TRANSVAAL FIRST INNINGS

A. Gabru lbw Kleinveldt		1
C. Vergie b Kleinveldt		16
S. Nana c Isaacs b Kleinveldt		9
S. Gabriels b Kleinveldt		3
R. Begg c & b Van Oordt		16
A. Manack lbw Jabaar		50
O. Visser b Jabaar		10
F. Kimmie c & b Jabaar		14
I. Bhaghalia b Davids		33
N. Edwards c & b Davids		6
D. Parbhoo not out		0
	EXTRAS	14
	TOTAL	172

FALL OF WICKETS: 1/2; 2/21; 3/23; 4/30; 5/55; 6/81; 7/114; 8/149; 9/170

BOWLING: R. Magiet 12-2-43-0; Kleinveldt 8-1-37-4; Van Oordt 6-1-23-1; Jabaar 12-1-38-3; Davids 6,3-3-17-2

TRANSVAAL SECOND INNINGS

C. Vergie st Isaacs b Doman		15
A. Gabru c R. Magiet b Doman		12
S. Nana c Davids b Jabaar		14
A. Manack lbw Davids		36
R. Begg c Isaacs b Jabaar		12
S. Gabriels c Doman b Van Schalkwyk		70
F. Kimmie c Davids b Jabaar		0
O. Visser run out		27
I. Bhaghalia lbw Van Oordt		0
N. Edwards c sub b R. Magiet		36
D. Parbhoo not out		2
	EXTRAS	13
	TOTAL	237

FALL OF WICKETS: 1/22; 2/27; 3/66; 4/82; 5/102; 6/102; 7/153; 8/158; 9/217

BOWLING: Kleinveldt 9-3-12-0; Van Oordt 14-4-26-1; Jabaar 28-5-80-3; R. Magiet 7-1-20-1; Doman 8-0-46-2; Z. Davids 9-0-36-1; Van Schalkwyk 0,6-0-4-1

WP FIRST INNINGS

+E. Isaacs c Visser b Kimmie		34
R. Musson lbw Gabriels		98
MZ. Allie lbw Gabriels		10
F. Solomons c Manack b Gabriels		3
M. Doman b Gabriels		1
*C. van Schalkwyk c Visser b Manack		5
A. Jabaar lbw Kimmie		2
G. van Oordt c Edwards b Kimmie		11
R. Magiet not out		57
Z. Davids not out		32
	EXTRAS	23
	TOTAL	276/8 dec

FALL OF WICKETS: 1/67; 2/93; 3/103; 4/117; 5/133; 6/143; 7/171; 8/202

BOWLING: Kimmie 16-3-50-3; Manack 10-0-40-1; Gabriels 22-4-71-4; Parbhoo 4-0-31-0; Edwards 12-0-46-0; Nana 1-0-15-0

WP SECOND INNINGS

R. Musson not out		64
E. Isaacs b Kimmie		15
MZ. Allie st Visser b Gabriels		6
F. Solomons c & b Gabriels		23
M. Doman not out		18
	EXTRAS	10
	TOTAL	136/3

BOWLING: Kimmie 5-0-31-1; Manack 2-0-10-0; Gabriels 10-2-24-2; Edwards 3-0-14-0; Parbhoo 7-0-28-0; Nana 2-0-12-0; Bhaghalia 1,4-0-7-0

WP WON BY 7 WICKETS

More Musson magic for Western Province spells misery for Natal

RASHAAD MUSSON'S bountiful summer continued at Elfindale, with another scintillating innings – this time against Natal.

After falling lbw to Seraj Gabriels when just two runs short of what would have been a deserved maiden first-class century, in Western Province's last game against Transvaal, Musson again came tantalisingly close to three figures. This time, inept batting by most of his team mates, saw him high and dry on an undefeated 90, when the innings closed on 209.

Natal's batsmen showed a distinct lack of fight, although their wickets did not fall to Western Province's penetrative opening attack, but to the friendly medium-pace of Zak Davids (4/29).

With a lead of exactly 100, Western Province were given a rollicking start to their second innings by Braima Isaacs, who scored the lion's share of an opening partnership of 106. For once, Musson failed – falling to the bowling of Jugoo Govender for 28. After declaring at 145/4, Western Province bowled the Natalians out for 192, to secure victory by 53 runs.

WP FIRST INNINGS

+E. Isaacs c J. Govender b Compton 24
R. Musson not out 90
MZ. Allie lbw Compton..8
F. Solomons lbw Sathar 12
M. Doman lbw Compton...11
S. Magiet c Julius b Khan..20
*C. van Schalkwyk c Sathar b Khan...........................4
A. Jabaar lbw Khan..6
Z. Davids c Vahed b Khan 2
J. Kleinveldt c Vahed b Khan....................................16
V. Barnes b Khan 0

EXTRAS..............16
TOTAL..............209

FALL OF WICKETS: 1/32; 2/49; 3/72; 4/93; 5/147; 6/163; 7/174; 8/184; 9/204

BOWLING: M. Govender 8-0-26-0; Compton 17-2-72-3; Khan 19,4-5-55-6; Sathar 7-3-15-1; Francois 2-0-8-0; J. Govender 4-0-17-0

WP SECOND INNINGS

E. Isaacs c J. Govender b Khan 73
R. Musson c Francois b J. Govender 28
MZ. Allie lbw Khan 5
F. Solomons b J. Govender 0
M. Doman not out...16
S. Magiet not out 14

EXTRAS................9
TOTAL.....145/4 dec

FALL OF WICKETS: 1/106; 2/110; 3/112; 4/114

BOWLING: M. Govender 5-0-25-0; Compton 6-1-20-0; Sathar 1-0-7-0; Francois 5-1-25-0; Khan 13-2-39-2; J. Govender 8-1-20-2

NATAL FIRST INNINGS

G. Francois b Van Schalkwyk.....................................8
K. Hiraman c Davids b S. Magiet 0
M. Vahed b Jabaar...39
R. Julius lbw Van Schalkwyk.......................................6
Y. Moorad run out..0
M. Khan c Doman b Davids 34
F. Hassim c Kleinveldt b Jabaar 4
R. Compton b Davids 4
J. Govender not out 1
A. Sathar b Davids 0
M. Govender lbw Davids 4

EXTRAS................9
TOTAL..............109

FALL OF WICKETS: 1/0; 2/30; 3/41; 4/47; 5/85; 6/98; 7/101; 8/105; 9/105

BOWLING: Barnes 8-6-3-0; S. Magiet 12-5-22-1; Jabaar 10-3-18-2; Van Schalkwyk 9-1-14-2; Kleinveldt 4-0-9-0; Davids 9,4-1-29-4; Doman 2-0-5-0

NATAL SECOND INNINGS

G. Francois c Davids b Barnes 11
K. Hiraman lbw Barnes..4
M. Vahed b Barnes 1
R. Julius c Musson b Barnes.....................................16
M. Khan c Musson b Jabaar 16
J. Govender c Davids b Jabaar....................................5
Y. Moorad not out 55
F. Hassim c S. Magiet b Kleinveldt 32
R. Compton b Van Schalkwyk...................................11
M. Govender c Musson b Jabaar 0
A. Sathar b Van Schalkwyk...5

EXTRAS...............36
TOTAL..............192

FALL OF WICKETS: 1/16; 2/22; 3/29; 4/44; 5/58; 6/71; 7/139; 8/170; 9/173

BOWLING: Barnes 16-6-30-4; S. Magiet 5-2-5-0; Jabaar 24-3-72-3; Davids 5-0-16-0; Doman 2-0-6-0; Kleinveldt 7-1-22-1; Van Schalkwyk 5-2-5-2

WP WON BY 53 RUNS

Ton-up Musson keeps the Western Province juggernaut rolling on

IF RASHAAD MUSSON keeps on batting like this, who the heck is going to care about Western Province's brittle middle order?

Against the luckless Transvaalers, it was a case of third time lucky for Musson. After two near misses, he finally got that elusive century – 108 to be exact. And the most impressive feature of his innings, was his willingness to concentrate for long periods – and his excellent shot selection.

The only other innings of note in Western Province's total of 263/9 declared was a well played 66 by Armien Jabaar.

Transvaal's erratic batting again proved their downfall. With Jabaar and Johnny Kleinveldt taking three wickets each, the Transvaalers were bundled out for 102. Asked to follow on, they performed only marginally better, reaching 156, and thus losing the game by an innings and five runs.

WP FIRST INNINGS

+E. Isaacs b Bhaghalia		25
R. Musson c & b Nana		108
S. Hendricks b Bhaghalia		0
M. Doman b Manack		7
S. Magiet b Variawa		18
A. Katts b Baghalia		4
A. Jabaar c Parbhoo b Manack		66
J. Kleinveldt c Baghalia b Parbhoo		6
*C. van Schalkwyk c Variawa b Manack		12
V. Barnes not out		0
EXTRAS		17
TOTAL		263/9 dec

FALL OF WICKETS: 1/43; 2/45; 3/76; 4/128; 5/137; 6/221; 7/228; 8/260; 9/263

BOWLING: Variawa 12-2-57-1; Bhaghalia 15-0-51-3; Manack 8,7-1-28-3; Parbhoo 15-1-73-1; Nana 10-1-37-1

TRANSVAAL FIRST INNINGS

C. Vergie c Hendricks b Doman		17
D. Nagin run out		13
G. Okkers c Hendricks b Doman		0
S. Nana lbw Kleinveldt		10
A. Manack c Barnes b Van Schalkwyk		7
M. Jajbhai b Kleinveldt		5
I. Bhaghalia b Kleinveldt		12
R. Khan b Jabaar		13
E. Choonara b Jabaar		1
D. Parbhoo not out		6
A. Variawa c Katts b Jabaar		2
EXTRAS		16
TOTAL		102

FALL OF WICKETS: 1/27; 2/30; 3/40; 4/51; 5/64; 6/64; 7/90; 8/94; 9/94

BOWLING: Barnes 4-0-12-0; Magiet 4-1-6-0; Van Schalkwyk 8-0-19-1; Jabaar 10-3-14-3; Doman 5-0-11-2; Kleinveldt 8-1-24-3

TRANSVAAL SECOND INNINGS

(FOLLOWED-ON)

C. Vergie b Davids		21
D. Nagin c Barnes b Jabaar		7
G. Okkers c Isaacs b Kleinveldt		17
S. Nana st Isaacs b Doman		13
A. Manack c Kleinveldt b Doman		15
M. Jajbhai c Davids b Jabaar		31
I. Bhaghalia c Magiet b Jabaar		7
R. Khan b Barnes		11
D. Parbhoo run out		0
E. Choonara b Jabaar		9
A. Variawa not out		4
EXTRAS		21
TOTAL		156

FALL OF WICKETS: 1/33; 2/42; 3/62; 4/84; 5/94; 6/103; 7/120; 8/120; 9/151

BOWLING: Magiet 8-2-7-0; Barnes 8-1-27-1; Jabaar 22,4-5-43-4; Doman 11-1-22-2; Z. Davids 10-1-19-1; Kleinveldt 5-2-17-1;

WP WON BY AN INNINGS AND 5 RUNS

Abdullah gives a demonstration of pure batting class as Eastern Province flounder

WP vs EP 17-19 January 1981 at Elfindale Cape Town

WHEN MUNSOOR Abdullah hits the type of batting form he displayed against Eastern Province, he is one of the most watchable cricketers in the country.

Playing his shots all round the wicket, he strode to 81, before falling to Edwin Frans. Arthur Katts, who also looks a very useful cricketer indeed, hit 40 and the flamboyant Johnny Kleinveldt a quickfire 43, as Western Province reached 256/9. Eastern Province were never comfortable against the blistering pace of Vincent Barnes (3/32). But, in compiling 153, they did not appear all that comfortable against spin either. Armien Jabaar took advantage of the fact that South African batsmen seldom use their feet, to claim 3/19 in one ball short of eight overs.

It was back to familiar territory for Western Province in their second innings. A number of their batsmen reached the twenties or high teens, but none of them could make a hundred, with the end result being a moderate 158. The Eastern Province second innings was destroyed by Vincent Barnes (6/31)

WP FIRST INNINGS

+E. Isaacs ret hurt	19
R. Musson c Govindjee b J. Frans	12
M. Abdullah c J. Frans b E. Frans	81
M. Doman st Abrahams b Govindjee	17
S. Magiet lbw Govindjee	6
A. Katts run out	40
A. Jabaar c Sandan b E. Frans	21
*C. van Schalkwyk b Draai	1
G. van Oordt lbw E. Frans	1
J. Kleinveldt b Govindjee	43
V. Barnes not out	1
EXTRAS	14
TOTAL	256/9

FALL OF WICKETS: 1/31; 2/96; 3/109; 4/171; 5/201; 6/202; 7/203; 8/216; 9/256

BOWLING: J. Frans 7-0-34-1; E. Frans 13-2-56-3; Draai 12-1-47-1; Govindjee 17,6-3-63-3; A. Frans 3-0-7-0; Jacobs 8-1-30-0; Lorgat 1-0-2-0; Majola 1-0-3-0

WP SECOND INNINGS

A. Jabaar c Jacobs b Govindjee	7
R. Musson lbw E. Frans	10
M. Abdullah lbw Draai	17
M. Doman b E. Frans	27
S. Magiet c Draai b E. Frans	29
E. Isaacs lbw E. Frans	12
A. Katts lbw E. Frans	9
*C. van Schalkwyk b E. Frans	7
G. van Oordt c Lorgat b Jacobs	29
J. Kleinveldt b J. Frans	0
V. Barnes not out	5
EXTRAS	6
TOTAL	158

FALL OF WICKETS: 1/13; 2/29; 3/45; 4/91; 5/106; 6/114; 7/ 117; 8/124; 9/131

BOWLING: E. Frans 15-6-35-6; J. Frans 10-1-33-1; Draai 9-1-23-1; Govindjee 13-1-37-1; A. Frans 4-0-20-0; Jacobs 1,3-0-4-1

EP FIRST INNINGS

J. Sandan c Barnes b S. Magiet	7
G. Cuddembey b Barnes	3
D. Jacobs c Kleinveldt b Barnes	0
K. Majola lbw Van Oordt	48
H. Lorgat lbw Van Schalkwyk	21
A. Frans b Barnes	20
F. Abrahams c Doman b Jabaar	16
D. Govindjee lbw Jabaar	0
E. Frans run out	1
S. Draai not out	4
J. Frans c Van Oordt b Jabaar	0
EXTRAS	33
TOTAL	153

FALL OF WICKETS: 1/10; 2/10; 3/22; 4/66; 5/115; 6/131; 7/132; 8/133; 9/153

BOWLING: Barnes 14-2-32-3; S. Magiet 12-3-32-1; Kleinveldt 4-1-12-0; Van Schalkwyk 3-0-17-1; Jabaar 7,5-1-19-3; Van Oordt 7-3-8-1

EP SECOND INNINGS

J. Sandan c Kleinveldt b Barnes	4
G. Cuddembey c Doman b Barnes	11
S. Draai c Isaacs b S. Magiet	1
D. Jacobs b S. Magiet	9
K. Majola c Jabaar b Barnes	0
H. Lorgat not out	12
A. Frans c Katts b Barnes	7
F. Abrahams c Isaacs b S. Magiet	0
E. Frans c Kleinveldt b Barnes	6
D. Govindjee b Van Oordt	0
J. Frans b Barnes	2
EXTRAS	35
TOTAL	87

FALL OF WICKETS: 1/4; 2/27; 3/48; 4/48; 5/48; 6/63; 7/63; 8/81; 9/83

BOWLING: Barnes 15,6-3-31-6; S. Magiet 13-6-19-3; Jabaar 1-1-0-0; Van Oordt 2-1-2-1

WP WON BY 174 RUNS

Natal vs WP
20-22 February
1981
in Durban

Great bowling by Georgie van Oordt does not make up for poor WP batting

IN A MATCH in which the bowlers shone, Georgie van Oordt guided Western Province to within a whisker of snatching an unlikely victory against the home side.

Van Oordt's eight-wicket haul – 4/32 in the first innings and 4/25 in the second – was not quite enough for WP to pick up the lion's share of the points. Once again, the batting from both sides was poor – and WP's batsmen, in particular, were guilty of a lack of application. Only Neil Fortune (46), in the middle of the batting order, looked remotely like a batsman in any sort of form. The next highest score was Braima Isaacs' 15.

An opening stand of 75 between Graham Francois and Enver Mall, set Natal up for a massive reply. But once they had been removed, the rest of their batting lineup fell quickly and cheaply – thanks to the bowling of Van Oordt, Barnes (3/27) and Kleinveldt (2/23). Having bowled Natal out for 170, Western Province needed a big second innings score. They didn't get one. Another poor batting display saw them being dismissed for 136. Natal scored the winning runs for the loss of eight wickets.

WP FIRST INNINGS

+E. Isaacs lbw E. Govender		15
R. Musson lbw Pentiah		13
M. Abdullah lbw Pentiah		4
M. Doman c Pentiah b M. Govender		1
A. Katts c P. Pillay b M. Govender		13
N. Fortune c P. Pillay b Pentiah		46
A. Jabaar lbw M. Govender		5
*C. van Schalkwyk c Pentiah b Francois		7
G. van Oordt c M. Govender b Pentiah		13
J. Kleinveldt not out		14
V. Barnes run out		1
EXTRAS		5
TOTAL		137

FALL OF WICKETS: 1/25; 2/34; 3/35; 4/37; 5/55; 6/67; 7/76; 8/113; 9/123

BOWLING; M. Govender 16-4-38-3; E. Govender 12-3-33-1; Pentiah 20-6-44-4; Khan 1-0-7-0; Francois 5-1-10 -1

WP SECOND INNINGS

E. Isaacs c Moorad b E. Govender		5
R. Musson run out		27
M. Abdullah st Moorad b Khan		31
M. Doman c Moorad b Francois		1
J. Kleinveldt c Pentiah b E. Govender		23
G. van Oordt c Khan b E. Govender		0
N. Fortune b Khan		9
A. Katts b E. Govender		2
A. Jabaar not out		12
C. van Schalkwyk b E. Govender		20
V. Barnes c M. Govender b E. Govender		0
EXTRAS		6
TOTAL		136

FALL OF WICKETS: 1/9; 2/41; 3/55; 4/92; 5/92; 6/92; 7/99; 8/109; 9/136

BOWLING: M. Govender 6-1-14-0; E. Govender 12-1-30 -6; Pentiah 8-2-24-0; Francois 7-2-30-1; Khan 7-0-32-2

NATAL FIRST INNINGS

G. Francois lbw Van Oordt		40
E. Mall b Van Oordt		23
E. Govender b Barnes		29
F. Hassim c Abdullah b Van Oordt		6
S. Govender c Jabaar b Van Oordt		1
Y. Moorad c Musson b Jabaar		6
M. Khan c Isaacs b Kleinveldt		12
P. Pillay b Barnes		1
N. Moodley c Isaacs b Kleinveldt		12
M. Govender c Isaacs b Barnes		8
Pentiah not out		0
EXTRAS		32
TOTAL		170

FALL OF WICKETS: 1/75; 2/76; 3/84; 4/ 88; 5/118; 6/ 121; 7/123; 8/158; 9/170

BOWLING: Barnes 18-6-27-3; Kleinveldt 10-2-23-2; Jabaar 14-0-48-1; Van Oordt 15-6-32-4; Van Schalkwyk 6-0-8-0

NATAL SECOND INNINGS

G. Francois c Isaacs b Van Schalkwyk		44
E. Mall c Katts b Kleinveldt		5
E. Govender c Fortune b Van Oordt		16
M. Govender b Van Oordt		1
Y. Moorad run out		0
F. Hassim lbw Van Oordt		12
S. Govender b Van Oordt		0
M. Khan b Van Schalkwyk		0
N. Moodley not out		7
P. Pillay not out		6
EXTRAS		14
TOTAL		105/8

FALL OF WICKETS: 1/14; 2/40; 3/49; 4/50; 5/71; 6/77; 7/78; 8/97

BOWLING: Barnes 10,6-2-36-0; Kleinveldt 6-2-21-1; Van Oordt 7-0-25-4; Van Schalkwyk 3-0-9-2

NATAL WON BY 2 WICKETS

Great bowling by Magiet – but, somehow, WP contrive to throw away the points

EP vs WP
14-16 March
1981
in
Port Elizabeth

SAAIT MAGIET (5/22) and his new ball partner, Ebrahim "Baby" Damon (3/36), sent Eastern Province crashing to 85 all – but just when they should have been winding themselves up for the knockout blow, they allowed their Eastern Cape rivals all the opportunities they needed to steal the game.

WP's first innings scorecard made for incredible reading: Michael Doman hit 53, before being run out, while Charlie van Schalkwyk struck 50 – out of a total of 143! The portly Steven Draai, who over the years has had a tendency to make merry against the Capetonians in Port Elizabeth, again showed his liking for bowling to WP batsmen, claiming 5/44.

Eastern Province, though, seemed intent on giving the match to WP, when they limped to 150 in their second innings.

Left with the relatively easy task of making 93 for victory, Western Province were bundled out by Edwin Frans (7/37) for 83.

EP FIRST INNINGS

J. Sandan b Damon	1
G. Cuddembey b Damon	11
Z. Hendricks c Isaacs b Magiet	0
K. Majola c Van Schalkwyk b Damon	5
H. Lorgat c Isaacs b Magiet	1
I. Hendricks b Magiet	5
S. Draai b Magiet	1
A. Frans c Musson b Magiet	6
C. Africander c Doman b Jabaar	4
D. Govindjee c Damon b Theron	28
E. Frans not out	2
EXTRAS	21
TOTAL	85

FALL OF WICKETS: 1/2; 2/6; 3/18; 4/21; 5/35; 6/35; 7/41; 8/48; 9/55

BOWLING: Damon 12-3-36-3; Magiet 12-4-22-5; Theron 2,4-0-2-1; Jabaar 1-0-4-1

EP SECOND INNINGS

J. Sandan b Theron	31
G. Cuddembey b Theron	0
Z. Hendricks lbw Theron	0
K. Majola c & b Theron	41
H. Lorgat b Magiet	0
I. Hendricks c Theron b Magiet	6
S. Draai b Magiet	3
A. Frans c Katts b Jabaar	20
C. Africander st Isaacs b Jabaar	23
D. Govindjee run out	8
E. Frans not out	1
EXTRAS	17
TOTAL	150

FALL OF WICKETS: 1/15; 2/15; 3/50; 4/51; 5/67; 6/76; 7/102; 8/128; 9/146

BOWLING: Damon 7-0-34-0; Magiet 12-3-27-3; Theron 21-1-52-4; Jabaar 5,4-0-20-2

EP WON BY 9 RUNS
WP WON THE HOWA BOWL

WP FIRST INNINGS

+E. Isaacs c Majola b E.Frans	0
R. Musson c E. Frans b I. Hendricks	12
A. Jabaar run out	1
M. Abdullah lbw I. Hendricks	11
N. Fortune c Africander b Draai	1
M. Doman run out	53
S. Magiet b Draai	1
A. Katts lbw Draai	0
*C. van Schalkwyk b Draai	50
M. Theron c I. Hendricks b Draai	0
E. Damon not out	1
EXTRAS	13
TOTAL	143

FALL OF WICKETS: 1/0; 2/6; 3/24; 4/29; 5/37; 6/42; 7/44; 8/141; 9/142

BOWLING: E. Frans 7-0-32-1; Draai 15-3-44-5; I. Hendricks 8-2-21-2; Govindjee 5-0-14-0; A. Frans 5-1-19-0

WP SECOND INNINGS

E. Isaacs lbw E. Frans	0
R. Musson c Majola b Draai	5
M. Abdullah b E. Frans	15
N. Fortune lbw E. Frans	5
M. Doman c Cuddembey b E. Frans	0
A. Katts c sub b I. Hendricks	32
A. Jabaar lbw E. Frans	0
S. Magiet c Sandan b E. Frans	10
C. van Schalkwyk lbw E. Frans	8
M. Theron run out	2
E. Damon not out	1
EXTRAS	5
TOTAL	83

FALL OF WICKETS: 1/0; 2/12; 3/22; 4/22; 5/35; 6/35; 7/48; 8/72; 9/78

BOWLING: E. Frans 14-4-37-7; Draai 5-2-11-1; I. Hendricks 9,2-3-16-1; Majola 1-0-14-0

WP Cricket Board First Class Averages 1980/81

BATTING

Name	Matches	Inns	NO	HS	Runs	Ave	50	100
Rashaad Musson	6	11	2	108	467	51,89	3	1
Zak Davids	3	2	1	32*	34	34,00		
Munsoor Abdullah	3	6	0	81	159	26,60	1	
Ebrahim Isaacs	6	11	1	73	222	22,20	1	
John Kleinveldt	5	6	1	43	102	20,40		
Michael Doman	6	11	2	53	152	16,89	1	
Saait Magiet	4	7	1	29	98	16,33		
Neil Fortune	2	4	0	46	61	15,25		
Armien Jabaar	6	9	1	66	120	15,00	1	
Arthur Katts	4	7	0	40	100	14,29		
Charles van Schalkwyk	6	9	0	50	114	12,66	1	
George van Oordt	3	5	0	29	54	10,80		
Faghme Solomons	2	4	0	23	38	9,50		
MZ Allie	2	4	0	10	29	7,25		
Vincent Barnes	4	6	3	5*	7	2,33		
Mervyn Theron	1	2	0	2	2	1,00		

***Also batted: Rushdi Magiet 57*, Stuart Hendricks 0, Ebrahim Damon 1* and 1*, Mervyn Theron (0 and 2)

FIELDING:

Wicketkeeper: 14 – Ebrahim Isaacs (11ct and 3st.)

Catches:

7 – Zak Davids; 5 – John Kleinveldt, Rashaad Musson; 4 – Michael Doman, Arthur Katts; 3 – Armien Jabaar, Vincent Barnes; 2 – George van Oordt, Stuart Hendricks, Saait Magiet, Mervyn Theron; 1 – Neil Fortune, Rushdi Magiet

BOWLING

Name	Overs	Mdns	Wkts	Runs	Ave	Best Bowling	5i	10m
Charles van Schalkwyk	34,6	3	9	76	8,44	2/5 v Natal		
George van Oordt	51	15	12	116	9,67	4/25 v Natal		
Saait Magiet	78	26	13	140	10,76	5/22 v EP	1	
Mervyn Theron	23,4	1	5	54	10,80	4/52 v EP		
Vincent Barnes	94,4	24	17	198	11,64	6/31 v EP	1	
Armien Jabaar	131,3	22	25	356	14,24	4/43 v Tvl		
Zak Davids	39,7	5	8	117	14,63	4/29 v Natal		
John Kleinveldt	61	13	12	177	14,75	4/37 v Tvl		
Michael Doman	28	1	6	90	15,00	2/11v Tvl		
Ebrahim Damon	19	3	3	70	23,33	3/36 v EP		
Rushdi Magiet	19	3	1	63	63,00	1/20 v Tvl		

Jabaar, Gabriels put Eastern Province in a spin as Western Province coast to victory

MUNSOOR ABDULLAH looked really good in compiling 52 for Western Province against Eastern Province in this Howa Bowl match at Avonwood Park in Elsies River – and other useful contributions from Braima Isaacs (47), Michael Doman (27) and Armien Jabaar (25 not out) took the home side to 175 all out in their first innings.

In reply, EP looked less than convincing against the slower stuff. Both Seraj Gabriels (3/31, in just over 20 overs) and Armien Jabaar (3/34 in 20 overs) bowled with deadly accuracy – and penetration – and played major roles in helping to bowl Eastern Province out for 136.

The WP second innings was shored up by Neil Fortune (44) and Ebrahim Isaacs, who followed up his first innings 47, with a well-played, undefeated 56. Bowled out for 126, the visitors again struggled against the spin of Jabaar (3/30) and Gabriels (3/45), although Charlie van Schalkwyk (4/15) was the most successful WP bowler.

WP FIRST INNINGS
+E. Isaacs c & b Majola......47
R. Musson lbw J. Frans......0
N. Fortune c Z. Hendricks b Draai......11
M. Doman run out......27
M. Abdullah lbw Lorgat......52
S. Magiet c Lorgat b Majola......8
S. Gabriels c A. Frans b Majola......0
*C. van Schalkwyk b J. Frans......0
A. Jabaar not out......25
E. Damon lbw Draai......1
V. Barnes b Draai......0
EXTRAS......4
TOTAL......175

FALL OF WICKETS: 1/5; 2/30; 3/80; 4/86; 5/105; 6/105; 7/108; 8/161; 9/175
BOWLING: J. Frans 29-8-55-2; E. Frans 12-3-26-0; Draai 11,5-4-16-3; I. Hendricks 6-1-12-0; Lorgat 8-4-15-1; Majola 19-4-47-3

WP SECOND INNINGS
R. Musson lbw Lorgat......11
S. Gabriels b J. Frans......0
N. Fortune b J. Frans......44
M. Doman c & b Majola......6
M. Abdullah run out......10
E. Isaacs not out......56
S. Magiet lbw Draai......7
A. Jabaar lbw Draai......17
C. van Schalkwyk run out......1
E. Damon b Draai......1
V. Barnes not out......1
EXTRAS......10
TOTAL.....164/9 dec

FALL OF WICKETS: 1/3; 2/29; 3/44; 4/66; 5/88; 6/103; 7/140; 8/144; 9/154
BOWLING: J. Frans 21-5-40-2; E. Frans 6-2-15-0; Majola 8-1-19-1; Lorgat 9-4-13-1; I. Hendricks 16-3-44-0; Draai 13-2-23-3

EP FIRST INNINGS
J. Sandan lbw Barnes......2
G. Cuddembey lbw Jabaar......34
Z. Hendricks lbw Damon......0
H. Lorgat b Gabriels......36
K. Majola c Isaacs b S. Magiet......10
A. Frans c Isaacs b Gabriels......1
I. Hendricks b S. Magiet......5
F. Abrahams c Barnes b Jabaar......13
S. Draai c Abdullah b Jabaar......9
E. Frans b Gabriels......4
J. Frans not out......0
EXTRAS......22
TOTAL......136

FALL OF WICKETS: 1/13; 2/14; 3/88; 4/89; 5/89; 6/105; 7/109; 8/131; 9/133
BOWLING: Barnes 12-6-12-1; Damon 12-5-17-1; Gabriels 20,3-8-31-3; S. Magiet 17-6-20-2; Jabaar 21-5-34-3

EP SECOND INNINGS
J. Sandan c Gabriels b Jabaar......15
G. Cuddembey c Musson b Gabriels......0
Z. Hendricks st Isaacs b Van Schalkwyk......30
H. Lorgat b Van Schalkwyk......19
K. Majola lbw Van Schalkwyk......1
A. Frans c sub (Z. Davids) b Van Schalkwyk......9
I. Hendricks lbw Jabaar......12
F. Abrahams c Magiet b Jabaar......8
S. Draai c Isaacs b Gabriels......2
E. Frans not out......1
J. Frans b Gabriels......12
EXTRAS......17
TOTAL......126

FALL OF WICKETS: 1/1; 2/16; 3/67; 4/68; 5/71; 6/88; 7/105; 8/112; 9/112
BOWLING: S. Magiet 5-3-5-0; Barnes 6-5-1-0; Gabriels 31,5-12-45-3; Jabaar 18-4-30-3; Doman 4-0-13-0; Van Schalkwyk 17-9-15-4

WP WON BY 77 RUNS

Transvaal vs WP
26-28 December
1981
in Johannesburg

Skipper Van Schalkwyk leads the charge as Western Province crush Transvaal

OVER THE years, a number of Western Province batsmen have shown a great liking for the batting wickets and bone-hard outfields of the Transvaal.

And so it proved in the latest match between these two sides. Western Province gave little hint of what was to come in their first innings, which realised just 175 runs. The best performance was produced by the skipper – the pugnacious Charlie van Schalkwyk – who cracked a confident 56. Others who showed glimpses of form were Neil Fortune (27) and Seraj Gabriels (30).

Transvaal struggled against both pace and spin in their knock. Vincent Barnes (3/26) and legspinner Armien Jabaar (4/32) were the main WP destroyers in their innings of 162.

WP scored an encouraging 306/9 declared in their second knock, thanks to fine efforts from Neil Fortune (70), Van Schalkwyk (51) and Gabriels and Stuart Hendricks (both of whom made 45). Transvaal, set to make 320 for victory, were bowled out for 141.

WP FIRST INNINGS

S. Hendricks lbw Manack	13
*E. Isaacs lbw Kolia	8
N. Fortune lbw Manack	27
M. Doman c Nagin b Manack	4
M. Abdullah c Nagin b Manack	8
S. Gabriels run out	30
A. Jabaar c Choonara b Amod	16
*C. van Schalkwyk c Variawa b Gokal	56
M. Theron run out	0
E. Damon c Variawa b Manack	0
V. Barnes not out	3
EXTRAS	10
TOTAL	175

FALL OF WICKETS: 1/16; 2/28; 3/46; 4/60; 5/71; 6/121; 7/144; 8/144; 9/145

BOWLING: Variawa 6-1-16-0; Kolia 8-3-14-1; Manack 20-7-43-5; Gokal 19-6-61-1; M. Mangera 5-2-24-0; Amod 2-0-7-1

WP SECOND INNINGS

E. Isaacs b Kholia	29
S. Hendricks lbw Amod	45
N. Fortune c Variawa b Manack	70
M. Doman c & b Variawa	16
M. Abdullah c Amod b Variawa	2
S. Gabriels c Visser b Gokal	45
C. van Schalkwyk not out	51
A. Jabaar c Choonara b Amod	33
M. Theron st Choonara b Gokal	1
E. Damon c Visser b Gokal	0
V. Barnes not out	0
EXTRAS	14
TOTAL	306/9 dec

FALL OF WICKETS: 1/42; 2/86; 3/125; 4/127; 5/185; 6/252; 6/255; 8/290; 9/296

BOWLING: Variawa 9-0-47-2; Kolia 9-1-44-1; Manack 17-3-64-1; Amod 15-2-55-2; Gokal 16-2-43-3; M. Mangera 8-0-39-0

TRANSVAAL FIRST INNINGS

E. Amod lbw Damon	3
D. Nagin st Isaacs b Jabaar	55
A. Dinath c Isaacs b Jabaar	11
O. Visser c Doman b Jabaar	11
A. Manack st Isaacs b Jabaar	21
S. Mangera lbw Theron	3
M. Mangera c Hendricks b Barnes	23
A. Kolia c Gabriels b Damon	14
E. Choonara c Isaacs b Barnes	0
A. Variawa c Isaacs b Barnes	19
M. Gokal not out	0
EXTRAS	2
TOTAL	162

FALL OF WICKETS: 1/23; 2/61; 3/75; 4/82; 5/83; 6/114; 7/136; 8/136; 9/162

BOWLING: Barnes 11-3-26-3; Damon 13.1-4-34-2; Theron 19-3-36-1; Gabriels 7-2-24-0; Jabaar 18-2-32-4; Van Schalkwyk 3-1-8-0

TRANSVAAL SECOND INNINGS

D. Nagin c Doman b Barnes	4
E. Amod lbw Jabaar	8
A. Dinath c Hendricks b Theron	8
O. Visser c Jabaar b Theron	11
A. Manack c & b Jabaar	34
S. Mangera c Jabaar b Theron	6
M. Mangera c Doman b Theron	9
A. Kolia b Gabriels	15
E. Choonara c Fortune b Jabaar	0
A. Variawa not out	24
M. Gokal c Isaacs b Gabriels	10
EXTRAS	12
TOTAL	141

FALL OF WICKETS: 1/9; 2/24; 3/39; 4/39; 5/55; 6/72; 7/103; 8/108; 9/108

BOWLING: Damon 10-4-15-0; Barnes 8-4-5-1; Jabaar 18-2-51-3; Theron 14-0-35-4; Gabriels 10,4-1-23-2

WP WON BY 178 RUNS

Nail-biting triumph for Natal as Western Province collapse in their second innings

**Natal vs WP
30 Dec 1981-
1 Jan 1982
in Durban**

WESTERN PROVINCE were kicking themselves after allowing Natal to snatch victory from under their noses in this Howa Bowl match.

And if Neil Fortune (53) and Georgie van Oordt (51), the standout batsmen in the WP first innings, had aimed some choice words at their less successful colleagues, well, who would have blamed them? The WP first innings of 201 seemed a sufficient deposit to push for victory when a far from impressive Natal huffed and puffed their way to 176.

The Western Province second innings of 115 was a disaster. Of the three batsmen who reached double figures, two made 10. The other, the classy Munsoor Abdullah, struck an impressive 68. His team mates found the seamers of Elvis Govender too hot to handle.

Set to make 141 for victory, the Natalians were never comfortable against the pace of Vincent Barnes (5/61), but somehow they managed to pass the winning total with one precious wicket to spare.

WP FIRST INNINGS

S. Hendricks run out	12
+E. Isaacs c Hansa b E. Govender	0
N. Fortune b M. Khan	53
M. Abdullah run out	11
S. Gabriels c Pentiah b M. Khan	14
*C. van Schalkwyk c Mall b M. Khan	22
A. Jabaar c Moorad b M. Khan	11
G. van Oordt c S. Govender b E. Govender	51
V. Barnes lbw E. Govender	0
M. Theron b M. Khan	20
E. Damon not out	0
EXTRAS	7
TOTAL	201

FALL OF WICKETS: 1/0; 2/32; 3/73; 4/77; 5/105; 6/122; 7/151; 8/152; 9/185

BOWLING: E. Govender 20.1-7-49-3; Mansoor 6-0-22-0; Pentiah 6-0-18-0; Naidoo 5-1-26-0; M. Khan 27-6-62-5; R. Khan 4-1-17-0

WP SECOND INNINGS

E. Isaacs c R. Khan b E. Govender	9
S. Hendricks c Moodley b Mansoor	0
N. Fortune c Naidoo b Mansoor	0
M. Abdullah c Moorad b S. Govender	68
S. Gabriels c Moorad b E. Govender	10
A. Jabaar b E. Govender	7
C. van Schalkwyk b M. Khan	0
G. van Oordt lbw M. Khan	10
M. Theron c Moorad b M. Khan	4
E. Damon c R.Khan b E. Govender	5
V. Barnes not out	1
EXTRAS	1
TOTAL	115

FALL OF WICKETS: 1/1; 2/1; 3/39; 4/85; 5/95; 6/95; 7/97; 8/102; 9/112

BOWLING: Mansoor 4-1-22-2; Pentiah 5-1-9-0; E. Govender 13,4-7-21-4; S. Govender 5-1-24-1; M. Khan 16-2-38-3

NATAL FIRST INNINGS

E. Mall b Jabaar	7
I. Hansa c Abdullah b Theron	28
S. Govender c Barnes b Van Schalkwyk	29
E. Govender c Van Schalkwyk b Barnes	1
RL. Naidoo c Theron b Damon	1
M. Khan c Jabaar b Damon	1
M. Moodley c Van Schalkwyk b Theron	20
Y. Moorad c Abdullah b Gabriels	28
R. Khan not out	29
S. Mansoor b Gabriels	5
C. Pentiah c & b Gabriels	6
EXTRAS	21
TOTAL	176

FALL OF WICKETS: 1/18; 2/68; 3/69; 4/74; 5/74; 6/77; 7/128; 8/150; 9/163

BOWLING: Barnes 13-3-33-1; Damon 6-3-4-2; Jabaar 17-3-30-1; Gabriels 10,5-1-26-3; Theron 15-4-35-2; Van Schalkwyk 7-3-16-1; Van Oordt 12-5-11-0

NATAL SECOND INNINGS

E. Mall c Isaacs b Barnes	5
I. Hansa c Isaacs b Barnes	3
S. Govender b Barnes	47
E. Govender run out	5
RL. Naidoo b Barnes	10
Y. Moorad c Isaacs b Gabriels	13
M. Khan c Jabaar b Van Oordt	3
M. Moodley lbw Van Oordt	0
R. Khan not out	19
C. Pentiah b Barnes	10
S. Mansoor not out	4
EXTRAS	22
TOTAL	141/9

FALL OF WICKETS: 1/7; 2/52; 3/63; 4/76; 5/83; 6/86; 7/86; 8/105; 9/132

BOWLING: Barnes 29-11-61-5; Damon 11-3-22-0; Van Oordt 24-9-29-2; Gabriels 6-1-7-1

NATAL WON BY ONE WICKET

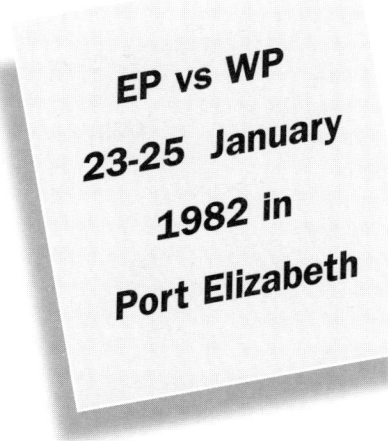

Crucial first innings contributions set up WP victory against EP

HOPING TO at least match a rather moderate Eastern Province first innings total of 191, Western Province were in all sorts of trouble at 141/8. And then, along came their captain, Charlie van Schalkwyk (46), and Armien Jabaar (44 not out) to launch a breathtaking rescue act, with a ninth-wicket stand of 90. Their batting helped Western Province to get to 234 – a precious lead of 43.

The Eastern Province batting, which in recent seasons, has often been even more unpredictable than that of Western Province, hit the gutters in their second knock, collapsing to 107 all out.

Western Province's victory target – 65 – should have been a doddle. But Van Schalkwyk's charges again showed that they seldom take the simple route.

After a reasonable start of 23 by Rashaad Musson and Stuart Hendricks, they did not seem overly concerned about losing 3/28 shortly afterwards.

But they were on the verge of panic when the total reached 60/7. Fortunately, Van Schalkwyk and Saait Magiet had enough big match temperament to steer them safely home.

EP FIRST INNINGS

A. Jordaan c Fortune b S. Magiet 7
G. Cuddembey c Isaacs b Barnes............................4
Z. Hendricks lbw Jabaar 28
H. Lorgat c Isaacs b Van Schalkwyk 17
W. Fischer c Fortune b Gabriels 4
V. Malgas c Van Schalkwyk b S. Magiet 58
J. Smith c Fortune b S. Magiet 16
F. Abrahams c Abdullah b S. Magiet 32
G. Koen c Barnes b S. Magiet 4
S. Draai c Abdullah b Jabaar.....................................2
T. Kadi not out 0

EXTRAS..............19
TOTAL...............191

FALL OF WICKETS: 1/12; 2/28; 3/58; 4/71; 5/79; 6/107; 7/177; 8/181; 9/189

BOWLING: Barnes 15-3-45-1; S. Magiet 20-5-37-5; Gabriels 13-3-48-1; Van Schalkwyk 5-1-18-1; Jabaar 6,3-2-24-2

EP SECOND INNINGS

A. Jordaan b S. Magiet..4
G. Cuddembey c Barnes b S. Magiet.......................8
Z. Hendricks b Barnes..4
H. Lorgat c Abdullah b Barnes 11
W. Fischer b S. Magiet 0
V. Malgas c Van Graan b Jabaar 21
J. Smith lbw S. Magiet 5
F. Abrahams b Jabaar 13
G. Koen c Jabaar b Barnes..6
S. Draai not out 10
T. Kadi c Van Schalkwyk b Jabaar..........................16

EXTRAS................9
TOTAL...............107

FALL OF WICKETS: 1/10; 2/17; 3/19; 4/29; 5/31; 6/44; 7/65; 8/80; 9/80

BOWLING: S. Magiet 17-6-24-4; Barnes 14-5-37-3; Jabaar 13,4-1-35-3; Gabriels 1-0-2-0

WP FIRST INNINGS

R. Musson c Cuddembey b Kadi 14
S. Hendricks run out 17
N. Fortune c sub b Malgas......................................22
+E. Isaacs lbw Malgas...23
M. Abdullah lbw Draai 41
S. Gabriels run out 5
S. Magiet c Abrahams b Kadi 6
R. van Graan c Abrahams b Kadi 0
*C. van Schalkwyk b Smith.....................................46
A. Jabaar not out 44
V. Barnes c Malgas b Lorgat.....................................0

EXTRAS..............16
TOTAL...............234

FALL OF WICKETS: 1/33; 2/35; 3/72; 4/101; 5/114; 6/136; 7/136 8/141; 9/231

BOWLING: Draai 22-5-53-1; Kadi 12-2-64-3; Malgas 14-0 -45-2; Lorgat 12-4-16-1; Koen 10-3-29-0; Smith 4-1-11-1

WP SECOND INNINGS

R. Musson c Lorgat b Draai 8
S. Hendricks lbw Smith 14
N. Fortune lbw Draai 13
M. Abdullah b Draai 1
S. Gabriels c Smith b Draai 6
R. van Graan b Draai 7
S. Magiet not out...6
E. Isaacs lbw Draai 0
C. van Schalkwyk not out 5

EXTRAS................5
TOTAL.............65/7

FALL OF WICKETS: 1/23; 2/27; 3/28; 4/40; 5/47; 6/60; 7/60

BOWLING: Draai 10-1-29-6; Kadi 5-2-3-0; Smith 2-0-11-1; Lorgat 3,3-0-17-0

WP WON BY 3 WICKETS

Exasperating Western Province turn it on after a poor first innings effort

WP vs Transvaal
20-22 February
1982
at Elfindale
Cape Town

WHEN THE Western Province openers, Stuart Hendricks (41) and Rashaad Musson (27) put on 75 runs for the first wicket, the home fans began licking their lips in anticipation of a run feast.

They ought to have known better. In the Western Cape, a run feast has often become a run famine in a matter of moments. Certainly, without skipper Charlie van Schalkwyk's little contribution of 21, near the bottom of the order, and the gratefully accepted 25 extras, Western Province would have done far worse than their 138.

And if Western Province supporters were muttering words such as "under-achievers" under their breath, spare a thought for the poor souls who support Transvaal. They were blasted out by Seraj Gabriels (4/9), Jabaar (2/3) and Vincent Barnes (2/9).

The Western Province second innings was a one hundred percent improvement on their first. In a run charge led by Neil Fortune (65) and Munsoor Abdullah (58), they reached 225/4 declared. Aboo Manack (102) fought a lone battle as Transvaal slumped to 183 all out in their second innings – to lose the match by 142 runs.

WP FIRST INNINGS

S. Hendricks lbw Manack		41
R. Musson st Begg b Manack		27
N. Fortune b Manack		0
M. Abdullah b Gokal		3
+E. Isaacs c Rajah b Manack		5
S. Magiet b Gokal		5
S. Gabriels b Manack		1
R. van Graan c Kolia b Gokal		10
*C. van Schalkwyk c Kolia b Gokal		21
A. Jabaar c Begg b Gokal		0
V. Barnes not out		0
EXTRAS		25
TOTAL		138

FALL OF WICKETS: 1/75; 2/76; 3/85; 4/85; 5/93; 6/94; 7/103; 8/117; 9/127

BOWLING: Variawa 8-2-22-0; Ganchi 7-4-12-0; Kolia 8-4-16-0; Gokal 26-11-34-5; Manack 19-8-29-5

WP SECOND INNINGS

R. Musson lbw Variawa		26
S. Hendricks b Ganchi		21
N. Fortune st Begg b Gokal		65
M. Abdullah c Dinath b Vairawa		58
E. Isaacs not out		20
S. Magiet not out		20
EXTRA		15
TOTAL		225/4 dec

FALL OF WICKETS: 1/42; 2/56; 3/171; 4/185

BOWLING: Variawa 24-5-69-2; Ganchi 11-1-29-1; Gokal 21-4-49-1; Kolia 10-1-28-0; Manack 4-0 35-0

TRANSVAAL FIRST INNINGS

C. Vergie c Isaacs b Barnes		9
D. Nagin c Isaacs b Barnes		6
A. Rajah c Abdullah b S. Magiet		2
A. Dinath b Gabriels		4
Y. Begg b Gabriels		4
A. Manack c Van Schalkwyk b Jabaar		1
M. Jajbhai st Isaacs b Gabriels		1
A. Kolia not out		7
A. Variawa c Jabaar b Gabriels		0
M. Gokal b Jabaar		1
A. Ganchi run out		1
EXTRAS		2
TOTAL		38

FALL OF WICKETS: 1/14; 2/19; 3/21; 4/29; 5/30; 6/31; 7/31; 8/32; 9/35

BOWLING: Barnes 10-5-9-2; S. Magiet 12-3-15-1; Gabriels 7-0-9-4; Jabaar 5-2-3-2

TRANSVAAL SECOND INNINGS

D. Nagin c Musson b Gabriels		3
A. Rajah b Gabriels		18
A. Manack not out		102
A. Dinath b Van Graan		2
M. Jajbhai b Gabriels		0
Y. Begg c Abdullah b Van Graan		0
A. Kolia c Isaacs b Jabaar		30
A. Variawa c Barnes b Gabriels		13
C. Vergie st Isaacs b Gabriels		6
M. Gokal c & b Jabaar		4
A. Ganchi c Van Graan b Gabriels		0
EXTRAS		5
TOTAL		183

FALL OF WICKETS: 1/8; 2/32; 3/35; 4/36; 5/39; 6/111; 7/136; 8/157; 9/182

BOWLING: Barnes 7-1-7-0; S. Magiet 9-0-15-0; Jabaar 34-13-40-2; Gabriels 43,5-3-59-6; Van Graan 22-5-53-2; Van Schalkwyk 3-2-4-0

WP WON BY 142 RUNS

Fortune's ton puts Western Province in the driving seat against Natal

NEIL FORTUNE, Western Province's most consistent batsman of recent times, struck a sublime 143 as his side posted an imposing 263/9 declared against Natal.

But the supporting cast are still struggling to put their act together: Saait Magiet compiled a typically aggressive 37 and Braima Isaacs looked good until he was trapped leg before wicket for 25. But far too many of the rest of the batting continue to fire blanks.

There's nothing wrong with the Western Province attack though – even taking into account Natal's batting frailties. Saait Magiet provided yet another demonstration of his allround value to the team with 4/23. Left-arm spinner, Mervyn Theron, had a day he won't forget in a hurry – his stint of 6,3 overs cost him just five runs and earned him three wickets. Impressive.

And what can you say about Vincent Barnes? Ten overs for four runs – and two wickets – is impressive bowling. Natal's second innings was only marginally better than their first – thanks mainly to a knock of 41 by Elvis Govender. But they couldn't play the spin of Armien Jabaar (7/38) and Theron (3/21) and were dismissed for 102 – to give Western Province victory by an innings and 122 runs.

WP FIRST INNINGS

R. Musson lbw E. Govender		2
S. Hendricks b Mansoor		3
N. Fortune run out		143
M. Abdullah b Khan		15
+E. Isaacs lbw Mansoor		25
S. Gabriels lbw Mansoor		6
S. Magiet c S. Govender b E. Govender		37
*C. van Schalkwyk c K.Govender b E.Govender		11
A. Jabaar not out		3
M. Theron b Mansoor		0
	EXTRAS	18
	TOTAL	263/9dec

FALL OF WICKETS: 1/7; 2/7; 3/52; 4/116; 5/132; 6/246; 7/254; 8/261; 9/263

BOWLING: Mansoor 24.1-8-48-4; E. Govender 32-9-62-3; M. Khan 25-6-58-1; Pentiah 10-2-22-0; R. Khan 5-2-29-0; Naidoo 2-0-26-0

NATAL FIRST INNINGS

E. Mall not out		11
K. Govender c Theron b Barnes		2
P. Pillay ret hurt		1
S. Govender c Hendricks b S. Magiet		10
E. Govender c sub b Barnes		0
G. Hoosen b S. Magiet		2
RL. Naidoo b S. Magiet		0
R. Khan c Fortune b S. Magiet		1
S. Mansoor b Theron		3
C. Pentiah c Barnes b Theron		0
M. Khan b Theron		2
	EXTRAS	7
	TOTAL	39/9

FALL OF WICKETS: 1/7; 2/22; 3/22; 4/26; 5/26; 6/32; 7/37; 8/37; 9/39

BOWLING: Barnes 10-7-4-2; S. Magiet 13-3-23-4; Theron 6,3-3-5-3; Gabriels 3-3-0-0

NATAL SECOND INNINGS (FOLLOWED ON)

E. Mall b Jabaar		0
K. Govender b Jabaar		7
S. Govender c Fortune b Theron		1
E. Govender st Isaacs b Jabaar		41
P. Pillay b Jabaar		18
RL. Naidoo lbw Theron		19
R. Khan c S. Magiet b Jabaar		6
M. Khan b Theron		0
G. Hoosen st Isaacs b Jabaar		6
S. Mansoor b Jabaar		0
C. Pentiah not out		0
	EXTRAS	4
	TOTAL	102

FALL OF WICKETS: 1/0; 2/3; 3/9; 4/41; 5/82; 6/92; 7/92; 8/101; 9/101

BOWLING: Jabaar 23,1-9-38 -7; Theron 12-3-21-3; Gabriels 10-1-38-0; Fortune 1-0-1-0

WP WON BY AN INNINGS AND 122 RUNS
WP WON THE HOWA BOWL

WP Cricket Board First Class Averages 1981/82

BATTING

Name	Matches	Inns	NO	HS	Runs	Ave	50	100
Neil Fortune	6	11	0	143	448	40,72	3	1
George van Oordt	1	2	0	51	61	30,50	1	
Charles van Schalkwyk	6	10	2	56	213	26,63	2	
Armien Jabaar	6	9	3	44*	156	26,00		
Ebrahim Isaacs	6	11	2	56*	222	24,67	1	
Munsoor Abdullah	6	11	0	66	269	24,45	3	
Stuart Hendricks	5	9	0	45	166	18,44		
Saait Magiet	4	7	2	37	89	17,80		
Michael Doman	2	4	0	27	53	13,25		
Rashaad Musson	4	7	0	27	88	12,57		
Seraj Gabriels	6	10	0	45	117	11,70		
Randall van Graan	2	3	0	10	17	5,67		
Mervyn Theron	3	5	0	20	25	5,00		
Vincent Barnes	6	8	5	3	5	1,67		
Ebrahim Damon	3	6	1	5	7	1,40		

FIELDING:

Wicketkeeper: 22 – Ebrahim Isaacs (15ct and 7st.)

Catches:

8 – Munsoor Abdullah, Armien Jabaar; 6 – Neil Fortune, Vincent Barnes; 5 – Charles van Schalkwyk, 3 – Michael Doman, Seraj Gabriels, Stuart Hendricks; 2 – Rashaad Musson, Saait Magiet, Mervyn Theron, Randall van Graan

BOWLING

Name	Overs	Mdns	Wkts	Runs	Ave	Best Bowling	5i	10m
Saait Magiet	93	26	16	139	8,69	5/37 v EP	1	
Mervyn Theron	66,3	13	13	132	10,15	4/35 v Tvl		
Charles van Schalkwyk	35	16	6	61	10,17	4/15 v EP		
Armien Jabaar	174	43	30	317	10,57	7/38 v Natal	1	
Vincent Barnes	135	53	19	204	10,73	5/61 v Natal	1	
Seraj Gabriels	164,4	50	23	312	13,56	6/59 v Tvl	1	1
Ebrahim Damon	53,1	19	5	92	18,40	2/4 v Natal		
George van Oordt	36	14	2	40	20,00	2/29 v Natal		
Randall van Graan	22	5	2	53	26,50	2/53 v Tvl		

Also Bowled: Michael Doman 4-0-13-0; Neil Fortune 1-0-1-0

Western Province blown away – again – by the medium-pacers of EP's Steven Draai

TO SAY WP were embarrassed by EP in the season opener would be putting it mildly. The game started well enough for WP, who limited EP to a first innings total of 210, with left-arm spinner Mervyn Theron claiming 4/62.

What followed was nothing short of catastrophic – WP were bundled out for a record low total of 41 in only 28,3 overs. It would have been even worse had skipper Charlie van Schalkwyk and Vincent Barnes not added 13 runs for the last wicket.

In essence, WP were once again unable to cope with the swing of Steven Draai,who emphasised his mastery over Western Cape batsmen with a fine spell of 4/8 in 9,3 overs.

Although Munsoor Abdullah (65) and Neil Fortune (29) threatened to play their side back into the game with a 5th wicket stand of 77, the burly Draai again proved too much for the WP batsmen, finishing with 6/59 as the visitors reached 188 in their second innings.

EP knocked off the required 20 runs for victory, to get their Howa Bowl campaign off to the perfect start.

EP FIRST INNINGS

G. Cuddembey b Barnes	9
G. Abrahams lbw Theron	13
Z. Hendricks c Fortune b Theron	52
H. Lorgat lbw I. Hendricks	1
V. Malgas b I. Hendricks	4
D. Reid b Barnes	4
D. Govindjee st Isaacs b Theron	42
F. Abrahams c Barnes b Van Schalkwyk	8
S. Draai not out	27
M. Abrahams lbw Van Schalkwyk	4
J. Frans lbw Theron	20
EXTRAS	26
TOTAL	210

FALL OF WICKETS: 1/27; 2/62; 3/72; 4/84; 5/102; 6/134; 7/156; 8/172; 9/177

BOWLING: Barnes 15-4-32-2; I. Hendricks 23-5-65-2; Theron 27-6-62-4; Jabaar 2-0-9-0; Van Schalkwyk 4-0-16-2

EP SECOND INNINGS

G. Cuddembey not out	5
G. Abrahams st Musson b Jabaar	2
Z. Hendricks lbw Theron	0
H. Lorgat not out	14
EXTRAS	0
TOTAL	21/2

FALL OF WICKETS: 1/3; 2/4

BOWLING: Jabaar 4,3-1-10-1; Theron 4-0-11-1

WP FIRST INNINGS

R. Musson lbw J. Frans	0
I. Dagnin b Draai	9
MZ. Allie lbw J. Frans	2
N. Fortune lbw M. Abrahams	1
+E. Isaacs run out	7
M. Abdullah b Draai	0
I. Hendricks lbw Govindjee	0
*C. van Schalkwyk run out	13
A. Jabaar b Draai	2
M. Theron c J. Frans b Draai	0
V. Barnes not ou	6
EXTRAS	1
TOTAL	41

FALL OF WICKETS: 1/0; 2/2; 3/8; 4/19; 5/19; 6/20; 7/22; 8/25; 9/25

BOWLING: J. Frans 7-2-8-2; M. Abrahams 6-2-9-1; Draai 9,3-6-8-4; Govindjee 6-0-15-1

WP SECOND INNINGS (FOLLOWED ON)

I. Dagnin b Draai	8
R. Musson c Frans b Draai	3
MZ. Allie lbw Govindjee	5
E. Isaacs b Lorgat	35
N. Fortune st F. Abrahams b Lorgat	29
M. Abdullah c F. Abrahams b Draai	65
I. Hendricks c & b Draai	5
C. van Schalkwyk c F. Abrahams b Draai	3
A. Jabaar not out	13
M. Theron lbw Draai	0
V. Barnes c F. Abrahams b Lorgat	4
EXTRAS	18
TOTAL	188

FALL OF WICKETS: 1/17; 2/24; 3/26; 4/68; 5/145; 6/157; 7/167; 8/172; 9/172

BOWLING: J. Frans 15-6-15-0; M. Abrahams 10-2-16-0; Draai 24-4-59-6; Lorgat 13,2-3-30-3; Govindjee 24-3-50-1

EP WON BY 8 WICKETS

New-look Western Province coast to victory against an outclassed Natal

*WP vs Natal
28-30 December
1982
at Westridge
Cape Town*

FOLLOWING THE debacle in Port Elizabeth, the WP selectors pressed the panic button, making six changes, including the choice of four new caps, for the match against Natal.

With the exception of new cap, Yunus Thomas, who made a typically hard-hitting 42, the WP batting once again failed miserably against a moderate Natal attack, scraping together 110 in their first innings.

Vincent Barnes (5/30) and Armien Jabaar (3/31) bowled WP back into the match by restricting the visitors to a lead of only 19. With the WP top order failing again in the second innings, it was left to Neil Fortune (59) and Nasser Antulay (64) to salvage matters with a 4th wicket stand of 106 as WP eventually reached 208 in their second innings. Natal were never comfortable against the pace of Baby Damon (4/36) and Barnes (3/35), and slumped to 24/5 in search of 190 for victory. They were dismissed for 102, to give WP victory by 87 runs.

WP FIRST INNINGS

S. Martin b Mansoor	0
N. Arendse c Hoosen b E. Govender	1
N. Fortune c Moorad b Mansoor	4
M. Abdullah c Moorad b E. Govender	5
N. Antulay b E. Govender	12
A. Jabaar c Dadabhay b Mansoor	2
Y. Thomas c Moorad b Khan	42
*C. van Schalkwyk b E. Govender	8
+N. White c & b Hoosen	6
V. Barnes c Munsoor b E. Govender	6
E. Damon not out	18
EXTRAS	6
TOTAL	110

FALL OF WICKETS: 1/0; 2/4; 3/6; 4/11; 5/18; 6/24; 7/35; 8/57; 9/67

BOWLING: Mansoor 16-7-29-3; E. Govender 18-3; 47-5; Hoosen 7-3-8-1; Khan 3,4-0-17-1; Dadabhay 2-1-3-0

WP SECOND INNINGS

S. Martin b Hoosen	8
N. Arendse c Mall b Mansoor	2
N. Fortune c sub b E. Govender	59
M. Abdullah c Mall b Hoosen	8
N. Antulay c Hoosen b Khan	64
Y. Thomas b E. Govender	21
A. Jabaar c Dadabhay b Khan	0
C. van Schalkwyk b Khan	8
N. White not out	2
V. Barnes c Moodley b E. Govender	1
E. Damon b Khan	20
EXTRAS	15
TOTAL	208

FALL OF WICKETS: 1/3; 2/18; 3/38; 4/144; 5/161; 6/163; 7/184; 8/184; 9/186

BOWLING: Mansoor 5-2-7-1; E. Govender 26-9-49-3; Khan 33-9-79-4; Hoosen 15-6-31-2; Dadabhay 5-0-27-0

NATAL FIRST INNINGS

E. Mall c White b Thomas	35
T. Narrandas c & b Damon	3
E. Govender b Barnes	2
S. Govender b Jabaar	36
M. Moodley c Van Schalkwyk b Jabaar	6
M. Khan c White b Barnes	12
Y. Moorad b Barnes	5
L. Maharaj c Abdullah b Jabaar	0
G. Hoosen b Barnes	9
S. Mansoor c Abdullah b Barnes	10
O. Dadabhay not out	0
EXTRAS	11
TOTAL	129

FALL OF WICKETS: 1/4; 2/14; 3/83; 4/87; 5/93; 6/101; 7/104; 8/109; 9/123

BOWLING: Barnes 23,2-5-30-5; Damon 13-2-22-1; Van Schalkwyk 4-0 16-0; Jabaar 17-3-31-3; Arendse 3-0-12-0; Thomas 6-4-7-1

NATAL SECOND INNINGS

E. Mall b Damon	1
C. Narandas c Thomas b Damon	4
E. Govender c Thomas b Barnes	2
S. Govender c White b Damon	4
N. Moodley c Thomas b Barnes	59
L Maharaj c van Schalkwyk b Barnes	1
M. Khan c Antulay b Damon	4
Y. Moorad st White b Jabaar	16
G. Hoosen c Arendse b Jabaar	2
S. Mansoor c Damon b Jabaar	3
O. Dadabhay not out	4
EXTRAS	2
TOTAL	102

FALL OF WICKETS: 1/6; 2/9; 3/9; 4/19; 5/24; 6/49; 7/81; 8/87; 9/100

BOWLING: Barnes 18,4-5-35-3; Damon 17-5-36-4; Jabaar 15-7-20-3; Thomas 3-1-9-0

WP WON BY 87 RUNS

WP vs Transvaal
1-3 January
1983
at Elfindale
Cape Town

New WP captain Armien Jabaar starts his reign with a tense victory over Transvaal

DESPITE THEIR comfortable win over Natal, the selectors once again rang the changes – the most significant being the axing of Charlie van Schalkwyk, who was replaced as skipper by Armien Jabaar. Hassiem Price, one of the new caps, and Braima Isaacs became the third new opening pair in as many matches. With the unpredictable bounce of the Elfindale wicket proving problematic, both sides were dimissed for moderate first innings totals. WP can thank the 4th wicket stand of 60 between Nasser Antulay (35) and Harris (43) for their first innings lead of 16.

Jabaar made the inspired choice of giving the ball to Yunus Thomas in the second innings, and the Hottentots Holland allrounder, bowling slow medium-pacers, responded by taking an incredible career-best 6/5 in 8 overs to help dimiss the visitors for 120.

Jabaar's debut as captain seemed set to start on a false note when WP slumped to 18/5 in pursuit of a modest victory target of 105 – but the experience of Braima Isaacs, who made a match-winning unbeaten 42, guided the side to a tense 2-wicket victory.

TRANSVAAL FIRST INNINGS

S. Mohammed c Isaacs b Barnes	16
A. Bhabha lbw Barnes	0
A. Rajah c Abdullah b Barnes	20
O. Visser c Fortune b Barnes	2
M. Jajbhai b Damon	6
N. Edwards c Isaacs b Barnes	29
J. Kleinveldt b Damon	0
Y. Begg c Damon b Jabaar	2
A. Kholia b Benjamin	19
A. Variawa b Jabaar	9
R. Galant not out	4
EXTRAS	8
TOTAL	115

FALL OF WICKETS: 1/0; 2/34; 3/38; 4/39; 5/57; 6/57; 7/62; 8/80; 9/107

BOWLING: Damon 18-5-43-2; Barnes 19-8-26-5; Jabaar 23-9-36-2; Benjamin 2,1-0-2-1

TRANSVAAL SECOND INNINGS

S. Mohammed lbw Jabaar	6
A. Babha b Barnes	11
A. Rajah run out	8
M. Jajbhai lbw Thomas	24
N. Edwards c Thomas b Benjamin	13
O. Visser c sub b Thomas	36
Y. Begg c Harris b Thomas	2
J. Kleinveldt b Thomas	3
A. Kholia lbw Thomas	0
A Variawa not out	0
R. Galant st Isaacs b Damon	1
EXTRAS	16
TOTAL	120

FALL OF WICKETS: 1/15; 2/24; 3/31; 4/52; 5/58; 6/96; 7/108; 8/108; 9/119

BOWLING: Barnes 12-3-26-1; Damon 11,3-2-21-1; Benjamin 12-2-29-1; Jabaar 13-2-22-1; Thomas 8-5-6-5

WP FIRST INNINGS

+E. Isaacs b Variawa	7
H. Price b Variawa	0
N. Fortune c Rajah b Kleinveldt	1
E. Harris b Edwards	43
M. Abdullah lbw Kholia	11
N. Antulay run out	35
Y. Thomas b Variawa	4
*A. Jabaar not out	14
E. Damon b Edwards	4
V. Barnes b Edwards	0
F. Benjamin b Edwards	0
EXTRAS	2
TOTAL	131

FALL OF WICKETS: 1/1; 2/6; 3/12; 4/42; 5/102; 6/106; 7/112; 8/125; 9/131

BOWLING: Variawa 17-6-30-3; Kleinveldt 11-2-26-1; Kholia 16-3-32-1; Galant 7-1-19-0; Edwards 7,5-1-12-4

WP SECOND INNINGS

H. Price lbw Kleinveldt	2
N. Fortune c Begg b Kleinveldt	2
M. Abdullah c Begg b Variawa	1
E. Harris c Edwards b Variawa	6
N. Antulay c Begg b Kleinveldt	0
E. Isaacs not out	42
Y. Thomas b Edwards	10
A. Jabaar b Variawa	9
E. Damon c & b Variawa	8
V. Barnes not out	0
EXTRAS	25
TOTAL	105/8

FALL OF WICKETS: 1/10; 2/11; 3/12; 4/12; 5/18; 6/67; 7/84; 8/98

BOWLING: Kleinveldt 16.3-9-17-3; Variawa 26-15-26-4; Edwards 17-6-26-1; Galant 6-4-4-0; Kholia 2-0-7-0

WP WON BY TWO WICKETS

Barnes grabs eight wickets in a career-best bowling stint, to set up an easy WP victory

**Natal vs WP
22-24 January 1983
in Durban**

FOR ONCE WP got off to a good start as the recalled opening pair of Rashaad Musson (31) and Stuart Hendricks (40) put on 79 for the first wicket. While most of the middle-order did the hard work of getting started, they failed to convert their double figures into substantial scores.

Munsoor Abdullah (49), Eddie Harris (15), Nasser Antulay (18), Saait Magiet (26) and Yunus Thomas (44) all seemed set for substantial scores before being dismissed at vital stages. WP were, nevertheless, able to top 200 for the first time in seven innings.

The WP total of 244 suddenly took on match-winning proportions as Vincent Barnes claimed career-best figures of 8/29 in an unchanged spell of 17,2 overs to skittle Natal for a paltry 61. As has been the case so many times in the past, the Natal batsmen had no answer to the pace and bounce of Barnes.

Although the home side fared slightly better in their second innings to reach 100, it wasn't enough to prevent WP from scoring a crushing innings and 83-run victory.

WP FIRST INNINGS

S. Hendricks c Mansoor b Hoosen	40
R. Musson b Khan	31
N. Fortune c Seedat b Khan	1
E. Harris b Khan	15
M. Abdullah b E. Govender	49
N. Antulay lbw Khan	18
S. Magiet run out	26
Y. Thomas c E. Govender b Hoosen	44
*A. Jabaar b Khan	1
+E. Isaacs run out	1
V. Barnes not out	0
EXTRAS	18
TOTAL	244

FALL OF WICKETS: 1/79; 2/81; 3/82; 4/113; 5/151; 6/171; 7/220; 8/226; 9/236

BOWLING: Mansoor 10-1-35-0; E. Govender 9-4-15-1; Chetty 5-0-18-0; Hoosen 24-3-68-2; Khan 26-4-85-5; Moses 1-0-5-0

NATAL FIRST INNINGS

E. Mall c Isaacs b Barnes	10
G. Moses c Abdullah b Barnes	0
S. Govender b S. Magiet	3
G. Hoosen c Musson b Barnes	4
M. Moodley c Hendricks b Barnes	9
M. Khan c Isaacs b Barnes	1
A. Chetty b Jabaar	6
L. Maharaj c Isaacs b Barnes	2
E. Govender c Jabaar b Barnes	5
S. Mansoor not out	4
GH. Seedat c Fortune b Barnes	1
EXTRAS	16
TOTAL	61

FALL OF WICKETS: 1/2; 2/16; 3/24; 4/26; 5/28; 6/41; 7/49; 8/55; 9/57

BOWLING: Barnes 17,2-5-29-8; S. Magiet 13-9-6-1; Jabaar 5-0-10-0

NATAL SECOND INNINGS (FOLLOWED ON)

E. Mall c Musson b Barnes	0
G. Moses c Barnes b S. Magiet	5
S. Govender run out	25
G. Hoosen b S. Magiet	12
N. Moodley b Barnes	27
M. Khan run out	1
A. Chetty b Barnes	10
L. Maharaj c & b Jabaar	6
E. Govender c Isaacs b Jabaar	0
S. Mansoor run out	4
G. Seedat not out	0
EXTRAS	10
TOTAL	100

FALL OF WICKETS: 1/0; 2/29; 3/35; 4/45; 5/57; 6/84; 7/91; 8/94; 9/98

BOWLING: Barnes 12-1-23-3; S. Magiet 18-6-32-2; Jabaar 21,2-8-33-2; Thomas 2-1-2-0

WP WON BY AN INNINGS AND 83 RUNS

WP vs EP
19-21 February
1983
at Rocklands
Cape Town

Sweet revenge for Western Province as EP flounder against Barnes

REVENGE WAS the word on everyone's lips in the WP camp for the return game against EP. To emphasise their determination to repay the visitors in kind, Rocklands with its lively emerald green wicket, was chosen as the venue.

The visitors, with the exception of Garth Cuddembey, who was unbeaten on 34, could not cope with the pace of the fiery Vincent Barnes, who followed his 8/29 against Natal with the spectacular figures of 7/19 on a wicket tailor-made for pace bowling.

After dismissing EP for a meagre 83, WP did well to make 159, thanks to a solid 50 by Eddie Harris, 35 by Stuart Hendricks and a valuable 27 by Yunus Thomas. Although EP coped much better with Barnes in the second innings, they found the support cast of Saait Magiet, Mervyn Theron and Armien Jabaar equally difficult to handle, and were dismissed for 123.

WP knocked off the required 48 for the loss of two wicket to gain sweet revenge for their first round embarrassment in Port Elizabeth. More importantly, they launched themselves into pole position to retain the Howa Bowl.

EP FIRST INNINGS

G. Abrahams c S. Magiet b Jabaar	16
J. Sandan c Isaacs b S. Magiet	4
Z. Hendricks c Fortune b Barnes	0
H. Lorgat c S. Magiet b Barnes	0
G. Cuddembey not out	34
D. Reid st Isaacs b Jabaar	0
S. Draai b Barnes	15
A Peters b Barnes	0
R. Dolley c Thomas b Barnes	0
D. Govindjee c Isaacs b Barnes	3
J. Frans c Isaacs b Barnes	0
EXTRAS	11
TOTAL	83

FALL OF WICKETS: 1/11; 2/14; 3/14; 4/31; 5/31; 6/64; 7/76; 8/76; 9/83

BOWLING: Barnes 12-4-19-7; S. Magiet 10-4-19-1; Theron 7-5-7-0; Jabaar 8-3-26-2; Thomas 2-1-1-0

EP SECOND INNINGS

J. Sandan b Thomas	15
G. Abrahams c Isaacs b S. Magiet	0
Z. Hendricks c Jabaar b Barnes	8
H. Lorgat run out	8
G. Cuddembey c Harris b Theron	26
D. Reid b Jabaar	14
S. Draai lbw Jabaar	2
A. Peters st Isaacs b Jabaar	1
R. Dolley c Isaacs b Barnes	6
D. Govindjee c Barnes b S. Magiet	20
J. Frans not out	7
EXTRAS	16
TOTAL	123

FALL OF WICKETS: 1/10; 2/18; 3/36; 4/37; 5/80; 6/82; 7/83; 8/84; 9/102

BOWLING: Barnes 13-3-33-2; S. Magiet 12-4-24-2; Theron 14-4-26-1; Thomas 5-2-4-1; Jabaar 6-1-20-3

WP FIRST INNINGS

S. Hendricks c Draai b Govindjee	35
R. Musson c Draai b Frans	5
N. Fortune lbw Draai	2
E. Harris c & b Draai	50
M. Abdullah c Govindjee b Lorgat	12
S. Magiet c Dolley b Lorgat	0
+E. Isaacs b Reid	2
Y. Thomas c Hendricks b Draai	27
*A. Jabaar run out	9
M. Theron st Cuddembey b Govindjee	12
V. Barnes not out	0
EXTRAS	5
TOTAL	159

FALL OF WICKETS: 1/6; 2/15; 3/61; 4/76; 5/80; 6/85; 7/137; 8/138; 9/159

BOWLING: Frans 12-3-21-1; Draai 15-3-30-3; Dolley 2-0-14-0; Lorgat 16-3-38-2; Govindjee 10,4-2-26-2; Abrahams 1-0-2-0; Reid 5-2-15-1; Peters 3-0-8-0

WP SECOND INNINGS

S. Hendricks c Sandan b Frans	2
R. Musson not out	20
N. Fortune c Cuddembey b Draai	2
E. Harris not out	16
EXTRAS	9
TOTAL	49/2

FALL OF WICKETS: 1/9; 2/22

BOWLING: Draai 9-1-16-1; Frans 5-0-11-1; Lorgat 4-2-3-0; Govindjee 1-1-0-0; Sandan 1-0-5-0; Hendricks 0,5-0-5-0

WP WON BY 8 WICKETS

Record-breaker Barnes powers WP to their fourth Howa Bowl triumph in succession

Transvaal vs WP 12-14 March 1983, in Johannesburg

DESPITE A solid half century by Rashaad Musson the WP top order woes continued as they slumped to 30/3 before t Munsoor Abdullah (40) helped them get to 192 in their first innings.

Bolstered by the inclusion of two former WP players, Michael Doman and Johnny Kleinveldt, Transvaal were dismissed for 164 as Vincent Barnes claimed his 4th five wicket haul of the season. When he bowled Faizel Kimmie for 31, Barnes claimed his 41st scalp to beat the record of 40 wickets in a season set by the great Lefty Adams in the 1979/80 season.

With the Howa Bowl in sight, Munsoor Abdullah (79) and Yunus Thomas (59) flayed the Transvaal bowling with a 5th wicket stand of 125 in even time to leave Transvaal with the stiff task of scoring 304 for victory. They were dismissed for 113, to give WP their fourth successive Howa Bowl title.

WP FIRST INNINGS

R. Musson c Kleinveldt b Variawa 52
S. Hendricks b Kleinveldt 0
+E. Isaacs c Begg b Variawa 5
E. Harris c & b Kimmie...3
N. Fortune c Edwards b Kimmie 15
M. Abdullah lbw Variawa...40
S. Magiet c Visser b Kleinveldt................................14
Y. Thomas c Dinath b Kimmie 16
*A. Jabaar lbw Kleinveldt 18
M. Theron b Kimmie 3
V. Barnes not out..4
　　　　　　　　　　　EXTRAS...............22
　　　　　　　　　　　TOTAL...............192

FALL OF WICKETS: 1/5; 2/18; 3/30; 4/67; 5/104; 6/140; 7/140; 8/180; 9/188

BOWLING: Variawa 15-4-54-3; Kleinveldt 15-5-33-3; Kimmie 10,1-2-31-4; Galant 6-1-25-0; Edwards 6-0-27-0

WP SECOND INNINGS

R. Musson c Mohammed b Edwards 18
S. Hendricks lbw Kleinveldt 8
N. Fortune c Galant b Edwards 25
E. Harris ret hurt 3
M. Abdullah b Kimmie 79
S. Magiet c Begg b Galant...2
Y. Thomas c Dinath b Kimmie 59
E. Isaacs c Mohammed b Doman 4
A. Jabaar c Begg b Kimmie......................................12
M. Theron not out 15
V. Barnes c Variawa b Edwards 24
　　　　　　　　　　　EXTRAS...............26
　　　　　　　　　　　TOTAL............275/9

FALL OF WICKETS: 1/12; 2/51; 3/54; 4/73; 5/198; 6/217; 7/217; 8/235; 9/235

BOWLING: Variawa 10-1-41-0; Kleinveldt 9-0-44-1; Kimmie 17-1-55-3; Edwards 17-2-45-3; Galant 15-3-54-1; Doman 5-3-10-1

TRANSVAAL FIRST INNINGS

S. Mohammed b Thomas 30
A. Rajah c Magiet b Barnes.......................................1
M. Doman b Magiet 4
O. Visser c Magiet b Jabaar 42
A. Dinath b Thomas 16
N. Edwards c Isaacs b Barnes 3
Y. Begg b Barnes 17
F. Kimmie b Barnes 31
J. Kleinveldt st Isaacs b Magiet 0
A. Variawa c Fortune b Barnes 5
R. Galant not out 1
　　　　　　　　　　　EXTRAS...............14
　　　　　　　　　　　TOTAL...............164

FALL OF WICKETS: 1/10; 2/17; 3/78; 4/98; 5/103; 6/111; 7/144; 8/147; 9/163

BOWLING: Barnes 15.3-0-57-5; Magiet 15-6-36-2; Jabaar 9-2-26-1; Theron 2-1-9-0; Thomas 12-4-22-2

TRANSVAAL SECOND INNINGS

S. Mohammed st Isaacs b Theron 33
A. Rajah run out 14
M. Doman b Jabaar 5
A. Variawa lbw Theron 2
R. Galant run out 0
Y. Begg c Barnes b Jabaar..0
O. Visser c Barnes b Jabaar....................................16
A. Dinath c Isaacs b Theron....................................10
N. Edwards b Jabaar...25
F. Kimmie c Thomas b Jabaar...................................1
J. Kleinveldt not out 4
　　　　　　　　　　　EXTRAS.................3
　　　　　　　　　　　TOTAL...............113

FALL OF WICKETS: 1/33; 2/37; 3/38; 4/38; 5/54; 6/60; 7/76; 8/94; 9/101

BOWLING: Barnes 4-2-8-0; Magiet 4-0-16-0; Jabaar 21,5-2-60-5; Theron 21-7-26-3

WP WON BY 190 RUNS
WP WIN HOWA BOWL FOR 4TH YEAR IN A ROW

WP Cricket Board First Class Averages 1982/83

BATTING

Name	Matches	Inns	NO	Hs	Runs	Ave	50	100
Yunus Thomas	5	8	0	59	223	27,88		
Edward Harris	4	7	2	50	136	27,20	1	
Munsoor Abdullah	6	10	0	79	270	27,00	2	
Nasser Antulay	3	5	0	64	129	25,80	1	
Rashaad Musson	4	7	1	52	129	21,50	1	
Stuart Hendricks	3	5	0	40	85	17,00		
Ebrahim Damon	2	4	1	20	50	16,67		
Ebrahim Isaacs	5	8	1	42*	103	14,71		
Neil Fortune	6	11	0	59	141	12,82	1	
Saait Magiet	3	4	0	26	42	10,50		
Armien Jabaar	6	10	2	18	80	10,00		
Vincent Barnes	6	10	5	24	45	9,00		
Ivan Dagnin	1	2	0	9	17	8,50		
Charles van Schalkwyk	2	4	0	13	32	8,00		
Nazeem White	1	2	1	6	8	8,00		
Mervyn Theron	3	5	1	15*	30	7,50		
Shadley Martin	1	2	0	8	8	4,00		
MZ Allie	1	2	0	5	7	3,50		
Imraan Hendricks	1	2	0	5	5	2,50		
Norman Arendse	1	2	0	2	3	1,50		
Hassiem Price	1	2	0	2	2	1,00		

Also batted; Fuad Benjamin (0)

FIELDING:

Wicketkeepers: 20 – Ebrahim Isaacs (14ct and 6st), 6 – Rashaad Musson (4ct and 2st), Nazeem White (3ct and 1st)

Catches:

8 – Munsoor Abdullah; 6 – Yunus Thomas; 5 – Vincent Barnes; Neil Fortune; 4 – Edward Harris, Saait Magiet; 3 – Michael Doman, Ebrahim Damon, Armien Jabaar; 2 – Charles van Schalkwyk, Norman Arendse, Nasser Antulay; 1 – Stuart Hendricks

BOWLING

Name	Overs	Mdns	Wkts	Runs	Ave	Best Bowling	5i	10m
Yunus Thomas	38	18	9	51	5,67	5/6 v Tvl	1	
Vincent Barnes	161,4	44	41	318	7,76	8/29 v Natal	4	1
Armien Jabaar	183,2	38	24	303	12,63	5/60 v Tvl	1	
Ebrahim Damon	59,3	14	8	122	15,25	4/36 v Natal		
Fuad Benjamin	14,1	2	2	31	15,50	1/2 v Tvl		
Mervyn Theron	75	22	9	141	15,67	4/62 v EP		
Charles van Schalkwyk	8	0	2	32	16,00	2/16 vs EP		
Saait Magiet	72	29	8	133	16,63	2/24 v EP		

Also bowled: Imraan Hendricks 23-5-65-2; Norman Arendse 3-0-12-0

WP and EP play to a first innings tie – then rain intervenes

AFTER THE bowlers had done their job by dismissing EP for a modest 171, the WP top order got into their customary bad habit of failing to lay a foundation for their powerful middle order. The top four were back in the hut with only 25 on the board, and although Munsoor Abdullah and Braima Isaacs retrieved the situation somewhat with a fifth wicket stand of 51, it was left to a defiant ninth-wicket stand, coincidentally also of 51, between Armien Jabaar and Vincent Barnes to add respectability to the WP innings.

True to the tradition of the tussles between these two sides, the first innings finished tied when Jabaar was trapped lbw by Haroon Lorgat with the WP total on 171. Rain intervened with EP on 46/2 in their second innings, but there way enough time for Braima Isaacs to take his only first-class wicket.

After the game, stalwart allrounder Georgie van Oordt announced his retirement from provincial cricket, citing dissatisfaction with the way he had been treated by the selectors over the years as the reason for his decision.

EP FIRST INNINGS

G. Cuddembey c Antulay b Jabaar 52
G. Abrahams lbw Barnes 2
M. Van Eck b Magiet 4
H. Lorgat b Barnes 4
A. Frans c Harris b Jabaar 18
F. Abrahams c & b Jabaar 8
K. Majola b Barnes 12
D. Jordaan c Antulay b Theron 16
G. Koen not out 22
M. Abrahams b Van Oordt 1
J. Frans b S. Magiet 12

EXTRAS 20
TOTAL 171

FALL OF WICKETS: 1/3; 2/10; 3/15; 4/58; 5/85; 6/106; 7/122; 8/148; 9/152

BOWLING: Barnes 17-5-26-3; S. Magiet 10.4-4-15-2; Theron 26-8-42-1; Van Oordt 11-3-20-1; Jabaar 26-7-48-3

EP SECOND INNINGS

G. Abrahams not out 22
G. Cuddembey c Dawson b Barnes 3
M. Van Eck c Dawson b Isaacs 17

EXTRAS 4
TOTAL 46/2

FALL OF WICKETS: 1/11; 2/46

BOWLING: Barnes 8-1-22-1; Magiet 3-2-1-0; Jabaar 2-1-1-0; Theron 6-1-12-0; Van Oordt 3-3-0-0; Isaacs 3,3-0-6-1

WP FIRST INNINGS

H. Dawson c F. Abrahams b J. Frans 1
S. Hendricks lbw Majola 5
N. Antulay b J. Frans 10
E. Harris lbw J. Frans 0
M. Abdullah lbw Majola 26
+E. Isaacs c J. Frans b Majola 24
S. Magiet c Jordaan b M. Abrahams 7
*A. Jabaar lbw Lorgat 70
M. Theron c Jordaan b Majola 4
V. Barnes c F. Abrahams b J. Frans 10
G. Van Oordt not out 1

EXTRAS 13
TOTAL 171

FALL OF WICKETS: 1/2; 2/18; 3/18; 4/25; 5/76; 6/83; 7/87; 8/118; 9/169

BOWLING: J. Frans 14-9-27-4; M. Abrahams 13-5-20-1; A. Frans 8-4-28-0; Majola 13-0-47-4; Lorgat 15,2-10-14-1; Koen 10-4-18-0; Jordaan 4-3-4-0

MATCH DRAWN; FIRST INNINGS TIED

Record-breakers Abdullah and Thomas steer WP to big innings victory

WP vs Transvaal 27-29 December 1983 in Johannesburg

FOR ONCE the Transvaal batsmen, led by a solid 83 from opener Ahmed Rajah, and 58 by Neil Edwards, made the WP bowlers work hard as Vincent Barnes, unusually for him, failed to take a wicket. With the exception of these two, however, the rest of the home side's batting crumbled against the WP spin twins, Armien Jabaar and Seraj Gabriels – and they were dismissed for 233 (after having been 170/4 at one stage).

Despite yet another poor start, WP went on to make their highest first-class score of 431, with the stylish Munsoor Abdullah (107) and Yunus Thomas (85) putting on a record 112 for the 5th wicket.

As was the case in the first innings, Jabaar and Gabriels bowled marathon spells of 37 and 39 overs respectively, and shared five wickets in the home side's total of 182, to help WP to victory by an innings and 16 runs

TRANSVAAL FIRST INNINGS

A. Rajah c Thomas b Gabriels	83
M. Kota c Antulay b Gabriels	18
E. Amod c Thomas b Gabriels	15
A. Wadvalla c Abdullah b Jabaar	13
N. Edwards b Damon	58
M. Jajbhai lbw Thomas	2
S. Cassim b Jabaar	1
Y. Begg c Abdullah b Jabaar	0
R. Galant c Solomons b Jabaar	0
F. Kimmie b Damon	13
A. Variawa not out	10
EXTRAS	20
TOTAL	233

FALL OF WICKETS: 1/52; 2/83; 3/124; 4/164; 5/171; 6/183; 7/187; 8/194; 9/210

BOWLING: Barnes 14-4-31-0; Damon 15.1-4-39-2; Jabaar 26-7-58-4; Gabriels 36-6-71-3; Thomas 9-4-14-1

TRANSVAAL SECOND INNINGS

A. Rajah c Damon b Gabriels	32
M.Kota st Isaacs b Gabriels	6
E. Amod lbw Jabaar	1
A. Wadvalla c Solomons b Jabaar	30
N. Edwards b Gabriels	34
M. Jajbhai b Gabriels	9
S. Cassim c Solomons b Gabriels	23
Y. Begg c Antulay b Jabaar	4
R. Galant st Isaacs b Jabaar	10
F. Kimmie not out	23
A. Variawa b Jabaar	1
EXTRAS	9
TOTAL	182

FALL OF WICKETS: 1/15; 2/16; 3/68; 4/104; 5/114; 6/123; 7/132; 8/154; 9/181

BOWLING: Barnes 7-0-17-0; Damon 13-4-27-0; Jabaar 37,1-15-49-5; Gabriels 39-8-78-5; Thomas 2-1-2-0.

WP FIRST INNINGS

H. Dawson b Cassim	3
R. Musson c & b Cassim	16
N. Antulay c Variawa b Edwards	48
F. Solomons c & b Amod	67
M. Abdullah lbw Edwards	107
Y. Thomas lbw Variawa	85
S. Gabriels ht wkt b Edwards	1
+E. Isaacs c Begg b Variawa	8
*A. Jabaar not out	43
V. Barnes c Wadvalla b Variawa	24
E. Damon b Variawa	2
EXTRAS	27
TOTAL	431

FALL OF WICKETS: 1/9; 2/34; 3/107; 4/197; 5/309; 6/327; 7/345; 8/376; 9/412

BOWLING: Variawa 20.2-3-67-4; Cassim 9-2-31-2; Galant 16-0-63-0; Kimmie 21-3-82-0; Amod 16-3-70-1; Edwards 17-2-75-3; Jajbhai 4-0-16-0

WP WON BY AN INNINGS AND 16 RUNS

SA CRICKET

2003/4 SEASON

GRAEME SMITH

MARK BOUCHER

PAUL ADAMS

NICKY BOJE

ALAN DAWSON

BOETA DIPPENAAR

HERSCHELLE GIBBS

ANDREW HALL

JACQUES KALLIS

GARY KIRSTEN

NEIL MCKENZIE

ANDRE NEL

MFUNEKO NGAM

MAKHAYA NTINI

ROBIN PETERSON

SHAUN POLLOCK

ASHWELL PRINCE

JACQUES RUDOLPH

MARTIN VAN JAARSVELD

MONDE ZONDEKI

SA CRICKET

2003/4 SEASON

GRAEME SMITH

MARK BOUCHER

PAUL ADAMS

NICKY BOJE

ALAN DAWSON

BOETA DIPPENAAR

HERSCHELLE GIBBS

ANDREW HALL

JACQUES KALLIS

GARY KIRSTEN

NEIL McKENZIE

ANDRE NEL

MFUNEKO NGAM

MAKHAYA NTINI

ROBIN PETERSON

SHAUN POLLOCK

ASHWELL PRINCE

JACQUES RUDOLPH

MARTIN VAN JAARSVELD

MONDE ZONDEKI

Mean Vincent Barnes batters Natal with a record-breaking analysis of 9/46

Natal vs WP
31 Dec 1983-
2 Jan 1984
at
Ladysmith

THIS GAME, played in faraway Ladysmith, will always be remembered for Vincent Barnes' record-breaking bowling analysis of 9/46 in the Natal second innings. Having gone wicketless in the previous encounter against Transvaal, Barnes returned with a bang to post the best-ever bowling figures in SACB first-class competition, beating his 8/29 against the same opposition in the corresponding fixture of the previous season.

Natal did well enough to reach 211 in their first innings. With WP struggling at 74/6, it was left to the experienced Armien Jabaar (39) and Seraj Gabriels (56) to do the business with the bat. Their combined effort enabled WP to take a slender first innings lead of 11.

The Natal second innings turned into the Vincent Barnes show as the paceman once again cast his spell over the home side's batsmen. The Natal batsmen had no answer, as Barnes, returning for his second spell, ripped through the rest of the batting to dismiss the home side for 156 . WP comfortably reached their victory target of 146 with four wickets in hand.

NATAL FIRST INNINGS

E. Mall b Thomas	27
G. Moses c Isaacs b Damon	1
E. Govender c Isaacs b Barnes	27
Y. Moorad c Barnes b Abdullah	7
S. Govender c Isaacs b Barnes	40
M. Moodley st Isaacs b Damon	21
M. Khan c Jabaar b Barnes	38
L. Maharaj b Jabaar	6
G. Hoosen lbw Jabaar	0
M. Govender b Damon	16
M. Rampersad not out	0
EXTRAS	28
TOTAL	211

FALL OF WICKETS: 1/2; 2/43; 3/72; 4/74; 5/130; 6153; 7/160; 8/164; 9/211

BOWLING: Barnes 17-6-36-3; Damon 19.1-5-51-3; Jabaar 16-5-28-2; Gabriels 7-0-21-0; Thomas 14-4-31-1; Abdullah 3-1-16-1

NATAL SECOND INNINGS

E. Mall c Isaacs b Barnes	49
G. Moses c Antulay b Barnes	3
E. Govender b Barnes	2
Y. Moorad c sub b Barnes	26
S. Govender c Isaacs b Barnes	10
M. Moodley b Barnes	0
M. Khan c Isaacs b Barnes	18
L. Maharaj c Isaacs b Damon	0
M. Govender c Isaacs b Barnes	26
G. Hoosen b Barnes	1
M. Rampersad not out	1
EXTRAS	20
TOTAL	156

FALL OF WICKETS: 1/22; 2/25; 3/92; 4/92; 5/96; 6/

BOWLING: Barnes 29.4-10-46-9; Damon 18-4-34-1; Jabaar 20-6-26-0; Gabriels 11-1-27-0; Thomas 4-2-3-0

WP FIRST INNINGS

R. Musson b Rampersad	0
N. Antulay c M. Govender b E. Govender	43
E. Harris c Moorad b Khan	20
F. Solomons run out	4
+E. Isaacs c Maharaj b Rampersad	2
Y. Thomas run out	1
*A. Jabaar lbw M Govender	39
S. Gabriels c Hoosen b Khan	56
M. Abdullah c Hoosen b Rampersad	26
V. Barnes b Hoosen	12
E. Damon not out	1
EXTRAS	18
TOTAL	222

FALL OF WICKETS: 1/6; 2/50; 3/60; 4/67; 5/72; 6/74; 7/144; 8/187; 9/214

BOWLING: Rampersad 17-4-39-3; M. Govender 11-1-54-1; E. Govender 18-4-46-1; Khan 21,3-9-45-2; Hoosen 13-6-20-1

WP SECOND INNINGS

R. Musson lbw E. Govender	22
N. Antulay b Khan	29
E. Harris c Moodley b Khan	15
F. Solomons st S. Govender b Khan	17
Y. Thomas lbw Hoosen	0
S. Gabriels b E. Govender	21
A. Jabaar not out	35
E. Isaacs not out	0
EXTRAS	7
TOTAL	146/6

FALL OF WICKETS: 1/48; 2/60; 3/87; 4/88; 5/88; 6/145

BOWLING: Rampersad 7-3-16-0; M. Govender 6-1-12-0; Khan 20-9-41-3; E. Govender 17-6-50-2; Hoosen 13,2-6-20-1

WP WON BY 4 WICKETS

Magiet and Jabaar ease WP to a fifth successive Howa Bowl triumph

ALTHOUGH THERE were still three matches to play, both sides knew the outcome of this match, played at bowler-friendly Rocklands, would determine the destiny of the Howa Bowl. WP virtually ensured that the trophy would remain in Cape Town for a fifth successive season when the pace of Saait Magiet (5/29) and the spin of Armien Jabaar (4/18) combined to dismiss EP for a meagre 93 in their first innings.

EP made the perfect response when they reduced WP to 36/3, but a magnificent 102 by Munsoor Abdullah snuffed out any hopes the visitors may have had of dismissing the home side cheaply. Abdullah guided his side to a respectable 205, which gave them a match-winning lead of 112. Jabaar's guile and variation once again proved too much for the EP batsmen in the second innings. He claimed the second seven-wicket haul of his career, to finish with outstanding match figures of 11/58 as EP were dismissed for 142.

Stuart Hendricks and Eddie Harris had no trouble in reaching the victory target of 31.

EP FIRST INNINGS
G. Cuddembey c Solomons b Magiet	3
G. Abrahams lbw Jabaar	14
H. Lorgat c Solomons b Magiet	3
A. Peters c Thomas b Magiet	19
A. Frans lbw Magiet	0
K. Majola c Abdullah b Magiet	7
F. Abrahams cThomas b Jabaar	2
S. Draai c Magiet b Jabaar	11
E. Frans run out	3
J. Frans not out	14
M. Abrahams b Jabaar	7
EXTRAS	10
TOTAL	93

FALL OF WICKETS: 1/3; 2/7; 3/37; 4/41; 5/42; 6/47; 7/55; 8/67; 9/74

BOWLING: Barnes 13-2-36-0; Magiet 15-5-29-5; Jabaar 12.2-5-18-4

EP SECOND INNINGS
G. Cuddembey c Harris b Jabaar	23
G. Abrahams b Magiet	7
H. Lorgat c Gabriels b Jabaar	19
A. Peters b Jabaar	9
A. Frans b Jabaar	20
K. Majola c Isaacs b Jabaar	14
F. Abrahams c Magiet b Jabaar	1
S. Draai c Abdullah b Gabriels	27
E. Frans c Solomons b Jabaar	7
J. Frans c Isaacs b Gabriels	4
M. Abrahams not out	0
EXTRAS	11
TOTAL	142

FALL OF WICKETS: 1/18; 2/47; 3/62; 4/65; 5/92; 6/94; 7/123; 8/131; 9/142

BOWLING: Barnes 6-0-22-0; Magiet 6-2-4-1; Jabaar 29,3-12-40-7; Thomas 4-0-12-0; Gabriels 27-8-41-2; Abdullah 6-2-12-0

WP FIRST INNINGS
+E. Isaacs b A.Frans	13
S. Hendricks lbw E. Frans	1
N. Antulay c Lorgat b J. Frans	9
F. Solomons c F. Abrahams b E. Frans	4
M. Abdullah c Peters b Majola	102
E. Harris c Lorgat b A. Frans	18
Y. Thomas c Majola b A. Frans	7
S. Gabriels c F. Abrahams b Draai	17
S. Magiet c F. Abrahams b E. Frans	12
*A. Jabaar c Lorgat b E. Frans	2
V. Barnes not out	0
EXTRAS	20
TOTAL	205

FALL OF WICKETS: 1/9; 2/13; 3/36; 4/95; 5/114; 6/145; 7/173; 8/198; 9/205

BOWLING: E. Frans 13.2-2-29-4; J. Frans 7-2-15-1; Draai 10-3-32-1; A. Frans 25-7-57-3; M. Abrahams 4-0-8-0; Majola 19-4-44-1.

WP SECOND INNINGS
S. Hendricks not out	12
E. Harris not out	19
EXTRAS	3
TOTAL	34/0

BOWLING: Cuddembey 2-0-8-0; M. Abrahams 1-0-2-0; G. Abrahams 1-0-5-0; Majola 2-0-5-0; Peters 1-0-1-0; Lorgat 1-0-1-0; A. Frans 1-0-5-0; E. Frans 0,1-0-4-0

WP WON BY BY 10 WICKETS

A maiden century by Thomas is the highlight of an easy WP victory against Transvaal

WP vs Transvaal
18-20 February
1984
at Rocklands
Cape Town

AFTER MUCH recounting by the scorers, Yunus Thomas recorded his first Howa Bowl century, making exactly 100 not out against a team whose bowling he has taken a liking to over the past few seasons. Thomas put on 131 for the seventh wicket with his captain, Armien Jabaar (61), just two runs short of the record for this wicket set by Saait Magiet and Gertjie Williams in 1972.

Eddie Harris (58) and Faghme Solomons (68), at the top of the order, laid the foundation for big-hitters such as Jabaar and Thomas to cart the Transvaal bowling to all parts of Rocklands.

With Seraj Gabriels (6/40) at his best, the bamboozled Transvaal batsmen succumbed for 121 in their first innings. In their second innings, it was Jabaar's turn to mesmerise the opposition ; he claimed 5/25 to skittle the visitors for 94 – which gave WP victory by an innings and 128 runs

WP FIRST INNINGS

N. Antulay c Dindar b Dawood 4
E. Harris lbw Ganchi..58
N. Fortune c Dindar b Amod 18
F. Solomons c Mohammed b Edwards 68
M. Abdullah c & b Edwards 10
S. Gabriels run out 3
Y. Thomas not out 100
F. Davids c Choonara b Ganchi 0
*A. Jabaar c Choonara b Edwards.........................61
+G. Petersen b Ganchi 7
E. Damon not out 0

EXTRAS..............14
TOTAL.....343/9 dec

FALL OF WICKETS: 1/4; 2/42; 3/141; 4/161; 5/165; 6/169; 7/172; 8/303; 9/341

BOWLING: Dawood 9-0-44-1; Ganchi 17-2-73-3; Amod 14-1-79-1; Galant 15-3-52-0; George 3-1-12-0; Edwards 19,2-3-69-3

TRANSVAAL FIRST INNINGS

E. Amod c Fortune b Gabriels 32
S. Mohammed run out..20
A. Rajah b Thomas..0
M. Desai c Petersen b Gabriels 0
N. Edwards c Petersen b Davids............................29
D. George b Jabaar 19
N. Dindar c Jabaar b Gabriels.................................3
E. Choonara c Abdullah b Gabriels 5
R. Galant c Antulay b Gabriels 0
A. Ganchi not out..1
A. Dawood b Gabriels..0

EXTRAS..............12
TOTAL...............121

FALL OF WICKETS: 1/57; 2/57; 3/58; 4/63; 5/100; 6/110; 7/116; 8/116; 9/120

BOWLING: Damon 14-6-16-0; Davids 8-3-12-1; Jabaar 22-10-22-1; Thomas 17-11-19-1; Gabriels 23,4-8-40-6

TRANSVAAL SECOND INNINGS

(FOLLOWED ON)

S. Mohammed b Davids..0
E. Amod run out...1
A. Rajah lbw Damon...13
M. Desai c Petersen b Jabaar 29
N. Edwards c Thomas b Damon 0
D. George b Gabriels 26
N. Dindar b Davids 5
E. Choonara not out 8
A. Ganchi b Jabaar 0
R. Galant st Petersen b Jabaar..................................1
A. Dawood lbw Jabaar 6

EXTRAS.................5
TOTAL.................94

FALL OF WICKETS: 1/1; 2/5; 3/19; 4/21; 5/66; 6/71; 7/77; 8/77; 9/77

BOWLING: Damon 9-2-9-2; Davids 14-2-26-2; Thomas 10-4-15-0; Gabriels 4-0-14-0; Jabaar 13,4-5-25-5

WP WON BY AN INNINGS AND 128 RUNS

Even without several of their stalwarts, WP are still too strong for Natal

AN INCIDENT in a limited overs playoff match against Primrose resulted in the suspension of key Montrose players Armien Jabaar, Munsoor Abdullah, Vincent Barnes and Nasser Antulay. However, the depth of talent in WP was such that old hands such as Zak Davids and Goolam Allie – and new caps, Cecil Felix and Randall Cupido, were able to fill the gaps with hardly any disruption.

Under the new leadership of Saait Magiet, WP brushed Natal aside with ease. Cupido got his first-class career off to a good start by scoring 62, and then taking five catches and making two stumpings in the match, to lay his claim to being Braima Isaacs' permanent successor.

Zak Davids smashed a quick, unbeaten 55, while Faghme Solomons and Seraj Gabriels also posted half-centuries, which enabled Magiet to declare at 302/9.

The Natal batsmen could not cope with the spin of Gabriels, who finished with match figures of 12/83, as WP cantered to an innings and 121-run victory – and thereby ensuring that the Howa Bowl remained in Cape Town for yet another year.

WP FIRST INNINGS

C. Felix c E. Govender b Mahara	27
E. Harris run out	1
N. Fortune c R. Govender b Omar	0
F. Solomons c R. Govender b Khan	52
S. Gabriels c Kolia b R. Govender	50
*S. Magiet b Khan	19
Y. Thomas b Omar	0
+R. Cupido c R. Govender b E. Govender	62
Z. Davids not out	55
G. Allie c Omar b Khan	19
E. Damon not out	0
EXTRAS	17
TOTAL	302/9 dec

FALL OF WICKETS: 1/7; 2/9; 3/79; 4/85; 5/114; 6/127; 7/200; 8/226; 9/294

BOWLING: E. Govender 17-7-31-1; Omar 25-7-58-2; Khan 34.3-9-105-3; LD. Naidoo 7-1-22-0; Maharaj 11-2-26-1; Mall 3-0-9-0; R.L. Naidoo 4-1-23-0; R. Govender 3-0-11-0

NATAL FIRST INNINGS

E. Mall c Cupido b Damon	0
Y. Omar b Gabriels	10
A. Jadwat c Fortune b Gabriels	3
M. Moodley c Cupido b Magiet	3
E. Govender b Damon	5
P. Maharaj c Cupido b Magiet	0
M. Khan b Gabriels	14
R. Govender b Allie	22
R.L. Naidoo st Cupido b Gabriels	2
A. Kolia c & b Gabriels	0
LD. Naidoo not out	0
EXTRAS	8
TOTAL	67

FALL OF WICKETS: 1/0; 2/6; 3/17; 4/17; 5/17; 6/33; 7/57; 8/59; 9/67

BOWLING: Damon 9-3-16-2; Magiet 11-4-14-2; Gabriels 8-0-27-5; Allie 5,4-3-2-1

NATAL SECOND INNINGS (FOLLOWED ON)

E. Mall c & b Gabriels	6
Y. Omar c & b Gabriels	25
A. Jadwat st Cupido b Gabriels	27
M. Moodley c Cupido b Gabriels	0
E. Govender b Thomas	9
M. Khan c Thomas b Gabriels	3
P. Maharaj b Allie	6
R. Govender c Gabriels b Allie	0
R.L. Naidoo st Cupido b Gabriels	4
A. Kolia c Fortune b Gabriels	15
L.D Naidoo not out	10
EXTRAS	9
TOTAL	114

FALL OF WICKETS: 1/27; 2/38; 3/38; 4/55; 5/72; 6/81; 7/81; 8/87; 9/92

BOWLING: Damon 4-1-14-0; Magiet 5-3-3-0; Allie 9-1-10-2; Gabriels 26-5-56-7; Thomas 12-3-17-1; Davids 4-3-5-0.

WP WON BY AN INNINGS AND 121 RUNS

WP Cricket Board First Class Averages 1983/84

BATTING

Name	Matches	Inns	NO	Hs	Runs	Ave	50	100
Armien Jabaar	5	6	2	70	250	62,50	2	
Munsoor Abdullah	5	5	0	107	271	54,20		2
Yunus Thomas	5	6	1	100*	193	38,60	1	1
Faghme Solomons	5	6	0	68	212	35,33	3	
Seraj Gabriels	5	6	0	56	148	24,67	2	
Nasser Antulay	5	6	0	48	143	23,83		
Edward Harris	5	7	1	58	131	21,83	1	
Vincent Barnes	4	4	1	24	46	15,33		
Saait Magiet	3	3	0	19	38	12,67		
Rashaad Musson	2	3	0	22	38	12,67		
Ebrahim Isaacs	4	5	1	24	47	11,75		
Stuart Hendricks	2	3	1	12*	20	10,00		
Neil Fortune	2	2	0	18	18	9,00		
Ebrahim Damon	4	4	3	2	3	3,00		
Hilary Dawson	2	2	0	3	4	2,00		

Also batted; Zak Davids (55*), George van Oordt (1*), Randall Cupido (62), Faiek Davids (0), Cecil Felix (27), Goolam Allie (19), Grant Petersen (7), Mervyn Theron (4)

FIELDING:

Wicketkeepers: 13 – Ebrahim Isaacs (10ct & 3st), 4 – Grant Petersen (3ct & 1st), 3 – Hilary Dawson (3ct)

Catches:

6 – Faghme Solomons, Nasser Antulay, Yunus Thomas; 5 – Munsoor Abdullah, Seraj Gabriels; 3 – Armien Jabaar, Neil Fortune; 2 – Edward Harris, Saait Magiet; 1 – Ebrahim Damon, Vincent Barnes

BOWLING

Name	Overs	Mdns	Wkts	Runs	Ave	Best Bowling	5i	10m
Goolam Allie	14,4	4	3	12	4,00	2/10 v Natal		
Saait Magiet	50	20	10	66	6,60	5/29 v EP	1	
Armien Jabaar	204,1	59	31	315	10,16	7/40 v EP	3	1
Seraj Gabriels	181	36	28	375	13,39	7/56 v Natal	4	1
Faiek Davids	22	5	3	38	12,67	2/26 v Tvl		
Vincent Barnes	111	27	16	236	14,75	9/46 v Natal	1	1
Ebrahim Damon	101,2	29	11	206	18,73	3/51 v Natal		
George van Oordt	14	6	1	20	20,00	1/20 v EP		
Yunus Thomas	72	29	4	113	28,25	1/14 v Tvl		
Mervyn Theron	32	9	1	54	54,00	1/42 v EP		

Also bowled: Ebrahim Isaacs 3,3-0-6-1; Munsoor Abdullah 9-3-28-1; Zak Davids 4-3-2-0

Gabriels in run-out drama as WP and EP play to the first tie in SACB history

AFTER PRODUCING a first innings tie in the previous season, WP and EP once again provided excitement and tension as their encounter at Elfindale produced the first, and only, tied result in the history of Sacboc and SACB first-class cricket.

Barney Mohammed made a dream debut for WP, taking 5/33 in 23 overs to help dismiss EP for 109. However, WP fared even worse. Steven Draai (5/20) routed them for 97.

Mohammed (4/23) and Goolam Allie (6/45) gave their side a great chance of victory when they dismissed EP for 109, for a second time. This left WP to get 122 for victory. WP finished the second day on 110/5, needing 12 runs for victory with ample batting to come.

But Draai, together with Jeff Frans and Haroon Lorgat, took four quick wickets for only 7 runs to bring their side to the brink of victory. Seraj Gabriels was run out trying to take a suicidal single in search of the winning run, with the WP score on 121.

EP FIRST INNINGS

G. Cuddembey c White b Mohammed	16
J. Sandan run out	8
M. van Eck c Hendricks b Jabaar	12
H. Lorgat b Jabaar	8
A. Peters b Allie	37
A. Frans lbw Mohammed	8
K. Majola c Antulay b Mohammed	4
S. Draai b Allie	0
J. Frans b Mohammed	4
F. Abrahams not out	2
D. Van Vuuren b Mohammed	0
EXTRAS	10
TOTAL	109

FALL OF WICKETS: 1/26; 2/35; 3/49; 4/81; 5/99; 6/99; 7/103; 8/103; 9/107

BOWLING: Mohammed 23-9-33-5; Allie 13-4-20-2; Miller 7-1-17-0; Jabaar 15-6-22-2; Gabriels 8-4-7-0

EP SECOND INNINGS

J. Sandan not out	39
G. Cuddembey b Mohammed	0
M. van Eck c White b Allie	13
H. Lorgat c Antulay b Allie	4
A. Peters c White b Allie	2
A. Frans b Mohammed	28
K. Majola b Allie	0
F. Abrahams c Miller b Mohammed	0
S. Draai c White b Allie	0
J. Frans c White b Allie	5
D. Van Vuuren b Mohammed	2
EXTRAS	16
TOTAL	109

FALL OF WICKETS: 1/1; 2/25; 3/30; 4/32; 5/81; 6/83; 7/84; 8/88; 9/102

BOWLING: Mohammed 17,2-6-23-4; Miller 3-0-8-0; Jabaar 8-1-14-0; Allie 22-6-45-6; Gabriels 3-1-3-0

WP FIRST INNINGS

S. Hendricks c Cuddembey b Majola	5
R. Musson lbw Van Vuuren	1
N. Antulay v Van Vuuren b Draai	42
F. Solomons b Draai	9
M. Abdullah run out	0
S. Gabriels b Lorgat	6
*A. Jabaar b Draai	3
G. Miller c Abrahams b J. Frans	8
+N. White not out	8
E. Mohammed b Draai	5
G. Allie b Draai	0
EXTRAS	10
TOTAL	97

FALL OF WICKETS: 1/3; 2/15; 3/38; 4/39; 5/65; 6/71; 7/77; 8/90; 9/97

BOWLING: J. Frans 6-2-14-1; Van Vuuren 3-2-3-1; Majola 7-3-10-1; Lorgat 25-7-40-1; Draai 20,4-9-20-5

WP SECOND INNINGS

S. Hendricks lbw J. Frans	10
R. Musson lbw Lorgat	0
N. Antulay lbw J. Frans	22
F. Solomons c Draai b Lorgat	34
M. Abdullah c Draai b Lorgat	36
G. Miller lbw J. Frans	0
S. Gabriels run out	7
A. Jabaar lbw Draai	1
N. White lbw Draai	2
E. Mohammed c Abrahams b Lorgat	0
G. Allie not out	0
EXTRAS	9
TOTAL	121

FALL OF WICKETS: 1/4; 2/20; 3/48; 4/107; 5/107; 6/111; 7/114; 8/116; 9/117

BOWLING: J. Frans 12-2-23-3; Van Vuuren 3-1-8-0; Majola 7-3-14-0; A. Frans 9-2-19-0; Lorgat 13-4-21-4; Draai 14-4-27-2

MATCH TIED

Whirlwind batting by WP's top allrounders, Magiet and Jabaar, blows away Transvaal

WP vs Transvaal 26-28 December 1984 at Green Point Track

HOOSAIN AHMED, playing for the lower league Combine side, was a surprise choice as opening batsman to replace Rashaad Musson, as WP tried to get their show on the road following their tie against EP.

With Saait Magiet and Vincent Barnes also back in harness, WP took only 45 overs to dismiss Transvaal for 85, with Barnes (3/13) and Armien Jabaar (4/13) doing most of the damage.

Magiet (61) and Jabaar (26) then shared in a whirlwind sixth wicket stand of 80 – to enable WP to declare at 200/9, a lead of 115.

Although Faizel Kimmie (20) and Yassien Begg (12) provided brief resistance with an eighth wicket partnership of 30, it wasn't enough to prevent their side from being skittled for 90, to give WP victory by an innings and 25 runs.

TRANSVAAL FIRST INNINGS

A. Bhabha c Solomons b Barnes	8
A. Mentor c Magiet b Mohammed	4
A. Rajah b Allie	23
A. Moola lbw Jabaar	4
M. Desai c Allie b Jabaar	9
N. Edwards run out	1
F. Kimmie b Barnes	25
Y. Begg c Magiet b Jabaar	0
M. Abed b Jabaar	0
AH. Manack not out	1
A. Variawa b Barnes	0
EXTRAS	10
TOTAL	85

FALL OF WICKETS: 1/6; 2/16; 3/31; 4/47; 5/49; 6/77; 7/77; 8/77; 9/85

BOWLING: Barnes 9,2-4-13-3; Mohammed 9-4-12-1; Magiet 11-4-14-0; Jabaar 7-3-13-4; Allie 9-1-23-1

TRANSVAAL SECOND INNINGS

A. Bhabha b Barnes	4
A. Mentor c Hendricks b Mohammed	12
A. Rajah lbw Allie	7
A. Moola c & b Mohammed	8
N. Edwards c Cupido b Allie	7
M. Desai b Mohammed	1
Y. Begg c Solomons b Jabaar	12
F. Kimmie b Barnes	20
AH. Manack st Cupido b Jabaar	4
M. Abed not out	0
A. Variawa st Cupido b Jabaar	4
EXTRAS	11
TOTAL	90

FALL OF WICKETS: 1/10; 2/22; 3/33; 4/35; 5/36; 6/50; 7/80; 8/81; 9/86

BOWLING: Jabaar 13.4-4-24-3; Barnes 11-7-12-2; Mohammed 13-7-25-3; Allie 13-6-14-2; Magiet 4-3-4-0;

WP FIRST INNINGS

S. Hendricks c Begg b Kimmie	27
H. Ahmed b Kimmie	19
N. Antulay c Begg b Kimmie	2
F. Solomons st Begg b Edwards	20
M. Abdullah lbw Kimmie	12
S. Magiet c Mentor b Manack	61
*A. Jabaar c Desai b Abed	26
+R. Cupido run out	7
G. Allie not out	0
V. Barnes run out	1
E. Mohammed not out	1
EXTRAS	24
TOTAL	200/9 dec

FALL OF WICKETS: 1/45; 2/53; 3/58; 4/80; 5/102; 6/182; 7/190; 8/198; 9/199

BOWLING: Variawa 10-2-38-0; Manack 13,4-3-27-1; Kimmie 14-3-38-4; Edwards 13-4-50-1; Abed 6-1-23-1

WP WON BY AN INNINGS AND 25 RUNS

Natal's cricketing lambs are slaughtered by Jabaar and his WP team mates

YACOOB OMAR'S hapless Natal side were next to be led to slaughter by Armien Jabaar's mean machine when they visited the Green Point Track.

Omar (17) and Elvis Govender (25) were the only Natal batsmen to reach double figures as Vincent Barnes, Goolam Allie and Jabaar each claimed three wickets to dismiss the visitors for 94.

The WP top order failed against the seam bowling of Rampersad and Omar, collapsing to 66/5, before Yunus Thomas and the reliable Jabaar restored respectablity to their innings by putting on 71 for the seventh wicket. Barney Mohammed, with some lusty hitting in his cameo innings of 21, saw his side to a first innings lead of 112.

Barnes, Mohammed and Jabaar, who claimed yet another five-wicket haul against Natal, proved too much for the visitors, who were dismissed for a meagre 117. This left WP with the formality of getting six runs for victory.

NATAL FIRST INNINGS

Y. Omar c Cupido b Allie		17
E. Mall c Antulay b Barnes		2
G. Moses c Hendricks b Barnes		3
M. Moodley b Barnes		3
M. Khan b Allie		6
E. Govender c & b Jabaar		25
L. Maharaj b Jabaar		9
T. le Roux b Allie		0
LD. Naidoo c Allie b Jabaar		6
M. Rampersadh not out		8
S. Kushor b Mohammed		1
	EXTRAS	14
	TOTAL	94

FALL OF WICKETS: 1/12; 2/18; 3/28; 4/38; 5/51; 6/77; 7/77; 8/77; 9/93

BOWLING: Barnes 12-3-14-3; Mohammed 11.1-4-16-1; Allie 13-7-18-3; Jabaar 13-3-32-3; Thomas 1-1-0-0

NATAL SECOND INNINGS

Y. Omar lbw Barnes		25
E. Mall b Jabaar		18
G. Moses lbw Jabaar		1
M. Moodley b Barnes		3
M. Khan b Jabaar		6
E. Govender c Thomas b Barnes		5
L. Maharaj b Mohammed		6
T. le Roux b Jabaar		4
LD. Naidoo b Jabaar		11
M. Rampersad c Antulay b Mohammed		16
S. Kushor not out		0
	EXTRAS	22
	TOTAL	117

FALL OF WICKETS: 1/42; 2/52; 3/59; 4/68; 5/74; 6/74; 7/82; 8/92; 9/115

Bowling: Barnes 15-8-19-3; Mohammed 13-2-37-2; Allie 6-2-9-0; Jabaar 20-6-29-5; Thomas 5-4-1-0

WP FIRST INNINGS

S. Hendricks c & b Omar		15
H. Ahmed c Kushor b Govender		6
N. Antulay c Kushor b Omar		17
F. Solomons c Naidoo b Khan		5
M. Abdullah b Omar		12
Y. Thomas b Rampersad		35
*A. Jabaar c Kushor b Rampersad		49
+R. Cupido c Omar b Rampersad		2
G. Allie c Kushor b Rampersad		0
E. Mohammed b Omar		21
V. Barnes not out		13
	EXTRAS	31
	TOTAL	206

FALL OF WICKETS; 1/13; 2/43; 3/44; 4/64; 5/66; 6/137; 7/149; 8/160; 9/167

BOWLING: Rampersad 17-4-39-4; Govender 19-4-46-1; Omar 15-3-36-4; Khan 10-2-32-1; Le Roux 5-1-22-0

WP SECOND INNINGS

S. Hendricks not out		1
H. Ahmed not out		5
	EXTRAS	3
	TOTAL	9/0

BOWLING: Naidoo 1-0-1-0; Mall 1-1-0-0; Moodley 1-1-0-0; Kishore 1-0-1-0; Moses 0,1-0-4-0

WP WON BY TEN WICKETS

Poor batting by WP allow victorious EP to put in a strong bid for Howa Bowl honours

EP vs WP 19-21 January 1985 in Port Elizabeth

WITH BOTH sides having won their subsequent two matches after their dramatic first round tie, WP's trip to PE shaped up as the Howa Bowl decider.

Their hopes of retaining the Howa Bowl for a sixth successive season faded when EP posted a commanding 280/8 in the first innings. Seamers Lorgat (5/36) and Steven Draai (4/26) once again combined, like they did in the first round game in Cape Town, to give the WP batsmen a torrid time. Only Saait Magiet (33), new cap Mark Haupt (20) and Randall Cupido (22) managed to reach double figures as WP were bundled out for a paltry 103. Although they coped much better with Lorgat and Draai in their follow-on innings, it was the turn of Khaya Majola to wreck WP with his left-arm spin. Bowling a marathon spell of 41 overs, Majola claimed 8/96 as WP batted much more resolutely to reach 253.

Although EP had a few hiccups on their way to their victory target of 77, the experienced Garth Cuddembey and Lorgat managed to steady the ship with an unbroken sixth wicket stand of 40 to put their side in pole position to win the Howa Bowl for the first time since 1978/79.

EP FIRST INNINGS
S. Kruger b Jabaar......7
G. Cuddembey b Jabaar......47
M. van Eck run out......8
M. Majola run out......69
A. Peters b Allie......17
A. Frans lbw Allie......19
H. Lorgat c Ahmed b Jabaar......63
K. Majola lbw Jabaar......18
F. Abrahams not out......3
S. Draai not out......1
EXTRAS......28
TOTAL......280/8 dec

FALL OF WICKETS: 1/18; 2/39; 3/118; 4/158; 5/166; 6/172; 7/274; 8/278

BOWLING: Barnes 17-2-58-0; Magiet 23-8-40-0; Jabaar 33-6-69-4; Allie 22-6-52-2; Davids 4-0-24-0; Thomas 1-1-0-0; Haupt 3-0-9-0

EP SECOND INNINGS
S. Kruger lbw Magiet......5
G. Cuddembey not out......32
M. van Eck lbw Jabaar......0
M. Majola st Cupido b Jabaar......6
A. Peters c Hendricks b Thomas......12
A. Frans c Magiet b Thomas......2
H. Lorgat not out......19
EXTRAS......2
TOTAL......78/5

FALL OF WICKETS: 1/7; 2/10; 3/24; 4/44; 5/48

BOWLING: Barnes 4-1-7-0; Magiet 12-3-18-1; Jabaar 12-4-17-2; Allie 7-2-13-0; Thomas 6-2-10-2; Solomons 2,3-1-9-0; Hendricks 1-0-2-0

WP FIRST INNINGS
S. Hendricks c Peters b Lorgat......6
H. Ahmed b Lorgat......0
F. Solomons b Lorgat......6
M. Haupt c Cuddembey b Lorgat......20
F. Davids c Cuddembey b Lorgat......5
S. Magiet c Peters b Draai......33
*A. Jabaar c Cuddembey b Draai......1
Y. Thomas c K.Majola b Draai......2
+R. Cupido run out......22
V. Barnes lbw Draai......0
G. Allie not out......0
EXTRAS......8
TOTAL......103

FALL OF WICKETS: 1/2; 2/11; 3/26; 4/37; 5/54; 6/69; 7/76; 8/89; 9/103

BOWLING: J. Frans 15-7-23-0; Lorgat 23-11-36-5; K. Majola 4-1-10-0; Draai 18-9-26-4

WP SECOND INNINGS (FOLLOWED ON)
S. Hendricks b K. Majola......56
H. Ahmed c Abrahams b K. Majola......39
F. Solomons lbw K. Majola......19
M. Haupt c A. Frans b K. Majola......36
F. Davids b K. Majola......18
S. Magiet c Abrahams b Draai......6
Y. Thomas c Abrahams b K. Majola......7
A. Jabaar c Kruger b K. Majola......30
R. Cupido not out......27
V. Barnes run out......0
G. Allie b K. Majola......0
EXTRAS......15
TOTAL......253

FALL OF WICKETS: 1/64; 2/114; 3/117; 4/153; 5/170; 6/183; 7/205; 8/251; 9/251

BOWLING: A. Frans 4-0-9-0; Lorgat 24-8-50-0; J. Frans 3-1-11-0; Draai 21,2-6-66-1; K. Majola 41-4-96-8; M. Majola 1-0-6-0

EP WON BY 5 WICKETS

WP vs Transvaal
16-18 February
1985 in
Johannesburg

Barnes and Magiet bowl brilliantly for determined WP

THE WP pace duo of Vincent Barnes (5/17) and Saait Magiet (4/24) routed Transvaal for 57. Only Ebrahim Amod (19) and Ahmed Bhabha (10) managed to reach double figures.

A brilliant spell of seam bowling by the youthful Jack Manack, who took 7/61, restricted WP to 134 in reply. Magiet, who made a fighting 75, and Barnes once again did the trick for WP – this time with the bat. The pair put on a crucial 44 for the last wicket, with Barnes contributing a mere single to the stand..

WP then dismissed the home side for 158, with Barnes (3/28), Seraj Gabriels (4/45) and Armien Jabaar (2/39) being the pick of the bowlers. Munsoor Abdullah, with a fluent unbeaten 34, guided his side to a comfortable seven-wicket win – a win that offered WP a mathematical chance of catching EP at the top of the log.

TRANSVAAL FIRST INNINGS

A. Mentor ht wkt b Magiet	0
E. Amod c Thomas b Barnes	19
A. Bhabha c & b Magiet	10
A. Rajah c Hendricks b Magiet	6
A. Odendaal c Jabaar b Magiet	0
A. Moola c Hendricks b Barnes	2
A. Manack c Harris b Barnes	6
I. Akoojee c Cupido b Barnes	7
Y. Begg c Hendricks b Barnes	1
M. Mangera c Cupido b Gabriels	0
AH. Manack not out	1
EXTRAS	5
TOTAL	57

FALL OF WICKETS: 1/0; 2/11; 3/18; 4/19; 5/31; 6/42; 7/47; 8/50; 9/51

BOWLING: Barnes 14.4-5-17-5; Magiet 12-5-24-4; Jabaar 3-0-5-0; Gabriels 4-0-6-1

TRANSVAAL SECOND INNINGS

A. Bhabha lbw Gabriels	16
S. Amod run out	14
A. Mentor c Cupido b Barnes	9
A. Rajah c Thomas b Barnes	24
A. Odendaal lbw Barnes	24
A. Moola b Jabaar	11
A. Manack st Cupido b Gabriels	3
I. Akoojee not out	18
Y. Begg b Gabriels	10
M. Mangera st Cupido b Jabaar	10
AH. Manack st Cupido b Gabriels	2
EXTRAS	17
TOTAL	158

FALL OF WICKETS: 1/16; 2/36; 3/80; 4/95; 5/100; 6/111; 7/113; 8/134; 9/152

BOWLING: Barnes 19-7-28-3; Magiet 7-1-17-0; Jabaar 20-4-39-2; Gabriels 25,1-6-45-4; Thomas 6-0-12-0

WP FIRST INNINGS

S Hendricks c Akoojee b AH Manack	5
H. Ahmed lbw AH Manack	3
M. Abdullah c Mangera b AH Manack	0
E. Harris c Mentoor b AH Manack	15
F. Solomons c Odendaal b AH Manack	8
Y. Thomas lbw AH Manack	0
S. Magiet c Odendaal b Mangera	75
S. Gabriels c Bhabha b A. Manack	5
*A. Jabaar b AH Manack	0
+R. Cupido c Mentoor b Mangera	5
V. Barnes not out	1
EXTRAS	17
TOTAL	134

FALL OF WICKETS: 1/9; 2/11; 3/12; 4/34; 5/34; 6/41; 7/42; 8/73; 9/90

BOWLING: AH Manack 15-3-61-7; Akoojee 6-1-18-0; Mangera 5-2-14-2; A. Manack 4-1-24-1

WP SECOND INNINGS

H. Ahmed c Begg b AH Manack	3
S. Gabriels c Begg b Mangera	17
M. Abdullah not out	34
E. Harris lbw Amod	16
F. Solomons not out	7
EXTRAS	9
TOTAL	86/3

FALL OF WICKETS: 1/11; 2/36; 3/66

Bowling: AH Manack 10-5-23-1; Akoojee 6-3-7-0; Mangera 10-4-23-1; Amod 11-4-24-1

WP WON BY 7 WICKETS

Great batting by Gabriels and several others is not enough to win the Howa Bowl

ARMIEN JABAAR'S side reserved their best performance for the last game of the season – against Natal in Tongaat, as their batsmen finally delivered the goods.

Useful contributions down the order saw WP reach a respectable first innings total of 269.

Although not bowling at the pace of a few years ago, Saait Magiet more than compensated for this with his ability to swing the ball, as he took 4/11 off 11 overs to help dismiss Natal for 176.

In the second innings, Seraj Gabriels registered his maiden first-class century (101*), in the process of adding 103 for the first wicket with Stuart Hendricks, who made a polished 54.

Jabaar was able to declare at 245/5, leaving Natal to score a challenging 338 for victory. Although WP's 208 run win was their biggest ever margin of victory, it wasn't enough to prevent EP from winning the Howa Bowl.

WP vs Natal
16-18 March 1985 in Tongaat

WP FIRST INNINGS

S. Hendricks b Govender	1
S. Gabriels c Haffejee b Le Roux	58
+R. Cupido b Govender	20
F. Solomons run out	35
N. Antulay c Sewmungal b Ramsaroop	7
M. Abdullah b Hoosen	38
S. Magiet c Patel b Le Roux	2
N. Booysen c Naidoo b Govender	37
*A. Jabaar c Patel b Govender	29
V. Barnes b Le Roux	19
E. Mohammed not out	12
EXTRA	11
TOTAL	269

FALL OF WICKETS: 1/8; 2/49; 3/107; 4/117; 5/126; 6/136; 7/176; 8/213; 9/253

BOWLING: Govender 19,4-4-65-4; Pentiah 8-0-21-0; Le Roux 23-3-69-3; Hoosen 11-1-54-1; Ramsaroop 13-1-49-1

WP SECOND INNINGS

S. Hendricks b Hoosen	54
S. Gabriels not out	101
R. Cupido c sub b Singaram	4
N. Antulay lbw Singaram	13
F. Solomons c Patel b Singaram	1
M. Abdullah c Patel b Hoosen	41
S. Magiet not out	9
EXTRAS	22
TOTAL	245/5 dec

FALL OF WICKETS: 1/103; 2/116; 3/144; 4/146; 5/218

BOWLING: Govender 9-1-37-0; Pentiah 14-2-51-0; Le Roux 3-0-23-0; Hoosen 11-1-35-2; Singaram 11-0-49-3; Naidoo 2-0-28-0

NATAL FIRST INNINGS

M. Patel b Mohammed	8
R. Ramsaroop c Gabriels b Jabaar	33
AH. Haffejee c Mohammed b Gabriels	7
J. Sewmungal b Gabriels	16
M. Bhigjee ht wkt b Mohammed	16
E. Govender c Cupido b Mohammed	13
C. Naidoo b Magiet	19
G. Hoosen b Magiet	9
T. le Roux b Magiet	0
C. Pentiah c Mohammed b Magiet	10
P. Singaram not out	0
EXTRAS	45
TOTAL	176

FALL OF WICKETS: 1/27; 2/50; 3/78; 4/80; 5/124; 6/135; 7/161; 8/161; 9/164

BOWLING: Barnes 23-10 -33-0; Jabaar 14-4-28-1; Mohammed 16-3-34-3; Booysen 7-2-14-0; Magiet 8,2-3-11-4; Gabriels 11-5-11-2

NATAL SECOND INNINGS

M. Patel c & b Jabaar	28
J. Sewmungal b Jabaar	2
AH. Haffejee run out	0
E. Govender b Magiet	9
C. Naidoo c Magiet b Jabaar	29
M. Bhigjee c Antulay b Gabriels	0
G. Hoosen c Abdullah b Gabriels	13
T. le Roux b Barnes	13
C. Pentiah c Abdullah b Barnes	19
P. Singaram not out	0
R. Ramsaroop absent injured	0
EXTRAS	17
TOTAL	130/9

FALL OF WICKETS: 1/18; 2/19; 3/29; 4/55; 5/62; 6/95; 7/97; 8/130; 9/130

BOWLING: Magiet 10-3-32-1; Barnes 9-3-15-2; Jabaar 13-3-40-4; Mohammed 3-1-7-0; Gabriels 6-1-18-1; Booysen 1-0-1-0;

WP WON BY 208 RUNS
EP WIN HOWA BOWL

WP Cricket Board First Class Averages 1984/85

BATTING

Name	Matches	Inns	NO	Hs	Runs	Ave	50	100
Seraj Gabriels	3	6	1	101*	194	38,80	1	1
Saait Magiet	4	6	1	75	186	37,20	2	
Munsoor Abdullah	5	8	1	41	173	24,71		
Stuart Hendricks	6	10	1	56	180	20,00	2	
Nasser Antulay	4	6	0	42	103	17,67		
Armien Jabaar	6	8	0	49	139	17,38		
Faghme Solomons	6	10	1	35	144	16,00		
Randall Cupido	5	7	1	29*	89	14,83		
Ebrahim Mohammed	4	5	2	21	39	13,00		
Hoosain Ahmed	4	7	1	39	75	12,50		
Yunus Thomas	3	4	0	35	44	11,00		
Vincent Barnes	5	6	2	19	34	8,50		

Also batted: Rashaad Musson (1 and 0), Gerry Miller (8 and 0), Nazeem White (8* and 2), Goolam Allie 4 matches (0, 0*, 0*,0, 0*,0), Eddie Harris (15 and 16), Neville Booysen (37), Mark Haupt (20 and 36), Faiek Davids (5 and 18)

FIELDING:

Wicketkeepers: 12 – Randall Cupido (6ct and 6st), 6 – Nazeem White (6ct)

Catches:

6 – Stuart Hendricks; 5 – Nasser Antulay, Saait Magiet; 3 – Ebrahim Mohammed, Yunus Thomas, Armien Jabaar; 2 – Goolam Allie, Fagmie Solomons, Munsoor Abdullah; 1 – Eddie Harris, Gerry Miller, Hoosain Ahmed, Seraj Gabriels

BOWLING

Name	Overs	Mdns	Wkts	Runs	Ave	Best Bowling	5i	10m
Ebrahim Mohammed	105,3	36	19	187	9,84	5/33 v EP	1	
Vincent Barnes	135	50	21	216	10,28	5/17 v Tvl	1	
Seraj Gabriels	57,1	17	8	90	11,25	4/45 v Tvl		
Armien Jabaar	171	44	30	342	11,40	5/29 v Natal	1	
Goolam Allie	105	34	16	194	12,13	6/45 v EP	1	
Saait Magiet	87,2	30	10	160	16,00	4/11 v Natal		

Also bowled: Stuart Hendricks 1-0-2-0; Faghme Solomons 2.3-1-9-0; Gerry Miller 10-1-15-0; Yunus Thomas 25-8-40-2; Faiek Davids 4-0-24-0; Mark Haupt 3-0-9-0; Neville Booysen 8-2-15-0

WP off to a bad start on the road against EP – and it got worse

WESTERN PROVINCE should have beaten EP in a low-scoring tussle at the Adcock Stadium on a difficult wicket, but allowed an eight-wicket stand of 40 between Khaya Majola (28) and wicketkeeper Faghme Abrahams (15 not out) to swing the game in the final innings.

EP needed 152 to win after facing a 13-run first innings deficit, and lost their ninth wicket on 151, but got the vital single in the end. Bright spots for WP were Faizel Ebrahim's 70 in the second innings, and five-wicket hauls in EP's first innings from Faiek Davids and Goolam Allie.

Apart from Ebrahim's knock and 34 from Nasser Antulay in the first innings, the top seven batsmen contributed only 54 in total.

Armien Jabaar's run of 16 matches as captain ended after this defeat, although their attack kept WP in the match and one of the side's worst seasons could have been so different had they managed to win a match that was there for the taking.

**EP vs WP
16-18 November
1985
in Port Elizabeth**

WP FIRST INNINGS

S. Hendricks b E. Frans 8
A. Coericius c J. Frans b E. Frans 3
F. Ebrahim c K. Majola b J. Frans 0
N. Antulay c A. Frans b Lorgat 34
+H. Dawson c Miller b J. Frans................................0
A. Odendaal c Miller b E. Frans 3
F. Davids b J. Frans...6
S. Gabriels b A. Frans...27
S. Magiet c Abrahams b Lorgat 10
*A. Jabaar c Cuddembey b Lorgat 5
G. Allie not out..9

EXTRAS...............15
TOTAL 120

FALL OF WICKETS: 1/20; 2/21; 3/21; 4/22; 5/29; 6/36; 7/80; 8/99; 9/106

BOWLING: J. Frans 11-4-13-3; E. Frans 9-3-32-3; Lorgat 10-4-31-3; K. Majola 7-1-22-0; A. Frans 2.3-0-7-1

WP SECOND INNINGS

S. Hendricks c A. Frans b J.Frans 15
A. Coericius lbw J. Frans...1
F. Ebrahim c Abrahams b Lorgat 70
N. Antulay c Miller b Coericius 2
H. Dawson c Miller b J. Frans 16
A. Odendaal lbw J. Frans...0
F. Davids c Abrahams b Lorgat 0
S. Gabriels c M. Majola b Lorgat 0
S. Magiet not out...27
A. Jabaar b Lorgat..1
G. Allie c J. Frans b Lorgat.......................................0

EXTRAS................6
TOTAL 138

FALL OF WICKETS: 1/5; 2/18; 3/23; 4/46; 5/55; 6/60; 7/65; 8/136; 9/138

BOWLING: J. Frans 11-2-26-4; E. Frans 4-1-18-0; Coericius 6-1-20-1; K. Majola 1-0-7-0; Peters 1-0-1-0; Lorgat 16-4-43-5; A. Frans 6-0-17-0

EP FIRST INNINGS

G. Cuddembey c Davids b Allie 4
G. Coericius b Davids 15
A. Peters c Davids b Allie...10
A. Frans c Magiet b Davids 5
M. Majola c Dawson b Davids 6
K. Miller b Davids 15
H. Lorgat c Antulay b Davids 41
K. Majola b Allie...10
F. Abrahams c Jabaar b Allie 0
J. Frans c Davids b Allie 0
E. Frans not out ....

EXTRAS................1
TOTAL 107

FALL OF WICKETS: 1/16; 2/27; 3/31; 4/35; 5/42; 6/69; 7/106; 8/106; 9/106

BOWLING: Magiet 1-0-5-0; Davids 17.3-5-57-5; Allie 16-5-30-5; Jabaar 2-0-4-0; Ebrahim 2-0-10-0

EP SECOND INNINGS

G. Cuddembey c Magiet b Allie 7
G. Coericius lbw Gabriels..9
A. Peters b Antulay 2
M. Majola c Magiet b Allie 0
K. Miller run out 61
A. Frans c Ebrahim b Davids 15
H. Lorgat b Jabaar..9
K. Majola c Antulay b Jabaar...................................28
F. Abrahams not out 15
J. Frans b Jabaar 1
E. Frans not out 0

EXTRAS................5
TOTAL............152/9

FALL OF WICKETS: 1/8; 2/13; 3/14; 4/28; 5/75; 6/109; 7/110; 8/150; 9/151

BOWLING: Antulay 10,1-5-16-1; Allie 8-1-37-2; Jabaar 18-6-38-3; Gabriels 9-4-15-1; Davids 16-2-41-1

EP WON BY 1 WICKET

Natal vs WP
28-30 December
1985
in Durban

Allie takes the reins, but Natal tailenders frustrate victory aspirations

SERAJ GABRIELS, promoted to open, was not a great success, but he recorded a career-best 8/53 (11/121 in the match) to set up a potential innings victory.

WP, showing four changes from the combination which lost against EP, compiled a formidable 328/9 declared, batting first.

Attacking opener Stuart Hendricks (49), Munsoor Abdullah (86) and Nasser Antulay (69) got the lion's share of the runs, and, thanks to Gabriels' eight-wicket haul, WP asked Natal to follow on183 runs behind. WP had lost the services of fast bowler Vincent Barnes, who had moved to Transvaal, and, as against EP in the first match of the season, they missed him.

Natal, who had a highest individual score of 28 in their first innings of 145, salvaged a draw thanks to a valiant last-wicket stand in their second knock of 216/9.

WP captain Goolam Allie did not bowl in the Natal second innings, the new ball being shared by Faiek Davids and debutant Shukri Conrad.

WP FIRST INNINGS

S. Gabriels b Omar	18
S. Hendricks lbw Omar	49
F. Ebrahim run out	5
N. Antulay b Khan	69
M. Abdullah lbw Le Roux	86
S. Conrad b Naidoo	15
Y. Thomas c Moodley b Khan	2
F. Davids lbw Le Roux	19
+H. Dawson not out	29
L. Roberts c Moodley b Khan	4
*G. Allie not out	8
EXTRAS	24
TOTAL	328/9 dec

FALL OF WICKETS: 1/40; 2/53; 3/112; 4/172; 5/204; 6/213; 7/258; 8/303; 9/308

BOWLING: Le Roux 22-2-82-2; Pentiah 5-1-23-0; Omar 15-4-35-2; Moodley 7-1-21-0; Khan 24-3-73-3; Hoosen 9-0-25-0; Naidoo 14-2-45-1

NATAL FIRST INNINGS

Y. Omar c Dawson b Gabriels	22
E. Mall c Conrad b Gabriels	18
M. Patel c Dawson b Gabriels	5
C. Naidoo lbw Ebrahim	11
J. Sewmungal b Gabriels	22
M. Khan c Dawson b Gabriels	2
N. Moodley c Dawson b Gabriels	28
G. Hoosen c & b Gabriels	6
T. Le Roux not out	18
R. Soobramoney lbw Gabriels	0
C. Pentiah c Abdullah b Thomas	1
EXTRAS	12
TOTAL	145

FALL OF WICKETS: 1/50; 2/65; 3/79; 4/84; 5/103; 6/103; 7/119; 8/125; 9/125

BOWLING: Davids 8-3-14-0; Allie 9-3-16-0; Roberts 4-2-5-0; Gabriels 21-3-53-8; Ebrahim 12-2-31-1; Thomas 3,1 -0-14-1

NATAL SECOND INNINGS
(FOLLOWED ON)

Y. Omar c Ebrahim b Davids	0
M. Patel c Abdullah b Gabriels	15
B. Sewmungal c Dawson b Thomas	29
N. Moodley b Conrad	23
T. Le Roux b Conrad	18
E. Mall c sub (Benjamin) b Roberts	11
M. Khan c Antulay b Gabriels	16
C. Naidoo c Abdullah b Ebrahim	22
G. Hoosen not out	41
R. Soobramoney c Thomas b Gabriels	16
C. Pentiah not out	9
EXTRAS	16
TOTAL	216/9

FALL OF WICKETS: 1/1; 2/46; 3/63 4/89; 5/97; 6/115; 7/139; 8/162; 9/191

BOWLING: Conrad 12-2-39-2; Davids 8-1-16-1; Thomas 7-3-11-1; Ebrahim 16-0-48-1; Gabriels 25-5-68-3: Roberts 12-5-18-1

MATCH DRAWN

Barnes turns foe to rout WP for second lowest total in three-day history

*Transvaal vs WP
1-3 January
1986
in Johannesburg*

FACING A fair Transvaal first innings total of 245, Western Province learnt just what it had been like for other teams facing them when they had speed demon Vincent Barnes in their ranks.

Transvaal won by four wickets despite a good fightback from WP in their second innings.

Sixty all out in their first innings would have looked even worse had top scorer Faiek Davids (18) not been dropped early in his innings, and had Extras not added 15 to the total. Barnes (8/29) and Abdul Haq Manack (2/16) shot out WP for a paltry 60 in 16,4 overs.

The follow-on innings – WP were 185 runs behind – began disastrously when Hilary Dawson (0) fell with the score on one, but WP showed plenty of backbone to build a formidable 351 all out.

A lot of the runs came late, as WP were not quite safe on 172/6. Yunus Thomas, batting at No 8, made a career-best first-class score of 116 at that point, and Transvaal were set 167 to get for their first home victory over WP in first-class cricket. Barnes ended the match with 12/99.

Transvaal had a bit of a wobble in reaching 41/4, but the middle order stabilised affairs.

TRANSVAAL FIRST INNINGS

A. Rajah c Antulay b Gabriels	63
M. Desai c Dawson b Davids	8
M. Saleh c Dawson b Conrad	10
A. Dinath c Dawson b Gabriels	45
N. Dindar c Abdullah b Benjamin	38
N. Edwards c Thomas b Benjamin	9
F. Kimmie b Davids	24
Y. Begg c Gabriels b Roberts	8
V. Barnes lbw Thoma	10
AH. Manack c Ebrahim b Davids	8
R. Galant not out	1
EXTRAS	21
TOTAL	245

FALL OF WICKETS: 1/14; 2/36; 3/138; 4/145; 5/180; 6/194; 7/215; 8/231; 9/243

BOWLING: Allie 4-0-20-0; Davids 9.3-1-36-3; Gabriels 16-3-41-2; Conrad 8-1-32-1; Roberts 15-4-33-1; Benjamin 19-6-48-2; Thomas 8-3-14-1

TRANSVAAL SECOND INNINGS

A. Rajah run out	23
M. Desai c Benjamin b Roberts	8
M. Saleh run out	29
A. Dinath c Dawson b Thomas	0
N. Dindar c Dawson b Roberts	5
N. Edwards run out	49
F. Kimmie not out	15
Y. Begg not out	23
EXTRAS	18
TOTAL	170/6

FALL OF WICKETS: 1/32; 2/35; 3/35; 4/41; 5/125; 6/130

BOWLING: Allie 7-1-12-0; Roberts 28-12-61-2; Gabriels 7,4-0-27-0; Thomas 9-4-18-1; Antulay 3-1-14-0; Conrad 2-0-12-0; Davids 1-0-8-0

TRANSVAAL WON BY 4 WICKETS

WP FIRST INNINGS

+H. Dawson c Begg b Barnes	0
S. Gabriels b Manack	1
FE. brahim c Rajah b Barnes	9
N. Antulay c Dinath b Barnes	4
M. Abdullah c Begg b Barnes	1
S. Conrad c Saleh b Barnes	0
F. Davids b Manack	18
Y. Thomas c Begg b Barnes	4
L. Roberts b Barnes	7
*G. Allie c Rajah b Barnes	0
F. Benjamin not out	1
EXTRAS	15
TOTAL	60

FALL OF WICKETS: 1/0; 2/7; 3/17; 4/26; 5/26; 6/30; 7/38; 8/57; 9/57

BOWLING: Barnes 8,4-1-29-8; Manack 8-3-16-2

WP SECOND INNINGS

(FOLLOWED ON)

H. Dawson c Begg b Barnes	0
S. Gabriels c Kimmie b Barnes	31
F. Ebrahim c Rajah b Dindar	42
S. Conrad c Begg b Barnes	23
N. Antulay b Manack	1
M. Abdullah lbw Kimmie	36
F. Davids c Barnes b Manack	58
Y. Thomas run out	116
L. Roberts run out	6
F. Benjamin c Manack b Barnes	3
G. Allie not out	1
EXTRAS	34
TOTAL	351

FALL OF WICKETS: 1/1; 2/72; 3/106; 4/107; 5/108; 6/172; 7/282; 8/307; 9/334

BOWLING: Barnes 31,4-10-70-4; Manack 32-11-63-2; Galant 19-4-40-0; Kimmie 17-2-70-1; Dindar 15-3-47-1; Edwards 8-1-27-0

WP vs EP
18-20 January
1986 at
Green Point Track
Cape Town

EP make history against WP – two wins in same season on way to the title

SET 311 TO win in the final innings, WP had a good stab at it, but fell 19 runs short. Victories against arch-rivals WP – home and away – represented the only time a side had achieved this in the same season.

EP's first innings total of 177 did not seem threatening, although WP were pushed to use eight bowlers in dismissing them. In reply WP slumped from 69/1 to 147 all out.

The Cape Town side stayed in the game by bowling out half the EP line-up for a mere 58 runs in their second innings. But then, enter Haroon Lorgat (121) and Ashwell Frans (83). The pair added 134 for the sixth wicket, and EP ended with 280 all out. For WP, Faiek Davids (81) and Saait Magiet (61) added a record-equalling 114 for the fourth wicket.

EP FIRST INNINGS

G. Cuddembey	c Khan b Davids	14
K. Majola	c Hendricks b Thomas	22
M. Majola	c Dawson b Thomas	11
K. Miller	lbw Thomas	0
H. Lorgat	run out	27
C. Kisten	c Khan b Ravens	28
A. Frans	lbw Damon	22
F. Abrahams	b Ravens	1
R. Dolley	c Khan b Davids	15
J. Frans	c Davids b Benjamin	5
E. Frans	not out	9
	EXTRAS	23
	TOTAL	177

FALL OF WICKETS: 1/25; 2/57; 3/57; 4/82; 5/108; 6/146; 7/147; 8/148; 9/157

BOWLING: Damon 21-6-46-1; Magiet 5-2-11-0; Davids 9,1-0-24-2; Thomas 12-0-30-3; Antulay 1-0-2-0; Benjamin 6-1-19-1; Ravens 7-1-17-2; Gabriels 4-1-5-0

EP SECOND INNINGS

G. Cuddembey	c Davids b Gabriels	16
K. Majola	b Davids	0
M. Majola	c Khan b Davids	0
K. Miller	st Khan b Gabriels	17
C. Kisten	b Gabriels	0
H. Lorgat	c Hendricks b Davids	121
A. Frans	lbw Antulay	83
R. Dolley	lbw Davids	16
F. Abrahams	c Magiet b Davids	0
J. Frans	run out	10
E. Frans	not out	0
	EXTRAS	17
	TOTAL	280

FALL OF WICKETS: 1/12; 2/18; 3/31; 4/35; 5/58; 6/192; 7/250; 8/250; 9/279

BOWLING: Damon 19-5-62-0; Davids 19.4-7-50-5; Gabriels 27-7-60-3; Thomas 11-4-22-0; Benjamin 8-3-35-0; Ravens 3-2-3-0; Magiet 2-0-13-0; Ebrahim 3-0-11-0; Antulay 3-0-7-1

WP FIRST INNINGS

S. Hendricks	c Abrahams b Lorgat	38
S. Gabriels	c Abrahams b Lorgat	24
F. Ebrahim	run out	14
F. Davids	c E. Frans b Dolley	0
+G. Khan	c Cuddembey b Lorgat	3
N. Antulay	c K. Majola b J. Frans	25
Y. Thomas	not out	25
C. Ravens	run out	0
F. Benjamin	c & b Lorgat	2
E. Damon	c K. Majola b Lorgat	9
*S. Magiet	absent	
	EXTRAS	7
	TOTAL	147/9

FALL OF WICKETS: 1/40; 2/69; 3/73; 4/78; 5/105; 6/111; 7/111; 8/115; 9/147

BOWLING: J. Frans 19-4-41-1; E. Frans 5-1-14-0; K. Majola 6-2-8-0; Lorgat 28,5-9-57-5; Dolley 9-3-20-1

WP SECOND INNINGS

S. Hendricks	st Abrahams b K. Majola	10
S. Gabriels	c Lorgat b E. Frans	1
G. Khan	c K. Majola b Lorgat	52
N. Antulay	c Abrahams b J. Frans	41
F. Davids	c A. Frans b K. Majola	81
S. Magiet	c & b A. Frans	61
Y. Thomas	b A. Frans	0
C. Ravens	c Abrahams b Lorgat	30
F. Ebrahim	not out	6
E. Damon	lbw Lorgat	0
F. Benjamin	b Lorgat	0
	EXTRAS	9
	TOTAL	291

FALL OF WICKETS: 1/2; 2/32; 3/104; 4/108; 5/222; 6/222; 7/273; 8/287; 9/291

BOWLING: J, Frans 17-1-66-1; E, Frans 3-0-9-1; K, Majola 10-0-45-2; Dolley 11-0-58-0; Lorgat 18-2-76-4; A, Frans 7-0-28-2

EP WON BY 19 RUNS

Unconvincing WP outshone by Natal – unhappy summer continues

*WP vs Natal
22-24 February
1986 at
Green Point Track
Cape Town*

TOP-ORDER INCONSISTENCY continued to plague WP, as recalled Shukri Conrad (54), batting at six, fared best with the bat for the host province in yet another average first innings score of 177.

But even with such a low score, Western Province must have been reasonably confident that they would beat the visitors.

Natal, hardly one of the better sights in the competition. rubbed salt into the wounds by taking an 18-run first innings lead, despite leg-spinner Seraj Gabriels' 8/64 – his second eight-wicket haul in an innings for the season.

Trying to salvage something out of a disastrous season, WP declared on 150/7 in their second innings, with Conrad again best with 49 before becoming one of former Capetonian Trevor le Roux's four victims.

Gabriels (2/16) was able to complete 10 wickets in the match, but Natal, who reached 44/2, would have been happy with a rare draw in Cape Town – it was only the second time they had avoided defeat in the Mother City.

Natal opening batsman Enver Mall (60) picked up one of two half-centuries in the low-scoring match.

WP FIRST INNINGS

S. Hendricks c & b Le Roux......................................34
S. Gabriels c Patel b Ramnarain 4
F. Ebrahim c Mall b Ramnarain...............................10
N. Antulay c Le Roux b Omar...................................13
F. Davids c Sewmungal b M. Khan 22
S. Conrad b Ramnarain...54
*S. Magiet c Pillay b Ramnarain 16
Y. Thomas c Le Roux b Omar 4
C. Ravens not out...0
+G. Khan c Moodley b Omar 5
F. Benjamin c M. Khan b Ramnarain 2

EXTRAS..............13
TOTAL..............177

FALL OF WICKETS: 1/13; 2/34; 3/51; 4/92; 5/95; 6/149; 7/166; 8/168; 9/175

BOWLING: Ramnarain 15.3-3-61-5; Omar 21-7-36-3; Le Roux 8-0-40-1; Khan 8-1-27-1

WP SECOND INNINGS

S. Hendricks lbw Ramnarain 19
G. Khan c Patel b Omar...7
N. Antulay c Pillay b Ramnarain 4
Y. Thomas c Ramnarain b Le Roux..........................37
F. Davids c Patel b Le Roux......................................21
S. Conrad c Maharaj b Le Roux 49
S. Magiet c Ramnarain b Le Roux..............................4
C. Ravens not out...1

EXTRAS.................8
TOTAL......150/7 dec

FALL OF WICKETS: 1/16; 2/21; 3/32; 4/72; 5/110; 6/120; 7/150

BOWLING: Ramnarain 11-0-53-2; Omar 5-0-46-1; Le Roux 5,3-0-43-4

NATAL FIRST INNINGS

E. Mall lbw Gabriels..60
Y. Omar c Hendricks b Gabriels 19
M. Patel lbw Davids..11
P. Pillay c Ebrahim b Gabriels 0
N. Moodley c Conrad b Gabriels 36
J. Sewmungal b Gabriels..0
L. Maharaj st Khan b Gabriels....................................0
M. Khan c Antulay b Gabriels...................................27
C. Naidoo c Thomas b Davids.....................................6
T. le Roux st Khan b Gabriels.....................................6
N. Ramnarian not out...9

EXTRAS..............21
TOTAL..............195

FALL OF WICKETS: 1/45; 2/75; 3/78; 4/125; 5/125; 6/128; 7/154; 8/176; 9/184

BOWLING: Ravens 6-1-11-0; Davids 17-3-39-2; Gabriels 35,5-6-64-8; Conrad 16-4-32-0; Benjamin 5-1-18-0; Magiet 4-1-4-0; Thomas 6-3-6-0

NATAL SECOND INNINGS

E. Mall c Antulay b Gabriels 5
Y. Omar not out..28
M. Patel c Magiet b Gabriels 0
N. Moodley not out...9

EXTRAS.................2
TOTAL..............44/2

FALL OF WICKETS: 1/23; 2/29

BOWLING: Conrad 3-1-8-0; Davids 1-0-4-0; Gabriels 7-2-16-2; Benjamin 5-0-14-0

MATCH DRAWN

**WP vs Transvaal
15-17 March
1986 at
Green Point Track
Cape Town**

WP rout Transvaal for first victory but it means little in title chase

GOOLAM ALLIE, restored to the team and the captaincy, picked up four wickets and Reggie February three as WP mowed down Transvaal for 53 in their first innings.

Allie would have been pleased with WP's first innings effort of 223 – and the lead of 170 – although the consistent Shukri Conrad (44) was the closest thing to a half-century. Debutant Ismail Behardien, like Conrad a player whose father (Taliep) had also represented WP, was next best with 32. Vincent Barnes (1/68) had a quiet time compared to the first-round match, although new-ball partner Abdul Haq Manack claimed 4/68 and 2/11 in the two innings.

Leg-spinners Armien Jabaar (5/48) and Seraj Gabriels (2/60) did the heavy work as Transvaal improved to 199 in their second innings, and it was a simple task for WP to knock off the 30 they needed for their first victory of the season, in the last match.

Eastern Province, though, were good value for their second successive Howa Bowl success.

Gabriels, one of only two players to play in all six matches in the season, finished with a total of 30 wickets at an average of 14,07, with Faiek Davids next best with 19 at 15,21.

TRANSVAAL FIRST INNINGS

A. Rajah c Jabaar b Allie	13
M. Moosajee c Behardien b February	5
M. Saleh c Behardien b February	1
A. Dinath c Behardien b Allie	0
N. Dindar not out	1
N. Edwards c White b Allie	2
F. Kimmie c White b February	0
Y. Begg b Gabriels	21
E. Mohammed b Allie	2
AH. Manack b Jabaar	0
V. Barnes c Conrad b Jabaar	4
EXTRAS	4
TOTAL	53

FALL OF WICKETS: 1/10; 2/21; 3/22; 4/22; 5/25; 6/29; 7/34; 8/39; 9/53

BOWLING: Conrad 4-0 -5-0; February 13-7-12-3; Allie 10-1-18-4; Jabaar 2,3-1-1-2; Gabriels 2-1-13-1

TRANSVAAL SECOND INNINGS

A. Rajah b Allie	5
M. Moosajee c Petersen b February	1
M. Saleh c February b Jabaar	31
A. Dinath b Gabriels	25
F. Kimmie b Gabriels	44
F. Edwards b Jabaar	1
N. Dindar c Gabriels b February	22
Y. Begg not out	42
E. Mohammed b Jabaar	15
AH. Manack b Jabaar	0
V. Barnes c White b Jabaar	1
EXTRAS	12
TOTAL	199

FALL OF WICKETS: 1/2; 2/23; 3/48; 4/93; 5/110; 6/112; 7/158; 8/193; 9/197

BOWLING: Allie 10-3-19-1; February 23-6-51-2; Jabaar 31,3-8-48-5; Gabriels 26-8-60-2; Conrad 3-0-9-0

WP FIRST INNINGS

S. Hendricks lbw Manack	7
S. Gabriels run out	2
F. Ebrahim c Barnes b Edwards	21
I. Behardien c Barnes b Edwards	32
S. Conrad c Dinath b Manack	44
A. Jabaar c Rajah b Manack	20
N. White lbw Manack	27
+G. Petersen c Rajah b Barnes	15
A. Burns not out	9
R. February b Kimmie	30
*G. Allie c Moosajee b Kimmie	0
EXTRAS	16
TOTAL	223

FALL OF WICKETS: 1/7; 2/11; 3/63; 4/83; 5/133; 6/177; 7/177; 8/185; 9/223

BOWLING: Barnes 26-5-68-1; Manack 29-4-68-4; Edwards 9-2-35-2; Mohammed 4-2-4-0; Kimmie 15-5-32-2

WP SECOND INNINGS

A. Jabaar c Rajah b Manack	5
S. Hendricks b Manack	5
F. Ebrahim not out	6
S. Gabriels not out	7
EXTRAS	8
TOTAL	31/2

FALL OF WICKETS: 1/6; 2/11

BOWLING: Barnes 4-0-12-0; Manack 3,1-1-11-2

**WP WON BY 8 WICKETS
EP WON HOWA BOWL FOR SECOND
SUCCESSIVE SEASON**

WP Cricket Board First Class Averages 1985/86

BATTING

Name	Matches	Inns	NO	HS	Runs	Ave	50	100
Munsoor Abdullah	2	3	0	86	123	41,00	1	
Yunus Thomas	4	7	1	116	188	31,33		1
Shukri Conrad	4	6	0	54	185	30,83	1	
Saait Magiet	3	5	1	61	118	29,50	1	
Faiek Davids	5	9	0	81	225	25,00	2	
Faizel Ebrahim	6	10	2	70	183	22,88	1	
Nasser Antulay	5	9	0	69	193	21,44	1	
Stuart Hendricks	5	9	0	49	185	20,56		
Gameem Khan	2	4	0	52	67	16,75	1	
Clinton Ravens	2	4	2	30	31	15,50		
Seraj Gabriels	6	10	1	31	119	13,22		
Hilary Dawson	3	5	1	29*	45	11,25		
Armien Jabaar	2	4	0	20	31	7,75		
Goolam Allie	4	6	3	9*	18	6,00		
Leon Roberts	2	3	0	7	17	5,67		
Fuad Benjamin	3	5	1	3	8	2,00		

Also batted: Ismail Behardien (32), Reggie February (30), Nazeem White (27), Grant Petersen (15), Ashraf Burns (9*), Ebrahim Damon (9 and 0), André Odendaal (3 and 0) and Anthony Coericius (3 and 1)

FIELDING:

Wicketkeepers: 12 – Hilary Dawson (12ct), 7 – Gameem Khan (4ct and 3st), 3 – Nazeem White (3ct), 1 – Grant Petersen (1ct),

Catches:

6 – Nasser Antulay; 5 – Saait Magiet, Faiek Davids; 4 – Faizel Ebrahim, Munsoor Abdullah; 3 – Stuart Hendricks, Saait Magiet, Shukri Conrad, Yunus Thomas, Ismail Behardien, Seraj Gabriels; 2 – Armien Jabaar; 1 – Fuad Benjamin, Reggie February

BOWLING

Name	Overs	Mdns	Wkts	Runs	Ave	Best Bowling	5i	10m
Armien Jabaar	54	15	9	91	10,11	5/48 v Tvl	1	
Reggie February	36	13	5	63	12,60	3/12 v Tvl		
Goolam Allie	64	14	12	152	12,67	5/30 v EP	1	
Seraj Gabriels	180,3	40	30	422	14,07	8/53 v Natal	2	2
Faiek Davids	106,4	22	19	289	15,21	5/50 v EP	2	
Yunus Thomas	56,1	17	7	115	16,43	3/30 v EP		
Leon Roberts	59	23	4	117	29,25	2/61 v Tvl		
Fuad Benjamin	43	11	3	134	44,67	2/48 v Tvl		
Shukri Conrad	48	8	3	137	45,67	2/39 v Natal		
Faizel Ebrahim	33	2	2	90	45,00	1/31 v Natal		
Ebrahim Damon	40	11	1	108	108,00	1/46 v EP		

Also bowled: Saait Magiet 12-3-33-0; Clinton Ravens 16-4-31-2; Nasser Antulay 17,1-6-39-2

WP vs EP
22-24 November
1986
at Florida Park
Cape Town

Barnes is back and puts WP on road to recovery

WESTERN PROVINCE got off to the best possible start against the defending champions, making light of a 10-run first innings deficit.

Vincent Barnes, back from his sojourn with Transvaal, made an immediate impression, adding 7/41 in the EP second innings to his first innings catch of 4/48 to record a match haul of 11/89. Taking 10 or more wickets in a match was a feat Barnes would accomplish four times in his career for WP; only spinner Seraj Gabriels (5 times) would do better in the period before unity.

Barnes, who would reap 42 wickets in the season to beat his own record of 41, and Neville Booysen (3/35) bowled unchanged for 25 overs as EP struggled to make a game of it in their second innings.

WP openers Stuart Hendricks (51 not out) and Gabriels (42 not out), the first duo to serve in that capacity in all six matches in a season since Braima Isaacs and Rashaad Musson had done so five years previously, knocked off the 102 required for victory. The margin of victory – 10 wickets – was a good omen as WP sought to wrest the Howa Bowl title from EP.

EP FIRST INNINGS

G. Cuddembey c White b Magiet	19
S. Kruger c Behardien b Barnes	54
M. Majola c Davids b Barnes	4
A. Peters c Hendricks b Gabriels	7
F. Abrahams c Abdullah b Magiet	16
A. Frans c Allie b Barnes	1
K. Majola not out	43
S. Draai c Behardien b Barnes	0
R. Dolley c Behardien b Booysen	8
J. Frans b Gabriels	41
S. Abrahams lbw Gabriels	0
EXTRAS	31
TOTAL	224

FALL OF WICKETS; 1/41; 2/52; 3/81; 4/98; 5/112; 6/119; 7/119; 8/142; 9/224

BOWLING: Booysen 11-4-27-1; Barnes 21-4-48-4; Magiet 19-5-47-2; Allie 16-2-38-0; Gabriels 10,5-6-9-3; Thomas 2-0-6-0; Davids 2-0-18-0

EP SECOND INNINGS

G. Cuddembey c White b Barnes	6
S. Kruger c White b Barnes	0
M. Majola c Abdullah b Barnes	17
A. Peters c Thomas b Booysen	2
F. Abrahams b Barnes	3
A. Frans b Booysen	11
K. Majola c Abdullah b Barnes	22
S. Draai c Magiet b Barnes	5
R. Dolley c White b Barnes	1
J. Frans c Behardien b Booysen	1
S. Abrahams not out	8
EXTRAS	16
TOTAL	92

FALL OF WICKETS: 1/1; 2/11; 3/27; 4/35; 5/40; 6/66; 7/76; 8/78; 9/79

BOWLING: Barnes 13-1-41-7; Booysen 12-3-35-3

WP FIRST INNINGS

S. Hendricks c A. Frans b Draai	8
S. Gabriels c Dolley b J. Frans	28
I. Behardien c F. Abrahams b Draai	33
M. Abdullah c Kruger b J. Frans	0
F. Davids b Dolley	15
*S. Magiet c Dolley b Draai	60
+N. White c S. Abrahams b K. Majola	39
Y. Thomas c Cuddembey b K. Majola	9
N. Booysen b Draai	2
G. Allie lbw Draai	0
V. Barnes not out	0
EXTRAS	20
TOTAL	214

FALL OF WICKETS: 1/23; 2/65; 3/67; 4/88; 5/118; 6/193; 7/209; 8/214; 9/214

BOWLING: J. Frans 11-4-26-2; S. Abrahams 18-5-50-0; Draai 21-6-50-5; Dolley 9-0-30-1; K. Majola 8,2-3-19-2; A. Frans 5-0-19-0

WP SECOND INNINGS

S. Hendricks not out	51
S. Gabriels not out	42
EXTRAS	10
TOTAL	103/0

BOWLING: Draai 6-0-20-0; J. Frans 5-0-12-0; K. Majola 3-1-9-0; Dolley 6-1-17-0; A. Frans 8-2-23-0; Peters 1-0-4-0; Cuddembey 0,5-0-8-0

WP WON BY 10 WICKETS

Abdullah and Magiet guide WP to record-breaking total – and second win

WP vs Natal
27-29 December 1986 at
Florida Park
Cape Town

NATAL BOWLING kingpin Mustapha Khan went wicketless in the face of blistering batting from Munsoor Abdullah (109) and Saait Magiet (100 not out), whose contributions helped set up WP's biggest first-class total of 436/6 declared – and ultimately a convincing win by an innings and 102 runs. It was allrounder Magiet's maiden first-class century, and Ismail Behardien (72) and Yunus Thomas (43) were also among the runs.

A shell-shocked Natal could only muster 110 in their first innings, and even a more than 100 percent improvement to 224 in their second attempt proved ineffective.

The batting highlight of the second innings was veteran Yacoob Omar's polished 107.

WP wicketkeeper Nazeem White turned in a splendid performance, helped by the team's penetrative pace attack. He picked up seven catches and two stumpings in the match, a major slice of the record-breaking 27 victims (23 catches and four stumpings) he would pick up for the season.

WP FIRST INNINGS

S. Hendricks run out	26
S. Gabriels c Moses b Le Roux	17
I. Behardien c Omar b Le Roux	72
M. Abdullah st Moses b Mall	109
F. Davids b Mall	31
*S. Magiet not out	100
Y. Thomas c Mall b Ramnarain	43
+N. White not out	14
EXTRAS	24
TOTAL	436/6 dec

FALL OF WICKETS: 1/31; 2/58; 3/199; 4/269; 5/278; 6/386

BOWLING: Ramnarain 16-2-64-1; Le Roux 20-4-80-2; Omar 15-2-69-0; Wadvalla 6-1-37-0; Khan 14-1-77-0; Naidoo 3-1-21-0; Mall 9-1-64-2

NATAL FIRST INNINGS

E. Mall c White b Booysen	3
G. Moses c White b Booysen	3
P. Nair c Hendricks b Barnes	5
M. Patel c White b Booysen	12
Y. Omar b Magiet	27
M. Khan c Barnes b Magiet	24
RL. Naidoo c White b Gabriels	10
K. Hiraman c Behardien b Allie	5
S. Wadvalla b Gabriels	5
T. le Roux not out	5
N. Ramnarain st White b Gabriels	0
EXTRAS	11
TOTAL	110

FALL OF WICKETS: 1/8; 2/14; 3/23; 4/36; 5/82; 6/83; 7/94; 8/98; 9/110

BOWLING: Barnes 13-3 -34-1; Booysen 15-5-29-3; Gabriels 10,4-3-22-3; Allie 8-6-3-1; Magiet 7-2-11-2

NATAL SECOND INNINGS (FOLLOWED ON)

E. Mall b Booysen	1
G. Moses c Hendricks b Booysen	5
P. Nair c White b Barnes	0
M. Patel run out	19
Y. Omar c Barnes b Booysen	107
M. Khan c White b Barnes	19
K. Hiraman c Davids b Barnes	19
RL. Naidoo st White b Gabriels	18
S. Wadvalla c White b Barnes	0
T. le Roux c Davids b Allie	18
N. Ramnarian not out	0
EXTRAS	18
TOTAL	224

FALL OF WICKETS: 1/3; 2/7; 3/7; 4/74; 5/134; 6/186; 7/186; 8/187; 9/222

BOWLING: Barnes 28-12-40-4; Booysen 20-3-61-3; Gabriels 18-3-45-1; Allie 11,3-3-22-1; Thomas 1-0-2-0; Behardien 1-0-2-0; Magiet 12-4-24-0; Davids 2-0-10-0

WP WON BY AN INNINGS AND 102 RUNS

WP vs Transvaal
1-3 January
1987 at
Green Point Track
Cape Town

Low-scoring affair, but WP stay on track for glory with third win in succession

VINCENT BARNES turned on his teammates of the season before, to pick up 6/45 as he bowled almost unchanged in the Transvaal first innings of 111.

Only two batsmen reached double figures for the visitors, and although WP weren't much better, they did secure a vital 40-run first innings lead thanks to the heroics of left-arm quick bowler Neville Booysen (38) in the last of his three matches for the season.

Booysen and Barnes cleaned up the Transvaal top order in their disastrous second innings, but the deadly finisher proved to be captain Saait Magiet, with 5/16 – one of the seven occasions the master allrounder collected five or more wickets in an innings in his first-class career.

Transvaal, without Barnes, were showing signs of becoming "cakewalk" opposition again, as their total of 73 suggests. WP's 10-wicket victory was clinched by Stuart Hendricks and Seraj Gabriels, who cruised past the 34 needed.

With three wins out of three, WP were shaping well to reclaim the Howa Bowl from Eastern Province, although the men from Port Elizabeth weren't doing too badly themselves.

TRANSVAAL FIRST INNINGS

E. Amod c Abdullah b Gabriels	36
A. Rajah c Behardien b Barnes	0
AH. Manack c White b Barnes	9
A. Dinath c White b Magiet	7
H. Lorgat c Behardien b Barnes	8
M. Saleh c Hendricks b Allie	7
N. Dindar run out	22
I. Khan c Thomas b Barnes	2
E. Mohammed b Barnes	3
Y. Begg c Booysen b Barnes	3
F. Patel not out	0
EXTRAS	14
TOTAL	111

FALL OF WICKETS: 1/4; 2/17; 3/31; 4/42; 5/54; 6/88; 7/98; 8/105; 9/109

BOWLING: Barnes 21,2-3-45-6; Booysen 9-2-19-0; Magiet 5-1-9-1; Allie 9-2-17-1; Gabriels 7-3-7-1;

TRANSVAAL SECOND INNINGS

E. Amod c Hendricks b Booysen	0
A. Rajah b Booysen	7
R. Khan c Behardien b Barnes	18
A. Dinath c White b Barnes	9
H. Lorgat c Davids b Magiet	3
M. Saleh c Behardien b Magiet	8
N. Dindar c Allie b Barnes	2
AH. Manack not out	6
E. Mohammed c Barnes b Magiet	4
Y. Begg b Magiet	3
F. Patel c Gabriels b Magiet	0
EXTRAS	13
TOTAL	73

FALL OF WICKETS: 1/6; 2/27; 3/46; 4/48; 5/54; 6/56; 7/60; 8/68; 9/72

BOWLING: Barnes 17-6-21-3; Booysen 9,2-3-23-2; Magiet 12-6-16-5;

WP FIRST INNINGS

S. Hendricks run out	18
S. Gabriels c Rajah b Manack	6
I. Behardien c Lorgat b Mohammed	2
M. Abdullah c Begg b Lorgat	16
F. Davids c Begg b Manack	5
*S. Magiet b Patel	7
+N. White b Mohammed	29
Y. Thomas c Begg b Lorgat	0
N. Booysen c Dinath b Manack	38
V. Barnes c Dindar b Manack	1
G. Allie not out	8
EXTRAS	21
TOTAL	151

FALL OF WICKETS: 1/24; 2/33; 3/34; 4/43; 5/55; 6/84; 7/84; 8/87; 9/119

BOWLING: Manack 21,5-8-35-4; Mohammed 12-3-31-2; Patel 10-1-36-1; Dindar 2-1-3-0; Lorgat 11-2-25-2

WP SECOND INNINGS

S. Hendricks not out	14
S. Gabriels not out	17
EXTRAS	4
TOTAL	35/0

BOWLING: Manack 3-0-13-0; Mohammed 2-0-12-0; Khan 0,5-0-6-0

WP WON BY TEN WICKETS

Into the lion's den, and WP emerge with severely wounded aspirations

THIRTY-EIGHT wickets fell for only 408 runs in a game between the top two teams in the competition – a disappointing return, with not one half-century recorded.

Eastern Province struck early to have their visitors reeling on 22/4, and only Saait Magiet (32) and Faiek Davids (17) made any headway. Magiet, enjoying one of his best seasons with the bat, eventually became one of veteran trundler Steven Draai's three victims.

Seamers prospered in the conditions, and Goolam Allie (4/33) and Vincent Barnes (3/37) maintained WP's interest in the game by shooting EP out for 95 – a first innings deficit of four runs. There was no batting recovery for WP, though. The only batsman to contribute anything significant in their second innings was Munsoor Abdullah, whose 34 at least helped to push WP into three figures, and set EP 107 runs to win.

In a see-sawing climax, WP had the champions on 79/8, but Richard Dolley (14 not out) and Draai (17 not out) kept their heads, though, to steer EP home by two wickets in a nailbiter.

WP FIRST INNINGS
S. Hendricks c V. Frans 0
S. Gabriels c V. Frans b Draai 8
I. Behardien c Peters b J. Frans 1
M. Abdullah b A. Frans.............7
C. Martin b Dolley 9
F. Davids c Cuddembey b K. Majola.....17
+N. White c K. Majola b V. Frans 7
* S. Magiet c Abrahams b Draai 32
Y. Thomas c K. Majola b V. Frans 5
V. Barnes c Abrahams b Draai 1
G. Allie not out 1
EXTRAS.............11
TOTAL 99

FALL OF WICKETS: 1/0; 2/7; 3/22; 4/22; 5/39; 6/50;7/71; 8/81; 9/98

BOWLING: V. Frans 16-8-19-3; J. Frans 8-5-10-1; A. Frans 6-2-12-1; Draai 19,3-6-41-3; Dolley 5-2-3-1; K. Majola 2-0-3-1; Peters 1-1-0-0

WP SECOND INNINGS
S. Hendricks c Peters b J. Frans 0
S. Gabriels c V. Frans b J. Frans 12
I. Behardien b Dolley................16
M. Abdullah c M. Majola b K. Majola 34
C. Martin c Peters b Dolley 4
S. Magiet c Abrahams b J. Frans 4
F. Davids b Draai....................6
N. White c Abrahams b K. Majola 1
Y. Thomas b K. Majola 4
V. Barnes c Kruger b Dolley..........6
G. Allie not out....................11
EXTRAS.............4
TOTAL 102

FALL OF WICKETS: 1/9; 2/30; 3/38; 4/43; 5/48; 6/73; 7/76; 8/85; 9/85

BOWLING: V. Frans 5-1-14-0; J. Frans 18-7-25-3; Dolley 11,2-4-20-3; Draai 9-3-17-1; K. Majola 10-2-22-3

EP FIRST INNINGS
G. Cuddembey c Magiet b Barnes 0
S. Kruger c Gabriels b Barnes 2
M. Majola c White b Allie 12
A. Peters c White b Barnes 31
K. Majola c Magiet b Allie 5
J. Frans b Magiet..................13
F. Abrahams c Hendricks b Allie 0
A. Frans c Martin b Magiet 20
R. Dolley run out 0
S. Draai c Behardien b Allie 2
V. Frans not out 1
EXTRAS.............9
TOTAL 95

FALL OF WICKETS: 1/1; 2/4; 3/32; 4/56; 5/66; 6/66; 7/89; 8/89; 9/91

BOWLING: Barnes 12-1-37-3; Magiet 8-2-15-2; Thomas 2-1-1-0; Allie 12-4-33-4

EP SECOND INNINGS
G. Cuddembey lbw Barnes 4
S. Kruger c Behardien b Allie 10
M. Majola b Barnes 0
A. Peters b Allie 40
K. Majola c Barnes b Allie 4
J. Frans c Martin b Barnes 7
F. Abrahams c White b Allie 0
A. Frans lbw Allie 8
R. Dolley not out 14
S. Draai not out 17
EXTRAS 8
TOTAL............112/8

FALL OF WICKETS: 1/4; 2/4; 3/30; 4/48; 5/59; 6/63; 7/74; 8/79

BOWLING: Barnes 17-1-51-3; Magiet 6-0-18-0; Allie 14-2-33-5; Gabriels 1-0-2-0

EP WON BY TWO WICKETS

Natal vs WP
21-23 February
1987
in
Pietermaritzburg

Skipper Magiet hits second century, but Natal hold WP at bay

A MORE significant first innings total would have given WP better prospects, but none of the batsmen could oblige with a bigger score than the consistent Munsoor Abdullah's 40, although Ismail Behardien (35) was not far behind.

Natal, thanks to Jessie Chellan's 74, compiled 165 for a first innings deficit of only 10 runs.

WP captain Saait Magiet moved up the order to speed things up in the second innings and recorded his second century of the season in typically aggressive fashion. The bludgeoning Magiet, who took 13 wickets in the six-match programme, picked up 335 run too.

The declaration on 209/7 left Natal 220 to chase, but there was not enough time for WP to bowl them out again and a frustrating draw did not do the Cape side's title chances any good.

Vincent Barnes knocked over the first three Natal wickets before they closed up shop, to finish with 5/60 in the match, and Goolam Allie claimed 4/38 in all against his former province.

Despite missing an opportunity to pick up a fourth victory, WP would have reason to thank Natal later in the season.

WP FIRST INNINGS

S. Hendricks c Khan b Le Roux	2
S. Gabriels c Patel b Y. Omar	13
I. Behardien c Soobramoney b Khan	35
C. Martin c Soobramoney b Le Roux	27
M. Abdullah c Soobramoney b Le Roux	40
*S. Magiet lbw Ramnarain	2
G. Miller b Ramnarain	7
+N. White c Mall b Khan	19
A. Jabaar c Mall b Ramnarain	0
V. Barnes lbw Khan	2
G. Allie not out	13
EXTRAS	15
TOTAL	175

FALL OF WICKETS: 1/4; 2/45; 3/59; 4/112; 5/115; 6/128; 7/132; 8/144; 9/148

BOWLING: Ramnarain 14-5-25-3; Le Roux 23-10-30-3; Y. Omar 15-6-25-1; Chellan 7-2-21-0; Khan 12-3-37-3; R. Omar 4-0-22-0

WP SECOND INNINGS

S. Hendricks b Ramnarain	20
S. Gabriels b Le Roux	14
I. Behardien run out	16
M. Abdullah c Mall b Naidoo	0
S. Magiet not out	100
G. Miller c Soobramoney b Chellan	14
C. Martin run out	8
N. White b Khan	6
A. Jabaar not out	26
EXTRAS	5
TOTAL	209/7 dec

FALL OF WICKETS: 1/24; 2/43; 3/51; 4/58; 5/86; 6/120; 7/133

BOWLING: Ramnarain 10-3-21-1; Le Roux 11,5-1-52-1; Khan 7-0-51-1; Naidoo 7-0-52-1; Chellan 6-1-28-1

NATAL FIRST INNINGS

E. Mall c Hendricks b Magiet	7
J. Chellan c Gabriels b Allie	74
P. Nair lbw Barnes	3
Y. Omar c & b Gabriels	26
M. Patel c White b Miller	4
M. Khan b Allie	14
RL. Naidoo run out	5
R. Omar b Barnes	0
R. Soobramoney lbw Jabaar	3
T. le Roux not out	14
N. Ramnarain lbw Allie	0
EXTRAS	15
TOTAL	165

FALL OF WICKETS: 1/11; 2/24; 3/75; 4/94; 5/138; 6/141; 7/147; 8/149; 9/158

BOWLING: Barnes 13-2-35-2; Magiet 6-2-8-1; Jabaar 15-2-32-1; Allie 19,3-8-30-3; Gabriels 12-2-27-1; Miller 6-0-18-1

NATAL SECOND INNINGS

E. Mall c White b Barnes	0
J. Chellan c Gabriels b Barnes	6
P. Nair c White b Barnes	4
Y. Omar b Allie	25
M. Patel not out	4
L. Naidoo not out	30
EXTRAS	5
TOTAL	74/4

FALL OF WICKETS: 1/0; 2/4; 3/17; 4/64

BOWLING: Barnes 8-2-25-3; Allie 8-5-8-1; Gabriels 5-1-21-0; Miller 6-0-15-0

MATCH DRAWN

Big ton from Hendricks knocks out Vaal; EP lose to relinquish the crown

Transvaal vs WP 14-16 March 1987 in Johannesburg

ATTACKING OPENING batsman Stuart Hendricks (137) got WP off to the best possible start with his maiden first-class century.

Fellow opening bat Seraj Gabriels (50) also came to the party, as did Munsoor Abdullah (61), as WP fashioned a 223-run first innings advantage over their hosts. Gabriels (6/27), himself a former regular for Transvaal, had been the chief destroyer when Transvaal, batting first, were skittled for 119. On 41/7 in their second knock, Transvaal were on a hiding to nothing, until Moosa Mangera, batting at No 9, smashed 66 to help move the total to a more respectable 159.

He could not avert an innings defeat, though, as Vincent Barnes took his quota of Transvaal wickets for the season to 15/115 with a second innings bag of 5/30. Gabriels' 4/37 meant a match-haul of 10/64. His 19 wickets cost 10,37 runs each, just a shade behind the 10,11 Barnes "paid" for his 42 victims. The best news of the weekend was Natal's home five-wicket victory over EP, which was sufficient to hand the Howa Bowl back to WP after two seasons.

TRANSVAAL FIRST INNINGS

A. Mentor c Martin b Allie	27
M Desai c Magiet b Gabriels	17
D. George c Abdullah b Gabriels	8
A. Rajah c White b Gabriels	4
H. Lorgat c Miller b Allie	5
I. Khan cWhite b Gabriels	1
I. Munshi c Hendricks b Gabriels	8
E. Mohammed b Barnes	24
Mos Mangera b Gabriels	0
A. Kolia run out	17
Moh Mangera not out	1
EXTRAS	7
TOTAL	119

FALL OF WICKETS: 1/41; 2/54; 3/61; 4/67; 5/67; 6/76; 7/83; 8/84; 9/118

BOWLING: Barnes 7,5-1-19-1; Magiet 3-0-16-0; Miller 4-0-15-0; Allie 14-5-30-2; Gabriels 19-5-27-6; Jabaar 4-1-5-0

TRANSVAAL SECOND INNINGS

A. Mentor c White b Barnes	15
M. Desai b Barnes	0
D. George st White b Gabriels	10
A. Rajah c Hendricks b Barnes	0
H. Lorgat lbw Barnes	40
I. Khan c Hendricks b Gabriels	2
I. Munshi c sub b Gabriels	0
E. Mohammed b Barnes	1
Mos Mangera st White b Gabriels	66
A. Kolia not out	6
Moh Mangera b Jabaar	0
EXTRAS	19
TOTAL	159

FALL OF WICKETS: 1/4; 2/28; 3/28; 4/28; 5/40; 6/40; 7/41; 8.114; 9/158

BOWLING: Barnes 15-3-30-5; Magiet 3-0-10-0; Gabriels 16-6-37-4; Jabaar 8,4-1-22-1; Allie 8-4-12-0; Miller 3-0-29-0

WP FIRST INNINGS

S. Hendricks c Mohammed b Lorgat	137
S. Gabriels b Mos Mangera	50
I. Behardien c Moh Mangera b Khan	0
C. Martin b Mos Mangera	9
M. Abdullah c Mohammed b Mos Mangera	61
* S. Magiet c Khan b Lorgat	30
G. Miller run out	1
A. Jabaar c Moh Mangera b Lorgat	8
+N. White c Moh Mangera b Mos Mangera	8
V. Barnes not out	11
EXTRAS	27
TOTAL	342/9 dec

FALL OF WICKETS: 1/99; 2/102; 3/123; 4/237; 5/292; 6/294; 7/316; 8/320; 9/342

BOWLING: Mohammed 9-0-42-0; Kolia 7-2-34-0; Lorgat 19-2-97-3; Mos Mangera 23-5-61-4; Khan 6-0-22-1; Munshi 2-0-14-0; George 11-0-45-0

WP WON BY AN INNINGS AND 64 RUNS. WP WON THE HOWA BOWL

WP Cricket Board First Class Averages 1986/87

BATTING

Name	Matches	Inns	NO	Hs	Runs	Ave	50	100
Saait Magiet	6	8	2	100*	335	55,83	1	2
Stuart Hendricks	6	10	2	137	276	34,50	1	1
Munsoor Abdullah	6	8	0	109	267	33,38	1	1
Goolam Allie	6	5	4	13*	33	33,00		
Seraj Gabriels	6	10	2	50	207	25,87	1	
Ismail Behardien	6	8	0	72	175	21,88	1	
Neville Booysen	3	2	0	38	40	20,00		
Nazeem White	6	8	1	39	122	17,42		
Armien Jabaar	2	3	1	26*	34	17,00		
Faiek Davids	4	5	0	31	74	14,80		
Yunus Thomas	4	5	0	43	61	12,20		
Cyril Martin	3	5	0	27	57	11,40		
Gerry Miller	2	3	0	14	22	7,33		
Vincent Barnes	6	6	1	12*	22	4,40		

FIELDING:

Wicketkeepers: 27 – Nazeem White (23ct and 4st)

Catches:

11 – Ismail Behardien; 10 – Stuart Hendricks; 5 – Seraj Gabriels, Munsoor Abdullah, Faiek Davids; 4 – Saait Magiet, Vincent Barnes; 3 – Cyril Martin; 2 – Yunus Thomas; 1 – Gerry Miller, Goolam Allie, Neville Booysen

BOWLING

Name	Overs	Mdns	Wkts	Runs	Ave	Best Bowling	5i	10m
Vincent Barnes	186,2	39	42	425	10,11	7/41 vs EP	3	1
Seraj Gabriels	99,3	29	19	197	10,37	6/27 vs Tvl	1	1
Goolam Allie	120	41	18	226	12,56	5/33 v EP	1	
Saait Magiet	81	23	13	174	13,38	5/16 v Tvl	1	
Neville Booysen	76,2	20	12	194	16,17	3/29 v Natal		
Armien Jabaar	27,4	4	2	59	29,50	1/23 v Tvl		
Gerry Miller	19	0	77	1	77,00	1/18 vs EP		

Also bowled: Faiek Davids 4-0-28-0; Yunus Thomas 5-1-9-0

Runs at last in Port Elizabeth and WP are quick out of the blocks

**EP vs WP
21-23 November
1987 in
Port Elizabeth**

DEFEATS IN low-scoring affairs there in successive seasons were banished from their minds as Western Province showed they meant business with a three-wicket win in Port Elizabeth – the first time they had won in the Friendly City in six years.

André Peters (73) was the backbone of the Eastern Province first innings effort of 236, although EP should have done better after being 161/5 at one stage.

The WP top order collaborated well in reply, contributing 228 runs out of a total of 272 – representing a vital first innings lead of 36. Opener Seraj Gabriels got the ball rolling with 62, while Faiek Davids contributed 51 at No 6 in the order.

Only two scores in the 40s in their second innings for EP meant they had left WP the comparatively easy task of making 138 to win, a feat they accomplished in 59,2 overs, after looking shaky on 99/7. Gabriels ground out a second half-century in the match, and with Reggie February (11 not out), added an unbroken stand of 39 for the eighth wicket to get WP home.

EP FIRST INNINGS

S. Kruger b Barnes	21
G. Cuddembey c Behardien b Barnes	7
A. Coetzee c Behardien b February	5
M. Majola c Behardien b Benjamin	27
A. Peters b Benjamin	73
V. Malgas c Magiet b Benjamin	1
K. Majola c White b February	16
R. Dolley not out	26
S. George b Barnes	23
V. Frans c Davids b Magiet	11
S. Abrahams c Davids b Benjamin	1
EXTRAS	25
TOTAL	236

FALL OF WICKETS: 1/31; 2/36; 3/38; 4/111; 5/123; 6/161; 7/172; 8/209; 9/226

BOWLING: Barnes 24-7-55-3; February 14-4-34-2; Benjamin 22,2-2-69-4; Gabriels 14-2-26-0; Davids 2-0-8-0; Conrad 3-0-15-0; Magiet 2-0-4-1

EP SECOND INNINGS

G. Cuddembey c February b Gabriels	47
S. Kruger c Benjamin b February	7
M. Majola c Magiet b February	0
A. Peters c White b February	0
V. Malgas c Benjamin b Gabriels	15
K. Majola c Barnes b Gabriels	25
R. Dolley b Magiet	44
S. George c Behardien b Barnes	9
V. Frans c Kemp b Barnes	1
A. Coetzee not out	5
S. Abrahams b Magiet	1
EXTRAS	19
TOTAL	173

FALL OF WICKETS: 1/19; 2/19; 3/23; 4/56; 5/91; 6/112; 7/162; 8/166; 9/172; 9/173

BOWLING: Barnes 17-4-28-2; February 17-4-34-3; Gabriels 19-2-52-3; Benjamin 11-2-27-0; Magiet 8.5-2-13-2

WP FRST INNINGS

S. Hendricks c K.Majola b George	26
S. Gabriels c Abrahams b George	62
+N. White c Kruger b K. Majola	27
S. Conrad c sub b K. Majola	31
I. Behardien c sub b K. Majola	31
F. Davids run out	51
D. Kemp st Kruger b K. Majola	1
*S. Magiet c Cuddembey b Dolley	15
R. February not out	8
V. Barnes c George b Dolley	4
F. Benjamin run out	0
EXTRAS	16
TOTAL	272

FALL OF WICKETS: 1/91; 2/95; 3/152; 4/162; 5/233; 6/244; 7/249; 8/263; 9/271

BOWLING: Abrahams 10-2-29-0; V. Frans 8-0-39-0; K. Majola 27,2-3-89-4; George 16-4-34-2; Dolley 24-6-65-2

WP SECOND INNINGS

S. Hendricks c Peters b George	10
S. Gabriels not out	56
I. Behardien c K.Majola b George	7
S. Conrad c V. Frans b Abrahams	6
F. Davids lbw V. Frans	7
D. Kemp b Abrahams	17
S. Magiet c Peters b Abrahams	4
N. White c Coetzee b Abrahams	0
R. February not out	11
EXTRAS	20
TOTAL	138/7

FALL OF WICKETS: 1/36; 2/42; 3/48; 4/65; 5/93; 6/99; 7/99

BOWLING: V. Frans 7,2-2-23-1; Abrahams 28-7-48-4; George 12-1-26-2; Dolley 12-5-21-0

WP WON BY 3 WICKETS

**Natal vs WP
29-31 December
1987 in
Pietermaritzburg**

Acrimonious ending as WP walk off in response to umpire's decision

A SPIRITED fightback by Natal came to nought as, 202 runs to the good in their second innings, they had their visitors troop off the field in protest at a not out decision against home captain Mustapha Khan, on 99.

Reggie February (4/28) made early inroads in the Natal first innings of 148, and Nilton Muller chipped in with 3/14. Ismail Behardien got his only half-century of a disappointing season as WP replied with 272; four scores in the 30s bolstered the effort.

Natal, in turn, only managed to wipe out the first innings deficit of 124 with five wickets down, but then Khan's exemplary stand began. The score had reached 326/8, with an amazing contribution of 66 from Extras, when WP took their unusual action in response to what they felt was a poor umpiring call, and the game was abandoned.

Extras in the less than three completed innings in the match contributed 116 runs in all.

NATAL FIRST INNINGS

E. Mall c Kemp b February		13
J. Chellan c Cupido b February		4
P. Nair lbw Barnes		7
M. Patel c Cupido b Muller		8
S. Govender c Gabriels b Muller		15
M. Khan c Muller b February		39
RL. Naidoo st Cupido b Gabriels		18
M. Rampersad c Abdullah b Barnes		0
R. Soobramoney c Cupido b Muller		8
N. Ramnarain b February		2
V. Kistnasamy not out		0
	EXTRAS	34
	TOTAL	148

FALL OF WICKETS: 1/8; 2/31; 3/36; 4/67; 5/77; 6/100; 7/115; 8/141; 9/148

BOWLING: Barnes 17-1-26-2; February 18-5-28-4; Magiet 3-1-6-0; Gabriels 12-5-26-1; Benjamin 6-1-14-0; Muller 10,4-2-14-3

NATAL SECOND INNINGS

E. Mall b Muller		19
J. Chellan c Cupido b Muller		14
P. Nair c Kemp b February		23
M. Patel c Cupido b Muller		1
S. Govender b February		38
M. Khan not out		99
RL. Naidoo b Davids		58
M. Rampersad c Cupido b Davids		3
R. Soobramoney b Magiet		5
V. Kistnasamy not out		0
	EXTRAS	66
	TOTAL	326/8

FALL OF WICKETS: 1/38; 2/45; 3/49; 4/98; 5/124; 6/259; 7/275; 8/310

BOWLING: Barnes 23-3-55-0; February 24-3-66-2; Gabriels 10-4-15-0; Benjamin 12-2-41-0; Muller 13-3-31-3; Davids 14-3-32-2; Magiet 8-3-15-1; Kemp 2-0-5-0

WP FIRST INNINGS

S. Gabriels c Rampersad b Ramnarian		16
+R. Cupido c Ramnarian b Khan		38
I. Behardien lbw Khan		50
M. Abdullah lbw Ramnarain		6
D. Kemp c Ramnarain b Rampersad		33
F. Davids c Naidoo b Khan		10
N. Muller lbw Khan		35
*S. Magiet c Khan b Rampersad		11
R. February c Soobramoney b Rampersad		37
V. Barnes run out		19
F. Benjamin not out		1
	EXTRAS	16
	TOTAL	272

FALL OF WICKETS: 1/29; 2/66; 3/81; 4/143; 5/149; 6/163; 7/187; 8/239; 9/271

BOWLING: Ramnarain 19-4-58-2; Kistnasmay 13-1-47-0; Rampersad 16,1-3-60-3; Khan 19-1-67-4; Chellan 10-5-20-0; Mall 2-0-4-0

MATCH ABANDONED AFTER WP DISPUTED AN UMPIRING DECISION AND WALKED OFF, FORCING THE GAME TO BE ABANDONED.

Runs, runs, runs – but Transvaal show character to earn draw

Transvaal vs WP
2-4 January
1988
in
Johannesburg

WESTERN PROVINCE put in some excellent batting performances in the summer, and their 350/8 declared was the first in a sequence of three first innings totals of 350-plus runs.

This time four batsmen in the top five delivered half-centuries – Seraj Gabriels, Randall Cupido, Munsoor Abdullah and Deon Kemp. The problem for WP on this occasion was that the home side's batsmen also took a liking to the friendly conditions, and replied with 298.

Faiek Davids then hit an undefeated 107 – his first of two centuries in the season – to help set up a declaration on 257/7 and leaving Transvaal the task of scoring 310 for victory.

It was a target which seemed beyond them, but despite Gabriels getting among the wickets with 4/45, Haroon Lorgat and Hussein Manack held out for a draw, with a final score of 150/7. With only one win in the first three matches of the season, WP's plans were not quite working out, considering their strength in depth, but for Transvaal, so often a soft touch, a draw was an excellent result.

WP FIRST INNINGS

S. Gabriels c Khan b Patel 58
+R. Cupido c Kemp b Lorgat 52
I. Behardien c Kemp b H.Manack 22
M. Abdullah b Patel 51
D. Kemp c AH Manack b Jajbhai 57
F. Davids c Desai b Mohammed 13
N. Muller c Kemp b H. Manack 29
*S. Magiet c Dinath b Jajbhai 9
R. February not out 16
F. Benjamin not out..1
               EXTRAS 42
               TOTAL ....350/8 dec

FALL OF WICKETS: 1/99; 2/129; 3/153; 4/242; 5/259; 6/279; 7/303; 8/333

BOWLING: AH Manack 14-4-36-0; Dindar 6-0-32-0; H Manack 20-6-63-2; Patel 19-6-67-2; Lorgat 12-1-55-1; Mohammed 9-3-24-1; Jajbhai 9-0-31-2

WP SECOND INNINGS

S. Gabriels lbw AH Manack 2
N. Muller c Patel b Dindar..2
D. Kemp c Kemp b AH Manack 30
+R. Cupido c Kemp b Mohammed 29
I. Behardien b AH Manack 7
M. Abdullah b Jajbhai..37
F. Davids not out 107
*S. Magiet c AH Manack b Patel.............................6
R. February not ou 12
               EXTRAS...............25
               TOTAL.....257/7 dec

FALL OF WICKETS: 1/4; 2/4; 3/67; 4/80; 5/110; 6/187

BOWLING: AH Manack 23-9-39-3; Dindar 5-1-15-1; H. Manack 15-2-50-0; Mohammed 6-1-16-1; Lorgat 4-2-14-0; Patel 11-2-39-1; Khan 4-1-16-0; Jajbhai 7-1-43-1

TRANSVAAL FIRST INNINGS

N. Kemp b February 1
M. Desai run out 24
I. Khan c Davids b Gabriels......................................9
H. Manack b Muller..28
A. Dinath b Magiet 32
H. Lorgat c Davids b Barnes 17
M. Jajbhai not out 61
N. Dindar c Gabriels b Benjamin 61
AH. Manack c Kemp b Benjamin 0
E. Mohammed b Barne 29
S. Patel b Barnes 0
               EXTRAS...............36
               TOTAL 298

FALL OF WICKETS: 1/5; 2/21; 3/66; 4/107; 5/119; 6/148; 7/251; 8/251; 9/272

BOWLING: Barnes 17.3-3-50-3; February 14-5-28-1; Gabriels 21-5-48-1; Benjamin 10-1-71-2; Muller 10-1-51-1; Magiet 7-1-14-1

TRANSVAAL SECOND INNINGS

N. Kemp b Gabriels 16
M. Desai b February 15
I. Khan c Cupido b Muller.......................................37
A. Dinath c Behardien b Gabriels...........................10
N. Dindar b Gabriels..1
AH. Manack c Behardien b Gabriels........................2
H. Lorgat not out..27
M. Jajbhai c Cupido b Barnes 1
H. Manack not out..6
               EXTRAS 35
               TOTAL............150/7

FALL OF WICKETS: 1/33; 2/56; 3/68; 4/80; 5/88; 6/104; 7/125

BOWLING: Barnes 15-7-17-1; February 12-2-29-1; Gabriels 15-3-45-4; Benjamin 5-0-19-0; Muller 5-3-5-1

MATCH DRAWN

Davids hits second ton in two games to set up slaughter of EP

FAIEK DAVIDS battered his way into the record books with a second hundred in successive innings for WP – his 146 out of a total of 367/5 declared was the third best individual first-class score for the province before unity.

The fifth-wicket partnership of 216 between Davids and Munsoor Abdullah (78 not out) was also a WP record, although it was broken three seasons later. The impact of Davids on the game can be seen from the fact that Abdullah, himself no tortoise in the scoring stakes, went in at No 3 and still ended up 68 runs behind Davids, the regular No 6.

EP, reeling after being tired out in the field, could only manage 98 in reply, with Seraj Gabriels weaving a web in which he caught four victims, at a cost of 31 runs. In the follow-on innings Gabriels was again given licence to turn and flight, and again he trapped four, this time for 82 runs. EP's much-improved performance realised 297, but the WP openers had only 29 to chase, to give WP a 10-wicket victory.

WP FIRST INNINGS

S. Gabriels c George b K. Majola...........................40
S. Hendricks c Cuddembey b K. Majola 70
I. Behardien run out 0
M. Abdullah not out 78
D. Kemp c Kruger b J. Frans 1
F. Davids lbw K. Majola 146
N. Muller not out...18

EXTRAS..............14
TOTAL.....367/5 dec

FALL OF WICKETS: 1/100; 2/100; 3/121; 4/123; 5/339
BOWLING: V. Frans 16-0-75-0; J. Frans 26-8-51-1; S. George 9-3-35-0; R. Dolley 9-0-46-0; K. Majola 30-7-106-3; E. Van Vuuren 3-0-28-0; Peters 1-0-12 -0

WP SECOND INNINGS

S. Hendricks not out..17
S. Gabriels not out 11

EXTRAS.................1
TOTAL 29/0

BOWLING: V. Frans 3-0-12-0; K. Majola 5-1-7-0; J. Frans 3-1-3-0; Cuddembey 1,4-0-6-0; Peters1-1-0-0

EP FIRST INNINGS

G. Cuddembey c Barnes b February.........................2
A. Jordaan b February...1
S. Kruger b Barnes..3
A. Peters c Cupido b February..................................0
K. Majola c Behardien b Barnes..............................33
R. Dolley c Behardien b Gabriels 13
A. Coetzee c Hendricks b Gabriels 0
J. Frans lbw Barnes..24
E. van Vuuren c Hendricks b Gabriels 3
S. George not out 0
V. Frans c Kemp b Gabriels 0

EXTRAS...............19
TOTAL.................98

FALL OF WICKETS: 1/4; 2/7; 3/7; 4/8; 5/49; 6/50; 7/93; 8/98; 9/98
BOWLING: Barnes 17-7-19-3; February 13-3-10 -3; Muller 6-1-16-0; *Magiet 3-1-3-0; Gabriels 12,3-3-31-4

EP SECOND INNINGS (FOLLOWED ON)

G. Cuddembey c Cupido b Muller..........................30
A. Jordaan c Behardien b February 56
S. Kruger c Kemp b Gabriels 27
A. Peters c Cupido b February................................20
K. Majola c Magiet b Gabriels................................42
R. Dolley b February...0
A. Coetzee c Hendricks b Barnes 35
J. Frans st Cupido b Gabriels....................................2
E. van Vuuren c Magiet b Gabriels 2
S. George b Magiet 25
V. Frans not out..18

EXTRAS..............40
TOTAL..............297

FALL OF WICKETS: 1/57; 2/119; 3/142; 4/159; 5/159; 6/229; 7/244; 8/244; 9/254
BOWLING: Barnes 20-5-45-1; February 23-8-65-3; Muller 10-4-25-1; Gabriels 32-7-82-4; Davids 7-2-11-0; Hendricks 2-0-8-0; Magiet 5,4-1-21-1

WP WON BY TEN WICKETS

Woeful Natal can't halt run-hungry WP's march to the title

IT WAS like an average club side taking on a well-oiled provincial unit, when Natal came to town.

It wasn't pleasant to watch – in fact, only four Natal batsmen made double figures in the match, and the highest individual score in two innings was Stanley Govender's 20 in a paltry first innings score of 78.

After the visitors were bundled out within 40,4 overs in their first innings, it was really just a question of how big WP's victory margin would be. On cue, the batting served up some exciting stuff, despite Mustapha Khan's 5/71, to carve out a first innings lead of 340.

Munsoor Abdullah fell six runs short of a century, and there were contributions all the way down the order, the best being 54 from Deon Kemp and 40 from Ismail Behardien.

Natal were even worse in their second knock, with Seraj Gabriels (6/17) picking up his best figures of the season, as the visitors crumbled to 69 all out– and defeat by an innings and 271 runs. Vincent Barnes, who finished the season with the most wickets again – 26 this time, the same number as Reggie February – took 6/28 in the Natal first innings.

WP vs Natal 20-22 February 1988 at Florida Park Cape Town

NATAL FIRST INNINGS

E. Mall lbw Magiet	8
K. Govender c Cupido b Barnes	8
P. Nair lbw Davids	6
J. Chellan c Kemp b Barnes	8
S. Govender c Cupido b Davids	20
M. Khan c Kemp b Barnes	0
RL. Naidoo lbw Barnes	3
R. Soobramoney b Magiet	3
LD. Naidoo b Barnes	0
V. Kistnasamy c Magiet b Barnes	1
N. Ramnarain not out	0
EXTRAS	21
TOTAL	78

FALL OF WICKETS: 1/14; 2/27; 3/47; 4/50; 5/65; 6/66; 7/77; 8/77; 9/78

BOWLING: Barnes 15,4-2-28-6; February 7-3-13-0; Magiet 11-5-10-2; Davids 6-4-4-2; Gabriels 1-0-2-0

NATAL SECOND INNINGS

E. Mall run out	3
P. Nair c Barnes b February	4
K. Govender c February b Gabriels	11
J. Chellan c Cupido b Gabriels	0
S. Govender c & b Gabriels	2
M. Khan lbw Gabriels	2
RL. Naidoo b Magiet	8
R. Soobramoney c Davids b Gabriels	0
LD. Naidoo c Abdullah b Gabriels	15
V. Kistnasamy not out	11
N. Ramnarian c Abdullah b Conrad	0
EXTRAS	13
TOTAL	69

FALL OF WICKETS: 1/6; 2/22; 3/22; 4/29; 5/30; 6/41; 7/41; 8/41; 9/67

BOWLING: Barnes 4-1-4-0; February 6-3-9-1; Davids 3-2-1-0; Magiet 9-4-18-1; Gabriels 10-3-17-6; Conrad 1,1-0-7-1

WP FIRST INNINGS

S. Hendricks c S.Govender b Ramnarain	17
S. Gabriels b Khan	28
I. Behardien c S. Govender b L. Naidoo	40
M. Abdullah c Soobramoney b Khan	94
D. Kemp lbw Mall	54
F. Davids c & b Kistnasamy	10
S. Conrad c M.Naidoo b Chellan	25
*S. Magiet c Soobramoney b Khan	32
+R. Cupido not out	37
R. February c Chellan b Khan	31
V. Barnes c S.Govender b Khan	26
EXTRAS	24
TOTAL	418

FALL OF WICKETS: 1/24; 2/83; 3/90; 4/186; 5/203; 6/248; 7/316; 8/319; 9/353

BOWLING: Ramnarian 10-0-42-1; Kistnasamy 18-0-75-1; L.D. Naidoo 23-1-95-1; Chellan 8-0-52-1; Khan 28,2-11-71-5; RL.Naidoo 3-0-9-0; Mall 10-2-50-1

WP WON BY AN INNINGS AND 271 RUNS

WP vs Transvaal
19-21 March 1988
at
Green Point Track
Cape Town

Davids and Magiet set up a lead; February plays major role in title success

TRANSVAAL PUT together a decent first innings total of 190, but with no sign of top order strength. Reggie February took all the wickets that mattered in his 6/73, to end the season with 26 scalps at a handy average of 17,23.

Then it was up to the WP batsmen. The top five contributed a mere 62 in a rare failure for the season, but allrounders Faiek Davids and captain Saait Magiet both hit 85 to ensure a sizeable first innings lead of 64 runs.

With a highest individual score of 32 in their second innings, Transvaal were nowhere near setting WP a challenging target, and the home side cruised to a seven-wicket win, and a second successive Howa Bowl triumph. This came despite boardroom upheavals, with long-serving president Hassan Howa ousted during the season.

Davids topped the averages with 429 runs overall, including two centuries and two fifties, while next best Munsoor Abdullah had an average of 54, with three half-centuries.

Seraj Gabriels, third in the batting stakes with 268 runs at 45,5, also picked up 23 wickets at 15,00 each, for third spot in the bowling averages.

TRANSVAAL FIRST INNINGS

N. Kemp c Kemp b February	6
M. Desai c Cupido b Barnes	4
A. Rajah c Barnes b February	1
I. Khan c Behardien b February	8
A. Dinath c Behardien b February	41
H. Lorgat c Kemp b February	5
N. Dindar c Cupido b Davids	18
M. Jajbhai c Cupido b February	58
AH. Manack run out	1
Y. Begg not out	13
E. Mohammed b Barnes	9
EXTRAS	26
TOTAL	190

FALL OF WICKETS: 1/9; 2/13; 3/13; 4/55; 5/79; 6/79; 7/130; 8/137; 9/177

BOWLING: Barnes 17,2-6-40-2; February 26-5-73-6; Magiet 8-2-15-0; Benjamin 12-4-20-0; Davids 6-1-16-1

TRANSVAAL SECOND INNINGS

N. Kemp c February b Barnes	8
M. Desai lbw Conrad	32
A. Rajah run out	9
I. Khan b Benjamin	8
A. Dinath b Barnes	16
H. Lorgat c Cupido b Davids	29
N. Dindar c Behardien b Barnes	3
M. Jajbhai b Davids	11
AH. Manack not out	16
Y. Begg c Magiet b Davids	2
E. Mohammed b Barnes	1
EXTRAS	21
TOTAL	156

FALL OF WICKETS: 1/16; 2/37; 3/65; 4/77; 5/107; 6/117; 7/125; 8/133; 9/151

BOWLING: Barnes 19,3-5-26-4; February 17-1-44-0; Benjamin 19-1-41-1; Conrad 8-4-16-1; Davids 4-1-8-3

WP FIRST INNINGS

S. Hendricks c & b Manack	9
+R. Cupido c Begg b Mohammed	0
I. Behardien c Dinath b Manack	15
M. Abdullah st Begg b Manack	4
D. Kemp c Dindar b Manack	34
F. Davids c Dindar b Manack	85
S. Conrad c Kemp b Manack	0
*S. Magiet c Dindar b Lorgat	85
R. February c Rajah b Lorgat	2
V. Barnes b Lorgat	0
F. Benjamin not out	5
EXTRAS	15
TOTAL	254

FALL OF WICKETS: 1/1; 2/25; 3/30; 4/107; 5/107; 6/192; 7/192; 8/229; 9/229

BOWLING: Mohammed 15-3-57-1; Dindar 11-2-50-0; Manack 26-5-82-6; Lorgat 13,5-3-50-3

WP SECOND INNINGS

S. Hendricks c Begg b Manack	36
R. Cupido c Dindar b Lorgat	41
I. Behardien c Kemp b Lorgat	0
D. Kemp not out	5
F. Davids not out	0
EXTRAS	13
TOTAL	95/3

FALL OF WICKETS: 1/69; 2/70; 3/91

BOWLING: Manack 12,5-5-19-1; Mohammed 2-0-8-0; Dindar 2-0-10-0; Jajbhai 3-0-17-0; Lorgat 12-6-12-2; Khan 3-0-16-0

WP WON BY 7 WICKETS
WP WON HOWA BOWL

WP Cricket Board First Class Averages 1987/88

BATTING

Name	Matches	Inns	NO	Hs	Runs	Ave	50	100
Faiek Davids	6	9	2	146	429	61,29	2	2
Munsoor Abdullah	5	6	1	94	270	54,00	3	
Seraj Gabriels	5	8	2	62	268	44,67	3	
Randall Cupido	5	6	1	52	197	39,40		
Reggie February	6	7	4	37	117	39,00		
Stuart Hendricks	4	7	1	70	185	30,83	1	
Deon Kemp	6	9	1	57	232	29,00	2	
Nilton Muller	3	4	1	35	84	28,00		
Saait Magiet	6	7	0	85	162	23,14	1	
Ismail Behardien	6	9	0	50	172	19,11	1	
Shukri Conrad	3	4	0	31	62	15,50		
Vincent Barnes	6	4	0	26	49	12,25		
Fuad Benjamin	4	4	3	5*	7	7,00		

Also batted: Nazeem White (27 & 0)

FIELDING:

Wicketkeepers: 20 – Randall Cupido (18c and 2st), 2 – Nazeem White (2c)

Fielders Catches:

12 – Ismail Behardien; 10 – Deon Kemp; 5 – Saait Magiet, Faiek Davids; 4 – Vincent Barnes; 3 – Stuart Hendricks, Seraj Gabriels, Reggie February, Munsoor Abdullah; 2 – Fuad Benjamin; 1 – Nilton Muller

BOWLING

Name	Overs	Mdns	Wkts	Runs	Ave	Best Bowling	5i	10m
Faiek Davids	42	13	8	80	10,00	3/8 v Tvl		
Saait Magiet	65,3	20	9	120	13,33	2/10 v Natal		
Seraj Gabriels	146,3	34	23	345	15,00	6/17 v Natal	1	
Vincent Barnes	206,4	51	26	406	15,62	6/28 v Natal	1	
Nilton Muller	54,4	13	9	145	16,11	3/18 v Natal		
Reggie February	151	46	26	448	17,23	6/73 v Tvl	1	
Fuad Benjamin	97,2	14	7	303	43,29	4/69 v EP		

Also Bowled: Shukri Conrad 12,1-4-38-2; Deon Kemp 2-0-5-0; Stuart Hendricks 2-0-8-0

WP vs EP
26-28 November
1988
in
Port Elizabeth

Rain comes to the rescue of EP after a Barnes blast put WP in the driving seat

RAIN PREVENTED Western Province from getting their campaign off to a perfect start against arch-rivals EP in Port Elizabeth. Playing under a new captain, Vincent Barnes, following the retirement of Saait Magiet, WP made a solid 285 in their first innings thanks to an aggressive 89 by Faiek Davids and a polished 60 from opener Seraj Gabriels.

Together with left-hander Ismail Behardien (40), Gabriels added a vital 73 for the second wicket to lay the foundation for the big-hitting Davids to tear into the EP bowling.

It was only a defiant 62 from André Peters and 37 extras that helped the home side to reach 163 after Barnes (6/32) had destroyed the EP top order with his pace and aggression.

WP raced to 162/5 declared, leaving EP ample time to reach their victory target of 285. When the rain came EP were battling at 139/5.

WP FIRST INNINGS

S. Gabriels b K. Majola	60
S. Hendricks c Coetzee b Paul	28
I. Behardien c R.Dolley b K.Majola	40
N. White c Coetzee b R. Dolley	21
F. Davids b Paul	89
D. Kemp c Coetzee b R. Dolley	2
Y. Thomas c Coetzee b K. Majola	13
G. Miller c Coetzee b K. Majola	2
+R. Cupido c M. Majola b K. Majola	12
R. February c Coetzee b K. Majola	2
*V. Barnes not out	0
EXTRAS	16
TOTAL	285

FALL OF WICKETS: 1/40; 2/113; 3/164; 4/164; 5/166; 6/195; 7/203; 8/259; 9/277

BOWLING: Paul 14-1-58-2; V. Frans 3-0-15-0; George 17-1-47-0; R.Dolley 27-9-48-2; K. Majola 37-7-92-6; A. Frans 3-1-9-0

WP SECOND INNINGS

S. Hendricks run out	63
S. Gabriels c Coetzee b V. Frans	13
I. Behardien c Paul b R. Dolley	17
F. Davids c A. Frans b George	47
D. Kemp not out	2
N. White c R. Dolley b V. Frans	1
Y. Thomas not out	10
EXTRAS	9
TOTAL	162/5 dec

FALL OF WICKETS: 1/37; 2/83; 3/140; 4/150; 5/151

BOWLING: V. Frans 12-2-38-2; Paul 4-0-15-0; R. Dolley 15-5-51-1; K. Majola 10-3-22-0; George 3-0-27-1

EP FIRST INNINGS

K. Majola run out	1
G. Cuddembey c Kemp b Barnes	4
M. Majola b Barnes	25
A. Peters b Barnes	62
R. Dolley lbw Barnes	1
G. Dolley b Barnes	2
A. Coetzee c & b Barnes	2
A. Frans b Davids	21
G. Paul run out	5
S. George not out	3
V. Frans c Davids b Gabriels	0
EXTRAS	37
TOTAL	163

FALL OF WICKETS: 1/10; 2/10; 3/100; 4/107; 5/121; 6/121; 7/127; 8/153; 9/153

BOWLING: Barnes 23-10-32-6; February 26-10-44-0; Miller 5-0-10-0; Gabriels 11,1-5-16-1; Davids 14-5-24-1

EP SECOND INNINGS

K. Majola c Cupido b Miller	47
G. Cuddembey lbw David	13
M. Majola c Cupido b Davids	1
A. Peters b Miller	10
R. Dolley not out	14
G. Dolley run out	0
A. Frans not out	27
EXTRAS	27
TOTAL	139/5

FALL OF WICKETS: 1/54; 2/60; 3/66; 4/96; 5/98

BOWLING: Barnes 14-7-23-0; February 19-10-25-0; Gabriels 17-3-44-0; Davids 11-6-12-2; Miller 5-3-2-2; Hendricks 1-0-6-0

MATCH DRAWN

Kemp smashes 148 for WP – and then Barnes does the rest against a poor Natal side

THE NATAL first innings scorecard resembled a long telephone number with no batsman being able to reach double figures in a miserable total of 49.

As has been the case so often in the past, Vincent Barnes was once again the scourge of the Natal batsmen, taking an incredible 5/11 off 13 overs. Newcomer Salie Green gave him solid support, chipping in with a tidy 2/9.

Deon Kemp smashed a career-best 148 as WP declared at 296/7 just after lunch on the second day. Faced with a first innings deficit of 247, Natal once again couldn't cope with the pace of Barnes, who claimed 5/22 to finish with a match analysis of 10/33 in 24 overs.

Munoj Patel (33) was the only Natal batsman to provide any resistance as they were bundled out for 65 – to give WP an easy victory by an innings and 182 runs, with more than a day to spare.

WP vs Natal 27-29 December, 1988 at Florida Park Cape Town

NATAL FIRST INNINGS

S. Sarang c Cupido b Barnes 3
M. Ameen run out 9
LD. Naidoo c Cupido b Barnes................................0
M. Badat c Ebrahim b Barnes..................................8
S. Govender c Galant b Barnes 2
M. Khan c Hendricks b Barne 0
M. Patel run out...0
S. Kushor c Galant b Green 1
M. Rampersad c Hendricks b Green.........................3
S. Jeram not out...6
V. Kistnasamy c White b Gabriels 4
     EXTRAS...............13
     TOTAL 49

FALL OF WICKETS: 1/15; 2/15; 3/24; 4/27; 5/28; 6/30; 7/33; 8/33; 9/41

BOWLING: *Barnes 13-6-11-5; Kemp 3-0-9-0; Galant 3-1-4-0; Green 8-4-9-2; Gabriels 1,3-0-3-1

NATAL SECOND INNINGS

S. Sarang lbw Barnes 0
M. Ameen b Barnes 10
M. Patel c Ebrahim b Gabriels 33
M. Badat c Cupido b Barnes....................................2
S. Govender c Cupido b Green 1
M. Khan c Cupido b Barnes 1
LD. Naidoo c Ebrahim b Barnes 0
S. Kushor c Barnes b Green.....................................1
M. Rampersad c Cupido b Green 4
S. Jeram not out 2
V. Kistnasamy c Hendricks b Gabriels 0
     EXTRAS...............11
     TOTAL 65

FALL OF WICKETS: 1/10; 2/21; 3/23; 4/24; 5/33; 6/35; 7/36; 8/59; 9/65

BOWLING: Barnes 11-1-22-5; Green 13-3-26-3; Gabriels 3,3-0-6-2

WP FIRST INNINGS

S. Hendricks c Jeram b Khan..................................35
S. Gabriels lbw Khan 35
F. Ebrahim b Rampsersad 14
N. White c Kushor b Khan......................................14
D. Kemp not out 148
N. Antulay b Khan 10
Y. Thomas b Khan..2
M. Galant run out 14
+R. Cupido not out...5
     EXTRAS...............19
     TOTAL 296/7dec

FALL OF WICKETS: 1/74; 2/90; 3/100; 4/124; 5/164; 6/185; 7/259

BOWLING: Rampersad 18-4-59-1; Kistnasamy 10-1-42-0; Jeram 4-0-27-0; Naidoo 16-3-57-0; Khan 27-5-92-5

WP WON BY AN INNINGS AND 182 RUNS

WP vs Tvl
31 Dec 1988
-2 Jan 1989 at
Green Point Track
Cape Town

Barnes leads from the front, but Transvaal hold on for a draw

DESPITE THE uneven bounce of the Green Point Track pitch, which saw opener Stuart Hendricks being struck on the ear by Jack Manack who claimed 6/34, WP managed to reach a respectable first innings total of 234, thanks to a defiant 53 by opener Seraj Gabriels and a valuable 9th wicket stand of 43 between Yunus Thomas (56) and Reggie February (21*).

After Barnes, who claimed his third consecutive five wicket haul, had removed the Transvaal top order, Haroon Lorgat (61) and Nazeer Dindar (54) added 102 priceless runs for the 5th wicket to enable the visitors to recover well enough to finish one run short of the WP first innings total.

The tricky pitch made run-scoring difficult – and Barnes made a token declaration after tea at 192/5 to leave Transvaal the impossible task of getting 194 for victory in just over 30 overs. The match was abandoned as a draw 11 overs into the Transvaal innings.

WP FIRST INNINGS

S. Hendricks c Begg b Parbhoo	16
S. Gabriels c Begg b Manack	53
I. Behardien b Manack	7
N. White c Ramnarain b Muller	14
F. Davids b Manack	4
D. Kemp c Begg b Manack	1
Y. Thomas b Manack	56
+R. Cupido c sub b Ramnarain	13
M. Galant b Dindar	14
R. February not out	21
*V. Barnes b Manack	2
EXTRAS	33
TOTAL	234

FALL OF WICKETS: 1/26; 2/89; 3/99; 4/114; 5/114; 6/115; 7/137; 8/179; 9/222

BOWLING: Ramnarain 21-10-29-1; Manack 23-9-34-6; Lorgat 26-8-41-0; Dindar 21-7-60-1; Muller 12-2-30-1; Parbhoo 7-1-7-1

WP SECOND INNINGS

S. Hendricks lbw Lorgat	28
S. Gabriels c Khan b Manack	1
I. Behardien c Munshi b Lorgat	44
N. White b Parbhoo	0
F. Davids not out	50
D. Kemp c Khan b Ramnarain	51
EXTRAS	18
TOTAL	192/5 dec

FALL OF WICKETS: 1/6; 2/83; 3/84; 4/96; 5/192

BOWLING: Ramnarain 8,3-2-21-1; Manack 7-1-11-1; Dindar 2-0-12-0; Lorgat 17-5-46-2; Muller 3-0-9-0; Parbhoo 18-2-64-1; Munshi 2-0-11-0

TRANSVAAL FIRST INNINGS

M. Desai b Barnes	6
I. Munshi run out	10
I. Khan lbw February	9
M. Abdullah b Barnes	16
H. Lorgat c Cupido b Barnes	61
N. Dindar c Behardien b Gabriels	54
AH. Manack c Cupido b Barnes	32
N. Muller lbw Barnes	0
Y. Begg run out	9
D. Parbhoo lbw Barnes	6
N. Ramnarain not out	4
EXTRAS	26
TOTAL	233

FALL OF WICKETS: 1/19; 2/21; 3/47; 4/54; 5/156; 6/191; 7/195; 8/217; 9/222

BOWLING: Barnes 28.2-3-53-6; February 32-10-68-1; Gabriels 19-2-58-1; Davids 8-2-13-0; Galant 4-1-15-0

TRANSVAAL SECOND INNINGS

M. Desai ret hurt	8
I. Munshi b February	4
I. Khan not out	13
M. Abdullah not out	5
EXTRAS	4
TOTAL	34/1

FALL OF WICKETS: 1/10

BOWLING: Barnes 2-0-7-0; February 3-0-12-1; Gabriels 4-1-7-0; Thomas 2-0-4-0

MATCH DRAWN

Big-hitting Davids clobbers the EP attack to lead WP to an exciting victory

THE RETURN game against EP proved to be yet another exciting clash between the two top teams in SACB, as WP scraped to a tense five-wicket victory with only seven balls to spare.

Yet WP seemed to be strolling to an easy victory after taking a commanding first innings lead of 201. Barney Mohammed, recalled to the side to replace Vincent Barnes who had quit as captain, claimed 5/30 to help dismiss EP for a paltry 120. Solid middle order contributions from Faiek Davids (64) and Deon Kemp (66) saw WP make a potentially match-winning 321 in their first innings.

But EP, led by a patient 96 from opener Roderick Yearwood, replied with a resolute 333 in their second innings, but more importantly, batted until after tea on the final day. Set to score 133 in 15 minutes and 20 overs, WP reached their target in 21,5 overs thanks to a pugnacious unbeaten 63 from Davids who clobbered 23 in one over from Ashwell Frans.

EP FIRST INNINGS
G. Miller c Cupido b Seconds 20
R. Yearwood c Kemp b Mohammed 0
S. Abrahams c Rasmus b Mohammed 2
A. Peters c Davids b Seconds 6
V. Frans c Cupido b Davids 11
K. Majola c Seconds b Mohammed 16
R. Dolley c Adams b Mohammed 10
P. Hufkie c Kemp b Mohammed 16
G. Paul c Seconds b Gabriels 17
S. George c Davids b Gabriels 3
M. Mali not out 2
EXTRAS.....17
TOTAL.....120

FALL OF WICKETS: 1/1; 2/4; 3/20; 4/31; 5/43; 6/71; 7/94; 8/98; 9/117

BOWLING: Mohammed 15-3-30-5; February 15-8-20-0; Seconds 7-1-16-2; Davids 10-3-34-1; Gabriels 4-2-3-2

EP SECOND INNINGS
G. Miller c Mohammed b Davids 32
R. Yearwood c sub b Gabriels 96
S. Abrahams st Cupido b Gabriels 9
A. Peters c Mohammed b Gabriels 0
V. Frans c February b Seconds 45
K. Majola c & b Gabriels.....24
R. Dolley b Dyason.....26
P. Hufkie st Cupido b Gabriels 43
S. George c Cupido b Gabriels 13
G. Paul c Adams b Davids 5
M. Mali not out 1
EXTRAS.....39
TOTAL.....333

FALL OF WICKETS: 1/69; 2/80; 3/81; 4/170; 5/233; 6/242; 7/279; 8/325; 9/331

BOWLING: Mohammed 22-8-27-0; February 22-7-38-0; Gabriels 41-16-47-6; Seconds 15-1-34-1; Davids 28,4-5-95-2; Thomas 3-0-7-0; Dyason 11-1-46-1

WP FIRST INNINGS
Y. Adams b Mali.....15
*S. Gabriels c Hufkie b Dolley 13
C. Dyason c Abrahams b Dolley 30
D. Kemp c Dolley b Paul 66
F. Davids c sub b Paul 64
M. Rasmus run out 23
Y. Thomas c Yearwood b Mali 43
+R. Cupido b Mali 29
E. Mohammed b Mali 11
R. February lbw Frans.....1
T. Seconds not out.....6
EXTRAS.....20
TOTAL.....321

FALL OF WICKETS: 1/27; 2/43; 3/104; 4/139; 5/202; 6/234; 7/295; 8/310; 9/311

BOWLING: Mali 32.1-4-96-4; Paul 26-4-125-2; Majola 7-1-23-0; Dolley 28-11-40-2; George 3-0-5-0; Frans 6-2-12-1

WP SECOND INNINGS
Y. Adams run out.....22
C. Dyason b George 10
D. Kemp b Mali 12
F. Davids not out 63
Y. Thomas c Hufkie b Mali 5
E. Mohammed b Mali 0
R. February not out 11
EXTRAS.....11
TOTAL.....134/5

FALL OF WICKETS: 1/37; 2/38; 3/51; 4/75; 5/85

BOWLING: Mali 11-0-47-3; George 6-0-35-1; Frans 3-0-30-0; Dolley 1,5-0-11-0;

WP WON BY FIVE WICKETS

WP vs Natal
18-20 February
1989
in
Durban

New Cap Hendrikse helps steer WP to an easy away victory over Natal

STELLENBOSCH ALL ROUNDER Charles Hendrikse made an impressive entry into the senior side with a fine allround performance at Tills Crescent. He troubled the Natal batsmen with his guile and accuracy, taking 3/16 in as many overs, as the home side were dismissed for 163 in their first innings

Hendrikse showed his allround ability with a fluent unbeaten 31 to allow Seraj Gabriels to declare at 226/8, giving WP a handy first innings lead of 63.

The bearded Stellenbosch all rounder's stakes continued to rise as he claimed career-best figures of 6/20 in the Natal second innings, to finish with the impressive match figures of 9/36. The home side were dismissed for 171, leaving WP the easy task of scoring 109 for victory.

NATAL FIRST INNINGS

E. Mall c Cupido b February	8
G. Mohamed c Hendrikse b February	23
LD. Naidoo st Cupido b Dyason	8
S. Govender lbw Hendrikse	3
M. Khan b Hendrikse	4
S. Kushor b Hendrikse	0
F. Suleman b Gabriels	44
Sh. Moodley run out	17
Sa. Moodley not out	32
S. Jeram c Kemp b February	0
V. Kistnasamy lbw Davids	13
EXTRAS	11
TOTAL	163

FALL OF WICKETS: 1/17; 2/39; 3/42; 4/50; 5/50; 6/58; 7/111; 8/116; 9/117

BOWLING: Mohammed 11-4-17-0; February 22-8-30-3; Davids 15,1-5-18-1; Gabriels 27-7-56-1; Hendrikse 16-8-16-3; Dyason 10 -3-15-1

NATAL SECOND INNINGS

E. Mall lbw Hendrikse	57
G. Mohamed st Cupido b Davids	7
L. Naidoo lbw Hendrikse	51
S. Kushor b Hendrikse	0
M. Khan c Rasmus b Gabriels	1
S. Govender c Cupido b Davids	27
F. Suleman c Gabriels b Hendrikse	5
Sh. Moodley b Hendrikse	0
Sa. Moodley not out	6
S. Jeram run out	0
V. Kistnasamy lbw Hendrikse	0
EXTRAS	17
TOTAL	171

FALL OF WICKETS: 1/12; 2/97; 3/97; 4/98; 5/155; 6/163; 7/163; 8/166; 9/169

BOWLING: Mohammed 10-3-17-0; February 18-6-23-0; Davids 18-3-41-2; Gabriels 22-3-38-1; Dyason 5-0-9-0; Hendrikse 15,2-3-20-6; Thomas 4-2-6-0

WP FIRST INNINGS

Y. Adams lbw Khan	26
*S. Gabriels c Kushor b Jeram	4
C. Dyason run out	40
D. Kemp c Kushor b Khan	24
F. Davids c Suleman b Sh Moodley	4
M. Rasmus c Kushor b Khan	31
Y. Thomas c Kushor b Khan	17
E. Mohammed b Sa Moodley	28
C. Hendrikse not out	31
+R. Cupido not out	3
EXTRAS	18
TOTAL	226/8 dec

FALL OF WICKETS: 1/15; 2/62; 3/98; 4/103; 5/115; 6/158; 7/163; 8/212

BOWLING: Sa Moodley 12-2-35-1; Jeram 9-1-19-1; Sh Moodley 20-3-71-1; Khan 26-5 -57-4; Kistnasamy 5-0-!! -0; Naidoo 3-1-15-0

WP SECOND INNINGS

Y. Adams run out	9
R. Cupido b Khan	17
S. Gabriels not out	38
D. Kemp c sub b Sh Moodley	31
F. Davids not out	7
EXTRAS	8
TOTAL	110/3

FALL OF WICKETS: 1/16; 2/51; 3/97

BOWLING: Jerram 4-1-7-0; Sa Moodley 4-0-9-0; Naidoo 6-1-18-0; Khan 7-1-24-1; Sh Moodley 8-0-23-1; Suleman 6-1-21-0

WP WON BY 7 WICKETS

Highveld thunderstorm – and some defiant batting by Davids – helps WP to a draw

WP vs Tvl 11-13 March 1989 in Johannesburg

TRANSVAAL WERE in the driving seat when rain intervened on the final day to scupper the match as a contest.

Haroon Lorgat, who took 6/53 with his seamers, was instrumental in helping to dismiss WP for a moderate 194. Nazeer Dindar then scored a fine 132 to guide his side to a commanding first innings lead of 124.

After Reggie February and Faiek Davids had removed the first four Transvaal batsmen for only 60, Dindar and Lorgat, as was the case in the first-round game, seized the initiative with a 5th wicket stand of 95, to lay the platform for their solid first innings total of 312.

WP were struggling at 88/5 in their second innings, before Faiek Davids (62*), who scored his fifth half century in as many matches, and Yunus Thomas (6*) were able to negotiate the Transvaal bowling until the heavens opened.

WP FIRST INNINGS

*S. Gabriels b Manack	8
Y. Adams c Dindar b Lorgat	31
C. Dyason b Lorgat	10
+R. Cupido c Begg b Lorgat	2
D. Kemp b Mangera	4
F. Davids c Khan b Lorgat	46
M. Rasmus c Dindar b Lorgat	9
Y. Thomas c Khan b Ramnarain	28
C. Hendrikse c Ramnarain b Lorgat	14
E. Mohammed not out	25
R. February c Begg b Mangera	4
EXTRAS	13
TOTAL	194

FALL OF WICKETS: 1/20; 2/48; 3/58; 4/61; 5/80; 6/103; 7/122; 8/149; 9/184

BOWLING: Manack 16-2-44-1; Ramnarain 8-1-14-1; Lorgat 25-7-53-6; Dindar 4-1-12-0; Mangera 7,4-0-32-2; Jabaar 11-2-26-0

WP SECOND INNINGS

Y. Adams c Begg b Manack	4
R. Cupido lbw Lorgat	18
C. Dyason c Abdullah b Lorgat	11
D. Kemp b Manack	0
F. Davids not out	62
M. Rasmus run out	11
Y. Thomas not out	6
EXTRAS	12
TOTAL	124/5

FALL OF WICKETS: 1/25; 2/36; 3/41; 4/41; 5/88

BOWLING: Manack 11-5-27-2; Ramnarain 10-3-22-0; Lorgat 10-3-28-2; Jabaar 5-1-16-0; Mangera 5,4-1-19-0

TRANSVAAL FIRST INNINGS

E. Amod b February	2
I. Munshi c Cupido b February	4
I. Khan c Cupido b Davids	17
M. Abdullah c Cupido b Davids	14
N. Dindar not out	132
H. Lorgat c Cupido b February	43
AH. Manack c Cupido b Hendrikse	4
A. Jabaar c Hendrikse b Dyason	31
M. Mangera b Hendrikse	22
Y. Begg c Kemp b February	0
N. Ramnarain c Adams b Dyason	14
EXTRAS	35
TOTAL	318

FALL OF WICKETS: 1/4; 2/20; 3/41; 4/60; 5/135; 6/157; 7/218; 8/265; 9/281

BOWLING: Mohammed 18-2-62-0; February 21-4-63-4; Davids 23-2-76-2; Hendrikse 16-2-48-2; Gabriels 9-2-29-0; Dyason 1,5-0-5-2

MATCH DRAWN
WP WON HOWA BOWL

WP Cricket Board First Class Averages 1988/89

BATTING

Name	Matches	Inns	NO	Hs	Runs	Ave	50	100
Faiek Davids	5	10	4	89	436	72,67	5	
Deon Kemp	6	11	2	148*	341	37,88	2	1
Stuart Hendricks	3	5	0	63	170	34,00	1	
Seraj Gabriels	6	9	1	60	225	28,13	2	
Ismail Behardien	2	4	0	44	108	27,00		
Yunus Thomas	6	9	2	56	180	25,71	1	
Ebrahim Mohammed	3	4	1	28	64	21,33		
Clinton Dyason	3	5	0	40	101	20,20		
Mark Rasmus	3	4	0	31	74	18,50		
Yusuf Adams	3	6	0	31	107	17,83		
Randall Cupido	6	8	2	29	99	16,50		
Reggie February	5	5	2	21*	39	13,00		
Nazeem White	3	5	0	21	50	10,00		

Also batted: Gerry Miller (2), Vincent Barnes (0* and 2), Mogamat Galant (14 and 14) Faizel Ebrahim (14), Nasser Antulay (10), Trevor Seconds (6*), Charles Hendrikse (31* and 14).

***Salie Green played in one match but did not bat

FIELDING:

Wicketkeepers: 23 – Randall Cupido (19 ct and 4st)

Catches:

5 – Deon Kemp; 4 – Faiek Davids; 3 – Stuart Hendricks, Faizel Ebrahim, Yusuf Adams; 2 – Seraj Gabriels, Vincent Barnes, Mogamat Galant, Ebrahim Mohammed, Trevor Seconds, Mark Rasmus, Charles Hendrikse; 1 – Ismail Behardien, Nazeem White, Reggie February

BOWLING

Name	Overs	Mdns	Wkts	Runs	Ave	Best Bowling	5wi	10m
Vincent Barnes	91,2	27	22	148	6,73	6/32 v EP	4	1
Charles Hendrikse	47,2	13	11	84	7,64	6/20v Natal	1	
Seraj Gabriels	155,1	41	15	307	20,47	6/47 v EP	1	
Faiek Davids	128	31	11	313	28,45	2/12 v EP		
Ebrahim Mohammed	75	20	5	153	30,60	5/30 v EP	1	
Reggie February	178	63	9	323	35,89	4/63 v Tvl		

Also bowled: Deon Kemp 3-0-9-0; Yunus Thomas 9-2-17-0; Nilton Muller 10-3-12-2; Mogamat Galant 7-2-19-0; Salie Green 21-7-35-5; Trevor Seconds 22-2-56-3; Clinton Dyason 16,5-3-29-3

Great debut for Manack – but WP have to fight hard to earn a draw against EP

WP vs EP
25-27 November 1989 in Cape Town

JACK MANACK, who had moved to Cape Town from Johannesburg, made an outstanding debut for WP when he took 5/39 off 28,5 overs to help dismiss EP for a modest 190. Left-arm paceman Neville Booysen grabbed 3/36 to help reduce EP to 70/6 before André Peters (70) and Richard Dolley (29) added an invaluable 90 for the 7th wicket.

The experiment of using wicketkeeper Randall Cupido as an opening batsman failed. He failed to score – and with fellow opener, Seraj Gabriels, also being cheaply dismissed, WP slumped to 65/8 in their first innings. Manack (27) and Charles Hendrikse (27) spared the home side's blushes with a face-saving 9th wicket stand of 42, but EP would still have been happy with their first innings lead of 69. EP then set WP a victory target of 272 in even time. But, although Faiek Davids made a typically agressive 91 in just over an hour, he received little support. In the end, WP were forced to play out a tense draw.

EP FIRST INNINGS

G. Miller c White b Manack	2
R. Yearwood c Manack b Davids	23
A. Coetzee c Behardien b Booysen	9
S. Abrahams b Manack	10
A. Peters c Gabriels b Manack	70
P. Hufkie b Manack	0
K. Majola c Cupido b Muller	15
R. Dolley b Booysen	29
G. Koen b Booysen	0
R. Bergins c Cupido b Manack	3
M. Mali not out	0
EXTRAS	29
TOTAL	190

FALL OF WICKETS: 1/12; 2/35; 3/50; 4/63; 5/64; 6/70; 7/160; 8/160; 9/189

BOWLING: Booysen 23-6-36-3; Manack 28,5-11-39-5; Gabriels 12-8-9-0; Hendrikse 17-10-22-0; Davids 10-3-28-1; Thomas 1-0-1-0; Muller 13-5-26-1; Dammert 1-1-0-0

EP SECOND INNINGS

G. Miller c Cupido b Manack	28
R. Yearwood b Gabriels	7
K. Majola b Booysen	12
S. Abrahams c Cupido b Booysen	4
A. Peters b Manack	18
P. Hufkie b Davids	38
A. Coetzee lbw Hendrikse	38
R. Dolley not out	17
G. Koen c Behardien b Hendrikse	14
R. Bergins c Cupido b Gabriels	0
M. Mali c Muller b Gabriels	0
EXTRAS	16
TOTAL	192

FALL OF WICKETS: 1/19; 2/32; 3/39; 4/76; 5/79; 6/139; 7/164; 8/185; 9/185

BOWLING: Manack 21-7-44-2; Booysen 15-2-24-2; Muller 5-0-21-0; Gabriels 16.5-2-33-3; Hendrikse 17-9-22-2; Dammert 2-0-9-0; Davids 6-1-23-1

WP FIRST INNINGS

*S. Gabriels b Mali	2
+R. Cupido c Coetzee b Bergins	0
I. Behardien c Yearwood b Koen	29
N. White c Coetzee b Mali	9
F. Davids st Coetzee b Koen	1
B. Dammert c Yearwood b Dolley	10
Y. Thomas c Coetzee b Koen	3
N. Muller c Coetzee b Dolley	4
AH. Manack b Dolley	27
C. Hendrikse lbw Mali	27
N. Booysen not out	3
EXTRAS	6
TOTAL	121

FALL OF WICKETS: 1/4; 2/5; 3/25; 4/28; 5/56; 6/56; 7/59; 8/65; 9/117

BOWLING: Mali 20-10-28-3; Bergins 9-4-11-1; Koen 22-10-33-3; Dolley 18,2-6-43-3

WP SECOND INNINGS

S. Gabriels b Bergins	12
B. Dammert c Coetzee b Mali	19
N. Booysen b Bergins b Mali	19
F. Davids c Majola b Mali	91
I. Behardien c Bergins b Majola	11
N. Muller c Peters b Dolley	4
C. Hendrikse run out	7
Y. Thomas b Mali	6
AH. Manack run out	3
N. White not out	7
R. Cupido not out	1
EXTRAS	11
TOTAL	191/9

FALL OF WICKETS: 1/24; 2/41; 3/66; 4/87; 5/121; 6/155; 7/167; 8/173; 9/181

BOWLING: Mali 20-3-81-4; Bergins 3-0-20-1; Majola 7-1-45-1; Dolley 9-2-34-1

MATCH DRAWN

Another fine allround display by Davids guides WP to an innings victory over Transvaal

A SUPERB allround performance by the in-form Faiek Davids enabled WP to comfortably beat Transvaal by an innings and 66 runs at Lenasia.

Coming to the wicket with his side struggling at 21/3 Davids struck a superb 106 – his third Howa Bowl century – and together with Barry Dammert (57), added 175 for the 5th wicket.

An unbeaten 6th wicket stand of 97 between Yunus Thomas (59*) and Nilton Muller (28*) enabled Seraj Gabriels to declare on a healthy 305/6.

Davids then grabbed four wickets in each innings to end with a match analysis of 8/40, and together with Jack Manack, who finished the match with 8/75 against his former team mates, was instrumental in helping to dismiss the home side cheaply twice within the space of a day to score a vital win.

WP vs Transvaal 27-29 December 1989 in Johannesburg

WP FIRST INNINGS
*S. Gabriels c Abdullah b Dindar 1
F. Ebrahim c Lorgat b Dindar 7
I. Behardien c Mangera b Sarang 5
+N White c & b Dindar..............................4
F. Davids b Manack.................................106
B. Dammert c Jabaar b Kolia....................57
Y. Thomas not out....................................59
N. Muller not out.......................................28
EXTRAS..............38
TOTAL ....305/6 dec
FALL OF WICKETS: 1/3; 2/21; 3/21; 4/27; 5/202; 6/208
BOWLING: Sarang 9-3-21-1; Dindar 10-1-29-3; Lorgat 24-2-63-0; Jabaar 15-3-38-0; Manack 13-3-55-1; Kolia 18,2-5-61-1

TRANSVAAL FIRST INNINGS
M. Jajbhai lbw Barnes................................22
I. Munshi b Davids.....................................30
I. Khan c Behardien b Manack 0
M. Abdullah c Hendrikse b Barnes 6
H. Lorgat c Gabriels b Davids 7
N. Dindar lbw Hendrikse 7
H. Manack c Behardien b Davids.................0
A. Jabaar c White b Manack.......................27
A. Kolia c Behardien b Davids......................2
M. Sarang c Behardien b Manack 4
M. Mangera not out......................................1
EXTRAS..............28
TOTAL 134
FALL OF WICKETS:
1/48; 2/49; 3/64; 4/73; 5/89; 6/89; 7/93; 8/116; 9/133
BOWLING: Barnes 10-0-38-2; Manack 11,4-3-27-3; Davids 10-2-11-4; Gabriels 2-0-16-0; Ebrahim 1-1-0-0; Hendrikse 7-2-14-1

TRANSVAAL SECOND INNINGS
(FOLLOWED ON)
M. Jajbhai c White b Manack 5
I. Munshi c White b Manack......................25
I. Khan c White b Barnes 1
M. Abdullah c Behardien b Manack 26
H. Lorgat c White b Davids 6
N. Dindar c Ebrahim b Davids.....................7
H. Manack b Manack 7
A. Jabaar c Behardien b Manack 11
A. Kolia c Ebrahim b Davids........................0
M. Sarang c Dammert b Davids....................0
M. Mangera not out......................................0
EXTRAS..............17
TOTAL 105
FALL OF WICKETS: 1/10; 2/15; 3/61; 4/73; 5/73; 6/88; 7/93; 8/95; 9/105
BOWLING: Barnes 7-1-10-1; Manack 18-3-48-5; Davids 12-4-29-4; Hendrikse 1-0-1-0

WP WON BY AN INNINGS AND 66 RUNS

Behardien's maiden century turns WP's match against Natal into a doddle

**WP vs Natal
1-3 January
1990
in Durban**

THE AWAY double-header against Transvaal and Natal provided a rich harvest of points for WP as they strolled to a comfortable eight-wicket win against whipping boys Natal in Durban.

After dismissing the home side for a moderate 180, WP took a commanding first innings lead of 92, thanks to a maiden Howa Bowl century by Ismail Behardien who made a polished 108. Together with the stylish Nazeem White, who made 72, Behardien added 164 for the third wicket as WP took control of the game.

Fuad Benjamin then destroyed the Natal second innings batting with his off breaks to finish with career-best figures of 6/35 as the home side were dismissed for a meagre 115, leaving WP with the easy task of making 24 for victory.

NATAL FIRST INNINGS

E. Mall b Barnes 6
Sa. Govender b Manack 6
M. Patel lbw Benjamin 10
E. Govender c Manack b Benjamin 41
F. Suleman c White b Muller 27
S. Govender c Davids b Hendrikse 46
P. Moodley c Kemp b Benjamin 4
R. Soobramoney b Barnes 15
LD. Naidoo b Barnes 1
S. Moodley not out 2
V. Kistnasamy b Hendrikse 2

EXTRAS 20
TOTAL 180

FALL OF WICKETS: 1/14; 2/18; 3/57; 4/81; 5/128; 6/138; 7/171; 8/175; 9/175

BOWLING: Barnes 23-11-31-3; Manack 13.2-4-24-1; Hendrikse 3,2-1-12-2; Benjamin 24-4-48-3; Davids 5-0-14-0; Ebrahim 9-1-17-0; Muller 5-0-14-1

NATAL SECOND INNINGS

E. Mall c Dammert b Benjamin 14
Sa. Govender b Barnes 0
M. Patel run out 39
E. Govender c White b Barnes 23
S. Moodley st White b Benjamin 0
S. Govender c Behardien b Benjamin 2
F. Suleman c White b Benjamin 6
P. Moodley c sub (Thomas)b B'jamin 0
R. S'bramoney c Behardien b B'jamin 6
LD. Naidoo not out 3
V. Kistnasamy lbw Hendrikse 4

EXTRAS 18
TOTAL 115

FALL OF WICKETS: 1/5; 2/32; 3/83; 4/85; 5/86; 6/89; 7/89; 8/101; 9/105

BOWLING: Barnes 17-6-25-2; Davids 4-1-8-0; Hendrikse 8,1-1-19-1; Benjamin 20-6-35-6; Ebrahim 2-0-7-0; Muller 2-1-3-0

WP FIRST INNINGS

F. Ebrahim c Patel b S.Moodley 0
B. Dammert lbw Kistnasamy 6
I. Behardien run out 108
+N. White c Patel b E. Govender 76
F. Davids b E. Govender 27
D. Kemp c Soobramoney b Naidoo 0
N. Muller c & b P. Moodley 17
C. Hendrikse c Sa Govender b P.Moodley 21
*V. Barnes c Patel b Naidoo 0
F. Benjamin lbw Naidoo 2
AH. Manack not out 2

EXTRAS 13
TOTAL 272

FALL OF WICKETS: 1/10; 2/22; 3/186; 4/204; 5/204; 6/238; 7/253; 8/258; 9/270

BOWLING: S. Moodley 10-3-23-1; Kistnasamy 10-1-43-1; P. Moodley 22,2-0-76-2; Naidoo 20-4-45-3; E. Govender 14-2-47-2; Suleman 7-1-13-0; Mall 3-0-12-0

WP SECOND INNINGS

F. Ebrahim lbw P. Moodley 0
B. Dammert c & b P. Moodley 5
I. Behardien not out 14
N. White not out 5

EXTRAS 0
TOTAL 24/2

FALL OF WICKETS: 1/0; 2/17

BOWLING: P. Moodley 4-1-10-2; Patel 3.3-1-14-0

WP WON BY 8 WICKETS

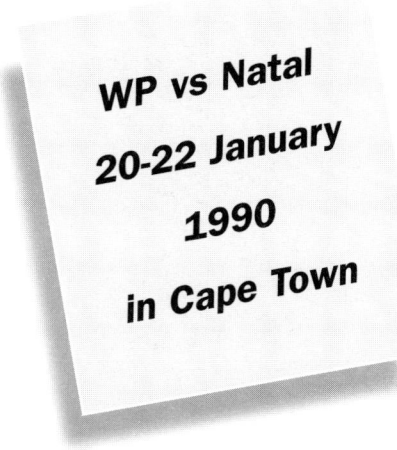

WP cruise to another victory against the Howa Bowl's whipping boys

NATAL WERE again soundly beaten, just three weeks after being crushed in their home match against Western Province.

This victory put Western Province firmly on the road to a fourth successive Howa Bowl title.

Vincent Barnes, who had returned from his self-imposed exile, grabbed yet another fiver, this time against the hapless Natalians, who managed to reach 142, thanks to a resilient, unbeaten 57 by Stanley Govender.

WP never looked back from the time newcomer Ebrahim Gafieldien (48) and captain Seraj Gabriels (52) added 107 for the first wicket. Solid contributions from the middle order saw the home side reach a first innings total of 326, giving them a commanding lead of 184.

Seamers Faiek Davids (3/27) and Nilton Muller (2/11) did most of the damage as Natal were dismissed for 162 in their second innings. It was WP's fourth successive innings victory over the visitors in Cape Town.

NATAL FIRST INNINGS

E. Mall c White b Muller	5
J. Chellan c White b Davids	0
M. Patel b Hendrikse	11
SA. Govender c White b Barnes	0
E. Govender c Hendrikse b Barnes	13
S. Govender not out	57
F. Suleman st White b Gabriels	15
Y. Moorad c White b Barnes	0
LD. Naidoo st White b Benjamin	2
P. Moodley c White b Barnes	3
S. Moodley c Gabriels b Barnes	5
EXTRAS	31
TOTAL	142

FALL OF WICKETS: 1/2; 2/14; 3/16; 4/43; 5/43; 6/101; 7/107; 8/114; 9/129

BOWLING: Barnes 18.3-6-23-5; Davids 14-4-28-1; Muller 6-3-9-1; Hendrikse 12-4-19-1; Benjamin 13-2-24-1; Gabriels 5-2-8-1

NATAL SECOND INNINGS

E. Mall c White b Davids	9
J. Chellan run out	32
M. Patel lbw Davids	0
SA. Govender run out	0
E. Govender c Barnes b Muller	12
S. Govender lbw Muller	4
F. Suleman b Benjamin	30
Y. Moorad c Thomas b Barnes	13
S. Moodley b Davids	0
L. Naidoo not out	9
P. Moodley st White b Gabriels	16
EXTRAS	37
TOTAL	162

FALL OF WICKETS: 1/33; 2/33; 3/33; 4/55; 5/68; 6/85; 7/115; 8/119; 9/141

BOWLING: Barnes 17-4-23-1; Davids 15-3-27-3; Hendrikse 9-3-21-0; Benjamin 11-4-14-1; Muller 9-3-11-2; Gabriels 17,1-5-28-1; Thomas 1-0-1-0

WP FIRST INNINGS

E. Gafieldien c Moorad b P. Moodley	48
*S. Gabriels st Moorad b P. Moodley	52
I. Behardien lbw Mall	17
+N. White c Suleman b P. Moodley	3
F. Davids c Patel b L. Naidoo	19
B. Dammert lbw P. Moodley	7
Y. Thomas c Sa. Govender b P. Moodley	30
N. Muller b Suleman	74
C. Hendrikse c Moorad b L. Naidoo	14
V. Barnes b P. Moodley	17
F. Benjamin not out	16
EXTRAS	29
TOTAL	326

FALL OF WICKETS: 1/107; 2/126; 3/130; 4/138; 5/145; 6/177; 7/201; 8/233; 9/270

BOWLING: S. Moodley 13-1-37-0; E. Govender 5-1-13-0; L. Naidoo 32-3-55-2; Suleman 9-1-27-1; P. Moodley 39-4-139-6; Mall 11-0-26-1

WP WON BY AN INNINGS AND 22 RUNS

WP old boy Jabaar helps Transvaal to a surprise away victory over WP

WP vs Transvaal 3-5 March 1990 at Florida Park Cape Town

AFTER THEIR crushing innings win in Lenasia, WP were confident of taking another step closer to retaining the Howa Bowl when they hosted Transvaal for the return encounter at Florida Park.

After helping to restrict WP to a moderate first innings total of 240 by taking 4/77 with his seamers, Hussein Manack then played a decisive innings of 72 to help his side to a first innings lead of 57. Together with former WP captain, Armien Jabaar, who made a valuable 38, Manack added a priceless 81 for the eighth wicket to wrest the initiative from the home side.

WP were stunned by an inspired opening spell from Mohammed Sarang and Haroon Lorgat, who reduced them to 12/5 in their second innings. Jabaar claimed three wickets with his leg spin to have WP facing the possibility of an innings defeat when they were tottering at 53/9. It was only a defiant 10th wicket stand of 60 between Yunus Thomas (52) and Vincent Barnes (16*) that restored respectability to the WP innings as they eventually reached 113. Transvaal comfortably reached their victory target of 57 to score only their second win in Cape Town – their first since 1975.

WP FIRST INNINGS

E. Gafieldien c Abdullah b Manack	15
*S. Gabriels c Jajbhai b Manack	11
I. Behardien b Sarang	38
+N. White b Begg b Sarang	6
F. Davids c Sarang b Manack	48
D. Kemp c Manack b Jabaar	31
AH. Manack c Mentor b Manack	11
Y. Thomas st Begg b Lorgat	41
N. Muller c Lorgat b Sarang	6
V. Barnes st Begg b Jabaar	5
F. Benjamin not out	10
EXTRAS	18
TOTAL	240

FALL OF WICKETS: 1/24; 2/45; 3/72; 4/79; 5/131; 6/163; 7/174; 8/193; 9/225

BOWLING: Sarang 25-1-47-3; Lorgat 37-12-68-1; Jabaar 25-12-30-2; Manack 27-5-77-4

WP SECOND INNINGS

E. Gafieldien c Y. Begg b Sarang	0
S. Gabriels b Sarang	0
I. Behardien b Jabaar	33
N. White b Y.Begg b Lorgat	1
F. Davids c Jabaar b Lorgat	1
D. Kemp b Lorgat	0
AH. Manack b Sarang	1
Y. Thomas b Munshi	52
N. Muller b Jabaar	2
F. Benjamin b Jabaar	0
V. Barnes not out	16
EXTRAS	7
TOTAL	113

FALL OF WICKETS: 1/0; 2/1; 3/2; 4/12; 5/12; 6/21; 7/43; 8/53; 9/53

BOWLING: Sarang 18-6-27-3; Lorgat 20-7-29-3; Jabaar 18-6-44-3; Munshi 2.4-0-6-1

TRANSVAAL FIRST INNINGS

M. Jajbhai c White b Barnes	8
I. Munshi b Barnes	29
I. Khan c Kemp b Benjamin	73
R. Begg c Gabriels b Barnes	3
M. Abdullah c White b Manack	4
A. Mentor c Behardien b Barnes	2
H. Lorgat c Manack b Gabriels	1
H. Manack st White b Gabriels	72
A. Jabaar b Gabriels	38
Y. Begg c Manack b Benjamin	19
M. Sarang not out	4
EXTRAS	44
TOTAL	297

FALL OF WICKETS: 1/27; 2/72; 3/84; 4/97; 5/108; 6/113; 7/177; 8/258; 9/273

BOWLING: Barnes 28-10-56-4; Manack 32-4-57-1; Davids 19-10-24-0; Benjamin 22,4-6-63-2; Gabriels 23-8-51-3; Thomas 1-0-2-0

TRANSVAAL SECOND INNINGS

M. Jajbhai b Manack	7
I. Munshi not out	27
M. Abdullah c White b Manack	0
I. Khan c & b Barnes	0
H. Lorgat not out	22
EXTRAS	2
TOTAL	58/3

FALL OF WICKETS: 1/25; 2/25; 3/30

BOWLING: Barnes 5-0-40-1; Manack 4-0-16-2

TRANSVAAL WON BY 7 WICKETS

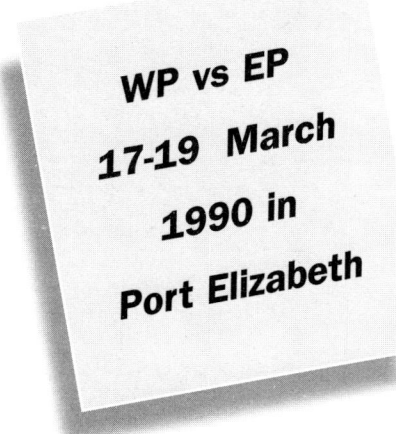

WP vs EP
17-19 March
1990 in
Port Elizabeth

Seconds and Gafieldien inspire WP to a fourth Howa Bowl triumph in a row

WITH EP still having an outside chance to win the Howa Bowl, provided they won outright, and picked up enough bonus points, they gambled by preparing a green top for the visitors.

The move backfired badly when Seraj Gabriels won the toss and a gleeful Jack Manack made merry, to claim a career-best 7/17 to help skittle the home side for 50.

With WP having gained enough bonus points to retain their title, Gabriels declared the first innings at 1/0, thereby denying EP any chance of picking up vital bonus points, which may have kept them in the hunt.

Left-arm seamer Trevor Seconds was the scourge of the EP batsmen in the second innings, claiming 6/47 as the home side were dismissed for 155. The victory target of 205 was a tough ask on a tricky pitch, but opener Ebrahim Gafieldien played magnificently for his 86 before being run out when he seemed set for a well-deserved century.

However, the platform was set as captain Seraj Gabriels (33*) and Jack Manack (10*) steered their side to a three-wicket victory inside two days, to give WP their fourth consecutive Howa Bowl title.

EP FIRST INNINGS

R. Yearwood c Barnes b Manack	2
M. Van Eck c White b Manack	0
K. Majola c White b Davids	6
A. Peters c White b Manack	5
S. Abrahams c Seconds b Manack	4
A. Coetzee b Manack	5
R. Dolley run out	0
D. Reid not out	9
M. Majola c sub (V Sch'wyk) b Manack	2
M. Mali c sub (V Sch'wyk) b Manack	0
T. Kadi c Kemp b Gabriels	8
EXTRAS	9
TOTAL	50

FALL OF WICKETS: 1/6; 2/7; 3/19; 4/19; 5/27; 6/31; 7/37; 8/37; 9/37

BOWLING: Barnes 6-3-7-0; Manack 15-7-17-7; Davids 9-4-14-1; Gabriels 0,4-0-3-1

WP FIRST INNINGS

R. Musson not out	0
E. Gafieldien not out	0
EXTRAS	1
TOTAL	1/0 dec

BOWLING: Mali 0.1-0-0-0

EP SECOND INNINGS

R. Yearwood b Seconds	8
M. van Eck c sub (V'Sch'wyk) b Barnes	3
K. Majola c White b Seconds	40
A. Peters c Gafieldien b Seconds	12
S. Abrahams c Gabriels b Seconds	1
A. Coetzee c White b Manack	10
R. Dolley c & b Barnes	1
D. Reid c White b Seconds	16
M. Majola not out	30
M. Mali b Seconds	1
T. Kadi run out	11
EXTRAS	22
TOTAL	155

FALL OF WICKETS: 1/10; 2/37; 3/57; 4/63; 5/90; 6/95; 7/100; 8/129; 9/131

BOWLING: Barnes 14-4-24-2; Manack 13.3-3-34-1; Seconds 19-6-47-6; Davids 6-2-8-0; Gabriels 9-1-20-0

WP SECOND INNINGS

R. Musson c Coetzee b K.Majola	15
E. Gafieldien run out	86
F. Ebrahim run out	20
+N. White st Coetzee b Abrahams	0
F. Davids b Abrahams	22
D. Kemp c Reid b Abrahams	6
Y. Thomas c K. Majola b Abrahams	1
*S. Gabriels not out	33
AH. Manack not out	10
EXTRAS	14
TOTAL	207/7

FALL OF WICKETS: 1/34; 2/91; 3/95; 4/144; 5/156; 6/158; 7/181

BOWLING: Mali 9-4-9-0; Kadi 5-1-15-0; K.Majola 18-6-40-1; Dolley 12-6-24-0; Abrahams 27-8-64-4; Reid 2-0-14-0; M. Majola 14-0-26-0; Peters 0,4-0-1-0

WP WON BY 3 WICKETS
WP WON HOWA BOWL FOR FOURTH SUCCESSIVE YEAR

WP Cricket Board First Class Averages 1989/90

BATTING

Name	Matches	Inns	NO	Hs	Runs	Ave	50	100
Faiek Davids	6	8	0	106	315	39,38	1	1
Ebrahim Gafieldien	3	5	1	86	149	37,25	1	
Ismail Behardien	5	8	1	108	255	36,42		1
Yunus Thomas	5	7	1	59*	192	32,00	2	
Nilton Muller	4	7	1	74	135	22,50	1	
Seraj Gabriels	5	7	1	52	111	18,50	1	
Barry Dammert	4	6	0	57	104	17,33	1	
Charles Hendrikse	4	4	0	27	69	17,25		
Nazeem White	6	9	2	76	111	15,86	1	
Fuad Benjamin	4	4	2	16*	28	14,00		
Abdul Haq Manack	5	6	2	27	54	13,50		
Vincent Barnes	5	4	1	17	38	12,67		
Deon Kemp	3	4	0	31	37	9,25		
Faizel Ebrahim	3	4	0	20	27	6,75		

Also batted: Randall Cupido (0 and 1); Neville Booysen (3* and 19); Rashaad Musson (0* and 15)

* Trevor Seconds played one match but did not bat

FIELDING:

Wicketkeepers: 29 – Nazeem White (24ct and 5st); 5 – Randall Cupido (5ct)

Catches:

11 – Ismail Behardien; 5 – Seraj Gabriels; 4 – Vincent Barnes, Abdul Haq Manack; 3 – Deon Kemp; 2 – Faizel Ebrahim, Charles Hendrikse, Barry Dammert; 1 – Yunus Thomas, Nilton Muller, Ebrahim Gafieldien, Rashaad Musson, Trevor Seconds, Faiek Davids

BOWLING

Name	Overs	Mdns	Wkts	Runs	Ave	Best Bowling	5i	10m
Abdul Haq Manack	157,2	42	27	306	11,33	7/17 v EP	3	
Neville Booysen	38	8	5	60	12,00	3/36 v EP		
Vincent Barnes	135,3	45	21	277	13,19	5/23 v Natal	1	
Fuad Benjamin	90,4	23	13	184	14,15	6/35 v Natal	1	
Faiek Davids	110	34	15	214	14,27	4/11 v Tvl		
Charles Hendrikse	73,5	29	7	130	18,57	2/12 v Natal		
Nilton Muller	40	12	5	84	16,80	2/11 v Natal		
Seraj Gabriels	85,4	26	9	168	18,67	3/33 v EP		

Also bowled: Barry Dammert 3-1-9-0; Yunus Thomas 3-0-4-0; Faizel Ebrahim 12-2-24-0; Trevor Seconds 19-6-47-6

WP vs Natal
17-19 November
1990 at
UWC
Cape Town

Great debuts for Meyer, Williams as WP crush Natal

PLAYING WITH a young new ball pairing of Adnaan Meyer and Henry Williams, WP were once again able to brush aside Natal with relative ease, inside two days.

Meyer made a great debut taking 5/22, while Williams also showed promise with 2/28 as the visitors were dismissed for a paltry 115 in their first innings.

Ismail Behardien (142) and Nazeem White (125*), both of whom made their second Howa Bowl centuries, came within one run of equalling the 3-day record WP partnership for any wicket of 232 set by Dickie Conrad and Viccie Moodie in 1973, when they put on 231 for the 5th wicket.

When Seraj Gabriels mercifully declared at 349/6, Natal faced a first innings deficit of 232, which they were unable to wipe out. Gabriels claimed 5/57 and Williams took 3/23 as Natal were dismissed for 104, to slump to their fifth innings defeat in as many years in Cape Town.

NATAL FIRST INNINGS

E. Mall c Conrad b Wiliams	18
E. Govender c Gabriels b Meyer	16
M. Patel c Kemp b Conrad	7
J. Chellan c White b Gabriels	4
S. Govender b Williams	25
F. Suleman b Meyer	26
R. Soobramoney c White b Meyer	1
LD. Naidoo run out	0
N. Ramnarain c White b Meyer	0
S. Jeram not out	1
A. Amra b Meyer	0
EXTRAS	19
TOTAL	117

FALL OF WICKETS: 1/32; 2/52; 3/57; 4/67; 5/112; 6/113; 7/115; 8/115; 9/116

BOWLING: Meyer 14.5-4-22-5; Williams 17-4-28-2; Hendrikse 11-3-20-0; Conrad 12-6-16-1; *Gabriels 9-3-12-1

NATAL SECOND INNINGS

E. Mall c White b Meyer	6
J. Chellan c Meyer b Conrad	13
M. Patel c Conrad b Gabriels	18
L.D Naidoo c Meyer b Williams	30
E. Govender c Gafieldien b Williams	6
S. Govender c Williams b Gabriels	19
F. Suleman b Williams	3
R. Soobramoney c White b Gabriels	0
A. Amra c Conrad b Gabriels	3
S. Jeram not out	0
N. Ramnarain st White b Gabriels	0
EXTRAS	6
TOTAL	104

FALL OF WICKETS: 1/11; 2/31; 3/48; 4/57; 5/97; 6/97; 7/98; 8/104; 9/104

BOWLING: Meyer 7-3-12-1; Williams 19-9-23-3; Conrad 6-3-6-1; Gabriels 17,4-3-57-5

WP FIRST INNINGS

E. Gafieldien c Naidoo b Ramnarain	0
F. Ebrahim c Soobramoney b Naidoo	22
I. Behardien lbw Naidoo	142
S. Conrad c E. Govender b Amra	13
D. Kemp c Naidoo b Ramnarain	13
+N. White not out	125
Y. Thomas c Amra b E. Govender	20
EXTRAS	14
TOTAL	349/6dec

FALL OF WICKETS: 1/8; 2/34; 3/51; 4/70; 5/301; 6/349

BOWLING: Ramnarain 18-7-35-2; Jeram 18-2-57-0; Naidoo 29-2-104-2; Amra 18-3-76-1; E. Mall 3-0-8-0; Patel 2-0-8-0; Suleman 8-0-41-0; E. Govender 5-0-6-1

WP WON BY AN INNINGS AND 128 RUNS

Fireworks by Conrad and Magiet as WP race to victory over EP

AFTER HIS satisfactory debut against Natal, Henry Williams was surprisingly omitted in favour of Trevor Seconds, while veteran Saait Magiet returned after coming out of retirement for the vital home game against EP.

By playing, Magiet set a record by being the only player to play in the first and last seasons of three-day non-racial cricket. Magiet announced his return with a typically belligerent 69, and together with the hard-hitting Yunus Thomas (70), rescued WP with a seventh wicket stand of 86, after WP had struggled to 59/6. Adnaan Meyer made a valuable 36 as WP stretched their first innings lead to 99.

Roderick Yearwood (58) provided the backbone of the EP second innings effort of 240, to leave WP to get 140 to secure an important victory against their perennial challengers.

Shukri Conrad (63) and Magiet (36*) smashed the EP bowling to all corners of Florida Park as WP sped to their victory target at a rate of 7 runs an over.

EP FIRST INNINGS

R. Yearwood b Seconds............15
G. Barry c Behardien b Seconds............8
K. Majola run out............3
A. Peters not out............77
S. Abrahams c White b Loggenstein............1
P. Hufkie c Behardien b Conrad............4
R. Dolley c White b Conrad............5
R. Blignaut b Conrad............4
R. Burgins ret hurt............1
F. Sarrahwitz c White b Conrad............1
M. Mali c Loggenstein b Gabriels............1

EXTRAS............21
TOTAL............141/9

FALL OF WICKETS: 1/25; 2/32; 3/43; 4/46; 5/55; 6/100; 7/120; 8/134; 9/141

BOWLING: Meyer 10-1-13 -0; Seconds 10-7-9-2; Loggenstein 12-1-41-1; Conrad 14-4-35-4; Magiet 6-0-17-0; Gabriels 0,5-0-5-1

EP SECOND INNINGS

R. Yearwood lbw Conrad............58
G. Barry c Conrad b Gabriels............17
R. Blignaut c Ebrahim b Seconds............0
A. Peters c Loggenstein b Seconds............27
S. Abrahams c White b Conrad............16
P. Hufkie c White b Loggenstein............33
K. Majola c Seconds b Gabriels............17
R. Dolley not out............27
R. Burgins b Magiet............16
F. Sarrahwitz c sub b Meyer............3
M. Mali b Meyer............0

EXTRAS............26
TOTAL............240

FALL OF WICKETS: 1/45; 2/52; 3/102; 4/121; 5/128; 6/180; 7/201; 8/230; 9/239

BOWLING: Loggenstein 20-5-38-1; Seconds 18-6-37-2; Meyer 9,4-3-24-2; Gabriels 26-5-56-2; Conrad 27-8-49-2; Magiet 8-3-10-1; Ebrahim 1-1-0-0

WP FIRST INNINGS

E. Gafieldien c Hufkie b Mali............0
F. Ebrahim lbw Mali............22
I. Behardien c Barry b Majola............20
*S. Gabriels c Dolley b Majola............5
+N. White c Hufkie b Majola............5
Y. Thomas c Barry b Majola............70
S. Conrad c Dolley b Mali............1
S. Magiet c Hufkie b Dolley............69
Q. Loggenstein b Majola............1
A. Meyer c Abrahams b Dolley............36
T. Seconds not out............6

EXTRAS............5
TOTAL............240

FALL OF WICKETS: 1/0; 2/37; 3/43; 4/51; 5/53; 6/59; 7/145; 8/148; 9/202

BOWLING: Mali 22-8-53-3; Sarrahwitz 8-1-27-0; Majola 27-10-81-5; Abrahams 3-2-5-0; Dolley 22,1-6-69-2

WP SECOND INNINGS

E. Gafieldien not out............27
F. Ebrahim c Abrahams b Burgins............2
S. Conrad c Burgins b Majola............63
S. Magiet not out............36

EXTRAS............15
TOTAL............143/2

FALL OF WICKETS: 1/4; 2/96

BOWLING: Mali 9.3-2-44-0; Burgins 8-0-38-1; Majola 3-0-24-1; Dolley 2-0-22-0

WP WON BY EIGHT WICKETS

WP vs Transvaal
5-7 January
1991
in Johannesburg

Great batting by Viljoen, White and Thomas earns WP a draw

THE BATTING efforts of new cap Andre Viljoen (48) and Nazeem White (57) stood out like beacons as the rest of the WP top and middle order succumbed to the pace and seam of Jack and Hussein Manack, who shared seven wickets between them.

After Viljoen and White had added 85 for the 3rd wicket, to lay a solid platform at 117/3, the rest of the WP batsmen failed to capitalise, collapsing to 168 all out.

At 150/4, the home side seemed set to take a substantial first innings lead, but Faiek Davids (4/28) triggered a middle-order collapse, which saw Transvaal lose their last six wickets for only 39 runs.

At 87/5 in their second innings, WP were in dire straits, but a record unbeaten sixth wicket stand of 122 between Yunus Thomas (75*) and Nazeem White (64*) guided the visitors to a secure 209/5 before rain intervened.

WP FIRST INNINGS

E. Gafieldien run out	1
A. Viljoen run out	48
I. Behardien c Begg b AH. Manack	6
+N. White c Jajbhai b Lorgat	57
F. Davids b H. Manack	0
Y. Thomas lbw H. Manack	0
S. Magiet c Jabaar b AH. Manack	11
*S. Gabriels c Khan b H. Manack	4
A. Meyer not out	2
Q. Loggenstein c Begg b AH Manack	12
V. Barnes c Khan b AH. Manack	11
EXTRAS	16
TOTAL	168

FALL OF WICKETS: 1/20; 2/32; 3/117; 4/124; 5/124; 6/125; 7/139; 8/141; 9/156

BOWLING: AH. Manack 21.3-8-49-4; Sarang 9-4-18-0; Lorgat 10-2-29-1; Jabaar 15-4-23-0; George 2-0-5-0; Jajbhai 1-0-6-0; H. Manack 12-4-22-3

WP SECOND INNINGS

E. Gafieldien c Begg b AH Manack	2
A. Viljoen c Begg b AH Manack	8
I. Behardien lbw Jabaar	48
F. Davids b H. Manack	1
N. White not out	64
Q. Loggenstein run out	0
Y. Thomas not out	75
EXTRAS	11
TOTAL	209/5

FALL OF WICKETS: 1/3; 2/20; 3/28; 4/87; 5/87

BOWLING: AH. Manack 15-3-37-2; Sarang 7-0-31-0; H. Manack 8-4-15-1; Lorgat 15-5-28-0; Jabaar 15-5-30-1; George 9-3-20-0; Jajbhai 4-1-28-0; Begg 1-0-9-0

TRANSVAAL FIRST INNINGS

M. Jajbhai b Meyer	2
I. Munshi c White b Meyer	22
I. Khan c Barnes b Davids	30
H. Manack c White b Barnes	12
M. Abdullah c White b Meyer	26
H. Lorgat c Thomas b Davids	13
AH. Manack c White b Davids	0
D. George lbw Davids	0
A. Jabaar run out	15
Y. Begg lbw Barnes	0
M. Sarang not out	3
EXTRAS	26
TOTAL	189

FALL OF WICKETS: 1/72; 2/79; 3/106; 4/135; 5/153; 6/153; 7/153; 8/174; 9/181

BOWLING: Meyer 20-3-53-3; Barnes 14-5-24-2; Loggenstein 8-1-25-0; Gabriels 18-4-28-0; Davids 15-5-28-4; Magiet 2-1-5-0

MATCH DRAWN

White's ton sees WP cruising to a clear lead at the top of the Howa Bowl log

WP vs Transvaal 26-28 January 1991 at UWC Cape Town

JACK MANACK exploited a damp UWC wicket to claim 5/26 as WP staggered to 43/7 before Adnaan Meyer (33*) and skipper Seraj Gabriels (11) nearly doubled the score with a crucial 8th wicket stand of 39.

Replying to WP's first innings total of 94, the visitors fared little better as they took a slender 11 run first innings lead at the close of the first day. With WP struggling at 10/2, Andre Viljoen (81), showing impressive powers of concentration, and Nazeem White (109), who cracked his second century of the season, regained the initiative with a record third wicket stand of 183 to allow Gabriels to declare at 282/9. This left the visitors to get a challenging victory target of 272 on the final day. Mohammed Jajbhai (67) and Hussein Manack (32) batted well, but after their dismissal, the innings quickly folded, with WP running out easy winners by 77 runs.

WP FIRST INNINGS

A. Viljoen c H. Manack b AH. Manack 2
E. Gafieldien run out................................0
I. Behardien c Begg b AH Manack..........................14
+N. White c Begg b AH. Manack...........................7
F. Davids c Jabaar b AH Manack 10
Y. Thomas c Begg b H. Manack 2
S. Magiet c Begg b AH Manack 3
*S. Gabriels c Jajbhai b H. Manack........................11
A. Meyer not out 33
V. Barnes c Munshi b Lorgat 1
F. Benjamin c Munshi b Lorgat 4

EXTRAS................7
TOTAL................94

FALL OF WICKETS: 1/2; 2/2; 3/24; 4/25; 5/34; 6/38; 7/43; 8/82; 9/84

BOWLING: AH Manack 15-6-26-5; Dindar 10-2-44-0; H. Manack 12-4-12-2; Jabaar 4-3-1-0; Lorgat 5-2-4-2

WP SECOND INNINGS

A. Viljoen c Dindar b Lorgat 81
E. Gafieldien b Dindar 0
I. Behardien handled ball 0
N. White run out 109
S. Magiet c Munshi b Lorgat 0
F. Davids c Begg b Lorgat 6
*S. Gabriels b H. Manack.............................14
Y. Thomas b H. Manack 42
A. Meyer c Jajbhai c H. Manack 6
F. Benjamin not out 1

EXTRAS...............23
TOTAL 282/9dec

FALL OF WICKETS: 1/5; 2/10; 3/193; 4/193; 5/202; 6/215; 7/263; 8/277; 9/282

BOWLING: AH. Manack 22-3-86-0; Dindar 12-6-26-1; H. Manack 9.1-1-18-3; Jabaar 15-2-44-0; Lorgat 34-12-68-3; George 3-0-13-0; Jajbhai 1-0-4-0

TRANSVAAL FIRST INNINGS

M. Jajbhai lbw Barnes 3
I. Munshi c Davids b Meyer 18
I. Khan b Barnes 0
H. Manack b Barnes...................................3
M. Abdullah b Davids 25
N. Dindar c Behardien b Gabriels........................13
D. Goerge st White b Gabriels 2
H. Lorgat c Barnes b Davids.........................12
AH. Manack c Behardien b Meyer 3
A. Jabaar c Benjamin b Meyer.........................0
Y. Begg not out 0

EXTRAS...............26
TOTAL...............105

FALL OF WICKETS: 1/6; 2/8; 3/14; 4/39; 5/79; 6/79; 7/90; 8/105; 9/105

BOWLING: Meyer 21.3-7-34-3; Barnes 8-3-13-3; Benjamin 3-1-8-0; Davids 10-5-11-2; Gabriels 6-3-10-2; Magiet 6-4-3-0

TRANSVAAL SECOND INNINGS

M. Jajbhai c Behardien b Meyer 67
I. Munshi c Thomas b Barnes 1
I. Khan c Behardien b Meyer..........................3
H. Manack c Benjamin b Gabriels........................32
M. Abdullah run out..................................11
N. Dindar c White b Benjamin 11
H. Lorgat c White b Meyer 5
AH. Manack not out...................................8
A. Jabaar c Viljoen b Barnes.........................20
D. George ht wkt b Meyer 12
Y. Begg b Barnes.....................................0

EXTRAS...............24
TOTAL...............194

FALL OF WICKETS: 1/6; 2/13; 3/86; 4/103; 5/127; 6/136; 7/168; 8/173; 9/191

BOWLING: Meyer 15-2-30-4; Barnes 14.3-0-47-3; Gabriels 11-1-28-1; Davids 5-1-17-0; Benjamin 11-2-40-1; Magiet 4-1-8-0

WP WON BY 77 RUNS

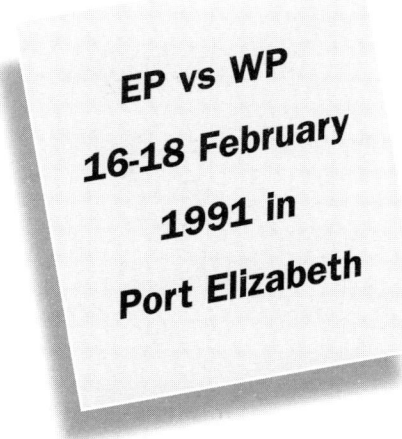

EP vs WP
16-18 February
1991 in
Port Elizabeth

Magiet's 97 is not enough to earn WP victory over their old rivals

AFTER SUFFERING two defeats and a draw in their past three encounters against WP in Port Elizabeth, EP were determined to resuscitate their title hopes by beating the champions in their last ever meeting in SACB cricket.

In a match befitting the tense encounters which these two sides had been involved in over the past decade (including a tie 1984), EP scraped to an exciting six-run victory, despite the efforts of Yunus Thomas (28), who battled gamely to lead his side to victory.

At 21/6 in their first innings WP seemed set to end with a substantial first innings deficit in reply to EP's total of 170, but a record seventh wicket stand of 136 between Saait Magiet, who was unluckily run out on 97, and Nazeem White (36), hauled WP back into the game.

However, there were no such heroics in the second innings as WP fell agonisingly short of their victory target of 102.

EP FIRST INNINGS

N.Ebrahim c Magiet b Gabriels	5
E. Van Heerden b Barnes	72
R. Yearwood b Kemp	14
A. Peters b Meyer	10
S. Abrahams c Benjamin b Barnes	23
R. Dolley c Gabriels b Barnes	5
K. Majola c Kemp b Barnes	10
P. Hufkie b Gabriels	0
F. Sarrahwitz c sub b Gabriels	0
V. Frans not out	0
B. Forbes b Barnes	1
EXTRAS	30
TOTAL	170

FALL OF WICKETS: 1/46; 2/81; 3/93; 4/127; 5/138; 6/157; 7/163; 8/166; 9/166

BOWLING: Meyer 21-9-30-1; Barnes 21,5-6-37-5; Magiet 10-7-11-0; Benjamin 10-2-18-0; Gabriels 12-4-19-3; Kemp 10-2-25-1

WP FIRST INNINGS

M. Isaacs c Majola b Dolley	5
A. Viljoen c Hufkie b Forbes	2
*S. Gabriels c Majola b Forbes	4
F. Davids c Hufkie b Dolley	6
D. Kemp lbw Forbes	0
+N. White c Hufkie b Van Heerden	36
Y. Thomas run out	2
S. Magiet run out	97
A. Meyer lbw Majola	1
V. Barnes not out	1
F. Benjamin st Hufkie b Majola	0
EXTRAS	7
TOTAL	161

FALL OF WICKETS: 1/11; 2/17; 3/19; 4/19; 5/19; 6/21; 7/157; 8/158; 9/160

BOWLING: Forbes 19-5-47-3; Frans 6-2-17-0; Dolley 16-7-31-2; Majola 13-4-42-2; Sarrahwitz 3-1-11-0; Van Heerden 3-0-6-1

EP SECOND INNINGS

N. Ebrahim b Barnes	7
E. Van Heerden run out	0
R. Yearwood b Meyer	33
S. Abrahams b Barnes	0
A. Peters lbw Barnes	6
R. Dolley b Magiet	12
K. Majola not out	14
P. Hufkie c Kemp b Meyer	0
F. Sarrahwitz lbw Meyer	0
V. Frans b Magiet	0
B. Forbes lbw Meyer	4
EXTRAS	17
TOTAL	93

FALL OF WICKETS: 1/3; 2/23; 3/23; 4/32; 5/61; 6/71; 7/73; 8/73; 9/78

BOWLING: Meyer 18-8-29-4; Barnes 10-3-21-3; Benjamin 3-2-3-0; Magiet 12-4-20-2; Gabriels 2-0-3-0

WP SECOND INNINGS

A. Viljoen lbw Forbes	0
M. Isaacs lbw Forbes	8
S. Gabriels c Hufkie b Forbes	2
N. White lbw Sarrahwitz	4
F. Davids b Sarrahwitz	28
D. Kemp c Hufkie b Sarrahwitz	8
S. Magiet c & b Sarrahwitz	5
Y. Thomas b Dolley	28
A. Meyer lbw Dolley	8
V. Barnes b Sarrahwitz	0
F. Benjamin not out	1
EXTRAS	4
TOTAL	96

FALL OF WICKETS: 1/0; 2/10; 3/15; 4/15; 5/31; 6/41; 7/58; 8/77; 9/90

BOWLING: Forbes 14-3-33-3; Peters 2-0-6-0; Sarrahwitz 22-10-40-5; Dolley 9,4-4-13-2

EP WON BY 6 RUNS

Heroics by Davids and Magiet – but rain has the last say

**Natal vs WP
9-11 March
1991 in
Durban**

WITH EP failing to beat Transvaal in Johannesburg, WP retained their Howa Bowl title for the fifth successive season – despite being held to a draw by Natal in Durban.

WP appeared to be on course for victory when they took a healthy first innings lead of 87, after making 179 in reply to Natal's first innings total of 92.

The WP first innings effort was built around a fast and furious fifth wicket partnership of 75 between Faiek Davids (62) and Saait Magiet (37), but after their departure the rest of the batsmen failed to make any impression, with the last five wickets falling for only 30 runs.

Although Natal fared much better in their second innings to reach 162/5, too much time had been lost to rain to enable either side to contrive a result.

NATAL FIRST INNINGS

E. Govender b Meyer	0
J. Chellan c Meyer b Benjamin	5
G. Moses c & b Benjamin	29
M. Patel run out	0
S. Govender c Benjamin b Meyer	6
M. Ameen c Gabriels b Meyer	21
I. Paruk lbw Barnes	0
LD. Naidoo not out	9
R. Soobramoney c Kemp b Benjamin	1
N. Moodley c & b Gabriels	4
N. Ramnarain st Cupido b Gabriels	0
EXTRAS	17
TOTAL	92

FALL OF WICKETS: 1/0; 2/31; 3/34; 4/49; 5/61; 6/62; 7/86; 8/87; 9/92

BOWLING: Meyer 15-6-27-3; Barnes 9-4-14-1; Davids 7-3-11-0; Benjamin 17-10-20-3; Gabriels 4,5-3-3-2

NATAL SECOND INNINGS

G.Moses c Gabriels b Barnes	5
J. Chellan c & b Cupido	37
M. Ameen st White b Gabriels	20
M. Patel lbw Meyer	16
E. Govender st White b Cupido	7
S. Govender not out	35
I. Paruk not out	23
EXTRAS	19
TOTAL	162/5

FALL OF WICKETS: 1/25; 2/64; 3/81; 4/89; 5/107

BOWLING: Meyer 7-1-16-1; Benjamin 19-2-40-0; Gabriels 16-3-40-1; Barnes 7-3-11-1; Kemp 4-0-12-0; Cupido 8-0-24-2

WP FIRST INNINGS

*S. Gabriels lbw Ramnarain	29
+R. Cupido lbw Moodley	0
I. Behardien c S'bramoney b Moodley	0
N. White b Moodley	0
F. Davids c S'bramoney b Moses	62
S. Magiet c Moodley b Naidoo	37
D. Kemp lbw Moses	6
Y. Thomas c Patel b Moses	0
A. Meyer lbw Naidoo	0
V. Barnes not out	5
F. Benjamin st S'bramoney b Moses	11
EXTRAS	29
TOTAL	179

FALL OF WICKETS: 1/9; 2/18; 3/22; 4/74; 5/149; 6/157; 7/157; 8/159; 9/163

BOWLING: Moodley 16-5-39-3; Ramnarain 9-3-26-1; E. Govender 8-3-23-0; Moses 12,5-1-47-4; Naidoo 6-2-15-2

**MATCH DRAWN
WP WON HOWA BOWL FOR FIFTH
SUCCESSIVE YEAR**

WP Cricket Board First Class Averages 1990/91

BATTING

Name	Matches	Inns	NO	Hs	Runs	Ave	50	100
Nazeem White	6	9	2	125*	407	58,14	2	2
Saait Magiet	5	8	1	97	258	36,86	2	
Ismail Behardien	5	7	0	142	230	32,86		1
Yunus Thomas	6	9	1	75*	239	29,88	2	
Shukri Conrad	2	3	0	63	77	25,67	1	
Andre Viljoen	3	6	0	81	141	23,50	1	
Adnaan Meyer	6	7	2	36	86	17,20		
Faiek Davids	4	7	0	62	113	16,14	1	
Faizel Ebrahim	2	3	0	22	46	15,33		
Seraj Gabriels	6	7	0	29	69	9,86		
Deon Kemp	3	4	0	13	27	6,75		
Vincent Barnes	4	5	2	11	18	6,00		
Fuad Benjamin	3	5	2	11	17	5,67		
Ebrahim Gafieldien	4	7	1	27*	30	5,00		
Quentin Loggenstein	2	3	0	12	13	4,33		

Also batted: Trevor Seconds (6*); Mishal Isaacs (5 and 8); Randall Cupido (0)

FIELDING:

Wicketkeepers: 19 – Nazeem White (15ct and 4st); 2 – Randall Cupido (1ct and 1st)

Catches:

6 – Seraj Gabriels, Ismail Behardien; 5 – Fuad Benjamin; 4 – Shukri Conrad, Deon Kemp; 3 – Adnaan Meyer; 2 – Yunus Thomas, Quentin Loggenstein, Vincent Barnes;1 – Ebrahim Gafieldien, Faizel Ebrahim, Saait Magiet, Henry Williams, Andre Viljoen, Faiek Davids

BOWLING

Name	Overs	Mdns	Wkts	Runs	Ave	Best Bowling	5i	10m
Vincent Barnes	84,2	24	18	167	9,28	5/37 v EP	1	
Henry Williams	36	13	5	51	10,20	3/23 v Natal		
Adnaan Meyer	159,2	47	27	289	10,70	5/22 v Natal	1	
Faiek Davids	37	14	6	67	11,17	4/28 v Tvl		
Trevor Seconds	28	13	4	46	11,50	2/9 v EP		
Shukri Conrad	59	21	8	106	13,25	4/35 v EP		
Seraj Gabriels	123,2	29	18	261	14,50	5/57 v Natal	1	
Saait Magiet	48	20	3	74	24,67	2/20 v EP		
Fuad Benjamin	63	19	4	129	32,25	3/20 v Natal		
Quentin Loggenstein	40	7	2	104	52,00	1/38 v EP		

Also bowled: Charles Hendrikse 11-3-20-0; Randall Cupido 8-0-24-2; Faizel Ebrahim 1-1-0-0; Deon Kemp 14-2-37-1

SFW Knockout competition 1974

Quarter-Final

WP VS GRIQUAS
WP (50 OVERS)

W. Hendricks c Palm c Saloojee 49
L. Jacobs c Connor b Saloojee.................................23
V. Moodie b Saloojee...10
R. van Graan c Williams b Jackson 41
M. Maclons lbw Williams...59
J. Lambert c & b Williams.......................................30
G. Williams not out 12
J. Neethling b Summers..0
J. Mahoney b Williams..10
B. Petersen c sub b Williams 0
A. Sonn b Williams 2

Extras...............14
Total...............250

FALL OF WICKETS: 1/63; 2/89; 3/100; 4/149; 5/215; 6/217; 7/217; 8/230; 9/249

BOWLING: Williams 8-0-46-5; Englebrecht 10-4-18-0; Saloojee 10-1-34 -3; Jackson 10-0-54-1; Jinnah 7-0-46-0; Summers 5-0-38-1

GRIQUAS (34,3 OVERS)

D. Jacobs c Maclons b Neethling 2
P. Salo run out 1
A. Hartzenberg b Mahoney.......................................0
H. Jinnah b Neethling 6
S. Saloojee c Hendricks b Williams.........................38
K. Connor st Maclons b Williams.............................31
A. Williams c Jacobs b Petersen 11
A. Jackson run out..9
R. Engelbrecht c Sonn b Lambert.............................6
G. Summers c Sonn b Lambert................................12
H. Palm run out 6

Extras...............13
Total...............135

FALL OF WICKETS: 1/3; 2/4; 3/7; 4/24; 5/85; 6/85; 7/109; 8/113; 9/123

BOWLING: Mahoney 7-2-21-1; Neethling 7-1-13-2; Petersen 9-0-36-1; Sonn 2-1-15-0; Williams 7-1-24-2; Lambert 1,3-0-8-1; Hendricks 1-0-5-0

WP WON BY 115 RUNS

Semi-Final

WP V EP IN PORT ELIZABETH,
WP (47,3 OVERS)

I. Dagnin c Abrahams b Williams............................1
L. Jacobs lbw Govindjee 19
V. Moodie b Draai..11
R. van Graan c Abrahams b D'Oliveira...................4
+M. Maclons c Francis b Draai 7
J. Lambert c & b D'Oliveira 27
K. van Graan c Abrahams b Hendricks 28
J. Neethling b D'Oliveira 0
B. Petersen lbw D'Oliveira 1
*G. Williams not out 1
A. Sonn b Williams 2

Extras...............10
Total...............111

FALL OF WICKETS; 1/2; 2/19; 3/27; 4/42; 5/48; 6/107; 7/107; 8/109; 9/109

BOWLING: Williams 8,3-2-15-2; I. Hendricks 10-4-24-1; D'Oliveira 9-3-14-4; Draai 10-4-16-2; Govindjee 10-1-32-1

EP (38,4 OVERS)

A. Douglas b Sonn 20
K. Barry run out 9
D. Jacobs c Williams b K. Van Graan......................9
N. Francis b Williams...3
B. D'Oliveira c K. van Graan b Petersen.................9
M. Wilson b Petersen 11
D. Govindjee lbw Neethling 2
I. Hendricks c Williams b Petersen..........................0
S. Draai lbw Petersen..2
F. Abrahams lbw Petersen...2
T. Williams not out...3

Extras...............6
Total...............76

Fall of wickets: 1/16; 2/36; 3/39; 4/55; 5/66; 6/66; 7/68; 8/68; 9/70
Bowling: Sonn 10-2-20-1; Neethling 10-4-17-1; Williams 7-3-10-1; K. van Graan 2-0-6-1; Petersen 9,4-3-17-5

WP WON BY 35 RUNS

Man of the Match: Basil Petersen

Other Results

WP B lost to Natal by 67 runs

Natal 125 (J. Govender 35, I. Ebrahim 26, G. Montgomery 25*, C. van Schalkwyk 4/20, A Kallis 2/9, H. Bergins 2/15)
WP B 58 (H. Arenz 21, Y. Omar 3/12, K. Barker 2/9, M. Patrick 2/11, L.S. Naidoo 2/17)

WP C lost to EP by 37 runs

EP 174 (D. Govindjee 93, D. Jacobs 31, I. Tromp 4/31, T. Le Cordeur 3/36)
WP C 137 (C. Kolbe 58, A. Katts 23, S. Snyders 21, T. Williams 4/27, D. Govindjee 2/24)

Final
WP VS TRANSVAAL
WP (48,7 OVERS)

L. Jacobs run out.......................................24
R. van Graan b Chotia................................8
V. Moodie c E. Bhamjee b Barnes................11
J. Lambert c E. Bhamjee b Chotia 1
+M. Maclons c A. Bhamjee b Rubidge 14
K. van Graan run out.................................46
J. Neethling c E. Bhamjee b Manack 14
J. Mahoney b Barnes..................................9
*G. Williams not out..................................15
A. Sonn b Ayob..7
B. Petersen b Rubidge................................5

EXTRAS..............25

TOTAL 179

FALL OF WICKETS: 1/39; 2/50; 3/53; 4/57; 5/96;
6/125; 7/146; 8/154; 9/168

BOWLING: Ayob 10-1-39-1; Manack 10-1-27-1;
Chotia 10-2-14-2; Barnes 10-3-32-2; Rubidge
6,7-1-26-2; Johannessie 2-0-16-0

TRANSVAAL (39,5 OVERS)

A. Bhamjee c Jacobs b Williams 5
A. Gabru b Mahoney.................................60
A. Barnes st Maclons b Willliams 11
Y. Snyders c Lambert b Williams 4
M. Mangera c Maclons b Williams..............24
S. Chotia lbw Williams 4
A. Manack c Jacobs b Sonn......................14
S. Rubidge b Mahoney..............................0
E. Bhamjee c & b Sonn 3
G. Johannessie c Lambert b Mahoney 1
H. Ayob not out......................................0

EXTRAS..............17

TOTAL 143

FALL OF WICKETS: 1/29; 2/47; 3/51; 4/113; 5/119;
6/125; 7/127; 8/134; 9/139

BOWLING: Mahoney 7-2-17-3; Neethling 6-0-28-0;
Sonn 6,5-1-15-2; Williams 10-1-32-5; Petersen
10-1-34-0;

WP WON BY 36 RUNS
Man of the Match Gertjie Williams

SFW Knockout competition 1975

Quarter-Final
NATAL VS WP
NATAL (60 OVERS)

G. Francois c Kolbe b Holder 36
M. Ebrahim b Mahoney 6
K. Barker c Abrahams b Petersen 18
Y. Omar b Witbooi.................................22
T. Roberts c Maclons b Abrahams............20
M. Patrick c Petersen 6
G. Govender not out..............................26
I. Ebrahim c sub b Witbooi 10
G. Allie c Maclons b Witbooi 12
LS. Naidoo not out................................13

EXTRAS.................6

TOTAL............175/8

FALL OF WICKETS: 1/15; 2/48; 3/70; 4/90; 5/104;
6/126; 7/143; 8/157

BOWLING: Mahoney 12-3-30-1; Witbooi 12-4-35-3;
Petersen 12-2-32-2; Holder 12-0-34 -1; Abrahams
12-1 38-1

WP (52,4 OVERS)

L. Jacobs run out 34
W. Hendricks c Williamson b Omar 14
C. Kolbe c Patrick b Allie 0
K. van Graan c Williamson b Patrick.........5
C. Abrahams c Francois b Patrick 17
A. Katts b Barker 24
+M. Maclons c Barker b Ebrahim 1
J. Mahoney b Ebrahim 1
J. Holder not out..................................5
R. Witbooi b Patrick...............................0
B. Petersen b Barker...............................0

EXTRAS..............14

TOTAL..............115

FALL OF WICKETS: 1/46; 2/49; 3/65; 4/65; 5/70; 6/99;
7/104; 8/109; 9/115

BOWLING: Barker 6,4-1-13-2; Naidoo 6-1-11-0; Allie
8-3-14-1; I. Ebrahim 10-5-17-2; Omar 10-2-25-1;
Patrick 12-3-21-3;

NATAL WON BY 60 RUNS

Benson & Hedges 1982/83

Quarter-Final
WP VS NATAL
WP (50 OVERS)

S. Martin c Dadabhay		12
N. Arendse b Khan		14
N. Fortune c Moorad b Hoosen		2
M Abdullah run out		43
Y. Thomas run out		11
C. van Schalkwyk b E. Govender		4
+E. Isaacs b E. Govender		13
*A. Jabaar not out		24
E. Damon not out		0
	EXTRAS	18
	TOTAL	141/7

FALL OF WICKETS: 1/25; 2/27; 3/42; 4/85; 5/99; 6/108; 7/141

BOWLING: Mansoor 10-3-33-0; E. Govender 10-3-20-2; Khan 10-5-27-1; Dadabhai 10-3-22-1; Hoosen 10-5-21-1

NATAL (49,5 OVERS)

E. Mall b Jabaar		21
T. Narandas st Isaacs b Damon		4
E. Govender b Damon		6
S. Govender c Martin b Thomas		28
L. Maharaj b Jabaar		0
M. Khan b Van Schalkwyk		5
G. Hoosen b Jabaa		0
Y. Moorad lbw Thomas		1
N. Moodley st Isaacs b Jabaar		12
S. Mansoor not out		2
O. Dadabhay b Jabaar		2
	EXTRAS	4
	TOTAL	85

FALL OF WICKETS: 1/9; 2/16; 3/61; 4/63; 5/63; 6/63; 7/64; 8/81; 9/81

BOWLING: Barnes 6-2-6-0; Damon 10-2-21-1; Theron 10-2-19-0; Thomas 10-5-12-2; Jabaar 9,5-3-11-5; Van Schalkwyk 4-1-12-1

WP WON BY 56 RUNS

Semi-Final
TRANSVAAL VS WP
TRANSVAAL (49,5 OVERS)

D. Nagin c Isaacs b Magiet		0
E. Amod run out		2
M. Doman c Magiet b Barnes		7
A. Wadvalla run out		6
D. George b Thomas		29
A. Manack c Antulay b Thomas		77
R. Khan c Harris b Magiet		8
Y. Begg not out		32
R. Galant c Musson b Barnes		0
Mather hit ball twice		0
I. Khan not out		5
	EXTRAS	18
	TOTAL	184

FALL OF WICKETS: 1/1; 2/12; 3/15; 4/20; 5/87; 6/120; 7/149; 8/160; 9/164

BOWLING: Barnes 9,5-3-28-2; Magiet 10-2-31-2; Jabaar 10-1-28-0; Theron 10-3-34-0; Thomas 10-0-45-0

WP (45 OVERS)

R. Musson b Khan		11
E. Isaacs not out		89
N. Fortune c Wadvallah b Amod		36
M. Abdulla not out		26
S. Magiet not out		17
	EXTRAS	6
	TOTAL	185/3

FALL OF WICKETS: 1/32; 2/125; 3/149

BOWLING: Khan 5-0-30-1; Mather 5-1-17-0; Manack 10-1-28-0; Galant 10-1-36-0; Amod 10-1-38-2; Doman 5-0-30-0

WP WON BY 7 WICKETS

Final:
WP VS EP
WP (50 OVERS)

R. Musson c F. Abrahams b Lorgat 13
+E. Isaacs b M. Abrahams 5
N. Fortune not out 46
M. Abdullah b Harrison 28
S. Magiet b Harrison 0
Y. Thomas c Reid b Harrison 5
A. Martin b M. Abrahams 7
*A. Jabaar run out 10
M. Theron not out 13
V. Barnes not out 7

	EXTRAS..............21
	TOTAL............155/8

FALL OF WICKETS: 1/12; 2/26; 3/89; 4/103; 5/111;
6/115; 7/127; 8/134
BOWLING: Draai 10-2-15-0; M. Abrahams 10-2-16-2;
Reid 6-0-35-0; Lorgat 9-1-19-1; Govindjee 9-1-26-0;
Harrison 6-0-23-3

EP (29,4 OVERS)

G. Abrahams b Theron 22
Z. Hendricks b Damon 1
H. Lorgat lbw Theron.............................10
F. Abrahams c Musson b Jabaar.............10
G. Cuddembey run out 0
D. Reid b Theron....................................0
D. Govindjee b Theron............................1
B. Nonganga b Jabaar 0
G. Harrison not out 2
M. Abrahams st Isaacs b Jabaar 0
S. Draai c Abdullah b Theron 9

	EXTRAS................4
	TOTAL.................59

FALL OF WICKETS: 1/6; 2/35; 3/40; 4/44; 5/44; 6/47;
7/47; 8/47; 9/48
BOWLING: Barnes 5-0-17-0; Damon 5-1-15-1; Jabaar
10-6-7-3; Theron 9,4-4-16-5;
Man of the Match: Mervyn Theron

WP WON BY 96 RUNS

Benson & Hedges 1983/84

Quarter-Final
TRANSVAAL B VS WP
TRANSVAAL B (46,2 OVERS)

Desai c Damon b Jabaar................................28
Kota c Abdullah b Magiet 4
Jajbhai c Damon b Abdullah 55
Dinath b Thomas 0
Naik c Thomas b Barnes 5
R. Khan b Thomas 2
Mangera c Isaacs b Magiet 10
Kolia c Isaacs b Barnes 5
I. Khan b Magiet 3
Dawood b Damon 0
Nawab not out 0

	EXTRAS...............24
	TOTAL 137

FALL OF WICKETS: 1/8; 2/58; 3/93; 4/93; 5/99; 6/105;
7/132; 8/136; 9/137
BOWLING: Barnes 10-2-22-2; Magiet 8,2-3-13-3;
Damon 6-0-26-1; Jabaar 10-1-30-1; Thomas
10-5-12-2; Abdullah 2-0-10-1

WP (25,2 OVERS)

N. Antulay c Kota b Dinath 33
E. Harris not out...48
N. Fortune not out...47

	EXTRAS...............13
	TOTAL............141/1

FALL OF WICKETS: 1/64
BOWLING: Dawood 2-0-10-0; I. Khan 3,2-0-22-0;
Kolia 7-0-28-0; Dinath 5-0-26-1; Nawab 6-0-26-0;
Desai 2-0-15-0

WP WON BY NINE WICKETS

Semi-Final
WP VS NATAL
WP (50 OVERS)

+E. Isaacs c & b Khan 22
E. Harris lbw E. Govender 1
N. Antulay c E. Govender b Omar 37
N. Fortune c Kholia b Omar 15
F. Solomons c & b Khan...1
M. Abdullah not out...76
S. Magiet c Mall b Gangat.......................................17
Y. Thomas b Gangat...0
*A. Jabaar c Morgan b Omar....................................1
V. Barnes not out..0

	EXTRAS 18
	TOTAL............212/8

FALL OF WICKETS: 1/4; 2/66; 3/74; 4/88; 5/88; 6/113;
7/113; 8/201
BOWLING: E. Govender 8-1-26-1; Gangat 10-5-23-2;
Khan 10-1-38-1; Omar 10-2-31-3; Hoosen
10-1-59-0; Mall 2-0-17-0

NATAL (48,3 OVERS)

Mall c Isaacs b Barnes 1
Omar b Magiet 40
E. Govender c Thomas b Damon 8
Khan b Barnes 31
P. Maharaj lbw Antulay...11
Hoosen c & b Barnes 10
L. Maharaj c Abdullah b Thomas 3
Kholia b Thomas 4
Morgan b Antulay 1
Gangat not out...0

EXTRAS	20
TOTAL	133

FALL OF WICKETS: 1/6; 2/21; 3/32; 4/82; 5/108;
6/122; 7/124; 8/128; 9/131

BOWLING: Barnes 10-3-15-3; Damon 10-3-21-1;
Jabaar 10-3-19-1; Magiet 10-1-40-1; Thomas
4,3-1-6-2; Antulay 4-0-12-2

WP WON BY 79 RUNS

Final
WP VS EP AT GREEN POINT TRACK
EP (49,2 OVERS)

G. Cuddembey c Magiet b Damon 0
G. Abrahams c Isaacs b Damon 7
H. Lorgat c Isaacs b Magiet.....................................2
A. Frans c Felix b Allie...5
W. Fischer c Isaacs b Magiet 0
I. Hendricks c Fortune b Allie................................6
K. Majola not out 39
F. Abrahams c Harris b Miller 8
S. Draai c Fortune b Thomas 5
J. Frans b Magiet...28
M. Abrahams run out 0

EXTRAS	36
TOTAL	136

FALL OF WICKETS: 1/0; 2/7; 3/9; 4/10; 5/23; 6/49;
7/66; 8/76; 9/135

BOWLING: Damon 10-2-13-2; Magiet 10-5-10-3;
Allie 9,2-2-26-2; Miller 10-3-21-1; Thomas 10-3-30-1;

RAIN STOPPED PLAY – TROPHY SHARED

Benson & Hedges 1984/85

Quarter-Final
NATAL VS WP B, DURBAN
WP (42 OVERS)

S. Hendricks c Patel b Pentiah 14
S. Gabriels c Haffejee b Ramsaroop......................56
F. Solomons c Soobramoney b Ramsaroop 31
M. Abdullah lbw Le Roux 34
S. Magiet not out...31
Y. Thomas not out 11

EXTRAS	29
TOTAL	206/4

FALL OF WICKETS: 1/33; 2/104; 3/122; 4/170

BOWLING: Pentiah 6-2-13-1; Naidoo 10-1-24-0;
Moodley 8-0-42-0; Le Roux 8-0-46-1; Ramsaroop 8-0-32-2; Sewmungal 2-0-20-0

NATAL B (35,3 OVERS)

Ramsaroop st Cupido b Jabaar.................................2
Limalia c Hendricks b Magiet 4
Haffejee b Allie 11
Patel c Harris b Jabaar..29
Sewmungal c Solomons b Allie 0
Moodley lbw Barnes 12
Govender lbw Allie 0
Le Roux c Jabaar b Barnes 2
Naidoo b Gabriels 0
Soobramoney not out 0
Pentiah b Barnes..0

EXTRAS	9
TOTAL	69

FALL OF WICKETS: 1/10; 2/15; 3/44; 4/48; 5/57; 6/62;
7/69; 8/69; 69

BOWLING: Barnes 8,3-4-5-3; Magiet 7-3-6-1; Jabaar
10-0-29-2; Allie 8-2-16-3; Gabriels 2-1-4-1

WP WON BY 137 RUNS

Semi-Final
EP VS WP
WP (49,3 OVERS)

S. Hendricks c Cuddembey b A. Frans 56
S. Gabriels b E. Frans 12
F. Solomons c A. Frans b Majola 2
N. Antulay run out...................................58
M. Abdullah c Majola b A. Frans 4
S. Magiet c Kisten b A. Frans 7
*A. Jabaar run out...................................1
N. Booysen run out 8
+R. Cupido c Kisten b Draai..........................8
V. Barnes not out 0
E. Mohammed b J. Frans 1

EXTRAS...............16
TOTAL 173

FALL OF WICKETS: 1/58; 2/73; 3/77; 4/91; 5/114;
6/139; 7/157; 8/169; 9/171
BOWLING; J. Frans 9,3-0-33-1; E, Frans 10-3-25-1;
Draai 10-2-33-1; Majola 10-1-33-1; A. Frans
10-4-33-3

EP (47 OVERS)

S. Kruger b Barnes...................................1
G. Cuddembey b Jabaar 14
K. Majola lbw Magiet 28
C. Kisten run out 5
A. Peters c Abdullah b Magiet 4
A. Frans c Booysen b Gabriels 21
D. Reid c Abdullah b Gabriels 16
S. Draai not out 10
J. Frans c & b Gabriels 3
B. Reid b Gabriels 6
E. Frans lbw Gabriels................................7

EXTRAS 13
TOTAL 128

FALL OF WICKETS: 1/7; 2/42; 3/43; 4/63; 5/64; 6/96;
7/104; 8/111; 9/118
BOWLING: Mohammed 8-1-31-0; Barnes 10-5-10-1;
Jabaar 10-2-18-1; Magiet 10-1-21-2; Booysen
1-0-3-0; Gabriels 8-0-32-5

WP WON BY 45 RUNS

Final
WP VS TRANSVAAL
WP (50 OVERS)

S, Hendricks c Begg b Edwards 25
S. Gabriels run out 57
F. Solomons lbw Edwards..............................4
N. Antulay b Mangera 2
M. Abdullah c Kimmie b Mangera 1
S, Magiet b A, Manack 73
*A. Jabaar b Kimmie 23
N, Booysen not out 12
+R. Cupido not out 2

EXTRAS...............26
TOTAL............225/7

FALL OF WICKETS: 1/53; 2/60; 3/65; 4/77; 5/118;
6/197; 7/212
BOWLING: AH Manack 10-4-32-0; Kimmie 10-0-60-1;
Edwards 10-0-28-2; Mangera 10-2-22-2; A, Manack
10-0-57-1

TRANSVAAL (50 OVERS)

Babha c Cupido b Barnes..............................6
Rajah run out..15
Mentor c Cupido b Barnes 0
Odendaal st Cupido b Gabriels 16
Edwards b Gabriels 27
Moosagie not out 44
Kimmie c Magiet b Gabriels...........................0
A, Manack ret hurt 9
Begg not out 8

EXTRAS 20
TOTAL............145/6

FALL OF WICKETS: 1/20; 2/25; 3/26; 4/40; 5/86; 6/98
BOWLING: Mohammed 7-4-16-0; Barnes 10-2-18-2;
Booysen 6-0-24-2; Magiet 7-1-14-0; Jabaar 8-0-24-0;
Gabriels 10-5-21-1; Solomons 1-0-5-0; Hendricks
1-0-3-0

WP WON BY 80 RUNS

Limited Overs Averages
BATTING

Name	Matches	Inns	NO	HS	Runs	Ave	50	100
Neil Fortune	6	5	2	47*	147	49,00		
Edward Harris	3	2	1	48*	49	49,00		
Ebrahim Isaacs	6	4	1	89*	129	43,00		
Seraj Gabriels	3	3	0	57	125	41,67	2	
Munsoor Abdullah	8	7	1	76*	212	35,3	3	
Nasser Antulay	5	4	0	59	131	32,75	1	
Stuart Hendricks	3	3	0	56	95	31,67	1	
Willie Hendricks	2	2	0	49	63	31,50		
Saait Magiet	8	6	1	73	145	29,00		
Keith van Graan	3	3	0	46	79	26,33		
Lawton Jacobs	4	4	0	34	100	25,00		
Mornay Maclons	4	4	0	59	81	20,25		
Joey Lambert	3	3	0	30	58	19,33		
Robbie Van Graan	3	3	0	41	53	17,67		
Armien Jabaar	8	5	1	24*	59	14,75		
Rashaad Musson	2	2	0	13	24	12,00		
Viccie Moodie	3	3	0	11	32	10,67		
Randall Cupido	3	2	1	8	10	10,00		
Neville Booysen	2	2	1	8	10	10,00		
Faghme Solomons	5	4	0	34	38	9,50		
Yunus Thomas	6	4	1	11*	27	9,00		
Jock Mahoney	3	3	0	10	19	6,33		
Coetie Neethling	3	3	0	14	14	4,67		
Archie Sonn	3	3	0	7	11	3,67		
Basil Petersen	4	4	0	5	6	1,50		

Also Batted: Gertjie Williams (12*, 1*, 15*), Ivan Dagnin (1), Clive Kolbe (0), John Holder (5*), Cecil Abrahams (17), Ronnie Witbooi (0), Arthur Katts (24); Mervyn Theron (13*), Ebrahim Damon (0*), Shadley Martin (13); Norman Arendse (14); Armien Martin (7); Charles van Schalkwyk (4); Ebrahim Mohammed (1); Vincent Barnes (7*, 0*, 0*).

* Cecil Felix and Gerry Miller played one game but did not bat

Bowling:

Name	Overs	Mdns	Runs	Wkts	Ave	B/bowling	5wkt	Econ
Gertjie Williams	24	5	66	8	8,25	5/32 v Tvl	1	2,75
Goolam Allie	17,2	4	42	5	8,40	3/16 v Ntl B		2,44
Saait Magiet	62,2	16	104	12	8,66	3/10 v EP		1,67
Vincent Barnes	69,2	21	121	13	9,30	3/5 v Ntl B		1,75
Armien Jabaar	77,5	16	166	13	12,76	5/11 v Ntl	1	2,14
Jock Mahoney	26	7	68	5	13,60	3/17 v Tvl		2,62
Mervyn Theron	20,5	9	69	5	13,80	5/16 v EP	1	3,37
Basil Petersen	40,4	6	119	8	14,88	5/17 v EP	1	2,95
Yunus Thomas	44,3	14	105	7	15,00	2/6 v Natal		2,37
Ebrahim Damon	41	8	96	6	16,00	2/13 v EP		2,34
Archie Sonn	18,5	4	50	3	16,66	2/15 v Tvl		2,70
Coetie Neethling	23	5	58	3	19,33	2/13 v Griquas		2,52

Also Bowled:

Willie Hendricks 1-0-5-0; Keith van Graan 2-0-6-1; Joey Lambert 1,3-0-8-1; John Holder 12-0-34-1; Cecil Abrahams 12-1-38-1; Ronnie Witbooi 12-4-35-3; Munsoor Abdullah 2-0-10-1; Nasser Antulay 4-0-12-0; Faghme Solomons 1-0-5-0; Stuart Hendricks 1-0-3-0; Charles van Schalkwyk 4-1-12-1; Neville Booysen 7-0-27-2; Ebrahim Mohammed 15-5-47-0

Fielding:

Wicketkeepers: 10 – Ebrahim Isaacs (7ct & 3st); 6 – Mornay Maclons (4 ct & 2 st); 4 – Randall Cupido (2ct & 2st)

Catches:

4 – Munsoor Abdullah; 3 – Lawton Jacobs, Archie Sonn; 2 – Gertjie Williams, Joey Lambert, Ebrahim Damon, Neil Fortune, Saait Magiet, Eddie Harris, Rashaad Musson; 1 – Willie Hendricks, Keith van Graan, Clive Kolbe, Cecil Abrahams, Vincent Barnes, Stuart Hendricks, Armien Jabaar, Faghme Solomons, Seraj Gabriels, Neville Booysen, Cecil Felix, Nasser Antulay, Shadley Martin

Batting averages (in order of top run scorers)

Name	Matches	Inns	NO	HS	Runs	Ave	50	100
Saait Magiet	64	100	12	100*	2397	27,24	13	2
Munsoor Abdullah	39	59	2	109	1854	32,53	11	3
Faiek Davids	32	51	6	146	1615	35,89	11	3
Seraj Gabriels	48	73	8	101*	1458	22,43	10	1
Ebrahim Isaacs	51	85	7	103	1458	18,69	5	1
Yunus Thomas	38	55	6	116	1320	26,94	7	2
Stuart Hendricks	33	59	5	137	1267	23,46	5	1
Armien Jabaar	44	67	11	70	1169	20,88	3	
Ismail Behardien	25	37	1	142	1034	28,72	3	2
Neil Fortune	25	45	3	143	1023	24,36	6	1
Rushdi Magiet	34	53	5	76	841	17,52	3	
Nazeem White	25	38	7	125*	762	24,58	3	2
Rashaad Musson	18	32	4	108	739	26,39	4	1
Viccie Moodie	17	24	1	100	665	28,91	3	1
Deon Kemp	18	28	3	148*	637	25,48	4	1
Charles van Schalkwyk	27	40	9	56	582	18,77	3	
Nasser Antulay	18	27	0	69	578	21,41	2	
Faghme Solomons	21	34	1	68	578	17,52	3	
Lawton Jacobs	15	28	3	50	538	21,52	1	
Dickie Conrad	8	13	0	166	524	40,30	1	2
Randall Cupido	19	25	4	62	448	21,33	2	
Willie Hendricks	18	32	3	60	424	14,62	2	
Robbie van Graan	15	25	2	67	424	19,27	2	
Mornay Maclons	17	29	3	75*	416	16,00	1	
George van Oordt	22	33	3	51	410	13,67	1	
Gertjie Williams	16	22	4	80	393	21,83	2	
Michael Doman	12	23	3	64	388	19,40	3	
Jock Mahoney	19	27	7	68*	377	18,85	2	
Shukri Conrad	9	13	0	63	324	24,92	2	
Vincent Barnes	53	59	24	41*	315	9,00		
Brian O'Connell	8	13	3	79	308	30,80	2	
Edward Harris	10	16	3	58	298	22,92	2	
Cyril Martin	13	20	2	66	297	16,50	3	
Joe Lambert	7	12	0	137	292	24,33		1
Faizel Ebrahim	12	18	2	70	270	16,88	1	
Coetie Neethling	11	18	5	53	263	20,23	1	
Winston Carelse	6	9	2	61*	232	33,14	1	
Nilton Muller	7	11	2	74	219	24,33	1	
Yusuf Adams	7	14	0	55	193	13,79	1	
Keith van Graan	9	15	1	44	191	13,64		
Reggie February	12	13	6	37	186	26,57		
Lefty Adams	23	30	16	39	180	12,85		
Ebrahim Gafieldien	7	12	2	86	179	17,90	1	
Noeg Martin	5	9	0	43	158	17,56		
Archie Sonn	10	14	2	28	148	12,33		

Name	Matches	Inns	NO	HS	Runs	Ave	50	100
John Kleinveldt	10	14	2	43	146	12,17		
Andre Viljoen	3	6	0	81	141	23,50	1	
Omar Henry	8	12	1	62*	128	11,64	1	
Shamiel Jassiem	6	9	3	43*	118	19,67		
Charles Hendrickse	6	6	1	31*	114	22,80		
Cecil Abrahams	5	8	1	40	111	15,86		
Arthur Katts	6	10	0	40	109	10,90		
Barry Dammert	4	6	0	57	104	17,33	1	
Ebrahim Mohammed	7	9	3	28	103	17,17		
Clive Kolbe	4	7	0	50	103	14,71	1	
Clinton Dyason	3	5	0	40	101	20,20		
Neville Booysen	5	5	1	38	99	24,75		
Hilary Dawson	9	14	2	29*	98	8,17		
Rashaad Salie	5	10	0	31	97	9,70		
Zak Davids	5	4	2	55*	89	44,50	1	
Abdurhaman Jakoet	3	5	0	64	89	17,80	1	
Adnaan Meyer	6	7	2	36	86	17,20		
Ebrahim Damon	14	22	7	20	86	5,73		
Howie Bergins	6	9	2	27*	83	11,86		
Mike Finnan	4	6	0	31	82	13,67		
Jumannah Khan	6	7	3	23*	80	20,00		
Reggie Simpson	2	4	0	43	76	19,00		
Hoosain Ahmed	4	7	1	39	75	12,50		
Mark Rasmus	3	4	0	31	74	18,50		
Goolam Allie	16	19	11	19	74	9,25		
Ismail Timol	2	3	0	29	67	22,33		
Gameem Khan	2	4	0	52	67	16,75	1	
Mervyn Theron	8	13	1	20	61	5,08		
Fuad Benjamin	15	19	8	16*	60	5,45		
Ivan Dagnin	4	7	0	19	58	8,29		
Abdul Haq Manack	5	6	2	27	54	13,50		
Ronnie Witbooi	2	3	1	28	46	23,00		
Vaughan Smith	4	8	0	14	46	5,75		
Kelvin Thomas	2	4	0	31	43	10,75		
MZ Allie	4	8	0	10	43	5,38		
Jacobus "Kosie" Williams	5	8	2	10	39	6,50		
Basil Petersen	3	5	2	17	36	12,00		
Terence Richards	3	5	0	19	34	6,80		
Gerry Miller	4	6	0	14	32	5,33		
Clinton Ravens	2	4	2	30	31	15,50		
Grant Petersen	2	2	0	15	22	11,00		
Randall van Graan	2	3	0	10	17	5,67		
Leon Roberts	2	3	0	7	17	5,67		
Owen Williams	2	3	2	9*	15	15,00		
Quentin Loggenstein	2	3	0	12	13	4,33		
Norman Arendse	2	4	0	3	6	1,50		
Aziz Wadvalla	2	2	0	5	5	2,50		
Noel Brache	2	3	0	3	5	1,67		

Also Batted:

Neville Lakay (14 and 0);

Marshall September (0);

Henry Arenz (0 & 10);

John Holder (3 and 4);

Cedric Miller (1 and 11);

Mohammed Ebrahim (19 and 10);

Sheraat Arnold (1*, 7*, 4*, 4*);

Yusuf Ebrahim (0 and 21);

Sa-at Galant (19 and 9);

Imraan Hendricks (0 and 5);

Shadley Martin (0 and 8);

Hassiem Price (0 and 2);

Nasser Kemp (3 and 3);

Mark Haupt (20 and 36);

Anthony Coericius (3 and 1);

Andre Odendaal (3 and 0);

Cecil Felix (27);

Ashraf Burns (9*),

Mogamat Galant (14 and 14);

Trevor Seconds (6* and 6*),

Mishal Isaacs (5 and 8);

Bowling averages (in order of top wicket takers)

Name	Overs	Mdns	Wkts	Runs	Ave	Best Bowling	5i	10m
Vincent Barnes	1400,3	404	250	2715	10,86	9/46 v Natal	19	4
Armien Jabaar	1131,4	280	188	2180	11,60	7/38 v Natal	11	2
Seraj Gabriels	1190,3	302	173	2477	14,31	8/53 v Natal	11	5
Saait Magiet	1109,3	331	169	2148	12,71	6/24 v Natal	6	
Lefty Adams	803	229	116	1702	14,67	6/7 v EP	8	3
Rushdi Magiet	594,5	185	97	1306	13,46	7/35 v Tvl	5	1
Faiek Davids	452,1	119	62	1053	16,98	5/50 v EP	2	
George van Oordt	438,1	135	58	898	15,48	5/50 v EP	1	
Goolam Allie	316,1	100	49	595	12,14	6/45 v EP	3	
Jock Mahoney	442	124	48	897	18,69	6/42 v EP	3	
Gertjie Williams	403,1	111	45	925	20,56	5/43 v Natal	1	
Reggie February	365	122	40	834	20,85	6/73 v Tvl	1	
Ebrahim Damon	330	89	37	735	19,86	4/21 v Tvl		
Howie Bergins	177,3	44	30	357	11,90	6/27 v Tvl	2	1
Fuad Benjamin	307,1	69	29	781	26,93	6/35 v Natal	1	
Mervyn Theron	198	46	29	381	13,14	4/35 v Tvl		
Adnaan Meyer	159,2	47	27	289	10,70	5/22 v Natal	1	
Abdul Haq Manack	157,2	42	27	306	11,33	7/17 v EP	3	
Willie Hendricks	174,4	45	27	356	13,19	5/9 v EP	1	
Charles van Schalkwyk	164	44	25	347	13,88	4/15 v EP		
John Kleinveldt	155	35	25	430	17,20	4/35 v Natal		
Ebrahim Mohammed	180,3	56	24	340	14,17	5/30 v EP	2	
Yunus Thomas	208,1	75	22	333	15,14	5/6 v Tvl	1	
Archie Sonn	195	62	21	407	19,38	4/57 v EP		
Winston Carelse	133	55	20	210	10,50	5/15 v Natal	2	
Charles Hendrikse	132,1	45	18	234	13,00	6/20 v Natal	1	
Neville Booysen	122,2	30	17	269	15,82	3/29 v Natal		
Coetie Neethling	167	32	17	463	27,23	5/52 v Natal	1	
Nilton Muller	94	25	14	229	16,35	3/18 v Natal		
Trevor Seconds	69	21	13	149	11,46	6/47 v EP	1	
Jacobus 'Kosie' Williams	120	39	13	237	18,23	3/21 v Natal		
Shukri Conrad	119,1	33	13	281	21,62	4/35 v EP		
Jumannah Khan	103,5	17	12	270	22,50	3/25 v Natal		
Michael Doman	62	1	10	202	20,20	2/11v Tvl		
Omar Henry	167,3	62	9	314	34,89	3/47 v EP		
Zak Davids	47,1	8	8	126	15,75	4/29 v Natal		
Shamiel Jassiem	54	12	8	145	18,13	4/27 v Tvl		
Cecil Abrahams	105	27	8	188	23,50	3/18 v Tvl		
Sheraat Arnold	74,2	12	8	216	27,00	4/50 v Natal		
Clive Kolbe	40,2	7	7	96	13,71	4/52 v Tvl		
Henry Williams	36	13	5	51	10,20	3/23 v Natal		
Keith van Graan	23,3	11	4	40	10,00	2/0 v Natal		
Leon Roberts	59	23	4	117	29,25	2/61 v Tvl		
Owen Williams	48,1	10	4	123	30,75	2/36 v Natal		
Basil Petersen	41,1	14	3	71	23,67			

Also Bowled:

Neville Lakay 1-0-5-0;

Marshall September 10-2-28-1;

Lawton Jacobs 3,4-1-5-2;

Brian O'Connell 6-1-28-1;

Viccie Moodie 4,3-0-30-0;

John Holder 16-6-33-0;

Robbie van Graan 12-4-17-2;

Dickie Conrad 1-0-1-0;

Ebrahim Isaacs 5,3-0-9-1;

Joe Lambert 11-1-36-5;

Cedric Miller 6-1-21-0;

Ronnie Witbooi 20,5-6-50-2;

Kelvin Thomas 14-4-39-0;

Noeg Martin 13-2-32-2;

Yusuf Ebrahim 6-0-40-0;

Cyril Martin 5-2-18-0;

Abdurahman Jakoet 1-0-2-0;

Neil Fortune 12-1-40-0;

Terence Richards 2-0-24-0;

Norman Arendse 5-1-15-0;

Munsoor Abdullah 9-3-28-1;

Stuart Hendricks 3-0-10-0;

Nasser Antulay 17,1-6-39-2;

Faghme Solomons 2,3-1-9-0;

Mark Haupt 3-0-9-0;

Clinton Ravens 16-4-31-2;

Deon Kemp 25-4-93-2;

Salie Green 21-7-35-5;

Mogamat Galant 7-2-19-0;

Clinton Dyason 16,5-3-29-3;

Barry Dammert 3-1-9-0;

Randall Cupido 8-0-24-2;

Name	Overs	Mdns	Wkts	Runs	Ave	Best Bowling	5i	10m
Gerry Miller	39	4	3	10	34,67	2/2 v EP		
Randall van Graan	22	5	2	53	26,50	2/53 v Tvl		
Imraan Hendricks	23	5	2	65	2,50	2/65 v EP		
Quentin Loggenstein	40	7	2	104	52,00	1/38 v EP		
Faizel Ebrahim	46	5	2	114	57,00	1/31 v Natal		

Fielding

Wicketkeepers:

161- Ebrahim Isaacs (119ct and 42st)

91 - Nazeem White (77ct and 14st)

62 - Randall Cupido (49ct and 13st)

54 - Mornay "Kulu" Maclons (39ct and 15st)

18 - Hilary Dawson (18ct)

7 - Gameem Khan (4ct and 3st)

6 - Rashaad Musson (4ct and 2st)

3 - Henry Arenz (2ct and 1st)

5 - Grant Petersen (4ct and 1st)

Fielders' Catches

60 - Saait Magiet

44 - Ismail Behardien

35 - Munsoor Abdullah

33 - Rushdi Magiet; Seraj Gabriels

32 - Vincent Barnes

31 - Stuart Hendricks

26 - Armien Jabaar

23 - Yunus Thomas

20 - Neil Fortune Faiek Davids, Deon Kemp

19 - Nasser Antulay

16 - Coetie Neethling, George van Oordt

14 - Viccie Moodie

13 - Lefty Adams, Charles van Schalkwyk

12 - Jock Mahoney, John Kleinveldt,

11 - Keith van Graan

10 - Faghme Solomons, Faizel Ebrahim

9 - Willie Hendricks, Cyril Martin, Michael Doman

8 - Lawton Jacobs, Omar Henry, Rashaad Musson, Fuad Benjamin,

7 - Gertjie Williams, Jumannah Khan, Brian O'Connell, Zak Davids, Eddie Harris, Shukri Conrad

6 - Robbie van Graan, Arthur Katts, Ebrahim Damon, Yusuf Adams,

5 - Ebrahim Mohammed, Reggie February,

4 - Archie Sonn,Cecil Abrahams, Mevyn Theron, Charles Hendrickse, Abdul Haq Manack

3 - Marshall September, Goolam Allie, Adnaan Meyer, Trevor Seconds

2 - Basil Petersen,Winston Carelse, Ismail Timol, Mike Finnan, Rashaad Salie, Sheraat Arnold, Terence Richards, Randall van Graan, Norman Arendse, Gerry Miller, Mogamat Galant, Mark Rasmus, Nilton Muller, Barry Dammert, Ebrahim Gafieldien, Quinton Loggenstein

1 - Owen Williams, Ivan Dagnin, Kosie Williams, Clive Kolbe, Reggie Simpson, John Holder, Howie Bergins, Cedric Miller, Rashaad Salie, Vaughan Smith, Yusuf Ebrahim, Noeg Martin, Shamiel Jassiem, Sa-at Galant, Hoosain Ahmed, Neville Booysen, Andre Viljoen, Henry Williams

Western Province First Class (3-Day) Records (1971/72-1990/91).

Partnerships.

1st Wicket: 111 - Dickie Conrad (99) and Ebrahim Isaacs (54) - vs Natal in Durban, February 1973.

2nd: 232 - Dickie Conrad (166) and Viccie Moodie (100) vs Transvaal in Cape Town, January 1973.

3rd: 183 - André Viljoen (81) and Nazeem White (109) vs Transvaal in Cape Town, January 1991.

4th: 114 - Stuart Hendricks (137) and Munsoor Abdullah (61) vs Transvaal in Johannesburg, March 1987.

5th: 231 - Ismail Behardien (142) and Nazeem White (125*) vs Natal in Cape Town, November 1990.

6th: 122* - Nazeem White (64*) and Yunus Thomas (75*) vs Transvaal in Johannesburg, January 1991.

7th: 136 - Saait Magiet (97) and Nazeem White (36) vs Eastern Province in Port Elizabeth, February 1991.

8th: 133 - Gertjie Williams (80) and Saait Magiet (89) vs Eastern Province in Port Elizabeth, January 1972.

9th: 93 - Rushdi Magiet (76) and Jock Mahoney (32) vs Eastern Province in Port Elizabeth, January 1975.

10th: 82 - Lefty Adams (39) and Vincent Barnes (41*) vs Natal in Cape Town, February, 1980.

Highest Partnership for any wicket: 232 - Dickie Conrad (166) and Viccie Moodie (100) vs Transvaal in Cape Town, December 1972.

Highest Total: 436/6 declared v Natal in Cape Town, December 1986 (Munsoor Abdullah 109, Saait Magiet 100*, Ismail Behardien 72).

Other High scores:

431 vs Transvaal in Johannesburg, December 1983 (Munsoor Abdullah 107, Yunus Thomas 85).

424/8 declared vs Transvaal in Cape Town, January 1973 (Dickie Conrad 166, Viccie Moodie 100).

418 - vs Natal in Cape Town, February 1988 (Munsoor Abdullah 94).

Lowest total:

41 - vs Eastern Province in Port Elizabeth, November 1982.

Other low totals:

60 vs Transvaal in Johannesburg, January 1986 (Vincent Barnes 8/29).

67 vs Transvaal in Cape Town, February 1976.

79 vs Eastern Province in Cape Town, March 1980.

83 vs Eastern Province in Port Elizabeth, March 1981.

Highest total against Western Province:

369 by Transvaal in Johannesburg, December 1971.

Lowest total against Western Province:

38 by Transvaal in Cape Town, February 1982 (Seraj Gabriels 4/9; Armien Jabaar 2/3; Vincent Barnes 2/9).

Other Low totals against Western Province:

39 by Natal in Cape Town, March 1982 (Saait Magiet 4/23; Mervyn Theron 3/5; Vincent Barnes 2/4).

42 by Eastern Province in Cape Town, March 1980 (Lefty Adams 6/7 and Saait Magiet 4/18).

50 by Eastern Province in Port Elizabeth, March 1990 (Abdul Haq Manack 7/17).

57 by Transvaal in Johannesburg, February 1985 (Vincent Barnes 5/17 and Saait Magiet 4/24).

61 by Natal in Durban, January 1983 (Vincent Barnes 8/29).

67 by Natal in Cape Town, March 1984 (Seraj Gabriels 5/27, Saait Magiet 2/14, Ebrahim Damon 2/16).

Most Runs in a season

492 by Dickie Conrad in 1971/73 season (highest score 166 vs Transvaal) * Includes match Western Province vs Rest of Sacboc

Other high run aggregates in a season

467 by Rashaad Musson in 1980/81

448 by Neil Fortune in 1981/82

436 by Faiek Davids in 1988/89

429 by Faiek Davids in 1987/88

407 by Nazeem White in 1990/91

Most Wickets in a season

42 by Vincent Barnes in 1986/87

Other leading wicket takers in a season

41 by Vincent Barnes in 1982/83

40 by Lefty Adams in 1979/80

Most dismissals by a wicketkeeper in a season

29 - (24ct and 5st) Nazeem White 1989/90

Most catches by a fielder in a season

12 by Saait Magiet in 1974/75 and Ismail Behardien in 1987/88.

Western Province captains 1971-1991 (3-day era)

Coetie Neethling (2 games: 1971-73).

Gertjie Williams (8 games: 1971-73 and 1974/75).

Lefty Adams (10 games: 1974/75 and 1979/80).

Dickie Conrad (5 games: 1971-73 and 1973/74).

Brian O'Connell (6 games: 1975/76).

Rushdi Magiet (12 games: 1977/78-1978/79).

Charles van Schalkwyk (14 games: 1980/81-1982/83).

Armien Jabaar (16 games: 1982/83 - 1985/86).

Saait Magiet (15 games: 1983/84 and 1985/86-1987/88).

Goolam Allie (3 games: 1985/86).

Vincent Barnes (4 games: 1988/89-1989/90).

Seraj Gabriels (14 games: 1988/89-1990/91).

Western Province captains in centralised Dadabhay tournaments

1961/62 Gasant "Tiny" Abed

1963/64 Owen Williams

1966 Salie "Lobo" Abed

1968 John "Coetie" Neethling

1969 John "Coetie" Neethling

Father and sons who played for Western Province

Three father and son combinations represented Western Province.

Dickie Conrad (1964-1975) & Shukri Conrad (1985-1991).

Taliep Behardien (1961-1970) & Ismail Behardien (1986-1991).

Ebrahim Isaacs (1968-1984) & Mishal Isaacs (1991).

Brothers who played for Western Province

Two sets of brothers played for Western Province in the same 3-day matches.

Rushdi and Saait Magiet.

Gertjie and Jacobus "Kosie" Williams.

*Robbie and Keith van Graan also played for Western Province but never in the same first-class match. They did, however, play in a limited overs provincial match.

The Ebrahim brothers - Mohammed (1978), Yusuf (1979) and Faizel (1988-1991) played in different periods, as did the Galant brothers - Sa-at (1980) and Mogamat (1989).

The Abed brothers - Tiny, Lobo and Dik played for Western Province in the Dadabhay centralised tournament, but not in first-class games.

Western Province players who played for Transvaal

Munsoor Abdullah

Vincent Barnes

Michael Doman

Seraj Gabriels

Armien Jabaar

Nasser Kemp

John Kleinveldt

Ebrahim Mohammed

Nilton Muller

Rashaad Musson

André Odendaal

Players from other provinces who represented Western Province

Ismail Timol, who started his career with Natal, played two games for Western Province in 1975/76.

Imraan Hendricks, of Eastern Province played one game for Western Province - against Eastern Province in November 1982.

Abdul Haq Manack of Transvaal played six games for Western Province in the 1989/90 season.

Goolam Allie, who started his career with Natal, played 16 games for Western Province including three as captain in 1985/86.

Zak Davids, who started his first class career with Eastern Province, played four games for Western Province between 1980 and 1981.

Aziz Samaai, who played for Transvaal, was 12th man for Western Province.

Aziz Wadvalla of Transvaal played 2 games for Western Province in 1978/79.

Centuries

166 - Dickie Conrad vs Transvaal, 30 December 1972-2 January 1973 in Cape Town.

148* - Deon Kemp vs Natal 27-29 December 1988 in Cape Town.

146 - Faiek Davids vs Eastern Province 23-25 January 1988 in Cape Town.

143 - Neil Fortune vs Natal 21-23 March 1982 in Cape Town.

142 - Ismail Behardien vs Natal 17-19 November 1990 in Cape Town.

139 - Dickie Conrad vs Transvaal 26-28 December 1971 in Johannesburg.

137 - Joey Lambert vs Eastern Province 16-18 November 1973 in Cape Town.

137 - Stuart Hendricks vs Transvaal 14-16 March 1987 in Johannesburg.

125* - Nazeem White vs Natal 17-19 November 1990 in Cape Town.

116 - Yunus Thomas vs Transvaal 1-3 January 1986 in Johannesburg.

109 - Munsoor Abdullah vs Natal 27-29 December 1986 in Cape Town.

109 - Nazeem White vs Transvaal 26-28 January 1991 in Cape Town.

108 - Rashaad Musson vs Transvaal 30 December 1980-1 January 1981 in Cape Town.

108 - Ismail Behardien v Natal 1-3 January 1990 in Durban.

107 - Munsoor Abdullah vs Transvaal 27-29 December 1983 in Johannesburg.

107*- Faiek Davids vs Transvaal 2-4 January 1988 in Johannesburg.

106 - Faiek Davids vs Transvaal 27-29 December 1989 in Johannesburg.

103 - Ebrahim Isaacs vs Natal 31 December 1979-2 January 1980 in Durban.

102 - Munsoor Abdullah vs Eastern Province 21-23 January 1984 in Cape Town.

101* - Seraj Gabriels vs Natal 16-18 March 1985 in Tongaat.

100 - Viccie Moodie vs Transvaal 30 December 1972-2 January 1973 in Cape Town.

100* - Yunus Thomas vs Transvaal 18 - 20 February 1984 in Cape Town.

100 - Saait Magiet vs Natal 27-29 December 1986 in Cape Town.

100* - Saait Magiet vs Natal 21-23 February 1987 in Pietermaritzburg.

Most Centuries

3 - Munsoor Abdullah and Faiek Davids.

2 - Saait Magiet, Dickie Conrad, Yunus Thomas, Ismail Behardien and Nazeem White.

Most Fifties

13 - Saait Magiet.

11- Munsoor Abdullah, Faiek Davids.

10 - Seraj Gabriels.

7 - Yunus Thomas.

6 - Neil Fortune.

5 - Ebrahim Isaacs, Stuart Hendricks.

4 - Rashaad Musson and Deon Kemp.

3 - Viccie Moodie, Rushdi Magiet, Armien Jabaar,Charles van Schalkwyk, Cyril Martin, Michael Doman, Nazeem White, Faghme Solomons, Ismail Behardien.

Batting average of 50 or higher in a season

Faiek Davids (1988/89) 436 runs - average 72,67.

Armien Jabaar (1983/84) 250 runs - average 62,50.

Dickie Conrad (1971-73) 492 runs - average 61,50.

Faiek Davids (1987/88) 429 runs - average 61,28.

Nazeem White (1990/91) 407 runs - average 58,14.

Saait Magiet (1986/87) 335 runs - average 55,83.

Munsoor Abdullah (1983/84) 271 runs - average 54,20.

Munsoor Abdullah (1987/88) 270 runs - average 54,00.

Rashaad Musson (1980/81) 467 runs - average 51,89.

Viccie Moodie (1971-73) 353 runs - average 50,42.

Ten wickets in a match

5 - Seraj Gabriels

4 - Vincent Barnes

3 - Lefty Adams

2 - Armien Jabaar

1 - Rushdi Magiet, Howie Bergins

Five wickets in an innings

19 - Vincent Barnes

11 - Armien Jabaar, Seraj Gabriels

8 - Lefty Adams

7 - Saait Magiet

5 - Rushdi Magiet

3 - Jock Mahoney, Goolam Allie, Abdul Haq Manack

2 - Howie Bergins, Winston Carelse, Faiek Davids, Ebrahim Mohammed

1 - Coetie Neethling, Gertjie Williams, Willie Hendricks, George van Oordt, Reggie February, Fuad Benjamin, Adnaan Meyer, Yunus Thomas, Charles Hendrikse, Trevor Seconds

Ducks on debut - players who made a duck in their first innings for Western Province

Clive Kolbe vs Eastern Province 8-10 January 1972 in Port Elizabeth.

Marshall September vs Transvaal 1-3 1973 in Cape Town.

Henry Arenz vs Natal 16-18 March 1974 in Durban.

Brian O'Connell vs Natal 16-18 March 1974 in Durban.

Howie Bergins vs Eastern Province 22-24 November 1975 in Port Elizabeth.

Hillary Dawson vs Natal 1-3 January 1976 in Cape Town.

Arthur Katts vs Natal 1-3 January 1976 in Cape Town.

Norman Arendse vs Eastern Province 26-28 November 1977 in Cape Town.

Aziz Wadvalla vs Transvaal 26-28 December 1977 in Johannesburg.

Vincent Barnes vs Eastern Province 18-20 November 1978 in Cape Town.

Noeg Martin vs Natal 26-28 December 1978 in Durban.

Yusuf Ebrahim vs Eastern Province 20-22 January 1979 in Port Elizabeth.

Zak Davids vs Eastern Province 15-17 March 1980 in Cape Town.

Stuart Hendricks vs Transvaal 30 December 1980-1 January 1981 in Cape Town.

Mervyn Theron vs Eastern Province 13-15 March 1981 in Port Elizabeth.

Seraj Gabriels vs Eastern Province 21-23 November 1981 in Cape Town.

Randall van Graan vs Eastern Province 23-25 January 1982 in Port Elizabeth.

Imraan Hendricks vs Eastern Province 20-22 November 1982 in Port Elizabeth.

Shadley Martin vs Natal 28-30 December 1982 in Cape Town.

Hassiem Price vs Transvaal 1-3 January 1983 in Cape Town.

Fuad Benjamin vs Transvaal 1-3 January 1983 in Cape Town.

Faiek Davids vs Transvaal 18-20 February 1984 in Cape Town.

Faizel Ebrahim vs Eastern Province 16-18 November 1985 in Port Elizabeth.

Clinton Ravens vs Eastern Province 18-20 January 1986 in Cape Town.

Ten Most Capped Players:

64 - Saait Magiet

53 - Vincent Barnes

51 - Ebrahim Isaacs

48 - Seraj Gabriels

44 - Armien Jabaar

39 - Munsoor Abdullah

38 - Yunus Thomas

34 - Rushdi Magiet

33 - Stuart Hendricks

32 - Faiek Davids

Batsmen who scored more than 1 000 runs

2 397 - Saait Magiet (average 27,23).

1 854 - Munsoor Abdullah (average 32,52).

1 615 - Faiek Davids (average 35,89).

1 458 - Seraj Gabriels (average 22,43).

1 458 - Ebrahim Isaacs (average 18,69).

1 320 - Yunus Thomas (average 26,94).

1 267 - Stuart Hendricks (average 23,46).

1 169 - Armien Jabaar (average 20,88).

1 034 - Ismail Behardien (average 28,72).

1 023 - Neil Fortune (average 24,36).

Bowlers who took more than 100 wickets:

250 - Vincent Barnes (average 10,86).

188 - Armien Jabaar (average 11,60).

173 - Seraj Gabriels (average 14,31).

169 - Saait Magiet (average 12,71),

116 - Lefty Adams (average 14,67).

Records against opposition:

Transvaal

- Home

played: 18 won: 14 lost: 2 drawn: 2

- Away

played: 18 won: 10 lost 1 drawn: 7

Natal

- Home

played: 18 won: 16 lost: 1 drawn: 1

- Away

played: 18 won: 7 lost: 4 drawn: 7

Eastern Province

- Home

played: 18 won: 12 lost: 1 drawn: 4

- Away

played: 18 won: 6 lost: 9 drawn: 3

*1 match was tied

Career records of players who represented WP at First Class level (1971-1991)

Abdullah, Munsoor

right-hand middle-order batsman; clubs: United, Montrose; debut vs EP in Port Elizabeth, 21-23 January 1978; 39 matches; 1 854 runs; average 32,53; highest score 109 vs Natal in Cape Town, December 1986; 3 x 100, 11 x 50; bowling figures 9-3-28-1; 35 catches.

Abrahams, Cecil

right-hand medium-pacer; middle-order batsman; overseas professional; debut vs EP in Cape Town, 23-25 November 1974; 5 matches, 111 runs; average 15,86; highest score 40 v Transvaal in Cape Town, January 1975; 8 wickets, average 23,50; best bowling 3/18 v Transvaal in Johannesburg, March 1975; 4 catches.

Adams, Abdurahman *"Lefty"*

left-arm spinner, lower-order batsman; clubs: Pirates, Primrose, WPCA, Metropolitan CA; debut vs Transvaal in Johannesburg, 26-28 December 1971; 22 matches, 10 as captain; 116 wickets, average 13,73; best bowling 6/7 vs EP in Cape Town, March 1980; 3 x 10 wickets in an innings, 8 x 5 wickets in an innings; 180 runs, average 13,84; highest score 39 vs Natal, February 1980; 13 catches.

Adams, Yusuf *"Gogs"*

left-hand opening batsman; clubs: Blue Bells, Primrose; debut vs EP in Port Elizabeth, 17-19 November 1979; 7 matches; 193 runs, average 13,79; highest score 55 vs EP, November 1979; 1 x 50); 6 catches.

Ahmed, Hoosain

right-hand opening batsman; clubs: Kenston, Montrose; debut vs Transvaal in Cape Town, 28-30 December 1985; 4 matches; 75 runs, average 12,50; highest score 39 vs EP in Port Elizabeth, January 1985; 1 catch.

Allie, Goolam

right-hand seamer; lower-order batsman; clubs: Primrose; debut vs EP in Cape Town 26-28 November 1977; 16 matches, 3 as captain; 49 wickets, average 12,14; best bowling 6/45 vs EP in Cape Town, November 1984; 3 x 5 wickets in an innings; 74 runs, average 9,25; highest score 19 vs Natal in Cape Town, March 1984; 3 catches.

Allie, Mogamat Zain *"Muis"*

right-hand top order batsman; clubs: Primrose, Montrose; debut vs Natal in Durban, 26-28 December 1978; 4 matches; 43 runs, average 5,38; highest score 10 vs Transvaal in Johannesburg, November 1980.

Antulay, Nasser

right-hand middle-order batsman; club: Montrose; debut vs Natal in Cape Town, 26-28 December 1982; 18 matches; 578 runs, average 21,41; highest score 69, vs Natal in Durban, December 1985; 2 x 50; bowling figures 17,1-6-39-2; 19 catches.

Arendse, Norman

right-hand top-order batsman; clubs: Metropolitan, Victoria; debut vs EP in Cape Town, 26-28 November 1977; 2 matches; 6 runs average 1,50; highest score 3, vs EP, Nov 1977, bowling figures. 5-1-15-0; 2 catches.

Arenz, Henry

right-hand opening batsman/wicketkeeper, clubs: St Augustines, Metropolitan CA; debut vs Natal in Durban 16-18 March 1974; 1 match; 10 runs; 3 dismissals (2 catches and 1 stumping).

Arnold, Sheraat

off-spinner, clubs: Hottentots Holland, Primrose; debut vs Natal in Durban 4-6 March 1978; 3 matches; 8 wickets, average 27,00; best bowling 4/50 vs Natal in Durban March 1978; 16 runs (no average – all not out); highest score 7* vs Natal in Durban, December 1978; 2 catches.

Barnes, Vincent

right-hand opening bowler, clubs: Victoria, Montrose; debut vs EP in Cape Town, 18-20 November 1978; 53 matches; 250 wickets average 10,86; best bowling 9/46 vs Natal in Ladysmith, January 1984; 4 x 10 wickets in an innings; 19 x 5 wickets in an innings; 315 runs, average 9,00; highest score 41 vs Natal in Cape Town, February 1980; 32 catches.

Behardien, Ismail

left-hand top-order batsman; clubs: Blue Bells, United; debut vs Transvaal in Cape Town, 15-17 March 1986; 25matches; 1034 runs, average 28,72; highest score 142 vs Natal in Cape Town, November 1990;(2 x 100, 3 x 50; 44 catches.

Benjamin, Fuad

off-spinner; club: Primrose; debut vs Transvaal in Cape Town, 1-3 January 1983; 15 matches; 29 wickets, average 26,93; best bowling 6/35 vs Natal in Durban, January 1990; 60 runs, average. 5,45; highest score 16* vs Natal in Cape Town, January 1990; 8 catches.

Bergins, Howard

right-hand opening bowler, clubs: Bellville, UWC, Maitland Parow CA; debut vs EP in Port Elizabeth 22-24 November 1975; 30 wickets, average. 11,90; best bowling 6/27 v Transvaal in Johannesburg, December 1975; 1 x 10 wickets in an innings, 2 x 5 wickets in an innings; 83 runs, average 11,86; highest score 27* vs EP in Cape Town, January 1976; 1 catch.

Booysen, Neville

left-hand opening bowler; lower-order batsman; club: Tigers; debut vs Natal in Tongaat, 16-18 March 1985; 5 matches; 17 wickets, average 15,82; best bowling 3/29 vs Natal in Cape Town, December 1986; 99 runs, average 24,75; highest score 38 vs Transvaal in Cape Town, January 1987; 1 catch.

Brache, Noel

left-hand top-order batsman; clubs: Ashtondale, Avendale, Metropolitan CA; debut vs EP in Port Elizabeth, 18-20 January 1975; 2 matches; 5 runs; highest score. 3 v EP in January 1975.

Burns, Ashraf "Astie"

left-hand middle-order batsman; club: United; debut vs Transvaal in Cape Town, 15-17 March 1986; 1 match; 9 runs; highest score 9* vs Transvaal.

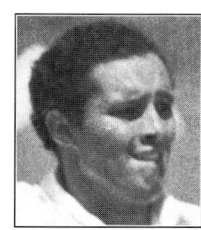

Carelse, Winston *"Pinky"*

right-hand medium-pacer, lower-order batsman; clubs: Wynberg, Cape District CA; debut vs EP in Port Elizabeth 22-24 November 1975; 6 matches; 232 runs, average 33,14; highest score 61* vs EP, January 1976 in Cape Town; 1 x 50; 20 wickets, average 10,50; best bowling 5/15 vs Natal in Cape Town, January 1976; 2 x 5 wickets in an innings; 2 catches.

Coericius, Anthony

right-hand top-order batsman; clubs: UWC, Tigers; debut vs EP in Port Elizabeth 16-18 November 1985; 1 match; 4 runs, average 2,00; highest score 3 vs EP in Port Elizabeth, November 1985.

*Conrad, Sedick *"Dickie"*

opening batsman; clubs: Vineyards, Primrose, WPCA, Wynberg CA; debut vs Transvaal in Johannesburg, December 1971; 8 matches, 5 as captain; 524 runs average 40,30; highest score 166 vs Transvaal in Cape Town, January 1973; 2 x 100, 1 x 50; bowling figures 1-0-1-0.

Conrad, Shukri

middle-order batsman, right-hand seamer; clubs: United, Montrose; debut vs Natal in Durban, 28-30 December 1985; 9 matches; 324 runs, average, 24,92; highest score 63 vs EP in Cape Town, December 1990; 2 x 50; 13 wickets, average 21,62; best bowling 4/35 vs EP in Cape Town, December 1990; 7 catches.

Cupido, Randall *"Joey"*

wicketkeeper, right-hand batsman; clubs: St Augustines, Metropolitan; debut vs Natal in Cape Town, 17-19 March 1984; 19 matches; 49 catches, 13 stumpings; 448 runs, average 21,33; highest score 62 vs Natal in Cape Town, March 1984; (2 x 50); bowling figures 8-0-24-2.

*Dagnin, Ivan

right-hand opening batsman; clubs: Silver Crowns, Wynberg CA, Peninsula; debut vs Transvaal in Johannesburg 26-28 December 1971; 4 matches; 58 runs, average 8,29; highest score 19 vs Natal in Cape Town, January 1972; 1 catch.

Dammert, Barry

right-hand middle-order batsman, medium-pacer; club: Bellville; debut vs EP in Cape Town, November 1989; 4 matches; 104 runs, average 17,33; highest score 57 vs Transvaal in Johannesburg, December 1989; 1 x 50; bowling figures 3-1-9-0; 2 catches.

Damon, Ebrahim *"Baby"*

right-hand opening bowler; club: United; debut vs Transvaal in Johannesburg 26-28 December 1977; 14 matches; 37 wickets, average 19,86; best bowling 4/21 vs Transvaal in Johannesburg, December 1977); 86 runs, average 5,73; highest score 20 vs Natal in Cape Town, December 1982; 6 catches.

Davids, Faiek

right-hand middle-order batsman, medium-pacer; clubs: Primrose, United; debut vs Transvaal in Cape Town, 18-20 February 1984; 32 matches; 1 615 runs, average 35,89; highest score 146 vs EP in Cape Town; 2 x 100; 11 x 50; 62 wickets, average. 16,98; best bowling 5/50 vs EP; 2 x 5 wickets in an innings; 20 catches.

Davids, Zak

all-rounder; clubs: United, Primrose; debut vs EP in Cape Town, 15-17 March 1980; 5 matches; 89 runs, average 44,50; highest score 55* vs Natal in Cape Town, March 1984; 1 x 50; 8 wickets, average 14,75; best bowling 4/29 vs Natal, December 1980; 7 catches.

Dawson, Hilary

right-hand top-order batsman, wicketkeeper; clubs: Ashtondale, Metropolitan CA, Westridge; debut vs EP 22-24 November 1975 in Port Elizabeth; 9 matches; 98 runs, average 8,17; highest score 29* vs Natal in Durban, December 1985; 18 catches.

Doman, Michael

right-hand middle-order batsman, leg spinner; club: Victoria; debut vs Transvaal in Cape Town, February 11-13, 1978; 12 matches; 388 runs, average 19,40; highest score 64 vs Transvaal in Cape Town, January 1980; 3 x 50; 10 wickets, average 20,20; best bowling 2/11 vs Transvaal in Cape Town, December 1980; 9 catches.

Dyason, Clinton

right-hand top-order batsman, leg spinner; club: Rivertonians; debut vs EP in Cape Town, 21-23 January 1989; 3 matches; 101 runs, average 20,20; highest score 40 vs Natal in Durban, February 1989; bowling figures 16,5-3-29-3.

Ebrahim, Faizel

left-hand top-order batsman, spinner; clubs: Elsies River, United, Primrose; debut vs EP in Port Elizabeth, 16-18 November 1985; 12 matches; 270 runs, average 16,88; highest score 70 vs EP in Port Elizabeth, November 1985; 1 x 50; bowling figures 45-5-114-2; 10 catches.

Ebrahim, Mohammed

right-hand top-order batsman; clubs: Elsies River, United; debut vs Transvaal in Cape Town, 11-13 February 1978; 1 match; 29 runs, average 14,50; highest score 19 vs Transvaal in Cape Town, February 1978.

Ebrahim, Yusuf

right-hand seamer, lower-order batsman; clubs: Elsies River, United, Primrose; debut vs EP in Port Elizabeth, 17-19 January 1979; 1 match; 21 runs, average 11,50; highest score 21 vs EP in Port Elizabeth, January 1979; bowling figures 6-0-40-0.

February, Reginald *"Koela"*

right-hand seamer, lower-order batsman; clubs: Stellenbosch, Montrose; debut vs Transvaal in Cape Town, 15-17 March 1986; 12 matches; 40 wickets, average 20,85; best bowling 6/73 vs Transvaal in Cape Town, March 1988; 1 x 5 wickets in an innings; 186 runs, average 26,57; highest score 37 vs Natal in Durban, December 1987; 5 catches.

Felix, Cecil

right-hand opening batsman; club: Rivertonians; debut vs Natal in Cape Town, 17-19 March 1984; 1 match; 27 runs, average 27,00; highest score 27 vs Natal in Cape Town, March 1984.

*Finnan, Mike

right-hand opening batsman; club: Victoria; debut vs EP in Cape Town, 26-28 November 1977; 4 matches; 82 runs, average 13,67; highest score 31 vs EP in Cape Town, November 1977; 2 catches.

Fortune, Neil

right-hand top-order batsman; clubs: Metropolitan, Victoria; debut vs Natal 17-19 February 1979 in Cape Town; 25 matches; 1 023 runs, average 24,36; highest score 143 vs Natal in Cape Town, March 1982; 1 x 100, 6 x 50; bowling figures 12-1-40-0; 20 catches.

Gabriels, Seraj

leg-spinner, top-order batsman; clubs: United, Primrose; debut vs EP in Cape Town, 21,23 November 1981; 48 matches, 14 as captain; 1 458 runs, average 22,43; highest score 101* vs Natal in Durban, March 1985; 1 x 100, 10 x 50; 173 wickets, average 14,31; best bowling 8/53 vs Natal in Durban, December 1985; 5 x 10 wickets in an innings, 11 x 5 wickets in an innings; 33 catches.

Gafieldien, Ebrahim

left-hand opening batsman; clubs: Hottentots Holland, Primrose; debut vs Natal in Cape Town, 20-22 January 1990; 7 matches; 179 runs, average 17,90; highest score 86 vs EP in Port Elizabeth, March 1990; 1 x 50; 2 catches.

Galant, Mogamat

right-hand middle-order batsman, seamer; club: United; debut vs Natal in Cape Town, 27-29 December 1988; 2 matches; 28 runs, average 14,00; highest score 14 vs Natal in Cape Town, December 1988; bowling figures 7-2-19-0; 2 catches.

Galant, Sa-at

right-hand. opening batsman; clubs: United, Primrose; debut vs Transvaal, 4-6 January 1980 in Johannesburg; 1 match; 19 runs, average 14,00; highest score 19 vs Transvaal in Johannesburg, January 1980; 1 catch.

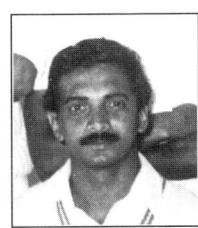

Green, Salie

left-hand opening bowler, lower-order batsman; club: United; debut vs Natal in Cape Town, 27-29 December 1988; 1 match; 5 wickets, average 7,00; best bowling 3/26 vs Natal in Cape Town, December 1988.

Harris, Edward

right-hand top-order batsman, club: Victoria; debut vs Transvaal in Cape Town, 1-3 January 1983; 10 matches; 298 runs, average 22,92; highest score 58 vs Transvaal in Cape Town, February 1984; 2 x 50; 7 catches.

Haupt, Mark

right-hand top-order batsman; clubs: Metropolitan, Victoria; debut vs EP in Port Elizabeth, 19-21 January 1985; 1 match; 56 runs, average. 28,00; highest score 36 vs EP in Port Elizabeth, January 1985; bowling figures 3-0-9-0.

Hendricks, Imraan

all-rounder; club: Primrose; debut vs EP in Port Elizabeth 20-22 November 1982; 1 match; 2 wickets, average 32,5; best bowling 2/65 vs EP in Port Elizabeth, November 1982; 5 runs, average 2,5; highest score 5 vs EP in Port Elizabeth, November 1982.

Hendricks, Stuart

right-hand opening batsman; club: Montrose; debut vs Transvaal in Cape Town, 30 December 1980-1 January 1981; 33 matches; 1 267 runs, average 23,46; highest score 137 vs Transvaal in Johannesburg, March 1987; 1 x 100, 5 x 50; bowling figures 3-0-10-0; 31 catches.

Hendricks, Willie

right-hand opening batsman, leg-spinner; clubs: Victoria, Wynberg CA; debut vs EP in Cape Town, 16-18 November 1973; 18 matches; 424 runs, average 14,62; highest score 60 vs Natal in Cape Town, January 1976; 2 x 50; 27 wickets, average 13,19; best bowling 5/9 vs EP in Cape Town, November 1974; 1 x 5 wickets in an innings; 9 catches.

Hendrikse, Charles

right-hand seamer, lower-order batsman; club: Stellenbosch; debut vs Natal in Durban, 18-20 February 1989; 6 matches; 18 wickets, average 13,00; best bowling 6/20 vs Natal in Durban, February 1989; 1 x 5 wickets in an innings; 114 runs, average 22,80; highest score 31* vs Natal in Durban, February 1989; 6 catches.

Henry, Omar

left-arm spinner, lower-order batsman; clubs: Excelsior, Stellenbosch CA; debut vs Natal in Durban, 16-18 March 1974; 8 matches; 9 wickets, average 34,44; best bowling 3/47 vs EP in Port Elizabeth, November 1975; 128 runs, average 11,64; highest score 62* vs Transvaal in Cape Town, February 1976; 1 x 50; 8 catches.

Holder, John

opening bowler, overseas professional; debut vs EP in Cape Town 23-25 November 1974; 1 match, bowling figures 16-6-33-0; best bowling 0/2; 7 runs; highest score 4 vs EP in Cape Town, November 1974; 1 catch.

*Isaacs, Ebrahim *"Braima"*

right-hand top-order batsman/wicketkeeper; clubs: Pirates, Primrose, Metropolitan CA, Wynberg CA; debut vs Transvaal in Johannesburg 26-28 December 1971; 51 Matches; 1 458 runs, average 18,69; highest score 103 vs Natal in Durban, December 1979; 1 x 100, 5 x 50; 119 catches, 42 stumpings; bowling figures 5,3-0-9-1.

Isaacs, Mishal

left-hand opening batsman; club: Primrose; debut vs EP in Port Elizabeth, 16-18 February 1991; 1 match; 13 runs, average 6,50; highest score 8 vs EP in Port Elizabeth, 1991.

Jabaar, Armien

right-hand middle-order batsman, leg-spinner; clubs: Arabian College, WPCA, United, Montrose; debut vs Natal in Durban, 14-16 December 1974; 44 matches; captained WP 14 times; 1 169 runs, average. 20,88; highest score 70 vs EP in Port Elizabeth, November 1983; 3 x 50; 188 wickets, average 11,60; best bowling 7/38 vs Natal in Cape Town, March 1982; 2 x 10 wickets in an innings, 11 x 5 wickets in an innings; 26 catches.

Jacobs, Lawton

right-hand opening batsman; clubs: Newtons, Elma, Stellenbosch CA, Maitland-Parow CA; debut vs Transvaal in Cape Town 16-18 February 1974; 15 matches; 535 runs, average 22,29; highest score 50 vs Rest of Sacboc in Stellenbosch, March 1976; 1 x 50; bowling figures 3,4-1-5-2; 8 catches.

Jakoet, Abdurahman

"Manie"

right-hand opening batsman; club: United; 3 matches; 89 runs, average 17,80; highest score 64 vs Transvaal in Potchefstroom, March, 1979; 1 x 50; bowling figures 1-0-2-0.

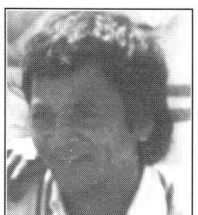

Jassiem, Shamiel

off-spinner, lower-order batsman; club: Ottomans; debut vs EP in Port Elizabeth, 21-23 January 1978; 6 matches; 118 runs, average 19,67; highest score 43* vs EP in Port Elizabeth, January 1978; 8 wickets, average 18,13; best bowling 4/27 vs Transvaal in Cape Town, December 1978; 1 catch.

Katts, Arthur

right-hand middle-order batsman; clubs: All Saints, Somerset West CA, Helderberg CC; debut vs Natal in Cape Town, 1-3 January 1976; 6 matches; 109 runs, average 10,90; highest score 40 vs EP in Cape Town, January 1981; 6 catches.

Kemp, Deon

right-hand middle-order batsman; clubs: Crusaders, St Augustines, Montrose; debut vs EP in Port Elizabeth, 21-23 November 1987; 18 matches; 637 runs, average 25,48; highest score 148* vs Natal in Cape Town, December 1988; 1 x 100, 4 x 50; bowling figures 25-4-93-2; 20 catches.

Kemp, Nasser

right-hand batsman, wicketkeeper; clubs: Blue Bells, United; debut vs EP in Port Elizabeth 16-18 November 1979; 1 match; 6 runs, average 3; highest score 3 vs EP in Port Elizabeth, November 1979.

Khan, Gameem

right-hand batsman, wicketkeeper; club: Ottomans; debut vs EP in Cape Town, 18-20 January 1986; 2 matches; 67 runs, average 16,75; highest score 52 vs EP in Cape Town, January 1986, 1x50; 4 catches, 3 stumpings.

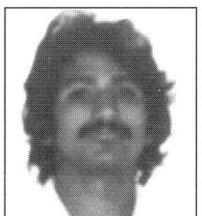

Khan, Jumannah

off-spinner; clubs: Silvertree, WPCA; debut vs EP in Port Elizabeth 27-29 January 1973; 6 matches; 12 wickets, average 20,00; best bowling 3/25 vs Natal in Cape Town, February 1975; 56 runs, average 14,00; highest score 23* vs Rest of SA in Cape Town, March 1973; 7 catches.

Kleinveldt, John

right-hand seamer, lower-order batsman; clubs: Metropolitan, Victoria, Montrose; debut vs EP 16-18 November 1979 in Port Elizabeth; 10 matches; 25 wickets, average 17,20; best bowling 4/35 vs Natal, December 1979 in Durban; 146 runs, average 12,17; highest score 43 vs EP in Cape Town, January 1981; 12 catches.

Kolbe, Clive

right-hand middle-order batsman, leg spinner; clubs: St Augustines, Metropolitan CA; debut vs EP in Port Elizabeth 8-10 January 1972 in Port Elizabeth; 4 matches; 103 runs, average 14,71; highest score 50 vs Transvaal in Cape Town, February 1974; 1 x 50; 7 wickets, average 13,71; best bowling 4/52 vs Transvaal in Cape Town, February 1974; 1 catch.

*Lakay, Neville

right-hand top-order batsman, medium-pacer; clubs: Oakdale, Cape District CA; debut vs Natal 1-4 January 1972 in Cape Town; 1 match; 14 runs; bowling: 1-0-5-0.
* Note: Lakay played in all five Dadabhay centralised tournaments between 1961 and 1970.

*Lambert, Joey

right-hand top-order batsman, leg spinner; clubs: Young Ideas, Primrose, St Augustines, WPCA, Wynberg CA; debut vs Transvaal in Johannesburg, 26-28 December 1971; 7 matches; 292 runs, average 24,33; highest score 137 vs EP in Cape Town, November 1973; 1 x 100; 5 wickets, average 7,20; best bowling 4/18 vs Natal in Cape Town, January 1974.

Loggenstein, Quentin

right-hand opening bowler, lower-order batsman; club: Rivertonians; debut vs EP in Cape Town, 8-10 December 1990; 2 matches; 2 wickets, average 52,00; best bowling 1/38 vs EP in Cape Town, December 1990; 13 runs, average 6,50; highest score 12 vs Transvaal in Johannesburg, January 1991; 2 catches.

*Maclons, Mornay *"Kulu"*

right-hand batsman, wicketkeeper; clubs: Elsies River, Somerset West CA, Maitland Parow CA; debut vs EP in Port Elizabeth 8-10 January 1972; 17 matches; 416 runs, average 16,00; highest score 75* vs Natal in Durban, March 1974, 1x50; 39 catches, 15 stumpings.

*Magiet, Rushdi

right-hand seamer, lower-order batsman; clubs: Combine, Primrose, Wynberg CA; debut vs Transvaal 26-28 December 1971 in Johannesburg; 34 matches, 12 as captain; 841 runs, average. 17,52, highest score 76 vs EP in Port Elizabeth January 1975; 2 x 50; 97 wickets, average 13,46; best bowling 7/35 vs Transvaal in Cape Town, December 1978; 1 x 10 wickets in an innings, 5 x 5 wickets in an innings; 33 catches.

Magiet, Saait

right-hand opening bowler, middle-order batsman; clubs: Primrose, Wynberg CA; debut vs Natal 1-4 January 1972 in Cape Town; 64 matches; 169 wickets, average 12,71; best bowling 6/24 vs Natal in Cape Town, February 1975; 6 x 5 wickets in an innings; 2 397 runs, average 27,24; highest score 100* vs Natal in Cape Town, December 1986; 2 x 100, 13 x 50; 60 catches.

Mahoney, Jock

right-hand opening bowler, lower-order batsman; clubs: St Augustines, UWC, Metropolitan CA; debut vs EP in Port Elizabeth 27-29 January 1973; 19 matches; 377 runs, average 18,85; highest score 68* vs Transvaal in Cape Town, January 1975; 2 x 50; 48 wickets, average 18,69; best bowling 6/42 vs EP in Port Elizabeth, November 1975; 3 x 5 wickets in an innings; 12 catches.

Manack, Abdul Haq *"Jack"*

right-hand opening bowler, lower-order batsman; club: Ottomans; debut vs EP in Cape Town, 25-27 November 1989; 5 matches; 27 wickets, average 11,33; best bowling 7/17 vs EP in Port Elizabeth, March 1990; 3 x 5 wickets in an innings; 54 runs, average 13,50; highest score 27 vs EP in Cape Town, November 1989; 4 catches.

Martin, Cyril

right-hand middle-order batsman; club: Primrose; debut vs EP in Cape Town, 26-28 November 1977; 13 matches; 297 runs, average 16,50; highest score 66 vs Transvaal in Johannesburg, 1980; 3 x 50; bowling figures 5-2-18-0; 9 catches.

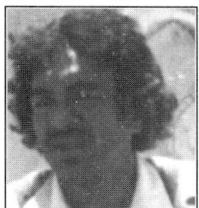

Martin, Noeg

right-hand top-order batsman, off spinner; club: Ottomans; debut vs Natal in Durban, 26-28 December 1978; 5 matches; 158 runs, average 17,56; highest score 43 vs Transvaal in Cape Town, December 1978; bowling figures 13-2-32-2; 1 catch.

Martin, Shadley

left-hand opening batsman; club: Primrose; debut vs Natal in Cape Town, 28-30 December 1982; 1 match; 8 runs, average 4,00; highest score 8 vs Natal in Cape Town, December 1982.

Meyer, Adnaan

right-hand opening bowler, lower-order batsman; clubs: Blue Bells, Montrose; debut vs Natal in Cape Town, 17-19 November 1990; 6 matches; 27 wickets, average 10,70; best bowling 5/22 vs Natal in Cape Town, November 1990; 1 x 5 wickets in an innings; 86 runs, average 17,20; highest score 36 vs EP in Cape Town, December 1990; 3 catches.

Miller, Cedric

right-hand batsman; club: Hands and Heart, Cape District CA; debut vs Rest of Sacboc in Cape Town, March 1976; 1 match; 12 runs, average 6,00; highest score 11; bowling figures 6-0-21-0; 1 catch.

Miller, Gerry

left-hand batsman, right-hand seamer; club: St Augustines; debut vs EP in Cape Town, 17-19 November 1984; 4 matches; 32 runs, average 5,33; highest score 14 vs Natal in Durban, February 1987; 3 wickets, average 34,67; best bowling 2/2 vs EP in Port Elizabeth, November 1988; 2 catches.

Mohammed, Ebrahim
"Barney"

right-hand opening bowler, lower-order batsman; clubs: Primrose, Ottomans; debut vs EP in Cape Town, 17-19 November 1984; 7 matches; 24 wickets, average 14,17; best bowling 5/30 vs EP in Cape Town, January 1989; 2 x 5 wickets in an innings; 103 runs, average 17,17; highest score 28 vs Natal in Durban, February 1989; 5 catches.

*Moodie, Viccie

right-hand top-order batsman; clubs: Elsies River, Maitland Parow CA; debut vs Transvaal in Johannesburg, 26-28 December 1971; 17 matches; 665 runs, average 28,91; highest score 100 vs Transvaal in Cape Town, January 1973; 1 x 100, 3 x 50; bowling figures 4,3-0-30-0, 14 catches.

Muller, Nilton

right-hand middle-order batsman, medium pacer; clubs: Stellenbosch, Montrose; debut vs Natal in Pietermaritzburg, 29-31 December 1987; 7 matches; 219 runs, average 24,33; highest score 74 vs Natal in Cape Town, January 1990; 1 x 50; 14 wickets, average 16,35; best bowling 3/18 vs Natal in Pietermaritzburg, December 1987; 2 catches.

Musson, Rashaad

right-hand opening batsman, occasional wicket-keeper; clubs: Victoria, United; debut vs Transvaal in Johannesburg, 15-17 November 1980; 18 matches; 739 runs, average 26,39; highest score 108 vs Transvaal in Cape Town, December 1980; 1 x 100, 4 x 50; 12 catches, 2 stumpings.

*Neethling, John *"Coetie"*

right-hand seamer, lower-order batsman; clubs: Elma, Elsies River, Maitland Parow CA; debut vs Transvaal, 26-28 December 1971 in Johannesburg; 11 matches; 215 runs, average 20,23; highest score 53 vs EP in Cape Town, January 1973; 1 x 50; 17 wickets, average 27,23; best bowling 5/53 vs Natal in Cape Town, January 1974; 1 x 5 wickets in an innings; 16 catches.

O'Connell, Brian

right-hand middle-order batsman, seamer; clubs: Melbourne, Cape District CA; debut vs Natal in Durban 16-18 March 1974; 8 matches, 7 as captain; 308 runs, average 30,80; highest score 79 vs EP in Cape Town, January 1976; 2 x 50; bowling figures 6-1-28-1; 7 catches.

Odendaal, André

right-hand top-order batsman; club: United; debut vs EP in Port Elizabeth, 17-19 November 1985; 1 match; 3 runs, average 1,50; highest score 3 vs EP in Port Elizabeth, November 1985.

Petersen, Basil

left-arm spinner; clubs: Ashtondale, St Augustines, Metropolitan CA; debut vs Natal in Cape Town 1-4 January 1972; 3 matches; 3 wickets, average 23,67; best bowling 1/3 vs Natal January 1974; 36 runs, average 12,00; highest score 17 vs Natal, January 1974; 2 catches.

Petersen, Grant

wicketkeeper, left-hand batsman; club: Primrose; debut vs Transvaal in Cape Town, 18-20 February 1984; 2 matches; 4 catches, 1 stumping; 22 runs, average 11,00; highest score 15 vs Transvaal in Cape Town, March 1986.

Price, Hassiem

right-hand opening batsman; club: Blue Bells; debut vs Transvaal in Cape Town, 1-3 January 1983; 1 match; 2 runs, average 1; highest score 2 vs Transvaal in Cape Town, January 1983.

Rasmus, Mark

right-hand top-order batsman; clubs: Stellenbosch, Montrose; debut vs EP in Cape Town, 21-23 January 1989; 3 matches; 74 runs, average 18,50; highest score 31 vs Natal in Durban, February 1989; 2 catches.

Ravens, Clinton *"Kosie"*

right-hand batsman, medium-pacer; clubs: Blue Bells, Montrose; debut vs EP in Cape Town, 18-20 January 1986; 2 matches; 31 runs, average 15,50; highest score 30 vs EP in Cape Town, January 1986; 2 wickets, average 16,50; best bowling 2/17 vs EP in Cape Town, January 1986.

Richards, Terence

right-hand top-order batsman, off spinner; clubs: Metropolitan, Victoria; debut vs EP, 16-18 November 1979; 3 matches; 34 runs, average 6,80; highest score 19 vs Transvaal in Johannesburg, January 1980; bowling figures 2-0-24-0; 2 catches.

Roberts, Leon

left-hand seamer, lower-order batsman; clubs: Stellenbosch, Montrose; debut vs Natal in Durban, 28-30 December 1985; 2 matches; 4 wickets, average 29,25; best bowling 2/61 vs Transvaal in Johannesburg, January 1986; 17 runs, average 5,67; highest score 7 vs Transvaal in Johannesburg, January 1986.

Salie, Rashaad

right-hand opening batsman; club: Ottomans; debut vs EP in Cape Town, 26-28 November 1978; 5 matches; 97 runs, average 9,70; highest score 31 vs EP in Cape Town, November 1978; 1 catch.

Seconds, Trevor

left-hand opening bowler; clubs: Rivertonians, Primrose; debut vs EP in Cape Town, 21-23 January 1989; 3 matches; 13 wickets, average 11,46; best bowling 6/47 vs EP in Port Elizabeth, March 1990; 1 x 5 wickets in an innings; 12 runs (no average – 2 not outs); highest score 6* vs EP in Port Elizabeth, January 1989), 3 catches.

September, Marshall

right-hand opening bowler, clubs: St Augustines, Metropolitan CA, debut vs Transvaal 1-3 January 1973, 1 match, bowling figures 10-2-28- 1; best bowling 1/15 vs Transvaal, January 1973, 0 runs, 3 catches.

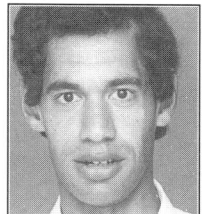

Simpson, Reggie

right-hand opening batsman; clubs: Victoria, Wynberg CA; debut vs Natal in Cape Town, 1-3 January 1973; 2 matches; 76 runs, average 19,00; highest score 43 vs Natal in Cape Town, January 1974; 1 catch.

Smith, Vaughan

right-hand opening batsman, clubs: Peninsula, Primrose; debut vs Transvaal in Cape Town, 11-13 February 1978; 4 matches; 46 runs, average 5,75; highest score 14 vs Transvaal in Cape Town, February 1978; 1 catch.

Solomons, Faghme

left-hand top-order batsman; clubs: Ottomans, Primrose; debut vs EP in Port Elizabeth, 21-23 January 1978; 21 matches; 578 runs, average 17,52; highest score 68 vs Transvaal in Cape Town, February 1984; 3 x 50; bowling figures. 2,3-1-9-0; 10 catches.

Sonn, Archie

allrounder; clubs: Bellville, Maitland Parow CA; debut vs Transvaal in Cape Town, 1-3 January 1973; 10 matches; 21 wickets, average 19,38; best bowling 4/57 vs EP in Cape Town, January 1973; 148 runs, average 12,33; highest score 28 vs Transvaal in Potchefstroom, March 1979; 4 catches.

Theron, Mervyn

left-arm spinner; club: Montrose; debut vs EP in Port Elizabeth, 13-15 March 1981; 8 matches; 29 wickets, average 13,14; best bowling 4/35 vs Transvaal in Johannesburg, December 1981; 61 runs, average 5,08; highest score 20 vs Natal in Durban, December 1981; 4 catches.

Thomas, Kelvin, Kashief

right-hand top-order batsman, spinner; clubs: St Augustines, Primrose; debut vs EP in Cape Town, 18-20 November 1978; 2 matches; 43 runs, average 10,75; highest score 31 vs EP in Cape Town, November 1978; bowling figures 14-4-39-0.

Thomas, Yunus

right-hand middle-order batsman, slow-medium bowler; clubs: Hottentots Holland, Primrose; debut vs Natal in Cape Town, 28-30 December 1982; 38 matches; 1 320 runs, average 26,94; highest score 116 vs Transvaal in Johannesburg, January 1986; 2 x 100, 7 x 50; 21 wickets, average 15,29; best bowling 5/6 vs Transvaal in Cape Town, January 1983; 1 x 5 wickets in an innings; 23 catches.

Timol, Ismail

right-hand middle-order batsman, wicketkeeper; clubs: Primrose, Wynberg CA; debut vs Natal in Durban 13-15 March 1976; 2 matches; 67 runs, average 22,33; highest score 29 vs Natal in Durban, March 1976; 2 catches.

Van Graan, Keith "Kitty"

right-hand middle-order batsman, medium-pacer; clubs: St Athens, Metropolitan CA; debut vs Transvaal in Cape Town, 1-3 January 1975; 9 matches; 191 runs, average 13,64; highest score 44 vs EP in Cape Town, January 1976; 4 wickets, average 10,00; best bowling 2/0 vs Natal in Cape Town, January 1976; 11 catches.

Van Graan, Randall *"Jacko"*

off-spinner, lower-order batsman; clubs: Victoria, Westridge, Montrose; debut vs EP in Port Elizabeth, 23-25 January 1982; 2 matches; 17 runs, average 5,67; highest score 10 vs Transvaal in Cape Town, February 1982; 2 wickets, average 26,5; best bowling 2/53 vs Transvaal in Cape Town, February 1982; 2 catches.

Van Graan, Robbie

right-hand top-order batsman; clubs: St Athens, Metropolitan CA; debut vs Transvaal in Cape Town 1-3 January 1973; 15 matches; 424 runs, average 19,27; highest score 67 vs Transvaal in Cape Town, February 1974; 2 x 50; 6 catches.

Van Oordt, George

right-hand middle-order batsman, medium-pacer; clubs: Tigers, St Augustines, Maitland Parow CA, Metropolitan CA; debut vs Rest of Sacboc in Cape Town, March 1976; 22 matches; 410 runs, average 13,67; highest score 51 vs Natal in Durban, December 1980; 1 x 50; 58 wickets, average 15,48; best bowling 5/50 vs EP in Port Elizabeth, January 1978; 1 x 5 wickets in an innings; 16 catches.

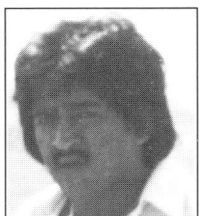

Van Schalkwyk, Charles

right-hand middle-order batsman, medium-pacer; clubs: Victoria, Wynberg CA; debut vs Rest of Sacboc in Cape Town, March 1976; 27 matches, captained WP 14 times; 582 runs, average 18,77; highest score 56 vs Transvaal in Johannesburg, December 1981; 3 x 50; 25 wickets, average 13,88; best bowling 4/15 vs EP in Cape Town, 1 x 50; November 1981; 13 catches.

Viljoen, Andre

right-hand opening batsman; club: St Augustines; debut vs Transvaal in Johannesburg, 5-7 January 1991; 3 matches; 141 runs, average 23,50; highest score 81 vs Transvaal in Cape Town, January 1991, 1x50; 1 catch.

Wadvalla, Aziz

right-hand top-order batsman; club: Primrose; debut vs Transvaal in Johannesburg, 26-28 December 1977; 2 matches; 5 runs, average 2,50; highest score 5 vs Natal in Cape Town, January 1978.

White, Nazeem

wicketkeeper/batsman, clubs: St Augustines, Montrose; debut vs Natal in Cape Town, 28-30 December 1982; 25 matches; 761 runs, average 24,55; highest score 125* vs Natal in Cape Town, November 1990; 2 x 100, 3 x 50; 77 catches, 14 stumpings.

*Williams, Garret, *"Gertjie"*

off-spinner, lower-order batsman; clubs: Valiants, Elsies River, Maitland Parow CA; debut vs Transvaal in Johannesburg 26-28 December 1971; 15 matches, 8 as captain; 393 runs, average 21,83; highest score 80 vs EP in Port Elizabeth, January 1972; 2 x 50; 45 wickets, average 20,56; best bowling 5/43 vs Natal in Durban, March 1974; 1 x 5 wickets in an innings; 7 catches.

Williams, Henry *"Bollie"*

right-hand opening bowler; club: Stellenbosch; debut vs Natal in Cape Town, 17-19 November 1990; 1 match; 5 wickets, average 10,20; best bowling 3/23 vs Natal in Cape Town, November 1990; 1 catch.

Williams, Jacobus *"Kosie"*

right-hand opening bowler; clubs: Valiants, Elsies River, Maitland Parow CA; debut vs Transvaal in Johannesburg 26-28 December 1971; 5 matches; 13 wickets, average 18,23; best bowling 3/21 vs Natal in Durban, March 1978; 39 runs, average 6,50; highest score 10 vs Natal in Cape Town, January 1972; 1 catch.

*Williams, Owen

left-arm spinner; clubs: Oakdale, Cape District CA; debut vs Transvaal in Johannesburg 26-28 December 1971; 2 matches; 4 wickets, average 30,75; best bowling 2/36 vs Natal in Cape Town, January 1972; 15 runs, average 15; highest score 9* vs Natal in Cape Town, January 1972; 1 catch.

Witbooi, Ronnie

right-hand seamer; club: Primrose; debut vs Natal in Durban, 26-28 December 1978; 2 matches; 2 wickets, average 25,00; best bowling 2/27 vs Natal in Durban, December 1978; 46 runs, average 23,00, highest score 28 vs Natal in Durban, December 1978.

***Note: Players marked with an asterisk (*) all played in Dadabhay tournaments prior to the start of the 3-day competition.
Prior to 1977/78 season players represented board teams in Super League.*

Index

* Page numbers in italics denote photographs